VENICE AND THE DEFENSE OF REPUBLICAN LIBERTY

PA X | VAN
TIBE | GELI
MAR | STA
CE E | MEVS

Venice and the Defense of Republican Liberty

Renaissance Values in the Age of the Counter Reformation

by William J. Bouwsma

UNIVERSITY OF CALIFORNIA PRESS
BERKELEY, LOS ANGELES, LONDON

University of California Press
Berkeley and Los Angeles, California

University of California Press, Ltd.
London, England

First Paperback Printing 1984
ISBN 0-520-05221-8

Library of Congress Catalog Card Number: 68-14642
Printed in the United States of America

1 2 3 4 5 6 7 8 9

TO MY WIFE

Acknowledgments

THIS work has been long in progress, and in the course of it I have accumulated numerous debts. Fulbright and Guggenheim Fellowships allowed me to make use of European libraries and provided opportunities for reflection, and a fellowship at the Center for Advanced Study in the Behavioral Sciences gave me time, under singularly favorable conditions, to write much of this book. I have also incurred many obligations to friends who read major parts of the work and offered encouragement and suggestions for its improvement, among them Stanley Chojnacki, Elisabeth Gleason, Peter Gay, and my colleagues Gene Brucker, Robert Brentano, and Randolph Starn. Felix Gilbert helped me to clarify my general understanding of Venetian development and saved me from many particular mistakes. But I must make special acknowledgment here to Hans Baron. Years ago he suggested that Paolo Sarpi might interest me, and he has given constant encouragement to my work. I owe to him not only many particular kindnesses but, above all, much in the way I have come to perceive what was crucial to the Italian Renaissance.

I have been helped from many directions in assembling by illustrations, and I must record here my indebtedness to the firms of Osvaldo Böhm in Venice, the Fratelli Alinari in Florence, and Albert Skira in Geneva; to the Bodleian Library at Oxford for permission to reproduce the only known portrait of Sarpi; and to Mr. Frank W. Kent, director of the E. B. Crocker Art Gallery in Sacramento, California, for the Carpaccio drawing. Michelangelo Muraro and Terisio Pignatti gave me important help; and Juergen Schulz, my fellow Venetian at Berkeley, aided me in many ways. I am particularly obligated to the generosity of Gaetano Cozzi for several illustrations; every historian of Venice will also discern the influence of his vast learning on almost every page of this book.

My relations with the staff of the University of California Press have been so pleasant and helpful that I must record here my general appreciation to it, and especially to my editors, Herbert F. Mann, Jr., and Max Knight, for their understanding and support. I am grateful too for the general design of Pamela Johnson, and the jacket, endleaf, and title-page designs of Wolfgang Lederer. They have succeeded remarkably in conveying a visual impression of what

I have tried to say in words. I must also thank Mark Phillips and Charles Wittenberg for the strenuous job of reading proofs, and Barbara Beckerman for preparing an unusually complicated index.

Finally I feel some obligation to note here that the later stages of my work were accomplished during the disorders that have agitated Berkeley since 1964, and these well-publicized events have taught me a good deal about the realities that underlie political discourse. They have required of me, as of other academic men, some direct participation in the *vita activa civile*; and they considerably deepened my understanding of the relationship between political liberty and intellectual vitality, of the contradictions between idealism and political accommodation, of the tension between freedom and order and the terrible anxieties this can generate in a crisis, and of the strain such anxieties impose on the sense of community. The relationship between my experience and my work also taught me something about the nature of the historical understanding, even perhaps when it attempts to grapple with events remote in both space and time.

W. J. B.

Contents

List of Plates

Abbreviations

Albèri	*Relazioni degli ambasciatori veneti al senato*, ed. Eugenio Albèri, 15 vols. (Florence, 1839–1863).
ASI	*Archivio storico italiano.*
AV	*Archivio veneto.*
BSV	*Bollettino dell'Istituto di Storia della Società e dello Stato Veneziano.*
Busnelli	Paolo Sarpi, *Lettere ai Protestanti*, ed. Manlio Diulio Busnelli, 2 vols. (Bari, 1931).
Componimento	*Per la storia del componimento della contesa tra la Repubblica Veneta e Paolo V (1605–1607): documenti*, ed. Carlo Pio de Magistris (Turin, 1941).
Cornet	*Paolo V e la Repubblica Veneta: giornale dal 22 ottobre 1605–9 giugno 1607*, ed. Enrico Cornet (Vienna, 1859).
Magistris	*Carlo Emanuele I e la contesa fra la Repubblica Veneta e Paolo V (1605–1607): documenti*, ed. Carlo Pio de Magistris (*Miscellanea di storia veneta*, Ser. 2, X) (Venice, 1906).
Pastor	Ludwig von Pastor, *The History of the Popes*, trans. F. I. Antrobus et al, 40 vols. (London and St. Louis, 1898–1953).
Pirri	*L'interdetto di Venezia del 1606 e i Gesuiti: silloge di documenti con introduzione*, ed. P. Pirri (Rome, 1959).
Raccolta	*Raccolta degli scritti usciti fuori in istampa, e scritti a mano nella causa del P. Paolo V. co'signori venetiani. Secondo le stampe di Venetia, di Roma, & d'altri luoghi*, 2 vols. (Coira, 1607).
RSI	*Rivista storica italiana.*
Scritti	Paolo Sarpi, *Istoria dell'interdetto e altri scritti editi ed inediti*, ed. Giovanni Gambarin, 3 vols. (Bari, 1940).
SG	Paolo Sarpi, *Scritti giurisdizionalistici*, ed. Giovanni Gambarin (Bari, 1958).
Smith	Logan Pearsall Smith, *The Life and Letters of Sir Henry Wotton*, 2 vols. (Oxford, 1907).
Ulianich	Paolo Sarpi, *Lettere ai Gallicani*, ed. Boris Ulianich (Wiesbaden, 1961).

Preface

THIS book is very different, in both size and scope, from the book I had intended when I began to work on it ten years ago. My original aim was quite limited; I proposed to write about Paolo Sarpi, who interested me both as a religious thinker and as a historian. It gradually became apparent to me, however, that Sarpi could only be understood historically as a product of the Venetian interdict of 1606–1607, and I had therefore to try to identify the essential issues in that massive confrontation. But since it takes two to quarrel, I had to study not only the long and slow development of the Venetian political consciousness but also the contrary ideals and purposes of the Counter Reformation, neither of which had yet, as I came to believe, stimulated any satisfactory general treatment. The final stage in the evolution of this book was reached, however, only when it dawned on me that I seemed to be dealing with a set of issues strikingly similar, *mutatis mutandis*, to those that had concerned the great Florentine political writers of the earlier sixteenth century. I began to comprehend then why some Venetians seemed occasionally to be haunted by the memory of Florence; and I also found myself looking at Machiavelli and Guicciardini, and even earlier Renaissance figures, in what were, for me, new ways.

Therefore, although this book deals mainly with Venice, it touches so frequently also on Florence and on Rome that it is in some sense a tale of three cities. For the Venetians of the sixteenth and seventeenth centuries with whom we shall chiefly be concerned, Florence was largely important as a feature of the past and a stimulus to thoughtful comparison and contrast, but Rome belonged in one sense to the past and in a different but related sense to the present. The origin in antiquity of the most effective imperialism the world had ever known, she was now the center of a renascent universalism directed perhaps even more against the impulses of the Renaissance than against Protestantism. Rome was thus the great adversary of Venice, the anvil against which her political consciousness was hammered out at last. Two traumatic papal interdicts very nearly set the chronological terms of the process. The interdict of Julius II in 1509 helped to launch the career of Venice as a self-conscious republic, a marvel about which men could write entire books; and the interdict of Paul V, almost a century later, brought that career to its dramatic climax. The fact that this was also the last great interdict to be imposed on a political community suggests something of its broader importance.

The story I shall tell covers more than a century, and some parts of it are already reasonably familiar to specialists, in Italy and elsewhere, on whose researches I have relied heavily at many points. My own primary investigations have been chiefly directed to the writings of Venetian statesmen, political thinkers, and historians, some of them well known, others relatively obscure. But beyond this I have been concerned to follow, through nearly its full course, the development of the Venetian political mind and of a body of historical writings, through which it found expression, that commanded the respect and admiration of Europe until, in the nineteenth century, Venice was eclipsed in the European imagination by Renaissance Florence. I hope that, through this larger perspective, my account will prove helpful to specialists as well as to readers interested both in the neglected place of Venice in the Italian Renaissance and in the contribution of Venice to the general culture of Europe.

My first chapter requires a word of explanation. Like most historians, I feel some embarrassment in the presence of such grand labels as "Renaissance" and "medieval" to designate comprehensive patterns of thought and attitude. It became increasingly apparent to me as this book progressed, nevertheless, that I could only understand the development of Venetian political and historical thought as a particular case of something more general, and that this development was in fact closely related to tendencies that have recently been identified as central to the Renaissance, particularly in Florence. It has seemed to me necessary, therefore, for the clarity of my presentation in later chapters, to identify as well as I could my own general approach to the Renaissance problem, in spite of the obvious dangers of committing oneself publicly on matters of such complexity and controversy. The first chapter is thus intended as a thematic index to what follows.

At the same time it does not, I believe, merely reflect what I have managed to digest out of the conclusions of other historians working chiefly from evidence supplied by Florence. I think that the Venetian experience reinforces these conclusions in some ways, but that it also clarifies dimensions of the Florentine Renaissance, suggests relationships that have been neglected, and points to some shifts in emphasis. My first chapter thus attempts to apply more broadly a number of general conclusions suggested by the development of Venice. Like many introductory statements to works of this kind, it was finished last; and a case might be made for reading it last. On the other hand, readers who regard a general essay of this sort as inappropriate to historical discourse may wish to disregard it. I hope they will find particularity enough to suit their taste in other parts of the book.

Renaissance Republicanism and the *Respublica Christiana*

THE age of the Renaissance has evoked many generalizations, of various degrees of ingenuity, that have failed to survive close scrutiny. I should like, nevertheless, to propose still another which, though closely related to some of its predecessors, may avoid some of their defects. To put the matter briefly, it is that between the thirteenth and the seventeenth centuries western Europeans, and perhaps Italians most directly and vividly, were torn between two largely antithetical modes of perceiving reality.

Some recognition of this is implied in much discussion of the Renaissance problem, but it has been regularly obscured by a difficulty in language. Since the Renaissance vision of reality is more like our own, it has generally appeared to us more "real" than the medieval, and historians have commonly contrasted the "realism" of the Renaissance, particularly in political matters, with the merely "theoretical" vision which it presumably replaced. This familiar way of posing the issue, however, begs the question. For the distinction between practice and theory is by no means the same (unless one prejudges the matter) as the distinction between a concern with "reality" and the absence of such concern. The medieval theoretician, however indifferent to "practicality," was a realist too, but in his own fashion. He simply defined "reality" in a different way and located it differently from the thinker of the Renaissance.

The present book is concerned with the tension between the medieval and Renaissance conceptions of reality as it was felt by articulate Venetians, particularly during the climactic sixteenth and early seventeenth centuries, as the result of a series of events comparable in importance to those in which Florence had figured earlier. Since the tension found general expression, at this relatively late date, in a substantial body of literature both in Venice and among her opponents, much of the exposition of its character and meaning may be left to later chapters. It will be necessary here, therefore, to describe it only in a rather general way.

To prevent kinds of misunderstanding that have too often hampered general discussion of the Renaissance, some basic points must be made at the outset. In view of the common tendency to divide the past into discrete periods, the first may appear somewhat paradoxical. It is that the medieval and Renaissance conceptions of reality should not be conceived, necessarily and without exception, as chronologically successive. I do not find altogether persuasive a recent suggestion that the medieval phase of Italian history generally followed rather than preceded the Renaissance.[1] There is a good deal of truth in the argument that the conventional contrast between Middle Ages and Renaissance, primarily devised by northern scholars, actually pits aspects of northern European civilization, and particularly of thirteenth-century France, against an Italy that had developed from a remote point along rather different lines. It is useful to recall that feudalism was not a significant feature of the Italian scene except in backward areas, and that scholasticism, imported into Italy only in the later thirteenth century, grew in influence (rather than declined) during the following centuries. But these were not the only vehicles of the medieval vision of reality. Another, of at least equal influence, had deep Italian roots. This was the papacy, together with the ecclesiastical hierarchy that to varying degrees depended on it, and the theologians and above all the canonists who promoted its claims. The experience of Venice was to reveal the importance of this agent of the medieval vision, and it was perhaps more significant even for Florence than has generally been recognized. Yet it remains true that the historian is confronted not so much with a distinct sequence of attitudes as with an almost perennial tension; and it is essential to recognize that each position enjoyed moments of dominance, now in one place and now in another, in a struggle without clear resolution, at least during the age of the Renaissance itself. The relative standing of the two fundamental attitudes in Italy by the end of the sixteenth century seems sufficiently to refute the simple view that a new vision of reality displaced that of the Middle Ages in the Renaissance.

A second caution must be directed against the temptation to classify men into distinct parties consistently contending against each other. The most common form taken by this mistake has been the unequivocal identification of scholasticism with medieval and of humanism with Renaissance attitudes.

[1] Jerrold E. Seigel, " 'Civic Humanism' or Ciceronian Rhetoric? The Culture of Petrarch and Bruni," *Past and Present*, No. 34 (July, 1966), 3–48, which relies particularly on the chronology proposed by Armando Sapori.

There is more truth in this identification, as I will argue shortly, than has been acknowledged by some of its recent critics; but it is also true that neither scholasticism nor humanism was monolithic, and neither schoolmen nor humanists were immune from the basic dilemmas faced by other men. It should not, therefore, be surprising to encounter men whose minds were formed in the schools taking up the defense of civic life, even (like Luigi Marsili) under quite concrete circumstances.[2]

This suggests a third caveat: that it may be misleading, and for the purposes of this discussion unnecessary, to insist on a direct and unambiguous movement on the part of individual men from one set of attitudes to another. Petrarch and Salutati evidently oscillated between fundamental alternatives according to circumstance or their own private needs; Machiavelli made no clear and absolute choice; nor, as we shall see, can Gasparo Contarini, Paolo Paruta, or even Paolo Sarpi, be finally categorized. All were to a degree, although we may discern in them a definite movement at some times in their lives, divided against themselves. This does not mean that they constantly exhibited signs of strain. Conflicting impulses often achieve a relative equilibrium, in individuals as well as in societies, which, however, is likely to break down in moments of personal or historical crisis. Such moments have often proved unusually illuminating for the historian, and they will be at least as useful for Venice as they have proved for Florence.

Finally it should be apparent in what follows that I am not immediately concerned with explaining the movement between the two visions of reality, and for the moment I shall describe them largely in ideal terms. This should not be taken to mean that an idealistic conception of historical change underlies this book. I firmly believe, with Frederic Lane, that the ways in which men support their material needs (a task that occupies most of their time) substantially determine their values and their attitudes to experience in general,[3] and I think it no accident that the vision of reality which I propose to associate with the Renaissance was first articulated in commercial republics. In addition, as the sequel will show, I think that political conditions can exert a powerful effect on the way men regard life in general.

Nevertheless, the relation between life and ideas is more complicated than these reflections may suggest; it can be observed, for example, that not all

[2] Cf. Jerrold E. Seigel, *Rhetoric and Philosophy in Renaissance Humanism: the Union of Eloquence and Wisdom, Petrarch to Valla* (Princeton, 1968), Ch. 8; and Frederic C. Lane *Venice and History* (Baltimore, 1966) 531–532.

[3] *Ibid.*, pp. 427–428.

commercial republics, but only some among the commercial republics of Italy, enunciated Renaissance values. Furthermore, ideas, once expressed, take on a variety of functions which give them a remarkable survival value. As the men of the Renaissance were perhaps the first to recognize in a general way, ideas can be used to disguise and to promote material interests of various kinds, albeit often unconsciously; and they may be kept alive and disseminated for this purpose in environments otherwise uncongenial. In addition ideas may serve psychological needs. Traditional ideas are often attractive simply because they are traditional; accepted as eternally true, they remove the need for independent thought and for adjustment to novelty, which is frequently frightening. They often served this purpose for Venice. And some patterns of ideas seem to provide security, or to serve other more obscure psychic needs, almost as a result of their own intrinsic character. Much in the development of Italian culture during the sixteenth century, an age of peculiar anxiety, will be seen to illustrate this point.[4]

The crucial difference between the two positions, between the medieval vision and that of the Renaissance, was an utterly different conception of the general nature of order; every other difference between them can be related to this. To put the matter in its simplest terms: in the medieval vision of reality, every dimension of the universe and every aspect of human existence were seen as part of an objective and cosmic system of order. But the Renaissance mind perceived nothing of the sort. Unable and frequently little caring to find coherence in the universe as a whole, it discerned only such limited and transient patterns of order as could be devised by man himself. Furthermore, the medieval vision identified a definite pattern in the universal order. All things appeared to be arranged in a hierarchy of complexity and value, an arrangement whose basis was ideal and therefore utterly static. In this conception some things were unalterably higher and therefore better, others were lower and thus inferior. But in the Renaissance vision there was no such hierarchy, and instead of stasis it saw merely, though often reluctantly, the incessant flux of things. The medieval vision attributed reality only to what was general and could therefore be related to the universal system. The Renaissance vision, sure only of the particular, located reality there. The medieval vision of reality, as a system comprehending all things, was closed; the Renaissance vision, comprehending very little and uncertain that anything had its definite place, was open.

[4] See below, esp. Chs. III and VI.

This description evidently contrasts ideal types, and accounts of such a kind are always likely to approach caricature. Nevertheless, what I have here represented as the "medieval vision" is useful to explain systematic descriptions of feudalism (if less so to expose how feudalism worked), to illuminate the major purposes of at least some schoolmen, and to understand the elaborate justifications of medieval theocracy. It may also be observed here that by the sixteenth century many expositions of the medieval position were hardly more nuanced than my own sketch of it, though they were often developed at great length. I am not aiming, however, for novelty; I wish here only to provide a brief preliminary for some comment on issues that fundamentally concerned the thinkers of the Renaissance.

Implicit in the medieval vision is a remarkable confidence in the intellectual capacities of man. It assumed not only the existence of a universal order but also a substantial capacity in the human mind to grasp this order. The intellectual optimism in this position is particularly notable; in an important sense medieval culture took a far higher view of some human capacities than did that of the Renaissance. Furthermore, the medieval position tended to identify man with his intellect, and his ability to apprehend the pattern of universal order was closely related to the ultimate purpose of human existence. By contemplating its perfect structure and ascending its stages, man could, with his mind, rise from what was good to what was better, and finally approach and seek to unite himself intellectually with what was best. Contemplation was thus the noblest of pursuits, the highest path of existence; activity in the world of men and particular things was not only inferior but could chiefly be justified only by its contribution to something superior to itself. Augustine might be cited on this point: "The active life is necessary not for its own sake but as preparation for contemplation." [5] The value attached to contemplation also led to contempt for the concrete and particular, which in this perspective evidently derived its "reality" only from participation in the general structure of things. Truth depended on first principles, not on immediate perceptions, and practice on theory rather than the reverse. Experience had little or no independent existence; it was required to conform to theory, not to determine it. That experience often failed to meet this obligation only proved its inferiority to the essential dimension of reality.

This general conception of reality was reflected in a characteristic political

[5] *Contra Faustum Manichaeum*, Ch. 53.

model that was almost the converse of the political model of the Renaissance. The essential feature of the medieval political ideal was its denial of the legitimacy of the particular, the autonomous, and the secular. Hence it rejected the propriety of such independent political entities as have been the primary subject of modern political discourse; it was concerned rather with the social (as well as spiritual) unity of all Christians in a single body, the *ecclesia* or *respublica christiana*, terms often used interchangeably. According to James of Viterbo, no community but the church could be considered a *vera respublica* since only the church could supply, in their true meaning, the benefits of government. The church alone was in direct contact with the ultimate source of all benefit, and nothing could be more clear than that the church was one.[6]

And like the larger dimensions of reality, the *respublica christiana* was necessarily organized as a hierarchical system in which lower ends were subordinated to higher, and inferior powers to superior; authority in the entire structure descended from above. Its systematic character meant that the clergy were superior to the laity and gave an ultimate supremacy, in temporal as in spiritual matters (since the former ranked lower in the hierarchy of values), to the pope. And as subordinate members of a universal system men could be seen to have no right to govern themselves, and states no right to determine their separate courses of action. Self-determination, in this view, could only appear, in the deepest sense, as a violation of the very structure of reality, and political duty appeared to consist only in patient submission and obedience. Man, in this system, was always and necessarily a subject; he could not be a citizen.[7] Thus the ideal had important ethical implications.

Political responsibility in this conception could only seem relatively contemptible, at best an ancillary necessity.[8] It was clearly better for any man, if he could, to leave it to such baser sorts as were incapable of rising to higher things, and himself to withdraw from the confusing and generally

---

[6] *De regimine christiano*, i. 4, p. 127: "Nulla communitas dicitur vera republica nisi ecclesiastica, quia in ea sola est vera iustitia et vera utilitas et vera communis," quoted by M. J. Wilks, *The Problem of Sovereignty in the Later Middle Ages* (Cambridge, 1962), p. 18.

[7] See generally the works of Walter Ullmann, *Principles of Government and Politics in the Middle Ages* (London, 1961) esp. pp. 21ff., and *The Individual and Society in the Middle Ages* (Baltimore, 1966); and cf. the interesting remarks of Nicola Abbagnano, "Italian Renaissance Humanism," *Journal of World History*, XI (1963), 269.

[8] Cf. Herbert A. Deane, *The Political and Social Ideas of St. Augustine* (New York, 1963), p. 7, generally contrasting classical and Christian conceptions of the state.

meaningless particularity of daily life to abide in the realm of the general and the unchanging. Related to this attitude was a substantial indifference to history, which was concerned with the inferior realm of change, from which (at best) general truths of a low and practical character could only occasionally be abstracted; there are no historians among the great ancients gathered around the fire in Dante's Limbo. The medieval conception of reality found expression not in historical compositions but in magnificent architectonic systems of thought, final answers in as final a form as possible to perennial questions, designed rather to close than to continue discussion.[9]

I am describing here a great vision rather than an actuality, and it will be unnecessary to discuss either its complex origins (more hellenistic than specifically Christian) or the long effort of the papacy to translate it into a reality, although it may be observed that this effort was not so successful as has often been supposed.[10] Its earlier protagonists were largely content to enunciate the ideal and to demand the world's conformity; the notion that the ideal had generally achieved acceptance would have required concrete political and historical evidence and a species of discourse which these men rarely found congenial. The historical claim came, on the whole, later, and largely during the period with which this book is concerned.

The spiritual leaders of the *respublica christiana* made, nevertheless, a considerable effort to impose their lofty conception on the refractory world; and to promote it they devised several techniques destined for particular importance, not only directly and practically during earlier episodes in the elaboration of the theocratic ideal but also because they stimulated the elaboration of a new political consciousness from the fourteenth century onward. These techniques included the excommunication of rulers, usually accompanied by a formal declaration of deposition; the release of subjects from obedience together with the encouragement of revolt as a sacred duty; and the interdiction of an entire political community as a means of bringing public pressure to bear on its government. Often used in combination, these

[9] See the excellent discussion of this point in Eugenio Garin, *Medioevo e Rinascimento: studi e ricerche* (Bari, 1961), pp. 202–204.
[10] For a different view see Walter Ullmann, *The Growth of Papal Government in the Middle Ages. A Study in the Ideological Relation of Clerical to Lay Power* (London, 1955), p. 1. I am evidently more impressed than Ullmann appears to be here by the slow development of papal claims, the difficulties impeding their implementation, and the long and effective history of resistance to them. It seems to me that Ullmann implies too positive an answer to his own question (p. 451): "How far were all these measures and actions ordered by the popes effective?"

devices gave a cutting edge to the spiritual sword. They were the instruments by which the superior spiritual authority enforced its will against the lesser members of the body politic. Their use implemented the general claim to sovereignty over the entire *respublica christiana;* submission to them implied the acceptance of this claim by the temporal power.[11] As a primary means for imposing theoretical requirements on political practice, the spiritual weapons wielded by popes were bound to provoke crises and thereby to stimulate reflection about the nature of human society and its organization. They had therefore a considerable role in developing the characteristic political attitudes of the Renaissance, particularly for Venice.

The antithesis of the *respublica christiana* was the Renaissance republic, a phenomenon whose importance for the remarkable achievements of Italy during the fourteenth, fifteenth, and sixteenth centuries has received some emphasis from modern scholars.[12] But the relation between republicanism and Renaissance culture was recognized long ago. Thus, toward the end of the sixteenth century, Giovanni Botero discussed it in an unusually general way; but he did so, as he generally sought to do in other connections, because it had already become a familiar sentiment. In the extended section on Venice in his *Relationi universali* Botero wrote:

> From good government derive all those good qualities in subjects that belong to civil and virtuous life, every means for doing good things, all the arts both of peace and war, of acquiring and saving, all polite customs, all noble manners, every honored form of politeness. For this reason free cities of great size surpass those that are subject to princes, at once in magnificence of buildings and in beauty of streets and squares, in multitude of people, in variety of arts, in refinement of manners, and in every kind of polity [*politia*] and humanity. Venice and Genoa prove it, and Florence and Siena did so in their time.[13]

[11] L. Godefroy, "Interdit," *Dictionnaire de Théologie Catholique,* VII: 2 (Paris, 1930), cols. 2280–2290; Edward B. Krehbiel, *The Interdict: Its History and Operation, with Special Attention to the Time of Pope Innocent III, 1198–1216* (Washington, 1909).

[12] Especially by Hans Baron, *The Crisis of the Early Italian Renaissance,* rev. ed. (Princeton, 1966), and Eugenio Garin, *L'umanesimo italiano* (Bari, 1958).

[13] P. 764 in the edition of Venice, 1640. The various *Relazioni* collected in this edition were first published in Rome between 1592 and 1596.

It had early become a commonplace that republican freedom made better men, supplied better government, and nourished a more brilliant culture than other kinds of government.

To appreciate the significance of the Renaissance republic, it is necessary to emphasize, however, that (like the *respublica christiana*) it was not simply a political construction; it rested, as an ideal, on specific assumptions, and it pointed to a set of general attitudes. Republicanism was intimately connected with powerful convictions about the nature of man that bore directly on his capacity to apprehend the structure of reality, though perhaps not so immediately with positive beliefs about its ultimate nature, a point on which republicanism was likely to be agnostic. The belief that a republic was the form of government most appropriate to the human condition, and therefore best suited to bring out the full potentialities of man, as Botero suggested, was thus a reflection of fundamental attitudes to experience as a whole.

Republicanism, to put the matter in its simplest terms, did not identify the essence of man with his intellect. It tended rather (though such modes of thought were not altogether congenial to it) to find man's essence in his will. Republicanism lacked, therefore, the confidence implicit in the medieval vision in the power of the human reason to grasp general patterns of order to which every element in creation, and notably man himself, must conform. It saw no absolute structure in the nature of things, no clear gradations of ultimate value, no ground for classifying some elements in the universe as higher and others as lower, no reason accessible to man for affirming that reality consisted of a system of unchanging forms and that the fluidity of common experience could be dismissed as meaningless. It accepted inconsistency, contradiction, and paradox as insurmountable.

The historical significance of Renaissance humanism lies in the fact that it reflected this set of essentially skeptical attitudes. Instead of attempting to coordinate classical texts into a system, it rejected the possibility of systematic knowledge in favor of a kind of intellectual pluralism. Renaissance humanism recognized that men filled various roles in society or had, in their personal lives, a variety of needs which might require a variety of intellectual postures. Humanistic culture was unsystematic and eclectic; it was prepared to range among alternative positions and to select whichever seemed appropriate to a particular set of circumstances. And a professional humanist was simply a man who made appropriate attitudes available for the use of others. From this standpoint it seems to make little difference whether a rhetorician employed by a government, like Salutati or Bruni, actually believed personally in what he wrote on its behalf. The attitude toward the nature of truth implied by his profession was itself utterly at odds with the systematic mentality attached to the medieval vision of reality. A man who believed one thing but wrote another, for whatever purpose, or who supplied an argument for one occasion utterly inconsistent with what he provided for another, was, against this background, perhaps a more striking phenomenon than one who simply deviated from traditional views on particular issues.[14] And it is particularly significant that the profession of rhetoric seems to have involved no great burden on the conscience.

A skeptical, antisystematic position generally characterized the great Florentines who first brought republican political discourse to a high level of articulation, although hints of it may be discovered (along with entirely contrary tendencies) at least as early as Petrarch and Salutati. Machiavelli and Guicciardini, the latter more consistently, rejected the abstract and general for the concrete and particular, the theoretical for the empirical. They did so from their understanding of the nature of man and in a spirit of profound disillusionment with the consequences of relying on the generalizing intellect. "Philosophers and theologians and all those who investigate the supernatural and the invisible," declared Guicciardini, "say thousands of insane things. As a matter of fact, men are in the dark about such matters, and their investigation has served and serves more to exercise the intellect than to find truth." [15] But the objection went beyond metaphysics to all general statements. The difficulty with any generalization was that it was all too likely to take on a life and a power of its own, to attempt to control the details it had been intended only to summarize, in effect (to paraphrase Walter Ullmann) to transform an ascending into a descending theme of intellectual authority. This is the meaning of Machiavelli's conviction that "in general men deceive themselves a great deal, in specific things not so much," on the basis of which he praised the Romans for their wisdom in disregarding a general principle of whose abstract truth they had been fully persuaded.[16]

---

[14] Cf. Seigel, " 'Civic Humanism' or Ciceronian Rhetoric?" esp. pp. 33–35. Seigel's own evidence seems to me to point to a considerably greater significance for humanism than he implies here.

[15] *Ricordi*, Ser. C, No. 125. I follow here both the numbering and the translations in Francesco Guicciardini, *Maxims and Reflections of a Renaissance Statesman*, trans. Mario Domandi (New York, 1965).

[16] *Discorsi*, Bk. I, Ch. 47. In citing Machiavelli I have relied (with occasional changes of my own) on the translations of Allan Gilbert, *Machiavelli, The Chief Works and Others* (Durham, 1965), and on Leslie J. Walker's edition of the *Discorsi* (London and New Haven, 1950).

From this perspective the life men lived, in contrast to an uncontrolled speculation about life in general, appeared to consist of discrete moments in particular situations; for all practical purposes (in the literal sense) this was the true nature of reality. Hence Guicciardini's sweeping prescription:

> It is a great error to speak of things of the world absolutely and indiscriminately and to deal with them, as it were, by the book. In nearly all things one must make distinctions and exceptions because of differences in their circumstances. These circumstances are not covered by one and the same rule. Nor can these distinctions and exceptions be found written in books. They must be taught by discretion.[17]

From a strictly intellectual point of view republicanism may thus appear deeply pessimistic, and its dim view of man's generalizing intellect was often extended to his capacity for virtue. But what republicanism yielded in this area it sometimes made up for in others. It assumed the existence of a wide range of positive values in the nonintellectual dimensions of human experience: in the infinite variety of the material world of place and time, in the various dimensions of the emotional life, in problems of moral choice, in creative expression, in the struggle (albeit so often tragic) between man and his destiny. And since it did not conceive of man primarily as an intellectual being, it freed him to engage in the active life as the mode of existence best suited to his complex nature. Social responsibility was valuable not only for society but for individual men as well because it meant exposure to a broad range of experiences.

Renaissance republicanism adapted this vision of man to politics; it tried to solve the problem of adjustment to a reality that was, in any general or ultimate sense, beyond human grasp. For the heart of republicanism, as Botero seems to have recognized, was the claim to liberty; and liberty meant the rejection of subordination. A true republic was in the first place a particular power, not a participant in a universal system directed by some superior authority; and it claimed the right to determine its own policies simply on the basis of its particular interest. Nor was its internal structure, in the medieval sense, systematic. It was directed not to a single end from above, by a prince, but by a body of citizens, who somehow represented the community and its interests, and who were related to one another by a principle very different from that of hierarchy.

[17] *Ricordi*, Ser. C, No. 6.

The first meaning of Renaissance liberty was thus the independence of the state;[18] the Renaissance republic was free because it belonged to no eternal system and acknowledged no earthly superior. The political universe, in this conception, was not a hierarchy but a congeries of discrete entities, each unique in origin and internal structure and each working out its particular destiny. The conception explains both the theoretical justification supplied by Bartolus for urban legal codes that lacked sanctions from above, and the preoccupation of the new Renaissance historiography with the careers of individual states. Machiavelli once put it into a remoter perspective by relating the evolution of Christian Europe to the four universal monarchies through which the political organization of the world had earlier passed. After the disappearance of the last, he declared, political *virtù* had been dispersed among various peoples, infidel as well as Christian. "Hence," he wrote, "after ruin had overtaken the Romans, there continued to exist in all these provinces and in all these separate units, and still exists in some of them, that virtue which is desired and quite rightly praised." [19] For Machiavelli the Christian era did not mark the culmination of universalism but evidently coincided—when one examined actualities rather than theories—precisely with its collapse.

There is, perhaps, a hint of nostalgia in Machiavelli, who (like many others) admired the Romans, though not necessarily their imperial predecessors, even while he recognized that in the modern world, and clearly for centuries, political competence had found practical expression only in "separate units." But many of those who wrote in favor of the Renaissance republic, among them in most moods Machiavelli himself, exhibited remarkably little regret for the systems of universal order alleged to have prevailed in the past. These writers do not give the impression of praising and serving their particular communities *faute de mieux*, but of a quite positive satisfaction and devotion. They made a point of discovering in their individual republics human values that even the Romans, as they discerned, had manifested only before their conquest of the world, when their own state had been small and particular.

---

[18] For general discussion of the meaning of Renaissance liberty, see Nicolai Rubinstein, "Florence and the Despots in the Fourteenth Century," *Transactions of the Royal Historical Society*, Ser. 5, II (1952), 21–45, and D. M. Bueno de Mesquita, "The Place of Despotism in Italian Politics," in *Europe in the Late Middle Ages* (Evanston, 1965), ed. John Hale *et al.*, pp. 303–312.

[19] *Discorsi*, Bk. II, Introduction.

The Renaissance conception of the political world as an agglomeration of particular communities also had fateful implications for international relations. Medieval universalism had provided, at least in theory, a solution to the problem of political conflict. Without particular states or nations, international collisions were by definition impossible. The disputes that arose between the members of the universal family were seen as no more than domestic quarrels which could properly be settled by the paternal authority of a hierarchical superior, on the basis of universal principles accepted by all. But political particularism seemed to leave the world without any way to maintain order among peoples. Unless the world could devise some new principle of order, particularism pointed to chaos.

This is the significance of the notion of balance of power, the characteristic Renaissance solution to the problem of international order; the conception of an equilibrium among discrete political units provided a natural alternative to the medieval ideal of an order supplied by a hierarchic system. Among the Florentines Bernardo Rucellai, an associate of Machiavelli, had first seen the issue clearly; and he attributed the relative tranquillity of Italy before 1494 to the preservation of a balance, through the wisdom of prudent statesmen, among the states of the peninsula.[20] Machiavelli, presumably on the basis of this conception, also hinted that international order had been effective, in the absence of universal subordination and hierarchical control, much earlier in Italian history. "Some of the new cities and new states born among the Roman ruins showed such great ability," he declared, "that although one of them did not master the others, they were, nevertheless, so harmonious and so well organized that they freed Italy and defended her from the barbarians." [21] Thus on quite practical grounds there was no cause to regret the medieval ideal, which had been patently unsuccessful in meeting precisely these national needs; the harmonization of independent states, balancing and cooperating with each other according to circumstance and their mutual necessities, was demonstrably a better instrument of political order. During the sixteenth century the conception of balance was steadily enlarged. As Italy was increasingly drawn into the struggles of the ultramontane powers, Italian political observers tended more and more to understand international relations as a series of problems in equilibrium.

[20] Felix Gilbert, *Machiavelli and Guicciardini: Politics and History in Sixteenth Century Florence* (Princeton, 1965), pp. 113–114.
[21] *Istorie fiorentine*, Bk. V, Ch. 1.

The internal structure of a state, according to the republican conception of political reality, followed the same general principles. Although often the focus of profound loyalty and affection, the state itself was not conceived organically, as a reality transcending those who composed it, but as the sum of its parts; the human interests within it appeared as discrete and self-determined, not coordinated from above. Monarchy (pejoratively labeled *tyranny* or *despotism*) was thus repugnant to the conception in principle; conversely, because it reflected a descending theme of authority, it was consistent with the medieval view of reality; the princes of Italy, unlike republican governments, generally sought imperial sanction for their authority.[22] But the Renaissance vision of the nature of things required self-government by citizens, through a process of self-assertion, accommodation, and balance roughly the same as the processes of international politics. The first meaning of Renaissance liberty, the independence of the state, was therefore closely related to its second meaning: self-government by citizens.

A merely independent state was thus not necessarily altogether free, as Poggio pointed out on behalf of Florence in 1438, in reply to the curious claim of the Milanese duke that the submission of the Republic to himself would mean no loss of liberty. The liberty of Florence, Poggio proclaimed, was "more solid and truer" than elsewhere because "not one or another man governs here, nor does the arrogance of optimates or noblemen command, but the people are called on the basis of equal right to perform public functions in the commonwealth. As a consequence, highly placed and humble persons, members of noble families and commoners, rich and poor, work together with a common zeal for the cause of liberty."[23] Machiavelli was also sensitive to this issue, which he dramatized in the confrontation between the Duke of Athens and the Florentine commune in his *Istorie fiorentine*. In the eyes of the Signoria the duke, who asserted that "it was not his purpose to take away the city's liberty, but to give it back again, because only disunited cities were slaves and united ones free," had in actuality aimed "to make a slave of a city that has always lived free."[24]

Poggio's rhetoric obviously exceeded the realities of Florentine politics,

[22] Felix Gilbert makes this point in "The Humanist Concept of the Prince and the 'Prince' of Machiavelli," *Journal of Modern History*, XI (1939), 454–455.

[23] Quoted by Baron, *Crisis*, p. 408. For similar sentiments in Leonardo Bruni, see also pp. 418–419.

[24] Bk. II, Chs. 34 and 35.

and his sentimentality should remind us of both the practical limits and the theoretical possibilities in the republican conception of citizenship. It is hardly necessary to observe that Renaissance republics were not democratic, and their vaunted equality prevailed only, and often irregularly, among certain groups; the status and rights of citizenship were always restricted. The *people* (*populus*, *popolo*) generally signified, in Renaissance discourse, the politically competent group in a state, Aristotle's middle party of practical order, indeterminate in size, between a minority of powerful men, ambitious to assume an absolute control and to rule from above, and the politically incompetent masses. Machiavelli also makes these distinctions clear in his instructive account of the Duke of Athens. Temporarily supported by the "nobles" and by the lower class, whose nature is "to delight in evil," he had overthrown a government of the "middle class." And opposition to his tyrannical rule had developed along the same lines: "Three distinct conspiracies were formed: one of the great, another of the people, and the third of the working classes." [25]

It may be observed, however, that Renaissance distrust of democracy, although it intensified in the later fifteenth and sixteenth centuries, was of a practical rather than a theoretical character; it had no metaphysical overtones. Distinctions were based on experience and interest, and these were presumably susceptible to change and redefinition by men as circumstances altered. Furthermore it was generally assumed that the right of citizenship depended on some correspondence, manifested by "the middle sort" alone, to the general interest; that class somehow represented the community as no other group could do. But the gulf between this conception of society and the hierarchical model of reality is clear in any case; Renaissance publicists were inclined to emphasize fraternal equality, not social subordination.[26] Finally the conception suggests an implicit pluralism. Behind it lies the general conviction that a number of heads and a variety of talents are, in political matters, always better than one.

The attention given to constitutional problems in Renaissance political speculation must also be understood in the light of the general perception of reality as an accumulation of particular entities and forces in need of coordination for the attainment of particular ends. The body of ordinances and

[25] *Ibid.*, Bk. II, Chs. 34 and 36.

[26] As in the letter of Bruni *ad magnum principem imperatorem* (1413), the text of which is given by Hans Baron, *Humanistic and Political Literature in Florence and Venice at the Beginning of the Quattrocento* (Cambridge, Mass., 1955), pp. 181–184.

institutions that regulated each political community was a complex mechanism created by men to maintain practical order and to secure the other purposes of their separate societies, in the absence of any ultimate and universal pattern of cosmic order to which every human community must conform. It might be well or badly devised to meet local needs, but it was long seen as a unique creation intended to serve the peculiar requirements of particular societies with special characteristics;[27] only in the later Renaissance were efforts made to generalize about constitutions, and to apply the characteristics discerned in the ordinances of one community to solve problems in others.

The Italian preference for constitutional government can be traced back at least to the thirteenth century;[28] and the discussions of Machiavelli and Guicciardini represent only a latter phase in Renaissance constitutionalism. Constitutions, in this tradition, were seen to serve a variety of important functions. For Machiavelli only a sound constitution could solve the problem posed by man's mortality; good institutions survived the men who made them.[29] They could also strengthen states against external attack and thus enable men to control their own destiny; by its internal structure, over which it has substantial power, a state could resist those perils over which it has none.[30] Above all, a constitutional polity served to restrain those special interests in the state which, if allowed to act unchecked, would destroy it; a constitution was thus the best guardian of freedom.[31] In looking back on the history of Florence, therefore, Machiavelli concluded that such greatness as she had achieved had resulted from the civil and military institutions "by which the Florentines established their liberty." [32] Conversely, he attributed all tribulations of the Republic to her constitutional defects. As he makes a Florentine patriot observe, "The laws, the statutes, the methods of government here always have been and now are managed not as required by free government but as required by the ambition of the dominant faction." [33] Instead of coordinating the various interests in the state, the Florentine

---

[27] Felix Gilbert, "The Venetian Constitution in Florentine Political Thought," *Florentine Studies*, ed. Nicolai Rubinstein (London, 1968).

[28] Cf. Nicolai Rubinstein, "Marsilius of Padua and Italian Political Thought of His Time," in *Europe in the Late Middle Ages*, pp. 50–55.

[29] *Discorsi*, Bk. I, Ch. 11.

[30] *Discorsi*, Bk. I, Ch. 34.

[31] *Discorsi* Bk. I, Ch. 58.

[32] *Istorie fiorentine*, Bk. II, Ch. 6.

[33] *Ibid.*, Bk. III, Ch. 5.

constitution had strengthened some at the expense of others; but the point was that it ought to and could have been better devised.

The ideal represented by Machiavelli is thus one of balance and pluralism. It recognizes political value in the various components of a society, and it aims to allow each to make its specific contribution to the governance of the whole. The theory of the mixed constitution, adapted from the ancients and destined for so prominent a place in later political discourse, was attractive to the republicans of the Renaissance precisely because it seemed to express this ideal. Thus Machiavelli saw clearly that leadership was essential to a republic, which must somehow provide for strong executive authority and prompt action to meet any crisis; but at the same time it had to be restrained by constitutional means from subverting the republic.[34] Only the nobility could supply qualities of valor and generosity, but its characteristic ambition had also to be kept in check. The people, finally, were devoted to liberty and equality; but since these were not the only political virtues, and could indeed degenerate through excess, this group too required control. Ideally, therefore, each of the three elements in political life would not only make a peculiar contribution to the whole but would also help to keep the other two within bounds.

It should again be apparent that the principle of order in this conception is not that of hierarchy but the idea of dynamic equilibrium. The mixed constitution thus occupies much the same place in the structure of internal politics as the balance of power in international affairs; its principle of operation is identical. The hierarchical ideal applied to internal politics, on the other hand, would seem from this point of view to spell disaster. For Machiavelli the rise of any of the three components of a well-ordered polity above the others would not only reduce their capacity to contribute those qualities which they alone could give to political life, but also by its own excesses stimulate a reaction to the opposite extreme. The result could only be that contrasting forms of government, each excessive and defective in its own way, would succeed each other in a constant and disorderly alternation. This truth had been tragically illustrated, he believed, by the history of Florence.[35]

But reality, as the Renaissance understood it, was not only particularized and ungraded; it was also fluid and subject to change. Mutability in this

[34] *Discorsi*, Bk. I, Ch. 34.
[35] *Istorie fiorentine*, Bk. II, Chs. 39–42; Bk. III, Ch. 1; Bk. IV, Ch. 1.

conception was not merely illusory and meaningless; it was a part of the true nature of things, insofar as men could apprehend them in this life. Change had to be acknowledged, reckoned on, adapted to, and provided for. Balance in external affairs and constitutional processes to solve domestic problems may thus be seen as devices to manage the omnipresent possibility of change in the realm of politics.

Change, to be sure, was not generally regarded as a pleasant dimension of reality, and the need to face it often produced a high degree of ambivalence and even anguish. The admission that all things must change suggests that the future will probably be as different from the present as the present is from the past. It means that such moments of peace and security as may fall to a man cannot last, and this awareness naturally produced anxiety. The thought of the Renaissance therefore not only exhibits the earliest efforts in the modern world to deal constructively with the nature of change in human affairs, but also exhibits correspondingly powerful impulses to escape from it into contemplation, or to transcend change by identifying the reliably constant principles that underlie the apparent flux. Conventional lamentations over the mutability of all earthly things and historical composition were thus two sides of the same coin. They may often be encountered in the same individual.

Machiavelli is, again, a notable case in point. He studied past events, he wrote history, and at times he seemed to take a kind of fierce joy in displaying the restless passions of men; but he also complained of "the malice of time" and denounced the infamy of those who proposed to accelerate change by subverting religions or republics.[36] Change, in certain moods, terrified him. Thus he brooded over the Roman collapse in the West:

> For if one will consider what a damage it might be to a republic or to a kingdom to change its prince or government, not through any external force but merely because of internal discords (by which we see that through little changes all republics and all kingdoms, even though very powerful, are overthrown), one can then easily imagine how much in those times Italy and the other Roman provinces suffered, for they not merely changed their government and their prince, but their laws, their customs, their way of living, their religion, their

[36] *Discorsi*, Bk. I, Introduction, and Ch. 10. For the hostility toward change in the generation before Machiavelli, see Felix Gilbert, "Florentine Political Assumptions in the Period of Savonarola and Soderini," *Journal of the Warburg and Courtauld Institutes*, XX (1957), 211.

speech, their dress, their names. Individually and still more together these things when merely thought about and not seen or suffered, are enough to terrify the firmest and steadiest mind.[37]

Even Guicciardini, although more resigned to the changeability of things, succumbed on occasion to the temptation to deny the reality of change. "Everything that has been in the past and is in the present will be in the future," he wrote. "But the names and appearances of things change, so that he who has not a discerning eye will not recognize them." [38] Such sentiments help to explain the attractions of Platonism during some phases of the Renaissance.

But although the Renaissance mind was sometimes afflicted with a nostalgia for permanence, it is significant chiefly for its attention to the fact of change, doubtless substantially aided by its perception of the political world as no more than a collection of particular states. Unlike a universal empire, whose permanence, being chiefly theoretical, was difficult to challenge, individual communes and principalities could be seen to alter and in some cases even to disappear; and since the fourteenth century, political instability had been widely discussed in Italy.[39] By the fifteenth century their conviction that political change was ubiquitous and inevitable stimulated the Florentines to reject with ripe scorn the boast of Venice (with which we shall be much concerned in later chapters) that she had ruled for a thousand years "without ever changing at all." [40] And by the sixteenth century the consciousness of change, aided increasingly by philological research, was extended from politics to other dimensions of human life; a genuine historical perspective now became general. Guicciardini, whatever he may have felt at other moments, acknowledged it more calmly than Machiavelli, in a statement which carries broad possibilities for social history. "If you observe well," he declared, "you will see that, from one age to another, there is a change not only in men's speech, vocabulary, dress, style of building, culture, and such things, but, what is more, even in their sense of taste. A food that was highly prized in one age will often be found far less appetizing in another." [41] And even Machiavelli was able on occasion

[37] *Istorie fiorentine*, Bk. I, Ch. 5.
[38] *Ricordi*, Ser. C, No. 76.
[39] Cf. Rubinstein, "Marsilius and Italian Political Thought," p. 59.
[40] See "Un frammento inedito della Cronaca di Benedetto Dei," ed. Giustiniano Degli Azzi, *ASI*, CX (1952), 110.
[41] *Ricordi*, Ser. C, No. 69.

to recognize that change might sometimes be positive. He admitted that the decline of Rome, however terrifying, had led to the emergence of new states, new languages, and new religions that were by no means necessarily deplorable. His beloved Florence had herself come into existence because the world had changed.[42]

But although the writing of history was a major vehicle of this growing historical consciousness, so that the popularity of history in the Italian Renaissance is significant evidence of developing interest in the world of time, historical composition should not be altogether identified with the Renaissance vision of reality. This is partly because history was traditionally a branch of rhetoric; and although the increasing prominence of professional rhetoricians facilitated the writing of history, the function of historical discourse in the rhetorical tradition was chiefly to generate admiration and abhorrence, or to persuade men to act in certain ways, rather than to provide any genuine insight into the true character of the past. Renaissance historiography was also hindered by the antihistorical tendencies in its ancient models: by their assumption of an unchanging substance underlying events, their concern with the eternal laws governing and manifested in all particular phenomena, and their preoccupation with the role of individual choice in history, which tended to divert attention from change itself to more general problems of ethics and political science.[43] And Renaissance historiography was generally inhibited by the personal reluctance of individual historians to abandon the pursuit of reliable norms in the welter of events.

It is necessary, therefore, to distinguish among the various types of historical interest in the Renaissance, some of which somewhat contradicted the Renaissance vision of reality. Among these the humanist conception of history as *magistra vitae* perhaps reflected that vision least. According to this view the past was to be utilized as a repository of moral and political instruction for individuals, especially rulers; history supplied them with examples to be imitated or avoided. Since war and other great actions provided the major occasion for such instruction, histories composed in this tradition were primarily concerned with military exploits, a preoccupation that considerably limited their scope.[44] This had been a major

---

[42] *Istorie fiorentine*, Bk. I, Ch. 5.

[43] Cf. R. G. Collingwood, *The Idea of History* (Oxford, 1946), pp. 20ff.

[44] See the discussion of this point in Myron P. Gilmore, *Humanists and Jurists: Six Studies in the Renaissance* (Cambridge, Mass., 1963), pp. 45–46.

concern of ancient historiography,[45] and the exploitation of the past in this fashion had also been sanctioned by Augustine.[46] Its effect, however, was to subordinate history to more general considerations; history, in this conception, was easily reduced to ethics or religion teaching by example. In addition, concerned primarily with practical results, it attached a particular value to style as a means of inciting to virtue and inducing abhorrence to vice; the actual structure of events was largely irrelevant to its purposes. History of this kind also tended to concentrate on antiquity—the most glorious chapter in man's past and the period most replete with heroic models—and on the importance of leadership. Man, in this view, was the subject of history rather than its object, a conception that made it generally impossible to discern the importance of large impersonal forces in human affairs.

Yet even exemplary historiography in some ways pointed toward more directly historical uses of the past. This became apparent when, as with Machiavelli, the search for examples shifted its emphasis from individual behavior to political situations that needed to be understood as a whole. When history was no longer ethics teaching by example but politics, the actual facts and their connections with each other became important: not only, furthermore, the facts about the past, which now required careful investigation and digestion, but also those pertaining to the present, to which the lessons of the past might hopefully be applied. Exemplary political history, because it aimed at comparison, thus stimulated a far closer analysis of particular situations. The reciprocal effect may be observed in Machiavelli's movement between the Roman Republic and the republics of his own experience, notably that of Florence. If, in describing the achievements of Rome, he was concerned to show "how well the institutions of that city were adapted to making it great," he was stimulated to do so by observing "how much other republics, which are different in their ways, deceive themselves."[47] The same concern also enlarged the scope of history. For although the ancients had perhaps a monopoly on heroic action and the Romans seemed particularly to have anticipated most of the problems of contemporary politics, antiquity clearly did not provide the only instructive models of political success or failure; and Machiavelli himself began also

[45] Cf. George H. Nadel, "Philosophy of History before Historicism," *History and Theory*, III (1964), 296–298.
[46] *De Civitate Dei*, Bk. V, Ch. 18.
[47] *Discorsi*, Bk. I, Ch. 36.

to scrutinize the political experience of other peoples, notably the Florentines.

Machiavelli's conviction that past experience provides useful models for the present required a new degree of attention to political actualities, and from this standpoint it supported the Renaissance vision of reality. But it also assumed the existence of regularities in all human experience which he proposed to identify and as far as possible to systematize; and this assumption was not altogether in keeping with the reservations he occasionally expressed about the possibility of generalization. But Machiavelli's inconsistency on this point was not shared by Guicciardini, who rejected the whole doctrine of imitation because he discerned no dependable uniformities in human experience. For Guicciardini, therefore, Roman practice could give no useful instruction to the present age. "How wrong it is to cite the Romans at every turn," he wrote. "For any comparison to be valid, it would be necessary to have a city with conditions like theirs, and then to govern it according to their example. In the case of a city with different qualities, the comparison is as much out of order as it would be to expect a jackass to race like a horse."[48] Every situation and problem was, in his view, unique. Hence, "to judge by example is very misleading. Unless they are similar in every respect examples are useless, since every tiny difference in the case may be a cause of great variations in the effects. And to discern these tiny differences takes a good and perspicacious eye."[49] Guicciardini had presumably reached this conclusion through his own careful scrutiny of particulars, but he had also examined these because he was already persuaded that essential reality was located in them. His own transition to history was therefore virtually complete; and he wrote history not from any great conviction of its utility either for action or for the reduction of events to a kind of system but simply because of his interest in the predicament of Italy. Venetian historiography was eventually to face the same issue.

But the historians of the Renaissance also engaged in another kind of enterprise that was closer in form, if not necessarily in spirit, to later historical composition than was the search for models of political action. This was the

---

[48] *Ricordi*, Ser. C, No. 110.

[49] *Ricordi*, Ser. C, No. 117. Cf. his *Storia d'Italia*, Bk. I, Ch. 14, in connection with the attempt of Piero de'Medici to follow the example of Lorenzo: "Ma è senza dubbio molto pericoloso il governarsi con gli esempli se non concorrono, non solo in generale ma in tutti i particolari, le medesime ragioni, se le cose non sono regolate con la medesima prudenza, e se, oltre a tutti gli altri fondamenti, non v'ha la parte sua la medesima fortuna."

rhetorical celebration of events, once more chiefly military, with the primary aim of glorifying political leaders or states, a purpose often combined with the thesis that these might be worthy of emulation. Frequently concerned with the recent exploits of generations still in power, accounts of this kind were a form of publicity with some immediate practical value. Intended, like the didactic histories of the humanists, primarily to produce an effect on the reader rather than to report the exact truth, such history was similarly preoccupied with questions of style and therefore drew heavily on ancient models. Yet this sort of history also made major contributions to the development of modern historical discourse. Since it was composed as narrative, it required attention to the continuities and relationships between discrete events, which were no longer classified according to static categories based on ethical or political values but understood as elements in a sequence, intricately connected in a network of causes and effects. In addition its concern with the perpetuation of past glories for the admiration of posterity, especially when it dealt with the exploits of republics rather than those of princes, contributed to the understanding of the political world as composed of particular communities working out their separate destinies in time.

Renaissance historiography, even in its Florentine phase, also hinted at a conception of general conditions and processes that, though intellectually apprehensible, transcend any particular decision or act, considerably limit human freedom, and substantially determine the trend of events. The conception is implicit (together with other impulses) in the idea of *fortuna*, to which Italians increasingly appealed as their helplessness to guide events became more obvious.[50] For fortune, which transformed man from the subject and actor in events into their object, only signified what was incalculable; and even Guicciardini, who so strongly emphasized the power of fortune, suggested that by closer study its precise significance might become accessible. Evidently concerned with his own role in history, he meditated on the accidental relation between a man's talents and the needs of his time. "Even if you attribute everything to prudence and virtue and discount as much as possible the power of Fortune," he wrote, "you must at least admit that it is very important to be born or to live in a time that prizes highly the virtues and qualities in which you excel. Take the example of Fabius Maximus, whose great reputation resulted from his being by nature hesitant. He found himself in a war in which impetuosity was ruinous, whereas

[50] Cf. Giuliano Procacci, "La 'fortuna' nella realtà politica e sociale del primo Cinquecento," *Belfagor*, VI (1951), 407–421.

procrastination was useful. At another time, the opposite could have been true. His times needed his qualities, and that was his fortune."[51] The effect was to shift the attention of the political analyst (or the historian) at least partly from the man to the general condition of the age. A similar tendency may be discerned in Machiavelli's attachment to the familiar political cycle, which meant not only that reform required a return to origins but also that both decline and renewal were the product of natural forces ultimately (though not altogether) beyond human control.[52] The Venetians were to face these issues too, though it must be recognized that no Renaissance historian was able to move very far in this direction.

Successful government depended, for the Renaissance observers, on accepting these political realities, themselves the reflection of what men could apprehend of the more ultimate character of reality. That the realities were often unpleasant was clear enough, but the problems of political survival (particularly after 1494) were too grave to permit the retention of such sentimental illusions as mankind had generally been tempted to indulge in. Men naturally wanted such comfort as could be provided by the notion of a cosmic order with a definite place for themselves; they craved (like Dante) a government that could supply the "peace and leisure" in which they might perfect themselves "in knowledge and wisdom";[53] they wanted to believe that good men and bad received their just deserts in this world and that the traditional virtues were consistent with an effective policy. But the facts were otherwise: there was no order beyond what men could create for themselves, no peace in which a responsible man could relax and address himself to allegedly higher things, no discernible justice in the course of events.

It became, therefore, a primary motive of Renaissance political discourse, pursued with a kind of zealous indignation, to reveal the truth on such matters. Hence Machiavelli repudiated his predecessors who had so futilely described republics that had never existed and propagated the myth that, in politics, virtue pays. On the contrary, he insisted, "there is such a difference between how men live and how they ought to live that he who abandons what is done for what ought to be done learns his destruction rather than his preservation, because any man who under all conditions insists on making it his

---

[51] *Ricordi*, Ser. C, No. 31.

[52] For Machiavelli's treatment of the political cycle, see *Discorsi*, Bk. I, Ch. 2, and *Istorie fiorentine*, Bk. V, Ch. 1. On his modification of its naturalistic implications, see Gennaro Sasso, *Niccolo Machiavelli, Storia del suo pensiero politico* (Naples, 1958), pp. 308ff.

[53] Dante, *De monarchia*, Bk. I, Ch. 4.

business to be good will surely be destroyed among so many who are not good. Hence a prince, in order to hold his position, must acquire the power to be not good, and understand when to use it and when not to use it, in accord with necessity."[54] Guicciardini found in Pope Alexander VI an apt illustration of the converse of Machiavelli's point: that wicked men by no means all come to bad ends. The Borgia pope had indeed been "a serpent who, with his immoderate ambition and abominable perfidy, giving every example of horrible cruelty, monstrous lust, and unheard of avarice, and making no distinction between sacred things and profane, had poisoned the whole world." But he had nevertheless "been exalted with the most rare and constant prosperity from early youth to the end of his life; always desiring the greatest things, he had obtained more than he desired." Alexander VI was thus "a potent example to confound the arrogance of those who, presuming to see into the profundity of divine judgments by the weakness of human vision, affirm that what happens to men, either prosperous or adverse, proceeds from their merits or demerits, as if every day one did not see many good men unjustly oppressed and many of wicked mind undeservedly exalted, or as if, interpreting this in another way, they would derogate from the justice and power of God, the breadth of which, not restricted to the brief terms of the present, will distinguish the just from the unjust in another place, with a liberal hand and eternal rewards and punishments."[55] The mixture of skepticism and piety in these remarks was to appear again in Paolo Sarpi almost a century later. The moral and political world of common experience, in this view, had no identifiable patterns of order, just as it had no neat boundaries and internal gradations. And the first condition of a successful politics was precisely the recognition of the true character of this world.

The second condition, given the uniqueness of every situation and the inevitability of change, was adaptability: the avoidance of excessively general principles and rigid views, an openness to the infinite variety of problems and conditions, and a willingness to alter policy according to circumstance. A ruler, as Machiavelli emphasized, must understand that the peculiar social character of his state determined what was politically possible; thus an aristocratic or feudalized society could only be governed as a principate, whereas an egalitarian society had to be organized as a republic; this

[54] *Il Principe*, Ch. 15.
[55] *Storia d'Italia*, Bk. VI, Ch. 4; cf. *Ricordi*, Ser. C, No. 92: "Never say 'God helped so and so because he is good, and that so and so was unsuccessful because he is evil.' For we often see that the opposite is true."

apparent commonplace points, in fact, to a whole set of attitudes.[56] Successful action also required flexibility. In foreign relations, for example, as Guicciardini observed: "It is impossible to give ambassadors instructions so detailed as to cover every circumstance; rather discretion must teach them to accommodate themselves to the end generally being pursued."[57] The same principle also meant the need, on occasion, to postpone an action that might be, in a general way, desirable—in short what men with a totally different attitude to human experience would condemn as an unprincipled opportunism. As Machiavelli remarked: "Men in their conduct, and especially in their actions, ought to think of the times and adapt themselves to them."[58] Guicciardini made the point more fully: "If you attempt certain things at the right time, they are easy to accomplish—in fact, they almost get done by themselves. If you undertake them before the time is right, not only will they fail, but they will often become impossible to accomplish even when the time would have been right. Therefore do not rush things madly, do not precipitate them; wait for them to mature, wait for the right season."[59] That ripeness is all was also to become one of the favorite sentiments of Renaissance Venice.

It should be apparent that although these prescriptions are based on a strong sense of the limitations of human intellectuality, they are by no means obscurantist. Although they reject abstract speculation, they imply the value and importance of a more concrete and immediate species of thought. As Guicciardini remarked in one of his more optimistic moments: "The more and better one thinks about things, the better they are understood and carried out."[60] There was thus a point to political study; by engaging in the right kind of reflection, it was evidently possible to add at least a cubit to one's political stature. Furthermore, a valid understanding of politics, by making issues clear and choice among genuine alternatives possible, also immeasurably increased the dignity of political acts. A statesman, in this light, was no longer limited to an obedient conformity with general principles external to the problems actually confronting him. He was now free, responsible, and creative, able to discern the possibilities in chaos and to impose order upon it—on a human rather than a cosmic scale. He might choose well or ill, but the choice was his own.

---

[56] *Discorsi*, Bk. I, Ch. 55.

[57] *Ricordi*, Ser. C, No. 2.

[58] *Discorsi*, Bk. III, Ch. 8.

[59] *Ricordi*, Ser. C, No. 78. For an interesting discussion of this general attitude in the Renaissance, see Edgar Wind, *Pagan Mysteries in the Renaissance* (New Haven, 1958), pp. 89–99.

[60] *Ricordi*, Ser. C, No. 83.

For Machiavelli, at any rate, this signified the importance of creative and energetic political leadership, a dimension of political life that would also one day interest the ruling group in Venice. Although he accepted the dominion of fortune over half of life,[61] in practice he held rulers responsible for even the most complicated predicaments. He attributed the fall of Rome to imperial neglect as well as to the barbarians who "overran the world," the Lombard conquest of Italy to bad administration, Rienzo's failure to his own timidity, and the fall of the restored Florentine Republic to the scruples of Soderini.[62] Even the catastrophe of 1494 might have been avoided if Italy "had been embanked with adequate strength and wisdom."[63]

But strength generally struck him as more important than wisdom, and with Machiavelli's conception of the political virtues we have returned once more to the Renaissance understanding of man, fitted by his nature for an active rather than a contemplative existence. He acknowledged, to be sure, that calculation should precede action,[64] but calculation was to be based on empirical realities and kept subordinate to action. And the energies applied to execute a policy, Machiavelli suggested, were a larger element in success than the policy itself; these infused the will, impelled men to action, insured the effect of almost any technique.[65] The value he attached to decisive action (so conspicuously absent among his contemporaries) meant in practice, among other things, a willingness to wage war. Machiavelli's insistence on the need to be ready to act may also be interpreted as a particular case of the demand for flexibility in a changing world. States had to be prepared for any eventuality, as Venice too would one day discover.

Since republicanism was not merely a political posture but an expression of general attitudes about the nature of man and reality, we may also expect to find some reflection of it in the religious preferences of the Renaissance. Historians have too often been disposed to assume that only the medieval perspective was genuinely "religious," and that the religious impulses which may be discerned after the fourteenth century should be interpreted largely as residues of a vision of things utterly different from that which characterized the Renaissance. I think, nevertheless, that there was a close connection between republicanism and typical religious attitudes and ecclesiastical

---

[61] *Il Principe*, Ch. 25.
[62] *Istorie fiorentine*, Bk. I, Chs. 1, 8, 31; *Discorsi*, Bk. III, Ch. 3.
[63] *Il Principe*, Ch. 25.
[64] Cf. *Discorsi*, Bk. I, Ch. 52.
[65] Cf. *Discorsi*, Bk. III, Ch. 21.

arrangements. This is why, particularly in the case of Venice, the pressures exerted by the traditional ecclesiastical authorities were peculiarly important in stimulating the republican consciousness.

The affinity between republicanism and characteristic modes of formulating Christianity is suggested by the close correspondence between the basic perceptions of Renaissance politics and Augustine's vision of the political world. It has been too little recognized that Machiavelli's picture of political reality is very nearly identical with that of Augustine, for whom the earthly city was patently neither orderly nor stable but (in an image destined to become a Renaissance cliché) "subject, like the tempestuous deep, to agitations from tempests."[66] In his *Confessions* the greatest of the Latin Fathers had also observed that "it is the nature of time to change," and Guicciardini might well have found congenial Augustine's practical conclusion from this inescapable fact: "Man's life on earth is short, and he cannot, by his own perception, see the connection between the conditions of earlier times and of other nations, which he has not experienced himself, and those of his own times, which are familiar to him. But when only one individual, one day, or one house is concerned, he can easily see what is suitable for each part of the whole and for each member of the household, and what must be done at which times and places."[67] For Augustine too secular business (and it is by no means clear that he believed this could be relinquished altogether before the end of the world) presumably could not be effectively conducted on the basis of large and comprehensive views. The central problem of Renaissance politics was precisely how to survive in the earthly city. Those who, like Machiavelli, preferred "politics" to "principle" (as the issue would be disparagingly represented by spiritual authority) were thus, perhaps, in an important sense on the side of Augustine.[68]

---

[66] *De Civitate Dei*, Bk. V, Ch. 22.
[67] Bk. III, p. 64, in the translation of R. S. Pine-Coffin (The Penguin Classics, 1961).
[68] Cf. Reinhold Niebuhr, "Augustine's Political Realism," in *Christian Realism and Political Problems* (New York, 1953), p. 133: "Augustine's conception of the radical freedom of man, derived from the biblical view, made it impossible to accept the idea of fixed forms of human behavior and of social organization, analogous to those of nature, even as he opposed the classical theory of historical cycles. Furthermore, his conception of human selfhood and of the transcendence of the self over its mind made it impossible to assume the identity of the individual reason with a universal reason, which lies at the foundation of the classical and medieval natural law theories. It is in fact something of a mystery how the Christian insights into human nature and history, expressed by Augustine, could have been subordinated to classical thought with so little sense of the conflict between them in the formulations of Thomas Aquinas."

On a certain level, therefore, the essential difference between medieval and Renaissance politics may be seen as a conflict over the implications of the Augustinian dichotomy, which, it may be suggested, was still an important influence on political discussion, even (and perhaps especially) when no one referred to it. Both positions appreciated the difference between the two cities, but they drew opposite conclusions. In accordance with its vision of reality as static, systematic, and orderly, the medieval mind could only regard the earthly city as essentially unreal; and it proposed to restore its reality by subordinating politics to spiritual direction. An awareness of the difference between heaven and earth, even when it most emphasized the sinfulness of the political realm, did not preclude their reconciliation in a visible hierarchical unity. But the Renaissance mind, with its very different perception of the problem, rejected the possibility of such accommodation. Reason of state, in this view, could not be derived from eternal reason because eternal reason, given the variety and changeability of things and the limitations of man, was inaccessible.

The correspondence between the Renaissance vision and certain tendencies in Augustine helps to explain the growing attraction, from the fourteenth century, of a Pauline-Augustinian spirituality. The Renaissance perception of reality was not merely compatible with positive religious values; to men of pious inclinations (by no means rare among the republicans of earlier centuries and almost certainly growing during the sixteenth) it required a restatement of Christianity, a shift of concern within the historic faith. The skepticism implicit in the republican vision, its emphasis on the particular and concrete, its elevation of will over intellect, meant that the content of the faith could no longer be conceived as a systematic and comprehensive body of general propositions that were objectively true and therefore required universal assent. It appeared even less probable than with humbler dimensions of reality that religious truth should be apprehensible to men in this form on earth; it could only be apprehended by each believer in his own way, as through a glass, darkly, and with divine assistance. The skepticism appropriate to man's humble posture in the universe thus substantially enhanced the importance of revelation and special acts of grace. So also did the individualism implicit in this vision. No longer viewing themselves as participants in a system of hierarchical gradations rooted in the nature of things, men not only felt a heightened sense of personal responsibility, both for what they did and what they believed, but yearned for immediate contact with the divine, with a longing which (given the limitations of man) only grace could appease.[69] And salvation itself, on the basis of the Renaissance understanding of essential human nature, had to be conceived as the transformation of a total personality through love, not as intellectual union with eternal wisdom. Thus the Christian life, like civic life, was interpreted as basically active rather than contemplative.[70]

The Renaissance also exhibited a characteristic ecclesiological bias, very different from that developed by medieval ecclesiology, which similarly corresponded to its general vision of reality. Here, however, we are immediately confronted with a paradox. The republicans of the Renaissance required the external structure of the church to conform to the fragmented structure of political reality, itself a reflection of the general nature of the universe as men could know it. But at the same time they frequently and passionately demanded a more spiritual church, a church radically different from the actual world. They appear to have wanted the church simultaneously to remain exactly as it had been and yet to be radically reformed.

The paradox will be resolved once it is recognized that they conceived of the church as existing on two levels with very different sets of requirements. In some ultimate and ideal sense the church was indeed assumed to be one and immutable. This was the church of faith, the immaculate Body of Christ, the true City of God; and its peculiar responsibilities, the preaching of the Gospel and the administration of the sacraments, were generally entrusted to the clergy under the spiritual leadership of the pope. But the essence of the church, on this, its highest, level, was precisely its spirituality. Only because it was absolutely spiritual, and only insofar as it remained spiritual, could it, in contrast to all earthly reality, claim both unity and invulnerability to change.

But to claim these attributes for it as a visible organization was to confuse the two cities. The visible world was fragmented, subject to constant alteration, and susceptible only to patterns of local organization based on pragmatic needs rather than ultimate conceptions of order; its limitations were, in visible terms, inescapable. Insofar as it required a visible body, the church had therefore to conform to these realities. The alternative to preserving the

---

[69] Cf. Heiko A. Oberman, "Some Notes on the Theology of Nominalism, with Attention to Its Relation to the Renaissance," *Harvard Theological Review*, LIII (1960), 61–62.

[70] Petrarch may be recalled in this connection: "It is better to will the good than to know the truth . . . . In this life it is impossible to know God in his fulness; piously and ardently to love him is possible," *De sui ipsius et multorum ignorantia*, trans. Hans Nachod, *The Renaissance Philosophy of Man* (Chicago, 1948), p. 105.

distinction between the spiritual and visible realms would expose the church as a spiritual entity to corruption, and the limited order of earthly society to subversion. This view of the problem may not, it is true, be altogether satisfactory from the standpoint of theology (itself traditionally concerned with the ultimate order of conceptions), but it explains a good deal in the ecclesiastical policies of the Renaissance republics, and indeed, though perhaps to a lesser degree, of other later medieval polities. Above all it explains the double meaning of religious reform in the Renaissance setting. From the standpoint of the local community reform meant an enlarged responsiveness to local needs; from the standpoint of the church universal it meant a reduction in visible organization and the promotion of spirituality. In extreme cases these tendencies aligned republicanism with the program of the heretical sects; even the staunchly pious Salutati, drawing momentarily on Joachimite doctrine, wrote of the need to destroy "the carnal church" and to replace it with "the third, spiritual church."[71] The ecclesiastical authorities, from an early point, had with some justification regarded the free communes with suspicion;[72] and this attitude persisted, as we shall see, into the seventeenth century to complicate the relations between Rome and Venice.

Whatever the theories about the nature of the church propounded at the Curia, the Italian church had long been organized, as a practical system, around particular urban communities;[73] and these tended to insist as vigorously on their ecclesiastical as on their political particularity.[74] Florence, whose conscious movement in this direction had been somewhat delayed by her long political alliance with the pope, began to display this tendency after the disintegration of the Guelph alliance.[75] The Florentine government, from the middle decades of the fourteenth century, was as aggressive as the monarchies beyond the mountains during an earlier period in protecting

[71] Marvin B. Becker, "Church and State in Florence on the Eve of the Renaissance (1343–1382)," *Speculum*, XXXVII (1962), 525. On Salutati's piety in general, see Berthold L. Ullmann, *The Humanism of Coluccio Salutati* (Padua, 1963), pp. 90–91. Ullmann speaks on p. 12 of papal charges of heresy against the Florentine Chancellor.

[72] Cf. Ullmann, *Principles of Government and Politics*, pp. 223–225, and Armando Sapori, *L'Età del Rinascita: Secoli XIII–XVI* (Milan, 1958), p. 446.

[73] On this point see, in general, the remarkable work of Robert J. Brentano, *Two Churches: England and Italy in the Thirteenth Century* (Princeton, 1968).

[74] This was, of course, the local variant of a European phenomenon. Cf. E. Delaruelle, et al., *L'Église au temps du Grand Schisme et de la crise conciliaire (1378–1449)* [*Histoire de l'Église*, vol. XIV] (Paris, 1962), II, 876–877.

[75] For what follows, see in general Peter Partner, "Florence and the Papacy, 1300–1375," in *Europe in the Late Middle Ages*, pp. 76–121.

native clergy against the financial demands of Rome and opposing the presentation of local benefices to outsiders,[76] practical gestures which had, nevertheless, broad implications for the general structure of the church. The effect of numerous piecemeal acts of resistance to central control, repeated locally in hundreds of places, was to define the visible church as a collection of loosely associated local or territorial bodies, and thus to bring it into conformity with the general structure of reality already reflected politically in the congeries of particular states. Conciliarism evidently reflected this attitude to the structure of the church universal. It aimed to coordinate, largely by constitutional principles much like those operating in politics, the various particular components of the visible church into a whole that was conceived not organically but in a way that preserved their discrete identities. Another important effect of this attitude was to strengthen the tendency, especially powerful in Italy, to conceive of the church—insofar as it was a dimension of man's experience in this world—not as a mystical body but as a species of government.[77] This tendency too was to play an important part in determining the emphasis of the papacy during the Counter Reformation.

Meanwhile the antihierarchical principle underlying the repudiation of superior authority in the larger organization of the visible church was also reflected in the treatment of the clergy within particular communities. They were denied special status, special privileges, or any ruling authority over their fellow believers. Indeed, as persons who had in some measure abandoned the visible world of affairs for spiritual things, they seemed perhaps less qualified than other men to understand it or to participate in its governance. Renaissance observers were regularly to comment on the political incapacity of popes and other prelates.[78] Meanwhile the kingdom of the clergy was literally not of this world; and insofar as they needed to inhabit the earthly city, they were obligated to obey its ordinances. In Florence a series of fourteenth-century statutes thus struck at a wide range of clerical privileges. The clergy were required to pay taxes to the civil government and brought under the jurisdiction of its courts; and other regulations restricted the power of inquisitors, rejected the demand that clerical creditors take priority over others, and even allowed appeals to the civil government from the decisions of church courts. It is also of some interest that measures of this kind were

[76] Becker, "Church and State," pp. 525–526.
[77] Cf. Delaruelle, I, ix, and 206ff.
[78] See, for example, Gilbert, *Machiavelli and Guicciardini*, pp. 123–128, on the Florentine view of Julius II.

generally the work of the more broadly based among the various Florentine governments during this turbulent century.[79]

The sustained denial of privileges and visible status to the clergy expressed too the later medieval tendency, also an underlying impulse in conciliarism, to repudiate too close an identification of the church with its clerical structure, and to conceive of it primarily as the whole body of the faithful. This position suggested the equal authority of laymen in the visible governance of the church, and clearly enhanced lay dignity. It implied that the clergy were properly servants rather than rulers over the ecclesiastical community, and perhaps also that clerical office was based not on a divine commission but on human choices and conventions. It also tended to mean in practice that the lay magistrate who governed the particular state on which the visible organization of the church was based had substantial responsibilities for ecclesiastical administration. Above all it suggested the right and duty of laymen to reform the church in time of need.

Implicit in these attitudes is a hostile judgment of the history of the medieval papacy destined for elaboration by Machiavelli and Guicciardini, and above all by Paolo Sarpi. For Fueter's assertion that the Renaissance historians ignored the "historical system of the Church" is not entirely correct.[80] The great Florentines, to employ Febvre's useful distinction,[81] were not on the whole *religious* historians, if only because they denied a history to religion itself; but they had a substantial interest in *ecclesiastical* history, which they treated with indignation precisely because it had turned out so badly, as they saw for themselves. For these historians the root of the problem lay in the fact that the visible world operates through the assertion of self-interest and the drive for power; and in condescending to act in the world the church, though declining the principle of balance which normally holds egotism in check and makes political order possible, had inevitably taken on worldly characteristics. Neither the Florentines nor Sarpi accepted the systematic arguments used to justify the ecclesiastical supervision of society; the former

[79] In addition to Becker, "Church and State," and the same author's "Florentine Politics and the Diffusion of Heresy in the Trecento: A Socio-Economic Inquiry," *Speculum*, XXXIV (1959), 60–75, see Richard C. Trexler, *Economic, Political and Religious Effects of the Papal Interdict on Florence, 1376–1378* (Frankfurt am Main, 1964), esp. p. 12.

[80] Eduard Fueter, *Histoire de l'historiographie moderne*, tr. Émile Jeanmaire (Paris, 1914), p. 14.

[81] Lucien Febvre, *Au coeur religieux du XVIe siècle* (Paris, 1957), p. 25.

ignored and the latter vigorously rejected them. Consequently the history of the papal church was exposed to exactly the same treatment that historians were increasingly according to secular states,[82] and from an early point individual popes were treated in humanist historiography to the same cool analysis given to other political leaders.[83] Machiavelli even erased the boundary between secular history and the presumably sacred events recorded in Scripture, depicting Moses (like Cyrus, Theseus, and Romulus) as a shrewd ruler who had recognized the unreliability of popular support and had therefore not scrupled to employ force.[84]

Ecclesiastical history was above all depicted, like much of secular history, as a long decline from an original perfection; on this point the later Renaissance historians were in agreement with a central conviction of the later medieval reform movement.[85] During the first centuries, they believed, the clergy had confined themselves to a spiritual ministry; and in temporal matters they had been properly obedient to secular authority. Before the arrival of the Lombards, as Machiavelli reported, the popes "obtained no other power than was given them through respect for their habits and their teaching. In secular things they obeyed the emperors and the kings, and sometimes were killed by them or employed as their servants in their administration."[86] Holiness, combined with historical accident, as Guicciardini argued, had also been a major element in the establishment of the Roman primacy:

> Pride and ambition not having yet entered into their breasts, the bishops of Rome, as successors of the apostle Peter, were recognized universally by Christians as superior to all churches and to the whole spiritual administration; and also because that city, through its ancient dignity and greatness, retained, as head of the others, the name and majesty of the empire, and because from it the Christian faith had been diffused into the greater part of Europe, and because Constantine, baptized by Silvester, had willingly recognized such authority in him and in his successors.

But the conversion of Constantine had also begun the corruption of the

[82] See, for example, Machiavelli's *Istorie fiorentine*, Bk. I, Chs. 30–36.

[83] The tendency can be traced as far back as the early fourteenth century Paduan humanist Mussato; cf. Manlio Dazzi, "Il Mussato storico," *AV*, Ser. 5, VI (1929), 361.

[84] *Il Principe*, Ch. 6.

[85] Cf. Delaruelle, II, 894–895, and 954–955, on Wyclif and Nicolas de Clamanges, to cite only two examples among many.

[86] *Istorie fiorentine*, Bk. I, Ch. 9.

church. His endowments (though not the Donation, which Machiavelli ignored and Guicciardini rejected) had first involved the church with the material and political world, and this had increased with the withdrawal of the emperors to the East. For this move had left the popes without the salutary restraints that only effective secular government could supply; and the unhappy engagement of the church with the political world had become definitive with the Frankish donations, since these were closely followed by the collapse of Frankish power. Guicciardini made the point in the passionate climax to his survey of medieval ecclesiastical history, in an extended passage expurgated from most early editions of his *Storia d'Italia*:

> On these foundations and by these means exalted to earthly power, the popes, gradually forgetting the salvation of souls and the precepts of God, and turning all their thoughts to worldly greatness, and no longer using spiritual authority except as the instrument and minister of temporal, began to seem secular princes rather than pontiffs. Their care and business began to be no longer holiness of life, no longer the increase of religion, no longer zeal and love for one's neighbor, but armies, and war against Christians, so that they made their sacrifices with bloody hands and thoughts and accumulation of treasure, with the devising of new laws, new arts, new tricks to collect money from everywhere, using spiritual arms for this purpose without respect, shamelessly selling both sacred and profane things for this end.[87]

In view of the general importance of spiritual weapons for the development of Renaissance republicanism, Guicciardini's reference to the uses of ecclesiastical censure should not go unnoticed.

Machiavelli, lacking Guicciardini's sense of religious outrage, concentrated on the political techniques of the papacy and their tragic consequences for Italy. Without sufficient armies to support their political ambitions, he reported, the popes had regularly invited barbarian hordes into the peninsula to serve their own secular purposes; and they had also regularly exploited spiritual weapons for political ends:

> The many wars that were carried on by the barbarians in Italy . . . were for the most part caused by the popes, and the many barbarians that flooded her were usually summoned by them. This sort of thing has

---

[87] *Storia d'Italia*, Bk. IV, Ch. 12. This section was deleted from early editions of the work; see V. Luciani, *Francesco Guicciardini and His European Reputation* (New York, 1936), pp. 14ff.

lasted even to our times; it has kept and now keeps Italy disunited and weak . . . . It will be evident that the popes, first with censures, and then with censures and arms at the same time, mixed with indulgences, excited fear and awe.[88]

Machiavelli typically discerned as well, in the history of papal policy, a regular alternation between the pope's need for powerful allies and his fear of powerful neighbors. As a result the papacy had been both a treacherous ally and a peculiar source of disorder, as she had been to Florence, for those states that had given the popes their most effective support. "Because the pontiffs always feared any man whose power in Italy had become great," he wrote, "even though it had grown up as a result of the church's support, and because they tried to reduce it, their policy caused the frequent disturbances and the frequent changes that took place in the country. The pontiffs fear of a powerful man caused a weak one to grow, and when he had grown strong, made them fear him, and since they feared him, made them try to bring him low."[89] This explained the unusual instability of Italy: "Thus the pontiffs, now through love for religion, now through their personal ambition, did not cease to provoke new dissensions in Italy and to stir up new wars, and when they had made a prince powerful, they repented of it and sought his ruin; thus that country which through their own weakness they could not hold, they did not permit any other to hold. Yet the princes were afraid of them because they always won, either fighting or running away."[90] Thus too the original relationship between the papacy and political authority had been overturned: "Whereas the pope had according to custom been confirmed by the emperor, the emperor, for his election, now had need of the pope; and the empire kept on losing its offices and the church gaining them. By these means continually there was an increase in her authority over the temporal princes."[91] Hierarchy was evidently replacing restraint.

And the catastrophe of 1494, though its causes were acknowledged to be complex, had been above all the consequence of this whole fatal development. Bernardo Rucellai, Machiavelli's friend, was perhaps the first to charge publicly that "the origin of the calamity" lay with Alexander VI, a pope "distinguished by crimes of every kind."[92] But Machiavelli seems to have

[88] *Istorie fiorentine*, Bk. I, Ch. 9.
[89] *Ibid.*, Bk. II, Ch. 10.
[90] *Ibid.*, Bk. I, Ch. 23.
[91] *Ibid.*, Bk. I, Ch. 11.
[92] Gilbert, *Machiavelli and Guicciardini*, p. 260.

had this view in mind in his emphasis on papal solicitation of barbarian invasion through the ages; and Guicciardini wove the charge into his account of the French invasion. The pope, he reported, had been "among the first to incite the king to concern himself with the things of Naples."[93] Thus the destruction of Italian liberty could be viewed as the consummation of the whole perverse medieval career of the Roman church.

Occasionally resentment at the political consequences of the papacy's involvement in Italian affairs found expression in hostility to the Christian faith, particularly apparent from time to time in Machiavelli. Thus Machiavelli noted that even the early church, in spite of its relative sanctity, by its establishment at the expense of other faiths, had been a source of disorder in the world. "But among all these changes," he wrote of the first centuries of the Christian era, "of not less importance was that in religion because, in fighting the established habits of the ancient faith with the miracles of the new, there sprang up very serious troubles and enmities between men." And matters had only become worse when divisions among the Christians themselves variously "afflicted the world."[94] Machiavelli also suggested a deep incompatibility between Christian values and the civic virtues he so highly esteemed, a point on which he would be echoed by Gibbon. "Our religion had glorified humble and contemplative men, rather than men of action," he wrote. "It has assigned as man's highest good humility, abnegation, and contempt for worldly things," whereas that of antiquity had identified the good "with magnanimity, bodily strength, and everything else that tends to make men very bold." The result had been to make the world "effeminate and Heaven powerless." A Christian education was specifically responsible, he declared, "for the fact that we see in the world fewer republics than there used to be of old, and that, consequently, in peoples we do not find the same love of liberty as there then was." The political consequences of Christianity evidently struck him, at least in some moods, as disastrous for what generally seemed most important.

But it should also be observed that having made the point, it apparently occurred to him that perhaps he had been describing not so much essential Christianity as a degenerate interpretation of it, the result, as he suggested, of "the worthlessness of men, who have interpreted our religion according to sloth and not according to vigor." In fact, he went on, a proper comprehension of Christianity "allows us the betterment and the defense of our

[93] *Storia d'Italia*, Bk. I, Ch. 17. Cf. also his treatment of papal tactics in Chs. 3 and 4.
[94] *Istorie fiorentine*, Bk. I, Ch. 5.

country" and "intends that we love and honor her and prepare ourselves to be such that we can defend her."[95] He did not elaborate, and it would be futile to dispute the general impression that Machiavelli's direct interest in religious matters was slight. But he appears to leave open the possibility that Christianity might be reformulated in a manner consistent with his civic values.

Elsewhere Machiavelli implied that the involvement of the church with the world had been nearly as disastrous for religion as for politics. It had destroyed the power of the church to improve mankind. Thus he noted the effect of the crusade of Boniface VIII against the Colonna: "This, though it somewhat injured them, injured the church still more, because that weapon which through love of the faith he might have used effectively, when through personal ambition it was turned against Christians, began to stop cutting."[96] The particular case illustrated a general principle: through "bad use of censures and arms" over the centuries, Machiavelli declared, the popes had "wholly lost awe, and as to fear they are in the power of others."[97] Their personal misconduct had contributed to the same result; and so Machiavelli remarked that if Giovampagolo Baglioni had taken advantage of his opportunity to murder Julius II, he "would have caused everyone to admire his courage and would have gained immortal fame, since he would have been the first to show prelates how little men are respected who live and rule as they do."[98] Thus, although Italy owed to the papacy those political divisions that had contributed so heavily to her ruin, "the first debt which we Italians owe to the church and to priests," Machiavelli declared, "is that we have become irreligious and wicked."[99]

His own view of the function of religion, as this sentiment may suggest, was primarily ethical and therefore political. Religion existed to make men better, and above all to improve them as social beings. For political reasons, therefore, he attached the highest importance to a vigorous religion. As he remarked in explaining the peculiar successes of ancient Rome: "Religion caused good laws; good laws make good fortune, and from good fortune came the happy results of the city's endeavors. And as the observance of religious teaching brings about the greatness of republics, so contempt for it brings about their ruin. Because where fear of God is lacking, it is necessary

[95] *Discorsi*, Bk. II, Ch. 2.
[96] *Istorie fiorentine*, Bk. I, Ch. 25.
[97] *Ibid.*, Bk. I, Ch. 9.
[98] *Discorsi*, Bk. I, Ch. 27. Cf. Guicciardini on the character of Innocent VIII, *Storia d'Italia*, Bk. I, Ch. 2.
[99] *Discorsi*, Bk. I, Ch. 12.

either that a kingdom fall or that it be sustained by fear of a prince which atones for what is missing in religion." But this was a poor substitute for genuine piety since, while princes die, religion endures from generation to generation.[100] There was, Machiavelli firmly asserted, "no greater indication of the ruin of a country than to see divine worship despised." It was therefore incumbent on every ruler "to preserve the foundations of the religion they hold. If they do this, it will be an easy thing for them to keep their state religious, and consequently good and united."[101] It is obvious, however, that this emphasis on the civic value of religion reinforces the conception of the church as a collection of local bodies based on the fragmented political world. It also attributes a primary role in ecclesiastical administration to the secular authorities.

Machiavelli's views were also common in Venice, and the general position may appear on first inspection to reflect a very different concern from that usually associated with Augustine. There was no necessary connection, as Machiavelli himself recognized clearly, between the utility of religion and its truth. He advised rulers that "whatever comes up in favor of religion, even though they think it false, they should accept and magnify. And so much will they do it as they are more prudent and have a better understanding of natural things."[102] We may detect here the influence of the obscure Averroist tradition which depicted the major religions as cynical fabrications of clever leaders for the purpose of holding the masses in subjection.[103] Religion, in this perspective, presents itself as a device by which a ruler, himself unbound, binds his subjects; and Machiavelli perhaps regarded traditional Catholicism in this light, as an instrument of essentially political control. So he represented the historical significance even of Saint Francis and Saint Dominic: "Having great influence with the people because of hearing confessions and preaching, they gave them to understand that it is evil to speak evil of the evil, and that it is good to live under the control [of prelates] and, if they err, to leave them to God for punishment."[104] The Venetians were to interpret the teachings of the Counter Reformation in much the same way. But recognition that religion could be exploited for political ends did not inevitably mean that it could not be true or even that its political exploitation was in all cases illegitimate. And although so utilitarian a view of the faith

[100] *Ibid.*, Bk. I, Ch. 11.
[101] *Ibid.*, Bk. I, Ch. 12.
[102] *Ibid.*, Bk. I, Ch. 12.
[103] Cf. Giorgio Spini, *Ricerche dei libertini. La teoria dell'impostura delle religioni nel Seicento italiano* (Rome, 1950), pp. 15–33. But see also Sasso, pp. 350–351.
[104] *Discorsi*, Bk. II, Ch. 1. See also his treatment of Savonarola, Bk. I, Ch. 11.

seems quite un-Augustinian, it did not prove incompatible with an Augustinian piety, as Venice would demonstrate in the later sixteenth century. It may be observed also how Machiavelli's view that civic virtue requires spiritual nourishment points to the dependence of works on faith.

It pointed in addition to the importance of religious reform, a matter which, if only because of its political significance, Machiavelli could not altogether ignore. And his recommendations for ecclesiastical reform wei, identical with his recommendations for political society, and indeed those of more directly religious reformers: a corrupt church, like a corrupted state, required rebirth. "I am speaking of mixed bodies, such as republics and religions," he wrote by way of introducing his general thesis; and the conception of a religion as properly, like a republic, a "mixed body," a composition of various and balanced elements rather than a monolithic unity, should be noticed. Of these he continued:

> I say that those changes are beneficial that take them back toward their beginnings. And therefore those are best organized and have longest life that through their institutions can often renew themselves, or that by some accident outside their organization come to such renewal. And it is clearer than light that if these bodies are not renewed they do not last. The way to renew them, as I have said, is to carry them back to their beginnings; because all the beginnings of religions and of republics and of kingdoms must possess some goodness by means of which they gain their first reputation and their first growth. Since in the process of time this goodness is corrupted, if something does not happen that takes it back to the right position, such corruption necessarily kills that body.

Machiavelli's prescription for ecclesiastical reform is thus posited, like that of his more spiritual contemporaries, on the vulnerability of the institutional church to historical alteration and decay. The church, like Florence herself, needed to "take on new life and new vigor and take up again the observance of religion and justice, which were getting corrupt." This process had to be repeated again and again; it was essential "that men who live together in any organization often examine themselves." Machiavelli's position also implied that exactly the same principles governed both ecclesiastical and secular institutions.[105]

While Machiavelli's program of religious reform concentrated on the visible aspect of the church, other reformers contemporary with him looked

[105] *Ibid.*, Bk. III, Ch. 1.

to the improvement of the church in its spiritual dimension. This is the significance of the Italian movement generally designated by the term Evangelism, which, though hardly identical with it, had profound affinities with republicanism and proved particularly attractive to pious Florentines and Venetians in the sixteenth century. Evangelism translated the Augustinian impulses of the period into a program of reform whose very vagueness, both on matters of doctrine and of institutional correction, suggests its connections with the general attitudes of the Renaissance. It neglected systematic doctrine because it shared the characteristic distrust of the Renaissance in the capacity of the human mind to grasp ultimate truths. Instead it emphasized the immediate spiritual insights and experience of the individual believer, and it conceived the Christian life as loving action in the world rather than contemplative withdrawal from it. It also attached greater weight to the operations of grace than to sacerdotal mediation; its spiritual universe was remarkably lacking in hierarchical gradations, and it was largely a movement of laity. Meanwhile its general distrust of formalism hinted at a strong bias toward a more spiritual church, and as institutional reformers the Evangelists demanded a reduction in the visible and bureaucratic functions of the church and above all in the jurisdictional power of the Curia; in its practical operations the church evidently seemed to them largely a local responsibility.[106]

Against this complex background of fundamental attitudes and values, a republic presented itself as the form of political organization best suited to man's nature, man's needs, and what man could grasp of the structure of reality itself. It provided room for all the ungraded variety that composed the actual social universe, it facilitated such tentative solutions for man's problems as seemed appropriate to the human condition, and it was flexible and open to change in accordance with man's fluctuating needs and interests.

A long series of republican spokesmen in Florence, from Salutati to Guicciardini, had therefore been at one in proclaiming the superiority of a republic to other forms of government. In accordance with the empirical bias of republicanism, however, they did so chiefly on practical rather than on

[106] See, in general, Delio Cantimori, *Eretici italiani del Cinquecento* (Florence, 1939); Eva-Marie Jung, "On the Nature of Evangelism in Sixteenth Century Italy," *Journal of the History of Ideas*, XIV (1953), 511–527; and Elisabeth G. Gleason, "Cardinal Gasparo Contarini (1483–1542) and the Beginning of Catholic Reform" (unpublished doctoral dissertation, Berkeley, 1963), esp. Ch. 1. For the prominence of Pauline-Augustinian impulses in the movement, cf. Hubert Jedin, *Papal Legate at the Council of Trent: Cardinal Seripando*, trans. Frederic C. Eckhoff (St. Louis and London, 1947), pp. 105–106.

theoretical grounds. Theory—systematic argument operating deductively—was likely to favor monarchy; but even Savonarola, whose early training had inclined him to prefer a monarch, had finally concluded that a republic worked best.[107] For Machiavelli republican government seems to have been the normal condition of political greatness. While subject to the emperor, he remarked, the Florentines "could not expand or do anything worth recording because of the power of those in authority over them."[108] But once Florence had achieved her liberty, she was able to blossom out, like Athens after her liberation from the tyrant Pisistratus and like Rome once she was rid of her kings. History itself proved the superiority of republics.

The explanation for their superiority, he argued, generally lay in the fact that in a republic the common good, which makes cities great, takes precedence over the good of individuals.[109] But this argument pointed to a deeper conviction: that "the populace is more prudent, more stable, and of sounder judgment than the prince."[110] This was true, however, largely because, in a collectivity, men of diverse abilities could pool their talents; the government of a republic could utilize the full range of human qualities and experience needed in its various and ever-changing tasks. The effectiveness of the Roman Republic had been due to its utilization of "different citizens with different opinions," and it was generally the case that "a republic has a fuller life and enjoys good fortune for a longer time than a principality, since it is better able to adapt itself to diverse circumstances, owing to the diversity found amongst its citizens, than a prince can do."[111] In addition Machiavelli considered a free and responsible citizenry superior in the keeping of agreements and more stubborn in the defense of liberty.[112] It was clear, therefore, why republics consistently proved more durable, more prosperous, and more populous than other states.[113]

Our description of the various manifestations of republicanism has thus far proceeded for the most part schematically, and the problems connected with its concrete historical development have been kept as much as possible

[107] Cf. Rudolph von Albertini, *Das florentinische Staatsbewusstsein im Übergang von der Republik zum Principat* (Bern, 1955), p. 25. On the affinities of Savonarola's movement to Florentine republicanism, see also Donald Weinstein "Savonarola, Florence, and the Millenarian Tradition," *Church History*, XXVII (1958), 291–311.

[108] *Istorie fiorentine*, Bk. II, Ch. 2.

[109] *Discorsi*, Bk. II, Ch. 2.

[110] *Ibid.*, Bk. I, Ch. 58.

[111] *Ibid.*, Bk. III, Ch. 9.

[112] *Ibid.*, Bk. I, Ch. 59; Bk. II, Ch. 2; Bk. III, Ch. 12.

[113] *Ibid.*, Bk. II, Ch. 2.

in the background. The illustrations most useful to display the nature of Florentine republicanism will nevertheless suggest, by their groupings in time, that some collective experiences proved especially stimulating to the republican consciousness. Some of these are well known, and it is unnecessary here to summarize the conclusions of Hans Baron about the impact of Milanese pressure on Florentine attitudes during the decades before and after 1400, or of the considerable group of historians, led by Federico Chabod and Felix Gilbert, who have concerned themselves with the effects of the crisis released by the French invasion of Italy. It may be observed, however, that these historians leave the impression that the decades between the two periods of crisis were an extended interval of relative quiescence between two critical moments of political and republican exaltation.

This interval has not been so thoroughly studied as other periods in Florentine history, but such tentative conclusions about it as now seem indicated will also be of some use for understanding some phases in the development of Venice.[114] During the long middle decades of the fifteenth century, the firm control of the Medici considerably altered the political and cultural climate of the Republic. The frustration of civic energies under what was a kind of disguised principate had a marked effect on political discourse, which degenerated into the construction of those ideal and utterly unrealistic schemes on the part of professional intellectuals against which Machiavelli was finally to react. And under Medici patronage the most respected minds in Florence turned once again to the construction of abstract systems of thought which, although different in detail from the scholastic systems of earlier generations, reflect much the same vision of reality. The Florentine Platonists too were contemptuous of the immediate world of appearances and change, and sought to leave it behind. The best life appeared to them to consist, once more, in the contemplation of eternal verities.[115] When the

---

[114] The following will be useful for this period: Lauro Martines, *The Social World of the Florentine Humanists, 1390–1460* (Princeton, 1963), esp. pp. 286ff.; the subtle piece of Francesco Adorno, "La crisi dell'umanesimo civile fiorentino da Alamanno Rinuccini al Machiavelli," *Rivista Critica di Storia della Filosofia*, VII (1952), 19–40; and the more general treatment by Franco Catalano, "La crisi italiana alla fine del secolo XV," *Belfagor*, XI (1956), esp. 398ff. For the academic quality of Florentine political discourse under the Medici, cf. Gilbert, *Machiavelli and Guicciardini*, pp. 89ff.

[115] Cf. the remarks of Ernst Cassirer on the significance of Florentine Neoplatonism, in *The Individual and the Cosmos in Renaissance Philosophy*, trans. Mario Domandi (Oxford, 1963), p. 61: "The retrogressive movement, the attempt at restoring Scholastic forms of thought, gradually gains more and more breadth and strength. The movement reaches its apex in the last decades of the fifteenth century, the epoch characterized by the ascendancy of the Platonic Academy in Florence."

Florentines were ready to undertake the reconstruction of the Republic, their civic consciousness had been remarkably diminished. Salutati, in what Garin has described as the heroic age of Florence,[116] had depicted her as the descendant and emulator of Rome, and a model for the imitation of other states. But by the end of the Quattrocento the leaders of the Republic had been reduced to proposing that Florence should emulate Venice—not because Venice was glorious but because she was quiet.[117]

The appearance of Machiavelli and Guicciardini not long after this indicates that Florence still had a good deal to say about politics; the Renaissance vision of reality had been only temporarily obscured and its full application to politics only temporarily delayed. But the Florentine Quattrocento will serve as a reminder that the movement from the medieval to the Renaissance vision was neither direct nor uninterrupted. We will see, in the case of Venice, a similar interruption which, indeed, was partly nourished by impulses emanating from Florence. For the first major cultural contacts between the two republics came during the height of Medici control over Florence.

Confrontations with other secular powers obviously had a large part in awakening Florence to the value of republican liberty in its various aspects. But they were, perhaps, not the only pressures moving her in this direction. If, as I have tried to suggest, republicanism was connected with a more general complex of attitudes, and developed in a kind of dialectical relationship with a contrary pattern (as demonstrably occurred in Venice), it seems at least possible that the papacy, as the primary agent in Italy of the medieval vision of reality, may have played a larger part in the development even of Florentine republicanism than has commonly been supposed.

The activities of the papacy in Italy during the fourteenth and fifteenth centuries have long been studied, however, chiefly in their most secular dimensions and as an element in the narrowly political struggles of the peninsula. The result has been almost to deprive Italy during this period, and indeed till the sack of Rome, of a genuinely ecclesiastical history intimately connected with other aspects of experience. The policies of Avignon and even of Rome have seemed only occasionally relevant to deeper Italian concerns, and so little attention has been paid to the papacy as the agent of a

[116] Eugenio Garin, "I cancellieri umanisti della Repubblica Fiorentina da Coluccio Salutati a Bartolomeo Scala," *RSI*, LXXI (1959), 199.

[117] In addition to Gilbert, *Machiavelli and Guicciardini*, pp. 9-10 *et passim*, and "Venetian Constitution," see Renzo Pecchioli, "Il 'mito' di Venezia e la crisi fiorentina intorno al 1500," *Studi storici*, III (1962), 451-492.

comprehensive vision of the world that the remarkable efflorescence of theocratic and hierocratic claims at the Curia in the later sixteenth century may seem rather anomalous. This development, however, will appear less mysterious when it has been recognized that the papacy, from its sojourn at Avignon to the sixteenth century, was neither so decadent as an institution and an ideological force, nor so irrelevant to the central movements of the Renaissance described in this chapter as has generally been assumed.

The discrepancy between *Unam sanctam*, as a last defiant protest from the dying past, and the realities of European power politics at the beginning of the fourteenth century has long been a pedagogical cliché. That it expressed defiance can hardly be denied; but if the values it represented were moribund, they took a remarkable time to die. And the extreme claims of the popes of Avignon, which were accompanied by a degree of administrative centralization beyond anything the church had known before, suggest that the pronouncements of Boniface marked the beginning of a new phase in ecclesiastical history quite as much as the end of an old one. A variety of movements, perhaps nowhere more directly than in Italy, had indeed, by the end of the thirteenth century, challenged the medieval vision of reality: the pressures of communal life, with its emphasis on flexible adjustment to concrete needs, its mobility, and its egalitarian bias; Roman law, with its general reluctance to acknowledge the hierarchical superiority of theology and the spiritual power;[118] the naturalism of Aristotle, only partly assimilated by the schools. Against this background theological, canonical, and administrative impulses toward unity and hierarchy during the fourteenth century are better understood as the vigorous reaction of an almost perennially attractive and vital ideal of order than as its last gasp.

The massive writings of Augustinus of Ancona, known as Augustinus Triumphus, are of particular value in suggesting the degree to which the assertions of the fourteenth century belonged as much to the future as to the past. For some years at Paris, and active in Padua, Naples, and his native Ancona, Augustinus composed, among other works, an enormous *Summa de potestate ecclesiastica*, completed in 1326 and dedicated to John XXII, which, as numerous manuscripts and early printings attest, was widely studied in the fourteenth and fifteenth centuries.[119] Its purpose was primarily to translate the medieval vision of reality into a comprehensive theory of

---

[118] Victor Martin, *Les origines du gallicanisme* (Paris, 1949), I, 137ff., is illuminating on this point.
[119] Wilks, pp. 4–11.

society, and in doing so Augustinus drew on and systematized the views of standard earlier writers, canonists as well as theologians. But his *Summa* is of special interest for the future because of its appeal to history. Against the growing tendency of reformers, orthodox as well as heretical, to discern a radical break in the history of the church, a shocking contrast between its earlier perfection and its present corruption,[120] Augustinus insisted on an unbreached and perfect continuity. History, in his view, was an expression of the divine will; God had decreed that the universe should be hierarchically organized under the pope; and therefore, he argued, the world had always been so organized. Accordingly he discovered in the Old Testament not only prototypes of papal governance but also the linear predecessors of the popes, and in the medieval past further examples that displayed not only how the Christian society should properly function but also that it had always functioned properly.[121] The bulk of his argument was systematic rather than, in this peculiar sense, historical; and a preference for directly systematic argument was to persist among later representatives of the hierocratic position. But Augustinus' special appeal to history to prove that what should be had always been was destined to play an important part in the ecclesiastical thought of later centuries. Its assumption of an underlying historical truth that must take precedence over the lesser truths derived from specific research was eventually to confront the very different historicism of the Renaissance.

The Schism and the challenge from conciliarism required some diminution of the ideological and bureaucratic pressures that had characterized the fourteenth century; and until about the middle of the fifteenth the Curia, though withdrawing none of its claims, exercised considerable restraint.[122] Signs of change were apparent, however, as soon as conciliarism no longer posed a practical danger. A steady stream of aggressive treatises, of which Torquemada's *Summa de ecclesia* was typical, proclaimed the succession of the pope to the legislative authority of Moses and the universal monarchy of Christ. Meanwhile Traversari's Latin translation of Pseudo-Dionysius (1431) made the world views underlying these hierocratic claims more widely available and emphasized their apparently primitive sanction.[123]

[120] Cf. Delaruelle, II, 521–522.
[121] Wilks, pp. 538–547.
[122] Cf. Delaruelle, I, vi; and Partner, p. 117.
[123] L. D. Ettlinger, *The Sistine Chapel before Michelangelo: Religious Imagery and Papal Primacy* (Oxford, 1965), esp. pp. 110ff., is particularly useful on this development. See also Delaruelle, II, 518–519, and Hubert Jedin, *Geschichte des Konzils von Trient*, 2nd ed. (Freiburg, 1951), I, 19–23.

Pius II's resurrection of the crusade ideal, together with the appearance of his bull *Execrabilis* in 1460, may be taken as marking the start of a new hierocratic offensive under the official direction of the pope. And it is also hardly a coincidence (and of particular interest from our standpoint) that this pope displayed a singular hostility to republics. An aristocratic enemy of the commune of his native Siena,[124] he was also convinced that (however they disguised their true sentiments) the great republics of Florence and Venice were hostile to his pontificate.[125] General attitudes, destined for long life in Rome, underlay his contempt for Florence, and his bitter denunciations of Venice for meddling in the affairs of the papal state. He attacked the Florentines "as traders and a sordid populace who can be persuaded to nothing noble";[126] and the Venetians, he wrote, had behaved "with the good faith characteristic of barbarians or after the manner of traders whose nature it is to weigh everything by utility paying no attention to honor." "But what," he asked rhetorically, "do fish care about law?" The answer was clear:

> As among brute beasts aquatic creatures have the least intelligence, so among human beings the Venetians are the least just and the least capable of humanity and naturally, for they live on the sea and pass their lives in the water; they use ships instead of horses; they are not so much companions of men as of fish and comrades of marine monsters. They please only themselves and while they talk they listen to and admire themselves. . . . They are hypocrites. They wish to appear Christians before the world but in reality they never think of God and, except for the state, which they regard as a deity, they hold nothing sacred, nothing holy. To a Venetian that is just which is for the good of the state; that is pious which increases the empire. . . . They are allowed to do anything that will bring them to supreme power. All law and right may be violated for the sake of power.

And the pope foresaw the decline and disappearance of Venice as a judgment on her impiety. We may discern here the enduring bias of churchmen against mercantile societies, to which was attributed a peculiar inclination to follow particular interests at the expense of the *universitas*, and already the charge of elevating politics above principle that was to be repeated for centuries; Machiavelli was by no means its first target. Pius II also

---

[124] Cf. *The Commentaries of Pius II*, trans. Florence A. Gragg (Northampton, 1937–1957) [Smith College Studies in History, XXII, XXV, XXX, XXXV, XLIII], Bk. I, 57.
[125] *Ibid.* Bk. I, 106–107.
[126] *Ibid.* Bk. XII, 829.

manifests the conviction, developed in the previous century by Augustinus Triumphus, that the course of history must ultimately illustrate the moral order decreed by God. This too we shall encounter again.[127]

It has also been recently suggested that the Sistine frescoes of Sixtus IV were intended to give pictorial expression to the revived hierocratic ideal.[128] They present, on opposite walls, scenes from the lives of Moses and Christ which illustrate the various dimensions of their institutional authority, as rulers, legislators, and priests, and at the same time emphasize continuities between the powers of the pope and God's first ordinances for the governance of mankind. From this standpoint it is apparent not only that the church (to cite the formula of Nicholas the Great) was the world, but also that its governance was ultimately identical with that of the world. As Domenico de' Domenichi declared in a typical pronouncement: "Papal power stems from God alone, but all legitimate temporal power depends on papal power."[129] Against this tradition of thought, therefore, it seems difficult to continue to view the popes of the later Renaissance as hardly more than local Italian princes. Not only did their own ambitions have a wider resonance (as the Venetians were perhaps the first fully to recognize), but they helped to transmit the articulated papalist tradition of earlier centuries to the Counter Reformation.

Nor were these claims so empty of practical effect as has generally been supposed. Occasional attempts were made to apply them to the states of Renaissance Italy by means of ecclesiastical censures that appeared sufficiently ominous to play some part in the maturation of republican values and attitudes. Excommunication and interdict, the practical devices by which ecclesiastical authority sought to maintain its direction of a unified and hierarchically organized society, made a considerable impact on the political imaginations of Italian republicans, as the references to spiritual censure by Machiavelli and Guicciardini clearly reveal. These weapons of the church also stimulated a general hostility to its interference in politics, encouraged radical ecclesiological impulses, and assisted in the development of a political and historical perspective on the church. The effects may be seen most clearly in sixteenth- and seventeenth-century Venice, but Florence also

[127] *Ibid.*, Bk. XI, 743–746. For charges that the Venetians were less than cooperative in his crusade projects, see also p. 776. For the deep roots of anti-Venetian sentiment at the Curia see Gina Fasoli, "Nascita di un mito," in *Studi storici in onore di Gioacchino Volpe* (Florence, 1958), I, 462–463.

[128] This is Ettlinger's general thesis in the work cited above.

[129] Quoted by Ettlinger, p. 129.

experienced them in several earlier encounters that contributed significantly to her political education.

Florence was frequently the victim of ecclesiastical censure. Her contiguity to the states of the church, especially after the consolidation of papal control by Cardinal Albornoz, brought numerous clashes of interest with the papacy; and Florence was under interdict during much of the first decade of the fourteenth century, again in 1331, in 1346–1347, in 1355, in 1361–1362, and most seriously during the period of the *Otto Santi* when, in the words of Machiavelli, her rulers "had little regard for the censures, stripped the churches of their property, and forced the clergy to celebrate the offices. So much higher did those citizens then value their city than their souls! They proved to the church that just as earlier, being her friends, they had defended her, so, being her enemies, they could distress her."[130] The friction between Rome and Florence then declined temporarily as the papacy faced more formidable enemies, but it revived in the latter part of the fifteenth century during the period when papal claims were being urgently renewed. Under Lorenzo the Magnificent Florence found herself at war with the pope three times in seven years, was again under an interdict, and saw her ruler excommunicated.[131] And both Alexander VI and Julius II, during a period when the fate of the Republic was already sufficiently precarious, also threatened her with censure.

It took some time for these unpleasant confrontations to produce any general effect on the Florentines. Villani, for example, appears to have accepted the legitimacy of ecclesiastical censure without serious question.[132] But a very different attitude had clearly emerged by 1376. Although on this occasion Florence for some time complied with the interdict (as Machiavelli failed to recognize), she chose eventually to defy the pope.[133] On the ground that the interdict had merely a political motive, the government, after fifteen months, reinstated the banned religious services. This argument is of considerable interest. It suggests not only the right of laymen to evaluate the tactics of ecclesiastical authority, but also a growing sense of the radical distinction between the two cities and the concerns proper to each. And

---

[130] *Istorie fiorentine*, Bk. III, Ch. 7.

[131] These events are well covered in Warman Welliver, *L'impero fiorentino* (Florence, 1957).

[132] Cf. Giovanni Villani, *Cronica*, Bk. VIII, Ch. 69, which seems to acknowledge the right of the ecclesiastical authorities to impose censure, and records the disasters falling on Florence as a result of the interdict of 1304.

[133] For what follows see, in general, Trexler, *Papal Interdict on Florence*.

Florence, in her moment of defiance, was swept by a wave of religious exaltation. She represented herself as the champion of true piety against the corruptions of the papal church, and her spokesmen questioned (as Venice would do much later) the very meaning of ecclesiastical censure. The Vallombrosian hermit Giovanni Dalle Celle wrote solemnly: "Excommunications are made for those who sin mortally, and it is certain that no innocent person can be excommunicated. If he were excommunicated, it would be worth nothing to God, who only confirms the sentences of pastors who bind justly and with legitimate cause." The influential Augustinian friar Luigi Marsili, who took much the same position, attacked the censures as an attempt by the pope to usurp secular power, and represented the Florentines as champions of a purified church.[134] Meanwhile the practical effect of the interdict was very different from what the papacy had intended. When religious services were not available from the clergy, the Florentines took care of their spiritual needs in other ways and discovered that intermediaries were less necessary than they had supposed; and the hostility of the pope reinforced their impression that their churches properly belonged to themselves. At the same time the other republics of Italy, as well as most of the monarchies of western Europe, generally disregarded the interdiction of Florence, some at the cost of censures imposed on themselves. The Florentine attitude to ecclesiastical actions of this kind was by no means unique.

In the fourteenth century an interdict could doubtless still produce a significant degree of anxiety; the medieval conception of reality retained a considerable hold over the consciences of men. But by the later fifteenth and early sixteenth centuries the spiritual impact of ecclesiastical censure had undergone a .significant decline, and the rulers of Florence appraised an interdict primarily from the standpoint of its impact on commerce.[135] Yet even Machiavelli, whose religious apprehension was presumably negligible, displayed a nervous concern on the point and a touch of indignation (as though the issue was not quite dead) at the intrusion of such irrelevancies into politics. He felt compelled to record his contempt for them, not only in connection with the *Otto Santi* but on other occasions as well. Thus the death of Frederick Barbarossa provided him with an opportunity to suggest his scorn: "And so the waters gave more aid to the Mohammedans than did the excommunications to the Christians, because the latter bridled his pride

---

[134] Garin, "Cancellieri," pp. 193–194; Gene A. Brucker, *Florentine Politics and Society, 1343–1378* (Princeton, 1962), pp. 301–303.
[135] Cf. Gilbert, *Machiavelli and Guicciardini*, p. 31.

and the former destroyed it."[136] And the humiliation of Henry I of England by a papal censure provided him with a measure of the progress of politics: "Thus so great a king subjected himself to that judgment which today a private citizen would be ashamed to submit to."[137]

By the third decade of the sixteenth century when Machiavelli was setting down these sentiments, the sense his words convey of the dignity of the lay estate, its proper independence from ecclesiastical meddling, and the outrageous irrationality of spiritual censure had apparently been firmly established. Yet less than a decade earlier Julius II had imposed an interdict on Venice that had apparently achieved devastating results. The century ahead was to prove that the pretensions of the church to supervise the political order, and the vision of reality on which they were based, possessed more vigor than Machiavelli was prepared to recognize.

[136] *Istorie fiorentine*, Bk. I, Ch. 19; cf. Bk II, Ch. 10, where he insists on treating a censure as no more than an act of vindictive passion.
[137] *Ibid.*, Bk. I, Ch. 19.

·II·

The Venetian Political Tradition

JACOB Burckhardt provided a classic view of Renaissance Venice, which he contrasted sharply with Florence. He depicted Florence as "the city of incessant movement, which has left us a record of the thoughts and aspirations of each and all." From a political standpoint, Florence was all volatility and articulateness. But Venice seemed very different: she was "the city of apparent stagnation and of political silence." Since Burckhardt's vision of Venice will be the point of departure (in both senses) for much in the present book, it may be useful to observe that he chose his language carefully. The "stagnation" of Venice, he implied, was only apparent; and he did not mean that Venice had no political conceptions, but only that she failed to give them expression. His conclusion, nevertheless, seems categorical: "No contrast can be imagined stronger than that which is offered us by these two, and neither can be compared to anything else which the world has hitherto produced."[1]

Yet contrast is only possible between entities in fundamental respects similar, and it is equally undeniable that Florence and Venice were in some ways alike. Even Burckhardt recognized this by treating them jointly in a single chapter which set them both apart from the princely states of Italy. Both were urban republics, both were largely controlled by businessmen, and both managed to dominate a considerable hinterland. Both, in addition, nourished a brilliant literary and artistic culture that has conventionally been considered "Renaissance." Therefore, the juxtaposition of Florence and Venice yields a somewhat equivocal impression: they were at once different and alike.

The present chapter is chiefly concerned with ways in which they appeared different, though I too am trying to choose words carefully and mean to suggest that the long absence of a sophisticated tradition of formal political discourse in Venice may obscure deeper similarities. On this point, nevertheless, Burckhardt seems to me still basically correct, even though his description of Quattrocento Venice certainly needs some modification and must

---

[1] *Die Kultur der Renaissance in Italien: Ein Versuch*, 10th ed., ed. Ludwig Geiger (Leipzig, 1908), I, 65.

always be taken not in an absolute sense but as one term of a comparison. The impression that Venice on the whole lacked spokesmen comparable to Salutati and Bruni, or to Savonarola and Machiavelli, depends on something more profound than the backwardness of our scholarship. It is a consequence of the fact that Venice was long spared such political crises as troubled Florence during the fourteenth and fifteenth centuries; lacking comparable stimuli, Venetian political expression was also relatively retarded. This chapter, therefore, which deals with the roots and the perennial elements in Venetian republicanism, will depend less on the testimony of theorists than on the broad outlines of Venetian policy, the structure and spirit of Venetian institutions, and the political values conveyed from generation to generation through various myths about the Venetian past.

But before the end of the fifteenth century conditions had begun to change, and for the subsequent period Burckhardt's vision is no longer adequate. The traditional values and institutions of Venice were exposed to increasing pressure from many directions, and her very existence seemed periodically in danger. She then began to articulate a set of political beliefs in which the central elements of Renaissance republicanism, earlier worked out by her Florentine predecessors, found perhaps their most mature form under somewhat different circumstances. Venice, therefore, as a self-conscious republic of the Renaissance type, was primarily a development of the sixteenth century, with a great climax as late as the first quarter of the seventeenth. Eventually this development was to produce a series of distinguished individual spokesmen whose reflections on politics, history, and religion would be cherished, along with the works of the great Florentines, by a large body of readers throughout Europe. And, as in Florence, political articulation was accompanied by a remarkable flowering of literary and artistic culture. Thus the difference between Florence and Venice, on a point now generally considered crucial to the meaning of the Renaissance in Italy, was less one of kind than of degree and time.

Both the actual peculiarities of Venetian history and certain fundamental assumptions of Venetian politics depended largely on geography. Isolated from the mainland and easily accessible only by sea, Venice had long needed no protection from major powers that might have required in return some surrender of her independence. It was true (contrary to one of her most cherished beliefs) that Venice had been originally a part of the Byzantine imperial system, and she had also been briefly incorporated into the empire of

Charlemagne. But imperial control over Venetian affairs had never amounted to much in practice, and by the second half of the ninth century phrases acknowledging some degree of subordination were already disappearing from the formulas employed by the rulers of the small Venetian state.[2] Thus Venice, from a remarkably early point in her history, was free in the first meaning of Renaissance liberty. Recognizing no political superior, she had been a discrete state of the Renaissance type long before the age of the Renaissance. She had also managed to remain remarkably aloof from the political struggles between medieval popes and emperors, and she took no interest in the claims on either side to a universal authority seemingly irrelevant to her own existence. When the emperor Henry VII descended into Italy, Venice, unlike most other Italian states, refused to swear fidelity to him. As a contemporary wryly observed, "I know no good reason for it, unless it be that they are of the fifth essence."[3] Venice, almost from the beginning, occupied a very special position in the political universe.

The geographical peculiarity of Venice and the various advantages it entailed provide one of the constant themes of Venetian political expression. The lonely islands in the lagoons, somehow detached from imperial jurisdiction as well as from the mainland, had been settled, as Venetians would repeat for centuries, by free men who in the troubles of the fifth century had valued liberty above all other earthly goods. The conception already figured prominently in the early eleventh-century chronicle bearing the name of Giovanni Diacono,[4] and it emerged full-blown in the humanist historiography of fifteenth-century Venice. Bernardo Giustiniani's *De origine urbis Venetiarum* particularly stressed the original and perpetual liberty of Venice, denying vigorously that she had ever been subject to the empire of either East or West, or to any other mainland power. Venice, he argued, owed her political existence solely to the virtuous exertions of men who had freely settled territory over which all imperial rights had been allowed to lapse. The islands had been there for anyone to take. "For where are the law and the right, the empire and the jurisdiction," he makes an early Venetian leader ask, "if not in this company and gathering of men who have established a covenant and laws by a mutual oath? If the jurisdiction were only in

---

[2] Giuseppe Maranini, *La costituzione di Venezia dalle origini alla serrata del maggior consiglio* (Venice, 1927), pp. 28ff.; Roberto Cessi, *Le origini del ducato veneziano* (Naples, 1951), pp. 1–6, 26ff.

[3] Nicolò da Butrinto, as quoted by Fasoli, "Nascita di un mito," p. 470.

[4] Ibid., pp. 453ff., for the general importance of this chronicle. See also Franco Gaeta, "Alcune considerazioni sul mito di Venezia," *Bibliothèque d'Humanisme et Renaissance*, XXIII (1961), 60–61.

this or that place, surely it would have been there since eternity, nor would it ever change. If indeed the earth is unmoving and eternal, everything else is now subject to fortune. Empires are daily changed and transferred." But although the argument admits that change rules the world, it finally points to the long continuity of Venetian freedom, which was apparently more stable than any imperial authority. Above all it is intended to make the point that the liberty of Venice was not, like that of other Italian states, a novelty of recent institution. It was intimately connected with her origins.[5]

The place Venice assigned to herself in the political world was eloquently expressed in the myth that the Republic had arranged peace in 1177 between Frederick Barbarossa and Pope Alexander III. According to a story made familiar by generations of Venetian chroniclers, historians, and painters, the pope, fleeing in disguise from the emperor, had taken refuge in Venice, where he was recognized and promised succor by the doge. After a Venetian embassy had failed to reconcile the two antagonists, Venice pledged full support to the pope and proceeded to win a major naval victory over an armada commanded by the emperor's son. Taken prisoner by the Venetians and dispatched to his father as an envoy, the young prince at last persuaded the emperor to make peace. The doge then conveyed the pope through Ancona to Rome in a great triumphal procession. Meanwhile, at various times during these events, the grateful pope had bestowed a series of symbolic gifts on the doge: a candle, a sword, the right to seal documents with lead, the ring for the wedding of Venice with the sea, banners, and silver trumpets. Most significant of all was the pope's insistence, over the objections of the emperor as the two universal authorities sat beneath their umbrellas, that a third umbrella be produced for the doge so that he might sit with them as equals. The pope, the emperor, and the prince of Venice thus emerged as the three parallel potentates of Christendom.

The suggestion in this account that Venice owed to the pope the traditional insignia of her sovereignty, and even her dominion over the sea, may seem to give the story a somewhat equivocal ring. But in practice its function was clear. The tale was taken as a demonstration that the piety of Venice, her rule of the Adriatic, and her liberty were together recognized on Venetian

---

[5] For Giustiniani I have been guided throughout this chapter by the 1957 Radcliffe doctoral dissertation of Patricia Hochschild, "Bernardo Giustiniani: A Venetian of the Quattrocento." On this point see pp. 373-374, 395-398, 423-425. The quotation is from Book VI, Col. 67, in the edition of J. G. Graevius, *Thesaurus antiquitatum et historiarum Italiae* (Leyden, 1722), V. Cf. Marcantonio Sabellico, *Le historie vinitiane*, trans. Lodovico Dolce (Venice, 1554), sig. B2ʳ. For Machiavelli on the freedom of Venice, see *Istorie fiorentine*, Bk. I, Ch. 29.

terms by both universal powers. Beyond this the story represented Venice as patron of the pope and peacemaker for the world. Far from being a subordinate member in the hierarchical structure of the Christian Republic, Venice in some sense appeared to stand outside and above it.[6]

Already circulating in earlier chronicles, the legend was widely disseminated in the fourteenth century, partly through the chronicle of Andrea Dandolo and other writings,[7] partly by the first decorative scheme for the Hall of the Great Council, planned as early as 1319, executed after 1365, and generally retained in the later decorations of this huge room.[8] The Venetian victory over the imperial fleet was also celebrated annually, in connection with the marriage to the sea, on the Feast of the Ascension, with the usual Venetian pageantry.[9] Thus the story and the radical political claims it served to dramatize were held constantly before the minds of the Venetian patriciate. Venetian historians continued to retell the legend, and Venetian publicists regularly referred to it as proof of the Republic's status in the world.[10]

The long and jealous independence of Venice also gave a special character to Venetian law. Just as she had rejected absorption into the medieval empire, so she rejected the application of imperial law. As Paolo Sarpi maintained early in the seventeenth century, Venice had never been subject to any emperor, not even to Justinian. She had been ruled from her earliest beginnings only by local custom.[11] For Venetians, this had the virtues of flexibility and accommodation to local needs, which were evidently lacking in Roman law with its universal sanctions and applicability.[12] Venice had

---

[6] For the myth in general, see Fasoli, pp. 464–467, 473ff.; and Franz Wickhoff, "Der Saal des Grossen Rats zu Venedig," *Repertorium für Kunstwissenschaft*, VI (1893), 10–13.

[7] For various literary accounts, see Antonio Viscardi, "Lingua e letteratura," in *La civiltà veneziana del Trecento* (Florence, 1956), pp. 199–200. A fourteenth century version is printed by D. Urbani de Gheltof, "Leggenda veneziana di Alessandro III," *AV*, Ser. I, XIII, Pt. 2 (1877), 365–369.

[8] Wickhoff, pp. 2–3, 8ff. 20ff.

[9] Cf. Iason de Nores, *Panegirico in laude della Serenissima Republica di Venetia* (Padua, 1590), an oration composed for this occasion.

[10] For example Sabellico, sigs. F4ʳ–F6ʳ, though here presented with a certain scepticism; and Pietro Marcello, *De vita, moribus, et rebus gestis omnium ducum venetorum* (Venice, 1574), leaves 44–46 for the events of 1277. This work was first published in 1502.

[11] Letter to Jacques Leschassier, Jul. 8, 1608, in *Lettere ai Gallicani*, ed. Boris Ulianich (Wiesbaden, 1961), p. 18. Hereafter cited as Ulianich.

[12] Cf. Agostino Valier, *Dell'utilità che si puo ritrarre dalle cose operate dai Veneziani libri XIV* (Padua, 1787), p. 139: "Andrea Dandolo fu il primo che unì in volumi le leggi Venete, chiamate Statuti; le quali non sono già contrarie al gius Romano, ma le più accomodate ai Veneti costumi, e che sembrano al dritto naturale piu uniformi."

accordingly been indifferent to the twelfth-century revival of Roman law, and medieval Venetian jurists never cited Roman legal texts. The acquisition of mainland possessions where Roman law was in force eventually required Venetian administrators to familiarize themselves with it;[13] but Venice herself, according to the formula of a respected jurist, was always held to be *nullis legibus caesareis subiecta, propriisque legibus orta*.[14]

The security and independence afforded by Venetian isolation from the mainland probably long affected the attitudes of Venice to other states; so, at any rate, it was widely believed elsewhere. Venice, as Burckhardt put it a century ago, could ignore the immediate turbulence of the peninsula and decide important issues on their long-range merits rather than under pressure of emergency.[15] Guicciardini noted the conviction of "certain of the oldest and most reputable" members of the Venetian Senate that Venice enjoyed a particular advantage in her ability "to wait for the opportunity of times and the maturity of occasions."[16] From an early point, therefore, the conduct of Venetian affairs seemed to reveal a remarkable continuity based on settled principles and habits of rational calculation. In this respect too Venice hardly needed to become a "Renaissance state" during the Renaissance; she had behaved like one for centuries. In addition, the isolation of Venice relieved her of the need to cooperate with other powers, and she retained a deep antipathy to entangling alliances. But her coldly self-centered policies and her apparent disdain for the interests of other states were to contribute a good deal to the almost universal and nearly fatal detestation she had aroused by the early sixteenth century.

The location of Venice also contributed to the homogeneity of her population and hence to internal peace.[17] Cut off from the landed nobility of the mainland, a group elsewhere so destructive of domestic order, and able to dispense with a native military class, her easy access to the sea could be exploited jointly by all elements in Venetian society. Eventually the necessity to develop and maintain an elaborate system of canals, dikes, drainage projects, and other hydraulic works also required of the entire Venetian populace

---

[13] Carlo Guido Mor, "Problemi organizzativi e politica veneziana nei riguardi dei nuovi acquisti di terraferma," in *Umanesimo europeo e umanesimo veneziano* (Venice, 1963), pp. 5–6.

[14] On this point in general, Pier Silverio Leicht, "Lo stato veneziano ed il diritto comune," in *Miscellanea in onore di R. Cessi* (Rome, 1958), I, 203–211.

[15] I, 69.

[16] *Storia d'Italia*, Bk. III, Ch. 4.

[17] Cf. Machiavelli, *Discorsi*, Bk. I, Ch. 6.

a high degree of cooperation and a sophisticated set of administrative agencies dedicated to purposes all Venetians could respect and support and from whose activities all profited.[18] Thus, along with its other benefits, geography provided the social foundations for a unity based on common interests that goes far to account for the remarkable stability and continuity in Venetian political history. Venice during the Middle Ages experienced relatively few of those revolutionary moments that so frequently punctuated the histories of other Italian states, effecting radical changes in institutions and ruling groups, putting an end to one phase of development and starting another. There was development in the Venetian constitution, but its pattern and direction were consistent; and eventually, as though a natural goal had been reached, it largely ceased.

This development was, of course, toward an aristocratic republic. But it is important to recognize a major difference between the patriciate of Venice and other European aristocracies. As Machiavelli observed: "The gentlemen in that republic are so rather in name than in fact; they do not have great incomes from landed possessions, but their great riches are based on trade and movable property; moreover none of them holds castles or has any jurisdiction over men. Thus that name of gentleman among them is a name of dignity and reputation, without being founded on any of those things in other cities signified by the word *gentleman*."[19] Like Venice herself, the Venetian nobles recognized no superior, nor was there any legal hierarchy of status among them. Every noble was equal, and the members of the Great Council sat where they pleased, in no special order, at its meetings.[20] The collective status of the Venetian aristocracy was based on a political authority exercised in common, and distinctions among them were the product only of disparities in ability and wealth.

Nobility in Venice was thus the special mode employed by Venetian society to define active citizenship, a condition everywhere restricted in one fashion or another. When Paolo Paruta tried at the end of the sixteenth century to describe the Venetian nobility, he gave first place to this fact. "Among the Venetians," he declared, "those men are called nobles who

---

[18] Giovanni Botero also suggested that the canals of Venice contributed to internal order by impeding quick assemblage of the populace (*Della ragion di Stato*, Bk. V, Ch. 7).

[19] *Discorsi*, Bk. I, Ch. 55.

[20] Cf. A. Sagredo, "Leggi venete intorno agli ecclesiastici sino al secolo XVIII," *ASI*, Ser. 3, II (1865), 97.

participate in the governance of the Republic, that is, those who have authority to elect and who can be elected to public magistracies."[21] The Venetian aristocracy existed to serve the state, in governorships, embassies, major administrative positions, or naval commands. Europeans elsewhere regarded its sense of responsibility for the general welfare as a major cause for the relative tranquillity of the Venetian populace.[22]

Equally striking, as Machiavelli noticed, was the peculiar economic base of the Venetian nobility. Whatever its origins, the Venetian ruling group was soon committed to trade; and ancient lineage steadily gave way to wealth as a major source of political influence.[23] Some degree of wealth, though not necessarily enormous riches, was essential in Venice for a significant political career. Wealth was needed first for the extensive education prerequisite to holding the most important offices in the government, and it was even more necessary to hold the coveted ambassadorships and governorships in which expenses exceeded income and which were often essential to influence at home.[24] Thus by the fourteenth century the oldest Venetian families which claimed descent from the earliest settlers had virtually lost access to the office of doge, displaced by families with a more tangible claim to power.[25] Continuing respect for wealth also imparted a measure of mobility to the Venetian aristocracy. Long after the freezing of the Great Council, Venetian nobles regularly took lower-class wives to recoup their fortunes, and the sons of such marriages, unless they involved girls from the most menial class, entered the Great Council in the usual way and qualified for the highest positions in the state. It was long theoretically possible for the direct descendant of a poor fisherman to become doge of Venice.[26]

The Venetian nobility was also relatively numerous. During the sixteenth

[21] Paolo Paruta, *Historia vinetiana* (Venice, 1703), p. 488. This work was composed after 1580.

[22] For example Giovanni Botero, *Relazioni universali*, in the Venetian edition of 1640, p. 799.

[23] Cf. Margarete Merores, "Der venezianische Adel," *Vierteljahrschrift für Sozial- und Wirtschaftsgeschichte*, XIX (1926), 195–196.

[24] James Cushman Davis, *The Decline of the Venetian Nobility as a Ruling Class* (Baltimore, 1962), pp. 28–29.

[25] For the distinction between old (*longhi*) and new (*curti*) families, see S. Romanin, *Storia documentata di Venezia* (Venice, 1853–1869), IV, 420. Cf. Antonio Bonardi, "Venezia città libera dell'Impero nell'immaginazione di Massimiliano I d'Asburgo," *Atti e Memorie della R. Accademia di Scienze, Lettere ed Arti in Padova*, N.S., XXXI (1915), 134, 143–147, on this division in Hapsburg calculations.

[26] Giuseppe Maranini, *La costituzione di Venezia dopo la serrata del Maggior Consiglio* (Venice, 1931), pp. 71–77.

century, when the population of Venice was expanding rapidly, it amounted to somewhere between 4 and 5 percent of the whole, and earlier probably a good deal more.[27] In fact the Venetian patriciate was probably no smaller in proportion to the total population of the city than the politically active group in Florence. During the most democratic of the Florentine constitutional experiments, the Great Council included only three thousand from a total population of about a hundred thousand.[28]

The obvious difference between the nobility of Venice and the political class in other republics was its fixed membership. But the "closing" of the Great Council in 1297 was not the seizure of power by an ambitious oligarchy in a previously democratic commune. This action actually had the effect of enlarging the Venetian ruling class, and it was less palatable to aristocratic elements in the Republic than to the lower orders.[29] The exclusiveness of the patriciate was also somewhat mitigated by the existence of the rather more numerous body of *cittadini originari*, to which lower class Venetians and even foreigners might be admitted. This special category of citizens supplied essential personnel for the routine tasks of government, residents at all but the most important foreign courts, and even the chancellor, whose office carried with it heavy political responsibilities. Although these men did not share in legislative authority, they provided continuity in agencies of government whose patrician heads were frequently rotated, and they often had considerable influence in the formulation of policy. As in Florence humanistic attainments were prized among the citizen-secretaries who came from this group, and they participated on equal terms in the cultural life of the patriciate.[30] In all, therefore, about 10 percent of the Venetian population was active in public life.

Sovereignty in Venice resided in the Great Council. This had been so *de facto* since the thirteenth century and *de iure* since 1423, when the Great

[27] Daniele Beltrami, "Lineamenti di storia della popolazione di Venezia dal Cinquecento al Settecento," *Storia dell'economica italiana*, I (Turin, 1959), 517. The population of the city before the Black Death was about 100,000; and, having recovered rapidly from that catastrophe, it was approaching 150,000 by the end of the fifteenth century (Gino Luzzato, *Storia economica di Venezia dal XI al XVI secolo* [Venice, 1961], pp. 88–89, 231).

[28] Felix Gilbert, *Machiavelli and Guicciardini: Politics and History in Sixteenth Century Florence* (Princeton, 1965), p. 20. Cf. Frederic C. Lane, *Venice and History* (Baltimore, 1966), p. 530.

[29] Lane, p. 525; Gioacchino Volpe, "L'Italia e Venezia," in *La civiltà veneziana del Trecento*, p. 42.

[30] Roberto Cessi, *Storia della Repubblica di Venezia* (Milan, 1944), II, 14; A. Baschet, *Les archives de Venise: histoire de la chancellerie secrète* (Paris, 1870), pp. 131–146.

Council formally absorbed the rights of the long-quiescent popular assembly. The formality of popular approval for a newly selected doge was also dropped, and Venice shortly ceased to describe herself as *comune Venetiarum* and became in effect a *signoria* held, collectively, by a fixed group. But, since every noble over twenty-five (and occasionally younger men for a fee) belonged to the Great Council, and most attended its regular Sunday meetings, this large body was obviously too cumbersome for most political decisions. Therefore, although it technically retained sovereignty, its primary task became the election of other bodies to carry on the government. Its electoral responsibilities were carefully protected by a series of laws in the fifteenth and sixteenth centuries which were intended to guarantee Venice against degeneration into a narrow oligarchy.[31]

At the next level of decision was the Senate, a body of about three hundred, partly elected for terms of a year by the Great Council, partly *ex officio*. With the usual fine Venetian concern for continuity (unmatched by an equal respect for fact), the Great Council at the beginning of the fifteenth century had discovered origins for the Senate at the very birth of the republic; it actually began to emerge clearly only in the thirteenth century. The senators, known collectively as the *Pregadi* (literally, those summoned), exercised a general supervisory authority over all agencies of the state. They administered foreign policy, waged war and concluded peace, appointed military commanders and ambassadors, and decided on the replies to be given to the envoys of foreign powers; they dealt with taxation and other problems of internal policy; and they chose, as a kind of executive committee, various categories of *savi* or counsellors, who, meeting with the heads of the criminal judiciary and with the doge and his counsellors, composed the full College of the Senate. This body convoked the Senate, prepared and managed its agenda, received reports from agents and agencies of the government, and dealt directly with the representatives of foreign powers. It met almost daily.[32]

Standing somewhat apart from this hierarchy of bodies was the Council of Ten. Established early in the fourteenth century to deal with a particular

[31] Maranini, *Costituzione dalle origini*, pp. 150ff., 207ff.; *Costituzione dopo la serrata*, pp. 35 ff., 47–48; Cessi, *Storia*, II, 508. For a vivid, if somewhat idealized, description of the organization and procedures of the Great Council, see also Charles Yriarte, *La vie d'un patricien de Venise au XVIe siècle* (Paris, 1874), pp. 44–53. For a particularly detailed account of this and other agencies of the Venetian government, see Francesco Sansovino, *Del governo de' Regni e delle Repubbliche antiche e moderni* (Venice, 1583), leaves 151ᵛ–166ʳ.

[32] Maranini, *Costituzione dalle origini*, pp. 276ff.; *Costituzione dopo la serrata*, pp. 131ff.; Cessi, *Storia*, II, 8; Yriarte, pp. 54–73; Baschet, pp. 228ff.

crisis, it was not intended to be permanent. Nevertheless, the speed and secrecy made possible by its smaller size gave it obvious advantages for special categories of business; and, although constitutionally irregular, it became an alternative to the Senate and was regularly assigned certain tasks by the College. It came therefore to deal with urgent and extraordinary problems; and since these arose with increasing frequency after the middle of the fifteenth century, it then began a rapid growth in power. During the course of the sixteenth century its position was strengthened by the addition to it of a group of leading senators known as the *Giunta*. The extraordinary character of the Council of Ten made it an obvious focal point for controversy about the nature of the Venetian constitution and a possible opening for the modification of that constitution, or at least of the practical character of the government, in the direction of a narrower oligarchy.[33]

At the top of the constitutional pyramid was the doge, who represented the sovereignty of the Venetian state and was for this reason often described as "prince" of Venice. But the success of the Venetian nobility in preventing the conversion of the republic into a principate is well known.[34] By the *promissione ducale* and other devices, the doge had been excluded from genuine personal sovereignty, and during most of her history Venice was one of those cities described by Bartolus as "prince unto herself."[35] In one of Patrizi's dialogues on history, the partipants in which were chiefly Venetians, the distinction between other princes and the Venetian doge was clearly delineated. "I call a prince absolute who is unlimited master over laws and arms, whether he is prince by right or by force," Patrizi wrote. "But the prince of a republic is subject to the laws; and if he disposes of arms, he does so with the consent of the citizens and of the laws."[36] The restrictions on the doge thus became an important element in the Venetians' conception of their polity. For Francesco Sansovino the office had been instituted not to provide direction but to express, through election, the original demand of the Venetian settlers for liberty.[37] Agostino Valier was to see the post as essentially honorary.[38]

[33] Maranini, *Costituzione dopo la serrata*, pp. 387ff., 408; cf. Horatio Brown, *Venice: An Historical Sketch of the Republic*, 2nd rev. ed. (London, 1895), pp. 398ff.

[34] See, in general, Maranini, *Costituzione dalle origini*, pp. 172ff.

[35] Cf. Francesco Ercole, *Dal comune al principato: saggi sulla storia del diritto pubblico del Rinascimento italiano* (Florence, 1929), p. 256.

[36] Francesco Patrizi, *Della historia diece dialoghi* (Venice, 1560), sig. C3^v.

[37] *Venetia città nobilissima, et singolare; descritta già in XIII libri*, in the Venetian edition of 1604, sig. KKKKl^r.

[38] *Dell'utilità*, p. 124.

The doge was nevertheless a more important official than has sometimes been supposed. His ritual significance remained great. In the event of his physical death, as Wotton observed early in the seventeenth century, it was necessary to represent the continuing life of the body politic by other means: " . . . the first care is the ordering of the palace, where the Signory (represented by the Councillors and some others) are during the vacancy to reside in the rooms of the dead prince; thereby figuratively signifying (as they will have it) the immortality of the Commonwealth."[39] Beyond this it was also possible, in spite of all constitutional limitations, for a doge of ability and energy to wield great influence, particularly in times of crisis. Several powerful doges, long after the office had presumably been rendered harmless, demonstrated its continuing potentiality as an instrument of political leadership. After Michele Steno, Tommaso Mocenigo, and Francesco Foscari had made this clear in the first half of the fifteenth century, the alarmed patriciate initiated, as a general practice, the election of mediocrities or men of great age to the dogeship. But the potentialities in the office were to be demonstrated again from time to time, notably, as we shall see, in the early seventeenth century.

Venice had been celebrated for centuries, both at home and abroad, as a paragon of domestic tranquility. In the words of Sanuto: "This holy republic is governed with such order that it is a marvelous thing. She has neither popular sedition nor discord among her patricians, but all unite in promoting her greatness; and therefore, as wise men say, she will last forever."[40] By the fifteenth century this achievement was largely attributed to the Venetian constitution, which was identified with the mixed government idealized by the ancients and endorsed by Thomas Aquinas. The Greek scholar Trapezuntius had been perhaps the first to discern (though possibly on the basis of a suggestion by Vergerio) that the Venetian constitution fully realized the classical ideal. In a letter to Francesco Barbaro in 1452, he proposed to dedicate to the Republic his translation of Plato's *Laws*. So clear was the analogy between ancient constitutional theory and what Venice had created in practice, he claimed, that the Venetian achievement could only have come from a kind of Platonic inspiration. Trapezuntius was eventually rewarded for this insight by the Senate of the Republic, and the conception of Venice as a

[39] Letter to the Earl of Salisbury from Venice, Feb. 18, 1606, in Logan Pearsall Smith, ed., *The Life and Letters of Sir Henry Wotton* (Oxford, 1907), I, 343, hereafter cited as Smith.
[40] Quoted by Maranini, *Costituzione dopo la serrata*, p. 14.

model of the mixed state was henceforth a commonplace of Renaissance political discussion; it evidently corresponded to preconceptions about political organization that were now increasingly common. The Great Council was understood to represent the popular element in the constitution (though always in the limited sense in which Renaissance republicanism conceived of the *populus*), the Senate the aristocratic element, and the doge the monarchic. Wisely balancing each other and effectively coordinating particular interests to serve the general welfare, the relation of these three agencies was seen as the basic secret of Venetian political success.[41]

But the spirit animating the Venetian government was quite as important as the machinery of this admirable constitution. We may note first its secular bias. This found expression in the freedom Venetians generally enjoyed from such restrictions on the taking of interest as frequently hampered business elsewhere; money lenders were not prosecuted in Venice before the fourteenth century, and then only for charging excessive rates.[42] The Venetians also tended to justify their celebrated system for poor relief on political grounds; they saw public assistance not as a religious duty but as a useful device to prevent public disorder and insurrection.[43] But Venetian secularism was particularly reflected in an intense distrust of clerical influence on the government which found overt expression in fifteenth-century legislation. Nobles who received income from any ecclesiastical benefice were in 1498 excluded from membership in the Great Council and from all public office. The families of Venetians holding ecclesiastical positions were also suspect. Their members (labeled *papalisti*) who belonged to the various governing bodies of the state, by a series of laws beginning in 1411 were regularly excluded from all deliberations concerning ecclesiastical matters. Some appointments, such as the coveted embassy to Rome, were closed to these families altogether. No member of the clergy was allowed to serve the

[41] Gilbert, "Venetian Constitution," now provides the fullest account of early discussion about the Venetian constitution; see also Gaeta, "Mito di Venezia," p. 62; and Giorgio Candeloro, "Paolo Paruta," *RSI*, Ser. 5, I (1936), 83. But cf. Carlo Curcio, *Dal Rinascimento alla Controriforma. Contributo alla storia del pensiero politico italiano da Guicciardini a Botero* (Rome, 1934), pp. 106–107.

[42] Cf. Frederic C. Lane, "Recent Studies on the Economic History of Venice," *Journal of Economic History*, XXIII (1963), 315–316.

[43] Brian Pullan, "Poverty, Charity and the Reason of State: Some Venetian Examples," *BSV*, II (1960), 17–60.

Venetian state in any capacity, even as a clerk or notary, or to have access to the public archives.[44]

Loyalty to Venice was clearly to be undivided, and Venetian devotion to the state was long celebrated by observers. Thus in the middle of the thirteenth century a Paduan chronicler had exclaimed: "Oh happy commune of Venice, that happy city where the citizens, in their every manifestation, have the common interest so much at heart that the name of Venice is held as divine!"[45] Elsewhere during the Middle Ages men bestowed their worldly goods on the church, but Venetians gave them also to the state.[46] For Venice represented to the Venetians a realm of unique and abiding values which it was their particular obligation to conserve and to transmit from generation to generation.

The community of all Venetians, therefore, like the communion of saints, transcended the limits of time; and their sense of responsibility to carry on a cherished tradition contributed heavily to the much celebrated conservatism of Venice. Venetians were inclined to view all institutional change with suspicion and even to deny that it had occurred; as in the case of the Senate, they preferred to believe that nothing had ever really changed. Their respect for continuity also made them particularly respectful of old age as implying long saturation in the traditional wisdom of the state. On the other hand Venetian conservatism, however inconsistent with a true historical consciousness, was not altogether inimical to an interest in the past. Venetians were constantly concerned to study and follow the examples set by their ancestors, whose wise and glorious deeds had been recorded in the precious archives of the Republic. Thus they were interested in a kind of historical research.[47]

But the spiritual community of all Venetians in the state linked them to each other in the present as well as the past, and few societies in the West have had such success in defining the limits of individual autonomy. The solidarity of the Venetian patriciate can, of course, be exaggerated. There

[44] Maranini, *Costituzione dopo la serrata*, pp. 239–242; Bartolomeo Cecchetti, *La Repubblica di Venezia e la Corte di Roma nei rapporti della religione* (Venice, 1874), I, 133–134; Sagredo, pp. 95–104. Sarpi described some of this legislation in a letter to Leschassier, Mar. 2, 1610, Ulianich, p. 71.

[45] Quoted by Volpe, "Italia e Venezia," p. 44.

[46] Fasoli, p. 461.

[47] Cf. the remarks of Cessi, *Storia di Venezia*, II, 3; E. Besta, *Il Senato veneziano* (Venice, 1899), p. 43; Davis, p. 88; Fasoli, pp. 449–450.

were conflicts of economic interest and struggles for power within it as in other polities. Early in the seventeenth century a hostile critic noted its divisions and its changeability, and his observations have some validity for earlier periods as well. "The Republic of Venice," wrote the count of Bedmar, recently Spanish ambassador to Venice, "is a convent of nobles composed of so many humors, and of so much variety and mixtures of affects and inclinations, that, as in a gulf in which a variety of different winds are blowing, the navigation and course change." But he also identified an essential area of unity: "On one point alone is there agreement, and that is on the perpetuation of ruling. For the rest, almost every one follows his own passions." Between the lines of this acid description one may discern the peculiar Venetian balance between individual interests and common needs.[48] Venetian society was long characterized by a high degree of in-dividual freedom, its disorderly potentialities held in check by the discipline of the ruling nobility.

Comparison with other communities sets off the peculiar coherence of Venetian society. This coherence is evident not only in the relative absence of internal dissension but also in the relative scarcity of prominent individuals who achieved fame in Venetian history by their personal exploits. In the eighteenth century a distinguished Venetian noted the curious paucity of biography in Venetian literature, a circumstance he attributed to "the cautious and temperate genius of free cities, to which too explicit testi-monials of honor paid to an individual have never been congenial." [49] In spite of its title, Marcello's *Lives of the Doges*, first published at the beginning of the sixteenth century is less a collection of biographies than a chronicle of events conveniently organized according to the doges under whom they occurred; it invites comparison with Machiavelli's treatment of Florentine affairs or with Vespasiano's *Vite* in this respect. Meanwhile the commercial policies of the Republic prevented the accumulation of huge fortunes by individuals; the most profitable ventures were broadly collective, and the government retained ownership of the largest galleys. The pressures of close family life and of a whole culture based on group activity also supplemented the Venetian political tradition to reduce the prominence of individuals. It was common, as elsewhere, for children to continue to live together even after the death of the parents, and for agreements to be worked

---

[48] "Una relazione del Marchese di Bedmar sui veneziani," ed. Italo Raulich, *AV*, Ser. 2, XVI (1898), 20.

[49] Marco Foscarini, *Della letteratura veneziana* (Venice, 1854), pp. 314–315, 318. This work first appeared in 1752.

out among them, based on family convenience, about which should marry and which should serve the common interest in other ways; business, meanwhile, remained unusually dependent on family solidarity. The government recognized and exploited the solidarity of the Venetian family by holding all its members responsible for the misdeeds of an individual. And literature and other intellectual interests were typically cultivated not by isolated individuals of genius but in groups of men bound together by ties of friendship and common tastes. All these influences combined to produce an educational tradition whose remarkable power as an instrument for the formation of a clearly delineated character type left an indelible impression on every young Venetian. No student of Venetian history can escape being struck by the number of Venetians who can properly be described, even after close inspection, as *typical* of their society.[50]

With so much settled internally, the major problems and decisions in Venetian history concerned her external relations.[51] By the fifteenth century the most serious disagreements within the ruling group in Venice were over the direction to which her major energies should be pointed. The more traditional view began by noting that from her origins Venice had lived on commerce with the Levant, and it argued that her attention should remain fixed on the Orient and the sea. As a Venetian chancellor declared late in the fourteenth century, "the proper thing for Venice is to cultivate the sea and to leave the land alone."[52] Involvement on the mainland, according to this view, would only distract Venice from her essential business, and even endanger it by poisoning the good relations between the Republic and her customers. This position remained that of many Venetians long after Venice had committed herself to the land. Among them was the diarist Priuli, who deplored the interest of his contemporaries in the pleasures of life on the mainland; for Priuli every blessing came from the sea.[53] Machiavelli was thus expressing a classic notion of Venetian policy when he argued that the

---

[50] Gino Luzzatto, "L'economia," *La civiltà veneziana del Trecento*, p. 105; Lane, *Venice and History*, pp. 36–55; Davis, pp. 25–26, 63–64; W. Theodor Elwert, "Pietro Bembo e la vita letteraria del suo tempo," *La civiltà veneziana del Rinascimento* (Florence, 1958), pp. 129ff.

[51] For a lucid account of the general evolution of Venetian foreign policy, see Piero Pieri, *Intorno alla politica estera di Venezia al principio del Cinquecento* (Naples, 1934), esp. pp. 5–6.

[52] Raffaino Caresini, quoted by Vittorio Lazzarini, "Antiche leggi venete intorno ai proprietari nella terraferma," *AV*, Ser. 3, XXXVIII (1920), 19 n. 2.

[53] Girolamo Priuli, *I diarii*, ed. Roberto Cessi (Bologna, 1912–1938), IV, 50; see also p. 121.

greatness of Venice had come from the sea and that her glory had lasted only for so long as she had kept her attention fixed on it.[54]

The alternative was obviously that Venice should expand on the Italian mainland. But the choice of policies had never been so simple as it was often represented; Venice was never entirely free to choose between isolation and involvement. Concentration on trade had itself created problems for the Republic in her relations with other European powers as well as with the Turks. For the security of the sea was essential to a profitable commerce; and to the Venetians this had long meant control of the Adriatic, through which every Venetian ship had to pass, the seizure and maintenance of fortified points along its shores, and the suppression of other ports that might compete with Venice or on which hostile ships might be based. Venice had therefore to master the Adriatic, which, though already described as the Gulf of Venice in an Arab geography of the twelfth century, she did not fully control before the fifteenth. But a consequence of this achievement was persistent friction with the papacy. The port of Ancona suffered particularly from the brutal limitation of its activity by Venice, which responded to papal protests as early as the fourteenth century by claiming that her tactics were no more than "the conservation of the rights and jurisdiction acquired in the custody of the sea through the expenditure of so much blood and sweat on the part of our ancestors." The issue still embittered Venetian relations with the pope in the seventeenth century. Meanwhile the Adriatic question had also become a major cause of conflict between Venice and the Austrian Habsburgs.[55]

Eventually Venice had also to take into account the actions of other powers, and before the end of the fourteenth century ambitious despots on the mainland were compelling the Venetians to abandon their traditional isolation from Italian politics, if only because trade routes by land were necessary to complement trade routes by sea. The conquest of Padua and Verona first established Venice on the *terraferma,* and the possession of these territories in turn exposed her to the aggressions of Milan. The Venetian alliance with Florence in 1425 may be taken to mark the practical end of Venetian isolation, although it persisted as an ideal. From this date Venice,

---

[54] *Istorie fiorentine,* Bk. I, Ch. 29.

[55] Luigi Simeoni, *Le signorie* (Milan, 1950), I, 231; A. Battistella, "Il dominio del Golfo," *AV,* Ser. 3, XXXV (1918), 18ff., and "Venezia e l'Austria durante la vita della Repubblica," *AV,* Ser. 3, XXXI (1916), 283ff.; Roberto Cessi, *La Repubblica di Venezia e il problema adriatico* (Naples, 1953).

for better or worse, was clearly an Italian power, and Italian politics was henceforth of crucial importance to the Republic.[56]

The Italian policy of Venice in the later fifteenth century has been difficult to evaluate, partly because it has been chiefly interpreted to us by the unfriendly historians of Florence. Cosimo de' Medici's break with Venice in the middle of the century was followed by a sustained effort to blame the shift in Florentine policy on Venetian imperialism, and a standard account of Venetian aims was elaborated and widely circulated. Thus Machiavelli reported that the Venetians "did not respect the church; they did not find Italy large enough for them, and they imagined that they were going to form a monarchy like the Roman." He represented Venice as an ungrateful friend, an unreliable ally, and a major threat to the peace of Italy before the coming of the French. Her populace he depicted as morally deficient, insolent in prosperity, and abject in adversity.[57] Guicciardini, too, although he admired the Venetian constitution, blamed Venice for a selfish ambition that blocked Italian unity in the face of the foreigner;[58] and the same attitudes to Venice persisted among later Florentine historians, including that degenerate representative of the tradition, Scipione Ammirato.[59]

But historians have now begun to take a cooler view of Cosimo's place in the political history of Florence, and it is possible to raise the question whether Venice was, in fact, primarily to blame for the rupture of the republican alliance. As the most powerful Italian state, she could hardly have been expected to forego all opportunity for expansion; self-restraint of this kind was not usual among the states of Renaissance Italy, including Florence. In the political climate of the time Venice had reason enough for attempting to strengthen her Italian frontiers, and her fault seems to have lain primarily in an imprudent neglect of the hostility which her tactics were building up among the other states of the peninsula.[60]

[56] For a very clear account of the Venetian shift to the mainland, see Luzzatto, *Storia economica*, pp. 155ff. On the significance of 1425, cf. Hans Baron, *The Crisis of the Early Italian Renaissance: Civic Humanism and Republican Liberty in an Age of Classicism and Tyranny*, rev. ed. (Princeton, 1966), pp. 387ff.

[57] *Discorsi*, Bk. III, Ch. 31; *Istorie fiorentine*, Bk. V, Chs. 19–21; *Il Principe*, Ch. 11. Benedetto Dei, cited above, represents an earlier stage in the development of this attitude.

[58] *Storia d'Italia*, Bk. I, Ch. 1.

[59] *Istorie fiorentine* (Florence, 1647) II, 910A, for example.

[60] Nino Valeri, "Venezia nella crisi italiana del Rinascimento," *La civiltà veneziana del Quattrocento* (Florence, 1956), pp. 35ff.; Garrett Mattingly, *Renaissance Diplomacy* (Boston, 1955), pp. 93–94; Simeoni, I, 549–550.

Whatever her motives, Venice acquired a considerable empire on the mainland in the course of the fifteenth century; and although the expense and danger of conquering and maintaining it confirmed traditional opposition to the acquisition of an empire on land, the glory and eventually the profits of conquest stimulated the emergence of a substantial party which can roughly be described as the landed, in opposition to the mercantile, interest. For although Venetian publicists liked to represent the Serenissima as the liberator of the grateful communities of the *terraferma*, she imposed a firm control over their governments[61] and began to make up for the losses of overseas empire to the Turks by taking over, for her patriciate, the resources of the mainland. Ecclesiastical benefices were increasingly held by Venetians, and large amounts of land soon passed into their hands. By 1446 Paduans claimed (although this was probably an exaggeration) that a third of the Padovano was held by the Venetian nobility. The transformation of many Venetian patricians into a landed aristocracy was chiefly the work of the sixteenth century, but a social change of revolutionary implications had been started.[62] In addition the annexation by Venice of territories that had acknowledged imperial suzerainty, and which she ruled officially, after 1437, as imperial vicar, complicated her legal relationship to the rest of Christendom.[63]

Security, stability, conservatism, and deep-rooted agreement on essentials combined for a long while to inhibit the appearance in Venice of such creative and vigorous political discussion as the more turbulent history of Florence produced. In Venice, there seemed little to discuss, although from time to time some celebration of the Venetian achievement appeared appropriate. Disagreement over the proper direction of foreign policy was evidently hardly enough to stimulate much thought about politics in general. Nor do the Venetians appear to have learned much from Florence, where social and political disorders seemed only negatively instructive.

That Venetian politics had latent possibilities even in the Quattrocento for

[61] For Venetian administration of the terraferma, see Mor, *loc. cit.*; Daniele Beltrami, *La penetrazione economica dei veneziani in terraferma* (Venice, 1961), pp. 47–48; Simeoni, II, 578.

[62] Beltrami, *Penetrazione economica*, pp. 48–49; Stuart J. Woolf, "Venice and the Terraferma: Problems of the Change from Commercial to Landed Activities," *BSV*, IV (1962), 420ff.; Luzzatto, *Storia economica*, pp. 161–164.

[63] Cf. Ercole, p. 286 n. 1; and Antonio Bonardi, "Venezia e la lega di Cambrai," *AV*, Ser. 3, VII (1904), 126.

a development along Florentine lines is suggested, however, by the case of Francesco Barbaro, a leading member of the Venetian patriciate during the fateful decades of the earlier fifteenth century when Venice was beginning the conquest of her *terraferma* empire.[64] An enthusiastic humanist in his youth, Barbaro composed a treatise on marriage, which he praised both for its moral values and as the source of new citizens to serve the state. He was contemptuous, like the Florentines, of philosophical abstractions, and he praised the active life of civic responsibility. Eventually he became an enthusiastic proponent of the republican alliance as the most dependable guarantor of the *libertas Italiae*, by which he meant the maintenance of a federation of independent republics in a stable equilibrium.[65] Well before the Florentines, Barbaro appears to have formulated the idea of balance to govern relations among independent states.[66] At the same time he exhibited a typically Venetian caution about political decisions. He insisted that long and careful deliberation should precede any commitment to action, and he particularly deplored the impulsive resort to arms, seeing in war the abnegation of reason and the abandonment of politics to the mercy of fortune.

Yet the expression of such views by an individual patrician seems less striking than the scarcity of general political discussion in Venice. It may be that Barbaro's rare articulateness was the result of a youthful trip to Florence, where he probably came into contact with members of the ruling group.[67] In Venice he was exceptional. The Florentine alliance proved, after all, to be not the expression of mutual devotion to a community of conscious ideals but chiefly a practical arrangement to meet a passing need; and after Francesco Barbaro political discussion in Venice appears to have died away again.

As in Florence, but with deeper roots and therefore more stubborn consequences in practice, republican attitudes in Venice had profound

[64] See, for Barbaro, the excellent work of Natale Carotti, "Un politico umanista del Quattrocento: Francesco Barbaro," *RSI*, Ser. 5, II (1937), 18–37; and Gianni Zippel, "Lorenzo Valla e le origini della storiografia umanistica a Venezia," *Rinascimento*, VII (1956), 117–119.

[65] Baron, pp. 392–397.

[66] Carlo Morandi, "Il concetto della politica di equilibrio nell'Europa moderna," *ASI*, XCVIII (1940), 6.

[67] Cf. Eugenio Garin, "Cultura filosofica toscana e veneta nel Quattrocento," in *Umanesimo europeo e umanesimo veneziano*, p. 12.

implications for ecclesiology; and Venice developed characteristic ways of defining the relations between the spiritual and temporal authorities. That these patterns demonstrate the influence on Venice of Byzantine theory and practice (so easily despised in the Latin West, but so often without insight into their religious meaning) or of the views of Marsilio of Padua, has often been maintained; and such suggestions may indeed contain some truth. Venetian pronouncements about the church occasionally suggest a typically Eastern ideal of unity as the communion of local congregations rather than a unitary organization and a conception of the local church as a congregation of individual believers. But ecclesiastical arrangements, like political ideas, are not altogether autonomous. They often correspond to the more general features and needs of a given situation; and if Byzantine ways caught on in Venice, it was because they seemed appropriate in the beginning, and in the long run proved effective. It is thus more to the point to recall that Venice saw herself as an independent city-state; and it should hardly be surprising that she found congenial the manner of reconciling local particularity with Christian universalism that had been maintained in the eastern Mediterranean, far more than the West the direct heir to the ancient city-states.

The ancient habit of associating religion with the state, given the early appearance of their own city, very likely influenced the Venetians from the beginning. The "national Venetian church" was in some sense probably already in existence when the relics of Saint Mark arrived from Alexandria in 828, although this event undoubtedly contributed to the sense that Venice possessed some sacral character. The Serenissima was commonly described as "this holy republic," the participation of the doge and other officials of the government in great religious processions regularly dramatized the religious values inherent in the state, and the liturgy celebrated in Venice was made to incorporate a variety of specifically civic elements.[68]

Such an association between religion and the state can be variously interpreted. It could, for example, lead to the notion of the state as first servant of the faith, and the involvements of Venice with the Turks from time to time received this construction. Venice, according to this interpretation, was the defender of Christendom, the guardian of its eastern gateway. So the Venetian ambassador in London once indignantly replied to the taunts of a group of English, who had described his people as mere fishermen. He reminded them that fishermen had been the founders of the Christian faith, and went on to convert the description of Venetians as

[68] Fasoli, pp. 451–456. Cf. Burckhardt, I, 77–78.

fishermen into an elaborate metaphor of devotion to the defense of Christendom: "Our fishing boats have been galleys and ships; the hooks have been our money; the bait has been the flesh of our citizens who have died for the Christian faith. Our old histories are full of this, as are the recent memories of those still alive. The lands and states we have lost through defending the rest of the Christians ... are testimonials of this truth, and of the wars waged by us against the Turks." [69] On the whole, this was sentimental exaggeration for the benefit of foreigners. Yet that it formed a real part of the Venetian sense of what Venice stood for the later sixteenth and seventeenth centuries were also to demonstrate.

At the same time the close connection between religion and the Venetian state received a different, if not necessarily inconsistent, construction, as it facilitated the assumption, itself antique rather than Christian, that one of the functions of religion, if not necessarily its essential purpose, is social discipline. Both Francesco Barbaro and Bernardo Giustiniani, without any sense that such a position might offend religious sensibilities, well before Machiavelli expressed the common Venetian conviction that religion is a valuable instrument of government, singularly well adapted to keep subjects obedient to law.[70] The point may remind us again of the popularity at Padua of the Averroist view of the great world religions.[71]

This view suggested that a religious position might be assessed according to its social results rather than its substance and truth, and on this basis Barbaro had recommended gentle treatment of the Greek subjects of the Republic; the attempt to impose Latin Catholicism on them would have caused trouble.[72] Political expediency, no doubt mingled with simple indifference and the skeptical latitudinarianism of a well-traveled business community, promoted a remarkable degree of religious toleration in Venice herself, Crete, and other places; and the Venetian government from time to time protected its Greek subjects against pressures and propaganda emanating from Rome.[73] Such acceptance of "schism" was another long-standing cause of papal irritation against the Republic.

But the most important element in the Venetian ecclesiastical tradition

[69] Sebastiano Giustiniani to the Council of Ten, Apr. 1, 1516, quoted by Cecchetti, I, 324.

[70] Carotti, p. 33; Hochschild, pp. 417–418.

[71] Cf. Spini, *Ricerca dei libertini*, pp. 15ff.

[72] Carotti, p. 35.

[73] Cf. Deno J. Geanakoplos, *Greek Scholars in Venice: Studies in the Dissemination of Greek Learning from Byzantium to Western Europe* (Cambridge, Mass., 1962).

was the claim to a substantial autonomy that paralleled and reinforced Venetian political autonomy. Just as Venice insisted on her freedom from the emperor in temporal affairs, so she insisted—almost as firmly—on her freedom from the pope in the affairs of the church. This claim too found support in a myth: that Christianity had been planted in the Venetian lagoons by Saint Mark.[74] This legend, which was to become another of the pregnant commonplaces of Venetian historiography, gave to the Venetian church an independent and apostolic foundation paralleling that of Rome, and in some measure recognized even by the papacy. In the eleventh century Gregory VII himself attributed to the Venetian church, because of her relationship with Saint Mark, a position of leadership in the West second only to that of Rome herself.[75] Dandolo's chronicle began with the apostolate of Mark,[76] and the story of the saint's sojourn in what was to become the Venetian Republic figures prominently in the Venetian histories of the early Renaissance. Bernardo Giustiniani, in addition to giving a full account of Mark's mission in the neighborhood of Venice in his major history, composed a number of works to celebrate the relationship between Venice and Saint Mark;[77] and Sabellico, who also retold the story, expressed the common view that the presence of the saint's relics guaranteed the survival of the Republic forever.[78] Apostolic patronage made Venice, no less than Rome, an eternal city.

The ecclesiastical autonomy of Venice opened the way to a degree of control over the Venetian church by the lay government comparable to that exercised through the Middle Ages by lay authorities in the kingdoms of western Europe. Both the autonomy of the Venetian church and lay influence on its direction found expression in the peculiar status of the church of San Marco, where the bones of Saint Mark were thought to repose. San Marco was from the beginning the private chapel of the doge, and therefore not under the jurisdiction of the local hierarchy. The doge designated its clergy and also took a solemn oath to respect its privileges. For centuries no papal bulls or briefs were published in the church.[79] It is

---

[74] For what follows see, in general, Fasoli, p. 452.

[75] Maranini, *Costituzione dalle origini*, p. 59.

[76] The point is brought out by Enrico Simonsfeld, "Andrea Dandolo e le sue opere storiche," *AV*, Ser. 1, XIV, Pt. 1 (1877), 59.

[77] Discussed in some detail by Hochschild, pp. 430–437.

[78] At the end of the second book of his Venetian history, sigs. B4^v–B5^r.

[79] Fasoli, p. 459; A. Nürnberger, "Papst Paul V und das venezianische Interdikt," *Historisches Jahrbuch*, IV (1883), 202.

therefore particularly significant that San Marco, rather than the cathedral church of San Pietro di Castello, was the center of Venetian religious life.

The church, both in Venice and throughout her empire, was generally administered almost as though Rome did not exist, and also with little concern to preserve a distinction between clerical and lay responsibility. In Venice the nobility supervised ecclesiastical as well as secular administration. Numerous actions of the government, extending even into the eighteenth century, dealt with such sensitive religious questions as the acquisition and custody of relics, the content of sermons (when, for example, it seemed necessary to prohibit inflammatory preaching against the Greeks), the provision of religious services when prelates absented themselves from their posts, the administration of the mass and the cult of saints, the designation of religious festivals, parish administration, and conventual discipline. Examples may be found in every period of Venetian history.[80]

The method of designating Venetian bishops, from the patriarch down to the occupant of the humblest see, contributed heavily to patrician control of the church. The normal practice, prescribed by a law of 1391 but already probably long in effect, was nomination by the Senate (often with little regard to canonical qualifications) of a dependable Venetian, whose name the doge would then submit to the pope for confirmation. This right of nomination was maintained until 1510 for all Venetian bishoprics, and even after that date for the patriarchate of Venice and the archbishopric of Candia.[81] And although technically most Venetian bishops were directly appointed in Rome after 1510, most episcopal appointments were in fact still determined in Venice by the practice, easily arranged in so closely-knit a patriciate, of having an aged incumbent resign in favor of some predetermined person, usually a younger member of the same family, whose designation as bishop-elect was ratified by the pope.[82] Thus, for example, the Senate secured papal approval of Domenico Grimani as patriarch of Aquileia in 1497; and the benefice remained in the Grimani family, to the annoyance of Habsburg Austria, through the whole of the sixteenth

[80] Cecchetti, I, 81 ff., 115, 138–139.
[81] Cecchetti, I, 309, 399; Antonio Niero, *I patriarchi di Venezia da Lorenzo Giustiniani ai nostri giorni* (Venice, 1961), pp. 14–17; Gino Benzoni, "Una controversia tra Roma e Venezia all'inizio del '600: la conferma del patriarca," *BSV*, III (1961), 121, 125.
[82] The procedure is described by Giuseppe Alberigo, *I vescovi italiani al Concilio di Trento (1545–1547)* (Florence, 1959), pp. 52–53.

century.[83] Meanwhile the Senate wielded some additional control over major ecclesiastical appointments by retaining the right of investiture to the temporal endowments of benefices.[84] Under these conditions, although the papacy could at times block the appointment of a nominee favored by Venice, it was unable to obtain bishoprics for its own candidates against Venetian opposition. A dispute over the see of Padua in 1459, for example, resulted in the withdrawal of both the Venetian and the Roman choice and was finally settled by the designation of a third candidate acceptable to both sides. But the Senate had meanwhile insisted on its right to ratify all significant appointments to Venetian benefices, and a similar altercation over the same bishopric in 1486 resulted in a clear victory for Venice.[85]

Thus the upper clergy, both in Venice and her possessions, were generally in the first place Venetian nobles. Their education, their social world, and their attitudes both to the Venetian state and to the church were generally identical with those of the rest of the patriciate.[86] And even those rare prelates in the Venetian church during the sixteenth century, like Gian Matteo Giberti, bishop of Verona, who were not of Venetian origin, felt it wise to insist on their devotion to the Republic. In a letter to the doge in 1524, he paid tribute to Venice as the living representative of "the ancient greatness and the true liberty of Italy," indicated his belief that the pope had appointed him to serve Venice as well as the Holy See, and promised his continued service to the state as "a good son and subject."[87] His words may have been chiefly a diplomatic tribute to the traditional pattern of

---

[83] Pio Paschini, "La nomina del patriarca di Aquileia e la Repubblica di Venezia nel secolo XVI," *Rivista di Storia della Chiesa in Italia*, II (1948), 61–76.

[84] Simonsfeld, p. 59, discusses fourteenth century concern with maintaining this right. For later practice, see Pietro Savio, "Il nunzio a Venezia dopo l'Interdetto," *AV*, Ser. 5, LVI–LVII (1955), 89.

[85] Gaspare Zonta, "Un conflitto tra la Repubblica Veneta e la Curia Romana per l'episcopato di Padova (1459–60)," *Atti e memorie della R. Accademia di Scienze, Lettere ed Arti in Padova*, XL (1924), 221–238; Franco Gaeta, "Origini e sviluppo della rappresentanza stabile pontificia in Venezia (1485–1533)," *Annuario dell'Istituto Storico Italiano per l'Età Moderna e Contemporanea*, IX–X (1957–1958, 20–21). For other disputes (in which Venice also prevailed) during the early sixteenth century, see Ludwig von Pastor, *History of the Popes* (London and St. Louis, 1891–1953), VI, 301–302.

[86] Cf. Alberigo, pp. 79–80.

[87] The letter is given in an appendix to Angelo Grazioli, *Gian Matteo Giberti vescovo di Verona precursore della riforma del Concilio di Trento* (Verona, 1955), pp. 177–178. Giberti also attempted to arrange, to succeed himself, a Venetian patrician favored by the government. See Benedetto Nicolini, *Aspetti della vita religiosa, politica e letteraria del Cinquecento* (Bologna, 1963), pp. 73–75.

relationships, but they also demonstrate its power and the necessity for even the most devout of reformers to conform to it. Venetian cardinals, meanwhile, were regarded at home as representatives of the Republic rather than servants of the pope. Giustiniani reminded them that Venice was their true parent, the church merely their stepmother.[88]

Lay control over ecclesiastical office in Venice was also extended to the lesser clergy who were in direct contact with the populace; parish priests were traditionally elected by the property owners of each parish. This practice was sanctioned by Leo X in 1517 and more definitively in 1526 by Clement VII in the bull *Clementina*, but these acts only recognized (perhaps because there was no remedy) a long-established procedure for which there is clear evidence at least a century earlier. Although the patriarch of Venice, who found elections by the laity distasteful, received from the pope in 1557 the right to examine and reject parish priests chosen in this way, he was permitted to do so only with the approval of the Council of Ten.[89] Thus lay influence was maintained at the most local level of ecclesiastical organization in Venice as well as at the highest. Meanwhile the practice constituted another long-standing Roman grievance against Venice. Early in the seventeenth century a writer at the Curia expressed his horror at a situation in which "everyone who has a house [has] the vote, and he who has the most votes becomes priest; this is ordinarily he who has the most experience and friends." [90] We will perhaps also be able to detect the influence of Venetian practice at the parish level in Sarpi's views about the proper structure of the church.[91]

The Venetian government not only had a major hand in the selection of clergy; it also maintained a large measure of control over them after they

[88] In his "Responsio ad sacrum collegium cardinalium" (May 28, 1483), cited by Hochschild, p. 419.

[89] The arrangement is discussed at length in Vettore Sandi, *Principi di storia civile della Repubblica di Venezia dalla sua fondazione sino all'anno di N.S. 1700* (Venice, 1755-1756), III, Pt. 1, 470-488. For the *Clementina* see also the "Sommario della Relazione di Roma" of Marco Foscari, May 2, 1526, in *Relazioni degli ambasciatori veneti al senato*, ed. E. Albèri (Florence, 1839-1863), Ser. 2, III, 130-131. Like much else in the ecclesiastical structure of Venice, this was not absolutely unique but rather more consistent and deeply rooted than elsewhere; see Federico Chabod, *Per la storia religiosa dello Stato di Milano durante il dominio di Carlo V*, 2nd ed. (Rome, 1962), pp. 60-62.

[90] This was the author of the *Relatione dello stato, costumi, disordini et rimedi di Venetia*, printed in part in Federigo Odorici, "Paolo V e le città di terraferma," *ASI*, Ser. 2, X (1859), 171-180.

[91] See below, pp. 454ff., 578ff., 606ff.

were appointed. Venetian ecclesiastics were considered, as physical residents of the state, to be not privileged members of a supranational body but subjects of the Venetian government exactly like other men. They were expected to show constant loyalty to the government, and prelates might be banished for public statements considered hostile to its interests or for other offenses.[92] The subjection of clergy to the lay government was emphasized above all in their juridical status. In practice two tendencies may be discerned on this point, but both assumed that the Venetian government had primary responsibility for the discipline of clerical persons. One tendency was to leave the clergy to the disposition of local ecclesiastical courts administered by native clergy on whom the government could rely, but to forbid any appeal to Rome. At least as early as 1315 such appeals were prohibited. A decree emanating from the Great Council in 1402, which called for the banishment of any cleric who appealed to the Curia against the judgment of his superior, provides an unusually revealing statement of the grounds of this position. It began with a general invocation of the principle of equity. The decree was based, it stated, on the fact that "the principal cause of the conservation of this city is the solicitude of our ancestors, who wished every rank and condition whatsoever to be subject to laws and justice." In Venice it was thus assumed that even local ecclesiastical courts administered justice under the authority of the government. The other tendency was to treat the clergy precisely like other subjects; and in numerous instances they were dealt with directly by the secular courts. Policy was not uniform, and there were times when Venice did not attempt to assert a direct judicial authority over the clergy. The general Venetian bias in this matter is nevertheless clear.[93]

The Venetian government in various ways also asserted its rights to control ecclesiastical property. A series of laws going back at least to the early thirteenth century restricted the rights of the church to acquire property from laymen; and additional legislation, extending back to the fourteenth century, forbade the construction of churches and other ecclesiastical buildings in the city of Venice without the permission of the government. Laws of the fourteenth and early fifteenth centuries prohibited the possession of Venetian

---

[92] Cf., for example, the case described by Arturo Segre, "Di alcune relazioni tra la Repubblica di Venezia e la S. Sede ai tempi di Urbano V e di Gregorio XI," *AV*, Ser. 3, IX (1905), 204; and by Zippel, p. 93 n. 1.

[93] Cecchetti, I, 143–146, 263–266.

benefices by foreigners. As we have seen the right of investiture by the lay power was also vigorously maintained.[94]

The Venetian state was less successful in asserting its authority to tax clerical property at will. For centuries this right had been enforced in spite of regular protests, of a kind familiar elsewhere, by the local clergy to Rome. But in 1464, as part of a general effort to win Christian support against the Turks, now expanding at Venetian expense, Venice at last yielded to ecclesiastical pressure on this matter. Henceforth she generally accepted the practical need for papal consent before undertaking to tax clerical wealth, and her requests to do so constituted a major part of Venetian negotiations at the Curia from the later fifteenth century onward. Nevertheless this change was relatively recent and a break with tradition, and it is doubtful that Venice accepted it in principle.[95]

The Venetian government refused, finally, to acknowledge that the responsibility for dealing with heresy belonged solely to the spiritual authorities. As early as 1249 the *promissione ducale* included a pledge to appoint pious and upright men to investigate heresy; and the introduction of the Roman Inquisition into Venice in 1289, as Sarpi was to argue, was the result of a concordat rather than a unilateral action of the pope, and therefore subject to conditions.[96] Thus in 1301 the Doge Pietro Gradenigo, although pressed hard, refused to swear unconditional obedience to papal and imperial directives against heresy. Of particular importance was the presence of lay representatives of the state as regular participants in all proceedings of the Venetian Holy Office, and on the mainland lay governors intervened almost at will in the actions of the Inquisition. Neither local ecclesiastics nor the pope could end this arrangement; and, after centuries of futile protest, Julius III in 1551 at last sanctioned what could not be abolished. Venetian treatment of the Inquisition was in some respects even more significant than Venetian efforts to control the personnel and property of the church. The intervention of laymen in cases involving heresy was justified on political grounds, as necessary to protect the interests of the

---

[94] Cecchetti, I, 124–125, 295ff.; Aldo Stella, "La proprietà ecclesiastica nella Repubblica di Venezia dal secolo XV al XVII," *Nuova Rivista Storica*, XLII (1958), 52–53.

[95] Cecchetti, I, 128ff., 151ff.; R. Battistella, "La politica ecclesiastica della Repubblica Veneta," *AV*, Ser. 2, XVI (1898), 402. See below, p. 114.

[96] Paolo Sarpi, *Sopra l'officio dell'inquisizione*, in *Scritti giurisdizionalistici*, ed. Giovanni Gambarin (Bari, 1958), pp. 140, 184; hereafter cited as *SG*. In this work Sarpi provides a general account of Venetian procedure, emphasizing its traditional character.

government and of social order. It suggested, nevertheless, that the superiority of the spiritual over the temporal was not absolute, and thus it posed a challenge to the principle of hierarchy. But above all it allowed laymen to participate directly in decisions involving the content of the faith.[97]

The Venetian Republic attributed to the pope a general spiritual leadership and a primacy of honor in the church, but little authority to administer churches outside of Rome, and none in politics. Thus from the thirteenth century, beginning dramatically with Venetian "disobedience" on the occasion of the Fourth Crusade, the relations between Venice and the papacy were punctuated by a long series of disputes. The Republic was particularly stubborn in the face of papal interdicts, so regularly employed to enforce the superiority of the pope over the political order.

Her small respect for ecclesiastical censure was displayed even when it was imposed on other states. Thus at the time of the *Otto Santi* Venice refused to publish in her own state the interdict against her sister republic, and she offered to protect Florentine interests in Flanders and Ireland for as long as the censure was in effect. Venice pointed out to the pope her need to live in peace with neighboring states and to continue a trade which the interdict would have required her to cease. But she also suggested a more general motive by remarking that publication of the interdict would perpetrate "novelty in our land," a phrase which implies that interdiction was somehow antagonistic in principle to the Venetian way of life. Unable to have his way, Gregory XI could only attempt to have his interdict attached secretly and by night to the doors of San Marco.[98] Nor was this the only such episode. Even after relations between Venice and Florence had become rather cool, Venice gave nominal support and eventually minor military aid to Florence at the time of the Pazzi conspiracy, again defying a papal censure.[99]

During the later Middle Ages, Venice had also considerable experience of her own with interdiction. On each occasion she chose to respond with the claim that papal censure was only an instrument of political ambition and therefore illegitimate: a spiritual penalty, Venice insisted, could not properly be invoked for temporal ends. This had been her reaction in 1201 when Innocent III imposed an interdict for her seizure of Zara, and again in 1282 when Martin IV put her under an interdict for refusing to help in the

[97] Cecchetti, I, 16ff., 279; Savio, p. 66.
[98] Segre, pp. 207–208, 213–214. See also Trexler, pp. 72–73.
[99] Cf. Simeoni, I, 541–542.

Sicilian crusade. Her response had been the same in 1309, when Clement V censured her for the seizure of Ferrara.[100]

But these were only preliminaries to the more modern Venetian interdicts, of which the first, over the war of Ferrara (1482–1484), remarkably foreshadowed, in the tactics Venice adopted, the later and far more dangerous censures of the sixteenth and seventeenth centuries. In this war Sixtus IV had been allied with Venice; but, the conflict going badly in the Papal State, he suddenly made a separate peace, switched sides according to the easy habits of the age, and (over the opposition of his Venetian cardinals) placed Venice under an interdict when she refused to abandon her siege of Ferrara. When the text of the interdict reached the patriarch in Venice, he typically conveyed it to the government instead of publishing it; and the government directed him to keep the entire matter secret and to continue all religious services as usual. The patriarch complied. Meanwhile the government commissioned five canonists and several prelates to examine the question; leading Venetians like Bernardo Giustiniani began to defend the Venetian position in writing, attacking both the justice and validity of the papal action; and Venice formulated an appeal to a future council, sending it to be posted (necessarily in secret) on the doors of San Celso in Rome. Ambassadors were also dispatched to the emperor and to the rulers of France, England, and Burgundy to justify Venetian defiance. When Sixtus died and his successor revoked the interdict, it had not yet been published or acknowledged in Venice. The episode was to serve as a model for the future.[101]

In spite of the charges that would eventually be levied against Venetian society and the Venetian church during the Counter Reformation, there is little evidence that the quality of moral and religious life supported by this unusually autonomous church was inferior to what prevailed elsewhere in Italy.[102] Indeed, the reverse may have been true. That Venetian bishops were largely drawn from the patriciate of the Republic probably meant that the high standards of social responsibility among this group were applied to

[100] Giovanni Soranzo, *La guerra fra Venezia e la S. Sede per il dominio di Ferrara (1308–1313)* (Città di Castello, 1905), esp. pp. 114–160, 177–235. The interdiction of Venice on this occasion produced a particularly vivid impression on contemporaries (p. 131).

[101] Cecchetti, I, 309–310; Pastor, IV, 375; Hochschild, pp. 317–321. For the official documents in the case, see Giuseppe Dalla Santa, "Le appellazioni della Repubblica di Venezia dalle scomuniche di Sisto IV e Giulio II," *AV*, Ser. 2, XVII (1899), 216–242.

[102] Cf. Franco Gaeta, *Un nunzio pontificio a Venezia nel Cinquecento (Girolamo Aleandro)* (Venice, 1960), p. 88. Even Pastor (IV, 92–93) found the piety of Venice an impressive "paradox" in view of Venetian policy toward the church.

ecclesiastical as well as to secular office.[103] The attractions of Venetian life undoubtedly promoted absenteeism, although the problems this caused were mitigated by the small size of the Venetian state. But there were also model bishops among the prelates of Venice, for example the devout and conscientious reforming bishop of Belluno (and later Padua), Pietro Barozzi (1441–1507).[104] To foreigners the Venetian church seemed flourishing. Commynes, at the end of the fifteenth century, was impressed like other travelers not only by the numbers and magnificence of the churches in Venice but also by the devoutness of the Venetian people. "Though they may indeed have other faults," he wrote, "I believe God blesses them for the reverence they show in the service of the church." [105] Nor was Venetian religion merely external. A rich spiritual and theological culture characterized the monasteries of the Republic which, through their patrician heads, were in close touch with the general culture of the aristocracy.[106]

Signs may be detected at least as early as the fifteenth century of the special piety and the typical attitude to ecclesiastical reform that were to characterize much of the Venetian patriciate until well into the seventeenth century. The piety of Venice was essentially a local variant of later medieval Evangelism; and we have already noticed the affinities of this movement, with its indifference to dogmatic articulation, its openness to personal religious experience, and its emphasis on individual responsibility, with the culture of Renaissance republicanism. Venice had her own analogue to the *devotio moderna* in the circle of Ludovico Barbo (1381–1443), founder of the religious community of San Giorgio in Alga; and Lorenzo Giustiniani, the first patriarch of Venice, represented similar tendencies in the middle of the fifteenth century.[107]

But the peculiar ecclesiastical arrangements of Venice and her special interest in constitutional and administrative questions also fostered a particular Venetian concern, and eventually something like a regular program, for the reform of the institutional church. Generations of Venetian reformers

[103] Cf. Alberigo, pp. 51–53, 80ff.

[104] Franco Gaeta, *Il vescovo Pietro Barozzi e il trattato 'De factionibus extinguendis'* (Venice, 1958).

[105] *Mémoires*, ed. Joseph Calmette (Paris, 1925), III, 110.

[106] Giuseppe de Luca, "Letteratura di pietà," *La civiltà veneziana del Trecento*, pp. 217–218.

[107] Roberto Cessi, "Paolinismo preluterano," *Rendiconti dell'Accademia Nazionale dei Lincei, Classe di scienze morali, storiche e filologiche*, Ser. 8, XII (1957), 7–8; Hubert Jedin, "Gasparo Contarini e il contributo veneziano alla Riforma Cattolica," in *La civiltà veneziane del Rinascimento*, p. 107.

were to urge that the church could only be purified by a more spiritual conception of her own nature and mission, by comprehensive decentralization, and by the admission of laymen to a greater share in her direction. Some of these tendencies are already apparent, along with his strong papalism, in the reform proposals of Domenico de'Domenichi, a Venetian and bishop of Torcello and Brescia as well as prominent at the Roman Curia. Domenichi prepared for Pius II a memorial *De reformationibus Romanae Curiae* (1458) which denounced the papal court for putting its ambitions in the world ahead of the kingdom of God. This was finally published in 1495, not in Rome but in Brescia. In other works Domenichi warned against exaggerations of the *plenitudo potestatis*, and conversely he exalted the dignity of episcopal office.[108] Meanwhile the law faculty at Padua continued to support the conciliar view of the church which ascribed sovereignty ultimately to the *congregatio fidelium*.[109] Nor was the Venetian reform impulse confined, even in the fifteenth century, to ecclesiastics. Francesco Barbaro indignantly contrasted the corruption of the modern with the holiness of the primitive church, and exalted Franciscan poverty.[110] In Venice the obligation of the laity to supervise the church was assumed to include substantial responsibility for its reform.

The relative political reticence and the ecclesiastical autonomy of Venice were accompanied by some cultural peculiarities. Burckhardt, who found Venice dull, backward, and derivative in her response to the literary and artistic movements of the Renaissance, will again introduce us to what has long been the standard view of the matter. He remarked on the "scanty representation" of Venice in humanistic activity. He also noted that physicians and jurists, rather than grammarians and rhetoricians, received the highest salaries at the University of Padua; that Bessarion's library, bequeathed to Venice, narrowly escaped dispersion; that there was little Venetian poetry before the sixteenth century; and that Renaissance styles in art had to be imported into Venice from the mainland.[111] Later students of the Venetian past have been inclined to depict Venice, from a cultural standpoint, as an anachronism. In this perspective she has seemed still essentially "medieval," or at least aloof from all that was exciting in the period, during the age of the

---

[108] *Ibid.*, p. 109; Pastor, IV, 9–10; and, in general, Jedin, *Studien über Domenico de'Domenichi* (Mainz, 1958).

[109] Jedin, *Geschichte des Konzils von Trient*, I (Freiburg, 1951), 29.

[110] Carotti, pp. 34–35.

[111] I, 76–77.

Renaissance; and she became "Renaissance" only when the rest of Italy was entering into the baroque age.

This conception of Venetian cultural development is still influential and undoubtedly has some validity, perhaps especially for the history of art.[112] I am inclined to believe that it is particularly useful for the sixteenth century. But, although a thorough study of the subject as a whole is still lacking, it is fairly clear that the conception will not quite do for the development of Venetian humanism. Venetian humanism did not simply follow, at some distance in time, the humanism of Florence; it may, indeed, have been important rather earlier. The differences here are not so much chronological as qualitative. This was implied at the time by the comparison of Florence with Athens and Venice with Sparta, which suggested a striking difference in spiritual climate and yet appeared to recognize that they belonged to the same cultural world.[113]

Venice, in short, was exposed to humanism early, but she failed to respond to it with an enthusiasm comparable to what it aroused in Florence. Under the influence of the Paduan humanist Mussato, humanistic attainments found a useful place in the Venetian government early in the fourteenth century. But in spite of Petrarch's close ties with Venice (where he was chiefly admired not as a classicist but as a lyric poet in the vernacular) humanism remained, in fourteenth-century Venice, primarily the possession of the narrow class of secretaries associated with the chancery.[114] As a movement it failed to develop notable leaders comparable to the humanists of Florence after Petrarch, it continued to depend largely on foreign stimulation, and above all it failed to be taken up in any general way as the new culture of the patriciate.[115]

This is not to say that it aroused no interest among the nobles of Venice. Humanistic pursuits seem to have become steadily more popular, though

[112] It may be recalled that Berenson began his account of Renaissance painting in Florence with Giotto; for Venice he started at the end of the fifteenth century. On the point in general see Guido Piovene, "Anacronismo della Venezia quattrocentesca," in *La civiltà veneziana nel Quattrocento*, pp. 1–21. For art history see also Ridolfo Pallucchini, "L'arte a Venezia nel Quattrocento," pp. 147–177 in the same volume; and for literature, the remarks of Elwert, pp. 127–128.

[113] Garin, "Cultura filosofica," p. 11.

[114] For Petrarch and Venice, see Antonio Medin, "Il culto del Petrarca nel Veneto fino alla dittatura del Bembo," *AV*, Ser. 3, VIII (1904), 421–465; Lino Lazzarini, "Francesco Petrarca e il primo umanesimo a Venezia," in *Umanesimo europeo e umanesimo veneziano*, pp. 63–92; and Paul Oskar Kristeller, "Il Petrarca, l'umanesimo e la scolastica a Venezia," in *La civiltà veneziana del Trecento*, pp. 147–178.

[115] Lino Lazzarini, *Paolo de Bernardo e i primordi dell'umanesimo in Venezia* (Geneva, 1930); Roberto Weiss, *The Spread of Italian Humanism* (London, 1964), p. 17.

probably also rather slowly, especially as contacts with the mainland increased in the course of the fifteenth century; the concerns of Francesco Barbaro and several generations of the Giustiniani make this clear. Even these figures, nevertheless, seem to have remained primarily devoted to politics and business; and if their humanistic interests were occasionally keen, they were compelled (which perhaps means that they chose) to spend most of their attention on other matters. In Venice one misses much of the fervor that elsewhere idealized the study of the classics as the "pursuit of eloquence," the source of an elevated new life style, the key to a new wisdom, and a source of hope for rebirth in all human affairs. This is probably why, although important humanists like Vittorino da Feltre, Guarino, and Filelfo were from time to time in Venice or her territories on the mainland, they did not remain long or leave any deep marks of their presence.[116]

The intellectual life of Venice remained largely attached, instead, to the conservative philosophical traditions of the University of Padua,[117] whose dominance over the education of the patriciate was carefully protected by the government for political reasons that further suggest the lack of any official concern with the new culture. In 1434, to prevent the economic decline of an important community that had ceased to be the center of a princely state after its subjection to Venice, the Senate forbade Venetians to attend any other university and declared void all academic titles obtained elsewhere.[118] Padua had a long interest of its own, side by side with its philosophical concerns, in the educational values of humanism, but there is little evidence that Paduan humanism had much general influence on the youthful patricians of Venice. Meanwhile the protection of Padua was accompanied by official indifference to the development of educational institutions in Venice. Efforts to establish a new university in the city were discouraged; and not till 1443, a century after Florence had given public support to humanistic studies, did the Great Council of Venice vote support for instruction in grammar and rhetoric. Even then it did so only with an eye to the requirements of the chancellory.[119]

[116] Cf. Hochschild, esp. pp. 111–112.

[117] Cf. Garin, "Cultura filosofica," pp. 25–26.

[118] Bruno Nardi, "Letteratura e cultura veneziana del Quattrocento," in *La civiltà veneziana del Quattrocento*, p. 117.

[119] *Ibid.*, pp. 118ff. For education in Venice during the fifteenth century in general, see also the same author's "La scuola di Rialto e l'umanesimo veneziano," in *Umanesimo europeo e umanesimo veneziano*, pp. 93–139. Vittore Branca, "Ermolao Barbaro e l'umanesimo veneziano," in the same volume, p. 193, provides a useful analysis of the stages of Venetian humanism.

Venice at last became a true center of humanistic activity in the later fifteenth century, but this was less the result of any deep (if delayed) attraction to humanistic culture than of the needs of the growing printing industry. From the presses of Venice came numerous editions of classical authors which required the services of large numbers of textual scholars; and Venetian humanism, previously pursued mainly by a few patrician amateurs, now became highly professionalized and academic, the occupation of critical philologists rather than the new culture of citizens. Its typical representatives were the orthographer Merula or Ermolao Barbaro, sponsor of the new Aristotle based directly on Greek texts instead of the standard medieval transmitters.[120] Industrial needs, therefore, pushed Venetian humanism in much the same direction as that in which humanism was being impelled by the new political climate of later fifteenth century Florence. Ermolao Barbaro was understandably an admirer of Poliziano.[121]

There are two major reasons, I think, for the relatively shallow influence of humanism in Venice and (compared with Florence) its small impact on her political culture. The first is the comparative stability of Venetian society. Its ruling group, remarkably homogeneous, dedicated to the conservation of an established rather than the creation of a new order, and continuously active both in business and public affairs, found little attraction in change, variety, or experiment. It tended, therefore, to view learning and the arts either as diversions that had always to be sacrificed in favor of more serious matters, or else in a narrowly practical light. It did not require humanistic expression for new values because it found nothing exceptionable in its traditional ways and beliefs.

The continuity of the Venetian attitude to intellectual and esthetic culture from generation to generation is notable. In the middle of the fifteenth century Bernardo Giustiniani expressed it in an oratorical commonplace: "The purpose of learning and the reward of true philosophy is not to make a man more learned but to make him better." [122] A century later, when Venetians had perhaps grown more self-conscious, a participant in one of Sperone Speroni's dialogues is made to doubt that a Venetian would study

[120] W. Theodor Elwert, *Studi di letteratura veneziana* (Venice, 1958), pp. 11ff.; Pier Giorgio Ricci, "Umanesimo filologico in Toscana e nel Veneto," in *Umanesimo europeo e umanesimo veneziano*, pp. 159–172; Weiss, pp. 45, 57–58; Branca, pp. 193–212.

[121] Cf. Arnaldo Della Torre, "La prima ambasceria di Bernardo Bembo a Firenze," *Giornale Storico della Letteratura Italiana*, XXXV (1900), 258–333; Garin, "Cultura filosofica," pp. 27ff.

[122] Quoted by Hochschild, pp. 18–19, from an oration of 1458.

philosophy "for any other purpose than to be useful to his Republic." [123] Even the Sagredo whom Galileo was to make famous as a champion of the new science sounded the same note:

> I am a Venetian gentleman, and I have never hoped to be known as a literary man. I am well disposed to literary men and have always protected them. But I do not expect to improve my fortunes or to acquire praises or reputation by becoming famous for my knowledge of philosophy and mathematics, but rather from my integrity and good administration in the magistracies and the governance of the Republic, to which I applied myself in my youth, according to the custom of my ancestors, all of whom wore themselves out and grew old in it. My studies are directed to the knowledge of those things which as a Christian I owe to God, as a citizen to my country, as a noble to my family, as a social being to my friends, and as an honest man and true philosopher to myself. [124]

Sagredo's pragmatism is clearly related to an important motive in some forms of humanism, in spite of his patronizing (and perhaps slightly aristocratic) attitude to "literary men." It also suggests much good sense. But it smacks, too, of self-complacency, narrowness of vision, and a limited capacity for intellectual or esthetic enthusiasm. A powerful inertia, related at once to practical needs and a massive self-respect, long impeded the full engagement of Venice with the new culture of the Renaissance.

Yet the conservatism and narrow practicality of Venice do not entirely explain the relatively superficial influence of humanism on Venetian culture. Another and deeper cause was also at work. Elsewhere enthusiasm for the classics depended largely on a vast admiration for Roman virtues and exploits, on a nostalgic conception of the order and stability of Roman society, and on hopes for personal and social renewal through imitation of the ancients. But their peculiar vision of the past excluded the Venetians from any general participation in this positive estimate of antiquity, especially of ancient Rome. Venice, according to Venetian tradition, had not been founded by the virtuous Romans in the course of their vigorous

[123] Quoted by Arturo Pompeati, "Le dottrine politiche di Paolo Paruta," *Giornale Storico della Letteratura Italiana*, XLVI (1905), 346.
[124] Letter to Marco Welser, Apr. 4, 1614, in Galileo Galilei, *Opere* (Florence, 1890–1909), XII, 45.

expansion throughout Italy. On the contrary: she owed her existence to successful detachment from a Roman world whose disintegration proved that it had been, in some ultimate sense, a political failure. Furthermore Venice had managed to endure essentially unchanged, both orderly and free, for a thousand years; her history was in remarkable contrast to that of turbulent and militaristic Rome. Venetians therefore were unable to view themselves as the degenerate descendants of glorious Latin antiquity now called upon, after centuries of barbaric darkness, to resume a noble heritage. Commynes noted that the Venetians venerated Livy not because he expounded Roman virtue (the reason Machiavelli esteemed him) but rather because Livy had "acquainted them well with the defects of the Roman government," which, through his instruction, they had the better managed to avoid.[125] Their disapproval of the ancient Romans promoted a marked bias in favor of Greek studies over Latin. Eventually it also stimulated Venetian suspicion of ecclesiastical Rome and contributed to anticipations of the idea of progress.[126]

The relative shallowness of Venetian humanism, its failure to be assimilated with civic values, and the absence of the perspective on antiquity that had proved so stimulating to Florentine historiography were all reflected in a comparative slowness to take up the new humanist historiography on ancient models that had so long served as a vehicle for the republican idealism of Florence. From a historiographical standpoint, this was not altogether a loss. The abiding preoccupation of the Venetians with the deeds of their ancestors found expression in a rich body of chronicles that were often far superior in accuracy and concreteness to the works of the humanists who so scorned them, and annalistic treatment of the Venetian past persisted through the fifteenth century and beyond.[127] Although this literature has not yet received careful study, we have already found it useful to illustrate some fundamental Venetian attitudes.[128] It is also significant in that, unlike most other medieval writings in this genre, the Venetian chronicles almost never attempted to place the history of the Republic in a universal context by starting with the Creation; they almost invariably

[125] *Mémoires*, III, 114.

[126] The Venetian bias against ancient Rome is discussed in Giuseppe Toffanin, *Machiavelli e il tacitismo: la politica storica della Controriforma* (Padua, 1921), pp. 11–14.

[127] See Gaetano Cozzi, "Cultura politica e religione nella 'pubblica storiografia' veneziana del '500," *BSV*, V–VI (1963–1964), esp. 218–219.

[128] Cf. above, pp. 54–56.

began with an episode directly related to the particular career of Venice. But, produced to meet the practical needs of particular patrician families or of a government that attached special value to discretion, the chronicles of Venice were not widely circulated, and they did not constitute a public corpus of historical literature like some Florentine chronicles.[129]

Only toward the middle of the century did Venetians begin to take an active interest in the new humanist history of the Renaissance. In about 1440 Francesco Barbaro commissioned Evangelista Manelmi to compose a humanistic account of the recent heroic defense of Brescia; and in the following decades several prominent patricians tried to interest the government in importing a distinguished humanist to write an official history of Venice. Several candidates, including Lorenzo Valla, Trapezuntius, and Filelfo the younger were proposed to the Senate after 1456; and Lodovico Foscarini attempted in 1463 to secure an appointment for Flavio Biondo, who had already demonstrated his fitness for the post by summarizing the references to Venice from his *Decades* into a work *De origine et gestis Venetorum*.[130] But these efforts came to nothing.[131] Although the Senate rewarded Marc'Antonio Sabellico (also an outsider) for his Venetian history some two decades later, it could not be persuaded to establish the position of official historian until the appointment of Andrea Navagero in the sixteenth century.[132] Yet the encouragement given Sabellico signified that Venice was perhaps at last ready to participate more fully in Renaissance culture. The publication of his work in 1487 and, posthumously, of Bernardo Giustiniani's account of the early centuries of Venetian history in 1492, mark the beginning of the Venetian transition from chronicle to history. Eventually, as in Florence, historical compositions were to play a large part in expressing the political consciousness of Venice.

[129] Auguste Prost, "Les chroniques vénitiennes," *Revue des questions historiques*, XXXI (1882), 528–529, which includes a useful catalogue of works of this kind; cf. Hans Baron, "A Forgotten Chronicle of Early Fifteenth Century Venice," *Essays in History and Literature Presented to Stanley Pargellis* (Chicago, 1965), esp. pp. 20–21.

[130] First printed at Venice in 1481.

[131] Foscarini, pp. 244–249; Zippel, pp. 93–133. Foscarini's judgment that Venice was relatively lacking in historical composition and that gestures of this kind were exceptional, however significant (p. 244), seems to me still valid, though it takes too little account of chronicle literature.

[132] Sabellico has often been treated as an official historian; but see Carlo Lagomaggiore, "L'Istoria veneziana di M. Pietro Bembo," *AV*, Ser. 3, VII (1904), 6–7. The distinction between encouragement by the government and official appointment may be only a matter of degree, but the difference between a tentative interest and the institutionalization of historiography is of some importance here.

The Venetian history of Sabellico, however, the first such work to be composed with the positive encouragement of the Venetian government, was a rather mediocre example of humanist historiography; and later generations of Venetians treated it with contempt.[133] Sabellico was neither a Venetian nor a man of affairs, and some of the defects in his work perhaps derived from insensitivity to Venetian values and attitudes and from political inexperience. Thus his conventional flattery of the Venetians as equal in military prowess to the Romans gave offense because it cast doubt on Venetian pacifism and suggested a similarity precisely where the Venetians took pride in difference.[134] He also revealed a remarkably un-Venetian scepticism in his treatment of the events of 1177.[135] The fact that Sabellico followed his work on Venice with a universal history[136] further illustrates, in spite of the place it gave to Venice, his remoteness from the attitudes of a true Venetian, and his inadequacies as a philologist contrast markedly with the precise scholarship now beginning to characterize Venetian humanism.[137]

He managed nevertheless, in a work tracing the history of Venice from her foundation in the fifth century down to 1487, to incorporate most of the commonplaces about the Venetian past we have already encountered. The earliest Venetians, he repeated, had been without exception free and worthy men; and he celebrated their simplicity, virtue, and piety. Wishing "to make sure that the liberty in which the city had been born should be perpetual," they had created a structure of "holy laws and ordinances" in order to provide "a form of life and of equal justice for all." And these happy institutions had been zealously protected by all subsequent generations. Venice, "if it should be possible for anything human," would be "perpetual and eternal." Nor did Sabellico omit the suggestion, in spite of his conventional use of the Roman model, that a good judge might plausibly find

[133] Donato Giannotti reflects this contempt in his *Libro della Repubblica de'Veneziani* (Opere [Pisa, 1819] X), 19, 56. See also Foscarini, p. 263, and the epistle to Ludovico Domenichi's translation of Marcello, *Vite de' prencipi di Vinegia* (Venice, 1557). For Sabellico in general, see Ruggiero Bersi, "Le fonti della prima decade delle *Historiae rerum venetarum* di Marcantonio Sabellico," *AV*, Ser. 3, XIX (1910), 422–460, and XX (1910), 115–162; and Gaetano Cozzi, "Cultura politica e religione nella 'pubblica storiografia' veneziana del '500," *BSV*, V–VI (1963–1964), 219–222.

[134] For example sig. B3^r. This may well be the passage referred to by Trifone Gabriele in his attack on Sabellico, in Giannotti, p. 19.

[135] Sigs. F4^r–F6^r.

[136] *Rapsodie historiarum enneadum ab orbe condito ad annum salutis humane 1504* (Venice, 1498–1504), discussed by Wallace Ferguson, *The Renaissance in Historical Thought* (Boston, 1948), pp. 16–17.

[137] Cf. Branca, pp. 196, 198, contrasting him with Ermolao Barbaro.

Venice more admirable than Rome "for sanctity of laws, for equity of justice, and for goodness." [138]

Otherwise there is little to distinguish Sabellico's work from humanist histories elsewhere, and in some respects it is inferior: for example in its discovery of the miraculous coincidence that Venice was founded on the same day of the year (the twenty-fifth of March) that God created Adam and Mary conceived Jesus.[139] Like other humanist historians Sabellico was convinced of the utility of historical composition, which could make the attentive reader "wise and prudent in all civil actions through the multitude of good examples." But he conceived of his task as rhetoric rather than research. For Sabellico the problem of the historian was to compose an attractive account from the raw material contained "in certain crude and disorderly old books." [140] Even here his success was limited. In spite of his pretensions to polish, his account hardly rises above the chronicles on which it is based. It is thus hardly surprising that his more sophisticated Venetian readers of the next century found his work neither rhetorically pleasing, precise enough to be politically useful, or sufficiently flattering to Venice. Yet it marked a beginning of a kind, even though Sabellico's claim—presented with some amazement—that "from whatever reason this proceeds" no one before him had written a history of the Venetians[141] was true only if it is taken to refer to formal humanist productions like his own.

Giustiniani's *History of the Origin of Venice*, which was composed at about the same time as Sabellico's work, though far narrower in scope, is both more satisfactory as history and more illuminating as a vehicle of Venetian attitudes. Both virtues may be attributed largely to Giustiniani's active career in the service of Venice; his broad experience in public affairs enabled him to bring a seasoned judgment to his sources. In addition, his reading was extensive, and he has long been admired as a pioneer of critical research.[142] Foscarini, who thought poorly of Sabellico, hailed Giustiniani as the "new father," after Andrea Dandolo, of Venetian history.[143] But Giustiniani's motives were those of a humanist historian. He shared the humanists' confidence in the exemplary uses of the past; his aim was to expose the

[138] Sigs. A1v–A2r.
[139] Sig. A3v.
[140] Sigs. A1r–A1v (Proemio).
[141] Sig. A1v (Proemio).
[142] Fueter, *Historiographie moderne*, pp. 136–139; Gilbert, *Machiavelli and Guicciardini*, p. 14. He relied particularly, as Sabellico had done, on the work of Biondo.
[143] P. 263.

founding fathers of Venice as models of devotion to liberty and general civic responsibility for the emulation of his own contemporaries.[144]

Much in his work reminds us that he was a Venetian, including his initial emphasis on the remarkable location of the city[145] and his preoccupation with the Turks as the perennial enemies of the Republic.[146] Some degree of aristocratic bias appears in his insistence that Venice possessed a great nobility from the beginning and in his approval of the reduction in the size of the ruling group during the Middle Ages.[147] Venice, he also believed, had been founded by providence as the refuge for a group of peculiarly devout and virtuous men in an age of general decline; and this saving remnant he saw as ordained by God to take the place of ancient Rome by establishing the most excellent polity in the world.[148] He also suggests the typical political pluralism of the Renaissance in his approval of the division of the ancient universal empire. "It must not be omitted," he declared, "that nature has constituted all things in appropriate numbers, and it does not wish the power of any kingdom to be infinite." The size and variety of the world, for Giustiniani, precluded effective government by a single authority.[149] It is true that, throughout his history he emphasized Venetian orthodoxy and religious zeal in a manner not generally characteristic of humanist histories,[150] but his piety was of a typically lay variety. Thus, like Guicciardini, he deplored the withdrawal of Constantine to the East (however beneficent its eventual political consequences) because of its unhappy results for the clergy. The removal of the restraints imposed by a strong temporal authority had the result, he wrote, that "avarice and envy, the common pestilences of human beings, invaded the minds of the priests."[151]

Thus in various ways Giustiniani reveals biases much like those of the great Florentine historians in the next century. This is also true of his sensitivity to the precarious condition of Italy in his own time and his brief analysis of its causes, in which he remarkably foreshadows Machiavelli.

[144] Hochschild, pp. 356–358, 385–389.
[145] Cols. 5–8 in the edition cited.
[146] Cols. 85–90.
[147] Hochschild cites Cols. 29, 32–34, 61, 71, 104, 106, 119.
[148] Col. 9.
[149] Col. 145: "Caeterum illud quoque non omittendum: Naturam omnia numeris suis constituisse, neque infinitam esse voluisse ullius regni potentiam. Universi autem orbis si quis populorum regnorumque multitudinem consideret, haud crediderim, ex unius arce mentis recte gubernari posse."
[150] Hochschild, pp. 416–418.
[151] Col. 14.

For Giustiniani Italy was weak because she had lost the military virtue of antiquity; and his alarm at the transfer of this quality to the peoples beyond the Alps suggests considerable prescience.[152] Aware of the crisis gathering over Italy, Giustiniani was inclined, in occasional moods, to lament the general mutability of things in the manner of the later Renaissance.[153] His concern for the future did not exclude Venice, and his exemplary use of the past seems to have been partly based on anxiety about the present condition and prospects of the Republic. There is in his history a hint, previously rather uncharacteristic of a Venetian, that even the happy institutions of Venice might be subject to decay and in need of periodic regeneration.[154] Venice, by the end of the fifteenth century, was perhaps at last on the verge of participating in the central Renaissance ideal of renewal.

Although Venice lagged considerably behind Florence in many dimensions of Renaissance culture, she had nevertheless long realized one major Renaissance ideal in abundance: her subjects enjoyed a high degree of personal liberty. In a society where an internalized conformity to the fundamental demands of the state was so dependable, much could be tolerated; and Venice managed to contain a wide range of individual difference, especially in matters of religious opinion, within a relaxed homogeneity secured by education rather than compulsion. Because agreement on essentials went so deep, freedom and difference (which the enemies of Venice called *license*) were possible to an unusual degree.[155]

Testimony to the personal freedom enjoyed by the inhabitants of Venice may be found at least as early as Petrarch, who claimed to be shocked by it. "Much freedom reigns there in every respect," he declared, "and what I should call the only evil prevailing—but also the worst—far too much freedom of speech." [156] For centuries Venice was an asylum for refugees of many kinds, to whose diverse ways of life and thought she granted a broad tolerance. The Greek delegation was impressed, on its way to the Council of Florence, by its warm reception in Venice, and many of its members eventually returned.[157] And, as we shall see, the free atmosphere of Venice was only slightly modified by the pressures of the tenser sixteenth century.

[152] Col. 24.
[153] As in Col. 53.
[154] Hochschild, pp. 400–406, particularly citing Cols. 57–59.
[155] Cf. Elwert, *Studi*, p. 57.
[156] *De suis ipsius et multorum ignorantia*, p. 121.
[157] Geanakoplos, pp. 34–35.

Marot, who did not feel safe enough with his patroness in Ferrara, took refuge in Venice. Aretino found in Venice a secure base from which to harry contemporaries with his wit. Postel, Le Roy, and Bodin—the last in spite of his attacks on the polity of the Republic—published their most radical works in Venice. Galileo, in a kind of tribute to the milieu that had nourished his boldest conclusions, set his great *Dialogo* in Venice.[158] The freedom of Venice provides another significant line of continuity in her history; we shall find it celebrated as enthusiastically at the end of the development with which this book is concerned as at the beginning, and in much the same terms. So Henry Wotton reported in 1606 to the Earl of Salisbury, as a point worth noting: "It is a State that whether it be in fear or otherwise, heareth all men speak willingly." [159] The point is even stronger as one term in a tragic comparison. Sagredo made it in a letter to his friend Galileo, written to warn the great scientist after his departure for Florence of the danger of depending on the promises of even so hopeful a patron as the young Grand Duke of Tuscany and to remind him of the advantages in the situation he had decided to abandon. "Where will you be able to find liberty and the right to rule your own life as in Venice?" he asked. "You are now serving your natural prince, who is great, full of virtue, young, and of singular promise; but here you command those who command and govern others, and you had only to serve yourself, as if you were the ruler of the universe." [160]

Thus, if Venice was in some respects less conscious and articulate about dimensions of political liberty that Florentines discussed with such appreciation, she was notably advanced in her realization of still another aspect of freedom that was, perhaps, her peculiar contribution to the Renaissance political achievement. And in an important respect freedom of thought and expression, so directly related to the Renaissance vision of reality as open and indefinite, was basic to the other dimensions of political liberty. As long as such freedom survived, it would still be possible to maintain, at least as ideals, the other kinds of freedom; but once this perished, all would be lost together. Her special attachment to this kind of liberty allowed Venice to continue to express Renaissance values of all kinds, and eventually to defend them in a world that found them increasingly uncongenial.

[158] Cf. Gaeta, "Mito di Venezia," p. 69.
[159] Letter of June 16, 1606, in Smith, I, 352.
[160] Aug. 13, 1611, in Galilei, *Opere*, XI, 170–172.

· III ·

Venice Preserved

ALTHOUGH the roots of Venetian republicanism went remarkably deep, and although during the fifteenth century Venice abandoned her long isolation from the political struggles of Italy, she had by the sixteenth century made no great advance toward the development of a native tradition of political and historical discourse such as had long been at work in Florence, nor had she yet committed herself fully to the new artistic and literary attitudes of the Renaissance. As long as the prosperity of the Republic was undiminished, as long as she felt secure and could still consider herself a world power, Venice was apparently destined to remain locked in the self-centered and relatively inarticulate complacency that had so long characterized her history. Before any serious transformation could occur, Venice needed to be shaken up.

Such a shaking was administered by the catastrophic events of the later fifteenth and early sixteenth centuries. Economic setbacks on several fronts, mounting Turkish pressure in the Levant, the domination of Italy by ultramontane powers too formidable to be either ignored or manipulated, and the hostility of a militant pope prepared both to ally with the invaders and to humiliate the Republic with spiritual weapons, combined to bring about a general crisis which substantially altered the circumstances of Venetian existence. The proud Republic, long confident that she could freely determine her own destiny in the world and that the greatness of the past could be extended indefinitely into the future, began accordingly to articulate views on the nature of political reality which subtly adapted her traditional assumptions to new and changing conditions.

The adaptation of Venice was gradual; and its first stage, which will be studied in this chapter, was often spiritually closer, in its abstractness and idealization, to the medieval vision of reality than to the realism of Machiavelli. Venetian political discourse, until well past the middle of the sixteenth century, was generally as remote from the dangerous world of modern politics as political discussion was now tending to be in the rest of Italy. It was superior only, perhaps, in energy and conviction. But Venice was compelled to pass, eventually, through further perilous adventures; and the preservation of her independence, her republican institutions, and the relative openness of her cultural atmosphere, all of which generally distinguished her now from the rest of Italy, enabled her political vision to develop from stage to stage. Thus the defensive idealism of Venice during the earlier sixteenth century became the point of departure for a more realistic political mentality in her later history.

It can hardly be denied that Venice in the long run did not, and probably could not, rise to the challenges with which she was confronted. By the second quarter of the seventeenth century her decadence was evident, though less so to contemporaries than to us. Yet her adjustment to novel conditions was more successful, and some of its incidental accomplishments were more significant for the future, than has often been recognized. To characterize the sixteenth century as the decadence of Venice is premature, at the least.[1] Venice retained her vigor through the sixteenth century, her European importance through the first half of the seventeenth, and, under improbable conditions, her independence until Napoleon. Meanwhile she was slowly taking her place, like Florence a century earlier, as an aggressively self-conscious republic in which explicit civic values developed in close conjunction with a brilliant native culture.

The economic difficulties of Venice during the later fifteenth and early sixteenth centuries were complex. Venetian shipping in the Mediterranean had been declining during the second half of the fifteenth century, though more from foreign competition than Turkish pressure. In addition, the first results of the Portuguese development of new trade routes to the Orient were disastrous. Within a few years the Venetian spice trade fell to a quarter of its previous level, and Venetian galleys gradually gave up the voyage to Flanders.[2] Meanwhile the end of the fifteenth century and the early years of the sixteenth brought a wave of bank failures, the result of heavy public expenditures for war combined with a lack of ready money; even the

---

[1] As in Roberto Cessi's standard *Storia della Republica di Venezia* (Milan, 1944), which covers the history of Venice from the beginning of the sixteenth century to the end of the Republic under the general title "La Decadenza." See also Brown, *Venice*, pp. 353–354. On the other hand the suggestion of Alberto Tenenti, *Cristoforo da Canal. La marine vénitienne avant Lepante* (Paris, 1962), xi, that Venice during this period missed a genuine opportunity to create a state of the modern type seems to me unrealistic.

[2] Cf. Lane, *Venice and History*, pp. 10–15; and Vitorino Magalhães-Godinho, "Le repli vénitien et égyptien et la route du Cap," *Hommage à Lucien Febvre: Éventail de l'histoire vivante* (Paris, 1953), II, esp. 285ff.

greatest Venetian banks succumbed.[3] Yet, although her economic reverses during this period no doubt affected the mood of the Republic in subtle ways, the importance of this dimension of the general Venetian crisis should not be exaggerated. Venice remained prosperous,[4] and the major blows she was compelled to absorb were not so much to her pocket-book as to her security and self-esteem. The crisis was above all moral and political.

The first damaging blows came from the East. Turkish attacks during the first half of the fifteenth century did little harm either to the empire or the commerce of Venice, but after the fall of Constantinople the Turks began to absorb Venetian possessions in the eastern Mediterranean. During the first great Turkish war of 1463–1479 Venice, still reasonably undistracted by events in Italy, could concentrate on the Levant; but even so she lost Negropont, to her great distress. The war of 1499–1503, occurring after the entrance of the great powers into Italy, was even more serious. It brought further heavy losses overseas, it distracted Venice from the struggles on the peninsula, and its heavy costs limited her role in Italy for the immediate future.[5] Criticism of Venetian policy during this period has not always considered the problem of the Republic in having simultaneously to play some role in Italy and to engage in a desperate series of holding actions against the Turks. The two areas of concern were related. Her enemies in Italy, pro-French Florence and Milan, encouraged the Turks to attack Venice; and the Venetian decision to accept harsh terms of peace with the Turks was based largely on the need to attend to matters closer to home.

Yet Venice, perhaps partly because her own territories were not immediately threatened, was remarkably slow to appreciate the full significance of the foreign presence in Italy. For some time, persisting in the narrowly self-seeking mentality of fifteenth-century politics, she viewed the new situation largely as an opportunity for making gains at the expense of her neighbors. Her participation in the alliance that expelled the first wave of French invaders thus indicated no general appreciation of the need for unity against a common danger. This shortly became clear with her aid in the effort of Pisa to throw off the rule of Florence, and even more when in 1499 she collaborated in the French conquest of Milan, accepted Cremona as her reward, and took

[3] Luzzatto, *Storia economica di Venezia*, pp. 189, 246–247; and, in more detail, Lane, pp. 78–83.

[4] Cf. Luzzatto, pp. 230–233.

[5] *Ibid.*, pp. 236–240.

advantage of the troubles of the Papal State by seizing territories in the Romagna.[6]

By such actions Venice managed both to isolate herself and to increase the universal resentment to which she was already exposed by her vast wealth. The general hostility of Europe at last took concrete form in the League of Cambray, concluded at the end of 1508, in which all the major powers, both in Italy and abroad, committed themselves to chastise Venice and to partition her empire. No doubt greed played the largest part in the formation of this alliance, but the obtuse expansionism of Venice allowed the allies to represent the war as a defensive, righteous, and almost judicial operation. The French ambassador at the imperial court described the Venetians, with at least feigned sincerity, as "merchants of human blood, traitors to the Christian faith, [who] have tacitly partitioned the world with the Turks, and already are thinking of throwing bridges across the Danube, the Rhine, the Seine, the Tagus, and the Ebro, aiming to reduce Europe to a province and to hold her in subjugation with their armies."[7]

The role of the pope first in sponsoring the League of Cambray and then in supplementing its military operations with spiritual weapons added another major dimension to the struggle which would be long remembered both in Rome and Venice. Almost immediately after his election, Julius II complained about the Venetian occupation of papal territory[8] and showed his displeasure by refusing to name any Venetian subject to the Sacred College.[9] He also spoke, as early as 1503, of a holy alliance against the Republic; and in February of the following year he was considering the wisdom of an interdict.[10] Venice defended her action with the argument that the pope was patently incapable of any direct rule over the lands in question and that the Republic should be permitted to rule in his behalf,[11] an argument perhaps ambiguously related to the Venetian preference for a spiritual church. On

[6] Cessi, II, 32ff., though this is perhaps too favorable to Venice; and Federico Seneca, *Venezia e Papa Giulio II* (Padua, 1962), *passim*.

[7] Quoted by Antonio Bonardi, "Venezia e la lega di Cambrai," *AV*, Ser. 3, VII (1904), 212. Over a century later Sarpi still recalled the ambassador's speech with resentment. See his *consulto, Sulla publicazione di scritture malediche contra il governo*, in *SG*, pp. 225–226. That belief in Venetian imperialism was widespread is also indicated by the remark of Commynes: "Et vous diz bien que je les ay congneüs si saiges et tant enclins à croistre leur Seigneurie, que, s'il n'y est pourveü tost, que tous leurs voisins en mauldiront l'heure." (*Mémoires*, III, 113).

[8] Antonio Giustinian, *Dispacci*, ed. P. Villari (Florence, 1876), II, 277 (dispatch of Nov. 2, 1503).

[9] *Ibid.*, II, 319–321 (dispatch of Nov. 30, 1503).

[10] *Ibid.*, II, 318, 430 (dispatches of Nov. 29, 1503, and Feb. 8, 1504).

[11] *Ibid.*, II, 402 (dispatch of Jan. 20, 1504), for example.

the papal side deeper grievances were also at work. Julius II, as heir to the renewed hierocratic militancy of the later fifteenth-century papacy, saw himself as the defender of all the claims of the church, ecclesiastical and spiritual as well as temporal. Thus he was concerned not only with the rights of the pope over the Romagna but also with his right, so long resisted by the Republic, to dispose of Venetian benefices. The bull by which he announced the excommunication of the Senate and the interdiction of the Venetian state specified both grievances.[12] Thus from the standpoint of Venice the issues in the war were not merely territorial. An important element in her traditional way of life, long considered an essential condition of Venetian liberty, was at stake.

The war opened with a major Venetian disaster. In the middle of May, 1509, in spite of a tardy effort to put a good face on her predicament by ordering the armies of the Republic to advance with the cry "Italy! Liberty!", the Venetian forces were badly defeated at Agnadello; and the remnant withdrew to the lagoons. As Machiavelli observed: "If their city had not been surrounded by the waters, we should have beheld her end." [13] Venice was saved by her location, but this totally unexpected defeat brought on a brief crisis of confidence which gave substance to foreign charges of Venetian inconstancy in the face of fortune. Contemporaries described how Venetians, ordinarily so dignified and grave, wandered erratically through the city exclaiming that all was lost.[14] Frantic attempts (later denied) were made to obtain help from the Turks.[15] Meanwhile an embassy was dispatched to the imperial court to sue for peace. It is likely, although the evidence is not altogether conclusive, that the Venetian ambassador offered, in return, to acknowledge the emperor's suzerainty, not only over Venetian territories on the mainland but also over the Serenissima herself.[16] The proposal, if actually made, suggested a radical moral and political disarray.

[12] Seneca, pp. 46, 105–106, 121, and *passim;* Niero, *I patriarchi di Venezia*, p. 55, notes his desire to take the designation of the patriarch away from the Senate.

[13] *Discorsi*, Bk. 2, Ch. 30. Cf. Bk. 1, Ch. 6, for Machiavelli's further reaction to the Venetian predicament.

[14] A particularly vivid account appears in Luigi da Porto, *Lettere storiche*, ed. Bartolommeo Bressan (Florence, 1857). p. 63.

[15] Bonardi, pp. 235–236, 243–244; Seneca, pp. 126–127.

[16] See Giucciardini, *Storia d'Italia*, Bk. VIII, Ch. 6; on the authenticity of this account cf. Luciani, *Guicciardini and his European Reputation* pp. 81ff. Machiavelli also insisted (*Discorsi*, Bk. III, Ch. 31) that the Venetians "made themselves tributary to the emperor." It may be significant that the emperor shortly afterward took the position that Venice was a free city of the Empire in the same class with such places as Hamburg and Lübeck; see Bonardi, "Venezia città libera dell'Impero", pp. 127–147. For Venetian denials, see Cessi, II, 66, 73.

But after the initial alarm Venetian morale began to improve; and it is some tribute to the coherence of a society often criticized as an oppressive oligarchy that the populace remained, in this many-sided crisis, generally united in support of the government. Private citizens pledged their fortunes to save the state, and the military situation began to improve.[17] The abandoned cities on the mainland, hoping to save themselves from pillage, had expelled their Venetian rectors and acknowledged new masters, French or imperial; but the disintegration of the mainland empire was finally halted at Treviso, and by the end of July the Venetians had reoccupied Padua. Its successful defense, supported by the lower classes in the town itself,[18] against a besieging force led personally by the emperor Maximilian, made the recovery of Venetian morale definitive.

Meanwhile Venice had been dealing with the danger posed by the pope's censures. She did so at home precisely as she had done earlier under similar circumstances, notably in the interdict of 1483. The government described the censures as politically motivated and therefore unjust, prohibited their publication, and prepared an appeal, secretly posted on the doors of Saint Peter's in Rome, to a future general council.[19] Venice also sponsored the preparation of a body of literature attacking the pope as a fomenter of war.[20] This defiance did not prevent her from sending an embassy to Rome to negotiate peace; but her ambassadors seemed in no great hurry to capitulate to the pope's demands, which were severe. Venice was prepared to surrender the disputed territories, but the disposition of benefices was a more difficult problem. Because the pope insisted that Venice must yield on this point, and also because he maintained for some time that his obligations to the whole

[17] In contrast to Machiavelli, Giovio discerned in the Venetians at this point a steadfastness superior to the Romans; cf. Carlo Volpati, "Paolo Giovio e Venezia," *AV*, Ser. 5, XV (1934), 152–153. But Seneca, p. 126, notes that Venetian solidarity was not total.

[18] This may be taken, at least in part, as a tribute to Venetian administration. On the tendency of the lower classes, both rural and urban, to support the Venetian side, see Bonardi, "Venezia e la liga," pp. 231–232, and, by the same author, *I padovani ribelli alla Repubblica di Venezia (a. 1500–1530)* (Venice, 1902), p. 304. For the general loyalty of the *terraferma* to Venice see also Valeri, p. 46; for the defense of Padua, see Polibio Zanetti, "L'assedio di Padova del 1509 in correlazione alla guerra combattuta nel Veneto dal maggio all'ottobre," *AV*, Ser. 2, II (1891), 5–168.

[19] Cecchetti, I, 315–316. For the Venetian case in favor of resistance, see Giuseppe Dalla Santa, "Il vero testo dell'appellazione di Venezia dalla scommunica di Giulio II," *AV* Ser. 2, XIX (1900), 349–361.

[20] Pastor, VI, 320.

alliance precluded lifting the interdict, the negotiations dragged on for six months.[21]

But at last, seeing no other way to break up the alliance against her, Venice agreed to the pope's terms. She relinquished the lands in the Romagna and also renounced her claims to Ferrara, and she promised to allow free passage in the Adriatic to the subjects of the pope. These concessions were merely political and, although painful, raised few issues of principle. But Venice was also compelled to renounce the right of presentation to most major benefices (though with the significant exception of the patriarchate itself), she promised to impose no tax on the clergy without the pope's permission, and she agreed to stop interfering with church courts. In addition she was forced to admit the justice of the papal censure (and thus in principle the validity of acts of this kind), and she renounced the right of appeal to a council.[22] The last capitulations were particularly serious because, if Venice adhered to them, her capacity for resistance in any future altercation with the pope would be seriously impaired. But, in appearing to surrender, Venice was following Cardinal Riario's advice: "Do what he wishes, and later, with time, do what you will."[23] She still hoped to install herself again in the Romagna, and she managed for the most part to avoid carrying out the other terms of the agreement. Even before the formal act of absolution, the Council of Ten secretly declared its conditions void because extorted by force. Eventually Venetians claimed, to the indignation of Rome, that no conditions had ever been imposed.[24] Venice had lost a battle but she was by no means ready to concede the war, and a century later she would resort to the same modes of resistance to ecclesiastical censure as in 1509.

Peace with the pope, nevertheless, served its immediate purpose. The inability of the allies to support or to coordinate their armies had delayed exploitation of the initial victory; and when Julius II now formed a new Holy League against the French in which Venice was included, her crisis of survival was clearly over. Furthermore when, in the new alliance, her papal and imperial allies showed little disposition to return to Venice the lands they had seized in 1509, she defied Leo X's threat of new censures and switched sides; and after Marignano she recovered nearly all that she had lost. The

[21] See the *Sommario della Relazione di Roma* of Paolo Cappello, Apr. 1, 1510, Albèri, Ser. 2, III, 17ff.; Seneca, p. 133.
[22] Cecchetti, I, 316–317.
[23] Quoted by Cessi, II, 61–62.
[24] Discussed by Seneca, pp. 146–147.

Peace of Bologna at the end of 1529, which brought an end to the Habsburg-Valois wars in Italy, confirmed this result.

The destruction of the last Florentine Republic in the following year underlined the dangers of this period for the freedom of all Italian states and doubtless contributed to the Venetian sense of isolation. This event was observed from Venice with mixed feelings. Venetians had felt little but hostility to the anti-Venetian Florence of the Medici, but a joint attack on the restored Republic by a Habsburg emperor and a Medici pope elicited a rather different reaction, in which the deeply rooted Venetian disapproval of Florentine disorder was accompanied by hints of sympathy. Although it repeated conventional criticism of Florence, the relation of Marco Foscari in 1527, after his Florentine embassy, had already suggested some respect for the republican followers of Savonarola, a group which, Foscari believed, included "almost all the first men of Florence for prudence, goodness, family, wealth, and every other sort of distinction."[25] And when the attack on the city began in 1529, the new Venetian resident, Carlo Capello, repeatedly described the resistance as a struggle for liberty. He also noted in it a strong religious impulse of a sort many sensitive Venetians may well have found congenial, and he communicated Florentine appeals for Venetian help, together with the argument that, if Florence fell, Venice would be next.[26] Gasparo Contarini expressed his pity for besieged Florence,[27] and a few years later the Venetian ambassador in Rome referred to her "harsh and shameful siege and overthrow."[28] But although Capello was authorized to encourage the Florentines "in the generous defense to conserve their liberty,"[29] Venice, already negotiating peace with the emperor, was in no position to help; and Florence fell. Her fate was taken by some Venetians as a warning. In a debate in the Senate shortly after, a leading patrician warned that what Clement VII had done to Florence he would now attempt against Venice.[30]

Nevertheless the downfall of Florence also served to dramatize the fact that Venice had survived the greatest crisis in her history, with both her liberty and her dominions on the mainland unimpaired. Assailed by nearly

[25] Albèri, Ser. 2, II, 42, 69.

[26] See his dispatches of Jul. 26, 1529, and Feb. 9 and 28, 1530, *ibid.*, Ser. 2, I, 179–180, 272, 275–276.

[27] In his *Relazione di Roma* of 1530, *ibid.*, Ser. 2, III, 299.

[28] *Relazione di Roma* of Antonio Surian, 1535, *ibid.*, p. 299.

[29] Capello's dispatch of Oct. 6, 1529, *ibid.*, Ser. 2, I, 230. There are many similar passages in these dispatches.

[30] See the exchange quoted by Gaeta, *Nunzio pontificio*, p. 61. For Venetian sympathy towards Florence in general, see Cessi, II, 90.

the whole of Europe, the Republic had miraculously endured; and until the last third of the century, her mood was in large measure a response to the miracle of Venice Preserved. On the surface this mood appears remarkably positive. Venetians, and indeed other Europeans, seemed generally persuaded that, having passed safely through so many perils, Venice could now endure anything. The pope himself compared Venice in 1531 to "a great ship which fears neither fortune nor commotion of winds, however great they may be." [31] Venice, to all appearances, was a rock of stability, a second Rome, superior to the first not only for domestic peace but in her capacity for survival. The miracle evidently justified enthusiastic self-congratulation, and it nourished expressions of confidence that went far beyond the more quiet assurance of earlier Venetians.

Yet the very extravagance of Venetian self-regard during the middle decades of the century suggests an underlying anxiety such as previous generations had not felt. In fact conditions had drastically altered, largely for the worse; and Venice, after the trauma of 1509, would never be able to regard either the surrounding world or herself in quite the same way. As the sequel would reveal, she began to acquire during this dangerous period a cautious sensitivity to complex political realities with which she had not previously been forced to cope, and above all to the dangers for republican liberty stemming both from the foreign presence in Italy and from the political and ecclesiastical ambitions of the pope. It was not only by way of celebration, but also because she was under pressure from an alien world, that Venice now began to articulate far more fully the republican values implicit in her history.

Thus the essential characteristics of the Venetian attitude toward political matters for the next half century was not so much confidence as a defensive conservatism in which the more measured complacency of previous generations was carried to extremes. Venice aimed chiefly to preserve what she had in a dangerous and unstable world; and in this respect she participated, for all her difference in other ways, in the weary passivity that had descended on the rest of Italy. Although her dedication to the preservation of a cherished heritage may have served the immediate political and psychological needs of the Republic, it also meant a growing rigidity and a resistance to change altogether contrary to the flexibility of Renaissance politics. The latter part of the century brought a considerable shift in this respect, but the reluctance of Venetians to adjust the admirable practices of the Republic to a world of constant change was to be a perennial defect of Venetian politics; Venice was

[31] As reported by Antonio Surian in his *Relazione* of 1531, in Albèri, Ser. 2, III, 286.

as notorious for procrastination and inflexibility as she was admired for prudence and gravity. As Sarpi described the problem a century after Agnadello, though with some exaggeration: "When an innovation is proposed, the whole Republic will certainly be opposed; but when something done ought to be undone, there will always be more in the council on the negative side than on the affirmative, and it will be said: let it go on, since it has begun." [32]

The revival of Venetian commerce after the first third of the sixteenth century, the expansion of other forms of economic activity, and a rapid growth in the population of the city, no doubt helped to sustain the conviction that all was well with the Republic. The Portuguese capture of the spice trade proved only temporary, and by 1550 Venice was again the leading purveyor of spices to the rest of Europe.[33] With the spice trade went a profitable commerce in other goods with the Levant, and Venice continued to enjoy the advantages of her location at the head of the Adriatic for trade with Germany, from which she drew rich profits until the Thirty Years' War.[34] A vigorous revival of Venetian shipbuilding after 1535 supplied the needs of her commerce.[35]

At the same time important shifts within the economy suggest, at least in this sector, more initiative than has conventionally been attributed to sixteenth-century Venice.[36] During the middle years of the century Venice became increasingly important as an industrial power. The production of woolens, for example, rose through the century, reaching a peak between 1560 and 1620, and by the end of the century Venice was producing far more woolen cloth than Florence or Milan, her nearest competitors in Italy.[37]

[32] In the discussion with Christoph von Dohna, reported by the latter on Aug. 4, 1608, in *Briefe und Akten zur Geschichte des 30 jährigen Krieges*, ed. M. Ritter et al. (Munich, 1870–1909), II, 81. See also Dohna's report three days later, p. 82; and cf. the remarks of William Bedell, letter to Adam Newton, Jan. 1, 1609, in *Two Biographies of William Bedell*, ed. E. S. Shuckburgh (Cambridge, 1902), p. 240.

[33] Lane, pp. 25–34; Gino Luzzatto, "La decadenza di Venezia dopo le scoperte geografiche nella tradizione e nella realtà," *AV*, Ser. 5, LIV–LV (1954), 162–181.

[34] Fernand Braudel, *La Méditerranée et le monde méditerranéan à l'èpoque de Philippe II* (Paris, 1949), pp. 423ff.; Hermann Kellenbenz, "Le déclin de Venise et les relations économiques de Venise avec les marches au nord des Alpes," *Aspetti e cause della decadenza economica veneziana nel secolo XVII* (Venice, 1961), pp. 111–112.

[35] Lane, pp. 11–12. Cf. Ruggiero Romano, "La marine marchande vénitienne au XVI siècle," *Les sources de l'histoire maritime en Europe, du moyen âge au XVIIIe siècle* (Paris, 1962), esp. p. 46.

[36] This is recognized by Tenenti, *Cristoforo da Canal*, viii–ix.

[37] See the figures in Domenico Sella, "L'industria della lana in Venezia nei secoli sedicesimo e diciassettesimo," *Storia dell'economica italiana* (Turin, 1959), I, 533.

Silk production was also beginning on the mainland,[38] and Venice herself manufactured in quantity a whole series of luxury goods for the international market: other fine textiles, books, glass, ceramics, sugar.[39]

But the most important shift in the Venetian economy was the relatively larger attention of the patriciate after the Italian wars to agriculture on the mainland. The movement of Venetian nobles to the land, already under way in the previous century, now began to increase, in a process that continued steadily into the next century. Its motives were various. Among its economic purposes was the need of Venice for a secure food supply, now a growing problem as her routes to the Black Sea and the Balkans, her customary sources of provision, were periodically endangered. The mainland was also now increasingly important as an outlet for Venetian manufactured goods, and perhaps above all, because opportunities in commerce were limited and eventually declined, as a new field for capital investment.[40]

Thus, although the familiar tendency to use commercial profits for purchases of land as a means of enhancing social status no doubt also affected Venice, we are not dealing here merely with a conventional symptom of decay, but also with a sound adaptation to new economic opportunities. The most powerful patrician families were aggressive in acquiring land and then energetic in its exploitation. By the early seventeenth century they had secured for themselves a large proportion of the arable land on the mainland: nearly 40 per cent in the Padovano and significant amounts elsewhere.[41] The process was assisted by the government, which began to regard common lands everywhere as legally its property, their use only conceded to local communities. In 1530 a special magistracy was established to supervise them, they were gradually surveyed in an operation that reached a climax in a great official survey of 1606, and their sale to individuals began.[42] More rational land administration was accompanied by other kinds of entrepreneurial enlightenment. Massive applications of capital made possible large-scale

[38] Domenico Sella, *Commerci e industrie a Venezia nel secolo XVII* (Venice, 1961), pp. 88–89.
[39] Fernand Braudel, Pierre Jeannin, Jean Meuvret, and Ruggiero Romano, "Le déclin de Venise au XVIIᵉ siècle," *Aspetti e cause della decadenza economica veneziana*, p. 51; Luzzatto, *Storia economica*, pp. 257–262, and "Decadenza," pp. 177–180.
[40] Aldo Stella, "La crisi economica veneziana della seconda metà del secolo XVI," *AV*, Ser. 5, LVIII–LIX (1956), esp. 20ff.; Beltrami, *Penetrazione economica*, pp. 54–55; Woolf, pp. 415–441.
[41] Beltrami, *Penetrazione economica*, p. 61.
[42] Daniele Beltrami, *Saggio di storia dell'agricoltura nella Repubblica di Venezia durante l'età moderna* (Florence, 1956), pp. 36ff.

reclamation projects and other improvements, and new crops were introduced. The cultivation of rice and corn in the Veneto dates from this period.[43]

Therefore, the Venetian nobles who went to the land were hardly the decadent aristocrats they are sometimes supposed but, on the contrary, hardbitten entrepreneurs, applying in a new area the energies that had long proved so effective in commerce. A hostile document of 1620, all the more revealing because of its late date, recognized the spirit in which they went about their business. The nobles, it declared, had bought up the best lands, and they lay in wait to fleece whoever fell into their hands. They traded, it continued, "in every quantity of goods, for example grain of every kind, wines, silk, wool, iron, wood, and even charcoal; and with abundance of money, but more with the authority they possess, they at certain times get their hands on goods and necessities for a small price, which they sell again at a greedy profit and with excessive distress to the poor." [44]

But although the economic benefits of this development were considerable, its social and political consequences were also of the greatest importance. The shift from Venice to the *terraferma*, from commerce to agriculture, accelerated the transformation of a segment of the patriciate from merchants into landed aristocrats with new tastes and somewhat different attitudes; we are in the presence of the Venetian form of the general "aristocratic revival" of the sixteenth century. It is closely related to other tendencies of this period. The life of the new Venetian country gentry tended to center in their handsome Palladian villas rather than in the city with its constant change and variety, their culture tended to lose its civic content and to grow more decorative and courtly, their minds grew rigid and less adventurous. Thus even the successful seizure of new economic opportunity strengthened conservative tendencies in sixteenth-century Venice. The landed nobility were also inclined to great caution in foreign policy since their estates were vulnerable to the depredations of war. Like more traditional landed aristocracies, this group began, too, to feel a heightened sense of class, accompanied by a special contempt and fear of the lower orders such as had not previously been characteristic of Venice. It was thus inclined to favor a more narrowly oligarchic government. In religion it was respectful of authority and particularly suspicious of novelty. In the long run, all these attitudes had serious political implications.

At the same time, although the conservative atmosphere of Venice

[43] *Ibid.*, pp. 11ff., 21ff., 30ff.; Sella, *Commerci e industrie*, pp. 87–88; Woolf, p. 419.
[44] Quoted by Sella, *Commerci e industrie*, p. 90.

allowed this group to exert particular influence during the middle decades of the century, its power should not be exaggerated. The Venetian nobility was by no means engaged in a massive retreat from commerce to the land. Only a minority was involved, chiefly consisting of members of the ruling group with sufficient capital for enterprises that, because of the magnitude of the expenditures required, only a few could manage; and even the families that participated did not entirely withdraw from commerce but continued to invest in trade when opportunities arose.[45] The vast majority of the Venetian nobility remained in the city, supporting themselves in traditional fashion, above all in commercial ventures in which many small capitalists could collaborate.[46] Although this larger group was not immune from the more cautious mood of these decades, it continued to live by venturing what it had, and it remained in close touch with the traditional ways and values of the Republic. It is possible to see in this period the beginnings of the sharp division apparent later in the century between *vecchi* and *giovani*,[47] but we are still dealing on the whole with broad tendencies that had not yet polarized into rival factions competing to control the state. Until the latter part of the century the two tendencies coexisted in a reasonably comfortable balance.

Venice, as the sixteenth century proved, had learned a great deal during the years after 1509 about the new realities of international politics. The devastation for the first time of territories on which she was heavily dependent for food, for men, and for access to her customers, taught her that she could no longer expect to make war in Italy at a comfortable distance and minimum expense. She had also discovered that she could never again afford to be caught alone in an aggressive posture. Both lessons suggested the need for caution. Venetian policy during most of the sixteenth century was thus relatively timid. Although the Republic did not entirely give up hope for further conquests if conditions changed, she was now chiefly concerned merely to retain her Italian possessions and what was left of her holdings in the Levant.

[45] Stella, "Crisi economica veneziana," p. 18, n. 1, points out how, in the case of the Priuli, a representative family, investment was directed to agriculture when commerce was poor but was returned to trade when conditions improved. The generalizations of Angelo Ventura, *Noblità e popolo nella società veneta del '400 e '500* (Bari, 1964), pp. 275–374, seem to me to apply chiefly to the minority of wealthy landholders, whose dominance over Venetian society was by no means secure, rather than to the nobility in general.

[46] Cf. Luzzatto, *Storia economica di Venezia*, pp. 252–253.

[47] Cf. Seneca, pp. 34ff., and the review of this work by Gino Benzoni, *BSV*, IV (1962), 396.

As Paolo Paruta observed before the century ended, in a document that testifies to the growing Venetian capacity for political and historical analysis,[48] the Italian policy of Venice during the sixteenth century had developed through two phases. During the first, which lasted as long as the French stayed in Italy, Venice promoted an equilibrium between the great powers and was thus able to retain some initiative. In practice this meant support for the French.[49] Since the French victory at Marignano had proved so profitable to herself, Venice hoped for the election of Francis I as emperor in 1519, loaned him money, and aided his Italian expeditions. But after the collapse of the League of Cognac and the exclusion of France from the peninsula, conditions were changed. Balance was no longer possible, and Venice could only accept Habsburg control of Italy. After a century of expansion, the neutral and passive policy of the following decades was humiliating; but, as Paruta plaintively asked: "After this, things being reduced to a universal quiet, what else could [Venice] do, or what ought she to have done, than to seek to maintain herself with this peace [of Bologna] in that condition and security which had been promised to her?" [50] In 1529 she was helpless to aid Florence, however active her sympathies. In 1536 she made no move to prevent the emperor's acquisition of Milan, although its retention by an Italian prince was thought crucial to Italian liberty.[51] In 1556 she refused to support the pope in his war with Spain.[52]

[48] The *Discorso sulla neutralità*, composed between 1592 and 1595, evidently to defend the passivity of Venetian policy against its Venetian critics, in his *Opere politiche*, ed. C. Monzani (Florence, 1852), II, 381–399.

[49] Cf. his *Historia vinetiana* (Venice, 1703), pp. 207–208, where Paruta reports a speech in the Senate by Domenico Trevisano, backing the French alliance in 1524: "Noi habbiamo sempre tenuta per costante, & risolute opinione, che una delle principali cose, con le quali in questi miseri tempi, ne'quali siamo incorsi, si possa conservare lo stato nostro, & la libertà d'Italia, sia il contrapeso, che si danno insieme le forze di questi due gran potentati, Francesco Re Christianissimo, & Carlo Imperatore: & che sia utile, & salutifero consiglio; poiche nè la potenza, ne le forze, nè la intelligentia de'Prencipi Italiani, non è tanta, ò tale, che basti à cacciarli tutti du fuori d'Italia, il procurare, che l'uno & l'altro vi habbia Stato; onde fra loro convengano essere emulationi, sospetti, gelosie perpetue; dalle quali cose sono costretti a far molta stima della Repub. procurare con ogni studio la nostra amicitia: perche quegli, che è congiunto con noi, si fa superiore all'altro, & sta piu sicuro di conservare ciò, che possede, & più confida d'acquistare ciò, che desidera."

[50] *Discorso sulla neutralità*, p. 396. Cf. Machiavelli's estimate of the Venetian position: "They have not regained their reputation or their military strength. Hence like all Italian princes they now live in the power of others." (*Istorie fiorentine*, Bk. I, Ch. 29.)

[51] This point is noted by Federico Chabod, "Venezia nella politica italiana ed europea del Cinquecento," *La civiltà veneziana del Rinascimento* pp. 42–43.

[52] Pastor, XIV, 151, 159.

So Venice, for decades regarded as the troublemaker of Italy, became a staunch advocate of peace. "Wars should always be avoided," Bernardo Navagero typically declared in his Roman *Relation* of 1558, "because they bring many troubles. And if they must be waged, make them by necessity and far from home; because friends and soldiers do worse damage in your state than the enemy, nor is there any remedy." [53] By the beginning of the next century the European reputation of Venice had completely changed. As Bedell wrote: "The world knows, the Venetians be noe hot undertakers in matters of warr; a people of the gown rather than of the Cloke; their Counsell, and commanders of that Age, which, even in them which have been brought up in the camp, curdleth the bloud and quencheth the heat of martial spirit. Their Arsenall indeed is a shop of warr; but it serveth them more for the guard of their peace with the opinion of it, than with the use." [54] After the Peace of Bologna the chief military action of the Republic in Italy was the construction of great fortifications to protect her possessions on the mainland, an enterprise perhaps as illuminating for the psychology of Venice as for her policy and tactics.[55] The same defensive mentality is also apparent in a contraction of the Republic's European horizons.[56] No doubt she was under pressure to abandon regular relations with the Protestant world, but this alone can hardly explain why a state that had taken so staunchly secular a view of external politics allowed her regular embassy with England to lapse. The last Venetian dispatches from England before the resumption of relations in 1603 were dated more than a year before the death of Mary and thirteen years before the excommunication of Elizabeth.[57]

But neutrality did not mean subservience to the emperor or to Spain. Venice meant to conserve her possessions, not to abandon them; and meanwhile she still had sufficient resources to compel respect from the distracted Habsburg states. Charles V's revival of imperial claims to suzerainty over Italy was not extended to Venice, whose "original liberty" he appears to

[53] Albèri, Ser. 2, III, 407–408. Note that Navagero here sounds much like Francesco Barbaro over a century earlier.

[54] Letter to Adam Newton, Jan. 1, 1608, in *Two Biographies*, p. 232.

[55] Cf. Paruta, *Historia vinetiana*, p. 154.

[56] See the remarks of Tenenti, *Cristoforo da Canal*, pp. 175–176.

[57] Cf. Nicolò Contarini's account of the opposition to an English embassy in his *Historie venetiane*, in the appendix to Gaetano Cozzi, *Il doge Nicolò Contarini: Ricerche sul patriziato veneziano agli inizi del Seicento* (Venice, 1958), pp. 371–372, which, emphasizing religious considerations, noted (for 1602) that forty-four years had elapsed without an embassy.

have acknowledged. He allowed the envoys of Venice at his court to style themselves *ambassadors*, a privilege he denied even to the representative of Florence.[58] Venice was also able to resist all pressures, from the pope as well as the emperor, to join the crusade against the Protestants of Germany.[59] Thus, whatever may have been its moral costs, neutrality during the middle decades of the century evidently worked. The effectiveness of Venetian policy was generally recognized abroad. Botero, that reliable purveyor of common opinion, remarked with some justice that "there has never been an empire in which mediocrity of power went with such stability and strength." But he was also quite clear that the Venetian achievement rested on a realistic acceptance of the limitations imposed by circumstance. "So long as the ruler recognizes the limits of mediocrity and is content to remain within them," he wrote, "his rule will be lasting." [60]

Venice was equally thrown on the defensive in the Adriatic and in her relations with the eastern Mediterranean, on which her economic existence still largely depended. New dangers presented themselves to her control of the Adriatic. Although she quickly abrogated the commitment of 1510 to allow the subjects of the pope to navigate freely in the "Gulf of Venice," papal and Habsburg legal theorists now carried on a growing offensive against Venetian claims. For the time being this paper attack was not backed by force, though the Venetians answered it in kind. But it indicated a new area in which vigilance was necessary.[61]

Having already suffered heavy losses in earlier wars with the Turks, Venice was inclined to caution in the eastern Mediterranean too. Botero also provided an apt description both of the Venetian problem here and the policy the Republic attempted to follow. "The Venetians have a common boundary with the Turk, on sea and on land, for many hundreds of miles," he wrote; "and they maintain themselves against him rather with the arts of peace than of war: with fortifying their places well, with avoiding the expense and the danger of war, with negotiation and with presents, finally

---

[58] This point was noted with pride by Vincenzo Fedeli in his *Relazione* from Florence in 1561, in *Relazioni degli ambasciatori veneti al Senato*, ed. Arnaldo Segarizzi (Bari, 1912–1916), III, Part 1, 172.

[59] See Paruta's remarks, *Historia vinetiana*, pp. 484–485; and Andrea Morosini, *Historia veneta ab anno 1521 usque ad annum 1615*, in *Degl'Istorici delle cose veneziane, i quali hanno scritto per Pubblico Decreto*, ed. Apostolo Zeno (Venice, 1719), V, 358–359.

[60] *Della ragion di Stato*, Bk. I, ch. 6. I follow the translation of P. J. and D. P. Waley, *The Reason of State* (New Haven, 1956).

[61] On this pressure see, in general, Cessi, *Venezia e il problema adriatico*, pp. 165ff., with massive bibliographies.

The Doge receiving the ceremonial umbrella from Pope Alexander III at Ancona in 1177 (*Carpaccio*).

Venice against Europe, an allegory of the seventeenth century. (Correr Museum, Venice.)

with doing everything to avoid coming to blows, preserving only liberty and the state. In truth, although they have money and munitions enough, they lack the provisions and the men for such an undertaking." [62] Accordingly Venice resisted as well as she could the imperial and papal solicitations to make war on the Turks; and, on the ground that the impending general council might antagonize this enemy since one of its official purposes was to consolidate Christendom for a general crusade, she refused to allow the council to be convened in Vicenza.[63] The Venetian policy toward the Turks was a constant source of friction with Rome.[64] But the consequences of the alternative were demonstrated between 1537 and 1540 when Venice, in response to Turkish aggression, reluctantly joined a new holy league with the pope and the emperor. The imperial fleet failed to give adequate support, the war went badly for Venice, and in the peace she lost more of her overseas empire and was compelled to pay a large indemnity.[65]

The same defensive attitudes, the same apprehension of change, are evident in the internal affairs of Venice during this period. The definition of noble status was made more rigid by laws requiring the official registration of patrician marriages and births and more rigorous proof of eligibility for admission to the Great Council.[66] Even more important was the tendency to centralize government in the College and above all the Council of Ten. Through these agencies and a system of clientage which, for the most part, effectively controlled the majority of lesser nobles in the Great Council, a few powerful families dominated the government; one of their leaders is said to have boasted, "*Sumus tot Reges.*" [67] Francesco Sansovino described the power of the Ten as equal to that of the Senate.[68] New agencies to facilitate state control were also established. The Inquisitors of State,

[62] *Relationi universali* p. 363.

[63] Paruta, *Historia vinetiana*, pp. 457–458; Paolo Sarpi, *Istoria del Concilio Tridentino*, ed. Giovanni Gambarin (Bari, 1935), I, 160.

[64] Cf. Pastor, VII, 215ff. and X, 195.

[65] Braudel, *Méditerranée*, p. 725.

[66] Sandi, III, Part 1, 11–29; Maranini, *La costituzione dopo la serrata*, pp. 61–63.

[67] Besta, pp. 144–145; Aldo Stella, "La regolazione delle pubbliche entrate e la crisi politica veneziana del 1582," *Miscellanea in onore di Roberto Cessi* (Rome, 1958), II, 157–158, 166–167; Cf. Cozzi, *Contarini*, pp. 7–9.

[68] *Regni, et republiche*, leaf. 165ᵛ; the epistle of this work is dated 1583, but it clearly describes the situation before the reforms of that year. Gasparo Contarini also recognized the recent enlargement of the powers of the Council of Ten in *De magistratibus et republica Venetorum*, written in 1524. I use the edition in Graevius, *Thesaurus antiquitatum et historiarum Italiae*, V, cols. 34–35 on this point.

previously only temporary, became permanent in 1539; these officers under-took secret investigation of alleged subversion or violations of law and reported to the Council of Ten.[69] Meanwhile tighter administration was imposed on all aspects of the government of the mainland. The increasingly statist mood of the period was also dramatized by the use of more elaborate ceremonial robes by the Venetian magistracy.[70]

It is possible that the narrowing of political responsibility had an adverse effect on the morale of the ruling class. There were scandals in the govern-ment: for example the instructions to the ambassador negotiating peace with the Turks in 1540 were sold to the French, who conveyed them to their Turkish allies with the worst possible consequences for the terms of the treaty.[71] The effectiveness of the Venetian fleet was also seriously reduced by the greed, luxurious tastes, and contempt for discipline of some of its noble officers:[72] one thinks of the English navy in the years when Pepys was trying to put it into condition. Yet it is unlikely that such cases were general; and the example of the naval reformer Cristoforo da Canal, as well as the reform movement in the last decades of the century, indicates that the long Venetian tradition of devoted responsibility to the state was still power-ful. The vigor and cogency of Canal's proposals, which appealed at once to experience and to ancient practice, reveal the persistence of a fresh and creative element in the Venetian political climate even when the protective attitude to established Venetian ways was most constricting. His sense of the relevance of republican Roman precedent to Venice, combined with a perception of occasions when the moderns had surpassed the ancients indicates a high state of morale.[73] Nevertheless the middle decades of the century were not generally characterized by political energy or freshness of vision.

We have described in previous chapters the tendency of Renaissance republicanism to consider the church under a double aspect. On the one hand, particularly as a universal body, the church was conceived as essentially spiritual, and the exercise of political and administrative responsibilities of any kind by its spiritual officers was regarded as profoundly inappropriate to its

[69] Noted by Romolo Quazza, *Preponderanza spagnuola (1559–1700)*, 2nd ed. (Milan, 1950), pp. 71–73.

[70] Simeoni, II, 949.

[71] Cessi, II, 95–96. Paruta tells the story, *Historia vinetiana*, pp. 450–451.

[72] Tenenti, *Cristoforo da Canal*, pp. 94ff.

[73] *Ibid.*, pp. 5, 7, 21.

nature. The function of the clergy, from this standpoint, was simply to preach the Gospel and administer the sacraments. But as a set of visible institutions the church was identified with the particular state in which it was established, whose government extended, in the divine economy, over all visible things. Thus the control of the ecclesiastical institution was vested in the lay authorities of the state, and coercive powers in the church were exercised chiefly in the interest of public order. Because of the importance of the church as a bulwark of society in general, its institutional structure could not be allowed to fall into disrepair, and republicanism was generally sympathetic to ecclesiastical reform, provided that reform was carried out under local auspices and posed no threat to the liberty of the state.

The autonomy of the churches within the several states also found a parallel on the personal level, particularly under the stimulus of later medieval Evangelism, in the acceptance of a substantial spiritual autonomy for individuals. So long as their beliefs did not weaken or disturb the established order, they might work out their own salvation as the spirit moved them. Indeed, because coercion had no place in the strictly spiritual realm, its use, without any political justification, could be interpreted as in principle subversive. Since religious solidarity was considered fundamental to the solidarity of society, the significance of this position should not be exaggerated. Nevertheless it inhibited dogmatism and facilitated emphasis on the internal workings of grace at the expense of external conformity. All these tendencies became more pronounced in the Venetian church of the sixteenth century.

The conservative instincts so apparent in other aspects of Venetian life are particularly evident in Venetian administration of the church. This was in part because, in a period of general danger, the role of religion as an instrument of social discipline seemed unusually important. Venetians, like other Europeans, simply assumed it. As Cristoforo da Canal reminded his fellow citizens: "Each of you knows how useful for civilization and the peace of men are not only the true but also the false religions." [74] Venice would thus have clung with special tenacity in any case to her traditional ecclesiastical arrangements. But, as the events of 1509–1510 seemed to reveal, there were now also special problems. Partly to extend a political empire inappropriate to his spiritual office, partly to destroy the ecclesiastical autonomy essential to the liberty of states, Julius II, as Venice believed, had plotted her destruction; and to bring about these ends he had shown a

[74] Quoted by Tenenti, p. 8.

willingness to use both spiritual and temporal weapons. Venetians could never forget this episode, which left a permanent residue of hostility and suspicion. Paolo Paruta, eight-five years after the event, still spoke, in tones of outraged innocence, of the "persecution" of Venice "with spiritual arms, although for an occasion of state and temporal things";[75] and a nuncio contemporary with him noted how Venetians regularly flared up still at any reference to the alleged concessions of 1510.[76] But they did so not only because Venetian memories were long, but also because the pressures dramatized by the action of Julius II were tending to grow steadier and more strong. The Renaissance papacy was increasingly the papacy of the Counter Reformation.

Under these conditions Venice clung as tenaciously as possible to her traditional authority over the church and its personnel; the Curia regarded Venice as the most difficult nunciature in Europe.[77] Although the Republic could not persuade the pope to let her nominate bishops in the old way,[78] the Curia generally found it prudent to respect her wishes.[79] Nearly all appointments continued to go to natives,[80] and the government persistently interfered in the administration of dioceses.[81] Nor did Venice retreat on the standard jurisdictional issues. Her government occasionally felt strong enough to tax the clergy without the pope's consent,[82] it continued to bring them to trial in its own courts in spite of the nuncio's protests,[83] and it firmly rejected clerical immunity in such matters.[84] Meanwhile a fateful

[75] Albèri, Ser. 2, X, 366.

[76] In the memorandum of Anton Maria Graziani, printed by Mario Brunetti, "Le istruzioni di un nunzio pontificio a Venezia al suo successore," *Scritti storici in onore di Camillo Manfroni nel XL anno di insegnamento* (Padua, 1925), p. 376.

[77] Gaeta, "Rappresentanza stabile pontificia in Venezia," pp. 7–8.

[78] For Venetian interest in recovering this privilege, see Paruta, *Historia vinetiana*, p. 321, and Morosini, V, pp. 254–255, 361–363. Cf. Pastor, X, 373–374, and the *Relazione di Roma* of Girolamo Soranzo in 1563, Albèri, Ser. 2, IV, 116.

[79] Gaeta, *Nunzio pontificio*, pp. 59–60.

[80] Cf. the *Relazione* of Soranzo, cited above, p. 116. Although Soranzo makes clear that the pope was appointing to most Venetian bishoprics, he concluded: "Ha proceduto con gran rispetto nel conferir i vescovati vacati a suo tempo in questo Serenissimo Dominio, avendoli dati tutti a gentilhuomini veneziani." Cf. Morosini, VI, 165.

[81] Cf. Niero, 55ff., 72ff., and *passim*.

[82] The Senate went on record on this point in 1561; for its resolution see Cecchetti, I, 130–131. For an occasion when the pope was angered by this, see Morosini, V, 372.

[83] As in the case of the disorderly abbot Lippomano, "guilty of grave transgressions" in 1578, described by Cecchetti, I, 265.

[84] Cessi, II, 115.

series of laws restricted the right of the church to own property. At the end of 1536 the Senate decreed that, "since it cannot be allowed that all real property of this city should go to ecclesiastics through legacies or donations *ad pias causas*, as a good part have gone," such property bestowed on the church must be sold after two years to a layman, the proceeds to go to the procurators of Saint Mark, the normal administrators of charitable bequests. This law was renewed three times before the end of the century, and ecclesiastical property in the city remained constant.[85]

Nevertheless, although she resisted all encroachments on her traditional control over the administration of the church, Venice was by no means indifferent to problems of institutional reform or the struggle against heresy. But she insisted on dealing with these matters through local agencies, in some instances apparently to forestall papal intervention but also because she was generally persuaded of the importance to her own social health of a purified church. Thus in 1521 she established a new secular magistracy to supervise monasteries, rejecting the pope's demand for conventual visitations by his own delegates as "dangerous novelty"; and in 1537 another set of magistrates was appointed to deal with blasphemy and related offenses. Both institutions were a continuing source of friction with Rome.[86] In 1531 the Council of Ten took on itself to prohibit pluralism.[87]

The Council of Ten also took a special interest in regulating the procedures of the Inquisition, whose activity was now increasing. In 1521 the Ten decreed that these must be in conformity with "maturity and justice" and (presumably because suspicions had been aroused) directed that "appetite for money should not be a cause for the condemning or shaming of anyone either guiltless or little at fault." It also made the significant observation that persons accused of heresy "have no less need for preachers with prudent instructions in the Catholic faith than for persecutors with severe punishments."[88] Laymen continued to be present at all sessions of the Holy Office in spite of vigorous opposition from Rome,[89] and a series

[85] Cecchetti, I, 126–127; Stella, "Proprietà ecclesiastica nella Repubblica di Venezia," p. 74. Venice also solidly resisted decrees against lay possession of ecclesiastical property; cf. Stella, *Chiesa e Stato nelle relazioni dei nunzi pontifici a Venezia: Ricerche sul giurisdizionalismo veneziano dal XVI al XVIII secolo* (Vatican City, 1964), p. 7.

[86] Antonio Battistella, *La Repubblica di Venezia ne' suoi undici secoli di vita* (Venice, 1921), pp. 587, 602; Sandi, III, Part 2, 514–518.

[87] Sandi, III, Part 1, 484; cf. Gaeta, *Nunzio pontificio*, pp. 80–81.

[88] Quoted in Cessi, II, 109.

[89] Cf. Pio Paschini, "L'Inquisizione a Venezia ed il nunzio Ludovico Beccadelli 1550–1554," *Archivio della R. Deputazione Romana di Storia Patria*, LXV (1942), 83ff.

of later decrees by the Council of Ten made clear its continuing sense of responsibility in cases of heresy.[90]

The regulation of printing, which involved major Venetian economic interests, is another case in point. Here too the Venetian government sought to mitigate the rigors of ecclesiastical control by undertaking some responsibility itself. As early as 1527 the Council of Ten undertook to censor books, but largely to frustrate the attempt of the clergy to do it.[91] But by the middle of the century an uneasy partnership between the ecclesiastical and secular authorities had developed. In May of 1548 Giovanni Della Casa, now the nuncio in Venice, drew up the first Italian list of prohibited books, whereupon the Council of Ten decreed harsh penalties for the printers and sellers of any work listed on it.[92] But Venetian publishers continued to produce works uncongenial to orthodoxy, and Rome was by no means satisfied with this arrangement.

Officially Venice professed as much zeal against heresy as any other state. Thus, as the nuncio reported in 1550, the doge, on being informed that Lutherans were living in Venetian territory, had responded appropriately: "When we see anyone who disturbs the state here, every man is indignant against him; but now that it is a question of those who make war on God, it seems we do not care. We must not behave like this but take vigorous action, and let it not be forgotten. I promise to deal with the matter quickly and properly." [93] Prosecutions for heresy in Venice increased markedly after about the middle of the century.[94] In 1562 the government went so far as to request the establishment of an inquisitor for Padua, where "many persons come from different places, of whom it is necessary in these most dangerous times to have diligent care so that they may live as Catholics and give no cause of scandal." [95] Nevertheless heresy was less likely to be prosecuted as such than because, in some forms, it seemed to threaten the

[90] Cf. Paolo Sarpi, *Sopra l'officio dell'inquisizione*, SG, p. 129.

[91] Giovanni Sforza, "Riflessi della Controriforma nella Repubblica di Venezia," *ASI*, XCIII (1935), 5ff.

[92] *Ibid.*, 27ff. Some information about early editions of the Index in Venice is also provided in Emmanuele Antonio Cicogna, *Saggio di bibliografia veneziana* (Venice, 1847), p. 124.

[93] Quoted by Paschini, "Inquisizione a Venezia," P. 76. Paschini provides evidence of the substantial cooperation of Venice with the papacy on religious questions during the middle decades of the sixteenth century.

[94] Pastor, XVII, 316. Cf. Lanfranco Caretti, "Giovanni Della Casa, uomo pubblico e scrittore," *Studi Urbinati*, XXVII (1953), 37–38.

[95] Quoted by Cecchetti, I, 20.

social order; and Venetian citizens were less likely to be turned over to the Inquisition than foreigners. Thus, while respectable Lutherans continued to study peacefully at Padua, lower-class Anabaptists and antitrinitarians were harshly suppressed.[96]

Antisemitic gestures of various sorts also testify to the somewhat more restrictive atmosphere of this period. Laws ordered Jews to be confined to a quarter of the city and then to withdraw to Mestre on the mainland;[97] and in 1550 a decree of the Senate expelled the Marranos and forbade commerce with them, to the satisfaction of the nuncio and the pope. Not long after the government cooperated in the papal campaign against Hebrew books, which were taken from their Jewish owners and burned, together with a newly printed edition of the Talmud.[98] Two decades later the employment of Jews in the printing industry was prohibited, along with the publication of Jewish books.[99] But such actions seem not to have expressed any consistent policy. The Jews expelled in 1527 were readmitted seven years later,[100] and it is significant that Francesco Sansovino took pride not in the severity of the Republic but in the liberality with which it treated Jews. They preferred Venice to any other part of Italy, he wrote, because there they were safe from the violence and tyranny to which they were exposed elsewhere, and could obtain justice against all. "Living in most singular peace," he concluded, "they enjoy this country almost like a true Promised Land." [101]

Nevertheless this rather selective deference to the pressures of the age for religious conformity was sufficient for the time being to satisfy the papacy, which had not yet passed into the most militant phase of the Counter Reformation; and the nuncios, although continuing to protest Venetian jurisdictionalism, were inclined to give a good report of Venetian Catholicism.[102] Venice was rewarded by the appointment, once again, of

[96] Cf. Cantimori, *Eretici italiani*, p. 55.
[97] For Venetian antisemitic legislation generally, see Sandi, III, Part 1, 434–450.
[98] Paschini, "Inquisizione a Venezia," pp. 71, 144ff.
[99] The decree, dated Dec. 18, 1571, is in Sforza, p. 45.
[100] Sandi, III, Part 1, 443–446.
[101] *Venetia citta nobilissima*, sig. SSS4ᵛ. Cf. Valier, *Dell'utilità*, pp. 358–9, which describes the refusal of the Senate in 1569 to order the expulsion of the Jews, although the author, an ecclesiastic, draws from the episode the moral that nothing is perfect and that it is sometimes necessary to tolerate lesser evils in the hope of avoiding greater. For Venetian policy to the Jews see also Ellis Rivkin, *Leon da Modena and the 'Kol Sakhal'* (Cincinnati, 1952), esp. pp. 18–39.
[102] Cf. Pastor, XIX, 300.

Venetian cardinals; Pius IV included six Venetians in his elevations of 1561 and 1565.[103] But Paruta, reviewing Venetian policy during the century and adding up the benefits of mollifying the pope, suggested how little it had come from a true change of heart:

> Truly it is a great trick and sound prudence to pursue these ways. For with very little, and often more with appearance than reality, showing a readiness to honor, obey, and respect the Apostolic See and its prelates, one may acquire true dominion and authority in the Curia itself, making oneself agreeable to all and acquiring a party of friends who then support any action of the prince who has known how to negotiate in this way. And this Republic, after having passed through the most grave dangers and experienced to its excessive damage the wrath, however unjust, of Julius II and of Leo X, has done everything it could, with the greatest study and much wise counsel, conserving its dignity and avoiding injury, to maintain itself in friendship and good intelligence with the Apostolic See, esteeming this one of the most important means by which it can be preserved in quiet and with greater dignity, in respect to those disturbances and troubles which can be born from Christian princes.

He concluded that friendship with the pope, "conserved with due means and reputation, can be seen to have always turned out to the great utility of those who have known how to maintain it." [104]

This combination of defensiveness, restriction, and cynicism, however, had its price, above all in the general failure of Venetians to grasp the significance of contemporary religious movements, both Protestant and Catholic. Thus, in spite of their Evangelical traditions and their larger opportunities for contact with northern Europe, their understanding of Protestantism remained as deficient as that of most other Italians. This was partly deliberate, though characteristically out of political rather than religious motives. Sarpi remarked in 1608 that Venetians knew as little of German affairs as they knew of what was happening in China; the reason, he explained, was that, "because of the war of Charles V and because of the reports that were spread about it, it was believed that the reformed religion brought with it war and mutation of state. Therefore it was decided to keep

---

[103] Valier took particular satisfaction in these elevations (p. 342).
[104] *Relazione di Roma*, Albèri, Ser. 2, X, 367–368.

it at a distance, and this opinion had deep roots in the hearts of this government." As a result, Sarpi said, "They know well here that the princes of Germany are Protestants, but no one knows their differences and disputes."[105]

Thus Venice preferred to regard the issues raised by Protestantism as essentially political and institutional, and Venetians persisted in regarding the Reformation and its causes in these terms. Girolamo Soranzo, who perhaps reflected also views prevailing at the Curia, attributed the Protestant revolt partly to the corruption of the Curia, partly to the ambitions of princes. Papal nepotism, he suggested, had given an example to secular princes, who sought in a similar way to secure the properties of the church for their families, and could only do so by breaking with Rome.[106] "In my opinion," he reported to the government after his Roman embassy in 1563, "the self-interest of the princes has had a much greater share in the alienation of Germany and England than the beliefs of Martin Luther or of Melanchthon; and your Serenity knows very well that the principal cause in the present disturbances in France has not been Calvin or Beza but particular enmities and the desire to govern."[107] Long habituated to view the institutional church as a dimension of politics, Venice could explain the religious behavior of others only in terms of such motives as had guided her own policy.

For the same reason she also continued to view Rome primarily as an element in the political scene; and the pope remained, in Venetian eyes, chiefly a political force, but unusually dangerous because of his peculiar claims over the world. For Bernardo Navagero, ambassador to Paul IV, papal greed for political empire, so long implemented by nepotism, was still a critical danger to Italy, as serious in 1558 as at the beginning of the century. The particular vice of Alexander VI, this passion to rule, Navagero believed, had persisted among his successors and "will always trouble this poor Italy."[108]

Retaining her suspicious and essentially political view of the papacy, Venice was generally as oblivious to the emergence of a serious reform movement in Rome as to religious developments elsewhere in Europe.

---

[105] Conversation with Christoph von Dohna as reported on Aug. 4, 1608, *Briefe und Akten*, II, 81–82.

[106] Albèri, Ser. 2, IV, 80–81.

[107] *Ibid.*, pp. 81–82.

[108] *Ibid.*, Ser. 2, III, 376. It may be recalled that the author of this reflection was made a cardinal not long after and served as papal legate at the last sessions of the Council of Trent.

It is hardly surprising, therefore, that she paid little attention to the Council of Trent in its earlier stages and that her eventual concern was limited largely to its political implications. Like other Italians, Venetians were suspicious of the pope's motives in first convening the Council, which appeared to them little more than a calculated move in the complex political game between Paul III and the great powers. Venice sent no diplomatic representative to either the first or second group of sessions and made little effort to secure the participation of Venetian bishops.[109] Although most of the seventy-eight Venetian dioceses were conveniently close to Trent, only twenty-one Venetians attended the first session; and of these only the bishop of Bergamo came from an important city. No Venetian bishops took an important part in the proceedings.[110]

But the attitude of Venice to the last phase of the Council was different. The doctrinal issues to which she was indifferent had now been largely settled, and the Council was ready to deal with questions likely to affect Venetian jurisdictional and political interests. Accordingly Venice was now well represented,[111] not only by prelates over whose conduct the government exercised close surveillance, but also by two lay ambassadors, Nicolò da Ponte and Matteo Dandolo, who kept in close touch with their government.[112] All were at Trent, from the standpoint of the Venetian government, primarily to prevent any modification in the traditional structure of the Venetian church. So da Ponte and Dandolo were instructed regarding their management of the Venetian bishops:

> Say to them that we do not propose anything detrimental to ecclesiastical authority and jurisdictions nor any impediment to the bishops in preaching the word of God to the people, in the distribution of alms according to the sacred canons, in the administration of the sacraments, and in similar things which truly belong to the spiritual realm. But where the authority and the interests of secular princes are at stake, and consequently our own, it seems appropriate that our prelates ought to have a proper respect to their natural prince; and they ought not try, on the pretext of religion, to injure the privileges, jurisdiction, and ancient customs we have always observed for so

[109] Jedin, "Contarini e il contributo veneziano," p. 120; Alberigo, p. 49.
[110] Alberigo, pp. 48ff.
[111] Jedin, "Contarini e il contributo veneziano," pp. 121–122.
[112] Their dispatches are printed by Cecchetti, II, 25–46.

many ages in the time of their predecessors, who for intelligence, goodness, and exemplary life are worthy of memory.

As representatives of the Republic, the Venetian bishops were not "to
burden their consciences nor be lacking in anything that is of the least
importance to the duty they have to their country, to whose honor and
benefit they are greatly obligated for many reasons and in many ways."
Da Ponte and Dandolo were required to report in detail on their negotiations
with each Venetian prelate and to indicate clearly his attitude to the desires
of the government.[113]

Venetian concern to defend the ecclesiastical *status quo* ironically allied the
Republic with that element in the Roman Curia which considered conciliar
reform an infringement on the prerogatives of the Holy See; and for its
support to the papalist party the Venetians were encouraged to believe that
Rome, once the Council had ended, would concede formal rights of
nomination to the major bishoprics of Padua and Verona.[114] Venice also
tended to see reform as a device by which alien political interests aimed to
control papal elections, a prospect which threatened her own security in
addition to suggesting a further reduction in the freedom of Italy.[115] The
Venetians therefore worked closely during the last session with the papalist
forces,[116] although this required stern treatment of several Venetian prelates
who proved sympathetic to the ultramontane reform proposals. On hearing
of their tendency to independence, the Council of Ten wrote to da Ponte
and Dandolo: "We are not a little offended by this, being amazed that these
men should have so little consideration and so little love for their country
that, motivated, as must reasonably be believed, by ambition and by greed
to increase their jurisdiction, *they wish to interpose themselves* and support a
thing so prejudicial to our dominion and so unsatisfactory to the other
Christian princes." The ambassadors were directed to interview the offending

[113] The instruction of Nov. 17, 1563 (in Cecchetti, II, 59–60), which includes the passages quoted here, gives full directions.

[114] See the letter of the Council of Ten to the Venetian ambassadors at Trent, Aug. 14,
1563, in Cecchetti, II, 53.

[115] See the letter of the Council of Ten, Sep. 22, 1563, in Cecchetti, II, 48, which treats
reform as a tool of Spanish interests attempting to take control of the papacy out of
Italian hands.

[116] Even Sarpi was compelled to recognize this fact, which he must have found somewhat distasteful; cf. *Concilio Tridentino*, II, 471, 483, 505, and III, 89. Jedin, "Contarini e
il contributo veneziano," p. 121, has noted the failure of the Venetian envoys to join the
other ambassadors in protesting the hurried treatment of reform.

bishops, to press them to comply with the wishes of the government, and to make clear that the resentment of the Republic would otherwise find appropriate expression.[117]

Venetian acceptance of the Tridentine decrees must be interpreted against this background. Formally this acceptance was complete and unconditional. On July 22, 1564, the Senate notified all rectors in its domain that, "for the glory of the Lord God, the service of Christendom, and the satisfaction of his Blessedness," it had determined to publish the decrees of Trent. The vote had been 161 to three. Several weeks later the doge wrote to the rectors again: "You must know the obligation of all Christian princes as obedient sons of Holy Church to accept and obey, and to procure acceptance and obedience in their kingdoms and states of, the decrees of the sacred general councils legitimately congregated by the authority of the Apostolic Holy See and celebrated with the assistance of the Holy Spirit, among which councils is that of Trent." [118] But such prompt support for a program of universal reform by a government so consistently jealous of its control over ecclesiastical affairs and so deeply suspicious of Rome proceeded, it may reasonably be supposed, from a conviction that the reforms of Trent were unlikely to have practical consequences. Venetians were inclined to believe, as the sequel would suggest, that the Council had accomplished nothing and that their own acceptance of its decrees implied no obligation to change anything. Two generations later this conviction was to provide a major thesis for Paolo Sarpi's *Istoria del Concilio Tridentino*.

But Venetian resistance to papal control over the institutional church, however interpreted in Rome, by no means implied a general indifference to spiritual realities; and in the course of the sixteenth century the Evangelical tendencies already for some time at work in patrician circles broadened out into a powerful current of personal piety and general ecclesiastical reform which, for a time, exerted an influence far beyond the Republic herself. This development was considerably aided by the relative freedom Venice still provided. For in spite of the restrictions we have noted, the Republic remained one of the most tolerant communities in Europe, particularly for native patricians. During the Council, for example, prohibited books were bought in Venice, where they were freely sold, for the inspection of the participants;[119] and Padua avoided requiring adherence to the Tridentine

[117] Nov. 3, 1563, in Cecchetti, II, 58–59; italics mine.
[118] In Cecchetti, I, 76–77.
[119] Pastor, XVI, 20.

profession of faith as a condition of the doctorate for Protestant students, who continued to frequent the university.[120]

The intellectual and spiritual mood created in Venice by her long crisis can perhaps best be approached through the career and thought of one of her most distinguished patricians, Gasparo Contarini. Contarini had much in common with earlier Venetians, notably his attachment to the Republic and its traditional ways. But he wrote about them and about their practical meaning to himself with a novel eloquence; and both his own pronouncements and the response they evoked suggest that recent events had deepened patriotic pride and strengthened the sense of civic responsibility. Contarini's spiritual development suggests that the Venetian ordeal, which in local eyes had so brutally dramatized the evil condition of Christendom, had meanwhile played some part in stimulating the Evangelical spirit in Venice. But, by evoking fear and insecurity the experience, as much of Contarini's mental outlook may suggest, also assisted in producing a kind of recoil, in some areas, from the more daring attitudes of the Renaissance toward which Venice had perhaps been moving, and a tendency to employ rather inappropriate systematic arguments and abstract formulas, such as had continued to occupy a large place in the education given at Padua, to support Renaissance values. The result was a state of peculiar tension in which a brave appearance of harmony and balance concealed serious potential conflicts.[121]

Born in 1483, Contarini early exhibited scholarly interests, above all an enthusiasm for philosophy. At the University of Padua, where he studied between 1501 and 1509, this meant primarily Aristotle, though Contarini was also open to other influences, and the problem of the soul and its relation to the material world as discussed by Pomponazzi and other masters. In theology Contarini became, on the whole, a Thomist. This early formation left him with a substantial confidence in the power of the human reason to order all things and an inclination toward a hierarchical vision of reality, tendencies which never left him. In some respects Contarini resembled Pico Della Mirandola far more than he did Machiavelli or Guicciardini, although the latter was born in the same year as himself.

Had his scholarly leisure been left undisturbed, it is possible that he would have enjoyed a moderately distinguished career as a speculative philosopher,

[120] *Ibid.*, XVII, 331.

[121] I should like to make a general acknowledgement here to Elisabeth Gleason, "Contarini and Religious Reform," for what follows. I have also made good use of Felix Gilbert, "Religion and Politics in the Thought of Gasparo Contarini," *Action and Conviction in Early Modern Europe: Essays in Memory of E. Harris Harbison* (Princeton, 1968).

more acceptable than Pomponazzi from a Christian standpoint but concerned like him with the nature of the soul and man's reason. His interest in these matters persisted, and as late as 1525 he assembled a *Compendium primae philosophiae* which, ranging from metaphysics to ethics, attempted to digest and systematize his philosophical views. But the onset of war in 1509 forced the closing of the University of Padua and sent Contarini home to Venice. More important, the events of the next few years compelled him to examine freshly his own life and values. The result was finally a fervent adherence to the Evangelical ideal in religion and a commitment to the active service of Venice which, nevertheless, did not displace the philosophical culture of his youth but merged a trifle uneasily with it.

In Venice, Contarini became a member of a circle of pious young nobles; and his partial conversion to a different pattern of values was considerably accelerated when, between 1510 and 1512, with the Republic still in grave danger, several members of the circle, including his particular friends Tommaso Giustiniani and Vincenzo Querini, abandoned the world for the strict Camaldolesian order. The world, to be sure, had undoubtedly presented itself recently as unusually full of moral ambiguity, frustration, and other unpleasantness; but young Venetians were commonly supposed to serve the Republic, especially in her hour of need, and the scandal in Venice was considerable. Contarini wrote to Querini that he had been compared to a soldier deserting his post.[122] For Contarini the event also produced an acute personal dilemma: his friends zealously pressed him to join them, urging on him the spiritual advantages of a religious life as compared with life in the world. He was confronted, in the deepest sense, with the problem of his vocation.

Then, on Holy Saturday of 1511, as he wrestled with this problem, he experienced a moment of illumination that Jedin has compared to Luther's epiphany in the tower. Henceforth, like Luther, he was fully convinced that salvation could not be won by any human act but was God's free gift; and, as in Luther's case, this conviction was accompanied by a perception that the monastery could not, for himself, procure an eternal blessedness. Free now from his doubts and trusting in God's mercy, he felt that he could be at once "religious" and active in the world. To Giustiniani he wrote: "You know better than I that, although the contemplative life may be nobler than the active, nevertheless the active life, which gives scope for helping

---

[122] Jedin, *Konzil von Trient*, I, 117–118; Carlo Dionisotti, "Chierici e laici nella letteratura italiana del primo Cinquecento," *Problemi di vita religiosa in Italia nel Cinquecento* (Padua, 1960), p. 176; Candeloro, p. 85.

one's neighbor in his spiritual life, is more meritorious than the contemplative. From greater love of God proceeds the willingness to deprive oneself at times of the sweetness of contemplating one's beloved so that his glory might be manifested in many ways." [123] Thus Contarini managed to reconcile a growing piety with service to Venice by means of a characteristically Evangelical insight.

He developed the point further in an eloquent letter to Trifone Gabriele which also reveals his concern to assimilate this new confidence in the value of the active life with his Paduan philosophical culture. In this letter, although he admitted that the speculative sciences (as Aristotle had held) were in some absolute sense superior to the moral virtues, Contarini argued that in particular respects virtue is superior to science: in respect to execution as good in itself (science being neutral), and above all as more appropriate to the nature of man. "Therefore every man ought rather to choose the good appropriate to his nature than something better to the privation of his nature," he declared. "Moral virtue and the active life are proper to man, contemplation to what is above man. Therefore the virtue appropriate to us is preferable, even with privation of the superior, to the superior with the privation of what is proper to us." [124]

It is thus hardly surprising that, although Contarini remained in principle a Thomist, he was not entirely comfortable with theological system-building; he once criticized even Augustine for claiming to understand too much.[125] He advised his fellow-Christians to eschew the presumption of "our new doctors" and rather "reverently to exclaim: 'Oh the depth of the riches of the wisdom and knowledge of God! How incomprehensible are his judgments and how unsearchable his ways!'" [126] Hence too his prescription, in a tract of 1530, for dealing with Protestantism: by pious example rather than argument:

We do not need councils, disputations, syllogisms, and excerpts from Holy Scripture to quiet the agitation of the Lutherans, but good will, love of God and neighbor, and humility of soul, as we put aside avarice and pride in our possessions and splendid domestic establishments, and

[123] Sep. 22, 1511, in Hubert Jedin, "Contarini und Camaldoli," *Archivio Italiano per la Storia della Pietà*, II (1959), 68. For Contarini's general decision, see Jedin, "Ein 'Turmerlebnis' des jungen Contarini," *Historisches Jahrbuch*, LXX (1950), 115–130.

[124] Quoted by Candeloro, pp. 86–87, from *Quattro lettere di Mons. Gasparo Contarini* (Florence, 1558), p. 38.

[125] Gleason, p. 202.

[126] Letter to Lattanzio Tolomei, in Aldo Stella, "La lettera del Cardinale Contarini sulla predestinazione," *Rivista di Storia della Chiesa in Italia*, XV (1961), 431.

convert our households to what the Gospel prescribes. This is necessary to extinguish the errors and tumults of the Lutherans. Let us not bring against them heaps of books, Ciceronian orations, subtle arguments; but uprightness of life and a humble mind cleansed of pride, only desiring Christ and the good of our neighbor. With these weapons, believe me, no dealing with the Lutherans, nay even with the Turks and Jews, could turn out badly. In this consists the duty of Christian prelates, and for this they should employ all their efforts. If they fail to do it, and rely instead on the favor of princes, arguments, authorities, and masses of books, they will, in my opinion, accomplish little. This is my firm conviction.[127]

These words are at once an eloquent statement of the Evangelical ideal of reform and a partial explanation of Contarini's failure in the work of reconciliation. Even the Lutherans required more than good example.

Yet such reform also depended entirely, for Contarini, on the grace of God; man could not accomplish it by himself. Thus his sense of the futility and helplessness of man's intellect is related finally, as with earlier and more consistent representatives of the Renaissance mentality in Florence, to a conviction of the general helplessness of man. As he wrote in his tract *De praedestinatione*, Christians should "seek to exalt as much as possible the grace of Christ and faith in him, and to humble as much as possible the confidence we feel in our works, our knowledge, and our will." [128] For Contarini justification was (though perhaps not exclusively) by faith: "No man is justified by his own works," he wrote to Giustiniani in 1523; "we must have recourse to God's grace, which we receive through faith in Christ." [129] In his last work, a commentary on the Pauline epistles, he emphasized again that salvation meant a renewal in which the initiative belonged wholly to God.[130] The problem of reform was thus primarily a problem of individuals, not of institutions: "True reformations are internal, which only God can accomplish, not merely external such as men can perform." [131]

---

[127] *Confutatio articulorum seu quaestionum Lutheranorum*, in Contarini, *Gegenreformatorische Schriften (1530c.–1542)*, ed. Friedrich Hünermann [Corpus Catholicorum, VII] (Münster, 1923), This passage was called to my attention by Elisabeth Gleason.

[128] Quoted by Stella, "Lettera del Cardinale Contarini," p. 441.

[129] Quoted by Jedin, *Konzil von Trient*, I, 305.

[130] Gleason, pp. 164ff.

[131] From a letter of Contarini to Alfonso Avalos, Mar. 29, 1542, in Alfredo Casadei, "Lettere del Cardinale Gasparo Contarini durante la sua legazione di Bologna (1542)," *ASI*, CXVIII (1960), 87.

Although he was more articulate than most other Venetians, the attitudes of Contarini were by no means exceptional. They expressed a general tendency now fed from many sources. Even the naturalism of Pomponazzi, which Contarini himself both respected and endeavored to refute,[132] became an ally of Evangelical piety and stimulated belief that the soul, dying naturally with the body, would rise with it again supernaturally at the Last Judgment. The consequence was to undermine belief in purgatory and the sacramental system attached to it.[133] For the most part this result remained rather as a tendency than an explicit heresy, but a hint of reserve on the sacraments and a special emphasis on grace were long to characterize an important element in the Venetian patriciate.

Nor were Evangelical impulses in Venice confined to the ruling circles. Popular preachers mediated between such cultivated patricians as Contarini and the masses, to the distress of the nuncio. In 1533 Aleander, then in this position, was directed from Rome to license preachers in Venice, but he was unable to obtain the cooperation of the government; and preachers like the Florentine Dominican Zaccaria continued to deliver attacks on the clerical establishment based on the vernacular Scriptures. His presence in Venice suggests some continuity between Venetian Evangelism and the reformist tradition of Savonarola.[134] Meanwhile Evangelical writings were being printed in Venice, where they circulated widely. The *Trattato del Beneficio di Gesù Cristo*, a popular vehicle of the piety associated with Juan de Valdés, was first printed in 1543 and sold forty thousand copies in Venice alone.[135] And as we shall see, the common view that Italian Evangelism had largely disappeared by the middle of the century[136] must be substantially modified in the case of Venice.

That the Italian reform movement in the first half of the sixteenth century was largely inspired by Evangelism has long been known, but the degree to which its practical energies were supplied by Venice has not been so clearly recognized. We have already noted the existence in Venice even in the fifteenth century of an ideal of reform that emphasized a more spiritual

---

[132] Étienne Gilson, "L'affaire de l'immortalité de l'âme à Venise au début du XVIe siècle," *Umanesimo europeo e umanesimo veneziano*, pp. 37–38.

[133] Cf. George Williams, *The Radical Reformation* (Philadelphia, 1962), p. 24.

[134] Gaeta, *Nunzio pontificio*, pp. 118–119. It may also be pointed out that numerous editions of Savonarola's works were printed in Venice.

[135] Gleason, pp. 217–222. The introduction to Ruth Prelowski's recent translation of this work makes its connection with the Venetian circle seem even closer (in *Italian Reformation Studies in Honor of Laelius Socinus*, ed. John A. Tedeschi [Florence, 1965], esp. pp. 23–28).

[136] As in Jung, "Evangelism in Sixteenth Century Italy," pp. 518–519.

church and at the same time demanded more autonomy for local churches. After the great Venetian political crisis of the earlier sixteenth century, in which the role of the pope seemed to expose the radical need for reform at the highest levels, this program became both more explicit and more insistent. The sack of Rome was to give it particular impetus.[137]

The first expression of this program in the new century came precisely from the young Venetians whose withdrawal into the strict Camaldolesian order had given Contarini such anguish. For, by leaving the world, Querini and Giustiniani hardly ceased to be Venetians; and their reformist *Libellus ad Leonem X*, submitted to the pope in 1513 during the Fifth Lateran Council, bears several marks of the Venetian bias in ecclesiastical matters. Blaming political activity and curial centralization for the corruptions of the church, it proposed reform not primarily through constitutional or administrative change but through the renewal of men. Accordingly it gave particular attention to the training of the clergy, through whom this renewal would have chiefly to be effected. It proposed to reduce the emphasis on scholastic theology in their training and to replace it with study of the Bible and the Fathers; in this way the clergy might learn about the holiness of the church preceding its medieval corruption. This educational reform was also intended to fit the clergy for the more regular preaching which the *Libellus* urged. In addition the *Libellus* perhaps reflected the special Venetian connections with the Levant by recommending a renewal of missionary action and reunion with the separated churches of the East. For the laity it favored Bible study too, in the vernacular when necessary. And in the governance of the church it advocated frequent local synods, the regular convocation of councils, and greater attention to their decrees; this demand seems a trifle pointed, perhaps, in view of the recent vain appeal of Venice against the pope to a council. It is hardly surprising that this reform program met with little favor in Rome.[138]

Meanwhile Contarini was translating his own Evangelical concerns into a program of ecclesiastical reform along much the same lines. He shared the common Renaissance vision of church history as a long decline primarily caused by ecclesiastical worldliness. His emphasis on the episcopacy as the proper agent of reform suggests the ecclesiastical particularism of the

---

[137] Cf. Cantimori, *Eretici italiani*, pp. 20–21.

[138] Jedin, *Konzil von Trient*, I, 103ff.; "Contarini e il contributo veneziano," pp. 110–115.

Venetian tradition;[139] and although for a Venetian he was unusually respectful of papal authority, he was also much concerned that the pope should be
restricted to a set of rather narrowly spiritual responsibilities. This position
evidently served the persistent efforts of Venice to control parts of the papal
state; and Contarini's exposition of his views when, as ambassador to the
pope, he tried to persuade Clement VII to relinquish Ravenna and Cervia
to the Republic might be difficult to accept as a reflection of his personal
opinions on the nature of the church. He argued, as Venetians had long done,
that the pope should confine himself exclusively to matters of the spirit.
"Your Holiness should not think that the riches of the church of Christ are
comprised within this little temporal state which she has acquired," he
declared. "Even before this state there was a church, and a most excellent
one. The church is the community of all Christians. This state is like that of
an Italian prince joined to the church. But your Holiness should above all be
concerned with the well-being of the true church, which consists in peace
and tranquility among Christians, and postpone for the moment the interests
of the temporal state." [140] But Contarini's suggestion that the pope could
better perform his spiritual mission by yielding his political state to Venice
was not altogether cynical. Thirteen years later, after he had been for some
time a cardinal of the church and had demonstrated his sincerity as a reformer,
he expressed the same views. "The temporal state," he wrote to Cardinal
Farnese from Regensburg, "is not the substance of the faith. The martyrs
lived at a time when the Christians had no temporal state, and then the faith
was most efficacious." He compared the temporal state to clothing which hid
the doctrinal body of the faith.[141] The example of Contarini should serve to
warn us against discounting Venetian reformism as no more than a transparent rationalization of Venetian interests. A partial, though unconscious,
rationalization it may have been, but it also coincided with the reforms
proposed by large numbers of other men. Nor was Contarini only concerned to limit the temporal action of the papacy. As a spiritual authority

---

[139] His episcopalianism is most prominent in his early *De officio episcopi* (1516), discussed by Gleason, pp. 65ff., but the emphasis on episcopal office recurs in Contarini's
later writings. Cf. Gleason, pp. 208ff.; it is clear that a similar emphasis on the office of
bishop characterized a whole circle of Venetian reformers.

[140] Quoted by Gleason, p. 57, from *Regesten und Briefe des Cardinals Gasparo Contarini*,
ed. Franz Dittrich (Braunsberg, 1881), p. 43. This argument was advanced in 1528.

[141] May 15, 1541, in Ludwig von Pastor, "Die Correspondenz des Cardinals Contarini
während seiner deutschen Legation," *Historisches Jahrbuch*, I (1880), 389.

too, he insisted, the pope was obligated to accept the limits imposed by divine precept, charity, and reason.[142]

Contarini was the leading spirit in a group of Venetians who, by about 1530, were meeting regularly in the garden of the Benedictine monastry on San Giorgio Maggiore.[143] Its members also included the abbot Gregorio Cortese and Reginald Pole, who was considerably influenced by his association with the Venetian reformers.[144] Carafa participated occasionally, but Aleander was not in touch with the group during his nunciature. Indeed he reported to Rome that Contarini left much to be desired from the standpoint of papal (i.e., jurisdictional) interests.[145] The anxieties of this group about the condition of the church had been considerably deepened by the imperial sack of Rome, a catastrophe that in Venetian eyes may well have seemed (however lamentable) a fitting retribution for the humiliation of Venice two decades before. It could hardly have escaped the attention of Venetians that God had visited on corrupt Rome a punishment he had spared their own city.[146] A year after the event, nevertheless, Contarini was complaining that although the pope talked about reform, he still did absolutely nothing to promote it.[147] From this standpoint it seemed likely that the emendation of the church could only come from Venice; and with the appointment of the leaders of the San Giorgio circle to the cardinalate in 1535 and 1536, the Venetian reformers at last had an opportunity to apply their views to the church universal.

The *Consilium de emendenda ecclesia* of 1538 was the climax of the effort to transform the ideals of the Venetian circle into an effective program of general reform.[148] Contarini dominated the commission that prepared this document and also recommended the appointment of several other members;

[142] Contarini's *De potestate pontificis in compositionibus epistola* is discussed by Gleason, pp. 139–141. Cf. Pastor, XI, 180–181.

[143] The circle is described by Gleason, pp. 158–159.

[144] Cf. Luigi Firpo's analysis of Starkey's *Dialogue between Pole and Lupset*, in *Appunti e testi per la storia dell'antimacchiavellismo* (Turin, n.d.), pp. 63–69.

[145] Gaeta, *Nunzio pontificio*, p. 115.

[146] Some hint of this emerges in Paruta's treatment of the sack of Rome. Though it was not otherwise closely related to his subject, he gave the event particular attention in his *Historia vinetiana*, pp. 242–243. After a dramatic description, he concluded: "Ecco come si stà la Città, ridotta in solitudine, senza popolo, fatta serva, quella, che soleva comandare à tutte le genti."

[147] *Relazione di Roma* of 1530, Albèri, Ser. 2, III, 265.

[148] Cf. Pastor, XI, 152ff., on the importance of the group. I do not mean to imply that these ideals were peculiarly Venetian in every case but only to emphasize their importance in Venetian circles.

among them were his friends Pole, Cortese, and Giberti, the bishop of Verona. Their report reflected in various ways the reformist bias of Venice, its distrust of papal monarchy, its anti-curialism, its concern to strengthen local ecclesiastical administration. The *Consilium* promptly identified the inflation of papal authority as the origin of all modern corruptions of the church. This, it noted, had found general expression in a tendency to regard the will of popes as the supreme law of the church and to consider popes as absolute masters of all benefices. "From this source, Holy Father," the *Consilium* declared, "there have erupted into the church of God, as from the Trojan horse, all those abuses and grave ills by which we, almost despairing of her salvation, now see her afflicted." [149] In its discussion of more specific problems, the document gave particular attention to abuses at the Curia, to the corruption of Rome itself, and to the need for more responsible appointments to all benefices, especially bishoprics.

The essential meaning of the *Consilium* was immediately recognized in Rome, where it was criticized and eventually suppressed. It was objectionable in principle to sincere papalists like the aged canonist Bartolomeo Guidiccione, who saw in it not the reformation but the destruction of the church as he understood it; and it was also seen as a tactical mistake which might play (as it did) into the hands of the Lutherans. But although its printing and sale were forbidden, it was published in numerous unauthorized editions, and its tenor was widely known.[150] Thus, largely under Venetian auspices, the authority of the pope and the possibility that the church had long been tending to tyranny became the subject of general debate. Possibly for this reason Contarini himself felt the need to prepare a careful new statement of his position on the matter. But his second little treatise *De potestate pontificis* could not have been altogether reassuring to Rome. Although it conceded that episcopal authority is derived through the pope (a position on which Contarini was later less obliging), it chiefly argued that legitimate papal authority is strengthened by more careful definition than it had lately received.[151] What remained from the whole discussion was thus chiefly the charge, which Venetians would take up again, that the church was in danger of degenerating into tyranny.

But although the Venetian ideal of reform met with so negative a response

[149] I use the edition in the *Concilium tridentinum*, 2nd ed. (Freiburg, 1963–1966), XII, 131–145; p. 135 for the passage cited.

[150] In addition to Gleason, see Jedin, *Konzil von Trient*, I, 341–343.

[151] Gleason, pp. 139–141. This short tract invites comparison with Contarini's earlier and more conventional work on the subject mentioned above.

in Rome, it received some practical application at home, above all through the famous reforms of Giberti in his diocese of Verona, which were eventually to exercise a considerable influence on Carlo Borromeo and so to enter the main stream of the Catholic Reformation by another route.[152] The educational and disciplinary reforms of Giberti, so consistent with a decentralized conception of ecclesiastical administration, were a matter of great pride to the Venetian reformers. In 1530 Contarini had praised him, noting that he had resisted pressures to reside at the Curia in order to attend to his diocese.[153] In 1532 a Venetian cardinal had also reported to the pope: "He has so regulated everything at Verona that, if all the other bishops did the same, there would be no need for a council." [154] Giberti, from the Venetian point of view, provided a practical demonstration that centralization was not only irrelevant but an obstacle to reform.

The Evangelical piety of Venice and her reservations about papal control, widely known abroad, were interpreted by Protestants to mean that Venice was ripe for conversion. Luther himself celebrated "with true joy" the news, in 1528, that Venice sought "the true word of God";[155] and Ochino, describing to a Venetian friend in 1542 his hopes for Italy, predicted that Venice would be "the door." [156] But such beliefs were a delusion. The hope of the Venetian reformers was that, without breaking her loose ties with Rome, Venice might convert papalists and Protestants alike to a true Evangelical faith in which dogmatic differences would dissolve, and the whole Christian church would be reorganized on the model of the church in Venice. Venetian reform aimed to conserve and to deepen, not to innovate. This is not to deny that there were occasional Venetian conversions to Protestantism,[157] but such cases must be carefully distinguished from those in which some individualistic implication of Evangelical piety was pushed to an unacceptable extreme;[158] and neither problem was

[152] Cf. Enrico Cattaneo, "Influenze veronesi nella legislazione di san Carlo Borromeo," *Problemi di vita religiosa in Italia nel Cinquecento*, pp. 123–166.

[153] *Relazione di Roma*, Albèri, Ser. 2, III, 269.

[154] Cardinal Cornaro in 1532, quoted in Grazioli, *Giberti*, p. x.

[155] Quoted by Federico Chabod, *La politica di Paolo Sarpi* (Venice, 1962), p. 127.

[156] Quoted by Edouard Pommier, "La société vénitienne et la Réforme protestante au XVIe siècle," *BSV*, I (1959), 4.

[157] For example a member of the important da Ponte family, mentioned by Cozzi, *Contarini*, p. 14.

[158] Such seems to have been the case with Vittore Soranzo, bishop of Bergamo, discussed by Pio Paschini, *Tre ricerche sulla storia della Chiesa nel Cinquecento* (Rome, 1945), pp. 92–151; and Giovanni Grimani, patriarch of Aquileia, also studied by Paschini in *Tre illustre prelati del Rinascimento* (Rome, 1957), pp. 131–196.

common. The essence of the Venetian position was dependence on local resources and the admission of substantial variety. Venice was no more inclined to accept the leadership of Geneva or Wittenberg than of Rome.

The initiative of Venetian Evangelism during this period suggests that the conservative and defensive posture of the Republic was compatible with a high degree of general creativity, and the political crisis of the early sixteenth century also initiated the great age of Venetian culture. In various areas of esthetic and literary expression Venetians now began to celebrate human and civic values much as Florentines had done in response to the critical moments of their own collective experience. But the achievements of the tardy Venetian Renaissance were of a character appropriate to their period. The works of Palladio and Titian, of Bembo and Contarini, aimed, for the most part, to realize ideals of balance and harmony which corresponded to the conservative mood of Venetian society.

The civic element in Venetian culture is particularly evident in architecture and painting, which were dedicated to the glorification of Venice almost in deliberate celebration of the miraculous preservation of the Republic amidst so many perils. Venice was the only city in Europe to compete in magnificance with Rome during the sixteenth century.[159] Most of the great Venetian palaces which, as Francesco Sansovino boasted, were more numerous than in any other city,[160] had been only recently constructed; Renaissance Venice was physically a product, for the most part, of this period.

The architectural embellishment of the city has been interpreted from an economic standpoint as a symptom of decline and socially as a sign of the triumph of wasteful aristocratic over bourgeois values,[161] and it is doubtless true that lavish construction diverts wealth from productive enterprise into economically sterile display. But the new buildings of Venice also served an important psychological and patriotic function. They expressed deep feelings about the dignity and importance of the community. When a Venetian family built a palazzo, it did so not only as a monument to its own eminence but also to enhance the magnificance of the city, in whose glories it took a deep pride. This collective sentiment also helps to explain the absence of abrupt discontinuities in architectural style. Individuality in Venice continued to be restrained by a sense of tradition; and even the classicism of

---

[159] Jean Delumeau makes this point in *Vie économique et sociale de Rome dans la seconde moitié du XVI*^e *siècle* (Paris, 1957–1959), I, 360–362.

[160] The short ninth book of his *Venetia città nobilissima* is devoted to describing them.

[161] Luzzatto, "Decadenza," p. 178; Davis, *Decline of the Venetian Nobility*, p. 41.

Palladio, however popular for mainland villas, was not entirely acceptable in the city itself. Thus, after a fire seriously damaged the Palazzo Ducale in 1577, a committee of architects, including Palladio, proposed to rebuild it on a new classical design; but the Senate insisted on the restoration of the old building exactly as it had been.[162]

Painting too flourished in a close relation to the Venetian community, whose official values it was called upon to represent. The subjects of the great series of paintings on the walls and ceilings of the ducal palace were determined by commissions of the state, not (like comparable works in Florence) proposed by the artists themselves.[163] This close relation to a stable society that idealized balance and was bent on conserving traditional values no doubt helps to explain the relatively small influence in Venice of mannerism,·now strong in other parts of Italy. The private responses, the apparent arbitrariness, the effect of disequilibrium that characterized the mannerist style were on the whole out of keeping with the Venetian mood, which demanded the representation of publicly accessible realities.

There was thus much work for architects and artists in Venice, which attracted them from many places. They came too to enjoy the advantages of republican liberty; Titian and Aretino persuaded Jacopo Sansovino, who had arrived after the sack of Rome, to remain for this reason;[164] and, while many of the best artists from other parts of Italy gravitated to Rome, Venetians on the whole stayed at home. Giorgione, Paolo Veronese, and Tintoretto were never attracted to the papal court, and Titian (who could have had the most magnificent patronage anywhere) left Venice only briefly.[165]

Musicians were also attracted to Venice, for the first time in considerable numbers. No more noted for her music in the previous century than for originality in the other arts, Venice began to develop as a musical center with the appointment of Adrian Willaert as *maestro di cappella* at San Marco in 1527; and a succession of distinguished figures succeeded him in this office in a line that culminated early in the next century with Gabrieli and Monteverdi. The presence of foreign musicians in Venice from a variety

[162] Pompeo Molmenti, *La storia di Venezia nella vita privata* (Bergamo, 1928), II, Part 1, 80.

[163] Cf. Bernard Berenson, *Italian Painters of the Renaissance* (London, 1952), p. 11.

[164] See the observations on the point by H. G. Koenigsberger, "Decadence or Shift? Changes in the Civilization of Italy and Europe in the Sixteenth and Seventeenth Centuries," *Transactions of the Royal Historical Society*, Ser. 5, X (1960), 10.

[165] Delumeau, I, 191.

of places insured a variety of musical styles that made her quite different from Rome, where the style of Palestrina was soon to be standard.[166]

Venetian literature during this period provides more ambiguous and in some respects more revealing evidence about the significance of this conservative phase in the mood of the Republic. Letters now tended to a more standardized usage and increasing refinement. Venetian printers, particularly Aldo Manuzio, established norms for the grammar and punctuation of Tuscan, thereby facilitating its acceptance as the common language of Italy. This accomplishment has been conventionally attributed to the practical needs of the printing industry,[167] but it perhaps also reflected the cult for stability so generally characteristic of this period. At the same time it suggests a growing academicism which, as it spread among elements in the patriciate, had dangerous implications for the republican tradition of active participation in civic life.

Pietro Bembo may be taken as the leading representative of these tendencies.[168] Born in 1470, he was introduced by his father Bernardo, ambassador to Florence, to the circle of Lorenzo the Magnificent; and the scholarly and philosophical interests of this group helped to determine a career rather different from what had been expected of a young Venetian. He quickly established his reputation as a literary figure, preparing Greek texts for Manuzio, aiding in the standardization of literary usage, and writing poetry in both classical languages and Italian. His Petrarchan lyrics and his praise of Platonic love in *Gli Asolani* (1505) qualified him to represent Platonism in Castiglione's *Il Cortegiano*. On the basis of his literary prestige he was invited to accompany Giulio de'Medici to Rome in 1513, remaining in his service as secretary after that ecclesiastic became pope. When this high patron died in 1521, Bembo retired to a villa at Padua, where he remained till his death in 1547, the central figure in the literary life of the Republic. He became official historiographer of the Republic in 1530 and later librarian of San Marco. The pope made him a cardinal in 1539, although he had never demonstrated much interest in either theology or ecclesiastical affairs, and conferred on him the bishoprics of Gubbio and Bergamo.

That an ecclesiastic and professional man of letters should have been

---

[166] Guglielmo Barblan, "Aspetti e figure del cinquecento musicale veneziano," *La civiltà veneziana del Rinascimento*, p. 59; Luigi Ronga, "La musica," *La civiltà veneziana nell'età barocca* (Florence, 1959), pp. 125–126.

[167] Elwert, *Studi di letteratura veneziana*, pp. 19ff.

[168] For a recent survey of Bembo's career, see Elwert, "Bembo e la vita letteraria del suo tempo," pp. 125–176.

regarded as the glory of Venice and heaped with honors puts this period in a somewhat new light. Bembo was doubtless popular with Venetians partly because he was known and admired abroad and therefore brought honor to his native city. But the quality of his culture is also instructive. As the philological and literary arbiter of his time, he was able to soothe, in one small but sensitive activity, the anxieties of a difficult age; Bembo represented order and authority, now increasingly attractive and finding expression in a host of written guides providing regulations for every aspect of conduct or belief His Platonism, with its promise of a dependable world of ultimate realities beyond the precarious realm of sense, also attracted a singularly insecure generation. But his influence points also to some weakening in the attractions of business and politics, the traditional foundations of Venetian life. Bembo did not see esthetic and intellectual culture as a flexible and dynamic response to the changing conditions of social existence but as a steady effort to grasp ideal forms elevated as far as possible above the ordinary world. And the most striking feature of his career was its detachment from the vital concerns of Venetian society.

Thus, considerably more than Querini and Giustiniani in the same generation, who assumed serious responsibilities in their new sphere of action, Bembo suggests a softening in the morale of the patriciate. It is true that he composed a patriotic canzone or two,[169] and some personal exchange on the subject may lie behind Castiglione's brief use of Bembo as a spokesman for republican liberty against government by princes.[170] But even as a papal secretary he found his duties uncongenial,[171] and he took almost no interest in politics; on the contrary, he associated the *vita activa civilis* with treachery, hypocrisy, and lust for power.[172] His attitudes emerged in connection with his appointment as historian of Venice. He responded to the first overtures of the Council of Ten with a show of reluctance that, from what we know of him otherwise, was probably sincere. He emphasized his inexperience: "I tell you that I am quite removed from the kind of life and the public actions that are largely the matter of history, both through choice in giving myself to study and because my ecclesiastical condition separates me from them." [173] He pointed to his age, suggesting that the scope and difficulty of

[169] Cf. *ibid.*, p. 152.

[170] In the fourth book of *Il Cortegiano*.

[171] Pastor, VIII, 196.

[172] This is emphasized by Carlo Lagomaggiore, esp. pp. 28–29. For Bembo as historian see also Cozzi, "Pubblica storiografia," pp. 231–236.

[173] Letter of Jun. 21, 1529, to Rannusio, Secretary of the Council of Ten, quoted by Lagomaggiore, VIII, 174.

the task made a younger man more appropriate. He pleaded his love of the tranquil and leisurely life afforded by his Paduan villa.[174] He seems also to have feared the enmities he might create for himself by writing honestly of recent events.[175]

Although he was finally persuaded to accept the post, he made clear that he consented only out of love for country and a sense of duty.[176] But his reservations about the task remained, as the opening sentences of the *Istoria viniziana* made clear: "I have begun to write the facts and things of the city of Venice my country which have happened in a period of forty-four years, not by my own will and judgment or because it was profitable or pleasing to me to do so, but pushed almost by fate or at least chance, which thus brought me to do this . . . being ashamed to refuse, I undertook this very various and complex and, as I can truly say, highly wearisome writing in the sixtieth year of my life." [177] But the chief reason for this doubtful tone was that Bembo had no confidence in the value of historical composition; even the Ciceronian clichés so dear to other humanist historians are absent from his work. The writing of history was, for him, a distraction. He took it up with a sigh and hoped to be released from it as quickly as possible.

With so negative a view of his task, Bembo's *Istoria* is a singularly undistinguished work for so distinguished an author. He was rarely capable of rising above a mechanically annalistic presentation. A single paragraph may string together promiscuously, as for the year 1488, a description of sumptuary laws, the birth of a two-headed baby in Padua, the Venetian visit of the queen of Dacia, and the assassination of Girolamo Riario in Forlì.[178] Bembo did better with military affairs, to which, in the Renaissance tradition, he devoted particular attention;[179] and he dramatized occasional episodes effectively. Caterina Cornaro's transfer of Cyprus to Venice, for example, is presented as a great scene, with moving speeches and tears in the eyes of the participants.[180] But Bembo's gifts were rhetorical rather than historical. He lacked a capacity for analysis, and he was unable to identify general themes around which to organize particular detail.

Nor did he feel any great obligation to factual truth; his primary aim was

[174] Lagomaggiore, VII, 15.
[175] *Ibid.*, VII, 354–355.
[176] *Ibid.*, VII, 15.
[177] *Della istoria viniziana libri dodici* (Milan, 1809), I, 33–34.
[178] *Ibid.*, I, 58–60.
[179] Lagomaggiore has noted this, VIII, 79.
[180] *Istoria viniziana*, I, 61ff.

to glorify Venice and to honor her leaders. Thus a revealing letter of complaint about his stipend pointed out that he deserved better treatment because he had put in the mouth of a doge a singularly effective speech, "the greater part of which his highness never thought of saying." [181] It has also been remarked that he was frequently less precise than the considerable sources available to him. He was admitted to the state archives by a special decree (necessary because he was an ecclesiastic), but he made little use of them, preferring to rely instead, though without acknowledgment, on the massive diary of Sanuto, which was furnished to him by the Council of Ten. In addition he had access to various chronicles as well as to oral testimony. His work, nevertheless, is chronologically imprecise, full of avoidable error, and weakened by such frivolous embellishments as senatorial invocation of the immortal gods.[182] Bembo was evidently correct in suggesting that his long indifference to public affairs was a serious disqualification from the writing of history.

There are some marks in the work of an emotional identification with Venice. Thus, although his explanation of the Republic's recovery after Agnadello as a direct effect of Venetian constancy and virtue may seem merely perfunctory, he appeared genuinely indignant at the interdict of Julius II and above all at the pope's delay in lifting his censures. This suggested to him that the pope and his supporters "enjoyed as their game and delight the indignities and humiliations of the Republic and the cruelty, indeed the savagery and monstrosity of their interdicts," [183] a judgment of particular interest from one who had seen service at the Curia not long after these events. On the other hand, he failed to recognize the danger to Venice in too candid an account of the negotiations with Maximilian, and his reference to an offer of perpetual tribute to the emperor had to be deleted by the Council of Ten.[184] Bembo was not only erratic about facts but also insensitive to their political meaning.

Bembo's inadequacies as a historian seem particularly significant when one recalls that he wrote the *Istoria viniziana* some time after the appearance of Machiavelli's works, and during almost the same years that Guicciardini was composing the *Storia d'Italia*. Venice was evidently still unable to support a mature historiography, and indeed the period with which we are now

[181] Quoted by Lagomaggiore, VII, 357, from a letter of Sep. 15, 1534.

[182] Lagomaggiore, IX, 88ff., 33ff., 48ff.; VIII, 175ff.

[183] *Istoria viniziana*, I, 94, 109, 130ff.

[184] E. Teza, "Correzioni alla Istoria Veneziana di P. Bembo proposte dal Consiglio dei Dieci nel 1548," *Annali delle Università toscane*, XVIII (1888), 90.

concerned by no means fulfilled the promise hinted at in the Venetian histories of the later fifteenth century. Thus the weakness in Bembo's historical understanding was not merely personal. It was symptomatic of the general political climate of the Republic. Venice felt too insecure to allow the publication of material excessively critical of other powers or damaging to herself, however instructive the truth might be; and the Council of Ten had no compunction about deleting from or adding to Bembo's work in any case where the interests of "the state and the quiet of the Republic" might be affected.[185] In addition the concern of Bembo's generation to preserve a set of permanent arrangements was hardly conducive to anything but the most conventional, mechanical, and selective reconstruction of the past. Venice still regarded history only as a means to glorify and shore up the state, not as a way to understand the political and social world.

This view of history was already apparent in the circumstances surrounding the designation of Andrea Navagero, Bembo's predecessor, as the first official historian of Venice. The action was taken in 1515 to commemorate the "constancy and invincible virtue" of the Republic in the recent crisis which still, perhaps, hardly seemed over;[186] the decree of appointment by the Council of Ten referred pointedly to the need of states for support "in times of turbulence." A historian's essential task, the decree suggested at the outset, was to promote the "reputation" of the state by preserving the memory of its actions, "not through compendious, uncertain, various, and crude chronicles and annals but with certain, authentic, elegant, and well-developed histories." He was not, certainly, to tamper with the truth; but his chief duty was to enhance the fame of those whose actions he described with all the resources of his eloquence.[187] But Navagero was unfortunately not up to the task. He executed at least part of his commission, but his work was so severely criticized—possibly because, as a man of some experience in public life, he understood politics too well for simple adulation—that (as it was reported) his will ordered that it be burned.[188]

The decree naming Bembo as his successor in 1530 suggests that the onset

---

[185] See the directive printed by Teza, pp. 77–78.

[186] The phrase is Daniele Barbaro's in his *Storia veneziana*, ed. Tommaso Gar, *ASI*, VII, Part II (1844), 951. On Navagero's appointment see also Cozzi, "Pubblica storiografia," pp. 222–229.

[187] The text of the decree, dated Jan. 30, 1515, is in Lagomaggiore, IX, 331–332.

[188] Morosini, V, 316, reports this. See also Sansovino, *Venezia città nobilissima*, sig. GGGGG4[r]. The story of the burning of this work apparently made a considerable impression on later generations.

of quieter times permitted, at least in theory, a broader view of history. This document again mentioned the contribution of history to the reputation of states, and it cited the ancients, whose heroes had been commemorated by historians. Venetians, it submitted, particularly through their exploits in the recent wars, were equally worthy of "immortal praise and commendation." But the decree also mentioned the value of history to instruct rulers in the management of their daily business and assist them "to foresee with greater prudence things to come." [189]

If Bembo proved of little use in this respect, his successor, Daniele Barbaro, promptly appointed after Bembo's death in 1547, should have been more helpful. Active in the affairs of the Republic, his political career was to culminate the next year in the important embassy to England. He had also been a friend, in his youth, of the Florentine historian Varchi. Although he managed to continue Bembo's narrative for only two years, therefore, he wrote history in a spirit very different from that of his predecessor. He seems to have been aware of this and in several places obliquely criticized Bembo. Thus, in discussing the appointment of Navagero, he noted that the Senate had intended the post of state historian to be held by a noble because only such a man knew the facts and sufficiently understood politics; in view of Bembo's deficiencies, the Polybian commonplace here seems a bit pointed. He also remarked that he had hesitated to succeed so elegant a writer as Bembo; but his doubt had changed to joy when he recalled that he would be recounting the experiences of his youth, which he could retell with authority: engagement with events was apparently a better qualification for the historian than a polished rhetoric.[190] Barbaro's Venetian history is accordingly a clear, disciplined narrative, chiefly of military campaigns, composed in a direct and simple style, with few speeches, classical allusions, or other embellishments.

The general theme of the work is the heroic struggle of Venice against "the malignity of the times and of men." [191] Through this long ordeal, as Barbaro remarks, the virtue of the Republic had been exercised, the prudence

---

[189] Dated Sep. 26, 1530, it is given in Lagomaggiore, IX, 332–334. On the rather different tone of this decree, see also Cozzi, "Pubblica storiografia," pp' 230–231.

[190] *Storia veneziana*, pp. 951–952. But since he was born in 1513, he did not in fact manage to come down to the period of his own experience. For Barbaro see, in general, Pio Paschini, "Daniele Barbaro letterato e prelato veneziano nel Cinquecento," *Rivista di Storia della Chiesa in Italia*, XV (1961), 73–107, though this does not treat Barbaro as historian. On this subject see Cozzi, "Pubblica storiografia," pp. 237–238.

[191] *Ibid.*, p. 1024.

of her senators made known, and the love of her citizens for their country praised.[192] But through the whole experience the most malignant of her enemies had been the pope; on this point Barbaro went far beyond Bembo. Julius II, who "desired to be arbiter of everything" and was filled with "insatiable desires to rule," had incited the princes to league against Venice, had "struck the innocent Republic with spiritual arms," had treated her ambassadors with brutality, and had tried to strip her of all her possessions in the peace. Furthermore the hostility of Julius was evidently, for Barbaro, no mere personal idiosyncracy. It persisted equally in Leo X, who was quite as ardently opposed to Venice's recovery of her possessions and had been primarily responsible for the ravaging of Venetian territory, "an impiety, I believe, such as has never been used before." [193] Thus Barbaro suggests again the depth of the Venetian feeling against Rome left behind by the League of Cambray.

Barbaro's work also gives other signs of political understanding. He was aware that the war imposed a serious financial burden on the Venetian state,[194] and he knew (like Giucciardini) that Italian affairs could be grasped only in a larger European context.[195] He gave particular attention to the value of the French alliance for Venice,[196] and he displayed a typically Venetian scepticism of crusades against the Turks.[197] But these particular insights are less interesting in his work than a tendency to view the realm of politics as one of constant and only partly comprehensible change. "The things of the world cannot truly remain long in the same condition," he wrote in connection with the recovery of Venetian fortunes in 1510. "Minds, occasions, destinies themselves change." [198] Like so many other political writers of the Renaissance, he saw war above all as the province of blind fortune, full of "uncertain events" and brutal acts of "cruelty and impiety against the miserable citizens." [199] From this vision of affairs he nevertheless seems to have been prepared to accept a number of conclusions. He hinted at the pacifism of Venice during the middle decades of the century by

[192] *Ibid.*, p. 951.
[193] *Ibid.*, pp. 964–965, 954–955, 957–958, 996–997. The last passage may have been added by Luigi Borghi, Secretary of the Senate; cf. Gar's introduction, p. xi.
[194] *Ibid.*, pp. 1015, 1031.
[195] *Ibid.*, pp. 1022–1024, for example, where he discusses the relevance to Italy of events in England, Scotland, and Burgundy.
[196] This is a major theme of the work, as on p. 994.
[197] Thus pp. 1053–1056, where he ridicules the "crusaders" gathering in Hungary.
[198] *Ibid.*, p. 959.
[199] *Ibid.*, p. 962.

recording the concern of the Senate to avoid the dubious chance of battle and to restrain its over-eager generals,[200] but he also several times invoked the familiar Renaissance doctrine of the occasion, with its suggestion that at least some moments may be fit for decisive action, that they must be awaited patiently, and that when they arrive they must be seized with energy.[201] Barbaro finally leaves the impression of one who has studied events with care and intelligence, has learned to respect the realities of power and change, but has by no means altogether lost confidence in the value of political calculation.

But Barbaro's pursuit of political understanding through history was by no means typical of Venice in this period, nor did he persevere in it himself. Three years after taking up his post as state historian, most of which had been spent in England, he abandoned his historical work to become co-adjutor to the patriarch of Aquileia.[202] But what is particularly striking is that the Venetian government failed to appreciate or to preserve what he had written. His manuscript was permitted to disappear, to be rediscovered only in the nineteenth century, and a generation later Francesco Sansovino was evidently unaware either of his official position or that he had written a history.[203] It is even more remarkable that for the next thirty years no official history of Venice was written at all. A series of patricians continued to receive appointment to the post of historiographer, but none actually wrote the history of the Republic.[204]

The collapse of official historiography in Venice during this period may be attributed in part to the fact that the immediate political crisis to which it had been a response was now receding into the past, and the Republic for the time being no longer needed weapons of this kind. But the neglect of

[200] *Ibid.*, pp. 998–999, 1008.

[201] For example, pp. 957, 960, 965, 967, 984, 1039.

[202] This is mentioned in Matteo Dandolo's *Relazione di Roma* of 1551, Albèri, Ser. 2, III, 348. See also Paschini, "Barbaro," pp. 81–82.

[203] In *Venezia citta nobilissima*, Sig, KKKKK2ʳ⁻ᵛ, Sansovino omits the *Storia* from his list of Barbaro's works and makes no reference to his appointment as historiographer. Valier, *Dell'utilità*, p. 404, mentioned the appointment but thought Barbaro had written nothing.

[204] A list is supplied by Apostolo Zeno at the beginning of the *Istorici delle cose veneziane*, I, xiii. In his dispatch of May 22, 1593, in *La legazione di Roma di Paolo Paruta, 1592–1595*, ed. Giuseppe de Leva (Venice, 1887), Paruta discussed the long gap between Bembo's work and his own: "E la Republica ha avuto in ciò così poca ventura, che, quantunque questo carico già il corso ormai di molti anni, sia stato in mano di diversi, non se ne legge però scrittura d'alcuno: onde è stato bisogno di ripigliare l'istoria così di lontano fin da'tempi, ne quali terminò il cardinale Bembo la sua."

Theft of the body of Saint Mark for conveyal to Venice *(Tintoretto).*

The Venetian political ideal of the mid-sixteenth century:
Venice between Justice and Peace *(Veronese)*.

historiography in the middle decades of the century also had deeper causes, I think. The whole climate of Venetian culture was now uncongenial to it. Thus, although a succession of citizen secretaries was ordered to keep vernacular annals, presumably against some future need, nothing was made public; the historical understanding, as a general instrument for coping with human experience, apparently no longer seemed worth cultivating. For history, which as Barbaro recognized, is a constant reminder that all things change, was peculiarly unattractive to a generation anxious to persuade itself that things would go on exactly as they had always been.

During this period, therefore, the most substantial formal work dealing with the Venetian past was Nicolò Zeno's quite unofficial *Origine de' barbari*,[205] which devotes one of its eleven books to the origins of Venice, a relatively safe subject. This is, however, essentially a work of erudition which the author passed off as a preliminary sketch he was too busy to refine.[206] Zeno expressed concern with the critical problem of sifting truth from conflicting evidence;[207] and his work is notable for recognizing the complexities of early migration from the mainland to the Venetian islands and for denying (though only implicitly) that the Republic had been always free.[208] But Zeno's critical sense was hardly consistent;[209] and his description of early Venetian society as egalitarian, ascetic, industrious, peaceful, and virtuous was not history but the projection of a static and utterly abstract ideal.[210] He also repudiated, with considerable indignation, the notion that the early settlers of Venice might have had any but the highest social origins.[211]

Zeno's work in these respects reflected the general tendencies of political discourse elsewhere in sixteenth-century Italy. So long disrupted, first by the internal and external struggles of the Renaissance states and then by foreign invasion, Italy longed for stability; and writers about politics were primarily concerned to describe ideal patterns of government that would

[205] *Dell'origine de' barbari, che distrussero per tutto'l mondo l'imperio di Roma, onde hebbe principio la città di Venetia libri undici* (Venice, 1557).
[206] See Francesco Marcolini's dedicatory epistle to this first edition, which was printed anonymously.
[207] In the opening lines, pp. 1–2. Foscarini particularly praised his critical sense, *Della letteratura veneziana*, pp. 294–295, 429–430.
[208] Cf. pp. 205–206, where he implies that Venice had been subject to the emperors in both East and West. He also fails to mention Saint Mark.
[209] Thus he accepted the mythical genealogies of Berosus, which were by no means universally considered authentic (pp. 3, 185).
[210] Pp. 194–195.
[211] Pp. 189–190.

perfectly exclude all disorder and change. At times they identified moments in the past that approached such perfection, but their essential method was rational rather than historical; with the aid of Plato, Aristotle, and Cicero, they constructed artificial and utopian systems. The conclusions based on this method were general and academic; and the political compositions of the period are less truly prescriptions for real political ills than symptoms of the anxiety provoked by long disorder. They have in common an exaggerated fear and contempt for the lower classes, a tendency to exalt law as the governor of passion, and an inclination once again to bind all things together into large, comforting systems of universal application. Thus the insights of Renaissance politics, its openness to immediate experience, its concreteness and flexibility, and its awareness of change as an inevitable condition of human existence gradually receded.[212]

Venice generally participated in these tendencies, but with some differences. The most striking was the conviction of Venetians that they had already attained the perfection to which other states still aspired. Thus while other writers were devising ideal constitutions, Venetians, along with admirers of Venice elsewhere, described Venice. In her alone, they insisted, the ideal and the real happily coincided. In addition Venice was still free; and although her mood had altered, she did not merely crave order and security. She was also resolved to cling to her traditional republican liberties. Thus her writers tended to combine familiar republican themes with the rather contrary tendencies of the age.

They wrote about Venice partly because the apparently miraculous preservation of the Republic during her recent terrible ordeal cried out for some explanation; partly to convince themselves that Venice, having survived this ultimate challenge, might now be expected to endure forever; and partly because the chaotic and unhappy world around her needed instruction in the political virtues she had so dramatically revealed. Thus the Venetian political tradition, powerful but still largely inarticulate, began to exhibit an explicit and characteristic pattern of political discourse. Its most famous early representatives were Gasparo Contarini's *De magistratibus et republica Venetorum*, and the *Libro della Repubblica de'Veneziani*, written partly from Venetian sources by the Florentine republican Donato Giannotti, works which are both much alike and yet significantly different. Contarini's treatise is largely a

---

[212] Albertini, *Das florentinische Staatsbewusstsein*, pp. 284ff., offers stimulating generalization about post-Renaissance political discourse in Italy. See also Curcio, *Dal Rinascimento alla Controriforma*, esp. pp. 1ff.

portrait of static perfection and offers a Venetian expression of the conservative idealism of the age. Giannotti's work adds impulses from the richer and more complex Florentine understanding of the political world. It hints at the inadequacies of Venetian thought at this stage and foreshadows some aspects of its future development.

Although Contarini's *De republica* was not published until 1543, it was written in 1523 or 1524 when his memory of recent perils was still vivid.[213] He noted in the course of the work that the pressures on Venice had come from two directions. First there had been the Turks, "whose attacks," he wrote, "we have endured to our great hurt for many years, holding back the fiercest enemy of all Christendom." But above all Contarini recalled how, fifteen years before, "almost all the Christian princes leagued to destroy our empire." Nevertheless, he went on, "thanks be to God, all their attacks were repelled; and, although we were at the point of collapse, all was restored." [214] Contarini was thus concerned to celebrate what had been so happily spared; but at the same time he appears to be seeking assurance that, in a world which had shown itself so universally and formidably hostile, such cherished values as Venice embodied could never perish from the earth.

His argument is based on an uneasy blend of Aristotelian commonplaces with the Venetian political myth, on most of whose scattered elements he draws; and the entire amalgam is occasionally modified by considerations drawn from his long personal experience. This mixed background creates tensions within his political vision which are never fully resolved. Following Aristotle (with Plato also obscurely in the background), Contarini is frequently eager to refer the perfections of Venice to nature, the basis of all political association, whose rational structure the Venetian founding fathers had evidently grasped, and which they had managed successfully to imitate. This tendency in his thought attributed the achievement of Venice to eternal principles and implied that she would last forever; its psychological function is obvious. But the Venetian myth, which Contarini could hardly relinquish, had a rather different basis. However indifferent to historical fact, it professed

---

[213] For what follows I should like to make a general acknowledgment to the dissertation of Elisabeth Gleason, esp. Ch. 3, and to her unpublished paper, "A Renaissance View of the Venetian State: Gasparo Contarini's *De magistratibus et republica Venetorum*," presented to the Northern California Renaissance Conference, Nov. 16, 1963; see also Gaeta, "Mito di Venezia," pp. 65–66. For the date of composition, see Felix Gilbert, "The Date of Composition of Contarini's and Giannotti's Books on Venice," *Studies in the Renaissance*, XIV (1967). Gilbert notes from internal evidence that Contarini touched up the work and that its final version was not completed before 1532.

[214] In the edition cited above, note 68, col. 47.

to identify the historical accomplishment of a particular society favored by concrete circumstances. It depicted the Venetians as wise, but the wisdom to which it pointed was largely empirical and practical rather than rational and speculative. Meanwhile Contarini's own political experience appears from time to time at cross purposes with both philosophy and myth. He seems scarcely to have recognized the problems arising from his attempt to combine these various types of political vision, but the ambiguity of his argument points up the strange dilemma of Venetian republicanism during its conservative phase. It sought to preserve the values of Renaissance politics by rejecting the perilous dynamic elements that had given them life.

Contarini's point of departure was as concrete as possible. He began with the more obvious wonders of Venice, noting the amazement of strangers at the quantities of goods passing through the city, at the many peoples from remote lands swarming over her quays and through her streets and canals, at the greatness of her empire, and above all at her exotic location, which so perfectly combined accessibility to trade with security from attack. But then he probed deeper to expose virtues of which a casual foreign observer could hardly be aware. The most marvelous feature of Venice was none of these visible wonders but the success of her government. For a city, as he remarked, is "not so much a wall and houses but the agreement and effective ordering of citizens . . . . This is the true basis and form of a republic, on which a happy life for men depends." [215]

Contarini's major thesis was thus that Venice was admirable because of an "order" which enabled her citizens to enjoy a good life. In this he believed that she excelled all other republics old and new. With obvious reference to both ancient Rome and modern Florence, he observed that all other republics had been plagued and finally destroyed by internal disorders, whereas, "in our city no popular tumult or sedition has ever occurred." [216] Contarini's understanding here of *order* is clear. He had in mind not conformity to some abstract pattern of universal order but the practical order provided by effective government. His meaning was precisely that of his less speculative contemporary Sanuto in recording the wonderful degree of "order" that characterized Venice and guaranteed her perpetuity.[217] Contarini concluded that no imaginary commonwealth invented by any philosopher had equaled the concrete reality of Venice.[218]

[215] Col. 3.
[216] Col. 58.
[217] Quoted above, p. 63.
[218] Col. 4.

But, living in so precarious a world, this did not fully satisfy him. A merely practical order consisting only in successful adaptation to circumstance did not seem likely to last forever, and the structure of the Venetian government had therefore to be seen as consonant with the eternal principles of philosophy. Thus, even though philosophers could not imagine so perfect a state as Venice, Contarini felt compelled, as though by the back door, to become a philosopher himself. Insisting dogmatically that "every human institution which seeks to be well regarded should imitate nature, the best mother of all things," [219] he repeatedly sought to explain what was admirable in Venetian practice as conformity to the general order of nature. As a result Contarini introduced the incongruous principles of unity and hierarchy into what was intended as the glorification of a republic. His political views are thus much like his religion, which mingled Evangelism with Thomistic theology.

The effect is slightly jarring, for example when, in explaining the function of the doge, he hints, albeit unconsciously, at a conception of authority rather alien from Venetian politics. "Truly," he wrote, "unity cannot be rightly maintained unless one is placed above the multitude of citizens and the body of magistrates to whom various functions are entrusted, and in a sense coordinates them, and brings them together. This the best philosophers and especially the investigators of nature have observed, both in the structure of the universe and in the animal microcosm." [220] His attempt to explain Venetian affection for the principle of seniority along similar lines is even more peculiar. Nature, he declared, "has so disposed the power and reason of the whole world that things devoid of sense and intellect are governed by those provided with understanding. The same principle must therefore be observed in this assemblage of men we call a city." But his conclusion clearly depends on a very different source than the relationships within the great chain of being. Contarini argues that a city should be ruled by its elders, "for old men excel younger men in prudence, are less subject to perturbations of mind, and are experienced in the ways of many things learned through longer life." [221]

But such weak excursions into systematic thought, however significant for this phase in the evolution of Venetian republicanism, by no means constitute the essential element in *De republica*, which is for the most part an idealized description of Venetian institutions, including much concrete detail.

---

[219] Col. 27.

[220] Col. 17.

[221] Col. 27. Here Contarini refers explicitly to Aristotle, though his debts to Aristotle are generally left implicit.

The missing link between philosophy and politics is supplied, for Contarini, by the fact that earlier generations of Venetians had been statesmen as well as sages; they had combined active with contemplative virtues. Venice had become great not only because of their wisdom but also through their devotion and self-sacrifice. "Without regard to their private interest and honor," he remarked, the ancestors of contemporary Venice had been "at one in their zeal to strengthen and enlarge their country." And their self-abnegation was still apparent in the striking absence of monuments to them of any kind, "although they carried out great exploits both at home and abroad and have deserved well of the Republic: no tombs, no statues of generals either on horseback or on foot, no prows of ships or standards taken from the enemy after great battles." [222]

But Contarini was far more interested in the peaceful virtues exhibited by his fellow-countrymen; and from this standpoint the greatest memorial to their ideal combination of reflective and practical wisdom was the Venetian constitution. Its principles of operation, however, were different from those of a unified, hierarchical, and essentially static natural order. It depended instead on the familiar Renaissance conception of a balance among forces sufficient to exclude either a monolithic uniformity in which all individuality would disappear or an anarchic struggle for power among opposing interests. Machiavelli had well understood this ideal and Contarini now proceeded to demonstrate that Venice was its perfect realization.

Venice, as he depicted her, had arrived at a perfect balance of the various interests and classes in society, and had effectively utilized the peculiar political talents of each for the good of the whole. "Such moderation and proportion characterize this Republic," he declared, "and such a mixture of all suitable estates that this city by itself incorporates at once a princely sovereignty, a governance of the nobility, and a rule of citizens, so that the whole appears as balanced as equal weights." [223] Even "the people," he noted, were "not entirely excluded but have been admitted to those offices which might be entrusted to them without detriment to the common welfare." [224] Venice had discovered the secret of maintaining equality among her various elements, the most dangerous problem of domestic polity. "No greater plague can infect a republic than when one part prevails over the others," he remarked

[222] Cols. 3–4.

[223] Cols. 7–8.

[224] Col. 58. Contarini appears to mean here, however, only the *cittadini*. Following both Aristotle and the actualities of Venetian practice, he rejected the political competence of "hirelings and artisans" (Col. 8).

generally. "For where equality is not preserved, a society cannot maintain any harmony among its citizens, which generally happens when many offices of a republic are combined in one." This was the key to social harmony: "Just as a mixture dissolves if any of the elements from which the body is composed surpasses the others, so all harmony becomes dissonance if you hear one instrument or voice more strongly. In the same way if you wish a city or a republic to last, it is above all necessary that no part should operate more powerfully than the others, but all, as far as possible, should participate in the public authority." [225]

But although the pleasing analogy to music here suggests a degree of idealization quite absent from Machiavelli's unsentimental treatment of constitutional balance, the difference is chiefly one of tone. Underlying Contarini's vision of harmony is the pessimism also basic to Florentine political thought. In spite of his praise for the virtue of earlier Venetians, Contarini was profoundly aware (as in his religious thought) that man is by nature selfish and limited. A mixed and balanced government was required by nature in this sense, which by the same token also taught that a republic is superior to a principate. On this point he chose to draw on a very different source of instruction from the philosophy to which he had elsewhere appealed. "Because the frail nature of man often changes for the worse and life is short," he wrote, "government by many citizens together is preferable. This experience, the master of all things, well teaches." [226] For the same reason Venice had always insisted that the serious business of the state should be conducted by groups of magistrates who, working together, could complement and check each other. [227] The same principle suggested that laws should be formulated by assemblies. Only in such bodies could men be sufficiently free from "hatred or friendship or any other perturbation of mind" to legislate in the common interest; in assemblies "many wise men meet who, taught by much experience and comparing the devices of others with earlier examples, at length and after long consultation, determine what has seemed best." [228] By such procedures Venetian law had been made severely impersonal, so that the sovereignty of the Venetian state could depend "on

[225] Col. 29. For a good discussion of the sources of the idea of the mixed constitution with particular reference to its transmission by Contarini, see Z. S. Fink, *The Classical Republicans: An Essay in the Recovery of a Pattern of Thought in Seventeenth Century England*, 2nd ed. (Evanston, 1961), pp. 2ff.

[226] Cols. 6–7.

[227] Col. 41.

[228] Cols. 5–6.

laws, not men." [229] Doubtless the conviction that law is in touch with the eternal order of things and is therefore superior to mere human whim as the basis of government was a major element in Contarini's esteem for the rule of law, as it had not on the whole been for Machiavelli. But Contarini's picture of the Venetian Senate at work suggests in addition a rather different set of considerations which align him rather more closely to later Florentine thought.

Considerable realism of this sort also characterizes Contarini's treatment of the Council of Ten, in which he evidently saw not the application of philosophical principles but an effective adaptation to particular dangers. He praised this body as "of the highest authority"; it "might properly be said to guarantee the security of the Republic." It was needed not only to suppress wickedness but also to prevent tyranny, the danger of which had been foreseen from the beginning by the founders of the Republic. The success of Venice in holding "such a monstrosity" at bay in a time when it had devoured nearly all the states around her was, for Contarini, a particular mark of the Venetian achievement. Nevertheless his satisfaction at the preservation of Venetian liberty when liberty was disappearing elsewhere suggested an acute sense of loneliness and special peril. Venice now needed, he was implying, to be particularly on guard.[230]

But the perfection of Venice, Contarini emphasized, consisted not only in her long duration as a free republic but also in the quality of life her government had provided for the entire populace. In his view the state did not exist merely to maintain peace and order and thus to perpetuate itself. "The whole purpose of civil life consists in this," he declared, "that, by the easiest way possible, the citizens may share in a happy life";[231] and it was one of the special glories of Venice that she effectively performed a whole series of welfare functions. Contarini praised the Venetian government for supplying food to the masses, often buying dear and selling cheap, sometimes at a great loss. The state made itself responsible for the control of contagious diseases. It provided support for the sick and aged, and pensions for employees of the arsenal no longer able to work.[232] Contarini also noted in passing the

[229] Col. 6.

[230] Col. 33. It is of some interest that Contarini, who had so little admiration for antiquity, saw the Council of Ten as the only Venetian institution that deliberately imitated the ancients.

[231] Col. 4.

[232] Cols. 50, 59. Contarini the success of these measures had been demonstrated by the loyalty of the lower classes in 1509 (Cols. 61–62).

responsibility of the magistrate for supervising Venetian religious life. Thus, he remarked, the procurators of Saint Mark "oversee the priests of this church and its maintenance, should any part need repair; and they see to it that God is worshipped in this church with piety and magnificence in accordance with the dignity of the city and the greatness of her patron, Saint Mark the Evangelist." [233]

This hint of independence from modern ecclesiastical Rome was accompanied by a conscious rivalry, throughout the book, with ancient secular Rome. A major thesis of the work is that the Venetian Republic was in essential respects superior to the Roman. Thus Contarini converted a bias at which earlier Venetians had hinted into a coherent argument destined for much elaboration by later Venetian writers.

His comparison between Venice and Rome sometimes lies just below the surface, as in his celebration of peace. "Although the praise of war and military discipline are necessary to cities for the conservation of liberty and the protection of frontiers, and also have much dignity and splendor," he wrote in connection with the purpose of government among men, "nevertheless the common sense of men denies that the office of war (by which the slaughter and ruin of mortals are especially procured) is desirable in itself and that all other civic functions should be related to it. And a man would be of a cruel disposition, indeed a hater of humanity, who desired battles, slaughter, burnings, only to be famous in military affairs." [234] Venice, Contarini was obliquely suggesting here, better understood the ends of civil government than the people who, as other Europeans long believed, had provided the most effective polity the world had ever known. The failure of ancient Rome to comprehend that peace must take priority over war had also, for Contarini, been the cause of her decline into tyranny. Venice had always recognized that, "since the nature of men constantly inclines to evil, citizens who have numerous troops and supporters may conceive arrogant ambitions." She had therefore avoided native armies and had happily remained a republic. But "this problem always troubled the Roman Republic, as can readily be grasped from the memorials of the ancients. It made many Roman citizens defy the laws of the Republic and the decrees of the Senate, and finally made Julius Caesar tyrant of the Roman Empire." [235] Furthermore (although again the

[233] Col. 52.
[234] Col. 5. Contarini's criticism of Roman militarism is also thoroughly Augustinian; cf. *De Civitate Dei*, Bk. V, Ch. 17.
[235] Col. 55.

point is left implicit) Venice had lasted far longer as a republic than Rome in any condition. Since her foundation, Contarini wrote, "the city of Venice (which we have read of no other city) has remained constantly free from conquest by any enemy for almost eleven hundred years." [236] But his insistence on the superiority of Venice to Rome emerges most dramatically in his discussion of the courts. He remarked that, whereas the Romans had left the prosecution of crime to private citizens, Venice employed a public prosecutor; and he made the remarkable suggestion that his own Republic had developed a superior understanding of public authority. "In this matter," he declared, "our ancestors must be seen as having better imitated the nature of things and more wisely provided for concord among the citizens than the Romans. For since anyone who commits a crime primarily harms the laws and the Republic, he should especially be punished by the Republic." [237] On no point is Contarini less in agreement with Machiavelli than in his estimate of Rome.

From the standpoint of the Renaissance political mentality there are significantly regressive elements in Contarini's ideal portrait of the Venetian government. Particularly prominent is the absence from his thought of any historical sense, his refusal to recognize change. His Venice is not the product of a long development; she seems to have been born already mature out of the almost supernatural wisdom of her founding fathers, and to have been maintained ever since in full vigor by the conservative dedication of successive later generations.[238] Yet there is also a curious ambiguity in Contarini's appeal to nature which points in a very different direction. Generally, to be sure, he meant by *nature* the eternal order of things; but he was also aware of some sense in which nature is far from stable. It is significant that this possibility occurred to him when he briefly abandoned philosophical description to consider the immediate plight of his beloved Republic. From this standpoint the prospect was less positive:

These ancient laws and customs endure even to our time, although certain young men, corrupted by ambition or luxury since the expansion of the empire, have neglected their country's institutions. In addition the number of citizens has so increased that through the inroads of war in our time and expenses at home, many more have become poor

236 Col. 3.
237 Col. 38.
238 Fink makes this point with some emphasis, p. 38.

than can be provided for by the benefit of this law [providing subsidies for maritime ventures]. For nature so works that nothing can be perpetual among men, but all things, however perfectly they may seem to have been established at the beginning, after some years, nature inclining to the worse, require restoration, just as the body, though sated with its lunch, cannot long remain sound unless dinner follows after some hours. Thus in everything it is necessary to assist declining nature and to renew her. May God also help us to follow reason in this and to devise a remedy, so that everything needful may be provided in our Republic.[239]

Nature, it appears, had two faces; and in the world of time (to which Venice after all belonged), she underwent inevitable cycles of decay and required regular renewal.

After such extensive demonstration to the contrary, this admission comes as a shock; but it reminds us of Contarini's long service to the state, which had taught him that, although eternal nature may be our universal mother, the *rerum omnium magistra* is still experience.[240] But Contarini's brief recognition of mutable nature is also significant because it suggests the applicability to Venice of the idea of renewal elsewhere central to the culture of the age. As an ecclesiastical reformer Contarini was about to apply it to the rehabilitation of the church, whose decline was more obvious than that of his own Republic. Since Venice still showed only small signs of decay and had never died, she could hardly be said to require rebirth; and this conception was never to occupy a prominent place in Venetian thought. But, under the pressure of her recent crisis, which had brought her very close to death, a somewhat paler version of the conception of renewal at last found some place in the Venetian ambience. Thus, after displaying the strength and wisdom of Venice over many pages, it was appropriate for Contarini to end with a prayer, as though human wisdom were finally not enough: "Let us pray God to preserve her long in safety." [241] In the end the preservation of civic values amidst so many trials and fluctuations depended, for Contarini, on God's grace; and his Evangelism was perhaps a better ally for his politics than his philosophy.

Giannotti's *Repubblica de'Veneziani* was written in the course of a sojourn

[239] Cols. 56–67.
[240] Cols. 6–7.
[241] Col. 63.

in Venice and Padua in 1525–1526,[242] during which he read widely about Venice and discussed her government with various Venetian acquaintances; Contarini was perhaps among them. From these sources he constructed a description of Venetian polity much like Contarini's, and his work reinforces that of Contarini on many points. But it also leaves a very different impression. It is less lofty and academic, less concerned to inspire feelings of awe, more concrete, more interested in practical detail. Above all Giannotti adds to Contarini's vision of static perfection a realistic awareness of historical development. Some of this difference may have come from his Venetian sources, but it seems likely that much of it was the contribution of the more highly developed republican consciousness of Florence to the understanding of Venice.

The contrast between the two works was also partly a result of differing purposes. Giannotti's aim was not to reassure himself about the future but to provide useful instruction for troubled Florence by a close analysis of stable Venice. Although Venetian practice had interested Florentine reformers for some time, Giannotti recognized that his own study challenged the contemporary prejudice in favor of ancient models, which he repudiated in an instructive preface. The rigid veneration of antique practice, he suggested, violated the practice of the ancients themselves; for they had been chiefly admirable as "curious investigators of all the customs that could be observed in their own times." Aristotle was thus instructive less for his substance than for his method: he had analyzed empirically the governments existing in his own age. And Giannotti denounced his own generation for having abandoned attention to living reality: "Very few can be found who are curious to understand the customs and governments of another man's city, and everyone thinks it enough to praise antiquity and condemn the present." He proposed for himself a different method. Instead of constructing an ideal polity from data supplied by the ancients, he would draw from contemporary practice "that fruit and that utility which can be derived from imperfect things." [243]

Giannotti's profession of openness to political reality is reinforced by the structure of his work. It is presented not as a didactic treatise, like Contarini's

---

[242] The best study of Giannotti is now in Randolph Starn's introduction to his new edition of Giannotti's letters, *Donato Giannotti and His Epistolae* (Geneva, 1968); see also Giuseppe Sanesi, *La vita e le opere di Donato Giannotti* (Pistoia, 1899), which covers his career to 1527 in some detail, with particular reference to his Venetian experience, and Gilbert, "Date of Contarini's and Giannotti's Books on Venice."

[243] *Libro della Repubblica di Venezia*, in *Opere* (Pisa, 1819), I, 2–3.

De republica, but as a dialogue between his Florentine friend, Giovanni Borgherini, and the Venetian man of letters, Trifone Gabriele, in the villa of Pietro Bembo. Giovanni is full of admiration for Venice and eager to learn how her government has managed to endure so long unchanged and unconquered.[244] Occasionally he asks sharp questions which Gabriele evades or refuses to answer,[245] but for the most part he is respectful and attentive, exhibiting a youthful relish in "the variety of the things" Gabriele imparts to him.[246]

Gabriele, an old friend of Contarini, may have been one of Giannotti's sources of information about Venice, but his career and interests make it unlikely that all the views Giannotti attributes to him were his own. Born in 1471, Gabriele was an almost exact contemporary of Bembo and typical of the literary and academic tendencies of Venetian culture in this period. Giannotti presents him as living peacefully in his Paduan villa, "far from every ambition, free from any administrative task in the Republic, removed from the many inconveniences of civil life." His favorite associates are not his uninspiring Venetian compatriots but "those ancient and noble spirits, Tuscan as well as Latin, such as Cicero, Vergil, Horace, Dante, Petrarch, Boccaccio, with whom he converses by reading their volumes." [247] He is also made to appear, at times, like a man of the study. Thus he asks, sounding a bit like Contarini: "Do not the Philosophers say that all sciences and doctrines must begin from the most universal things? . . . Painters and sculptors, if we look closely, follow in their arts the precepts of the Philosophers; for they too begin in their works from universal things." [248] The sentiment seems in character, but it suggests that the real Gabriele was hardly the most appropriate guide to the realities of Venetian politics.

But the Gabriele of the dialogue promptly drops this philosophic pose. There is less abstract discourse in his account of Venice than in Contarini's work, and he distinguishes more clearly between the ideal form of the Venetian government and its imperfect realization.[249] Even Gabriele's insistence

[244] Pp. 22–23.

[245] Giovanni asks, for example (p. 69), how it happened that so many Venetians accepted exclusion from the Great Council; and although he repeats the question (p. 76), he never receives an answer to this very Florentine inquiry. He also expresses scepticism about the value of the elaborate procedures for electing the doge (p. 149). It may be that Giannotti intended to deal with these matters in a continuation of his work.

[246] P. 225.

[247] P. 10.

[248] P. 34.

[249] P. 22, where the distinction is explicit.

on beginning with universals means, in practice, no more than mentioning first (like most other writers on the subject) the general advantages of the location of Venice before describing her constitution; and Gabriele emerges as rather more empirical than Contarini. This difference seems to reflect Giannotti's own very practical interest in the value of the Venetian model for Florence. Successful imitation required a concrete and detailed grasp of Venetian practice, as Giannotti makes Gabriele himself observe, but also an understanding of its deeper principles: "In the year 1494 you took the example of your Great Council from ours; and in 1502, in imitation of us, you made your Gonfaloniere perpetual. And would to God, for the sake of your country and for the honor of Italy, you had known how to imitate the institutions of our Republic which are not so clear and obvious as our Council and the perpetuity of the doge. Then your city would be kept free, nor would it have experienced those alterations which have brought it to the point of ruin." [250]

In spite of the more precise motive of the work, Gabriele's description of the Venetian government resembles Contarini's in major respects. He is equally pleased with the Republic and for the same reasons, above all for her effective maintenance of order. [251] He takes satisfaction in the equality among her citizens so that, as he remarks, every man, with few exceptions, sits where he pleases in the Great Council. [252] He points out the advantages of a broadly based government: where many share in public responsibility, many can seek glory in the service of the state. [253] Because the doge's authority is based on the laws of the Republic, Gabriele thinks him more honorable than other princes. [254] He is proud of Venetian courts because they mete out equal justice to the poor. [255] Like Contarini he testifies to the power of the Council of Ten, although he also sees it as an exceptional institution, an "annex" to the pyramid of political agencies devised for particular dangers and emergencies. [256] In spite of his own abandonment of political service, he celebrates

[250] Pp. 66–67.
[251] Cf. p. 17: "... la mia Repubblica ... è più perfetta ch'ella mai in alcun tempo fosse. La forma d'essa non può essere con miglior legge temperata, con maggior tranquillità e concordia retta, lontana dalle sedizioni intrinseche, e da tutte quelle cose, che rovinano le città; e quello che è bello, non manca di valorosi, e magnanimi spiriti, dalla cui prudenza, e virtù ella è felicemente governata.
[252] P. 95.
[253] P. 62.
[254] Pp. 153–154.
[255] Pp. 198–200.
[256] P. 168.

the moral values developed by active public life; for this reason he sees the patriciate of Venice as more noble than other aristocratic bodies.[257] Like Contarini he sees the Venetians as equal to the ancients in virtue,[258] and Venice as superior to Rome because of her dedication to peace.[259]

Much of this chiefly testifies to the fact that a specific image of Venice had been frozen into a convention; it is probably unrelated to the personal attitudes of Giannotti's protagonist. Yet there are occasional hints in Gabriele's discourses of a special point of view. He makes, for example, the odd claim (perhaps the result of his long association with the mainland) that, although Venice drew great incomes from both her overseas empire and her possessions on the mainland, her revenues from the latter source were much greater.[260] That a subtle shift in Venetian priorities and values was now under way may also be hinted at in his rather equivocal description of the Venetian *gentiluomini*, to whom he attributes not only the virtues developed through public service and a wealth whose origins are unspecified but also, like Zeno, ancient and noble lineage.[261] In addition his comprehension of the international scene seems somewhat limited. Gabriele is aware that Venice suffered great losses in 1509; but he believes that all has been restored, he expresses hope for the recovery of Italian liberty through the League of Cognac, and he generally seems to believe that Venice can still determine her own destiny as before.[262] Yet his sense of how this was now chiefly to be accomplished is revealing: he thinks that the fortification of the *terraferma*, a lesson from the events of 1509, has made the Venetian mainland impregnable.[263] He does not mention the possibility of danger from Rome, either political or spiritual.

While these elements in Gabriele's account were perhaps supplied by himself, others almost certainly came from Giannotti, notably a considerable historical sense such as was largely lacking in Contarini. Gabriele is made to attribute the character of Venetian institutions not to an original insight into the abstract structure of nature but to historical development. Indeed, he appears to exclude in principle a rational origin for political institutions by

[257] P. 42.

[258] Pp. 9, 17, 20. He includes the Greeks in his comparison as well as the Romans.

[259] P. 17. He goes on to criticize Sabellico and other earlier historians for comparing Venetian military prowess with that of Rome.

[260] P. 226.

[261] Pp. 40–41.

[262] P. 239. Giannotti's own realism on this point (though perhaps a product of his later experience) is emphasized by Albertini, pp. 162–163.

[263] Pp. 240–241.

emphasizing the difficulty of absolute innovation in human affairs. "Things that must be introduced without any precedent," he declares, "always encounter so many difficulties that they are many times abandoned as impossible. This happens because in human actions men do not approve arrangements whose utility they have not grasped through experience, their own or that of others; and there have never been many men able to discover new things and persuade others to accept them. Therefore in creating new institutions one should imitate old arrangements, both one's own and others." [264] Venice was thus so admirable not because of an original perfection but because she had learned from experience and could be happily numbered among "those republics that have changed for the better." [265] Venetian institutions were the product of history.

Gabriele therefore depicts the various agencies of the Venetian state as developing from inferior and more primitive forms, by stages, to better and more sophisticated forms. A notable example is his treatment of the Great Council, the basic institution of the government, in which the republicans of Florence had long felt a particular interest. He recognizes that the Great Council had not always existed. It had been preceded by a series of experiments, first with tribunes and then with an unrestricted dogeship which had worked out badly. It had achieved the supreme position in the state only in 1175, and the perfection of its machinery had taken over a century more.[266] Thus, although Gabriele is permitted to agree that Venice had been in continuous existence since the sixth century and had never known a master, he is compelled to acknowledge that she had by no means lasted over a thousand years the same. Her existence as a constitutional republic in which sovereignty was exercised by many and in which civic values had flourished was of relatively recent origin. This view of her career was doubtless far more encouraging to Florentine hopes than that of Contarini, but it was also closer to the truth.

Giannotti also attributes to Gabriele a remarkably Florentine conception of the general course of European history. Giovanni had detected some resemblance between Gabriele and Pomponius Atticus, the friend of Cicero who had withdrawn from public life in his own time. Gabriele promptly seizes on this opportunity to note that history repeats itself. There was, he

[264] P. 66.

[265] P. 77.

[266] Pp. 53ff. On p. 68 he distinguishes three stages in the development of the Great Council.

observes, a striking similarity between the condition of contemporary Italy and earlier phases in her history. Two evil moments in the past come particularly to his mind:

> One, which was the beginning of the ruin of Italy and of the Roman Empire, when Rome was oppressed by the Caesarian armies; the other, which was the height of Italian misfortune, when Italy was overrun and sacked by the Huns, Goths, Vandals, Lombards. And if we now consider the events that have recently occurred here, it may easily be seen that for those who live in Italy today the present is far worse than either of those times. But which of them ought to be considered the most horrible, I cannot now tell; because the second can be said to have been born out of the first, and from the second all that variation which has caused the world to assume the appearance we now see in our times and to lose all that which it had in the time of the Romans.[267]

This long historical perspective is of interest on several counts, and not least because it combines the idea of repetition, which permits the comparison of one age to another, with a sense of continuity, which made possible the ascription of present evils to past misfortunes. The republican idealism of Florentine historiography is also evident. Gabriele sees the overthrow of the republic as the ultimate cause first for the collapse of Rome and ultimately for the political disasters of the world around him.

The real Gabriele was an ardent enough republican to criticize his beloved Dante for treating Brutus and Cassius with such severity,[268] but the historical perception revealed by this passage hardly characterized Venice during this period, least of all the literary circles of Padua. Nevertheless Giannotti's work aroused considerable interest among his Venetian friends, and he finally published it in 1540 with some encouragement from Bembo himself.[269] In this way Giannotti's *Repubblica de' Veneziani*, which so curiously combined the political insights of Florence with the idealized political vision of Venice, became a part of the regular corpus of Venetian political literature. Furthermore Giannotti, permanently exiled from Florence after 1530, spent much of his time in Venice before his death in 1579 and continued on friendly terms with members of the patriciate.

---

[267] P. 15.

[268] Cf. Baron, *The Crisis of the Early Italian Renaissance*, p. 53.

[269] See Giannotti's letter of Aug. 13, 1540, in *Lettere a Piero Vettori*, ed. Roberto Ridolfi and Cecil Roth (Florence, 1932), p. 68.

Nor was he the only source of Florentine influence on Venetian politics. Venice was now from time to time a refuge for exiled Florentines, as she had so often been in the past for various political refugees. Some were artisans, but, besides Giannotti, other men of high status and sophisticated political culture visited Venice, including Varchi, Cavalcanti, and Nardi; their presence could only have been stimulating to their Venetian hosts.[270] For a long while they also nourished the hope that the liberty of Italy might yet be preserved and that of Florence restored through the action of the last great Italian republic.[271] Their impact on the Venetian understanding of politics was not immediately apparent, nor can the political revival Venice was to experience later in the century be attributed in any significant way to their influence. Nevertheless the empirical and historical attitudes of Florence indicated the direction in which Venetian thought would eventually move.

But for the time being Venetians were content to celebrate the ideal perfections of their Republic; and the works of Contarini and Giannotti, which were widely translated and went into many editions, were only the most important examples of a vast body of literature, both native and foreign, which for decades advertised the finished excellence of the Venetian constitution.[272] Venice was proclaimed as fatherland of the world, temple of justice, sun among the stars, the hope of Italy, a city constructed and ruled by philosophers, another Rome, greater than Rome.[273] Her good order and her survival seemed unimpeachable evidence of perfection in a world where all else was swirling flux. Ochino declared from a Venetian pulpit in 1539: "I look everywhere, but there is no longer a castle nor a city in Italy that is not perturbed. Only your city really remains standing, so that it seems to me that you contain in yourself the whole of Italy." [274] As the legend took deeper root, Botero, in spite of his devotion to Rome, was especially extravagant. "Among the many, many excellences and prerogatives which shine forth in the Republic of Venice," he declared, "there is none more marvelous than having been so long preserved, and maintained without notable alteration in the best condition. For since all things are subject to the moon, they are also

---

[270] Cf. Pecchioli, "Il 'mito' di Venezia e la crisi fiorentina," pp. 490–491.

[271] Albertini, pp. 143ff. See also Giorgio Spini, *Tra Rinascimento e Riforma: Antonio Brucioli* (Florence, 1940), p. 157.

[272] See the list of such works assembled by Rodolfo de Mattei, "Contenuto ed origini dell'ideale universalista nel Seicento," *Rivista Internazionale di Filosofia del Diritto*, X (1930), 398–399, n. 2.

[273] See Curcio, pp. 108–109.

[274] Quoted by Molmenti, II, Part 1, 8–9.

subject to instability, of which the moon, now full, now waning, is the cause. It seems a heroic accomplishment and more than human, indeed celestial and divine, to remain so many centuries, without change, in the same state." [275] Venice, though a small and independent state, evidently challenged Rome as the Eternal City of Christendom.

Venetians were not, of course, entirely taken in by such rhetoric. They kept a sufficient eye on sublunary affairs to look out for their own interests everywhere, as the reports of their envoys make sufficiently clear. The image of Venice as the immutable realization of an eternal ideal nevertheless provided welcome comfort in a terrifying world, and it continued to dominate the Venetian imagination during the middle decades of the sixteenth century. But since Venice did not after all inhabit a celestial sphere, conditions changed, both inside and outside. Indeed, the more things were declared the same, the more they in fact changed; and there would come a time when the disparity between image and reality would have to be faced. Soon enough Venice was compelled to awaken from her dream of security and perfection.

[275] *Relationi universali*, p. 771.

·IV·

The Awakening of Venice

THE myth that Venice ideally combined freedom and order and was therefore durable beyond any polity previously known to man stimulated the European imagination for almost three centuries. The Venetian constitution became a model for Englishmen in the seventeenth century as it had been for Florentines in the sixteenth, and the quality of life it appeared to guarantee both fascinated and encouraged the reformers of the Enlightenment.[1] The Venetians themselves also continued, from time to time, to celebrate the perfections of their Republic. But, within a generation after the works of Contarini and Giannotti had been published, Venice began to reveal hints of doubt that she would automatically last forever. During the last third of the century she moved in the direction of a more political and historical conception of herself and the world.

One cause of this change was doubtless a growing sense, once Venetian political discussion was properly under way, of the tension (which even Contarini could not altogether conceal) between abstract philosophy and practical experience. No Venetian directly attacked Contarini's vision of an ideal republic; but as the crisis of the early sixteenth century faded, Venetian political discussion increasingly referred to what Venetians had learned as shrewd observers and participants in political life. They displayed a growing awareness that the Republic was not a model of static perfection to be preserved intact but a dynamic reality, a system of shifting needs and interests whose existence could only be maintained through adaptation to a changing world.

The world, after the relatively tranquil middle decades of the century, was indeed visibly changing. Although Venice for the time being experienced no major crisis, signs of danger became increasingly apparent. They came notably from Rome, which the Republic had long identified as the chief enemy both of her independence and her traditional values. In Rome, after the concluding sessions of the Council of Trent, a new militancy was in the air; and what for the church universal signified reform seemed to promise,

---

[1] Fink, *The Classical Republicans*, pp. 28ff.; Felix Gilbert, "The 'New Diplomacy' of the Eighteenth Century," *World Politics*, IV (1951), 16.

for Venice, the renewal of old aggressions. In addition the danger represented by the papacy was associated with other perils by the circumstances surrounding the collapse of the Holy League after Lepanto in 1572. But that great victory, which the Venetians attributed largely to themselves, also affected the Republic much as the defeat of the Armada affected England. It produced an enthusiastic renewal of Venetian patriotism and republican values; and, raising the possibility once again of effective Venetian action in the world, it released latent political energies. Gradually leaving the static vision of Contarini behind, though never disowning it, Venetians began to reveal closer affinities with the mature republicanism of Florence.

At the University of Padua, the systematic attitudes expressed by Contarini had for some time been undergoing a subtle attack which perhaps prepared Venetians intellectually to engage in a more realistic political discussion. As Garin has pointed out, earlier Paduan Averroism, by carrying the static and rigid features of Aristotle to extremes, had opened the way to the criticism and rejection of abstract intellectuality;[2] and Pomponazzi in the earlier sixteenth century represented a different spirit. Behind his naturalism seems to lurk a characteristically Renaissance concern with the significance of the experience in this life, on the part of a soul itself conceived as mortal, of phenomena which are born, mature, and decline in time. Viewed rationally, even Christianity was, for him, no exception to the general rule that all things are subject to change and decay.[3] It seems hardly accidental that the followers of Pomponazzi a generation later began to add history to a culture that had before been largely philosophical.

This development, however slow in coming, seems also to have been peculiarly appropriate to the conditions of Venetian life, which provided a vivid experience with temporal affairs badly needing intellectual appropriation, as Vittorio Siri suggested in the opening page of his *Mercurio:* "I live in a city such as Plutarch desired for the habitation of a historian: that is, where a great court holds its residence, full of ambassadors and ministers. For in Venice, more than in any other city in the world, one sees a multitude of personages and gentlemen sent as ambassadors to all the courts of Europe.

[2] Garin, *Medioevo e Rinascimento*, pp. 30ff.

[3] Cf. Cassirer's interpretation of Pomponazzi, in *The Individual and the Cosmos in Renaissance Philosophy*, p. 108: "No form of faith may claim to stand, so to speak, as eternal truth *above* time; rather, each shows itself to be determined by time and bound to time. Faith, like all natural existence, has a period of blossoming and a period of decay, of rise and fall."

In Venice the nobles busy themselves with no other exercise than that of civic prudence, which is practiced by persons of the finest judgment well instructed in the affairs of princes." [4] Venetians had to learn to deal with the rich data provided by such an environment; and Padua, the traditional academy for the patriciate of the Republic, had happily been concerned for decades precisely with problems of intellectual method. During the sixteenth century, this concern was increasingly directed to the nature and methods of historical knowledge.[5]

During the decades when the antihistorical vision of Contarini dominated Venice, Paduan discussion concerning history amounted to little more than the paraphrasing of ancient commonplaces in conventional *Artes historicae* composed in the humanist manner. This genre continued to treat the past as a repository of examples to be exploited rhetorically for such lofty purposes as the historian might choose, including the glorification of rulers. A history employed in this way, as a Venetian secretary observed, was like a painting or a statue.[6] The hint of stasis in this image was realized even more clearly in the use of data from the past to convey ethical, political, or religious lessons. Thus Aldo Manuzio the Younger conventionally recommended historical study to noblemen because "we form the rule of our own actions from knowledge of the actions of others." [7] The effect was not only to deny the significance of historical change, which had to be squeezed out of events like a poison, lest it put the regularity of the universe into doubt, but also to deny the autonomy of the historical understanding. History thus became the handmaiden, at best, to a higher science. This was the view of history taken by such rhetoricians as Sperone Speroni, Giacomo Zabarella, Francesco Robertello, and others at Padua who, drawing their essential inspiration from Aristotle and Cicero, pressed historical phenomena into the construction of static orthodoxies.

But a rather different tendency was also operating in Padua, as became evident with the publication in 1560 of Francesco Patrizi's ten dialogues

[4] Quoted by Benedetto Croce, *Storia della età barocca in Italia*, rev. ed. (Bari, 1946), p. 100, n. 1.

[5] Paduan discussions of historial method are well treated in Giorgio Spini, "I trattatisti dell'arte storica nella Controriforma italiana," *Contributi alla storia del Concilio di Trento e della Controriforma* (Florence, 1948), pp. 109–136. For what follows see also Beatrice Reynolds, "Shifting Currents in Historical Criticism," *Journal of the History of Ideas*, XIV (1953), 471–492; and Nadel, "Philosophy of History before Historicism."

[6] Vincenzo Fedeli, in his Florentine *Relazione* of 1561, Segarizzi, III, Part 1, 147.

[7] *Il perfetto gentilhuomo* (Venice, 1584), p. 34.

Della historia.[8] This work purports to reflect discussions carried on by a whole circle of young Venetians, several of whom were destined for later prominence; and its dialogue form makes possible the expression of various points of view without any clear conclusion, as though positions were now tending to be rather fluid. Many speeches merely express the familiar concerns and commonplaces of the humanist manuals. Thus Patrizi and his young friends attempt to identify the essence of a history, although their indifferent success may be an oblique hint at the futility of so abstract an approach to the subject.[9] Several participants in the discussions also appear to be much impressed, in conventional fashion, with the value of history as a repository of examples for imitation, though by republics rather more than by individuals.[10]

But there are also suggestions in the work of a different attitude to history which seems to be related to the traditional distinction between philosophy and rhetoric, of which history was still generally considered a branch. The relationship between history and rhetoric implied that history could not be depended on (like philosophy) for ultimate wisdom. It meant that a historical proposition was not a dependable certainty but merely an opinion and therefore chiefly estimable because it might be useful, like other rhetorical productions. It belonged to the active rather than to the contemplative life. But since historical discourse, though never absolutely certain, evidently exhibited degrees of reliability, this suggested the possibility of imposing criteria to make it relatively more dependable, relatively more useful. Obscurely in the background here is perhaps also the familiar Averroist distinction between the certainties of faith and the conclusions of reason. A habit of distinguishing between kinds and levels of truth was clearly at work that would eventually assist history to develop a place and standards of its own.

These possibilities are approached most directly, in Patrizi's work, by the remarks of young Leonardo Donà, whom we shall meet again in a later stage of his career. Donà is made to insist on the distinction between philosophy and history as sources of political instruction. There are two ways by which cities may attain domestic peace, he observes, "that of the philosophers and that of the historians. The one teaches us by reasons, depending on universals,

---

[8] *Della historia diece dialoghi ne' quali si ragiona di tutte le cose appartenenti all'historia, & alloscriverla, & all'osservarla* (Venice, 1560).

[9] This concern is particularly apparent in the first three dialogues, sigs. A1^r–E3^r.

[10] See especially the eighth and ninth dialogues, sigs. L4^v–O2^r.

and the other by particulars and experience." And he concludes that "history, telling us how to direct our country to true peace and to such happiness as is possible through experience, should be held by us in the greatest and highest esteem, contrary to the opinion of those who read histories only for the sake of reasoning—an end which is useless and only a game." Donà does not here altogether deny the political value of philosophy, but he is prepared to insist on both the utility and the autonomy of history.[11] He seems already to have moved some distance from the position represented by Contarini.

A closely related element in Patrizi's work is its skepticism, which had a practical as well as a theoretical source. His circle has become aware, from the scrutiny of various historical compositions, that all testimony is shaped by a point of view, so that two observers of the same event are likely to describe it differently. As Patrizi himself remarks, this is not to deny all truth to history. Any historical account may be partly or wholly true, but the degree of its validity is beyond final proof. Furthermore, he observes, the historian sees only the surfaces of events; their causes are not accessible to him.[12] One of his friends is also allowed to suggest that it is impossible to determine whether any two historical situations are sufficiently similar for the lessons implicit in the one to be usefully applied to the other. Thus, he concludes, "we cannot, in our historical studies, employ the comparison between diverse ancient and diverse modern things, for everything is evidently irregular."[13] We may discern in these doubts something of the general skepticism of the later Renaissance, represented among others by Guicciardini, whose historical work would shortly be available for Venetian study and emulation. The discussion also reflects the growing concern among Venetians with the subversion of historical truth by writers who chiefly aimed to flatter princes.[14] But its primary function here was to drive deeper the wedge between history and philosophy, between the realms of contingency and certainty. Patrizi's argument meant that there could be no absolute history, no orthodox version of events not open to doubt.

Yet the argument did not conclude that history is worthless. As Agostino

[11] Sig. N3r.
[12] Sigs. G1v–G2r. On Patrizi's skepticism see also Julian H. Franklin, *Jean Bodin and the Sixteenth Century Revolution in the Methodology of Law and History* (New York, 1963), pp. 96–102, although Franklin over-emphasizes this aspect of Patrizi's thought.
[13] Sig. o1r–v.
[14] Cf. Fritz Saxl, "Veritas Filia Temporis," *Philosophy and History: The Ernst Cassirer Festschrift*, ed. Raymond Klibansky and H. J. Paton, new ed. (New York, 1963), pp. 199–200.

Valier remarks in the eighth dialogue, history gives a (presumably contingent) knowledge that is (as his companions agree) significantly useful for man's happiness;[15] and the work ends with the proposition that historical study is peculiarly appropriate to man.[16] In spite of his skepticism, therefore, Patrizi seems to regard history as a serious enterprise, and much of his book discusses how history should be conceived. Above all, having separated history from philosophy, the work recognizes that its major study should be to describe the development of societies through successive phases, since this is the actual pattern of earthly reality. The conception is expressed by Niccolò Zeno, whose own historical investigations apparently qualified him to express so important a doctrine. "History is written in the same way that human prudence, or the providence of God, or fortune, make things happen in the world," he declares. "And all things necessarily have a beginning to their existence, growth, maturity, decline, and end. The historian we are describing will consider closely all five things, distinguishing one from the other, so that man can look into the stages of things." Just as men grow in fortune, in size and strength of body, and in wisdom, so also cities increase "in public or private wealth, in population, in military discipline, in the prudence of their citizens, or in the quality of their government." And although Venice, he complained, had yet found no historian to identify the stages in her development, her career had been the same. Venice had developed through time; and if her present "mixture" was as perfect as the conditions of this life permitted, this had resulted from a long process of trial and error. As time passed, events had revealed which of her ordinances were good and which bad; and her wise legislators had constantly renewed the Republic by repealing some laws while confirming and altering others.[17] The notion of identifiable stages conforming to the structure of biological nature is still somewhat schematic, and residues in the work of the humanist-exemplary view of history indicate that the transition had not yet been completed; but for the circle of Patrizi Venice is clearly beginning to seem a part of the world of time.

Patrizi's work suggests a growing disposition among Venetians to view the world realistically and historically rather than ideally and systematically. But they were not quite ready (nor were they ever entirely pleased) to apply

[15] Sig. M1ᵛ. For Valier as a historian, see below, pp. 196–199.
[16] Sig. O4ᵛ.
[17] Sigs. H4ᵛ–I3ᵛ.

this new insight directly to their own Republic. They preferred to direct it first to the understanding of neighboring societies, notably those against which they felt some animus; for by historical analysis they could demonstrate the vulnerability of their enemies to change and thus magnify the significance of their own triumph over time. It was in this spirit that, even during the middle decades of the century, Venetians began to contemplate the career of Florence. The reports of the Venetian envoys to that unhappy city were increasingly filled with passages of political and historical analysis. The fate of Florence at once satisfied and obscurely troubled her sister republic.

The sympathy Florence had briefly aroused by her downfall soon subsided, and Venetians preferred to see in her chiefly an object lesson in what was likely to occur to a republic that did not sufficiently resemble their own. The Venetian envoys were inclined to interpret her present servitude as a divine judgment on her long history of faction, injustice, and violence. As Antonio Surian wrote in 1533: "It can truly be said that there is no health in any of the members of that Republic." [18] Venetians commonly attributed the failure of the Florentine Republic to two particular defects. One was an irrepressible political individualism. "The Florentines," according to Marco Foscari in 1527, "are not governed by the interest of the universal benefit of the city," but each one acts according to "the particular passions and needs of the faction to which he belongs." When a hostile army approached, Foscari noted, citizens with villas outside the city were less interested in resisting than in buying off the enemy. [19]

The second defect was an excess of democracy, the result of badly ordered institutions that allowed too much power to the incompetent, for men "who are engaged in the mechanic arts do not know the ways of true government." [20] In no context did Venetians appear so complacently patrician as when they described the ruling group in Florence. The chief men in the Florentine government, Foscari had reported with distaste, went daily to their shops and worked with their hands for all to see, in clear violation of the sound precepts of the ancients. [21] That too democratic a society had brought about the downfall of Florence became a highly satisfying dogma for Venetians. [22]

[18] Segarizzi, III, Part 1, 103.
[19] Albèri, Ser. 2, II, 22–23.
[20] This is Surian again, Segarizzi, III, Part 1, 101.
[21] Albèri, Ser. 2, II, 20–21.
[22] It is still prominent, for example, in Pier'Maria Contarini, *Compendio universal di republica* (Venice, 1602), esp. pp. 34–35, 38–39.

The disorders endemic in too popular a regime, however, had their too predictable result; and (according to the alternation Machiavelli had so well described) Florence had fallen into the power of men who, "having better fortune and greater support from outside" were able "to build their own greatness in the afflicted and defeated country." [23] Since the Florentines were evidently incorrigible, this outcome often appeared to the Venetian observers not only no better than they deserved but the best arrangement possible for them; and they were inclined to praise the government of the Medici grand dukes. As Vincenzo Fedeli reported in 1561, the terrible rule of the Florentine prince had at last reduced Florence to peace. He had suppressed faction, meted out equal justice, administered the finances of the state with care, developed a responsible and competent bureaucracy, and strengthened the authority of the church, that most effective pillar of the state. Withal he was a man of culture who (unlike other princes) lived a pure and simple life.[24]

At the same time the Venetians counted the cost of this success. They remarked again and again (as though the fact were peculiarly striking) that everything in Florence now depended solely on the will of the prince. As Fedeli observed, Florentines never said "the council has resolved" but always "the duke has decided the thing so." [25] A few years later Lorenzo Priuli noted that the duke dispensed with "any person of account" for advice.[26] Fedeli thought it "the greatest marvel" that a people so long accustomed to freedom "could tolerate and support the face of the prince" and that he "could rule and so easily and securely govern among so many of his open enemies." He attributed this achievement partly to the secrecy with which the duke's government was conducted, so that "even his movement from place to place is kept so secret that it is never known except by the sound of the trumpet," and partly to terrorism of the populace by means of spies and informers. The Florentines had become so demoralized that any man "might be a spy on another to win the duke's grace, so that there is no one who does not fear his closest relatives and most intimate friends." As a consequence

---

[23] Tomaso Contarini (1588), in Segarizzi, III, Part 2, 38–39. Tomaso Contarini's views generally correspond to a later phase in Venetian political development, which will be described in the next chapter; but I have chosen to deal with them here in order to reveal the full development of the Venetian attitude to Florence.

[24] *Ibid.*, Part 1, 127–129, 135–148. Cf. Tomaso Contarini, Part 2, 72–78.

[25] *Ibid.*, Part 1, 151.

[26] *Ibid.*, Part 1, 190. Cf. Andrea Gussoni (1576), *ibid.*, p. 220; and Tomaso Contarini, *ibid.*, Part 2, 67–68.

Florentines preferred to discuss any subject but politics.[27] Thus the contrasting roles of Florence and Venice had now been reversed: as Venice had commenced a more and more open discussion of politics, Florence had been compelled to give it up.

By 1566 the reservations left merely implicit in these Venetian descriptions were growing more explicit. Lorenzo Priuli, who had been badly received by the Florentine ruler, attributed his hostility directly to the fact that he was "tyrant of three republics" and "necessarily hates and abhors this most holy name of liberty." Priuli also suggested the disadvantage of dependence on a despot. The duke, he reported, though previously chaste, began after the death of his wife to take from his subjects the only thing of value they still possessed, the honor of their women; their wealth he already disposed of as his own. Priuli emphasized too the economic and moral decline accompanying the transition from republic to principate. An experienced person, he reported, had informed him that "the youth of the city, seduced by pleasures, willingly adopted the customs of the court rather than staying in their shops and attending to their business." Earning little and spending much, few Florentines now wished to marry because they had little to leave their children; and the population of the city was dwindling.[28] Florence had evidently swung from the democratic extreme to its opposite, which in Venetian eyes appeared perhaps even worse.

Meanwhile during the latter part of the century an important shift in the Venetian interpretation of Florentine history was also taking place. The destruction of Florentine liberty was no longer perceived merely as an inevitable judgment on political incompetence, but also as the deliberate effect of Medici skill and ambition, assisted by the papacy. The two interpretations could readily be coordinated by means of the idea that popular republics are easily seduced by ambitious men, and the vulnerability of Florence to tyranny could thus be made again to support the superiority of Venetian institutions. But a significant shift in emphasis was under way. As they contemplated Florence, Venetians were less doctrinaire and more historical.

While the memory of Florentine liberty was still fresh, Surian had remarked on the tendency of his Florentine hosts to consider the whole Medici domination a long tyranny.[29] And a generation later, writing in a rather different mood, Fedeli glorified the Medici as "a fatal house" and traced the greatness of the family from the prudent Cosimo of a century before to the

[27] *Ibid.*, Part 1, 168, 150–151.
[28] *Ibid.*, Part 1, 198, 190–191, 186.
[29] *Ibid.*, Part 1, 100.

present Cosimo, duke of Florence and Siena.[30] But the benignity with which Fedeli contemplated this succession was not so characteristic of his successors, notably Tomaso Contarini in 1588. The Medici, he declared, had always aspired to rule. "By hard work, by taking risks, and by spending money, they were steadily striving to realize their ambitions. They soothed the masses with gifts. With their buildings and memorable works they acquired reputation with all. They obligated their followers with rewards, and they quieted their opponents, sometimes with clemency and sometimes with terror. Partly by the fear of foreign arms, partly with benefits and kindness, they accustomed the free city to serve and remain subject." They had first allied with the lower orders to destroy the power of the nobility, and they had then found it simple to take away the privileges of the people. Contarini acknowledged that Florence under Medici dominion had at last been reduced to an admirable order, but the element of inevitability has disappeared from the process.[31]

This new sense that Florence had been deliberately subverted by the Medici was accompanied by an increasing tendency to emphasize the contribution of the papacy to the destruction of Florentine liberty. The Papal State, Contarini observed, had always been a source of disturbance in Italy, but for geographical reasons was particularly dangerous to Tuscany. Whenever that province had been under attack, the popes had somehow been to blame, and they had participated directly in the establishment of the Medici principate over Florence. The Venetian envoys remarked on the servility of Florentine rulers to the pope, and Contarini made an eloquent comparison on this point between the old Florentine Republic and the Florence of his own experience. "In those times the excommunications of the popes were despised," he declared. "Now all ecclesiastical censures are more feared, and consequently religion more venerated." [32]

Although the officials who offered these observations about Florence generally professed to find servility more appropriate than freedom to the nature of her people, their reports opened the way to a different construction of Florentine history. This found expression in the Florentine history of their compatriot, Gianmichele Bruto, published in 1562 at Lyons.[33] Bruto's work is best understood against the changing perspectives of the Venetian

---

[30] *Ibid.*, Part 1, 147–148. Cf. Gussoni, *ibid.*, p. 223.

[31] *Ibid.*, Part 2, 39, 41, 65–66.

[32] *Ibid.*, Part 2, 66, 89–90; 69. Cf. Gussoni, *ibid.*, Part 1, 230; and the *Relazione di Roma* of Paolo Tiepolo (1569), in Albèri, Ser. 2, IV, 189.

[33] *Florentinae historiae libri VIII:* I cite from the edition of Stanislao Gatteschi, *Delle istorie fiorentine* (Florence, 1838), which gives both the Latin text and an Italian translation.

envoys, on which it probably drew and to which it may well have contributed.

Little is known about the early life of this restless figure.[34] Born into an old Venetian family in 1517, he studied at Padua during 1539–1540. That he was well educated is clear; his works show an extensive knowledge of the classics as well as familiarity with contemporary authors and a careful style. Much of his life was spent in wandering through Europe. He was at various times in Germany, the Low Countries, England, and France; and he spent part of 1556 in Spain, where he was close to the Venetian ambassador Paolo Tiepolo. He then returned to Venice for several years, but he passed some months of 1561 in Florence.[35] In 1562 he was again in Venice, but three years later he fled to Lyons to escape prosecution for heresy.

The nature of his religious convictions is not altogether clear. He appears to have been a seeker who moved from vaguely Evangelical sympathies, with the help of Protestant associates in Lyons and elsewhere, to a position closer to Calvinism. He remained in Lyons till 1572 where, among other literary tasks, he prepared a new edition of Giannotti's *Repubblica*. Next he spent several years in Transylvania, and eventually he was appointed court historian to Steven Báthory, for whom he composed the first humanist history of Hungary. In 1588 he went to Prague as official historiographer for the emperor, Rudolf II, and here he died in 1592. As late as 1578 he still called himself a Catholic, and the charges of heresy against him were clearly insufficient to end his employment by Catholic rulers. But the ecclesiastical authorities refused to accept his protestations of orthodoxy, and he died without the public abjuration that would have permitted his formal reconciliation with the church.

Bruto was friendly with Florentine exiles in Venice and Lyons, especially Giannotti.[36] These friendships doubtless contributed to his tragic vision of Florentine history, and the undertone of satisfaction that may be discerned in

[34] For Bruto in general, see Mario Battistini, "Jean Michel Bruto, humaniste, historiographe, pédagogue au XVIe siècle," *De Gulden Passer*, XXXII (1954), 29–153; and Andrea Veress, "Il veneziano Giovanni Michele Bruto e la sua storia d'Ungheria," *AV*, Ser. 5, VI (1929), 148–178.

[35] The story that he became a Dominican and stayed at San Marco in Florence appears to be baseless; cf. Battistini, pp. 30–31.

[36] In his dedicatory epistle of the Florentine history, addressed to Piero Capponi, pp. xxix, xlvii, he speaks of Giannotti warmly, as of an old friend. But I am aware of no evidence that he wrote at the instigation of the Florentine exiles, as suggested by Fueter, *Historiographie moderne*, pp. 83–84. On the use made of Bruto's work by the Florentines, see Foscarini, *Della letteratura veneziana*, p. 421.

other Venetian discussions of Florence is notably absent from his work. His exposure to Florentine sentiments and documents may also account both for his particularly fervent republicanism and his unusual capacity (for a Venetian) to deal with historical data. But his Florentine history also bears the marks of its Venetian authorship. Close to important members of the patriciate, who regarded him highly,[37] Bruto combined his special sympathy for the fate of a sister republic with a range of characteristically Venetian attitudes. Much of the interest of his work derives from this fusion.

Bruto's general notions of historical composition were somewhat like the more advanced views expressed in Patrizi's work, with which he was probably familiar. Although he accepted in principle the rhetoricians' conception of history as a body of useful *exempla*,[38] he did not in practice moralize about the virtues and vices of individuals. His concern was politics, not ethics. And if history was to have political utility, he insisted, it must first of all tell the truth. This principle shaped his judgment of earlier historians, most of whom he found defective; like other Venetians, his respect for the ancients was limited. He praised the learning of Herodotus but criticized his frivolity. He admired Thucydides but thought him partial. But he reserved his most severe criticism for the Romans. He acknowledged that, among the historians of the Republic, Sallust had been scrupulously truthful; but he considered Livy little more than a fabler. And with the establishment of the Empire, he believed, historiography had become worthless. Historians continued to compose in a pleasing style, but increasing disorder made it impossible "to seek out and to examine documents on which to base their account." The historiography of his own age seemed to him worst of all. In spite of their increasing refinement, contemporary historians, in his eyes, were no more diligent in the search for truth than their medieval predecessors. They were venal, irresponsible, flatterers of princes; they badly needed "greater fidelity, or at least a certain diligence and more study." [39] Thus with Bruto history ceases to be primarily a species of oratory; it is now instead essentially a product of responsible research. Yet Bruto also distinguished between the historian and the pedant; he insisted on careful discrimination between petty detail and "things of great account." [40] The

[37] *Ibid.*, p. 425, for Bruto's reputation in Venice. Foscarini emphasizes Bruto's devotion to Venice.

[38] Preface, pp. xliii–xliv.

[39] *Ibid.*, pp. xxxi–xxxv. Bruto expressed similar views in his little treatise *De historiae laudibus* (Cracow, 1589); Spini mentions this work, "Trattatisti," p. 126.

[40] Preface, pp. xliv–xlv.

requirement was intended to restrict the historian to the classical themes of his art—wars and the acts of princes; but it supplied a necessary principle of formal control.

Bruto proposed to apply these views to the understanding of Florentine history because, Venice excepted, no other modern city in Italy was so worthy of attention as Florence, both for her greatness and for the changes through which she had passed.[41] The earlier history of Florence, he believed, was well enough known. But the case was different with her more recent past; hence "if ever any people had need of faithful writers, the people of the city of Florence has need of them today." For as accounts of Florentine history had moved closer to the present, they were increasingly filled with "perpetual praises of the Medici alone, with the most lying calumnies, with slanders, with villainies, with shameless falsehoods against the whole city." Giovio and Machiavelli (among others) had distorted truth in an effort to please the rulers of the city, and Bruto aimed to set the record straight with a true and republican account of Florence under the Medici.[42]

But Bruto's republican bias is constantly restrained both by a dependable sense of the complexity of human affairs and by respect for evidence; the *Istorie fiorentine* is no mere diatribe against the Medici. Certain that truth was on his side, Bruto exposed himself to a wide range of sources, including Poliziano, Valori, Sabellico, and Commynes, often treating them with remarkable coolness.[43] He also made heavy use of Machiavelli, in spite of his serious reservations about the great Florentine. "Machiavelli has written before me," he declared. "I attribute to him on the one hand eloquence, rare intelligence, a style that is excellent, erudite, grave, sententious, and tempered with an admirable sweetness. On the other hand I do not concede to him either care or study of his peers." [44] Thus he often followed Machiavelli's *Istorie fiorentine* closely, but he corrected details where his own evidence was superior and did not hesitate to go beyond him both in

[41] I, 4: ". . . nulla unquam in Italia civitas extitit, una aut altera excepta, quae simul aut magnitudine rerum, aut vicissitudine temporum, et conversione, commutationeque fortunae, quae res in omni libera civitate casus maxime memorabiles ac rerum eventa efficere consuevit, hac una superior videri possit." The identity of his exception seems obvious.

[42] Preface, pp. xxxv–xxxvi.

[43] For example II, 214 (where he criticizes Poliziano); I, 224ff. (where he compares Valori and Machiavelli); I, 86–87, 104–105, 328–329, 374.

[44] Quoted by Battistini, pp. 76–78, from Bruto's letter to Bacio Tinghi printed at the end of Federigo Alberti, *Le difese de' Fiorentini contro le false calunnie del Giovio* (Lyons, 1566) a work evidently based on Bruto.

information and tone. He regarded Machiavelli with a complex mixture of respect and blame as though, recognizing a kindred spirit, he was saddened to discover weakness.[45]

Various passages remind us of Bruto's Venetian loyalties. Against Machiavelli he insisted that Venice had displayed a steady constancy in moments of adversity, as well as a dignified moderation in prosperity.[46] He saw the defense of free cities and the protection of the unfortunate as a long Venetian tradition,[47] and he ascribed to a group of exiles from Medicean Florence in 1466 a tribute to Venice as the divinely chosen home of liberty.[48] He recalled that the cupidity of Julius II in Italy had ignited all Europe.[49] His suggestion that the discovery of a new world by Columbus proved the unreliability of traditional beliefs and the superiority of the moderns to the ancients may reflect the familiar Venetian coolness toward antiquity.[50]

The central theme of Bruto's work is the transformation of a free republic into a personal despotism, and his conception of both liberty and tyranny corresponded closely to that of earlier republicans. Liberty meant for him both the independence of the state and self-government according to law by a free citizenry; on such liberty the original greatness and dignity of Florence had been based.[51] Tyranny was simply government by men rather than by law, which he deeply venerated; law existed precisely to protect the weak from the strong: that is, to check tyranny. Without law life in society was intolerable for Bruto; a solitary existence was preferable to the rule of a tyrant.[52] Yet in spite of his respect for law, Bruto displayed, for a Venetian, remarkably little interest in the Florentine constitution, which may suggest

[45] Bruto's ambivalence towards Machiavelli emerges frequently. See, for example I, 124–125, where, discussing Machiavelli's treatment of the events following Cosimo's death, he acknowledges his debt to Machiavelli and expresses his admiration for him but at the same time notes the need to correct passages where he was defective in candor or exactness. See also I, 62–63, where Bruto describes Machiavelli as "vir non indisertus, obsequutus ingenio," and I, 42, 46, 52ff., 64, 110ff., 140, 214–216, 278, 284; II, 122, 214. It is fascinating to speculate that Bruto may have intended, under the influence of Giannotti, to correct those historiographical defeats at which Machiavelli had himself hinted to his young Florentine friend; cf. Felix Gilbert's introduction to the Torchbook edition of Machiavelli's *History of Florence* (New York, 1960), p. xiii.

[46] II, 414, in connection with the war of Ferrara.

[47] I, 276.

[48] I, 310.

[49] II, 492.

[50] II, 88.

[51] I, 2.

[52] He develops this position in the argument attributed to the anti-Medici group against the renewal of the Milanese alliance in 1465 (I, 160–164).

that what had seemed crucial to Contarini and Giannotti a generation earlier was no longer so compelling. If, for Bruto, Florence had followed the same unhappy course taken by the ancient republics of Athens and Rome, she was the victim not of an initial defect in her institutions or even of some congenital political incapacity on the part of her people, but of contingent actions and events. This view of the problem made possible a remarkably concrete historical analysis.

A good deal of this analysis resembles that of the Venetian envoys whose views of Florentine history we have already examined. Bruto identified two major causes for the destruction of Florentine liberty. The first was the struggle among social classes to control the government, to which Machiavelli, as well as the Venetian ambassadors, had given so much attention.[53] But Bruto gave particular emphasis to the ambitions of the Medici and to their skill in manipulating the tensions among the various elements in Florentine society to serve their own interests.[54] Free from any temptation to flatter princes, Bruto therefore undertook to show the real significance of Medici leadership for Florence. Tearing away all pious and patriotic disguises, he depicted the Medici as tyrants who, with remarkable determination and guile, had undertaken to undermine the Republic. Thus he leaves the impression at the end that, but for the machinations of the Medici, the social and political difficulties of Florence might well have found a happy resolution.

Bruto attributed to this "fatal house," to which he assigned an aristocratic rather than a popular origin,[55] a long effort to exploit Florentine social division, which had finally achieved success with Cosimo in the fifteenth century. For with Cosimo the conditions of historical greatness, so well understood by later Florentines, had been fully realized: circumstances had coincided with the appearance of an appropriate genius.[56] Bruto gave full

[53] I, 8, for his understanding of the Florentine class structure.

[54] Cf. his treatment (I, 18) of Salvestro de'Medici: "Princeps is in familia Medicum, optimatium ac populi discordiam visus in summo magistratu moliri, exemplus posteris prodidisse fertur, per infimorum hominum assectationem oppressa nobilitate, sibi viam ad Reipubl. imperium et ad dominationem struendi." Of the rise of Cosimo, Bruto says (I, 32): "Magistratum autem auctoritas omnis et vis, unius hominis cum infima multitudine coniunctione, aut fracta et debilitata, aut contempta plane abiectaque erat."

[55] His first reference to the Medici (I, 10) describes them as "nobilem quidem familiam et honestam."

[56] Cf. I, 32: "Itaque cum praeter patris memoriam gratiosi hominis, divitiarum copiam atque affluentiam, facultates ingenii maximas, in ea tempora incidisset: in eadem cum ceteris aequabilitate vivendo, cupiditatem dissimulando, multis privatim consulendo, ea

credit to Cosimo's abilities, paying him the equivocal compliment of comparison with Augustus.[57] Thus what seems so often implicit in Machiavelli's treatment of Cosimo now becomes explicit. In Bruto's version Cosimo is a typical Machiavellian prince, eager for power, capable of any amount of calculation, self-restraint, and dissimulation in its pursuit, a master at concealing his true motives. Bruto points out that Cosimo's pious benefactions were intended only to impress the multitude, and that even his services to learning aimed merely to secure a reputation for higher concerns behind which he could the more effectively destroy the Republic. Indeed, as Bruto noticed, the fact that letters were moribund in his time was a part of his good fortune, making it easier for him to appear their patron.[58] Bruto did not deny that these actions were good in themselves, but he insisted on distinguishing between the objective act and its shabby motives.[59]

Nor had Cosimo been the enemy merely of his own republic. Taking direct issue with Machiavelli, Bruto depicted Cosimo as actively pressing for war on Lucca, Florence's old republican ally; this, for Bruto, had been the most despicable action in his career.[60] To crush Lucca he had eventually formed a league with despotic Milan,[61] thereby initiating a particularly revealing association. For the discussions over renewing the Milanese alliance under Piero gave Bruto a useful opportunity to present the republican case against the Medici. Piero's opponents pointed out that renewal of the league would require heavy public expenditures and increase the presumption of those who sought to overthrow the Republic, and they followed these practical considerations with a series of general observations about the natural equality of men. Cities and laws had been devised, they submitted, because, without some restraints, the liberty and equality to which all men are born would surely end in disorder. The Florentine Republic, threatened by this alliance with a tyrant, must be preserved because a

---

posteris domesticae potentiae fundamenta constituit: ut illi quidem amplioris cuiusdam fortunae accessione, maiorum memoriam plane obscurare, ac Republ. de pristino statu convulsa, pervenire etiam ad civitatis imperium, huius gloriam, famaeque celebritatem, quamvis summis in imperiis positi, haud facile aequare, nulla unquam amplitudine honorum superare, nominisque maiestate potuerint.''

[57] I, 42, in connection with Cosimo's attitude to his opponents in Florence.

[58] I, 34.

[59] I, 36.

[60] I, 42.

[61] I, 88–90.

republic was the best instrument yet devised for resolving the tension between freedom and order.[62]

Even more interesting is Bruto's treatment of the altered moral climate of Florence under the Medici. Whereas frugality and parsimony had befitted a free city, the rise of the Medici had been accompanied by growing pomp and magnificence. Bruto followed Machiavelli's account of the degeneracy of the Florentines under Lorenzo and his suggestion that their corruption had been completed by the courtiers accompanying the duke of Milan on his ceremonial visit to Florence.[63] But Bruto made far more of these matters than his Florentine source. He presented the Milanese despot and Lorenzo the Magnificent as in every respect equals, and their encounter as a dramatic climax to the degeneration of Florence. Together they are made to speak of imposing a joint empire over Italy. Above all Bruto emphasized the civic meaning of the transformation in the Florentine atmosphere. If the brothels and taverns were full, it was because the palazzo and the piazza were now deserted. Private luxury, lasciviousness, effeminacy, corruption, and filthiness take on a larger public meaning in the neglect of the education and discipline appropriate to free men, in the betrayal of duty and faith.[64]

Bruto's approval of tyrannicide should therefore be no surprise, except that it comes so late. It found expression in his account of the assassination of Galeazzo Maria Sforza, an episode which, though it seems to have interested him a good deal, Machiavelli could only present as a dramatic instance of the folly of misrule and the consequence of reliance on the fickle mob.[65] Although Bruto admitted that the later sufferings of Italy had remotely originated in this bloody act, his feelings about the murder of this tyrant were direct and unambiguous. The young Milanese tyrannicides were heroes; and he was eager, as late as 1562, to celebrate their action at length. For him the conspirators had been moved by a deep devotion to liberty. He gave eloquent form to the exhortations of Cola Montano, treated so ambiguously by Machiavelli but for Bruto a genuine idealist who had recognized the close connection of virtue and glory with republican

[62] I, 154ff. Comparison with Machiavelli's treatment of this episode (*Istorie fiorentine*, Bk. VII, Ch. 12) is particularly revealing. Bruto has made into an extended direct discourse what in Machiavelli is only a rapid summary; the general remarks about equality, liberty, and law have no place in Machiavelli's account. Yet there is some irony here since Bruto does follow Machiavelli in his skepticism about the motives of most (if not all) the enemies of the Medici.

[63] *Istorie fiorentine*, Bk. VII, Ch. 28.

[64] II, 60ff.

[65] *Istorie fiorentine*, Bk. VII, Ch. 34.

government. Instead of condemning the folly of the assassins of Milan, Bruto asserted that none of the ancients had surpassed these noble youths in greatness of mind. Their hopes had been betrayed only by the failure of support from a populace which, no longer Machiavelli's fickle mob, had unhappily lost its native courage and vigor under the rule of a prince.[66]

Yet Bruto's direct treatment of Lorenzo the Magnificent was, after all this, surprisingly mild: rather kinder, indeed, than Machiavelli's. Although he gave a full account of the discontent that came to a head in the Pazzi conspiracy[67] and emphasized Lorenzo's lust for glory,[68] he praised his rule of Florence. To maintain the stability of the city and the liberty of the people (for Bruto admitted that it had in some degree survived), Lorenzo had carried out a double policy. Internally he had tried to preserve equality among the citizens so that none might rise above the others, while at the same time his equity and moderation prevented envy of himself. Meanwhile he had worked to maintain the peace of Italy by an alliance of Tuscan cities. Thus his death had been a profound misfortune for Florence, for his son had not inherited his abilities. Although the point may have been intended to reveal the defects of personal rule, a Florentine could hardly have dealt with Lorenzo himself more favorably.[69]

Two motives seem to account for this gentle treatment. One was Bruto's sense of the tension between liberty and order. Whatever the defects of his family, Lorenzo had apparently succeeded in coordinating these two needs of life in society. Furthermore Bruto was sufficiently realistic to recognize that the fine sentiments of their opponents were not always more genuine than the patriotic words of Cosimo and Lorenzo. Thus he noticed that good men supported Piero against the conspirators of 1465 out of love for peace and order and the sense that it was necessary to concede something to the times.[70] "It was not difficult to judge which side was defending the better cause," Bruto observed; but the interests of the Republic had to take precedence over every private consideration.[71] He displayed, therefore, rather less sympathy with the Pazzi than might have been expected. He was

[66] II, 150–176.

[67] II, 198–200. Bruto recounts, generation by generation, the crimes of the Medici against Florentine liberty; contrast with Machiavelli's briefer treatment, *Istorie fiorentine*, Bk. VIII, Ch. 1.

[68] II, 6.

[69] II, 494–500. Here, too, Bruto goes far beyond Machiavelli.

[70] I, 188.

[71] I, 246–248.

clear that the Pazzi conspirators should be judged differently from the tyrannicides of Milan; for, however ambitious they had been, the two Medici brothers had behaved with restraint and deserved well of many.[72]

A second motive for Bruto's gentle treatment of Lorenzo was his conflict with the pope, which placed him in a particularly sympathetic role from the standpoint of Venice. Bruto had hinted in an earlier passage at the remote origins of that association between the Medici and Rome ultimately so fatal to the Florentine Republic.[73] But Florence had meanwhile been placed under an interdict, and Lorenzo had been excommunicated by Sixtus IV; and to this episode Bruto gave an attention that suggests reminiscences of Julius II. Bruto treated Sixtus IV very harshly. A man of low birth, this unworthy pope, Bruto reported, had lacked any reputation either for virtue, understanding, or sanctity. He had been concerned only with improving the fortunes of his family, and rumor had it that the Riarii were closer to him than "nephews." [74] The identification of Sixtus IV with Julius II emerges most clearly in Bruto's obituary. He spoke of Sixtus's fierceness and ambition. The late pope, he charged, had sown wars among princes and dissension among the citizens of republics. His pontificate had been pernicious to the church but especially to the cities of Italy. His life had been devoted to war, and he died from chagrin when war ended with a peace he deemed little honorable.[75] All of this goes far beyond Machiavelli.

The identification of Florence and Venice was also apparent as Bruto's account of the clash unfolded. He noted the Florentine complaint at the injustice of imposing a censure normally invoked only for some enormous offense against the church,[76] and he offered a sardonic account of the pope's reaction to the resistance of Florence. In the pope's view the Florentines had behaved with shocking presumption in defying the warnings and corrections of the head of Christendom, the ruler of the entire world, whom the most powerful kings and emperors were obligated to obey. Hence he had had no alternative but to discipline so obstinate and arrogant a people. Bruto also

[72] II, 252.

[73] I, 142, where, in connection with the marriage of Lorenzo to Clarice degli Orsini, Bruto emphasized (as Machiavelli did not) that the Orsini were Romans. He also suggested as the view of those Florentines who saw "more deeply into things" that the motive behind the marriage was political ambition. Cf. Machiavelli, *Istorie fiorentine*, Bk. VII, Ch. 11.

[74] I, 400–404. Again Bruto goes considerably beyond Machiavelli; cf. *Istorie fiorentine*, Bk. VII, Ch. 31.

[75] II, 420–422.

[76] II, 160, 276–278.

described the pope's anger that Florence had ordered the clergy to celebrate mass during the interdict and had insulted the primacy of Peter by appealing to a council:[77] precisely the tactics Venice had employed under similar circumstances.

Bruto therefore entrusted Lorenzo with sentiments that might equally have come from any Venetian alert to the danger of papal meddling in politics. He described Lorenzo's accusation (in an effort to detach the Orsini from Sixtus) that the popes had persistently sowed discord among the Roman nobility, and he recorded Lorenzo's view of the insatiable ambitions of the clergy.[78] Lorenzo is also made to warn against putting any trust in Innocent VIII, however friendly that pope might for the moment appear; popes, for Lorenzo, were not only as susceptible to political greed as other men, but their power made them far more dangerous.[79] The deliberations of Lorenzo's council gave Bruto further opportunity to expose the dangers of papal policy for secular states, and again he went beyond Machiavelli. In doubt whether to come to terms with the pope or the king of Naples, the Florentines (according to Bruto) reflected that the papacy was not a hereditary principate but the gift of a few cardinals, who often acted thoughtlessly. Thus, since each pope was likely to repudiate the decisions of his predecessor, Rome lacked a coherent policy on which other states could calculate. Again, Lorenzo's counsellors considered, because the lofty position of a pope enabled him to act with impunity, no man was so great and obstinate a danger to the peace of Christendom. Thinking himself above all laws, a pope felt no obligation to keep faith; indeed, he counted on the awe inspired by his spiritual position to prevent any attempt to hold him to his word. From an alliance with the pope, therefore, no power could expect political benefits. Its only reward would be the pious satisfaction of having aided the church.[80]

Such passages suggest in Bruto a growing political realism along Florentine lines; and various sentiments in his *Istorie fiorentine* reinforce this impression. He noted that conspiracies in which many participate rarely succeed;[81] he observed that events seldom turn out according to our expectations;[82] he was aware that effective action depends on a proper reading of the times and

[77] II, 280–282.
[78] II, 466–468. These remarks, again, are missing in Machiavelli.
[79] II, 422ff.: another addition to Machiavelli.
[80] II, 324–326.
[81] I, 216–218.
[82] II, 408.

the ability to seize occasions;[83] and he knew that, in politics, men judge results, not motives.[84] He also had limited expectations of human behavior. Men, he remarked, are constantly tempted to wishful thinking and unreasonable hopes.[85] They are also little inclined to help each other. The languishing fortunes of the exiles from Medicean Florence reminded him that nothing declines more rapidly than compassion for the misfortunes of others when assistance promises to be expensive.[86] For Bruto the only dependable motives of human action were selfishness, ambition, and cupidity. His realism also found expression on a different level in an awareness (greater than Machiavelli's) of the European context of Italian affairs even in the fifteenth century.[87] In this respect he is closer to Guicciardini, whose *Storia d'Italia* had appeared the year before his own Florentine history.

Meanwhile, in a development of particular significance for the future of Venetian historiography, Venetian ambassadors to Rome were also showing a remarkable tendency to bring political and historical analysis to bear on the papacy. Earlier envoys to the Holy See, like Gasparo Contarini in 1530, had been content to provide a narrative of recent diplomacy and some account of personalities.[88] But soon after the middle of the century the Roman *Relazioni* began to probe more deeply into the character of the papal church and the way in which its institutions and policies had developed. The earliest and one of the most outspoken examples of this new perspective was provided by Bernardo Navagero in 1558. Navagero gives another broad hint of the interpretation of ecclesiastical history, earlier suggested by the *Consilium de emendenda ecclesia*, that was to reach a climax with Paolo Sarpi. His observations are also of some interest because of the distinguished ecclesiastical career on which he was soon to embark.

Navagero's historical perspective was based on a careful distinction, such as we have encountered earlier, between the church as a spiritual and invisible body and its institutional and political forms. In his view, only the latter could be historicized; but here, in its visible dimension, the church

---

[83] I, 36, where this gift is discerned in Cosimo.

[84] I, 150: ". . . ut fere semper res ex eventu non ex certa ratione aestimantur."

[85] I, 242: "Ut autem fere semper sunt homines acuti dubiis rebus in eam partem quo animi inclinant trahendis, suaque spe semper ulterius feruntur, quam quo res ipsa illos, si certam rationem ducem sequantur, perducere videatur."

[86] I, 372–374.

[87] For example, I, 404–406.

[88] Albèri, Ser. 2, III, 255–275.

had demonstrably developed, altered, and even shown a considerable capacity for error. And, like Machiavelli, Navagero was convinced that the deficiencies of the contemporary church had arisen from the confusion of the contingent and the essential; the church had so deplorably been allowed to change and therefore to have a history because popes had degenerated from spiritual leaders into temporal princes. Historical analysis thus became an instrument of reform. It displayed the tragic consequences of the failure to distinguish roles. "If we wish to consider the pope not as a prince with a state but as a head of religion," Navagero declared, "he is certainly head of all Christians, being successor of Peter, who was instituted vicar of Christ our Lord. If we wish, I say, to consider him in this way, it can be said that if the popes would pay attention to imitating the life of Christ and of the first Fathers, they would be much more terrible to the world with their excommunications and with their spiritual arms than they are now with leagues, armies, and temporal arms, which not many years ago they began to adopt openly to increase their possessions." [89]

But although this observation suggests a particular concern with recent events, Navagero also hinted at the deep roots of Roman ambition. He appears to have assumed that in some obscure sense papal Rome aspired to the political heritage of ancient Rome; and when he thought of the one, his mind automatically traveled back to the other. Only the means and the degree of success appeared to differ. Thus Navagero observed that in antiquity Rome had expanded by military conquest "and in six hundred years made herself mistress of the world." But "now that she has been reduced under the governance of the popes" she could maintain herself and increase in power only by the arts of peace.[90] Evidently papal Rome, for the time being, presented no serious danger to Venice; but it is significant that, for Navagero, the imperial universalism of Rome was still a living reality, and a potential threat to a society that took pride in its particularity.

Navagero believed that the political ambition of the papacy had become active only recently, perhaps when "Alexander VI of the Spanish nation first began openly plotting the greatness of Duke Valentino his son." He also discerned in it no deep ideological roots. It had been the result, in his view, of the existence of the papal state and the desire of individual popes to provide for their families. Since the popes were not "natural and hereditary princes" and could not "in a short time acquire and establish a new

[89] *Ibid.*, Ser. 2, III, 376.
[90] *Ibid.*, Ser. 2, III, 373–374.

state'' to leave to their heirs, he wrote, they could only "subordinate the world" by leaguing with various princes. This was the only means by which they could hope "to leave their families not as private men, as before they were popes, but with greatness and a new state, which cannot be done without wrong to others." But their resort to military alliances for political ends was, for Navagero, a scandal, since "nothing is more contrary to arms than the profession of religion." [91] For Navagero, as for earlier Venetians, religious reform and the security of Venice were complementary.

But Navagero's report is most suggestive where it touches on the constitutional development of the papacy, presumably a subject of natural interest to a Venetian. He displayed on this matter a considerable fund of information and a coolly secular attitude to ecclesiastical history. These qualities are particularly evident in his account of changes in the manner of electing the pope, a matter which he treated not with the awe due to a unique class of events but merely as a special mode of dealing with the common problem of political succession. He began by observing that "the creation of the pope has been different in different times," a point which might be supposed to suggest an arbitrary element in the constitutional structure of the church. Until 772, he believed, the Roman clergy and people had together selected the pope. But in that year the pope himself, "because, through the ambition that was beginning to hold sway, the election of the popes was done with seditions and murders," conferred on Charlemagne and his successors the right to appoint the pope. This arrangement had lasted till 817, when Louis the Pious restored the right of election to the Romans, though (as Navagero wished to make clear) "making no more mention of cardinals than of others." The substitution of election by cardinals for popular choice had been instituted only in 1059 by Nicholas II. But some popular role had persisted until 1274, when it was eliminated by Gregory X.[92]

Notable here is the vision, implicit in Navagero's rather dry reconstruction of this important evolution, of an original ecclesiastical constitution, from the outset and for many centuries based on popular election, which had been deprived of this essential condition of liberty by the popes themselves. Navagero does not labor the point. He is careful to recognize the primacy of the pope and his authority as vicar of Christ, whatever the means of his designation. He was so well regarded in Rome that the pope shortly made

[91] *Ibid.*, Ser. 2, III, 376, 374.
[92] *Ibid.*, Ser. 2, III, 371–373.

him a cardinal and employed him as legate at Trent. It is thus all the more remarkable that he too should have implied that the history of the church might be construed as the slow subversion of a republic, step by step, into an unregulated tyranny.

Navagero's immediate successors in the Roman embassy were less given to historical discussion, but they resembled him in other ways. The distinction between the pope as spiritual leader and as temporal ruler became a commonplace of the Roman *Relazioni*,[93] and in connection with the pope's latter role Girolamo Soranzo observed in 1563 that God had intended Rome always to possess a great worldly empire: the succession had been direct, he remarked, from the Roman Republic through the Empire to the Vicar of Christ.[94] And even when, as with Luigi Mocenigo in 1560, an ambassador took a broad view of the pope's spiritual authority, he was inclined to interpret Roman affairs realistically, as the product of political rather than spiritual motives. When papal conclaves seemed increasingly no more than struggles between the factions of France and Spain, Venetians analyzed the Sacred College and (like Navagero) elections to the Holy See with complete detachment.[95] But if, in these accounts, the Holy Spirit seems entirely absent from the Curia, the ambassadors also give regular expression to further reformist indignation. Soranzo, for example, attacked nepotism even more harshly than Navagero, tracing it down to his own time, pope by pope. Papal greed, he maintained, had long set a bad example to princes, whose ambitions had been chiefly responsible for the spread of heresy.[96]

Although Bruto's ardent republicanism found expression in connection with the Florentine past, his touches of political realism, his historical (rather than philosophical) presentation, and his preoccupation with the vulnerability of republican government may well be related to a growing uneasiness in Venice that was to be increasingly apparent during the next decades. Particularly significant is the absence from his work of the claim that Florence might have been saved from servitude by a constitution like that of Venice. Meanwhile the *Relazioni* of the various ambassadors to Rome at about this time were also suggesting a realistic and more historical conception

---

[93] So Luigi Mocenigo (1560), *ibid.*, Ser. 2, IV, 23; Girolamo Soranzo (1563), *ibid.*, Ser. 2, IV, 78–82.

[94] *Ibid.*, Ser. 2, IV, 83.

[95] Cf. Luigi Mocenigo, *ibid.*, Ser. 2, IV, 43–44; and Paolo Tiepolo (1569), *ibid.*, Ser. 2 IV, 182–183.

[96] *Ibid.*, Ser. 2, IV, 78–82.

of the political world, and particularly of the papacy. Neither Bruto nor the ambassadors suggested that these elements in their vision of politics had any relevance to Venice. But developments in the surrounding world shortly provided evidence of new dangers against which the alleged perfections of the Venetian constitution might provide insufficient protection. Two closely related events hinted at trouble ahead and gradually produced a clearer alteration in the Venetian outlook on politics. The first was a change in the atmosphere of Rome, in which Venice had long recognized a political and ideological enemy. The second was the victory of Lepanto and its ambiguous aftermath.

Venice had considered the Medici popes, Leo X and Clement VII, her enemies, not only because they had inherited the policies and ambitions of Julius II but also because they were Florentines.[97] But relations between Venice and Rome improved considerably during the middle decades of the century, if only because the Curia had more pressing concerns than the autonomy of the Venetian church, notably Protestantism, relations with the great powers, and the Council.[98] Clement VII had himself begun to recognize the value of a friendly Venice to the security of the papacy; but amicable relations between Venice and Rome reached a peak under Pius IV. Both sides contributed to the relaxation of tension. The Venetians had discovered that pleasing the pope was likely to pay well in benefits of various kinds,[99] and Pius IV had appeared remarkably respectful to secular rulers. He had openly declared that if the authority of princes were not maintained, it would be impossible to conserve that of popes; he seemed eager to confer favors on secular powers; and when he felt compelled to

[97] Cf. Luigi Gradenigo (1523), *ibid.*, Ser. 2, III, 69–70; he explains that Leo X was hostile to Venice "because of his country, since he was Florentine."

[98] This was the view of more than one ambassador. Thus Gasparo Contarini reported of Clement VII in 1530 (*ibid.*, Ser. 2, III, 265–266): "Dimostra di desiderare sommamente la pace d'Italia, la conservazione di essa, ed anche la riputazione d'Italia; nella quale non parendogli di vedere altro nervo che lo stato di Vostre Eccellenze, desidera grandemente di avere buona intelligenza con questa Serenissima Repubblica; perchè a questo modo gli pare che in Italia sariano tali forze, che non bisogneria dipendere in tutto da altri,cioè, ne da Francia, ne da Cesare." Cf. the relation of Marco Foscari (1526), *ibid.*, Ser. 2, III, 133, which speaks also of Luther and the Turks.

[99] Cf. the remarks of Girolamo Soranzo (1563), *ibid.*, Ser. 2, IV, 117: "Ma perchè io ho osservato nel tempo della mia legazione che quei principi che hanno dimandato ed ottenuto delle grazie, hanno anco gratificato la Beautitudine Sua e li suoi, però non voglio restar di recordare con la debita reverenza, che volendo ella dimandar e ricever delle grazie importanti, saria di suo servizio disponeri ancora lei a compiacere la Santità Sua in certe cose che si possono onestamente fare."

refuse a request, he did so with modesty and tact. To Venice he had seemed particularly gracious. He had decided for the Venetian ambassador in a dispute over precedence at the Curia with the Bavarian envoy, he had accepted Venetian nominations to benefices in Venetian territory, he had more than once allowed the government to tax the clergy, and he had promoted a suitable number of Venetians to the cardinalate, as the ambassador reported in 1563.[100] By 1565 there were seven Venetians in the Sacred College.[101]

This era of good feeling came to an abrupt end with the conclusion of the Council of Trent and the accession of Pius V in 1566. The end of the Council meant that Rome was at last relieved both of a serious distraction and a danger to papal authority, and the new pope resumed the long struggle to reduce the secular world to obedience. The Venetians felt they had understood Pius IV. He had seemed a part of the familiar world of Renaissance politics which, except for short intervals under Adrian VI and Paul IV, had so long dominated the Curia. He had been a man of the world, a practical statesman, a *politique* with whom one knew how to deal. But Pius V was, to the Venetians, shockingly different. He was austere, idealistic, devout, a pope at last of the Counter Reformation. He evidently required a good deal of study, and the Venetian ambassador, now Paolo Tiepolo, was of two minds about him. In comparison with his flexible and worldly predecessor, he seemed in a way admirable. A militant reformer, he met the high standards Venetians had long called for. But it was difficult to know how to do business with such a figure. It was true, Tiepolo had noticed, that Pius IV had changed his tone too as soon as the Council was over, but in a familiar way; his successor was an enigma:

> Asserting his own authority with firmness and vigor, Pius IV began [after the Council] to follow his own thoughts and inclinations more freely. Thus one could easily discern in him rather the attitude of a prince who was attending solely to his own interests than of a pope concerned about the benefit or the salvation of others. But Pius V, trusting in the upright will and conscience he appears to possess and in his blameless life, and little measuring things with human reasons,

[100] *Ibid.*, Ser. 2, IV, 115–117.
[101] This was observed by Giacomo Soranzo (1565), *ibid.*, Ser. 2, IV, 138. Only the Papal State and the Milanese, with twelve cardinals each, had more. In addition Cardinal Pisani, a Venetian, was dean of the Sacred College. It should be noted, however, that two of the Venetian cardinals were *personae non gratae* in Venice.

was from the beginning very vigorous in exercising his own authority. And although he has been warned many times in regard to what he does that he has to do not with angels but with men, and that he should consider the scandals and the harm that could ensue, . . . he has nevertheless never changed, saying that he has always found that his actions turn out well when directed to the good and favored by God. Thus it is universally believed that there is a good and holy intention in him, but that in judging and treating things he is often deceived . . . . Pius V does not at all understand *le ragioni di Stato*.

Apparently a zealous reformer made a bad administrator: the new pope was too severe, he ran to extremes, he failed to see that in remedying one disorder it was easy to fall into another.[102]

But worst of all Pius V did not confine himself to matters the Venetians considered spiritual. He made large theoretical claims: many times he informed Tiepolo that his authority extended over all states and that he possessed an absolute right of command in everything, alleging on the authority of Aquinas that Constantine had technically given nothing to the church but had merely restored to it its own. In making this point, Tiepolo wrote, the pope wished "to imply that there is nothing in the world that does not belong to the church." [103] Nor was this pope content to leave matters in the realm of theory. He had not hesitated to cite to Rome the duke of Mantua and leading officials of the Milanese, "and to make other great and important demonstrations against other princes without any sort of respect." Furthermore success in one affair did not satisfy him but only stimulated him to further exertions. For the pope was unhappily not alone in his ill-considered zeal. He was surrounded by men who, "without considering the circumstances of things and of the present times, continuously solicit and instigate him to continue, and to try to recover and increase the ancient authority and greatness of the church, alleging that if a man of such an exemplary and blameless life did not do it, it would be unthinkable for another pope." [104]

---

[102] *Ibid.*, Ser. 2, IV, 169ff. This relation of 1569 is largely organized as a study in contrast, Tiepolo having served under both Pius IV and Pius V. Criticism of the higher clergy for inexperience in worldly affairs is frequent with the Venetians. See for example the relations of Foscari and Surian, *ibid.*, Ser. 2, III, 138 (against Sadoleto) and 298 (against Cajetan). Andrea Morosini, *Historia veneta*, V, 84, made the same observation about Adrian VI.

[103] Albèri, Ser. 2, IV, 179.

[104] *Ibid.*, Ser. 2, IV, 180.

Generally suspicious of commercial republics because their citizens were constantly exposed to heresy through travel, Pius V seemed to feel a particular animus to Venice. Tiepolo attributed this to his years in the Inquisition, when his efforts to eradicate heresy seemed constantly thwarted by the Venetian government. He was convinced that Venice lacked either zeal for the faith or a proper respect for the Holy See and the person of the pope. "Thus," Tiepolo reported, "having succeeded to the pontificate, he began attentively to note, to reprove, and to impugn various procedures and operations by Your Serenity and your ministers." He continued to object to the laxity with which Venice treated heresy and in particular to the presence of laymen at the sessions of the Inquisition. He was perturbed by the whole range of Venetian jurisdictional arrangements, about which "he made so many complaints and raised so many difficulties that the time would not now suffice to go into them." In general he considered Venice selfishly indifferent to the needs of Christendom, since she had refused to support the Catholic cause against either the Turks or the Huguenots.[105] It also did not go unnoticed that this pope who was so hostile to Venice had personally crowned Cosimo de'Medici as grand duke of Tuscany, inscribing on the crown a tribute to the Florentine prince's zeal for the faith.[106] The gesture seemed to Venice a snub, and many in Rome thought that a break between the pope and the Venetian Republic was imminent.[107]

Even one unsympathetic pope created serious problems for Venice, but the election of Gregory XIII in 1572 revealed that the change in Rome was no mere temporary shift in mood. Tiepolo, again at the Holy See, observed that the new pope was even more devout than his predecessor, and (perhaps as a corollary) he rated his political understanding somewhat lower. Under Gregory's leadership, he remarked, possibly with a trace of irony, Rome was approaching "that perfection which human imperfection can receive." [108] Gregory XIII was also as hostile as Pius V to Venice. He snubbed the Venetian ambassadors immediately after his election; and when he decided that the representatives of all secular powers should be assigned lower places in the papal chapel, he began with the ambassador from Venice.[109] After having enjoyed so much favor in Rome, Venice now counted for nothing. Not one Venetian was made a cardinal during nineteen years.[110]

[105] Ibid., Ser. 2, IV, 190–192.

[106] Tiepolo described the event, ibid., Ser. 2, IV, 196.

[107] Ibid., Ser. 2, IV, 192.

[108] Ibid., Ser. 2, IV, 213, 215.

[109] Ibid., Ser. 2, IV, 232, 238–239.

[110] Lorenzo Priuli noted this in 1586, ibid., Ser. 2, IV, 298.

Meanwhile the papal nuncios in Venice were directed to push more vigorously for compliance with the pope's wishes on a wide range of issues. They demanded greater rigor against heresy, assimilation of the Greek subjects of the Republic into the Roman church, enforcement of the decrees of Trent, a larger role in the supervision of the Venetian clergy, and (again) an end to secular jurisdiction over churchmen. When in 1580 the archbishop of Spalato was convicted of misappropriating a legacy, the pope succeeded, by threatening censure and referring to the capitulations of Julius II, in forcing annulment of the judgment. In the same year he proposed a system of apostolic visitations for all Venetian monasteries.[111]

The danger these developments posed for Venice was in the meantime compounded by a renewal of war with the Turks. The new Holy League, sponsored by a more militant pope, dramatized the meaning of the changes in Rome; and the conduct of the war and its aftermath revealed in the ambitions of Spain a new cause for apprehension. At the same time the battle of Lepanto had been a great victory over the Turks, the first military triumph for decades in which Venice could take pride; and as a victory it had a positive effect on Venetian morale. The war of Cyprus exposed the perils which surrounded Venice, but it also strengthened her resolution to confront them.

She had been at peace since the end of the last Turkish war in 1540. Indeed she was now so accustomed to peace that the alternative had become almost unthinkable.[112] But Turkish pressure had been growing. In the year Pius V became pope, Venice had been alarmed by the intrusion of a great Turkish fleet into the Adriatic, although not yet to the point of making serious preparations for war.[113] She was thus unready for the Turkish demand that she cede Cyprus. When war began in February of 1570, Cyprus quickly fell, and the entry of Spain into the war was of no help to the Venetian position in the Levant. But by the spring of the next year the pope had formally organized the Holy League, a great armada was collected, and in October it decisively defeated a huge Turkish fleet off Lepanto. Largely because of disagreements among the major allies, however, the victory was not exploited. Spain proposed to attack her Moslem enemies in North Africa, while Venice naturally sought to recover Cyprus. And, increasingly

[111] Stella, *Chiesa e Stato*, pp. 23–33, 58–60.
[112] Cf. the remarks of Braudel, *La Méditerranée et le monde méditerranéen*, p. 912.
[113] *Ibid.*, pp. 865–866, 892, 911.

convinced that the alliance could never be induced to serve this aim, increasingly suspicious of Spain, and weary of a war that was enormously expensive to wage and required the suspension of her Levantine trade, Venice, after the most secret negotiations, concluded a separate peace early in the spring of 1573, abandoning Cyprus and paying an indemnity to the Turks.[114]

The reverberations of these events were profound. The pope (now Gregory XIII) was furious. He saw the abandonment of the common cause of Christendom as an additional proof of Venetian selfishness and indifference to the general good. When Paolo Tiepolo conveyed the news of the peace to the pope, he reported, the pontiff "was inflamed with anger and, without caring to listen to explanation, rose up from his seat, began to rage, and dismissed me from him in such a way that I was deserted by everyone in the place." There was again talk of excommunication.[115] But for Venice this reaction, which was followed by renewed pressure for Venetian participation in war against the infidel,[116] chiefly demonstrated the incompatibility of political needs with the militant idealism of the Counter Reformation. It posed the question how Venice could, in the long run, survive as a Catholic state. Matters were eventually smoothed over, on the surface, by a special embassy; and the dilemma did not require an immediate resolution. But, like so much else during these years, it was potentially alarming.

The alliance had also disclosed the hostility of Spain, whose ambitions in Italy now appeared increasingly dangerous. During the next few years boundary disputes with the Spanish authorities in Milan became more and more fierce, and Venice began to strengthen her mainland frontiers.[117] She was to be further disquieted by the Spanish acquisition of Portugal in 1580.[118] After the battle of Lepanto the Venetian ambassador in Rome also began to note with particular apprehension the strength of Spanish influence at the Curia. Sixteen of the fifty-four cardinals were "vassals" of the Spanish king, he reported in 1576, and the rest were all obligated to him.[119]

[114] On the motives of Venice for concluding a separate peace see, in addition to Braudel, pp. 963–964, Chabod, "Venezia nella politica italiana ed europea," pp. 45–46.

[115] *Relazione di Roma* of 1576, in Albèri, Ser. 2, IV, 226, 235–236.

[116] Cf. the instructions to the nuncio Alberto Bolognetti (1578), described by Stella, *Chiesa e Stato*, p. 19.

[117] Braudel, pp. 963–964; Gaetano Cozzi, "Politica e diritto in alcune controversie confinarie tra lo Stato di Milano e la Repubblica di Venezia," *Archivio Storico Lombardo*, LXXVIII–LXXIX (1951–1952), 7–44.

[118] Cf. Stella, *Chiesa e Stato*, pp. 34–35.

[119] Tiepolo, in Albèri, Ser. 2, IV, 223.

Spain and the papacy were now increasingly identified in the Venetian mind, and Venice grew increasingly anxious in her isolation.

The war also had important consequences within Venice herself. Some were unfavorable. The initial unpreparedness of the Republic, the abandonment of the alliance, and the damaging terms of the peace divided the patriciate and generally reduced confidence in the men who had so long dominated the government. Their cautious policies no longer appeared so effective. In addition, the great costs of the war left the Republic with serious financial problems. She was now burdened with a huge public debt, the interest on which absorbed a large share of her public revenues.[120]

Yet in the longer run the domestic effect of the war on Venice was positive. Braudel has reminded us how momentous an event Lepanto appeared to the whole of Christendom. After centuries of retreat before the infidel, this victory was, at first, literally incredible; and as the truth sank in, it was followed everywhere by a vast sense of relief and by enthusiastic celebration. The myth of Turkish invulnerability had been at last destroyed; after so many disasters the tide seemed finally to have turned. Nor was Lepanto a turning point only in this subjective sense. In spite of the failure of the allies to follow up their triumph, Lepanto marked the start of a rapid decay in Turkish power. The terrible danger that had so long hung over Europe began gradually to dissipate.[121]

What was so generally true for Europe as a whole was particularly true for Venice, which had so long been peculiarly exposed to Turkish pressure. Venice had seemed in terrible danger. At the start of the war, as Paolo Paruta declared in a public oration honoring those who had died at Lepanto, the sun appeared to be setting forever, a perpetual night seemed about to descend. But Lepanto had taught "that the Turks are not insuperable, as they were previously esteemed." [122] Above all, however, Venice was inspired by the conviction that the victory had been essentially her own.[123] It had demonstrated the prowess of the Republic, latent for so many decades; more forcefully than a thousand philosophical treatises, this single, great dramatic action had exposed the effective political virtue of the Republic. Paruta remarked that the Turks had been far more formidable as enemies than

[120] For the post-war problems of Venice, see Stella, "La regolazione delle publiche entrate," pp. 161–162, 170.

[121] Braudel, pp. 923ff.

[122] *Orazione funebre* in his *Opere politiche*, I, 28. Cf. Morosini, VI, 495, for a similar observation; Morosini too had lived through the event.

[123] Cf. Valier, *Dell'utilità*, pp. 376–379.

either the Persians or the Carthaginians. It was obvious, then, that the heroes of Venice had shown themselves superior to the greatest of the ancients.[124]

Lepanto thus seemed to have a joyful meaning for the whole future of the Republic. In Paruta's vivid image, the victory had restored the happy light of day; and the earth, feeling the rays of the sun once more, was turning unseasonably green and bursting into flower; the Republic had been impelled into a kind of rebirth.[125] The defeat of the Turk suggested that Venice could now hope to resume her ancient heritage as a great commercial republic dominating the sea routes to the east. More generally, in spite of the unfavorable terms of the peace, the sequel was to reveal a substantial quickening of Venetian political energy and a considerable change in outlook. During the generation after Lepanto a new leadership emerged which was resolved to prove that Venice had lost none of her old virtue during the decades of stagnation and that she could still hold her own with the great powers.

The combination of new dangers from Spain and Rome with the stimulus provided by Lepanto thus slowly brought to an end the long, passive phase in Venetian history during which the Republic had been able to think of herself, protected by her lagoons and her ideal constitution, as standing above the ravages of time and history. New men, devoted to the restoration of commerce, more open to ideas from the world beyond, more sensitive to danger and at the same time bolder and more confident, increasingly challenged those who had so long directed the Republic. A more dynamic formulation of Venetian republicanism now began to emerge. A decade after the war of Cyprus the *giovani*, as contemporaries described them in one of Europe's earliest associations of youth with a dynamic reform movement, had taken control of the Republic.

The division of the Venetian patriciate between *giovani* and *vecchi* in the later sixteenth century had been foreshadowed by earlier tensions over policy and differences in political and cultural attitudes. In the remote background of the split was the traditional division between those who insisted that the Republic should confine her energies to the sea and those who favored expansion on the land. But if the policy of the latter seemed initially

---

[124] *Orazione funebre*, pp. 26–27. Cf. Pietro Giustiniani, *Le historie venetiane*, tr. Gioseppe Horologgi and Remigio Fiorentino (Venice, 1576), sig. VVVVV4ʳ, which also compares Venetian valor at Lepanto with that of the ancients.

[125] *Orazione funebre*, p. 28. It appears that the weather had in fact been unusual.

more daring, it had resulted in the attachment of wealthier patricians to agriculture, begun their conversion into landed magnates with more aristocratic prejudices and a static ideal of politics, and made them more fearful of war and more apprehensive of offending the pope than many of their contemporaries. Thus, although in an exact sense the *giovani* were reactionaries, they looked to the past as a model in the manner of other reformers in an age when all salutary change was regarded as a return to the better condition of an earlier time. In practice they showed themselves more attentive to changing political circumstance, more flexible, more open to initiative. These differences have been discerned as early as the League of Cambray, and they manifested themselves occasionally, particularly over religious questions, during the middle decades of the century.[126] But the attitudes that were to be associated with the *giovani* began to crystallize into a genuine political program only in the decade after Lepanto. The years immediately after the war thus constituted a period of transition in which, while the *vecchi* continued to direct the government and their general views remained dominant, an opposition was gathering and growing increasingly articulate.

The transitional character of this period and the persistence of older attitudes are particularly evident in the historical works of Pietro Giustiniani and Agostino Valier. Giustiniani's *Rerum venetarum historia*,[127] composed between 1569 and 1575 when the author was in his eighties, begins with the foundation of the city; but it moves rapidly over the earlier phases of Venetian history to concentrate on the fifteenth and, above all, the sixteenth centuries down to the time of writing. Although he praised Biondo, Bernardo Giustiniani, and Sabellico (but not Bembo), the author regarded earlier Venetian historiography as thin; hence the need, as he wrote, to record many things omitted by his predecessors.[128] Much of the earlier part of the work is little more than an extended *laudatio* which preserves the familiar legends about the Venetian past; and Giustiniani's dedication (to the Council of Ten) suggests that he attributed no function to historical composition beyond the glorification of the exploits of the past "with the light of letters"

---

[126] On the remote backgrounds of this division, see Seneca, *Venezia e Papa Giulio II*, pp. 34ff.; the review of this work by Gino Benzoni, *BSV*, IV (1962), 396; and Stella, *Chiesa e Stato*, pp. 3–6.

[127] First published in 1576. I cite from the Italian translation (note 124 above), published the same year. For Giustiniani as a historian, cf. Cozzi, "Pubblica storiografia," p. 238.

[128] Sig. Al^v.

so that "the splendor of the Venetian name" might be made immortal. Although he was compelled to recognize that Venice had expanded through the centuries, his sense of development was entirely quantitative; for Giustiniani the Republic had undergone no qualitative or constitutional change, and her essential characteristics had been apparent since her origins.[129] The later sections of Giustiniani's narrative, particularly when based on his personal experience, are more concrete; but he was incapable of coherent organization and strung together a variety of events and anecdotes without discrimination. He was especially struck by prodigies and disasters: pious miracles, storms, conspiracies, crimes, the illnesses of rulers, the movements and atrocities of the Turks. He finally leaves the impression chiefly of a sentimental and garrulous old man.

Giustiniani is of considerable interest, however, for his respectful treatment of the papacy, which he accompanied with a rather un-Venetian admiration for the accomplishments of Roman antiquity. His manner even toward Julius II was remarkably restrained by Venetian standards;[130] he piously praised those more recent popes who had so puzzled the ambassadors in Rome;[131] and he unambiguously applauded "the love and diligence of the pope in aiding the Venetians" during the war of Cyprus.[132] Although he lamented the loss of the opportunity for final victory after Lepanto,[133] there is no hint in his work of tension within the Holy League. For the Council of Trent he expressed only the warmest approval.[134] And just as he seems to have accepted modern Rome as the source of all spiritual blessing, so he discerned in the institutions of pagan Rome the source of all political benefit. For Giustiniani, the Venetian constitution was not essentially an original creation based on a higher wisdom but, in its major agencies, a successful adaptation of Roman models. Earlier Venetians had admitted this for the Council of Ten, but in doing so they seemed to be suggesting a vague uneasiness about that institution. Giustiniani now represented the Senate, the Great Council, and "many other things" as mere imitations of Roman antiquity.[135] Thus, with this historian, Venice seems less

[129] Sigs. A2^r, A4^r.
[130] Treated in the eleventh book; see esp. sig. BBBB1^v.
[131] Sigs. NNNNN1^r, XXXXX3^v.
[132] Sig. QQQQQ2^v.
[133] Sig. XXXXX4^v.
[134] Sigs. BBBBB3^v, HHHHH2^r, LLLLL4^r.
[135] Sig. B3^v. For other instances of Venetian imitation of the Romans, sigs. MMMM1^v, QQQQ4^v. Lodovico Avanzo's epistle to the Italian edition also stresses the similarity between the Venetians and the Romans.

sensitive to the dangers represented by the pope, and the pride of the Republic in the peculiar structure of her government appears subtly diminished.

Agostino Valier's *Dell'utilità che si può ritrarre dalle cose operate dai Veneziani*,[136] which goes to 1580, was also composed after Lepanto. Once perhaps an associate of Patrizi, as we have noticed, Valier was a far better historian than Giustiniani. Where the latter had seen in historical composition only an opportunity for commemoration, Valier, as his title suggests, found knowledge of the past broadly advantageous. Even in citing the Ciceronian commonplaces he made clear that from history men might learn not only the principles of virtue but also (provided that it adhered closely to the truth) "the science of civil life." [137] He rated this form of knowledge (or, as he elsewhere described it, "this art of administering the Republic and conserving its government which is popularly called politics of the State")[138] very highly. He also combined a deep loyalty to his native city with a sense of the development of Venetian institutions which makes him seem quite different from most earlier Venetian writers about politics. He believed that the Venetian settlers had passed through an early period of anarchy; that the excellent aristocratic government of the Republic had been developed only "gradually after many years" following various experiments with popular and autocratic regimes such as other cities had also passed through; and that she had taken a long while to devise her admirable laws "because the ancient Venetians, not yet versed in the study of the sciences, would not have been able to imagine such marvelous laws as were needed to maintain the Republic so long." [139]

Valier did not attribute the progressive excellence of the Venetian constitution, like Pietro Giustiniani, to imitation of the Romans, toward whom he was fairly cool.[140] His sense of Venetian development also expresses a far clearer grasp of the nature of political formation than we have yet encountered in Venetian thought. But just as hostility first animated the Venetian efforts to view Florence and the papacy historically, so a subtly

[136] Composed in Latin for the edification of his nephews and published only in the Italian translation by Niccolò Antonio Giustiniani cited above. For Valier's importance as a historian see also Cozzi, "Pubblica storiografia," pp. 244–255.

[137] P. 286.

[138] P. 280.

[139] Pp. 24–25, 61.

[140] Cf. his opening lines (*p. 1*), where he contrasts the virtuous early settlers of Venice with the "uomini cattivi" who joined Romulus.

destructive impulse seems to have stimulated Valier. His work was directed, if not against Venice herself, at least against a certain way of regarding her; and its historical perspective suggests the influence during the period, even in Venice, of the Counter Reformation. For Valier was not only a Venetian. He was also bishop of Verona, a cardinal, and well regarded in Rome. He thought of himself, indeed, no longer as a Venetian but as one who, "summoned to the most weighty pastoral ministry," had abandoned his "sweet fatherland." [141] And his work must be read as an effort to reinterpret Venetian history, with a degree of love but also in the light of an ecclesiastical vision of politics. Valier could therefore not permit Venice to partake of eternity; she had to be reduced to the sublunary and inferior realm of alteration and decay.

His book was first introduced to Venetian readers in this sense by his close friend Silvio Antoniano, another high ecclesiastic. In the epistle he composed for the work, Antoniano, sounding remarkably like Machiavelli, pointedly attacked the tendency of "men little versed in the schools and academies" who "feigned imaginary cities, described their laws, their magistrates, and their rules of life, and dreamed of Republics come down from heaven and citizens who do not exist nor ever will." In some other context, these remarks might be taken to refer to the whole class of utopian writers in post-Renaissance Italy; but here one thinks immediately of Contarini. Thus Antoniano's conclusion seems equivocal. The truly learned, the "subtle investigators of things," he declared, recognized "that in every community there are great troubles" and that "this human life is full of many evils and many miseries." [142] Under these conditions Venice was merely the best polity possible; the ideal could find no earthly realization. As Valier himself observed: "Our fatherland is heaven, that is our home." [143] The reaction against Contarini clearly had widely different sources.

Much of Valier's work, furthermore, is directed to proving that the excellence of Venice and her long survival were the result neither of natural wisdom nor of political skill but of a steadfast devotion to the Christian religion and loyalty to the pope. In support of this thesis Valier presented the history of Venice as a record of unwavering devotion to the Holy See. "These islands were created," he wrote in connection with the Arian controversies, "to conserve the Christian religion and to defend the Holy

[141] See the preface to his nephews, pp. xiv–xv.
[142] P. vii.
[143] P. 121.

Apostolic See." [144] He exploited, in this sense, the story of Venetian support for the pope in 1177,[145] and he insisted that Venice had always fought with the Guelfs.[146] He also described the events of 1509–1510 almost without reference to ecclesiastical censure or the role of Julius II, whose alleged hatred against Venice he denied.[147] He represented the Venetians as enthusiastic supporters of the Council of Trent, which he warmly praised.[148] The most useful lesson that history can teach, he repeated, was that " a wise politics is never separate from Christian piety." [149] And as this had been the secret of Venetian success in the past, so it would insure her survival in the future:

> Sensible men often inquire to what should be attributed the fact that the Venetians have so long conserved the Republic. Some ascribe its cause to the convenience of the site, others to the prudence with which they have always been distinguished. Still others say that the Republic is sufficiently fortified and made impregnable by its great riches and its opulence, particularly from being a maritime city famous throughout the world, so that whoever sees her is never satiated. But we shall say that these defences are gifts God has given to the city of Venice. And believe me, my sons, nothing has ever been or ever will be more effective to conserve this beautiful Republic, which you also, I hope, may someday govern, than this: that the Senate should maintain itself, as in the past, in the Catholic faith and in its attachment to the Apostolic Holy See; that it should detest every novelty of doctrine in matters of religion; that it should flee heretics like the plague; that it should defend with its own blood, if necessary, the dogmas of the true religion; that it should lend due honors to Holy Mother Church, as did our ancestors, who were nourished with her milk and fortified with the divine word which she administered. In this way the Republic will always be conserved. Always observe this maxim: from the cult of the Triune God depends the beautiful liberty of the Republic, the moderation of her sweet laws, her amiable tranquility, and peace so dear.[150]

[144] P. 11.
[145] Pp. 90–98.
[146] P. 116.
[147] Pp. 251–258, 270.
[148] Pp. 315, 330, 350–351.
[149] P. 46. This sentiment is close to being the central theme of the work.
[150] P. 97.

Valier thus represents a systematic effort to reconcile Venetian patriotism with Counter Reformation piety, and his own political vision is utterly at odds with the political realism of the Renaissance. He glosses over embarrassing episodes in the Venetian past, he ignores the secular bias of republicanism, he perceives nothing dangerous to the Venetian tradition in the tendencies of the age, and his prescriptions for the future of the Republic lack both urgency and concreteness. It was precisely against attitudes of this sort, because they tended to compromise everything on which the greatness of the Republic had been based, that the *giovani* now began to react.

At the same time his interest in history, whatever impulses it reflected, had an important consequence for the development of Venetian political discourse. Valier was concerned at the long abeyance of official historiography and he was perhaps primarily responsible for the appointment in 1577, as historian of Venice, of his protégé Alvise Contarini, nephew of the great Gasparo. Perhaps under Valier's influence the decree appointing Contarini did not call on the new historian of Venice to glorify the Republic; instead it emphasized the need for fidelity, sincerity, and judgment, along with a "good and eloquent style." And Contarini set promptly to work, but he died two years later leaving only a sketch of the history of Venice from 1513 (where Bembo had ended) to 1570. The effective revival of Venetian historiography was thus left to his successor, Paolo Paruta, whose views on politics and history Valier would perhaps have found less congenial.[151]

Paruta, it may be supposed, had demonstrated his qualifications for this appointment in his extended dialogues *Della perfezione della vita politica*, published in 1579, which subtly document the tensions and changing attitudes of this period, but from a perspective rather different from that of Valier. Paruta's career closely followed the political and social changes experienced by his generation.[152] Born in 1540 into a lesser patrician family, he was brought up during the tranquil middle decades of the century. At Padua between 1558 and 1561, he received the usual education of his class in philosophy and rhetoric and then returned to Venice, where his house became the intellectual center for a group of cultivated nobles, both clerical and lay, several of whom were later prominent among the *giovani*. But his public career was for the time being slight. He served as a secretary during

---

[151] Cozzi, "Pubblica storiografia," pp. 250–256.
[152] For Paruta in general, see Candeloro, "Paruta," and Arturo Pompeati, "Per la biografia di Paolo Paruta," *Giornale Storico della Letteratura Italiana*, XLV (1905), 48–66.

the special embassy of Michele Surian to the imperial court; and when the ambassador's party stopped at Trent on its return journey in 1563, young Paruta had a brief view of the Council and its delegates. He was also elected to a minor office in 1565, but he served only briefly. During this period when the Venetian government was dominated by a few powerful families who were increasingly diverting their capital to agriculture, Paruta was one of the more numerous class of lesser nobles engaged in trade. Both his later career and his writings suggest an identification with the commercial interest. Lepanto stimulated him to his first public statement, the oration mentioned above, delivered in San Marco.

Paruta's *Vita civile*[153] is the eclectic work of a cultivated amateur in the world of ideas, and in this it is typical of the literary culture of the later Renaissance. It deals with a wide range of familiar topics, and it often appears little more than a tissue of ancient commonplaces. The second book, for example, is largely an amiable mixture of clichés drawn from the *Nicomachean Ethics*, Plato, and moral theology; and the third also relies heavily on Aristotle. But Paruta's work is more than an anthology of Renaissance platitudes. Below its surface may be discerned a fierce loyalty to Venetian values; it hints at a growing concern for the predicament of Venice in the real world, and it displays some insight into the nature of the dangers now gathering around her. Plato, Aristotle, and the Stoics supplied a common currency for political discourse which Paruta now exploited to analyze a complex of very real contemporary issues. He drew on them, especially on Aristotle, when they could be made to serve Venice; in other cases he departed from them, sometimes in favor of more serviceable authorities, sometimes on his own.[154]

The intellectual complexity of the work is also increased by its dialogue form; its many participants represent conflicting points of view, generally with eloquence and vigor on all sides. But this form is not merely intended to please the reader. It also reflects the author's distrust of dogmatism, not only as pedagogically ineffective but perhaps too as a violation of the dynamic and unfinished quality of human perception and finally of the dignity of the individual. Paruta claimed—though we need not take him altogether at his

[153] I cite the edition in his *Opere politiche*, I, 33–405.

[154] See on this point Arturo Pompeati, "Le dottrine politiche di Paolo Paruta," pp. 296–298. My own reading is more positive than that of Curcio, *Dal Rinascimento alla Controriforma*, p. 54, which finds Paruta's views largely derivative. I agree that Paruta relied on earlier authors, but I think that he used familiar materials for purposes of his own which were related to the peculiar circumstances of his time.

word—that he wished his reader, after a full exposure to opposing arguments, to make up his own mind.[155]

For the setting of this confrontation he went back to his youthful trip through Trent with Surian during the last session of the Council. According to Paruta, the Venetian ambassadors to the Council, Nicolò da Ponte and Matteo Dandolo, invited the traveling diplomats to a dinner with various other Venetians who were then in Trent, some of them ecclesiastics connected with the Council, others laymen. Paruta's book, then, purports to describe the extended conversation that followed this meal as reported to him (since he was unable to be present) by his friend Francesco Molino. It is thus presented as the record of an actual event; and since those alleged to be present were in every case real personages, some still alive when the work was published, it is likely that the book reflects, if not their actual words, the attitudes and opinions they were known to hold.[156] But whether some such discussion as Paruta describes really occurred in Trent in 1563 is less significant than his own interest, during the years after Lepanto, in the issues with which it is alleged to have dealt. And that these issues were of general concern is also indicated by the popularity of Paruta's work, which went through three Venetian editions before the end of the century.[157]

The discussion is important both for its substance and for Paruta's association of certain kinds of opinions with various classes of men. Its major subject is the validity of the entire range of Renaissance values: the active life of civic duty, love of country, modern accomplishments in the arts, the uses of history, the benefits of wealth, the dignity of women. Paruta depicts these values as under harsh attack by a number of the clergy present, as though he is beginning to suspect, a decade after the event, that the Council of Trent expressed tendencies not altogether friendly to the traditions and culture of his beloved Republic. Her defense is undertaken, on the other hand, chiefly by the Venetian diplomats present, wise and cultivated patricians with a long experience in the service of Venice. Thus Paruta's work may be interpreted as a dramatic ideological confrontation between the culture of the Counter Reformation, as Paruta was beginning to apprehend it, and that of the Renaissance, now represented with heightened self-awareness by the Venetian Republic. Paruta's own superior,

---

[155] P. 38.
[156] Candeloro insists on this point, "Paruta," p. 78. See also Gaetano Cozzi, "Paolo Paruta, Paolo Sarpi, e la questione della sovranità su Ceneda," *BSV*, IV (1962), 215–218.
[157] Candeloro, "Paruta," p. 95 and n. 2 for a list of editions.

Surian, is the chief spokesman of Renaissance values in the first section of the work. In the second, in which the division between the two sides is less sharp, Daniele Barbaro (now at the Council as patriarch-elect of Aquileia) analyzes the moral virtues. In the third, Nicolò da Ponte (with some assistance from the others) ranges over a number of issues of a more practical nature. Differences in tone, emphasis, and intellectual constitution may be detected among the various participants in the debate. They are presented as in-dividuals, and it is probably futile to identify Paruta's own position in an absolute sense with any of them. Yet the intention of the work is clear. Paruta aimed to supply an elaborate defense, at the deepest level, of the challenged values of Venetian life. But the participants in the debate, it may also be observed, are on both sides native Venetians. The challenge to Renaissance values was not altogether external; Paruta is in a sense dealing with a cleavage within Venice herself, and perhaps also within most Venetians.

The debate operates on various levels. Its participants seem to recognize that the *vita civile* is closely related to more general matters, and that whether one condemns or justifies it depends on assumptions concerning the nature of man, virtue, happiness, and even metaphysics and epistemology. Thus Paruta's work includes, in addition to some rather concrete reference to the achievements of Venice, a considerable systematic element. The mood that made Contarini's image of Venice so attractive was as much a part of his heritage as the new historicism of Patrizi or the elation following Lepanto. The mingling of elements in his work reveals again the transitional character of this phase in the history of Venice.

The issue between the two camps is joined in a belligerent speech by the count-bishop of Ceneda, Michele Della Torre, in real life a staunch champion of ecclesiastical jurisdiction with close ties to the Curia.[158] After listening impatiently as the ambassadors discuss their duties, their travels, and their experiences in various parts of Europe, he launches into a denunciation of their lives of worldly responsibility, contrasting the tedium of service to others with his own leisurely existence. He is eventually joined by others, and the case against the *vita activa civile* is developed along many fronts. The prelates represent it as inferior both relatively, in the degree of happiness it provides, and absolutely, in the values to which it is committed, than a life spent in contemplating eternal verities. The active life in society, they argue,

[158] Gregory XIII made him a cardinal in 1583. On this figure see Cozzi, "Paruta, Sarpi, e Ceneda," pp. 190–193.

means loss of privacy and servitude to others; it subordinates the wise man to the fickle crowd; since action is ruled by fortune, it means perpetual uncertainty. In addition it is morally pernicious. The active life is vulnerable to the passions, notably to ambition; the world is man's perpetual enemy and is constantly too powerful for him to resist. Above all the active life tempts man to subordinate the true good to mere utility, to prefer society (man's creation) to the wonders created by God, to place the interests of an earthly city—its precise identity hardly needs stating—above those of the City of God.[159] On the contrary the wise man perceives "that all men should be considered citizens of this great city of the universe, just as one same eternal law has been given for their governance and one same heavenly father, the source of those seeds from which we are all born, our one same head and ruler who governs us and gives us everything that is good among us, the best and greatest God. No other homeland have we than nature, no other law, no other family, no other prince." The wise man is at home whenever he is in the presence of virtue; or, better yet, man in this world is always a pilgrim, and every earthly city is rather an exile for him than a fatherland.[160]

Notable in this indictment is, first of all, its commitment to purely intellectual values and its assumption of the irrelevance to these of all mundane experience, sensible, social, or even moral. The archbishop of Cyprus, Filippo Mocenigo, sees "supreme virtue" as originating only "in the schools of the most wise." [161] Indeed, he seems essentially a dualist who argues that contemplation brings man closer to God than action because it alone is free from the "imperfections of matter." [162] It is of considerable interest that Paruta should now so clearly discern danger to the political life of Venice in the hellenistic intellectuality of the later Renaissance. But it is surprising that he attributes to a group of ecclesiastics at Trent this mixture of Platonism, Stoic withdrawal, and a vague theism. For the advocates of the contemplative life depicted here are not Christian mystics but philosophical recluses. Much of their case consists in depicting contemplation as the most comfortable way of life in a world of troubles; and, as it points to scientific or metaphysical interests, this conception of the *vita contemplativa* seems to reflect not so much its intensification or exaltation as its secularization.

[159] *Vita politica*, pp. 41–57.
[160] Pp. 214–216.
[161] P. 274.
[162] P. 138.

Paruta's rather curious view of the Counter Reformation perhaps reflects the general failure of the Venetian patriciate to comprehend its religious significance as well as his own need, as an amateur rhetorician, to recite all the platitudes usually adduced in discussions of this kind. Yet he also hints at some insight into the social meaning of recent developments. For access to higher truth through a life detached from immediate social responsibility was one ground for the ecclesiastical claim to a general right of direction over all Christians. And by exposing (and perhaps vulgarizing) these arguments, Paruta was preparing to contribute, in a time of growing tension, to the long Venetian struggle against clericalism. It could hardly have been an accident that he represented the archbishop of Cyprus not only as contemptuous of the entire realm of matter but also as a vigorous political Augustinian. The archbishop's deprecation of matter implied that the active life of political duty in the material world is inevitably corrupt. He was bent on reviving the view of society as a response to human depravity, as a mere instrument of discipline devoid of positive values. For this prelate all temporal activity had therefore to be subjected to spiritual direction; politics had ultimately to respond to clerical control.

All of this underlies his effort to minimize, in every possible way, the place of society in human existence. Thus he argues that love of country is a product not of nature but of convention: God arranged that man should be born free (an insidious suggestion to offer in Venetian company), and to represent him as naturally social is to make him inferior to the animals.[163] Again, the archbishop insists, the purposes of government are properly instrumental to higher ends and unworthy to be taken as ends in themselves.[164] The sting of the argument lies, for a Venetian, in the implication that the only human community with an independent basis for existence is the church. But the church is here understood not as any particular ecclesiastical community but only in its universal dimension. The ideal of life implicit in the whole conception would divest human existence of all particular attachments to places or to persons; it would deny the value of particular and concrete experience of any kind. As presented here the contemplative ideal is thus subversive of all aspects of Venetian political and cultural life.

The Venetian reply to this fundamental attack was equally many-sided, but it had first to deal directly with the contemplative ideal. This task Paruta

[163] Pp. 213–214.
[164] P. 49.

assigned to his master, Surian, the major protagonist of *Venezianità* in the first dialogue. Surian does not deny that the contemplation of eternal truth and direct experience of God are, in themselves, the highest good. But he sees the real issue as lying elsewhere. It has to do with the nature of man, created by God with limitations but also specific possibilities. Surian rejects emphatically the clerical identification of man's proper essence with his intellect. For him, man is the intermediate creature of Renaissance thought and therefore a complex mixture of elements appropriate to his middle position in the structure of the universe. He cannot and should not sever his connection with the world of matter, which is not dross to be purged away but an essential part of God's creation. By his very nature man is not fitted to exist exclusively, or even primarily, in the spiritual realm. However appropriate to metaphysical system-building, therefore, the contemplative ideal contradicts the actual nature of man. Contemplative man would be less than true man, would be indeed a kind of corruption, a betrayal of God's purpose. To put the matter in another way, the contemplative ideal represents a confusion of the church triumphant with the church militant. Any human being who proposed to devote this life to the contemplation of eternity would thus be guilty of presumption, of attempting to storm heaven prematurely. He would appear to be evading God's intention in giving him the great gift of earthly life, which is both good in itself and the means to every blessing.[165] Indeed the attitude to life is a fundamental issue in this dispute. To the ecclesiastics life is nothing but an exposure to misery, and the less of it the better. To Paruta and his friends it is filled with values of every description. For this reason Venetians properly rejoiced that their countrymen (as was notorious) tended to live longer than other men. Fullness of years meant fullness of blessings, and it was therefore one of the greatest benefits God could confer on men.[166]

It will be observed, then, that, in Surian's conception, human existence meant both limitation and opportunity. The limitation is primarily intellectual; and Paruta's Venetians display the same skeptical qualities we have

[165] Pp. 117–122. Much of Surian's argument here appears to follow Pomponazzi; cf. P. O. Kristeller, *Eight Philosophers of the Italian Renaissance* (Stanford, 1964), p. 82. Felix Gilbert has called my attention to the presence of similar views in Gasparo Contarini's *Compendium primae philosophiae*, first published in Paris in 1556 and included in two recent editions of Contarini's *Opera* (Paris, 1571, and Venice, 1578). The ideas Surian expressed were thus far from original. What gives them interest to me is not their originality but the situation in which they are developed.

[166] Pp. 281–284.

observed first among the Florentines and to a lesser degree in Contarini, but here raised to an even higher level of articulation. Surian, soundly Pauline, points out that man views the divine light only through a material veil.[169] Barbaro goes even further. He denies that the human mind, which cannot operate without the senses, can approach God by contemplation. "To use the light of the sciences to know God," he observes, "seems to me nothing but wanting to illuminate the face of the sun with the light of a tiny candle." [168] And when Giovanni Delfino, bishop of Torcello, suggests that doubt about man's ability to grasp general truth might be taken as an attack on all schools of philosophy, Surian neglects to contradict him. For Surian Prometheus was not the familiar benefactor of the human race but a prototype of intellectual man, eternally tormented by curiosity concerning matters hidden from him by his own intrinsic limitations and the human situation.[169]

But this sense of the limits of human understanding is closely bound up with a positive conception of man in other respects. If it means some reduction in the value attached to his mental capacity, this is the result of an effort to protect human experience as a whole. Thus Paruta's friends celebrate the life of the senses, the passions, and society as a necessary reflection of man's true essence. For Surian man's sensitive body is his indispensable equipment for all the knowledge of which he is capable in this life. "Although our intellect may be divine from its birth," he asserts, "nevertheless here below it lives among these earthly members and cannot perform its operations without the help of bodily sensations. By their means, drawing into the mind the images of material things, it represents these things to itself and in this way forms its concepts of them. By the same token it customarily rises to spiritual contemplations not by itself but awakened by sensible objects." [170] In Surian's rejection of the identification of man's essence with his intellect we thus begin to perceive more deeply the significance of Paduan discussions about the soul; the derivation of knowledge from sense appears less important as a denial of

[167] P. 123.

[168] P. 141.

[169] Pp. 118–120. This interpretation of Prometheus, again, follows Pomponazzi (cf. Kristeller, p. 77). Pomponazzi's comparison of the philosopher with Prometheus appears in his *De fato*, which was first published at Basel in 1567, that is four years after Paruta's dialogue is supposed to have occurred; but the comparison had probably long circulated at Padua.

[170] P. 116.

Venice as savior of Christendom: an allegory of the Battle of Lepanto *(Veronese)*.

Portrait of Paolo Paruta *(Tintoretto).*

pure intellectuality than as the affirmation of other dimensions of human existence. At the same time the whole position suggests that even the lofty realms inhabited by ecclesiastical contemplatives must rest finally on solid experience in the familiar lay world of time and space. The argument can also be interpreted, therefore, as an oblique attack on the special claims of the clergy.

Barbaro, somewhat further in the discussion, adds to Surian's claims for the life of the senses an argument for the priority of the passions over intellect. The bishop of Ceneda had maintained that the passions "are born from a corrupt judgment of reason concerning good and evil." For Barbaro this view too was based on an excessively simple notion of man. Adducing the power of music (to Venetians now a cherished experience) to arouse or to calm the passions, he insists that "if we will consider all the movements of our soul, it will be clear that the first impressions made there, which are properly affections, precede the discourse of reason . . . the appetitive power is the first to be moved," and reason comes into being only to regulate a set of prior motions.[171] Surian meanwhile has protested against the overly simple Stoic view of man as reducing him almost to "a cold and immobile stone." Man is warm flesh and blood as well as mind, and the two dimensions of his personality are inextricably mingled. To emphasize their complex interdependence Surian points to a variety of psychosomatic symptoms.[172]

The Venetians' understanding of philosophy and its proper function is thus made to depend on a complex analysis of the human personality; and Surian finally sounds remarkably like a man of the Enlightenment. "What, therefore, will be a more noble study, what a truer philosophy, than that which is directed to our human actions and teaches us to regulate well ourselves, our family, and our country?" he asks rhetorically. "Its task," he replies, "is to reawaken spirits and to make them better disposed and readier for civil operations. Thus, directed by it, we can devote ourselves more profitably to the common good."[173]

But our Venetians have dethroned intellect as queen of the soul only to

[171] Pp. 185–188.
[172] Pp. 98–100.
[173] P. 134. Cf. the memorial supplied by Paruta's sons after his death, quoted in V. Cian, "Paolo Paruta, spigolature," *AV*, XXXVII (1899), 121: ". . . stimava molto gl'huomini literati e i prudenti nel saper governar se stesso, et la casa sua, dicendo spesso, che questa era la più bella philosophia, che si potesse imparare; biasimando molto gl'huomini vitiosi, et imprudenti."

replace her with will; and Surian, if he makes the conventional analogy between the soul and a well-ordered city, expresses an ideal of psychological order quite different from Plato's. Reason is reduced to the role of a counsellor, although even in this capacity Surian suggests that she cannot speak with a single, unequivocal voice by likening her to a consultative body of citizens. The will, he declared, should always consult the "opinion of reason," but at the same time it must never abdicate its freedom and sovereignty.[174] For Surian man's virtue depends on his freedom.[175] And again it may be observed that this apparently general position had social and political implications. It implied that although a layman had some responsibility to listen to clerical counsel, he was ultimately responsible for his own acts. It also suggested the moral obligation of Venice to resist dictation from Rome.

If the primary human attribute is not reason but will, it is evident that man is essentially an active rather than a contemplative being; and he fulfills his true nature only in the *vita activa*, which alone affords expression to all elements in his complex personality. This is, indeed, Surian's first proposition, which is made more precise by placing activity directly in a social context. "What is our life but action?" he inquires. "And among our actions none is more noble or more perfect than that which is directed to the service of many. Therefore he who devotes himself to the government of the republic, rising out of indolence, the death of our soul, gives himself to a true and most happy life." [176] And since, for Surian, God himself is no unmoved mover contemplating his own perfections but the active principle of the universe, the active life proves also to be the best way to imitate him. "Man is placed in this world as in a theater in which God sits as spectator of his actions," Surian states; and man's "duty is to imitate the divine operations with his own, and with such imitation to seek as much as he can to resemble God." [177]

Before examining more precisely the meaning of this injunction for social thought, we may observe that Surian's position seems closely related to major tendencies in Venetian Evangelism. Thus in denying the superiority of contemplation Surian goes out of his way to reject any hierarchical ranking of human callings. For him virtue is to be measured by the general disposition of the soul, not by the specific circumstances and particular

[174] P. 179.
[175] As on pp. 80–81.
[176] P. 42.
[177] P. 134.

achievements of men.[178] One consequence of this view is that withdrawal from the particular temptations of active life is like applying an ointment to the surface of a body which is sick in its inmost parts. For it is not society that is evil. The problems of life arise from the fact that men are sinful and bring their wickedness with them to every condition, none of which is in itself better than others.[179] And Barbaro makes an even more direct application of Venetian skepticism to the religious life. He interprets the limitations of the intellect to mean that the intellect is useless for achieving unity with God. If man is to achieve this ultimate end of his existence, he must rather employ the most important and powerful of his faculties. He must endeavor to approach God through the disciplines of the active life, serving him in love through the exercise of will. Only in this way can the obstacles between man and divine grace be removed.[180]

Although (through Barbaro) Paruta invoked the Aristotelian view of society as natural because it is based on family groups biologically rooted in nature,[181] he preferred to argue for its natural character on the basis of the needs of man's complex nature. The full development of man, as God had created him, required a complex environment, which could nourish his senses, give adequate scope for his passions, and provide opportunities for a full moral experience. Therefore, effective government such as Venice provided was singularly valuable because it maintained precisely such an environment. It enabled men to live in a fully human way. Man for Surian was a social, if not essentially a rational, animal.[182]

Government in this conception obviously meant far more than the restraint of man's tendency to sin. It made possible that "civil felicity" so deeply cherished by generations of Venetians, by which they meant all the positive benefits of an advanced civilization. Civil life, as Surian remarked, had gradually developed to "that elegance in which we now see it, full of so many comforts, ornamented with so many virtues." Withdrawal from civil life meant the converse: return to a primitive and detestable barbarism.[183] With this sentiment we have come to an *apologia pro opera sua* of the Venetian patriciate. Surian's argument is that the ruling class in Venice, through

[178] Pp. 42–43, 57–58.
[179] P. 59.
[180] Pp. 139ff.
[181] P. 217.
[182] Surian develops the argument on pp. 42ff. See especially pp. 89–91.
[183] P. 91. On this ground Surian praises Alexander the Great for carrying civilization to the barbarians (p. 135).

service to the state, was engaged in the noble task of preserving the precarious values of higher civilization:

> Certainly, whoever considers the constant danger of a city controlled by wicked, crude, or inexpert men will know that, for their own safety and that of others, the best and wisest are bound to undertake the governance of the republic in order not to let it miserably sink, like a ship abandoned by the pilot .... We owe too great a duty to our country, which is a company of men not come together by chance for a brief time like a band of seafarers, but founded on nature, confirmed by election, always dear and necessary. When the city is in danger we do not risk merely a little merchandise, like the men of a ship, but all that we hold most dear. For the city alone contains in herself our goods, children, family, and friends; and in addition to these external things, our true and highest good, which consists in virtue.[184]

To reject such an obligation would make one "unworthy not only to be called wise but even a man." [185] The ancient commonplaces embedded in these remarks are thus made here to serve a stern practical function. Placed on the defensive, Venice was recalling her values and insisting on her resolution to defend them.

Yet these values are those of individual life. As Surian points out, every man has two basic needs corresponding to the two primary elements of his being: the need for physical comfort and the opportunity to exercise virtue as required by his moral nature. Only civil life satisfies both.[186] And Barbaro, so often a little more enthusiastic than Surian, bursts out: "What other benefit can be compared to what we receive, in every age of our lives, from our country? For it has produced us, nourished us, educated us; preserved for us riches, family, friends; given us honors, nobility, glory." [187] In short only the benefits of life in society supply the proper basis for human happiness. But it is important to notice again the qualification. As Surian declares in his conclusion, to reject the blessings of social existence is to reject humanity in favor of the perfection appropriate to some other nature: that of a beast or a god, but in either case unsuitable to man.[188]

Surian's analysis of man into material and moral elements in the first

[184] Pp. 44–45.
[185] P. 45.
[186] P. 89.
[187] P. 217.
[188] P. 90. Cf. Aristotle, *Politics*, I, 2.

dialogue also provides the basis for a remarkable defense of wealth, in which he joins da Ponte, in the third. For his argument suggests that ascetic renunciation is no more appropriate to human nature than a life of contemplation. Discussion of this subject arises in connection with the familiar problem of what constitutes true nobility, and da Ponte insists on the value of wealth to create an ideal human type. The good food wealth can buy, he argues, makes for a ready intelligence. Riches make possible the best education, the leisure for virtuous actions, liberality and magnificence. For although wealth is morally neutral in itself, it can be put to the highest uses and secure for man a wide range of goods both for the body and the soul. True wisdom, therefore, consists not in despising wealth but in employing it well.[189] At this point Surian enters the debate to make the point that the desire for wealth is rooted in nature and for this reason too is not to be despised:

> The desire to grow rich is as natural in us as the desire to live. Nature provides the brute animals with the things necessary for their lives; but in man, whom it makes poor, naked, and subject to many needs, it inserts this desire for riches and it gives him intelligence and industry to acquire them. Thus with these instruments alone he can procure all things necessary to him, not only to live as the animals do but *to live humanly:* that is to say, with a certain elegance and dignity as required by the civil life that is proper to man. Riches consist in those things that food, clothing, and houses gives us; from these things we not only sustain life and protect ourselves from cold and rain, but from our very necessities we also make to be born a certain delight and splendor, through which this life is more pleasing. Riches rule families and cities, increase good fortune, and prevent us from feeling the blows of bad; and to every action, both private and public, they impart a certain force and marvelous dignity. Wealth is, in a sense, the true mother of all the arts, for the reward it gives for works of art is the true nourishment that supports them. In the city where riches abound, therefore, the arts flourish. Remove the need of the artist and the payment for his works, and men will immediately decline into degraded indolence; but, one side stimulated by need and the other delighted with its precious acquisitions, artists will devote themselves to their varied, beautiful, and useful activities.[190]

[189] Pp. 335–338.
[190] Pp. 338–339; italics mine.

Thus wealth not only provides the necessary basis for human existence but also gives it an esthetic dimension. Surian is in fact offering an eloquent defense of the historic mercantile preoccupations of Venice against the attacks of Counter Reformation asceticism. His argument is that centuries of economic acquisition, centuries of commerce with the infidel, of buying cheap and selling dear, have had their justification in the wonderful city of the lagoons.

Da Ponte's discussion of economic questions also seems to touch on another contemporary preoccupation. His effort to define the nature of money, itself of some interest for the history of economic theory, leads him to distinguish among the forms of wealth; and in doing so he appears to touch on the relation between the agricultural and commercial sectors in the economy of Venice. His own position is conciliatory. He recognizes that, among the kinds of wealth, those are "more true and natural" which support life directly, for example the lands and flocks that produce food and clothing. Gold and silver, the instruments of commerce, he observes, have no virtue in themselves but constitute wealth in only a secondary and derivative sense. But although agriculture thus, in a sense, is closer to nature, da Ponte suggests that this advantage has been historically transcended. For cities and human wants slowly multiplied, and men wished increasingly to trade with other men. Money was therefore invented to facilitate the exchange of goods, themselves originating in nature. Thus in an indirect sense commerce too is natural, and its contribution to the quality of human life is beyond dispute. This is literally true; no member of Paruta's company takes issue with the point.[191]

But the major advantages of life in society for Surian and his friends are not material and esthetic but moral; the final justification of civil life is that it is the most virtuous life. Part of its superiority is that it supplies us with family and friends to love; Paruta's ecclesiastics, on the other hand, when they consider human ties, can think only of the troubles children bring on their parents and grief for the death of a loved one.[192] But civil life is superior above all because it actively exercises and tests man's capacity for virtue. This emerges as the true end of the rich variety of experience possible only in society. "Although any man who is well disposed to virtuous operations can be esteemed virtuous and happy," Surian declares, in this case sounding much like Aristotle, "nevertheless he who performs virtuously

[191] P. 346. Here the deviation from Aristotle is of particular interest; cf. *Politics*, I, 10.
[192] Pp. 352ff.

is more properly virtuous and happy. It is for this purpose that a man should be involved with his republic, that he should promote its dignity, that he should have friends, that he should possess riches, that he should keep himself in health." [193] And once more Barbaro (perhaps in tribute to his ecclesiastical status) is made to push his friend's view to a more exalted level. He reveals, in what for Surian needed no further justification, the preparation for an even higher form of life. He suggests that by accepting the responsibilities of society, the virtuous man is raised "to a nobler service" and approaching closer to God, becomes "fecund with truer virtues." A kind of Thomist rhapsody thus brings the first book to its climax; in God himself the natural virtues of civil life are perfected and reveal their ultimate direction.[194] So Venice ultimately serves a religious end.

Yet this is not, all the same, quite the end, and therefore perhaps not after all Paruta's own firm conviction. The last word in the substantive discussion (for what follows is merely transitional to the next book) is given to Paruta's friend Molino, who suggests the essential irrelevance of such speculation. We are still far from the blessedness envisaged by Barbaro, he remarks, and the way is tortuous and difficult. The immediate need is for practical guidance along the path of virtue in order to avoid the dangers of the road.[195] Thus if Paruta's Venetians, like Gasparo Contarini, have a theoretical bias towards Thomism, in practice they remain committed to the concrete and practical.

This commitment is also reflected in the appreciation Paruta's Venetian laymen exhibit for the variety revealed by experience. Their attitude contrasts sharply with the remoteness from the specific and the concrete which he attributes to his ecclesiastical spokesmen. Nature, Surian asserts, assigns different gifts to different men; and the harmony of the universe is itself a wondrous resolution of the variety of its components.[196] Furthermore peoples differ as well as people;[197] hence the form of government appropriate to one situation may be wrong for another.[198] Thus, although it is true that the whole earth has been given for the habitation of men, it does not follow that the same condition is as good (or bad) for all, or that each man must

[193] P. 98.
[194] Pp. 145–157.
[195] P. 148.
[196] P. 68.
[197] Note, however, that Surian rejects climatic determinism as the basis of such differences (pp. 80–81).
[198] Pp. 390–391.

constantly wander from place to place without a true homeland. Particular men require particular states in which to pursue their particular values. So Barbaro declares:

> It appears that nature herself, just as she has taught us to love most of all what is our own, has distinguished each country with qualities of its own because she wishes us to recognize one rather than another as ours, and to love and appreciate it. Manifestly every city, as though by some privilege of nature, has some things so much its own that the difference is apparent in the various tendencies, both physical and mental, of the men born there. It can be seen that in one place are generated persons of handsome appearance, great height, and vigorous strength, while in another persons who are ugly, short, and weak. Equally the citizens of one city all turn out of subtle intelligence and inclined to the arts and learning, while those of another are obtuse, unpolished, and lazy.[199]

Here Barbaro is evidently contrasting Venice with other human communities left nameless, but he is also making a larger point. Patriotism itself, he is suggesting, as the attachment to a particular place, is rooted in nature. This is proved first by its universality but more profoundly by its indispensability to civil life, itself a requirement of nature. "If the love of country should be destroyed," Barbaro asserts, "all the dignity of civil life would collapse, and all our strivings for the virtues would be in vain." [200] To the ecclesiastical critics of patriotism he is insisting on the right of every Venetian to love Venice.

The importance of Venice as the living reality behind all this apparently general and traditional discussion emerges with special force in the more obviously political sections of the discussion. Here the views of the clerical and lay spokesmen are again directly opposed. The antithesis appears clearly when one of the latter begins an eloquent defense of liberty, without which "man is scarcely a man, much less happy." Thus we are again confronted with the distinction between mere existence and what is appropriate to life as a man. "He who agrees to live according to the will of another," the speaker continues, "is deprived of the most excellent gift of humanity, and he may expect no true praise for his actions, no just reward. If liberty is

[199] P. 220.
[200] P. 216.

removed, every other good is worthless. Indeed virtue itself remains idle and of little value. As the principal condition for a man's becoming happy, therefore, it seems to me that he should ask to be born and to live in a free city in which, although he is not a prince, at least he is not forced to serve." [201] But the bishop of Ceneda immediately takes exception to this ideal of liberty. True liberty means, for him, something utterly different. It is a spiritual condition, a gift of God over which no external force can have effect; it is therefore by definition invulnerable to tyranny. Conversely the real tyrants man should fear are his own passions and worldly attachments.[202] The two sides are now clearly so far apart that they are hardly in communication.

The Venetian defense of liberty here depends on its value in enabling men to live humanly; liberty is by no means represented as an end in itself. Thus Dandolo's distinction between liberty and license, in which comparison between well-ordered Venice and chaotic Florence seems close to the surface, is also appropriate. "Just as it is a very wretched thing to obey the domination of the tyrant," he declares, "so to be subject to a good prince and to good laws cannot be called servitude. Nor is living free true liberty in every republic but often dissolute license which does not promote but harms living well. For good laws reveal the way of the virtues and make it easier." [203] As a means to the good life, nevertheless, liberty is essential.

The division between the two sides is equally sharp on the best form of government. The ecclesiastical preference is emphatically for monarchy, not however on the grounds of experience or appropriateness to human needs but, typically, for the abstract reason that human government should be modeled on the government of the universe, or because human government should conform to the metaphysical principle that perfection depends on the reduction of all things to "unity and to simplicity." [204] Surian is ready to meet this argument on its own terms by submitting that metaphysical perfection is complex rather than simple. "So the simplest elements are the most imperfect," he says; "and as for mixed things, each is the less perfect as it is uniform. And the human body, in order to have the most perfect form, that of the rational soul, was therefore composed of a most excellent mixture of all others." [205] Thus, it appears, the mixed constitution of Venice has some basis in ultimate reality.

[201] P. 371.
[202] P. 371.
[203] Pp. 372–373.
[204] Pp. 382–383.
[205] P. 383.

But Surian's primary defense of republicanism against monarchy is empirical and historical. Thus he insists on the superiority of collective to individual judgment. Perfection, he argues, is denied to any individual but is often conceded to a group. "The virtuous multitude is always more perfect, more wise, more prudent," he declares; "and when the right sort of group is entrusted with the responsibilities of government, marvelous results follow." [206] But his historical argument is of greater interest. He represents monarchy as appropriate to the primitive stage in human development; but, he maintains, with experience and the evolving needs of city life men eventually abolished monarchy in favor of a republic, "in which every good man would participate and could strive for the common good." [207] Not only does this scheme correspond in some degree to the actual development of Venice, but it also suggests that the transformation of Italian republics into principates during the recent past, measured by the natural course of social development, had been regression toward a barbarism once happily transcended. Surian thus implies as well that, as the last great republic in Italy, Venice alone was faithful to the cause of civilization. Against this background an incidental difference over events in Florence assumes some significance. When one of the party cites the expulsion of the Medici in 1494 as an instance of the vulnerability of republics to "the mutable wishes of the people," Surian corrects him: Piero de'Medici had in fact been ruined by his own immoderate ambition.[208] Paruta's friends appear to have absorbed something of Bruto's interpretation of Florentine history.

But on one significant point Paruta's republicans fail to meet the attack on Venetian ways with their customary assurance. When da Ponte, opening a conventional discussion of nobility, appears to suggest that (as in Venice) nobility is essentially a matter of birth, he is promptly challenged by the bishop of Ceneda. Branding da Ponte's position "a vain and fallacious opinion," the bishop attributes it to "the ambition of certain men who, having power in their hands, seek to pass it along to their posterity with this vain claim." On the contrary, he insists, nobility should be based solely on virtue; and his associates add that it might also come from public service or be acquired through education. The bishop of Cyprus, consistently with his earlier position, also proposes that intellectual distinction should be honored as a form of nobility. Thus pushed, da Ponte clarifies his position. Although

[206] P. 385.
[207] P. 380.
[208] Pp. 51, 56.

he insists that virtue tends to run in families, he admits that an old family may deteriorate and lose its claim to true nobility. He admits that public service is an element in nobility, and he notes a general agreement that some combination of virtue and wealth is basic to every definition of nobility. But his conclusion is ambiguous: that, other things being equal, old families are preferable to new.[209] As a defense of the social structure of Venice this seems hardly adequate.

The difficulty here was that argument from the nature of man in general was ill-adapted to justify what was in fact merely conventional. The definition of nobility in Venice was due to historical accident, not to philosophical insight; and the transitional quality of Paruta's work is suggested again by his ability to shift in the middle of debate to a more appropriate mode of discourse. But it is of some interest that this is done not by one of the diplomats but by the bishop of Torcello, who accepts the difficulty of defining nobility in the abstract and acknowledges that the various nobilities of Europe differed widely in actual character. Thus he notes that in France and England the nobility lived far from the cities, devoting themselves to hunting, arms, and the management of their estates. Spain associated nobility with elegance and a splendid mode of life, while in Germany it consisted in jurisdiction, often very petty. Italy, above all, revealed wide contrasts. In Naples and Lombardy, for example, nobility precluded engagement in trade; but "the Venetians, the Florentines, and the Genoese carry on commerce indifferently, so that the noblest among them are, for the most part, the most active merchants." The bishop concludes: "I do not see, therefore, how it is possible to give a general rule about such different customs." [210] Notable here is his insistence that the nobles of Venice are still essentially a mercantile class.

The extension of the dispute to the question whether women possess any capacity for nobility brings the two sides again into direct opposition. Da Ponte once more presents the argument from heredity, this time to rather better effect. He argues that women who are born into noble families inevitably participate in the nobility of their ancestors. The bishop of Ceneda, however, a conventional antifeminist, denies that women are capable of virtue; having only a material role in human reproduction, he argues, they are also incapable of transmitting any "true nobility" to their sons. Surian

[209] Pp. 315–328.

[210] Pp. 329–330. It is of some interest that the conventional Renaissance argument is here presented by an ecclesiastic, who follows Poggio's survey (cf. Burckhardt, II, pp. 79–80) but (in a larger political world) seems to pay more attention to noble classes outside Italy.

then closes the argument by making it more concrete. If women do not exhibit the same heroic forms of virtue as men, he declares, this is only because their responsibilities are different. In fact they are as capable of nobility as men and often excel their husbands "in elegance of manners, grace, and valor." [211]

It is clear that the defense of Venice developed in these pages is to a considerable degree philosophical. Even Surian, elsewhere so eloquent about the specific needs of man, seems to fall into a trap, of which neither he nor Paruta is aware, by appealing to nature as the fixed and ultimate structure of reality. To the charge that civil life implies contempt for the works of nature, a major focus of the contemplative life, Surian replies that, on the contrary, civil life requires the closest study of nature. Nature, he argues, is an essential source of instruction in the moral virtues. But beyond this the good government of the universe is the pattern for good government both in the individual man and in society, for the universe exhibits perfect order, strict obedience to law, and the infallible coordination of various elements for the benefit of the whole.[212] However effective as a debating point, the use of abstract nature as a political model no longer seems the best way to defend the specific character of the Venetian Republic.

The persistence of earlier attitudes is also displayed in the thoroughly conventional praise of the Venetian constitution offered by Dandolo. But although Dandolo adds nothing significant to Contarini's description of this perfect arrangement, on one point he reveals some advance: he is far more interested in governments elsewhere in Europe. He cites ancient examples: Rome and Athens, which had been less successful in preserving the proper mixture of elements; and Sparta, which had evidently done better. But he also points to contemporary examples. The kingdoms of France and Spain, and even more those of Poland and England, he informs the company, "are not simple and true royal governments" but mixed states, comparable to Venice if less perfect, in their balance of monarchy, aristocracy, and popular rule. Germany had done particularly well; there the three elements of good government, represented by "the emperor and various princes and republics," could be seen to "meet together in their diet to decide by common consent the most important things relating to the safety of the whole province." If they were only better regulated by an increase in the power of the emperor,

---

[211] Pp. 331–332. The discussion here has some similarities with that in the first book of Castiglione's *Il cortegiano*.
[212] Pp. 132–134.

Dandolo suggests, "I believe that we could expect marvelous proofs against the Turks from that most noble province, so abounding in men, in arms, and in riches, and in many parts well ordered." [213] The accuracy of Dandolo's description is less significant than his willingness to compare the Venetian constitution with other arrangements in the world of actual practice. He suggests a tendency to conceive of politics less as an abstract and philosophical study than as the empirical examination of concrete reality. Neither he nor Paruta has abandoned the old vision, but the period of its dominance was now drawing to a close.[214] Another set of political attitudes, in which such formulations had little meaning, was now taking shape.

And Paruta's work also suggests that Venetians in the generation following the battle of Lepanto, although without altogether abandoning systematic views, were tending increasingly to look to history for their understanding of human affairs. In an extended section of the second dialogue, those present (although with the significant exception of the more militant of the clergy, who are entirely silent on this subject) discuss a series of problems connected with historical study as though this subject was now much on their minds. It is introduced rather academically. The company had been dealing with particular virtues, and the discussion had turned to the formation of prudence. This is identified as a problem of education, an important matter for Venice;[215] and Barbaro, once a historian, turns the conversation to history. He remarks that, since the experiences of one lifetime are not enough to make a man fully prudent, he "should set himself to observe diligently the things of the past." Barbaro sees history as a vast repository of instructive experience; and thus, he concludes, "just as prudence is the beginning of all our good actions, so it can almost be said that history is the source of prudence." [216]

Furthermore Barbaro is primarily concerned with the political uses of prudence. He is familiar with conventional esteem for the ethical value of history which, he observes with some enthusiasm, is more effective than law to instruct men in virtue. "Laws only give the precepts for living well," he remarks, "but history confirms doctrine with example, which is of greater force in disposing us to embrace goodness." This is true enough but, he asks rhetorically: "How much greater fruit must one hope to obtain from it in

[213] Pp. 391–399.
[214] Cf. Gaeta, "Mito di Venezia," p. 369.
[215] Cf. Dandolo, in *Vita politica*, p. 402.
[216] Pp. 197–199.

ruling the republic well?" For in political life, "because of the diversity of governments and the variety of times, of customs, and of so many other circumstances, it is necessary for a man to have longer experience and of more things if he is to acquire a true prudence so that no situation appears new to him and no accident perturbs him, and so that he can demonstrate from his knowledge of the various human occurrences that he has learned to foresee and to provide for all things." And Barbaro cites examples of successful (but not necessarily virtuous) statesmen nourished by history: Alexander, who had read the Iliad, and Alfonso of Aragon, who (meaning that he read ancient history) claimed to have found his best counsellors among the dead.[217] This celebration of the value of history has, to be sure, a somewhat remote and theoretical quality; Barbaro here seems untroubled by the issues raised by Patrizi. Nevertheless he points to the increasingly important position of history, as the indispensable handmaid of politics, in the culture of the Venetian patriciate.

But Paruta's friends also exhibit a keen interest in the relationship between the form of historical composition and the purpose attributed to it, and this superficially rhetorical problem suggests a growing concern with the nature of historical thought and the problems of causation and generalization. These issues are opened up by Giovanni Grimani, patriarch of Aquileia, who proposes that in order to insure the utility of their work, historians should include frequent didactic passages. But Surian's sense of the proprieties is offended by this suggestion. Every art has its own principles, he argues, and the specific task of the historian is "simply to narrate things as they happened." He wishes to distinguish between the historian on the one hand and the legislator or philosopher on the other. Polybius, Xenophon, and Sallust, he insists, had been political scientists rather than historians, and he repeats Cicero's criticism of Thucydides for treating too much of causes.

The significance of Surian's narrow construction of the historian's function in the evolution of Venetian historicism is somewhat ambiguous. On the one hand it reflects the contemporary impulse to achieve systematic order by rigidly defining literary genres and determining the boundaries between disciplines, as though such delimitation had a place in the ultimate structure of reality. As Grimani suggests in objecting that Surian appeared to reject the distinction between history and annals, Surian's view also tended to impoverish history intellectually. But it freed the historian from the obligation to conform to the requirements of any other science, political, ethical, or

[217] P. 199.

theological; it allowed him to scrutinize events in a totally secular spirit and with complete impartiality. His duty consisted solely in the accurate representation of the past.

The debate between Grimani and Surian thus seems to touch on one of the perennial issues in European historiography; and, like most subsequent historians, Paruta appears to prefer a middle position. He allows Barbaro to resolve the disagreement by making a distinction between necessary and irrelevant *discorsi*, between those that bind a narrative together and those that interrupt it. Faithful history, Barbaro concludes, can train men in prudence, but only if historians expose their facts "not simple and naked but as though clothed in their causes and in all the conditions that accompany them." Although this happy figure suggests some concern with form, Barbaro means primarily that only through thoughtful generalization can the particularities of historical discourse be made to yield useful conclusions. If his view reopens the way from history to philosophy, it thus points also to an awareness of causes and processes in history.[218]

The serious importance of all this theoretical discussion is further revealed in the models of historical practice to which its participants refer. They have evidently read widely, but their favorite historians are Thucydides among the ancients and Guicciardini among the moderns. For Barbaro these two had best achieved the proper balance between narrative and generalization, although he found Guicciardini somewhat less praiseworthy for having included "the vain rumors of the crowd together with the most true causes of things." [219] But what is chiefly significant here is the evidence that, in spite of some lingering resentment at Guicciardini's treatment of Venice, Venetian patricians were now prepared to school themselves in the historical and political wisdom of Renaissance Florence.[220]

It is hardly surprising, therefore, that Paruta's protagonists from time to time engage in speculation reminiscent of Machiavelli. Dandolo, for example, reviewed the political cycle; Rome, he noted, had made the full circuit, from Tarquin to Caesar, in five centuries. "This easy changeability," he observed

[218] Pp. 199–203.
[219] P. 203. Cf. the remarks of Luigi Contarini, p. 200.
[220] For Paruta's own appreciation of Guicciardini, see also his *Discorsi politici*, in *Opere politiche*, II, 258, where he refers to Guicciardini as "per vero dire, in molte parti eccellente istorico." There were many Venetian editions of Guicciardini's *Storia d'Italia*, and his *Ricordi* were also printed in Venice in 1582. Valier, on the other hand, felt certain reservations about Guicciardini's "subtle pursuit of causes"; cf. Cozzi, "Pubblica storiografia," pp. 248–250.

without suggesting that there might be an exception, "is a kind of imperfection common to all states." [221] He makes this observation the point of departure for a description of the mixed constitution as an antidote to the universal weakness of states; but the remedy, after this, seems little more than a delaying action. Grimani, too, minimizes the power of fortune in human affairs. It is no more than an invention of the human intellect, he thinks, to conceal its ignorance of causes; he insists that, although all things are ruled by Providence, many can be controlled by prudence. "If a man knows how to make use of this," he concludes, "he need have little care for the favor of fortune." [222] To be sure, there is nothing novel about such speculation, but we have encountered little of it before in Venice.

In one respect, nevertheless, Venetian historical discourse retained its distinction. Although the Venetians could not altogether dismiss the cyclical view of history, their own long record of freedom, stability, and material improvement encouraged them, whatever the tribulations of less prudent peoples, to interpret history as a reasonably steady progress from barbarism to civilization. On this basis they continued to reject the imitation of antiquity as man's best hope for improvement. Thus when Barbaro denounces the literary and intellectual decadence of his own age, he is aiming at the slavish cult of the ancients. In fact, he declares, the imitation of antiquity will not do because times have changed.[223] And Surian makes a vigorous reply to the charge that the world has declined in magnificence and greatness since the fall of Rome, in which he combines the familiar idea of rebirth with a claim to the superiority of the modern world:

> I would not like us to have so debased a view of ourselves and our age, and I think it quite wrong. If the use of magnificence has varied in its particular operation through diversity in customs and the revolution of empires, this virtue is not in fact extinct. We see it shine forth very clearly among many princes and republics of this time. Indeed, whoever considers rightly may easily recognize that for some time now this noble virtue has been returned to the light of the world, together with various other arts and virtues, since its burial among the ruins of the barbarians; and the modern age can be compared in beauty to antiquity. If our contemporaries are not accustomed to build theaters, baths, or

[221] P. 391.
[222] Pp. 296–297.
[223] Pp. 63–64.

other such edifices, we have others to compare with them and perhaps
to surpass them, both in the greatness and durability of the work and
in the beauty and convenience they bring to the public.

He points in evidence to Venetian fortresses, as impressive in their way as
Roman aquaducts; to modern churches like St. Peter's in Rome, which rival
Roman temples; to modern tourneys, not only as colorful as ancient spec-
tacles but also nobler and more pleasing. But above all he takes pride in the
domestic architecture of his own time. "In private buildings and in domestic
magnificence," he asks, "what can be added to the usage of our age? There
is almost no city in Italy that is not embellished with many noble palaces.
In addition villas and numerous other noble buildings with delightful gardens
constructed by modern men give the truest evidence of magnificence, for
they serve not only necessity but also pleasure and the honor of families." [224]
We may observe again how the superiority of the modern age over ancient
Rome is based chiefly on the arts of peace, above all on such glories as are
peculiarly visible in Venice.

    Much in Paruta's dialogue, on both sides, is familiar and even trite, and
much of its interest comes only from its setting in place and time. His political
vision also has obvious limitations. It is still remarkably bookish and academic,
and in this respect clearly inferior to that of the great Florentines. In spite of
his admiration for Guicciardini, Paruta seems hardly yet to have registered
the impact of the great national monarchies on political life; his *homo politicus*
is still only the inhabitant of a small city state. Meanwhile his attempt to
justify civic life as the most virtuous form of existence, however useful to
meet contemporary attack, suffers badly, as realistic analysis, by comparison
with Machiavelli, against whom it was perhaps directed. Nevertheless the
naturalism at the heart of the argument points to the autonomy of the moral
life and of politics itself, and the deepening of Venetian historicism to which
Paruta attests hints at a major shift in perspective. Scattered through the book,
furthermore, is a succession of insights which suggest the slow growth of a
more sophisticated political consciousness than Venice had yet revealed.[225]

    Both the renewal of Venetian political energies after Lepanto and the am-
bivalence of this period also found expression in the redecoration of the

---

[224] Pp. 254–256.
[225] For the mixture of modern and traditional elements in Paruta, see Candeloro, pp.
95–96, and Pompeati, "Dottrine politiche," pp. 340ff.

Palazzo Ducale. In 1574 and 1577 fires swept through major sections of the building, leaving nothing but blackened walls; and its repair gave Venice an opportunity for a new declaration of the glories of the Republic. Plans for the walls and ceilings of the Great Council Chamber and the adjoining Hall of the Scrutinio were made with great care. Two nobles, Jacopo Contarini and Jacopo Marcello, were chosen, largely for their knowledge of history, to plan a series of paintings for these huge rooms with the help of the Florentine artist Girolamo Bardi. Great importance was attached to the work, which was rapidly pressed forward and engaged the most talented painters of Venice, among them Tintoretto, Paolo Veronese, and Palma Giovane. As an official statement the whole project lacked the subtlety and occasionally the political sensitivity of Paruta's work. Nevertheless it was judged significant enough to require systematic interpretation by Bardi, in a book published in 1587. Its long title conveys the spirit of the enterprise: *Declaration of All the Histories Contained in the Paintings Recently Placed in the Halls of the Scrutinio and Great Council of the Ducal Palace of the Most Serene Republic of Venice, in Which Is Contained Full Information about the Most Famous Victories Won over Various Nations of the World by the Venetians.*[226]

The new decorative scheme was thus conceived as a historical statement for the regular contemplation of the Venetian patriciate in its official place of assembly.[227] Its specific purpose was to provide examples of virtue and heroism from the past for imitation in the present, in the familiar manner of humanist historiography. Those entrusted with the plan were generally directed to choose episodes to demonstrate "how nobly the Republic has striven in all times and in every age." [228] Bardi's book was intended to make sure that the lesson would be lost on no one. He had written it, he explained, "in order that everyone may know everything that is contained in every picture . . . so that he can more easily imitate these famous heroes, and to leave an honored memorial of their operations to the posterity which will be born in future ages in this most Serene Republic." [229]

[226] *Dichiaratione di tutte le istorie, che si contengono ne i quadri posti novamente nelle Sale dello Scrutinio, & del Gran Consiglio, del Palagio Ducale della Serenissima Republica di Vinegia, nella quale si ha piena intelligenza delle più segnalate vittorie; conseguite di varie nationi del mondo da i Vinitiani.* For further indication of the importance with which the project was regarded by contemporaries, see the full notice in Morosini, *Historia veneta*, VI, 644–645.

[227] Patrizi, *Della historia*, sig. D2^r, with particular reference to the earlier paintings in the Great Council Chamber, had asked: "Et che altro è quella dipintura . . . che una historia?"

[228] *Dichiaratione*, sig. A2^r.

[229] Sigs. H7^v–H8^r.

Contarini and Marcello were instructed to include in the new scheme the effigies and insignia of the doges as before the fire, and also (as before) the full story of the events of 1177.[230] But the special attention given to Venetian exploits in battle seems to reflect the new spirit stimulated by Lepanto. Victories from every period of Venetian history are celebrated: the original defense of Venetian liberty against the Franks, victories over Genoa, successes against the Turks, triumphs over the tyrants of the mainland, the major victories after 1509, and Lepanto itself. The theme hints that in the years ahead Venice might no longer be so content with the passivity of the middle century. Some of the paintings were also intended to exalt Venetian republicanism. Thus the Serenissima is depicted as a liberator under whose benevolent rule existed various peoples "who, though they may nominally be deprived of communal liberty," as Bardi explains, "live once more secure from becoming the prey of cruel and avaricious tyrants." [231] Another work pictures the legendary eagerness of the citizens of Nuremberg to imitate the Venetian constitution.[232]

At the same time the curious piety in a number of the paintings suggests the mentality of Agostino Valier rather than of Paruta. A work in the Hall of the Scrutinio, for example, describes the resignation of the thirteenth-century doge Pietro Ziani to enter a monastery: a singular model in view of the traditional Venetian attitude to public service, even though Bardi explained that Ziani, as a religious, prayed for the salvation of Venice as well as his own.[233] Another work depicts the doge piously rejecting that Turkish aid against the League of Cambray which Venice had in fact actively solicited;[234] and still another holds up for admiration (and presumably emulation) the example of Pietro Zeno, a Venetian general who, with his entire household, was slaughtered at an altar by the Turks because he ignored warnings of approaching danger in order to finish his prayers.[235] In spite of its hints of assertiveness and its appeal to history, this iconographic scheme largely represents a period in Venetian history now drawing to a close.

The redecoration of the Palazzo Ducale reminds us that, although signs were mounting of a change in political climate both within Venice and in the surrounding world, the Venetian government altered little for a decade

[230] Described by Bardi, sigs. D7^{r}ff.
[231] Sig. H7^v.
[232] Sig. H4^v for Bardi's explanation.
[233] Sigs. D3^v–D4^r.
[234] Sigs. H4^v–H5^r.
[235] Sig. H1^v for Bardi's explanation.

after Lepanto. Still dominated by a small group of conservative families, Venice maintained her detachment from the great powers and the appearance of respect for the Holy See that seemed to have protected her so well for more than half a century. But, during the last two decades of the sixteenth century, the subtle and gradual modifications in the Venetian mood that had been gathering force for twenty years at last produced a major shift in Venetian politics. A new phase in the history of the Republic opened with the political crisis of 1582, which resulted in the overthrow of the conservative faction that had long dominated Venetian affairs and its replacement by new men with significantly different views. A majority of the patriciate chose to engage, at this point, in an open revolt against its old leaders. These men had managed the Republic primarily through the Council of Ten, and the revolt struck directly at that body by the refusal of the Great Council to designate a new *Giunta* to aid it in controlling the various agencies of the state. The Great Council then went on to strip the Council of Ten of responsibility for public finance, which was transferred to the Senate.[236]

This set of changes was as complex in its background as in its implications. The battle of Lepanto undoubtedly played an important part in its moral background, inspiring hope and thereby converting discontent into an active force. The struggle may also have been in some degree a product of tension between generations, a striking phenomenon in a society that had traditionally venerated the wisdom of age. Contemporaries were quick to note the predominance of younger men in the affairs of the Republic during the closing years of the century; and the papal nuncio was particularly inclined to attribute what, in his eyes, was an unfortunate course of events to the impulsiveness and inexperience of youth.[237] The reformers, from this standpoint, were *giovani*.

But older men were also prominent among the challengers. Together with their younger colleagues and partisans, they addressed themselves to issues of general interest, notably that of the Venetian constitution, whose traditional character, as they believed, was being slowly subverted in the direction of oligarchy. Both Paruta and Bardi had hinted at concern over this possibility during the previous decade. Paruta made Surian observe that tyranny can be exercised by a group as well as by an individual and that of the two kinds of despotism the collective sort might be the worse;[238] and among

---

[236] Stella, "Regolazione delle entrate e la crisi politica," pp. 166ff., for the course of events. See also Besta, *Il Senato veneziano*, pp. 146ff.

[237] Stella, "Regolazione delle entrate e la crisi politica," p. 161.

[238] *Vita politica*, pp. 387–388.

the directions to Contarini and Marcello for the decoration of the Great Council chamber was the stipulation that they must not appear to attribute the greatness of Venice only to a few families.[239] In the traditional language of Venetian politics, the mixed constitution with all its perfections, which had so long guaranteed the stability and survival of the Republic, had been endangered by recent developments.[240]

In addition recent shifts in the economy suggested, to substantial numbers among the patriciate, that the traditional sources of Venetian prosperity were being eroded. Members of the Great Council who were primarily engaged in trade in the eastern Mediterranean, including many of the lesser nobility, were alarmed by the increasing diversion of capital to agriculture and to Atlantic ventures.[241] Convinced that the economic future of Venice was unalterably tied to the Levant, their distrust of the recent conduct of Venetian affairs seemed born out by growing economic difficulties after Lepanto. Among the afflictions of the Republic had been the terrible plague of 1576, which took forty thousand Venetian lives;[242] the mounting activity of corsairs, especially the Uskoks, who preyed on Venetian commerce, with tacit Habsburg encouragement, from their island strongholds off the Istrian coast;[243] and the increasing competition of French and English merchants in the Mediterranean. Meanwhile, because timber for ship construction was becoming scarce and the expansion of the Arsenal with its higher wages discouraged private enterprise, Venetian shipbuilding, after flourishing during the middle decades of the century, began a serious decline; and Venetian cargoes after Lepanto were increasingly transported in vessels purchased abroad.[244] In addition the Republic was beset by a serious lack of capital. This had various causes. The needs of the government, especially for war, had tied up much Venetian capital in forced loans, and the general European price rise tended to reduce the value of the assets in Venetian banks, so that

---

[239] *Dichiaratione*, sig. A2ᵛ.

[240] On the constitutional significance of the reforms of 1582, see Maranini, *La costituzione dopo la serrata*, pp. 425–428; and Sandi, *Principi di storia civile*, III, Part 2, 492–497. Morosini, *Historia veneta*, VII, 6–15, saw these developments as the only important constitutional development of the century.

[241] Cozzi, *Contarini*, pp. 14ff.

[242] Morosini, *Historia veneta*, VI, 624–635, gives this catastrophe full treatment.

[243] Contemporary concern is reflected (among others) by Pietro Giustiniani, sig. MMMMM1ᵛ, and Morosini, VI, 193–194. For modern discussion see Gunther E. Rothenberg, "Venice and the Uskoks of Senj, 1537–1618," *Journal of Modern History*, XXXIII (1961), 148–156; and esp. Alberto Tenenti, *Venezia e i corsari, 1580–1615*. (Bari, 1961.)

[244] Lane, *Venice and History*, pp. 17–22; Romano, "La marine marchande vénitienne," pp. 46–47.

they were unable to supply safely the needs of Venetian commerce. Thus they were overextended, with the result that the second half of the century saw a series of bank failures which reached a climax with the collapse of the second Pisani-Tiepolo bank in 1583. Each failure increased the distress of the smaller commercial nobles, who lost both their small fortunes and their means of raising additional capital, while leaving untouched the agrarian fortunes of the minority of wealthy families. The special problems of Venice in this respect were also intensified by the general crisis of European capital after 1580; this helps to explain the particular timing of the Venetian political crisis. Men blamed the government for the general predicament, and in fact its financial adminstration was anything but perfect. Too many agencies collected too many levies; and the complexities and irrationalities of the fiscal system raised the level of collections without corresponding benefit to the state, permitted evasions of various sorts, and interfered with commerce so that foreign merchants were sometimes driven elsewhere.[245]

The sturdy traditionalism that found expression in demands for restoration of the constitution and more aggressive promotion of Venetian interests in the Mediterranean was also increasingly sensitive to the Italian position of the Republic. The *giovani* were far more concerned than those whom they displaced with the danger posed by Spain and by the aggressive papacy of the Counter Reformation.[246] Friction with Rome was increasing, and it reached a significant climax on the eve of the triumph of the *giovani*. Several incidents had recently aggravated this relationship. In 1578, for example, the pope denounced a proposal, which a number of Venetians were now beginning to support, for a renewal of regular diplomatic relations with England; and the doge had barely concealed his resentment. Anger at the pope's jurisdictional triumph of 1580 also increased Venetian sentiment in favor of a more vigorous policy toward the church; and in the same year the pope's demand that all Venetian monasteries be regularly inspected by his nuncio left further bad feeling. The issue was settled by a compromise; convents of nuns were excluded, and Venetian prelates were to be associated with the nuncio in his visitations to other monastic houses. But emotion had meanwhile run high on both sides. The pope had threatened spiritual censure, and some Venetians had begun to talk of secession from the Latin to the Greek rite as a protest against "a novelty so prejudicial to secular privileges." [247] To many

---

[245] Stella, "La crisi economica veneziana," 17–69.
[246] See, in general, Cozzi, *Contarini*, pp. 6ff.
[247] Stella, *Chiesa e Stato*, pp. 21–40.

Venetians the old government had failed to guard their most sensitive and vital interests.

Occasional expressions of discontent with those directing the state were heard even before Lepanto. Periodically during the century the Senate had attempted to limit the powers of the Council of Ten, though with little success.[248] The Ten were blamed for the unfavorable terms of peace with the Turks in 1540,[249] and in 1565 the Senate had tried unsuccessfully to assume the supervision of public finance.[250] In 1578 it made another attempt. With the support of the Great Council, it established a new magistracy to supervise public accounting; but the Council of Ten managed to frustrate this move by having the new officials chosen from its own ranks. Elections to the dogeship also gave some opportunity for protest against the policies of the ruling group. Thus in 1567, instead of being amicably arranged in advance by the dominant families as had happened for some time, the election was bitterly disputed. Seventy-six ballots in fourteen days having failed to designate a candidate, a compromise had finally to be arranged.[251] But the real turning point came in 1578, with the election as doge of Nicolò da Ponte, whom we have already met among Paruta's friends at Trent. Notoriously anti-Spanish and *persona non grata* at the Curia because of his staunch defense of Venetian jurisdiction, da Ponte presided over the events of 1582, which his election had foreshadowed.[252]

Da Ponte's republicanism and his views about the current plight of Venice afford some insight into the practical significance of the views Paruta attributed to the patricians at Trent. As doge, da Ponte proved an ardent defender of the traditional ways of the Republic. When the nuncio complained of Venetian delay in bowing to the pope's demands regarding the visitation of monasteries, da Ponte had pointed out firmly that the constitutional processes of Venice made her different from other states with which Rome might be accustomed to deal. In Venice, he declared, "the Prince could not say *sic volo, sic iubeo,* and not even the *Savi* could promise

[248] Maranini, *La costituzione dopo la serrata*, p. 418.

[249] Cozzi, *Contarini*, p. 17. Paruta, *Historia vinetiana*, p. 448, recorded in this connection the refusal of the Council of Ten to carry out an order of the Senate.

[250] Stella, "Regolazione delle entrate e la crisi politica," pp. 163–164. Valier, p. 385, noted the criticism of the Ten but declined to discuss its merits.

[251] Stella, pp. 159–165.

[252] For da Ponte's election and career, see Nardi, "La scuola di Rialto e l'umanesimo veneziano," pp. 133–137; Aldo Stella, "Guido da Fano, eretico del secolo XVI al servizio dei re d'Inghilterra," *Rivista di Storia della Chiesa in Italia*, XIII (1959), 234–235; and *Chiesa e Stato*, pp. 12–16.

anything firm on any matter whatsoever." In all matters, he said pointedly, it was necessary "to move a mechanism as great as the whole body of the Pregadi, where many participate and where each man is the free master of his own will." [253]

Shortly before his death in 1583, da Ponte prepared a memorandum for the Senate in which he sought to remind his countrymen of dangers which, he believed, had recently been too little heeded.[254] The document is primarily concerned with Spain, which da Ponte bitterly blamed for the Venetian loss of Cyprus. The Spanish king now aspired, he charged, to rule the whole of Italy; and he particularly accused Spain of a deep hatred for Venice: for da Ponte the Turk has been entirely replaced by Spain as the Republic's most dangerous enemy. Indeed da Ponte thought of Constantinople, along with France, chiefly as a prospective foe of Spain and thus a potential ally of Venice. He also blamed Spain, at least in part, for the growing pressure from Rome. The pope had refused Venice permission to tithe her clergy, he declared, because Venice would not serve the Spanish interest. In this precarious situation da Ponte advised his countrymen to seek peace with all Christian princes, but also (as though he judged the effort likely to fail) to maintain herself in a state of military readiness.

The views of da Ponte indicate that the opinions of the *giovani* were by no means limited to less prominent members of the patriciate. Their position found a number of eminent supporters, including some from families such as the Priuli with major agricultural interests. A high proportion of the leadership of the movement also came from families which claimed to go back to the earliest period of Venetian history. Some of these, for example the Morosini, had taken a leading part in trade with the Levant; but they had generally enjoyed little political influence since the fourteenth century.[255] Numerical support was provided, however, by lesser patricians in the Great Council who had for some time carried little weight in the government of the Republic. Among these was Paruta, whose rapid rise now suggested that the advent of the *giovani* had at last opened careers to new men of talent. So long without political employment, Paruta was suddenly elected to a minor

---

[253] Quoted by Stella, *Chiesa e Stato*, p. 36.

[254] Published under the title "Ricordi del doge da Nicolò da Ponte per il buon governo della Patria in pace ed in guerra," ed. N. Barozzi, in *Raccolta veneta. Collezione di documenti relativi alla storia, all'archeologia, alla numismatica*, I (Venice, 1866), 5–17.

[255] Stella, "Regolazione delle entrate e la crisi politica," p. 169, for a list of prominent *giovani* families.

office in 1581; and in November of 1582, just as the reform movement was gathering force, he was elevated to the College.[256]

The events of 1582 were hardly sufficient to restore the waning greatness of the Republic, whose basic problems were beyond local solution; and the shift of effective control from the Council of Ten to the Senate appears, in itself, of little significance.[257] But the impact of these changes on the conduct of Venetian policy and above all on the Venetian political consciousness was considerable, and for the next thirty years the government of the Republic was animated by a rather different spirit. The victory of the *giovani* ended the mixture of complacent isolation and passivity which had largely determined Venetian policy since the early decades of the century. By taking up the idea of reform, the *giovani* revealed some awareness that change and corruption were inescapable and that the survival of the state depended on constant vigilance, an unsentimental analysis of political forces, regular adaptation to circumstance, and a willingness to take initiative.

[256] Candeloro, pp. 51–52, links Paruta's public career directly to the triumph of the *giovani*.

[257] As has been argued by Stella, "Regolazione delle entrate e la crisi politica," pp. 168–171. Stella sees the affair as little more than a transfer of power from one narrow interest group to another.

· V ·

Venice Under the *Giovani*

THE triumph of the *giovani* during the winter of 1582–83 produced a general readjustment in Venetian policy both at home and abroad. The change was not absolute. The attitudes that had controlled the Republic during the middle decades of the century did not disappear, and they continued to find rhetorical and political expression in the next generation. The transition from one kind of political vision to another was still only partial; and most Venetians, including the new leadership of the Republic, lived uneasily between them. The new government of Venice was nevertheless animated by a rather different spirit from what had previously prevailed. It was at once more sensitive to the dangers surrounding the Republic and more firmly resolved to deal actively with them. Recognizing some decline in her status and prospects, it had less confidence in the survival of the Republic. At the same time it dreamed of restoring the glories of her past.

Early in his *Historia vinetiana* Paolo Paruta thoughtfully reviewed Venetian history during the decades since 1510 in a passage which, though it deals with an earlier period, nicely epitomizes the more sophisticated attitudes of the new generation. "All things human are ruled by a certain variety and change, so that they may be seen sometimes to increase and sometimes to diminish in a perpetual cycle," Paruta wrote. "The Republic had for a long time enjoyed a continuous prosperity, but now it was necessary to learn to tolerate adversity. When the condition of the times changed, she could easily revive her first reputation and recover her empire and her ancient glory. Meanwhile it was essential to employ much prudence and moderation rather than to do violence to the time and, by too much accelerating the reborn greatness of the Republic, conduct it to its final ruin." [1] In the same way the group that assumed the direction of the Venetian government during the last decades of the century recognized the vulnerability of the Republic to historical change and the particular precariousness of its own time. But it hoped too that, through some combination of sensitive calculation, firmness, and deliberate action, the decline of Venice might be stemmed and disaster averted. Perception of the past as alteration for the worse was also a necessary

[1] P. 9.

condition of aspirations for the political revival of the Republic, a possibility largely precluded by the ideal vision of Contarini and his followers.

The moral and political leader of the *giovani* was Leonardo Donà, whom we have previously encountered as a young man in the circle surrounding Francesco Patrizi. Born in 1536, Donà had received an extensive education based on the classics and history, in which he retained a profound interest. His family had long been engaged in the Mediterranean trade; but, finding commerce less profitable after Lepanto, it had recently concentrated on its extensive lands on the *terraferma*. The family had also been prominent in the service of the Republic. As a youth Leonardo had spent some time in Cyprus, where his father was governor. Even then he had been dismayed by the disorderly administration and weak defenses of the island, which appeared to invite attack. His brother Andrea was killed at Lepanto. His family had thus been intimately acquainted with the recent difficulties of the Republic.[2]

Leonardo's public career began in 1561 with his election as one of the *savi agli ordini*, a magistracy charged with administration of maritime affairs; it also brought membership in the College and was a considerable distinction for so young a man. This was the first in a series of major appointments both at home and abroad.[3] During the war of Cyprus, though still only in his thirties, he was ambassador to Spain; the peace ending the war seemed to him disgraceful and put him decisively in opposition to the old ruling group.[4] In 1577 he served as special ambassador to congratulate the new Habsburg emperor, Rudolph II. During the crucial months of the *giovani* revolt he was ambassador to Rome, where he defended Venetian jurisdictional claims with notable firmness as well as a remarkable legal and historical erudition.[5] Later, as a procurator of Saint Mark, he endeavored to breathe a new conscientiousness and order into the management of the charitable foundations

[2] Federico Seneca, *Il doge Leonardo Donà. La sua vita e la sua preparazione politica prima del dogado* (Padua, 1959), pp. 3–38; Cozzi, *Contarini*, pp. 18–20.

[3] For a synopsis of Donà's official career see *Paolo V e la Repubblica veneta. Giornale dal 22 Ottobre 1605–9 Giugno 1607*, ed. Enrico Cornet (Vienna, 1859), p. 13 n. 3; hereafter cited as Cornet.

[4] His dispatches from Madrid have been published under the title *La legazione di Madrid. Dispacci dal 1570 al 1573*, ed. Mario Brunetti and Eligio Vitale (Venice, 1963). For his opposition to the peace, see pp. xliv–xlvi.

[5] Cf. his preparation of the case for the authority of Venice over the patriarchate of Aquileia, described by Seneca, *Donà*, p. 132.

and endowments of the Republic.[6] This was the man who, on his return from Rome in 1583, was generally hailed as chief of the reformers.[7]

But Donà's influence over his contemporaries came less from his distinguished public service than from a moral and political constitution which, in the purest and most rigorous form, expressed the civic ideals of a whole generation of militant young Venetians. As a statesman and personality he brought to a climax the centuries-long evolution of a political type. He felt an almost sacerdotal devotion to public office, in which he aimed totally to submerge his private identity. In 1583 he wrote to the Senate: "I should like to be known in the Roman Curia as ambassador of Venice, which through the grace of God I am recognized and considered to be, and not as Leonardo Donà; and equally in Venice as senator of that fatherland, when it happens that I am called to serve her, and not by my private name. And when complaints are made of me, may they be of the ambassador and senator of your Serenity, that is of yourself, and not of my private person." [8] He probably kept a youthful vow of chastity to the end of his life,[9] a gesture with as much civic as religious meaning; and his prudence, self-discipline, and austerity of life were acknowledged even by his enemies. His friends held him up as a model for the imitation of young Venetians.[10] Both groups found him reserved, imperturbable, almost inhuman in his control; even Sarpi complained that "one never knows whether he loves or hates anything." [11] Such a personality infuriated his opponents, who sourly described him as "pedagogue of the Republic," [12] but it was also, with the new generation, one of the secrets of his leadership. To the younger nobles, according to a hostile source, he was particularly affable, spending much time discussing with them "the government of the republic, the preservation of liberty, political life, and reason of state, of which he was a great professional . . . . with his dignified appearance and white hair, and above all with his marvelous eloquence and with the reputation already acquired of being the Aristides of the Republic, he had so great an influence that the majority of

---

[6] See Mario Brunetti, "Il Diario di Leonardo Donà procuratore di S. Marco de citra (1591-1605)," AV Ser. 5, XXI (1937), 101–123.

[7] Seneca, Donà, pp. 161–162.

[8] Quoted by Seneca, pp. 229–230, n. 2.

[9] Cozzi, Contarini, p. 37.

[10] Ibid., p. 34. Agostino Valier, a close friend of his youth, dedicated educational treatises to him.

[11] Conversation with Christoph von Dohna, July 28, 1608, in Briefe und Akten, II, 78.

[12] Cozzi, Contarini, p. 33.

the young nobles of Venice, brought up in his school, considered him as Pythagoras and as an oracle." [13] Dona was evidently a man in whose judgment a generation that had long felt helpless and adrift could repose absolute confidence.

Nicolò Contarini, his younger associate, gives much the same impression. Born in 1553, Contarini came from a family of only moderate wealth. But it had also a long record of service to the state, and it was well connected; his mother was a Morosini, and he was distantly related to the Donà.[14] Attracted in his youth to mathematical and philosophical studies at Padua, Contarini had composed a speculative treatise *De perfectione rerum*, which he published in 1576.[15] But it was typical of his generation that Contarini soon moved from contemplation into political affairs, as Paolo Sarpi would also do;[16] the *giovani* seemed bent on reversing a tendency general in the later Renaissance, some Venetian examples of which we have already noticed. But, although Contarini was later embarrassed to recall his contemplative phase and pointed out that he had soon passed to "higher and more useful studies,"[17] the speculative element in his youthful work was hardly extreme. He had dedicated it to Donà, and in the epistle he observed (like a true Venetian) that philosophy finds its perfection only in utility to the state and to other human needs.[18] Soon after the reforms of the *giovani*, Contarini was converted altogether to the *vita activa*. During the last two decades of the century he served Venice in a series of magistracies, particularly those concerned with finances and hydraulic engineering. By 1601 he was in the College.

Paolo Paruta emerged during the period of the *giovani* as one of the most effective servants of the Republic and moved through a succession of increasingly responsible offices. By 1591 he was governor of Brescia, in 1592 he went to Rome as ambassador, in 1596 he became procurator of Saint Mark, and the next year he was made superintendent of fortifications. At the time of his death in 1598 he was considered a strong candidate for

---

[13] From the papalist *Historia delle differenze fra Paolo V e li Signori Venetiani* of Giuseppe Malatesta, quoted by Cozzi, pp. 39–40.

[14] For details concerning his family and early career, see Cozzi, pp. 53ff.

[15] Discussed by Alberto Tenenti, "Il 'De perfectione rerum' di Nicolò Contarini," *BSV*, I (1959), 155–166.

[16] This comparison has been made by Cozzi, *Contarini*, p. 57.

[17] As reported by Paolo Sarpi in a letter to Jacques Leschassier, Nov. 10, 1609, Ulianich, pp. 60–61.

[18] Tenenti, pp. 155–156.

doge. Appointed official historiographer in 1579, he also (unlike his predecessors in that office) finished substantial historical works, and he composed a series of political discourses, an interesting religious testament, and an unusually long account of his Roman embassy remarkable for its cool historical analysis and its undercurrent of republican indignation and reformist zeal. Paruta was not the most radical member of his generation, but he provides an illuminating expression of its attitudes and dilemmas.

The social and intellectual headquarters for the new leadership of the Republic was the house of the brothers Andrea and Nicolò Morosini, at San Luca on the Grand Canal.[19] The Morosini, one of the old families still devoted to commerce in the Levant, had taken a leading part in the changes of 1582, and Andrea had been a youthful associate of Paruta, whom he would eventually succeed as historian of Venice. The *ridotto Morosini* for some years brought together an extraordinary group of men: patrician statesmen, clergy, intellectuals. Among its participants were Donà, Contarini, and Antonio Querini, one of the major literary defenders of Venice at the time of the interdict; influential secretaries of various state agencies who shared their views like Agostino Dolce and Giambattista Padavino, eventually chancellor of Venice; learned monks such as Paolo Sarpi and his younger friend Fulgenzio Micanzio; and scientists, among them Galileo and Aquapendente. In spite of the variety in their social backgrounds, these men met and talked as equals, a point worth noting in a period when distinctions of class were generally more pronounced.[20] The group was also remarkable for its openness to ideas from all directions, especially from France. Sarpi first began to admire Gallicanism during this period,[21] and the Morosini circle was hospitable to Bruno on his return to Italy in 1591. Andrea Morosini, cited before the Inquisition in 1592 and questioned about his acquaintance with Bruno, defended the accused heretic; and Donà fought his extradition to Rome in the Senate.[22] Micanzio remembered the house of Morosini years later as "one of the most celebrated spots consecrated to the Muses." In it, he wrote, had "assembled a great part of those who made a profession of letters, not only of the nobility, all of whom present became

[19] For what follows see, in general, Antonio Favaro, "Un ridotto scientifico a Venezia al tempo di Galileo Galilei," *AV*, Ser. 2, V (1893), 199–209; and Cozzi, pp. 49–51.

[20] Fulgenzio Micanzio, *Vita del Padre Paolo dell'ordine de' Servi e theologo della Serenissima Republica di Venetia* (n.p., 1658), p. 45.

[21] See his letter to Jacques Gillot, Mar. 18, 1608, Ulianich, p. 127, where he says that he had first become interested in Gallicanism twenty years before.

[22] Luigi Firpo, "Il processo di Giordano Bruno," *RSI*, LX (1948), 572ff.

great senators and were like stars in the firmament of the most Serene Republic for goodness, religion, doctrine, and civil prudence; but there were also admitted every sort of talented men [*virtuosi*], both secular and religious. Indeed all the most cultivated personages who might arrive in Venice, from Italy or abroad, would have been found in this place." [23]

But Micanzio also made the special point that, although anyone present was free to introduce any subject, "the disputations had as their end the knowledge of truth." [24] The culture of this group was animated by the same seriousness about the actual operations of the world which had characterized the political writers of the later Florentine Renaissance and which we have seen developing more recently in Venice. The *giovani* notably combined literary with political interests in a way quite foreign to Bembo and his followers of an earlier generation. Personally engaged wholeheartedly in the active life whose claims had been so eloquently asserted by Paruta, they justified the *studio* largely on the ground of its value for society, like earlier representatives of republican culture. This concern is evident even among the most scholarly associates of the group, for example the philologist Domenico Molino, who called on foreign scholars to dedicate their works to contemporary human needs. He wrote in such terms to Casaubon in 1609, and again in 1622 to the Dutch classicist Jan Van Meurs, whom he urged to prepare an edition of Thucydides as a reply to those who, like Justus Lipsius, had recently exploited Tacitus on behalf of despotism. "But, sir," Molino wrote to Van Meurs, "if you labor so hard and so worthily on behalf of the inanimate rock of Athens, why should you show yourself less ready and less kind in giving a new spirit to, and reviving in the world, so worthy a citizen of that great mother of civil liberty? . . . Why should you not show your gratitude to Thucydides, an author to whom all of us who enjoy a free country owe so much? And if others have adorned the teachers of tyranny in such a grand manner, why, I beg, should a free man be grudging to the preceptor of our sweet, treasured liberty?" [25]

Nor did Venetian patriotism during this period express itself only through classical studies. It can hardly be a coincidence that the demand for a classicism relevant to political needs was accompanied by a revival of Venetian as a literary language. The triumph of Tuscan over Venetian as the vehicle of

---

[23] *Vita del Padre Paolo*, pp. 44–45.
[24] *Ibid.*, p. 45. Cf. Cozzi, *Contarini*, pp. 50–51.
[25] Quoted by Gaetano Cozzi, "Paolo Sarpi e Jan van Meurs," *BSV*, I (1959), 4, from a letter of August 19, 1622. Molino had written a similar letter to Casaubon in 1609.

polite expression was now far in the past, and it had been confirmed by Bembo's efforts to standardize linguistic usage. Venetian, nevertheless, had continued to be the only tongue common to all classes of society in the Republic, speeches were still delivered in Venetian in the Great Council, and laws were printed in it. And now, during the period of *giovani* dominance, a deliberate effort was made to revive Venetian literature in the language of the people. A whole group of poets sought in Venetian a simpler and more direct instrument for lyrical and patriotic expression. Among the neo-Venetian poets were members of patrician families such as Francesco Zano and Giovanni Querini, as well as humbler men.[26] Nor was the revival of literary patriotism confined to this perhaps slightly artificial movement. It was also an important element in the work of Celio Magno, secretary to a series of *giovani* ambassadors, to the Senate, and to the Council of Ten, and the most distinguished lyric poet in Venice during the later sixteenth century. Though he continued to write in Tuscan, love of Venice and enthusiasm for her exploits were major impulses in his work.[27] Thus while elsewhere in Italy literature was increasingly remote from life, in Venice it was being brought into closer relation with immediate human concerns.

The *giovani* had assumed control of the Venetian state in the conviction that decades of inaction and drift had exposed the Republic to increasing danger from both within and without. Subordination of the Council of Ten to the Senate and College had presumably blocked the slow subversion of the constitution through the concentration of power in the hands of a few families. But other factors in the apparent decline of the Republic also required urgent attention. Among these were the recent difficulties of Venetian commerce, a matter of particular concern to the lesser nobility who provided the broad support for the change in leadership. Thus the last decades of the century saw renewed insistence on the continuing importance of commerce for Venice, as well as an attempt to promote the recovery of trade. Paruta, who had a few years before described with some eloquence the place of wealth in the complex of Venetian values, suggests the general attitudes of the new generation.

For Paruta, the peculiarity of Venice, and the moral and political virtues

---

[26] Elwert, "Bembo e la vita letteraria," pp. 158ff. Marco Foscarini still admired these writings in the eighteenth century (*Della letteratura veneziana*, pp. 568–569).

[27] On Magno see, in addition to Elwert, pp. 152–153, G. Zanella, "Della vita e degli scritti di Celio Magno, poeta veneziano del secolo XVI," *Atti del Regio Istituto Veneto*, Ser. 5, VII (1880-1881), 1063-1075.

The redecoration of the Great Council Chamber: the Doge receiving the sword from Pope Alexander III in 1177 *(F. Bassano)*.

The redecoration of the Great Council Chamber: the Doge receiving the ring from Pope Alexander III in 1177 (*A. M. Vicentino*).

she so notably exhibited, depended on the historic devotion to commerce towards which both the wisdom of her founding fathers and her location had directed her:

> The ancient founders of the city and establishers of her laws took great care that her citizens should engage in voyages and traffic on the sea, and with their industry and virtue endeavor to increase their private resources and public wealth, making the Venetian name both known and famous among the most distant foreign nations. The site of the city invited this way of life and activity and almost by itself inclined its inhabitants to such thoughts. Since the city had no lands of its own through whose fertility and the diligence of men it could grow rich, and indeed lacked the things necessary to sustain life, its needs first of all stimulated industry, from which was then born the abundance of all things.

Her devotion to commerce, Paruta argued, had also profound consequences for the character of the Venetian people. It had required young Venetians to spend many years among foreigners, thus acquiring a rich and varied experience which could be utilized at home when they returned to participate in the government of the Republic. Commerce had also formed the Venetian character, planting in it a special diligence that safeguarded Venetians from the idleness and corruption of other ruling groups and inculcating the virtues of "frugality, modesty, goodness, and other honest customs." [28]

Paruta's identification of Venice with commerce emerged also as a part of the familiar Venetian comparison between Venice and ancient Rome, in which (perhaps as the challenge from modern Rome became more open) he engaged even more systematically than earlier Venetians. The commercial character of Venice was a major element in Paruta's explanation of her superiority to Rome. Her geography had made Rome essentially agricultural, and this difference he saw as the cause for the difference in their histories. "The Romans," Paruta wrote, "following pursuits appropriate to the location of their city, had a genius more inclined to express itself in a land army in war and the cultivation of the fields in peace. But the Venetians, invited to different things by the diversity of place, employed other means to defend liberty and to increase their wealth, using a navy for the former and dealing and trading for the latter." Yet a curiously defensive note also entered Paruta's

[28] *Historia vinetiana*, pp. 156–157.

argument, as though the historic pursuits of Venice were again under attack, as they had been attacked by Pius II. "Why should the Venetians be blamed for their trading, since this activity is so advantageous, and indeed as necessary to the site of Venice as agriculture was to the site of Rome?" he asked plaintively. "If the care of cultivating the land did not debase the minds of those ancient and venerable Romans, who have left to all other cities and nations such clear examples of every virtue, why is it likely that commerce should have caused any meanness in the minds of the Venetians, since on the contrary they have administered the Republic for so long a course of years so gloriously and with so much public benefit?" [29] Evidently there were now some, perhaps in Venice herself, who chose to question the propriety of her long commercial tradition.

At the same time Paruta was by no means insensitive to the contribution of agriculture to Venetian prosperity. The history of Venice suggested to him that she had become a great naval power capable of ruling a large commercial empire only after beginning to expand on the mainland. Lepanto in particular seemed to demonstrate that substantial territory was essential for "the men, the money, the supplies, and the other things necessary to maintain navies properly." [30] Paruta suggests that the *giovani* recognized the *terraferma* as an asset, but primarily in subordination to the historic commercial economy of the Republic.

Paruta's emphasis on commerce is reflected in the considerable attention— greater than in any previous Venetian history (and perhaps in historical writing elsewhere)—given the subject in his *Historia vinetiana*. He dealt in detail with commercial negotiations, the routes and commodities of Venetian trade, and its disturbance during the earlier part of the century, insisting also (as though uneasy at this departure from the conventional matter of history) on the need to deal with so unusual a topic.[31] He noted the seriousness of corsair damage to Venetian commerce,[32] and he remarked on the importance of trade with Germany and the benefits of treating German

---

[29] *Discorsi politici*, pp. 218–219; see also p. 228 for a good summary of this contrast. I cite from the edition in Paruta's *Opere politiche*, II, 1–371.

[30] *Ibid.*, pp. 216–217.

[31] Pp. 154–157. Paruta explained: "Ma poiche la cosa stessa mi ammonisce, hò stimato non essere dal mio instituto proponimento lontano, havendomi io preso à raccomandare alla memoria della lettere le cose de'Vinetiani, che ora essendomi à ciò offerta occasione, narri alcuna codelle loro maritime negotiationi, acciò i costumi delle nationi, & la principale cagione delle ricchezze della Città sia meglio conosciuta."

[32] For example, pp. 162 and 324.

merchants well.[33] He emphasized the necessity for Venetian commerce of peace and friendship with the Turks.[34] He also regretted, on commercial grounds, the failure of Venice at the end of the previous century to prevent the absorption of Pisa by Florence; the diversion of Italian commerce from Venice to Livorno was, this sentiment suggests, a matter of some concern among the *giovani*.[35]

Deeply committed to the restoration of commerce, the government took steps in the later years of the century to stem its decline. The transfer of fiscal responsibility from the Council of Ten to the Senate was in part intended to improve a system whose irrationality was particularly burdensome to merchants; and this was followed by additional measures. The most constructive was the establishment of the Banco di Rialto in 1587 as a public bank to fill the void left by the collapse of private banking in the previous decades. It proved helpful to both commerce and industry,[36] and Venice remained for some time an important money market, even after the decline in other sectors of her economy.[37] Although little could be done to revive Venetian shipbuilding because of the local dearth of materials, as an unsuccessful experiment with public subsidies revealed, the government relaxed its traditional prohibition against the purchase of foreign ships; fifteen large vessels were added to the Venetian merchant fleet in this way during the decade of the nineties. In addition, the ships of most nations were encouraged to touch at Venice by the reduction of port taxes. Thus, although an increasing proportion of her trade was in foreign ships, Venetian commerce showed a substantial rise.[38] Meanwhile, aided by mercantilist restrictions of industry on the mainland, industrial production in the city of Venice continued to rise.[39]

The renewal of Venetian prosperity toward the end of the century cannot be attributed entirely to the policies of the new government. Commerce increased in the eastern Mediterranean because the Portuguese route through the Atlantic was now increasingly harrassed by Dutch and English

[33] Pp. 486–487.
[34] Pp. 154–155.
[35] *Discorsi*, p. 243. He consoled himself with the hope that the Grand Duke of Tuscany would remain friendly so that commerce could always continue "open, secure, and free."
[36] Stella, "La crisi economica veneziana," p. 61.
[37] Kellenbenz, "Le déclin de Venise," p. 115.
[38] Lane, *Venice and History*, pp. 20, 156–157; Stella, "La crisi economica veneziana," pp. 56ff.; Sella, *Commerci e industrie a Venezia*, pp. 35–36.
[39] Sella, pp. 1ff.; cf. Beltrami, *La penetrazione economica dei veneziani in Terraferma*, p. 4.

corsairs. With the blockade of Antwerp, furthermore, Venice recovered her leadership in the German spice market; and Germany, at peace and relatively prosperous, bought a wide range of products in Venetian markets.[40] Nevertheless it seems likely that the greater sensitivity of the *giovani* to the needs of commerce contributed to the increased prosperity of the Republic during the latter part of the century. This in turn no doubt helped the new group to remain in control of the Republic.

But the *giovani*, as we have seen in the previous chapter, had been perhaps even more concerned with the international position of Venice: immediately with the growing pressure of the Habsburg powers in Italy and the Adriatic, particularly in view of what they regarded as the betrayal after Lepanto, and more generally with the declining power and authority of Venice among the states of Europe. Donà had been sufficiently impressed by the warnings of Nicolò da Ponte to copy out the latter's *Ricordi* in his own hand,[41] and suspicion of Spanish intentions became a primary influence on *giovani* foreign policy. This was clearly recognized in Madrid. As a Spanish ambassador to Venice declared on leaving his post early in the seventeenth century: "From the day that I took up my duties until the day of my departure, [the Venetian Republic] has always aimed at harming and depressing the Spanish name." [42] The *giovani* regarded the neutrality of the recent past as no more than the acceptance of a detestable Spanish preponderance, and they were vigilant for any opportunity to reduce Spanish power.[43] Meanwhile they were also aggressive in defending Venetian claims to control the Adriatic, an area of particular importance for commerce.[44] Here the Republic felt under growing pressure from both the papacy and the Habsburgs of Central Europe, who continued to view with benevolence the increasingly damaging Uskok depredations against Venetian shipping.

Paruta's reflections on Venetian policy since 1494, to which reference has already been made, suggest an inclination among the *giovani* to read contemporary preoccupations with Spanish power into the Venetian past, and

[40] Cf. Braudel et al., "Le déclin de Venise," pp. 74–75.

[41] The text printed in Barozzi's edition is taken from Donà's transcription. See p. 5 of Barozzi's introduction.

[42] Bedmar, "Relazione," p. 29.

[43] The general point is made by Cozzi, *Contarini*, pp. 17ff.

[44] For Donà's attitude on this question, see the dispatch of the nuncio in 1596, quoted by Mario Brunetti, "Schermaglie veneto-pontificie prima dell'Interdetto. Leonardo Donà avanti il dogado," *Paolo Sarpi ed i suoi tempi. Studi storici* (Città di Castello, 1923), p. 135.

in addition the development of a new sense of perspective, in which Venetian interests were increasingly identified with those of Italy as a whole. It pleased Paruta, in discussing the dealings of Venice with the invaders of Italy, to represent the Republic as the consistent champion of Italian independence. "To expel the foreigners from Italy," he observed, was "a thing desired by all Italians"; and he pointed out that the Venetians had been among the prime movers in driving Charles VIII from the peninsula.[45] For the good end of expelling the foreigner he was even prepared, for once, to accept the legitimacy of political action by the pope.[46] But he particularly insisted on the traditional opposition of Venice to the Italian designs of Spain. "To speak only of things of most recent memory," he exclaimed, "what concern the Republic has demonstrated for the common good! And therefore how much care she has taken for the liberty and glory of Italy by supporting, for so long a period, burdensome wars to keep the most noble states of Naples and Milan for Italian princes!" [47] Paruta was evidently confusing what Venice would have preferred with what she had been able actively to struggle for, but his concern for the general liberty of the Italian states appears to have been common among the *giovani*.[48]

Paruta accordingly looked back to the French invasion of 1494 with a grief that helps to explain the special interest of his generation in the history of Guicciardini. "Among those things whose memory remains bitter to Italy, indeed very bitter and, in a way, still recent," he wrote nearly a century after the event, "is the expedition of Charles VIII, king of France, to acquire the kingdom of Naples; because, from then on, the ultramontane nations have always maintained their empire in Italy. And the greatness of the Italian name, which was beginning to rise again in that age, with a hope of greater glory, since all the states of Italy were under the rule of our own Italian princes, began to decline again with this new shock; and it has not been able to resume its former majesty." [49] Notable here is Paruta's association of a renascent Italian glory—evidently the rebirth of antique greatness—with the liberty, under native rulers, of a series of particular states, as well as his grief at the apparent end, at least as a political phenomenon, of the Italian Renaissance. For Paruta the Italian Wars had destroyed the possibility of an active statecraft, the basis of political greatness.

[45] *Discorsi*, p. 265.
[46] *Ibid*., pp. 338–339.
[47] *Ibid*., p. 212. For similar passages see also pp. 238–240.
[48] Cf. Cozzi, *Contarini*, p. 81.
[49] *Discorsi*, p. 264.

His understanding of this change emerges with particular force in his treatment of the great Venetian reverses of 1509. In reply to Machiavelli's charge of Venetian inconstancy in the face of fortune (for Paruta a reflection of incomprehension as well as lack of proper sympathy), he pointed out that the coalition against Venice had been both unpredictable and too powerful to withstand. Thus Venice had deserved compassion rather than reproach. And the Senate, he argued, had in fact responded to the crisis with an admirable resolution and prudence. It had recognized the wisdom, for the weak, of playing for time, which has often been known to dissolve great armies, and of relative passivity when circumstances are altogether beyond control. "In so generally desperate a predicament," Paruta asked, "what else could be done than to yield and to let this dark cloud pass, against which it could be seen that no intelligence or counsel could make resistance? Thus, as sometimes happens in the greatest storms when the skill and exertions of the pilots are overcome by the evil of the weather and, the sails lowered, the ship is allowed to be carried wherever the sea may take it; so in the cases of great danger into which states sometimes fall, he who is at the head of the government must endure his fortune, however bad, until, when the fury of the tempests has passed, the kingdom or republic, beaten down but not overwhelmed, can rise up again and resume its previous greatness." [50] Yet Paruta's sense of helplessness is balanced by the suggestion that, just as every storm must finally pass, passivity too is appropriate only under certain political conditions. Occasionally required for moments of crisis, it is by no means the normal policy of states. In this sense, the *giovani* were committed to a restoration of normalcy. However dangerous the world might still appear, and to some degree even stimulated by danger, they were convinced that Venice could take at least a limited initiative and thus begin to resume her previous greatness.

The government of the *giovani* thus abandoned the isolation and passivity that had generally characterized Venetian policy since the peace of Bologna. Venice was not prepared altogether to give up her long neutrality, which Paruta staunchly defended as the basis of her freedom, in favor of active participation in a league of states. Her traditions and her recent experience were both against involvements of this kind,[51] and in any case the only league in which she might for the time being have found a place was a

[50] Pp. 245ff. For other passages on the wisdom of playing for time, see pp. 252, 256–257. For Paruta's reply to Guicciardini on the aftermath of Agnadello, see pp. 258ff.

[51] Cf. Paruta, *Discorsi*, pp. 139, 346.

project favored by the pope, to include Spain and the other Italian states, which in Venetian eyes would only have served the interests of her greatest potential enemies. As ambassador in Rome Paruta firmly opposed the pope's proposals to this end.[52] Instead Venice attempted to return to a policy of balance among the great powers which brought her once again actively into communication with the rest of Europe.

Paruta's identification of the most successful phase of Venetian policy in the recent past is of particular interest in understanding the considerations that underlay this shift. Venice had done best, he thought, during the long stalemate between the opposing forces of Charles V and Francis I. The causes of their *impasse*, he believed, had been complex—a relative equality in power being only one element among many. Elaborate systems of fortification had slowed down the speed of conquest. Artillery had made armies less mobile, and the skill required to use it had made battles more deliberate. Cavalry, increasingly used but more dependent on local conditions and supplies than infantry, had proved a less flexible instrument of war. In addition the savage methods of modern warfare made resistance more desperate and thereby prolonged it. For all these reasons a balance between the two forces had persisted for decades, and armies powerful enough to have made extensive conquests under other circumstances had been denied definitive victory in Italy. Furthermore a similar situation had prevailed on the frontiers between Christendom and Islam, where Charles V and Suleiman held each other at bay.[53] This situation, Paruta believed, had provided the best environment possible, under modern conditions, for an independent Venetian policy. It had been perfectly understood by the Venetian Senate, which had skillfully accommodated itself to the shifting fortunes of the great powers. Exploiting "the condition of things and times," Venice had often changed her friendships to balance between them; but "when an occasion arose to strike a blow at one without making the other too great," she had seized it, meanwhile standing "firm and constant, and opposed to any proposal to put down her arms." [54]

[52] See, for example, his dispatch of Dec. 12, 1592, *Legazione*, I, 39. He had represented Venice to the pope as wishing "to remain always in her neutrality and sincere friendship with all, indeed devoting all her thought rather to extinguish than to foment that fire which even now is sometimes lit in Italy." Leagues, he said, would only jeopardize peace, and he identified the proposal as a Spanish plan.

[53] *Discorsi*, pp. 294ff. The passage is really a contribution to the debate between the ancients and the moderns; Paruta is trying to explain why the moderns appear less glorious in war.

[54] *Ibid.*, pp. 347–348. Paruta also condemned Leo X for not pursuing a policy of this kind (pp. 343–345).

This analysis indicates something of the perspective on which the new Venetian policy was based, the experience to which it appealed. But it is important to recognize that the *giovani* understood balance of power not as a static confrontation between two equal systems of alliance but as a means by which the independence of lesser states might be protected. The necessary condition of political particularism, it left them free to change sides as interest dictated. Venice, for the *giovani*, was not to be bound by ties of clientage or sentiment to any great power, but was to be at liberty to modify any relationship which no longer served her needs.[55] The *giovani* were essentially neither anti-Spanish nor pro-French;[56] they were committed only to Venice. To promote her interests they were prepared to enter now into relationships with any European power, regardless even of religion. Thus in 1602, against the opposition of the pope and his closest adherents in Venice, the government sent a special envoy to England; and on the accession of James I the English embassy was again made permanent.[57]

But France had traditionally served to check the Italian ambitions of Spain, as Paruta clearly recognized; and the *giovani* were now chiefly interested in the possibility of French assistance. Accordingly they promptly began to cultivate the friendship of France, and the need for some degree of collaboration with France remained basic to Venetian policy for the next decades. As a contemporary Spanish diplomat observed: "The Republic was wont to pay particular respect to the king of France as the rival of this crown in balancing the things of Italy; and the Republic desired to be much esteemed in that court as being very powerful and of great influence in Italy, and above all for depending on no one and being entirely free." [58]

Unfortunately France, when the *giovani* took power, was paralyzed by civil war and promised to be of little use in Italian affairs. Accordingly Venice was acutely interested in bringing the French disorders to an end. As early as 1585 the French ambassador in Venice was reporting radical solutions advocated by some Venetian senators: either the acceptance of religious division so that France could present a united front on the political level

---

[55] Cf. *Discorsi*, p. 84, where Paruta implies the possibility of constantly shifting alliances.

[56] Paruta particularly blamed the French for disturbing the peace of Italy (p. 314). The French ambassador Philippe Canaye recognized the reluctance of Venice to enter into a formal alliance but explained it as the result of excessive caution. See, for example, his letters of 1602, in his *Lettres et ambassade* (Paris, 1635–1636), I, 196, 249, 292, 479.

[57] Morosini, *Storia*, VII, 269–276, 278–279; Nicolò Contarini, *Historie*, in Cozzi's Appendix, pp. 371–372.

[58] Bedmar, "Relazione," pp. 26–27.

against Spain and Rome, or a purely national settlement of the religious question.[59] But although these proposals indicate the presence in Venice of a considerable sympathy for both the *politique* and Gallican elements in the French kingdom, they had no practical effect. For Venice to make an effective contribution to French stability, she required, in the language of Renaissance politics, an opportunity.

Her opportunity came with the death of Henry III in 1589 and the appearance of Henry of Navarre as his legitimate successor. This situation gave Venice her first major opportunity to assert an independent foreign policy and to improve her international position.[60] She chose to ignore the excommunication against Henry (a point itself worth noting), and, the only Catholic power to do so, she immediately recognized him as king of France. She exchanged ambassadors with Henry, and acknowledged his right to the title of *most Christian king*—all of this four years before his abjuration of Protestantism, five before his reconciliation with the pope, and in the face of strong objections from Rome. The pope spoke of censures, and there was again talk at the Curia of enforcing the capitulations of Julius II. But Venice held firm. The Senate had been almost unanimous in approving recognition of the new French ruler, and papal pressure only converted a political decision into an issue of principle. When the nuncio decided to dramatize the disapproval of the church by withdrawing from the city, the Senate protested that such actions tended "to prejudice that liberty which, as the inherited and inestimable treasure of our Republic, has been defended and preserved with the greatest zeal, forever intact and inviolable during thirteen hundred years continuously." [61] For Venice the right of a state to act in accordance with its own interests without regard to any higher authority, was at stake. The government accordingly chose its most vigorous spokesman, Leonardo Donà, to present the Venetian case to the pope. He was presumably successful, and Sixtus V was finally content with a mild reproof, won over in part by the reflection that even the papacy might benefit by the presence in Europe of an effective counterweight to Spain.

The same concern for balance induced Venice to promote the reconciliation of Henry IV and the pope a few years later. Henry's conversion

[59] Cozzi, *Contarini*, p. 26.

[60] On what follows see, in general, Italo Raulich, "La contesa fra Sisto V e Venezia per Enrico IV di Francia, con documenti," *AV*, Ser. 2, IV (1892), 243–318; and Gina Fasoli, "Sulle ripercussioni italiane della crisi dinastica francese del 1589–95 e sull'opera mediatrice della Repubblica di Venezia e del Granduca di Toscana," *Memorie dell'Accademia delle Scienze dell'Istituto di Bologna: Classe di scienze morali*, Ser. 4, IX (1949), 1–64.

[61] Quoted by Seneca, *Donà*, p. 137.

opened the way; and Venice, now served in her Roman embassy by Paolo Paruta, exerted all her influence to secure its acceptance. As Paruta saw it, the problem was to persuade the pope to abandon the doctrinaire rigidity of theology and canon law, and instead to treat the problem politically. Paruta based his case on the practical need to protect the independence of the church, arguing that French arms were the only realistic guarantee of papal independence. The subtleties of the doctors, on the other hand, seemed to him only a transparent disguise for the Spanish interest.[62] And the success of Paruta and various other intermediaries on this matter facilitated even closer connections between Venice and France. A few years later Henry IV was made a patrician of Venice;[63] and with the internal recovery of France under his rule, Venice seemed at last to have found again a power that might give her support in time of danger.

The *giovani* were also compelled to defend the right of Venice to conduct an independent policy based on the interests of the state in another sector. During this period Rome exhibited a renewed enthusiasm for a general crusade, in which Venetian participation was considered essential.[64] But such an enterprise would have threatened the Republic from several directions. Her survival as a commercial power, and thus in a fundamental sense the recovery of her past greatness, depended, for the *giovani*, on peace in the eastern Mediterranean. At the same time it seemed clear to Venice that a successful crusade would substantially benefit her Habsburg enemies. Spain would no longer be distracted in North Africa, the emperor would be at peace in Hungary, and they could then together turn their full energies to the subjugation of Italy and the destruction of Venetian liberty.

Venice was not opposed in principle to war with the Turks. She had lost most of her empire to them, and the aspirations of the *giovani* for the recovery of past greatness suggested that, in time, Venice might be prepared to expand once again in the Levant. Paruta, who discussed the problem of a crusade at some length,[65] did not object to the idea of a holy war. But he

---

[62] See his dispatches of Dec. 18, 1593, Aug. 26, 1595, and Sep. 6, 1595, *Legazione*, I, 140, and III, 268–269, 281–282; and his *Relazione di Roma* of 1595, Albèri, Ser. 2, IV, 382. The negotiation is well described in Seneca, *Donà*, pp. 172ff.

[63] For the patent see Henri Hauser, *Les sources de l'histoire de France: XVIe siècle* (Paris, 1906–1915), IV, 194, no. 3166.

[64] Thus Giovanni Corraro reported in his *Relazione di Roma* of 1581 (Albèri, Ser. 2, IV, 281) that the dearest hope of Gregory XIII was to organize a new league against the Turks. Paruta reported this pressure regularly in his dispatches from Rome.

[65] In his *Discorso sopra la pace de'veneziani co' Turchi*, in *Opere politiche*, I, 427–448.

defended Venetian neutrality in this area on practical grounds, and his arguments suggest doubt that any general Christian campaign against the infidel could ever succeed. Lepanto, he believed, had demonstrated the impracticality of a crusade in the modern world. That famous victory had been, in the familiar sense, the supreme occasion for the destruction of the Turks. Every circumstance had been right; yet the Christian powers had allowed victory to slip through their hands, and the enemy had been given time to recover. Furthermore the prospects for any future crusade now seemed dark.[66] Turkish power was still formidable,[67] but in addition it seemed to Paruta highly unlikely that the Christian powers—states for the most part absorbed in their own affairs—could either unite or manage to fight effectively together.[68] The new advocates of a crusade seemed, to Paruta, to seemed lack any comprehension of what was possible.[69]

Venice, therefore, continued to insist on neutrality towards the Turks, and the *giovani* were even less inclined than their predecessors to heed papal appeals for a crusade. Although the emperor was actively at war with the Turks and receiving aid from elsewhere in the Catholic world for what seemed increasingly a major Christian effort, Venice withheld her support.[70] She merely watched, as the French ambassador to the Republic noted in 1601, "with folded arms." [71] Indeed she took advantage of the emperor's engagement with the Turks to build the great fortress of Palmanova in a disputed corner of Friuli.[72] She also refused to supply arms to the shah of Persia, who had offered to attack the Turks from the east; she rejected an opportunity to take the Albanians under her protection; and she refused passage through her territory to Christian forces on their way to fight the Turks.[73] During the same period Leonardo Donà was sent as extraordinary ambassador to Constantinople to renew the peace treaty of 1573.[74] Venice now had hardly even a sentimental attachment to the idea of Christendom.

---

[66] P. 431.

[67] Cf. *Discorsi politici*, p. 363.

[68] *Discorso sopra la pace*, p. 433.

[69] *Ibid.*, p. 440, where he speaks of "li quali mirando più a ciò che è desiderabile, che possibile."

[70] Cf. Tenenti, *Venezia e i corsari*, pp. 29ff.

[71] Canaye to the bishop of Evreux, Nov. 4, 1601, *Lettres et ambassade*, I, 27. Cf. Cornet, p. 3 n. 1.

[72] Quazza, *Preponderanza spagnuola*, p. 360.

[73] Ernesto Sestan, "La politica veneziana del Seicento," *La civiltà veneziana nell'età barocca*, p. 56.

[74] Seneca, *Donà*, pp. 221–229.

Just as the militant universalism of the Counter Reformation hampered the ability of Venice to base foreign policy on her own calculated interests, so its ecclesiastical centralism threatened her internal arrangements; and here too the *giovani* were firmly opposed to any concession. Donà was particularly intransigent on all matters of ecclesiastical jurisdiction. He was convinced that God had instituted secular government, that among its legitimate responsibilities was the administration of the institutional church, and that no spiritual authority could properly interfere in the operations of states. The alternative for Venice to these principles seemed to him sinister: "Dissension would easily be sown in the Republic, in the manner we see to have been done with such horrible results in the greatest governments of our time." He was in favor of the discipline, by secular government, of even the highest clergy. And from an early point in his career he was disposed to apply these views in practice. As *podestà* of Brescia from 1578 to 1580 he had vigorously resisted the attempt of Carlo Borromeo, in whose archiepiscopal jurisdiction that city lay, to control the property of its religious foundations. On that occasion he had distinguished, according to "most ancient custom," between the religious and civil spheres, and had expressed his resolve to prevent "any sort of alteration or novelty in the jurisdiction of the most Serene Dommion."[75]

He was particularly suspicious of the intentions of Rome in regard to secular states. A nuncio attributed to him a belief that "the Apostolic See behaves with such superiority that princes must keep their eyes wide open to its movements, else everything would be subordinated to the ecclesiastical power." [76] He also had no faith in the integrity of the Curia, where, he asserted, it was a "well-practiced dogma that it is praiseworthy to break promises in order to increase papal authority." [77] His strong opposition to the wearing of the Golden Rose, a papal decoration, by the wife of the doge was typical of his sensitivity to the pope's influence in politics.[78] He was even opposed to the creation of Venetian cardinals because in this way the political competence that should properly serve Venice would instead be disposed of by the pope.[79] He had asserted, as it was reported in Rome, that his obligation to his country came ahead of his duty to the church since he

[75] *Ibid.*, pp. 122–124, 185, 193.

[76] Quoted by Brunetti, "Schermaglie," p. 124.

[77] These words were attributed to him in Contarini's *Historie* and are quoted in Benzoni, "La conferma del patriarca," p. 132 n. 55.

[78] Discussed by Brunetti, "Schermaglie," pp. 140–142.

[79] Cozzi, *Contarini*, pp. 37–38.

had been born a Venetian before being baptized a Christian.[80] Donà's views clearly went somewhat beyond those of most of his compatriots, and the doge's wife was allowed to wear her Golden Rose; but such sentiments reflected a powerful impulse in later sixteenth-century Venice. It was hardly accidental that Donà was regularly appointed ambassador to Rome.[81]

The decades following the change in the Venetian government were filled, under such leadership, with tension over questions of ecclesiastical jurisdiction. To Venetians it seemed during these years that Rome was interested in nothing so much as impressing the world with the superiority of the clergy and enforcing their authority over laymen.[82] At the same time they assumed, as a point hardly requiring discussion, that this concern, and indeed all jurisdictional claims of the Curia, pertained to the temporal ambitions rather than the spiritual mission of the church.[83] Venetian intransigence was extended, under these conditions, even to such apparently minor matters as a proposal by Rome to establish a secular consulate in Venice; this would have freed the nuncio from minor temporal business and permitted him to concentrate on ecclesiastical questions. Donà and Paruta worked together to block this dangerous novelty.[84]

The new aggressiveness of Venetian jurisdictionalism took various forms during the later years of the sixteenth century. Donà felt strongly that the state should regulate closely all dealings of ecclesiastical courts with laymen, "ecclesiastical and lay jurisdictions being distinct by their nature";[85] and during this period the Venetian Senate insisted periodically and with vigor on due process in the proceedings of the Inquisition, including the presence of laymen representing the state. In a series of laws it attempted to define the authority of the Inquisition as narrowly as possible.[86] A special crisis also

[80] "Dokumente zum Ausgleich zwischen Paul V und Venedig," ed. A. Nürnberger, *Römische Quartalschrift für christliche Alterthumskunde und für Kirchengeschichte*, II (1888), 197. The report, dated May 30, 1606, referred to an earlier remark that, according to the nuncio, was widely known.

[81] Cf. Seneca, *Donà*, p. 308. In addition to his regular embassy in 1580–1583, he was chosen for special missions in 1589, 1592, 1598, and 1605, although on the last occasion he became doge before he could leave for Rome.

[82] Cf. Paruta, *Relazione di Roma*, pp. 374–375.

[83] Cf. Giovanni Gritti's *Relazione* of 1589, Albèri, Ser. 2, IV, 335.

[84] Brunetti, "Le istruzioni di un nunzio pontificio a Venezia," pp. 377–378, and "Schermaglie," pp. 137–140.

[85] See his statement to the nuncio in 1589, quoted by Seneca, *Donà*, p. 250.

[86] See Sarpi, *Sopra l'officio dell'inquisizione*, SG, pp. 123–127; and Battistella, *Repubblica di Venezia*, p. 602, for various measures by the government to maintain control over the inquisitors during this period.

arose in connection with the proposed Index of Clement VIII in 1595–1596. This Index, long in preparation, had been vigorously opposed in Rome by Paruta, chiefly on the grounds that it would damage the Venetian printing industry; he claimed that as a result of his protests the list of prohibited works had been considerably reduced.[87] But even the shorter form in which the Index finally appeared was objectionable in Venice on several counts. It included an oath of observance to be taken by all printers and booksellers, which gave offense because, as Donà argued, no Venetian should commit himself with an oath to any authority except his own prince. But above all the Index, imposed unilaterally, implied powers of control over their lives which the *giovani* could tolerate only in the government of the Republic. It suggested, too, that the Republic could not be trusted in religious matters; Donà complained that the pope was treating the Venetians almost like heretics. Therefore, the issues raised by the new Index had to be settled by a compromise which Venice generally considered a victory. The oath was dropped, and the Index was made to appear with a preface which represented it as the product of an agreement between contracting parties.[88] Sarpi was to interpret this as meaning that no book could be prohibited in Venice without the consent of the prince.[89]

Even more fundamental issues were raised by a papal decree of 1592 which required all Italian bishops to visit Rome before confirmation for a formal examination in theology and canon law. This had implications profoundly inimical to the view of episcopal office prevalent among the *giovani*. For Donà a bishop was primarily a civil functionary, not a theologian;[90] and the Senate, in protesting the papal decree, noted that a man who might please the pope as a theologian or preacher could well prove unsatisfactory to the government. The primary function of a bishop, from this point of view, was to keep the clergy in order and the city at peace: in short, to serve the needs of local administration. The Senate pointed out that men experienced in affairs of state and the things of the world had in the past proved "better prelates than those who have been taken from their books and from the cells of religious." [91] Venetians, it appears, saw the issue in relation to the familiar tension between activity and contemplation. Bishops, as agents of the government, from this standpoint, were properly men of action; and the *giovani* (in contrast to their predecessors) made a regular

---

[87] Dispatch of Aug. 14, 1593, *Legazione*, I, 296–298.
[88] Brunetti, "Schermaglie," pp. 124–133.
[89] Letter to Jacques Leschassier, Jul. 23, 1613, Ulianich, p. 124.
[90] Cf. Cozzi, *Contarini*, p. 222 n. 2.
[91] From a Senate deliberation of 1600, quoted by Benzoni, p. 127.

practice of choosing laymen for the patriarchate[92]—men, it may also be observed, whose previous careers might have made a formal examination in Rome rather difficult. But even more serious was the fact that such an examination would have given Rome an effective means to frustrate the will of the Senate. The primary issue in the matter was, again, local control of an autonomous Venetian church. Venice felt constrained to allow her other bishops to make the trip to Rome, but she delayed the visit of the patriarch.[93]

The tension between Venice and Rome was meanwhile generally exacerbated during these years by the growing influence of the Jesuits over some elements in the patriciate. Favored during its early years by Gasparo Contarini himself, the Society of Jesus had long maintained establishments in both Venice and Padua which had been, on the whole, regarded benignly by earlier Venetian governments. The influence of the Jesuits had been apparent in the establishment of various charitable foundations, and they had been instrumental in suppressing the Venetian theater.[94] Now, so closely identified with papal centralization, the Jesuits increasingly aroused the suspicions of the *giovani*, who exhibited toward them those almost paranoid fears of which the Society of Jesus has through the years been so often the object. Nicolò Contarini particularly abominated the Jesuits.[95]

Open conflict between the government and the Society first broke out in connection with the educational activities of the Jesuits in Padua, a sore point in view of the importance of the University of Padua in the education of the Venetian ruling class. The issue was forced by the University itself, in one of those disputes between established faculties and monastic intruders that had been a regular part of European academic life since the thirteenth century.[96] The University had never been pleased at the proximity of the Jesuit *studio* but had been unsuccessful in preventing its authorization by the

[92] Cf. Niero, *I patriarchi di Venezia*, pp. 15 and 88ff.

[93] Benzoni, p. 125.

[94] Gaetano Cozzi, "Appunti sul teatro e i teatri a Venezia agli inizi del Seicento. L'Interdetto e il teatro," *BSV*, I (1959), 187–192; and "L'Interdetto di Venezia e i Gesuiti," *AV*, Ser. 5, LXVI (1960), 170–171.

[95] Cozzi, *Contarini*, pp. 219–220. For the earlier unpopularity of the Jesuits in Venice, see also the remarks of *L'Interdetto di Venezia del 1606 e i Gesuiti: Silloge di documenti con introduzione*, ed. Pietro Pirri (Rome, 1959), p. 8; hereafter cited as Pirri.

[96] For what follows see, in general, Antonio Favaro, "Lo Studio di Padova e la Compagnia di Gesù sul finire del secolo decimosesto: Narrazione documentata," *Atti del Regio Istituto Veneto di Scienze, Lettere ed Arti*, Ser. 5, IV (1878), 401–535; and "Nuovi documenti sulla vertenza tra lo Studio di Padova e la Compagnia di Gesù sul finire del secolo decimosesto," *AV*, Ser. 3, XXI, Pt. 1 (1911), 89–100.

Senate. And the fears of the University seemed increasingly justified as the Jesuit establishment began to behave more and more like a rival university and competed for its students. Given a general right to confer academic decrees by Julius III in 1550, the Jesuits in Padua began formally to list courses in the manner of the University, and they were even presumptuous enough to signal classes, like the University, by the ringing of bells. Thoroughly alarmed, the University dispatched its most distinguished scholar, the philosopher Cremonini, to address the doge and Senate in 1591 and to demand redress for these damaging activities. Cremonini claimed that the University was being emptied by Jesuit competition. He suggested that the Jesuits were engaging in actions that had never been authorized by the Senate. And he raised the sensitive jurisdictional issue by pointing out that they were granting degrees on Venetian territory simply on the basis of bulls emanating from Rome. The cause of the University, he argued, was thus the cause of the government itself. "If these Fathers . . . claim that other princes can give them privileges and empower them in the Venetian state," he declared, "this touches your Serenity and is not only our cause." [97] Cremonini's plea succeeded, and the Senate prohibited the Jesuits from competing with the University. Yet the support for the Society which emerged in the course of this dispute must have alarmed the government and confirmed its fears. More than sixty Senators abstained from voting on the matter, and the Paduan commune repeatedly asked the Senate to restore the privileges it had taken from the Jesuits.

But while Venetian antipapalism and jurisdictionalism grew more vigorous, the persistent Evangelism that had so long accompanied it also deepened. The *giovani* were a peculiarly devout generation, combining the spiritualized ecclesiology and individualism of the Evangelicals with the austerity and moral rigor of Jansenism or the Puritans.[98] The peculiar piety of the *giovani*, so different now from what prevailed elsewhere in Italy, enabled them to preserve that cool perspective on the external history of the church which had for some time served to strengthen the Venetian argument for ecclesiastical autonomy. From this stance, still fiercely committed to their own ideal of reform, they also continued to stand in judgment on the Roman church, which appeared so different from their own. In Venice, as the French ambassador observed in 1604, *Catholic* and *papist* were not the

[97] Cremonini's oration is printed in *Le Mercure Iesuite: ou recueil des pieces concernant le Progres des Iesuites, leurs Escrits, & Differents* (Geneva, 1626), pp. 441–454.
[98] Cozzi, *Contarini*, p. 224 n. 1, has made the comparison with Jansenism.

same.[99] The English ambassador, at about the same time, described the Republic as "a Signory that with long neutrality of State is at length (as it seemeth) almost slipped into a neutrality of religion."[100]

This period saw no relaxation in Catholic practice, even among those most committed to the ideals of the *giovani*. The formal observances of the faith were an important element in the traditional way of life they cherished and proposed to preserve intact, and the papal nuncio had to admit that even Leonardo Donà was "a man of much conscientiousness in confessing and taking communion."[101] But the real sources of their devotion were private. Donà, for example, was devoted to the Scriptures and to various mystical and ascetic treatises, notably those of Luis of Grenada. Like Gasparo Contarini he also studied Thomas but rejected a primarily intellectual conception of the faith. A remarkable fragment in his hand gives an intimate insight into the personal quality of his religion. "The reading of the sacred scriptures and reflection about God works in us like green wood thrown on the fire," he wrote. "In the beginning, before it catches fire, it sends up vapors, black smoke, etc., and then it bursts into flame, but with great roarings, etc. And finally, every vapor consumed, the whole becomes fire. So, in the beginning, our intellect has much difficulty and conflict; but then, penetrating with labor and protest, it tastes the good. And finally persevering in its considerations, it is so much kindled by divine love that all burns most quietly." But for Donà the culmination of religious experience, the final test of its reality, lay in active service to God's will. In a religious sense the contemplative life seemed to him incomplete. "Devotion," he declared, "is a promptness to do good, with which man is always ready to do God's will. A devout man is he who is dedicated and ready in the service of God." He was therefore constantly concerned with the quality of his own obedience, systematically scrutinized his own conduct, and made resolutions for improvement.[102]

Nicolò Contarini, whose piety was equally personal, gave particular emphasis to man's dependence on divine grace. He had absorbed the conventional Paduan conception of religions as systems of law devised "by sagacious men" to serve political ends; but, as Pomponazzi had perhaps failed to do, he clearly excepted Christianity. For Contarini Christianity

[99] Canaye, *Lettres et ambassade*, II, Part 2, 158 (letter to De Thou, Mar. 10, 1604).
[100] Wotton, letter to Sir Robert Cecil, May 23, 1603, Smith, I, 318.
[101] Quoted by Cozzi, *Contarini*, p. 32 n. 1.
[102] Seneca, *Donà*, pp. 32ff. The quotations appear on pp. 34–35.

had a higher end. It could not be conceived as law, and man's salvation was therefore emphatically God's free gift. Contarini appears, indeed, to have been attracted by some of the more extreme expressions of Pauline-Augustinian piety. He followed closely the controversy *de auxiliis*, siding strongly with the Dominican defenders of Augustine and denouncing the Jesuits, whose theology, he declared, had provoked "a pernicious schism in the Catholic Church because they attributed much to human virtue, much to the works of men, going so far as to say that these works, aided by sufficient grace, which the Lord gives to each created soul, could justify it and make it worthy of eternal salvation." He also followed the disputes over grace in the Protestant world during his later years, favoring the Gomarists over the Arminians in the same way and finally taking satisfaction in the outcome of the Synod of Dort. The same impulse even inclined him to sympathize with Islamic predestinarianism. It was also calculated, as Cozzi has observed, to reduce dependence on the institutional church.[103]

But although the more fully articulated religious attitudes of Donà and Contarini indicate the direction in which the piety of the *giovani* was tending, the ambivalent and agonized position of Paruta is probably more representative of those who supported the policies of the government. His sincerity in rejecting the political and jurisdictional claims of Rome and his devotion to Venetian ecclesiastical usages is beyond doubt. Yet near the end of his life, during his Roman embassy, he composed a pious *Soliloquio* in which, perhaps in imitation of Augustine, he examined the course of his life in a manner which has been interpreted as a repudiation, under the influence of the devout atmosphere at the Curia, of the system of values expounded in his youthful *Perfezione della vita politica*.[104]

True, in this late work Paruta deplored the vanity of his youthful interest in rhetoric and philosophy. He condemned the personal ambition that had gone into his worldly career and admitted that it would have been better if he had studied holy things instead of history. He clearly opposed divine wisdom to the worldly wisdom of statesmen, he insisted on the dependence of all rulers on God and, most seriously of all, he expressed his regret that he had devoted himself to an active life in which he had been compelled to transact the world's business at the expense of the greater good of his soul. Rome, once queen of the universe and now in ruins around him, reminded him of the fate of all worldly success. Where now, he asked, were her

---

[103] Cozzi, *Contarini*, pp. 160–161, 212–221.

[104] For example by Candeloro, "Paolo Paruta," pp. 63–64; and by Cozzi, "Paruta, Sarpi, e Ceneda," p. 209. The work is included in Paruta's *Opere politiche*, I, 1–14.

treasures, her majesty, her victories, her pompous triumphs? Rome signified to him that all things (clearly including Venice) are the prey of time and death. The best life now seemed to him a holy leisure "given entirely to prayers and meditations: leisure which is the true business, the true transaction and the true nourishment of souls." [105]

Nevertheless, Paruta's *Soliloquio* is not so simple a work as concentration on these elements would suggest; it does not, I think, unequivocally reject, even momentarily, the civic values of his youth. Much of the work appears to be directed not against civic life as such but against some moral inadequacies incidental to his own career. Thus Paruta is explicit that the vanity and ambition which had spoiled his life in the world were in fact ubiquitous and equally to be encountered "in the hidden retreats of those who flee the world." [106] If monastic withdrawal struck him briefly as desirable for himself, this was not because he really considered it better in itself but only because of his personal failure to engage, in the proper spirit, with "love of children, governance of family, administration of property, and the business of the Republic." He saw all these as good in themselves, and his own sin only as having cared for them too much. Even here, however, he consoled himself that at least he wished to be better than he was, a sure sign that he had not been abandoned by grace.[107]

Nor should the reader be misled by other passages in the *Soliloquio*. Thus its denunciation of intellectuality and his insistence that the good is rather to be performed than to be grasped by the mind were rather more consistent with his earlier position than he seems himself to have realized. And if he ranked history lower than sacred studies, he nevertheless continued to describe it as "a good work, a worthy work." [108] Most striking of all is the prayer with which Paruta concludes this devout meditation on his life. The prayer is an eloquent reconciliation of the apparently conflicting sets of values he had been opposing to each other in his own mind, in a kind of dialogue similar to the calculated opposition between men or ideas in his earlier works. The prayer opens, indeed, with a conception of his political career as a religious calling:

> If I am called to this, to the duty of working in this situation, and to spend my talent in this civil life, help my weakness, Lord, with thy

[105] *Soliloquio*, p. 11.
[106] P. 5.
[107] P. 12.
[108] P. 6.

immense grace, so that I may give thanks for my happy moments to thee alone, author of all my good. To thee be all honor and praise; and from my labors in the world may I not lose that merit which thou desirest to be acquired through suffering in thy name and through directing all my labors to thee. Help me, Lord, that I may think of my mortal children in such a way that I do not forget thee. May I govern my faculties knowing that thou hast given them to me, that thou hast preserved them for me, and that my duty is to use well the gifts of thy grace. May I love my earthly country, but not so that I take less account of my celestial country. May I serve and obey my Republic with integrity of conscience, with the end of serving thee and not myself, for thy glory not for mine. She [Venice] is a marvelous work of thy hand, and must be recognized as thy workmanship alone, since she has been preserved for so long a course of years, as a unique example, in liberty, in dominion, in true religion. Therefore, if I cannot serve thee immediately with fervor of soul, help me at least that I may not be an unworthy and unprofitable servant to thee in this, the most excellent creation that thou hast made.[109]

Paruta's *Soliloquio* is eloquent testimony that the piety of the *giovani* was often tense and uncomfortable. It required painful self-examination and self-condemnation, and it imposed a constant responsibility to see clearly the relationship between civic and spiritual values. In individual cases, too, the adjustment of experience in this world to the requirements of God proved difficult for these men. Indeed Paruta hints that monasticism was enviable only because it looked easy; the true heroes of the spirit for him are by implication those who remain in the world, accepting its responsibilities and enduring its temptations. The *Soliloquio* can therefore hardly be read as an old man's capitulation at last to the Counter Reformation. It is rather a reexamination and finally a reassertion of civic values, but within a more serious religious framework appropriate to the increasing maturity and the deepening responsibilities of the Venetian reformers.

In view of the charges that would soon be heard from Rome that these men secretly favored Protestantism, it should also be recorded that, whatever the tendencies of their piety, the leaders of the *giovani* were consistently unsympathetic to concrete Protestant movements. Donà recorded his disapproval of Protestantism from time to time throughout his life, for

[109] P. 13.

example on the occasion of his embassy to Austria in 1577, which shocked him as a "sink of every sort of heretics." [110] Contarini was equally outspoken. He associated the Protestant Reformation with political disorder and insisted that it was an insult to God, "who wishes to be adored with the ancient, universal and united consent." [111] The democratic tendencies they discerned in Protestantism offended the aristocratic prejudices of the Venetians, but they were above all repelled by it as innovation, a conception that, whether in church or state, they found almost viscerally antagonistic.[112] Although they were concerned like their predecessors to prevent any extension of the powers of the Roman Holy Office in Venetian territory, they continued to suppress heresy.

On the other hand they appear to have been even less inclined than earlier Venetians to condemn the Greeks as heretics or even as schismatics, or to take action against their Greek subjects. Whether for religious reasons or because the Venetian position in the Levant after Lepanto particularly demanded peace within the remnant of their empire, their treatment of the Greeks was increasingly relaxed. The Greek colony in Venice grew in numbers (though a contemporary estimate of 15,000 in 1580 is probably too high), and it now enjoyed its period of greatest commercial and cultural prosperity. The Greek church in Venice was placed directly under the jurisdiction of the patriarch in Constantinople, to the distress of Rome; and the tolerance of Greeks by the Venetian government was a constant sore point in Venetian relations with the papacy.[113]

Like earlier reformers in the tradition of Italian Evangelism, the *giovani* professed a deep respect for the authority and leadership of the pope in all things *spiritual*. Paruta was emphatic on this point.[114] But, in view of the political and jurisdictional pressures emanating from the Curia, the distinction on which this profession was based was a more powerful element in the Venetian attitude to Rome during this period than sentiments of loyalty and obedience. This distinction, as we have seen, had made possible the first Venetian attempts to view the institutional church historically. And toward the end of the century the tendency to sort out the various roles combined in the papal office which had informed the relations of earlier

[110] Seneca, *Donà*, pp. 113ff.
[111] Quoted by Cozzi, *Contarini*, p. 211, n. 1, from the *Historie venetiane*.
[112] Cf. Cozzi, *Contarini*, pp. 112, 213–214.
[113] Cf. Geanakoplos, *Greek Scholars in Venice*, pp. 43ff.
[114] In his *Relazione di Roma*, Albèri, Ser. 2, IV, 361–362.

Venetian ambassadors to the Holy See grew sharper. It reached a climax with the lengthy *Relazione* by Paruta in 1595, one of the great documents of Venetian reformism.

Even Giovanni Corraro, the last ambassador in Rome before the *giovani* came to power, had made the familiar distinctions. "The pope, in my judgment, can be considered in three ways," he declared in his relation of 1581: "First as head of the church and patron in spiritual things; then as prince and ruler of his own state; and last as a prince who, in political affairs common to all states, can in various matters act as mediator among others." But Corraro had included in his description of the pope's spiritual office the power to levy taxes, and his conception of the pope as universal mediator implied a position of superiority over the entire political order.[115] The ambassadors dispatched to Rome by the *giovani*, more sensitive on such matters, somewhat altered the analysis. Thus, in 1589, Giovanni Gritti avoided the hint of any general papal supremacy in politics with his simpler formula. "The condition of His Holiness," Gritti declared starkly, "can be considered as spiritual and temporal." He was careful, in his discussion of these two dimensions of papal activity, to discuss the jurisdictional action of the pope only in connection with his temporal role.[116] Paruta followed this example. "The Roman pope," he noted, "can be considered in terms of the two persons he incorporates: that is, as head and universal pastor of all Christendom, and vicar of Christ and true successor of Peter in the Catholic and Apostolic Church; and then as temporal prince who holds a state in Italy." [117]

This analysis supplied the framework for Paruta's harsh indictment of the historical papacy, which in his view had deliberately blurred this essential distinction and had wantonly exploited the spiritual authority of the pope as vicar of Christ to promote his ambitions as an Italian prince. "The popes have sometimes been accustomed to take up spiritual weapons even for differences over temporal things," he asserted in explicit reference to Venetian experience. "Subjecting princes to censures and absolving subject peoples from their oath of fidelity and obedience, and by these means execrating and cursing princes and their states, they cause in them the greatest confusion and the most dangerous disorders; and many times the righteousness of the cause or late repentance do not suffice to free them." Ecclesiastical censure

[115] *Ibid.*, 284–285.
[116] *Ibid.*, pp. 334–335.
[117] *Ibid.*, p. 359.

had been effective, he explained, "because men generally judge things according to what seems clear on the surface to all, even though in reality they were of a different nature." [118]

Paruta's remarkable emphasis on the uses of ecclesiastical censure suggests that Venetian memories and apprehensions had been significantly revived by encounters with the more militant papacy of recent decades. But he may also have been stimulated to consider the subject by the attention he had given to the Italian policies of the papacy in the earlier parts of his *Historia vinetiana*. In this work he had attributed to Rome, over the course of many years, an all-consuming and illegitimate preoccupation with political aggrandizement, chiefly at the expense of Venice. At the same time he had developed, in the *Historia*, a consistent picture of the ineptness of papal interventions in the political arena which was also to color his historical vision. For Paruta, as for other Venetians, the failures of papal policy were almost as strong an argument for a spiritual church as the need to preserve the purity of its mission. Thus, in recording the death of Julius II, he had noted as the common view of contemporaries that its cause had been sheer mortification over political failure. "For certainly," he had remarked, "many signs reveal in Julius the greatest ferocity of mind, which neither age nor the dignity of his office was sufficient to correct or to temper. He could not observe measure or moderation, but was precipitately moved by his appetites like a blind man." [119] Paruta was aware that Leo X had displayed an admirable interest in high culture, but this pope was chiefly important for him because of his family ambitions and his unrelenting hostility to Venice. Fortunately his "arts" had everywhere deprived him of credit, so that his designs had come to nothing.[120] He depicted Clement VII as credulous, imprudent, and constantly oscillating between cupidity and fear,[121] and Paul III during his last years as moved by an imprudence that had brought his house, the church, and Italy close to ruin.[122] The popes of the earlier sixteenth century, as Paruta viewed them, were not religious leaders but merely defective politicians; and although he recognized the genuine concern of the contemporary papacy with ecclesiastical reform,[123]

[118] *Ibid.*, p. 366.
[119] *Historia vinetiana*, p. 11.
[120] *Ibid.*, pp. 30–31, 127, 176.
[121] *Ibid.*, pp. 237–238.
[122] *Ibid.*, pp. 496, 501.
[123] Cf. his dispatches of Nov. 21 and Dec. 5, 1592, and May 29, 1593, *Legazione*, I, 21, 34, 220. See also the *Relazione* of Lorenzo Priuli, Albèri, Ser. 2, IV, 305.

his vision of that institution was still largely determined by what had occurred in the past. Precisely when the dignity and authority of the pope's person and office were being deliberately exalted in Rome, Paruta, aided by the distinction between the pope as a prince and the pope as a spiritual authority, chose to emphasize his human limitations. In the eyes of a Venetian, the pope seemed, perhaps even more than other men, subject to passion and error.[124]

This humanization of individual popes was accompanied, among the ambassadors at the end of the century, by an acceleration in that historicization of the papacy already hinted at by some of their predecessors. Although Gritti had been little given to historical analysis, even he contributed to this tendency with a radical explanation for the origins of the Roman primacy. Rome had become the seat of the papacy, he calmly suggested, because she had previously been the temporal capital of the world. "The head of this noble state," he declared of the domains of the church, "is Rome which, having in other times been head of the world, deserves to have the Vicar of Christ maintain his habitation in her. For he too, through respect for religion, now extends his absolute dominion through all the provinces of the universe." [125] Gritti apparently thought it unnecessary to mention Saint Peter in discussing this question.

But the most comprehensive application of historical analysis to the papacy appeared in the *Relazione* of Paruta, by this time an experienced historian who, while in Rome, was still working on his official history of Venice. He aimed to show that the temporal power of the popes, so tragically confused with their proper spiritual authority, was based not on immutable divine right but on historical accident. "The pope only began to hold the name and authority of a temporal prince seven hundred years after Peter, the first pope, held this supreme grade of the priesthood," Paruta stated flatly. "That happened through the donations made to the church and to the Roman pontiffs by various princes, as a result of which various cities and provinces of Italy which had before obeyed the empire of the west and then

---

[124] Cf. the entry in the diary of Francesco da Molino, one of the younger supporters of the *giovani*, as quoted by Cozzi, *Contarini*, p. 30. Molino wrote in 1585: "As vicar of our Lord in spiritual things concerning the faith and the salvation of our souls, he ought to be obeyed and adored as an oracle; but as a prince in temporal things he must be considered a man, exposed to passions like others, so that it is legitimate to oppose him in unjust actions."

[125] In his *Relazione* of 1589, Albèri, Ser. 2, IV, 336.

for a while were occupied by northern barbarians, as happened to the rest of Italy, came under their dominion." [126]

But, like other Venetians, Paruta was interested above all in the constitutional development of the papal church. He discerned in it what, for a Venetian, could only have seemed a process of subversion: the gradual substitution of papal autocracy for an aristocracy traditionally exercised by the College of Cardinals. He knew that the church had not been originally ruled by the cardinalate; the Sacred College had come into existence, he admitted, no more than five centuries earlier.[127] Nor was he afflicted with any blind reverence for the cardinals as a group; he treated them with the same cool detachment he applied to the papacy. He emphasized the degeneration of the Sacred College from its original excellence. For, he declared, men had increasingly been appointed to that body "through blood, or particular friendship, or old and close service, or are closely related to popes, or are recommended and protected by the favor of princes, and many times without any distinction, either of age or of any condition of persons." The distressing result had been that, "although presumably there is a choice of the most excellent men from all the provinces of Christendom, since the door is open to all without any exception for birth or for any other respect, the excellence of the subjects included there does not correspond to the conception, if one has regard to most of them." [128] There was probably, in the back of his mind, some comparison with the Venetian Senate.

The authority of the cardinalate had almost inevitably declined as its quality had deteriorated. Paruta perceptively traced this process back to Pius II; since his pontificate the government of the church had steadily tended toward monarchy. "In previous ages," he wrote, "the cardinals were accustomed to be participants with the popes in the most important negotiations in that government, which were treated in Consistory by decision through the votes of the cardinals; and the resolutions were published as made, so it was said, *de consensu fratrum.* But for some time now, that is from the pontificate of Pius II until this age, everything has been more and more withdrawn to the supreme authority of the popes; and recently

---

[126] *Ibid.*, p. 360. Note that Paruta's chronology completely excludes from consideration the Donation of Constantine.

[127] P. 376.

[128] Pp. 376–377. Paruta noted also (p. 379) the practice of appointing one worthy man in order to make a group of other new cardinals tolerable.

this restriction of things has gone so far that now nothing is done in Consistory except the distribution of such churches as from time to time fall vacant." Essential business, Paruta reported, was now all transacted privately by the pope, who at best only communicated his decisions to the cardinals later. On the other hand, afraid to offend the pope by opposing him, they had been reduced "to adulation rather than free counseling." [129]

At the same time Paruta noted that the popes had steadily subverted the liberties of the Roman commune; his attention to this process, which had not been remarked by earlier ambassadors, probably also reflects a heightened republican sensitivity. The Roman people, as Paruta informed the Senate, had long been accustomed to designate a secular representative who bore the title of senator. But in 1389 Boniface IX had taken over the appointment of this officer and had in addition begun to choose other Roman magistrates. "Thus," Paruta concluded, "little by little everything has been absorbed by the single and supreme authority of the pope and now depends, as has been said, on his free and arbitrary will alone. And at present it can be said that there remains only the name and appearance of that ancient form of government in which the people had authority, since the pope gives this task and dignity of senator and conservator of the Roman people to persons of humble condition, who retain little authority and little dignity." [130]

Paruta was also struck by the unlimited authority of the pope in the governance of the papal state, a condition he evidently regarded as unprecedented:

> The pope commands the whole ecclesiastical state with supreme authority and with simple and absolute empire, the whole depending on his will alone. So that it can truly be said that it is a royal government, of a kind unusually free and immune from such strict control as various other royal states are subjected to by the great authority of councils or parliaments or the barons or the peoples, according to the customs and privileges of diverse provinces. But the pope ordains and disposes of all things with supreme and absolute authority, without any counsel but what pleases himself, and without receiving any impediment from any obviously opposing institution, as I have seen proved in many very important affairs and negotiations transacted during my time at that court.[131]

[129] Pp. 412–413.
[130] Pp. 414–415.
[131] P. 412.

No government could have differed more radically from that of Venice; in other words no government could be regarded, on theoretical grounds, as more defective than that operated by the pope.

Its theoretical deficiencies were reflected, as Paruta emphasized, in a general practical failure which, again, could be attributed largely to constitutional defects. The pope, Paruta pointed out, was an elected ruler; and in elective states consistent administration depended on regularly constituted bodies of magistrates to temper princely authority and maintain continuity. But in the papal state all arrangements depended on the whims of successive popes, each of whom created a whole new bureaucracy.[132] The consequence was what Paruta evidently considered one of the most inept governments in Europe. Papal administration, in spite of its severity and heavy taxes, was unable to maintain order, and bandits terrorized the countryside. Agriculture, once so productive, was as a result no longer sufficient to supply local needs. The nobility was irresponsible, extravagant, and heavily in debt, and the populace had generally lost the ability to use arms. There were few towns or persons of consequence outside Rome, and all elements in the population detested the government. "The ecclesiastical state," Paruta concluded, "is preserved and maintained not through good institutions or any of those internal things that generally make other states and empires secure and durable, but because there is nobody who wishes or ought to attempt anything against it." [133] Comparison with the admirable government of his own republic is implicit in Paruta's entire description of that provided by the pope and his ecclesiastical administrators. So is the familiar Venetian conviction that the clergy, incompetent in worldly affairs, should confine themselves to things of the spirit.

Thus in the course of its recent history the papacy had revealed a general hostility to republican and constitutional institutions in both church and state. Successful at least in destroying these, there were now no restraints on its ambitions; and Venice presumably had much cause for alarm. Strictly for political reasons, therefore, she favored reform of the church. But as men of piety, the *giovani* were also concerned with the need for reform on religious grounds. The developments Paruta recorded at such length disturbed them because they threatened to destroy the ability of the church to fulfill its spiritual mission.

Thus Paruta included in his *Relazione* a discussion of the general religious

[132] Pp. 419–420.
[133] Pp. 388–397.

decadence of the age. Religious zeal, he noted, had been generally greater in the past;[134] and, in spite of its larger pretensions in his own time, the actual authority of the pope had been much diminished. In earlier ages, Paruta remarked, "it extended more widely into many provinces, in some of which the name of the pope is no longer even known; and in others it is not only no longer esteemed as formerly but even extremely despised and abhorred." [135] It was clear that the increasing intrusion of the papacy into politics, its confusion of realms, its exploitation of the veneration due spiritual authority to promote its temporal empire, had been subversive of its evangelical mission.

Although none of the recent developments in Rome seemed so fundamentally objectionable to Paruta as the tendency to a general papal monarchy, he also offered other criticisms related to it. Thus his sense of the dignity of the lay estate was repelled by the clericalism of the Curia, above all its arrogance toward princes. This attitude, he asserted, encouraged the "impertinent operations" of ecclesiastics everywhere; and he described his own remonstrances to the pope about the inequities and disorders encouraged by clerical presumption. "When any disagreement arises between lay and ecclesiastical persons," he had told the pope, "greater consideration is given to the quality of the person, whether he is of the church or secular, than to the quality of the thing at issue or to knowing which side has the right or wrong. From these things are born notable disorders and very notable distaste in the minds of princes and also of peoples." Clement VIII, Paruta reported, "shows himself rather hot about these matters, not only through his own inclination but also through the many suggestions made to him emphasizing to him his own dignity and the reputation of the Holy See and of ecclesiastical things." [136] Paruta also professed to be shocked by the financial greed of the papacy, which in his view tended to reduce respect for religion.[137] He denounced as a "scandal" the employment of bishops in temporal offices, since this interfered with their proper duties.[138] And, like his predecessors, he attacked nepotism which, in spite of all papal

[134] P. 365.

[135] Pp. 360–361. Paruta noted gains in the Indies, but he considered these far less than the losses of the century.

[136] Pp. 375–376.

[137] See the remarks on p. 411, which conclude a long discussion of papal finances. Giovanni Gritti had been critical in much the same way in 1589 (Albèri, Ser. 2, IV, 337–338).

[138] P. 419.

disclaimers, he considered a continuing abuse in the administration of the church.[139]

But his disgust was particularly directed to the Curia, where he saw most sharply the contrast between the profession of sanctity and the flawed realities of politics, the almost inevitable results of the church's involvement in worldly affairs. The sense of this incongruity was hardly a novelty in Venice. In his *Relazione* of 1576, Paolo Tiepolo had noted the preponderance of lawyers at the Curia and the scarcity of theologians, "although theology ought to be the principal profession of priests." [140] Paruta now elaborated on this theme. Every issue was evaluated in Rome, he reported, according to its effect on the papal interest, and then settled not as a religious question but by factional pressures.[141] The political character of the Curia was sufficiently scandalous as it determined the general administration of the church, but (as previous ambassadors had also remarked) it was especially serious when it affected the choice of a new pope. Long before the death of an incumbent pontiff, the question of his successor became the object of intricate pressures and intrigues. Under these circumstances, Paruta suggested, the preservation of the papal church could only be interpreted as a divine miracle. "It certainly appears," he declared, "that the Lord God (to demonstrate effectively that the election of his vicar on earth does not depend on human effort and counsel) permits those who think about it most, and seek to attain it by human and often improper means, to achieve that dignity very rarely. And he allows the election to turn out, as it truly does, through divine inspiration and providence, differently from the thoughts of men and also of the wisest and most expert in the Curia. Thus, though it is not useless to understand these more general circumstances, so it would be presumptuous and vain to make any particular and more explicit judgment about them." [142] The balance in these remarks between piety and irony is difficult to assess.

But although the *giovani* were critical and suspicious of the papacy, they were resolved to maintain the traditional piety of the Republic. The doges of the later sixteenth century, for example Pasquale Cicogna (1585–1595), were esteemed for sanctity even in Rome. The story was told that one day a consecrated host, carried by a gust of wind, had been carefully deposited

[139] Pp. 420–421, 442.
[140] Pp. 222–223.
[141] P. 381, with particular reference to relations with France.
[142] P. 383.

on the altar before which Cicogna was praying.[143] Meanwhile the government was friendly to reform under local auspices. Lorenzo Priuli, the first patriarch chosen after the *giovani* came to power and at the time a layman, proved a vigorous reformer; and his decrees requiring examinations and residence for his clergy led them to protest to Rome.[144] A number of Venetian bishops during this period were distinguished as reformers in their dioceses.[145]

In any case, there is little evidence to support the charges which eventually came out of Rome that Venice was now entering into a serious moral and spiritual decline.[146] The impressions of foreigners at this time, indeed, give a rather different picture. Botero, writing in this period, remarked that "there is no place where the churches are more used, the sermons more frequented, sacred persons more respected, divine worship celebrated with more magnificence, feast days celebrated with more honor." [147] Henry Wotton in 1592 compared Florentine morality unfavorably with that of Venice; from Florence he wrote home: "I live here in a paradise inhabited with devils. Venice hath scarce heard of those vices which are here practised." [148] The French ambassador, Canaye de Fresnes, found the moral atmosphere of the city in 1602 considerably improved over what it had been thirty years before, the clergy better disciplined, and religious services more impressive. "In short," he declared, "everything that can be desired for the consolation of the soul abounds here as much as in any city in Christendom." [149] Even a contemporary Spanish ambassador agreed on this point.[150]

The more vigorous commercial policy of the *giovani*, their willingness to take a more active part in international affairs, and their heightened distrust of the monarchical papacy were accompanied by an acceleration of the movement away from the utopian and systematic political vision of the earlier sixteenth century, and toward a political and historical understanding resembling that of the mature Florentine Renaissance. Venetians were now

[143] Giuseppe de Luca, "Della pietà veneziana nel Seicento e d'un prete veneziano quietista," *La civiltà veneziana nell'eta barocca*, p. 223.

[144] Niero, pp. 102–104.

[145] Cf. the list in Pastor, XXIV, 190–191.

[146] Cessi, *Storia di Venezia*, II, 159.

[147] *Relationi universali*, p. 798. See his whole discussion of Venetian religion, pp. 794–800.

[148] Letter to Lord Zouche, June 25, 1592, Smith, I, pp. 280–281.

[149] Letter to Beaulieu, Jan. 19, 1602, *Lettres et ambassade*, I, 120.

[150] Francesco Vera, quoted in Nürnberger, "Paul V und das Interdikt," pp. 201–202.

increasingly interested in the political culture of Florence. If Giovanni Battista Leoni published in 1583 an extended refutation of Guicciardini's animadversions against Venice, he did so because of his general respect for the latter's knowledge and judgment;[151] and the Jesuit Possevino, now in Padua, wrote against Machiavelli (along with various French political writers) because young Venetians were displaying a growing interest in his ideas.[152] Paruta, as we shall see, was deeply (if not openly) interested in Machiavelli. But the growing Venetian application to Florentine thought must be understood as part of a more general shift in the political climate of the Republic.

Not all Venetians participated in this development. The rhetorical *Panegirico* of Iason de Nores, for example, was clearly intended to appeal to Venetians for whom the traditional static idealism still expressed essential political truth. For Nores Venice was still the eternal city, her perpetuity guaranteed by an original constitution that had achieved a perfect balance of social forces. He celebrated, to the satisfaction of his audience, the equality of her citizens, the justice of her laws, the freedom of her subjects, and the unqualified order insured by her government. There is no hint in this work that any change was taking place in the political mentality of the Republic.[153]

Considerably more interesting from this standpoint is the *Compendio universal di republica* of Pier'Maria Contarini,[154] which not only suggests that this period intensified the fearful and defensive attitudes of certain Venetians but also reveals how an extreme conservatism could itself be subversive of established practice. This work contains a good deal of incidental common sense which hints that even its author may have read Machiavelli. But although it is ostensibly in praise of republics, it deals with them primarily by advancing general and conventional maxims, based rather on antique than on contemporary practice. It is also considerably less interested in liberty—for more fervent republicans the essential condition of human greatness and dignity—than in security. Indeed it appears to define liberty *as* security; it declared that the purposes of liberty are first "against violence, that one man should not be oppressed by another," and second

---

[151] *Considerationi sopra l'Historia d'Italia di Messer F. Guicciardini* (Venice, 1583; reprinted in 1599 and 1600). For his admiration of Giucciardini, see p. 2 of the first edition. Even Pietro Giustiniani had read Guicciardini; see his *Historie*, sigs. PPPPr⁴-QQQQ1ʳ.

[152] J. Ledit, "Possevino," *Dictionnaire de Théologie Catholique*, XII: 2 (Paris, 1935), col. 2652.

[153] *Panegirico in laude della Serenissima Republica di Venetia* (Padua, 1590).

[154] Published in Venice in 1602.

"the enjoyment of the goods of Fortune without fear."[155] As a result of such anxieties, Contarini seems less concerned to extol republics than to celebrate aristocratic governments as best suited to keep the dangerous populous (which he abhorred) under control.[156] And although he praised Venice as a perfect mixture of social elements, its perfection consisted for him not in a genuine balance among them but in their subordination to one another in a regular hierarchy.[157] Among the various agencies of a republican polity, furthermore, he evidently preferred such bodies as the Council of Ten as most effective for the maintenance of order.[158] He distrusted senates because of the delays incident to their debates and the impossibility of keeping their proceedings secret, and in such bodies he particularly feared the influence of the young.[159] Even Pier'Maria Contarini's preference for a more narrowly aristocratic and even oligarchic government thus aided in the disintegration of the old ideal.

But the most articulate political writer of later sixteenth-century Venice, and probably again the best representative of the changing mood of the Republic, was Paolo Paruta. His attitudes are most fully revealed in his *Discorsi politici*[160] and to a lesser degree in his official histories. These works, composed during the most active period of his public service, exhibit at once continuities with the thought of earlier generations, some identification with the policies and concerns of the *giovani*, and (to a far greater extent than his youthful *Perfezione della vita politica*) an effort at realistic political analysis based on study of the concrete political and historical world.

He did not altogether abandon the static idealism of the earlier century. Venice, he declared at the beginning of the *Historia vinetiana*, was "a true image of perfect government," although he allowed some place for development by admitting that the intelligence of her founding fathers had been completed "by time and experience."[161] Nevertheless several passages in his work sound remarkably academic. He was attracted, for example, to the

---

[155] Pp. 24–25.

[156] So, p. 40, he concludes a lengthy discussion of the defects of popular government: "Il popolo in confusione è somigliato ad un Mostro pieno di confusione, e d'errore per le varie e incerte volontà de molti."

[157] Thus, p. 72, he concludes a discussion of the five (not three) elements in society: "Con tal temperamento, che sta un grado subordinato all'altro. Cosi tempra la Republica di Venetia la sua forma. Di cinque governi proportionati in un solo."

[158] Cf. p. 47.

[159] Pp. 59, 65.

[160] First published by his sons in 1599, shortly after his death.

[161] P. 3.

The redecoration of the Great Council Chamber: the Pope and the Doge allowing the Emperor's son to sue for peace in 1177 *(Palma Giovane)*.

The redecoration of the Great Council Chamber: the Doge receiving the ceremonial umbrella from Pope Alexander III at Ancona in 1177 *(Gambarato).*

image of a constitution as the soul of the body politic,[162] and he saw the question of its perfection as somehow independent of the practical fate of the state for which it had been devised. Too many external circumstances, too many adverse blows of fortune, he suggested, might damage or even destroy a state; but such misfortune could not, in itself, justify doubt of its perfection.[163] Paruta made this point, however, with specific reference to the Venetian reverses of 1509; and much of his academicism served to justify the realities of Venetian life. Thus he noted that "the right disposition of the orders and honors of the city requires geometrical proportion rather than arithmetical, so that the same things are not granted to all but to each what is most convenient for him. And certainly to institute a city with such a form that all citizens are equal would be exactly like composing a song with a single part. Just as the latter would produce no true harmony, so from the former no good concord would result. Therefore it is to be recommended that a state should keep every order from either rising too high or falling too low lest, like a tone that is either too flat or too sharp, it produce dissonance." [164] Although the mathematical and musical language in this passage comes from the study, its political meaning is altogether clear.

Much of his attention was thus directed to justifying the aristocratic government of Venice; the distance between his position and that of Pier'Maria Contarini was, on this point, perhaps slightly less than that between Machiavelli and Guicciardini. He drew on the classic arguments. Inequality, he pointed out, was the way of nature, and only some men were qualified to rule.[165] But most of his evidence came from history, which, he believed, proved that equality always produces disorder. It revealed that the ablest men are always likely to revolt against an unnatural equality, which could only be enforced by tyranny.[166] An excess of democracy, he argued, had been a basic defect of the Roman Republic, and a major cause of its instability.[167] No government could be secure, he declared, if it relied on "the will of the people which, by nature mutable, is moved to favor a foreign prince for the most trivial reasons and sometimes only through desire for novelty, which plots against the existing state with seditions and

[162] *Discorsi*, pp. 6,.8–9, 246–247.

[163] P. 247.

[164] Pp. 16–17. Paruta is explaining the defects in the Roman version of the mixed constitution.

[165] Pp. 203–204.

[166] Pp. 202–204.

[167] The point, developed at some length, is summarized on p. 228.

open force, and which gives both itself and the city into the power of another." [168] On the other hand his preoccupation with the problem of the too-mighty citizen suggests the concern of his generation with the possibility that Venice might decline into an oligarchy.[169]

Paruta displays a remarkable respect for the conservative political virtues, perhaps more than many of his contemporaries. Few Venetians would have disagreed with his sentiment that a man who preserves what has been previously acquired is as worthy of praise as he who acquires it,[170] a proposition fitting the Venetian case precisely; and none of the *giovani* would presumably have quarreled with his "general rule that states are conserved by proceeding along the same paths by which they were founded, since everything is preserved and maintained through what is similar to itself and is corrupted through what is contrary." [171] But perhaps not all of them would have entirely shared his admiration for circumspection. Paruta was opposed to taking risks; and it was appropriate that the discourses as printed by his sons should have concluded with the observation that caution is "a rule approved by the universal consent of men." Where the alternatives were doubtful, Paruta wrote, it was better to avoid action than to push ahead, since "after the act all repentance is too late and in vain; whereas, when things stay unresolved, there is still opportunity to take new counsel." [172] He was particularly dubious of the risks of war. He considered the courage of Hannibal a doubtful virtue,[173] and he recommended that too ardent a man should never be made a general.[174] Paruta's conservatism is thus also related to his pacifism, which was unusually prominent among his political attitudes; in nothing else was he so enthusiastically Aristotelian. Peace, for Paruta, was not only the natural condition of human society but the essential condition of "civil felicity" and thus of all the positive values of human existence.[175] He was clear that war was only justified as a means to peace.[176] Even more than earlier Venetians he rested the case for the superiority of Venice over ancient Rome

[168] P. 320.
[169] As pp. 198–207.
[170] P. 60.
[171] P. 167. A similar passage is on p. 140.
[172] P. 371.
[173] P. 71.
[174] P. 274. Paruta drew this lesson from the battles of Novara and Agnadello.
[175] Pp. 309, 105–106.
[176] Cf. *Sopra la pace*, p. 428.

on her long devotion to peace.[177] This emphasis suggests that Paruta had reservations about the new activism of his government.

But Paruta's conservatism was only one dimension of a singularly complex political vision which, indeed, seems to originate in a deep conviction of the complexity of all political experience and thus the need to view it from various directions at once. This conviction is generally reflected in the structure of the *Discorsi* which, though Paruta did not assign antithetical views to individualized spokesmen, are as dialectical as the *Perfezione della vita politica*. But in this case Paruta himself represented now one side and now the other on a variety of political questions, partly no doubt because he wished to determine the element of truth in each position, but partly also out of his willingness, as a man experienced in affairs of state, to recognize that political issues are almost always ambiguous and can rarely be resolved with absolute clarity. He usually tried, at the end of each of his internalized debates, to draw conclusions that would incorporate whatever might be valid on both sides, generally by distinguishing between situations.[178] His method occasionally makes it difficult to determine his final position on particular issues, but it is perhaps even more significant than his substantive conclusions as evidence of the change in political understanding through which his generation was passing. Gasparo Contarini had expressed himself in a very different manner.

Machiavelli's *Discorsi* had an important, if largely unacknowledged, place in the background of Paruta's discourses which, like those of his great Florentine predecessor, used Livy as the point of departure for a series of general reflections. Paruta wished to dissociate himself as far as possible from Machiavelli, no doubt partly because he feared that comparisons damaging to himself might be made. He declared rather unconvincingly that, in spite of "the curiosity of the subjects" Machiavelli had chosen to discuss, his works were now "buried in perpetual oblivion." Since they had been condemned by the pope, Paruta piously asserted, Machiavelli's writings were no longer even mentionable.[179] Accordingly he mentioned them very

---

[177] P. 211.

[178] So on the wisdom of making leagues, he concludes (pp. 287–288): "A conoscer, dunque, la verità tra queste diversità di ragioni e d'esempi, bisogna distinguere e separatamente considerare, per quali occasioni e con quali rispetti sia ciascuna lega fatta; quale fine sia stato in essa proposto; con quali patti e leggi sia stata congiunta: perocchè, da questi particolari, si potrà meglio conoscere ciò che di bene o di male partorir possa a collegarsi, e se abbia a riuscire di più breve o più lunga durazione."

[179] P. 209.

little. This disavowal, nevertheless, should not obscure the fact that his own political speculation was in large measure the consequence of a fruitful encounter with Machiavelli. Paruta's *Discorsi politici* marked the deliberate return to the main themes of Renaissance political discussion, three generations after Machiavelli, under the auspices of republican Venice.[180]

Paruta agreed with Machiavelli on various matters. He shared his view of the use of mercenaries, although he gave the subject less emphasis.[181] He also noted that "the operations of a prince should be measured by quite different rules from those of a philosopher." [182] But although he was also sharply critical of Machiavelli, he attacked him not because of his own respect for orthodoxy in faith and morals or because he was outraged by Machiavelli's novel political vision but, like Guicciardini, because Machiavelli had failed to go far enough. To Paruta, Machiavelli seemed too rational, too respectful of regularities, too optimistic; his thought had been too little based on the discrete, empirical, unpredictable, and uncontrollable realities of historical experience. Machiavelli had himself been too much the philosopher.

Paruta's most direct attack on Machiavelli was aimed against his use of the Roman model. Few Venetians could have responded favorably to Machiavelli's praise of Rome, but Paruta was not content to refute him merely by denouncing the Roman achievement. He did this with remarkable sophistication as we shall see, but he went beyond it to attack, like Guicciardini, the principle involved in extracting universal precepts from particular historical situations. Machiavelli, he declared, had failed "to distinguish between one thing and another, and between one time and another." Paruta wrote: "He praises and extols equally all the ordinances and all the actions of the Roman Republic in such a way, that he proposes as an example to all other princes and republics some things also that are more worthy of blame than of imitation and which were the cause of the ruin of the Republic of Rome itself." [183] There was, for Paruta, no universal political wisdom, accessible either to natural reason or to empirical investigation, that could guarantee the health or the survival of states.

His difference from Machiavelli on this fundamental issue usually appears less directly, but it is implicit in most of his political expression. In Paruta's

[180] On the relations between Paruta and Machiavelli, cf. Rodolfo de Mattei, *Dal premachiavellismo all'antimachiavellismo europeo del Cinquecento* (Rome, 1956), pp. 124ff.

[181] Pp. 228–229, 292–293.

[182] P. 240.

[183] P. 210.

vision all earthly experience presents itself as a chaos of unrelated and unstable impressions. Its contradictions sometimes appeared to distress him, and its variety occasionally gave him a wry delight;[184] but he was certain that it is absolutely beyond man's intellectual grasp. "So many accidents can occur," he remarked, "that it is not possible to comprehend every particular under the same rule." [185] The only general principle he was prepared to accept was a general prohibition against generalization: "The truest and most general rule is that not all things can be accommodated to all things. Nor in these operations of ours pertinent to civil life is there to be found that which is simply and for itself good (which would be in vain). But various things prove useful for various ends and for various persons, and ought to be accommodated to the condition of the times, to the nature of the customs, and to other particular circumstances. Therefore the same policies are not suitable to different princes, but different ways of proceeding in the government and conservation of their states." [186]

The practical meaning of this attitude is clear: politics must be approached not as a science based on general principles of the sort Machiavelli attempted to identify but as the art of adaptation to circumstance. "In ordering the republic, it is appropriate to adapt oneself in many things to necessity and to the quality of the times," Paruta observed.[187] Circumstances themselves were to be approached empirically. In the course of his negotiations in Rome for the reconciliation of Henry IV to the pope, Paruta had objected to the intrusion of "laws and doctors" into political matters;[188] and the *giovani* appear also to have attributed the political incapacity of the Florentines to an excessive intellectuality. "Subtle brains," Nicolò Contarini remarked in this connection, "are not good for republics." [189] For Paruta it was clear that

[184] Thus, p. 56, he concludes a discussion on a note of humorous scepticism: "Ma la verità di queste cose si può andar così con ragioni probabili discorrendo, per prendersi certo gusto e diletto di questa varietà di cose che ci si appresenta nel bilanciare le ragioni diverse che ponno concorrere in questi gran fatti; perchè a dover darne più certa sentenza, manca il fondamento di quei particolari de'quali non possiamo ora noi in cose tanto antiche aver notizia, e da quali soli ponno essere ben regolate le nostre operazioni, e massime le civili e militari a tante alterazioni soggette."

[185] Pp. 335–336, where he is discussing the reliability of fortresses and armies.

[186] Pp. 329–330, Cf. pp. 83, 365.

[187] P. 29.

[188] Dispatch of Aug. 26, 1595, *Legazione*, III, 268–269.

[189] A remark of 1628, quoted by Cozzi, *Contarini*, p. 89, n. 1. But this view of the Florentines appears to have become a cliché, perhaps going back to Petrarch's *ingenia magis acria quam matura*. Cf. Botero, *Relationi universali*, p. 33: "per la molta sottigliezza de gli ingegni, sono vissuti in perpetue discordie, le quali gli hanno rovinati."

"reasons ought not to prevail over experience," the source of man's "truest teaching." [190]

His repudiation of general principles affected his attitude to all political questions, even to those connected with the laws and constitutions of states, about which earlier Venetians had often been so rigidly "philosophical." Both laws and institutions, he maintained, must be adapted to the character of the particular peoples for whom they are devised; no utopian model could be applied to them all. The good legislator must therefore consider many circumstances over which he has no control; he must ask not only what is the best form of government in general but what would be best for his own city.[191] Furthermore laws, being themselves general, must be flexibly applied, lest they produce oppression and disorder.[192] On this basis Paruta ridiculed Machiavelli's belief that any set of constitutional arrangements, perhaps drawn from antiquity, could guarantee the stability and power of a state.[193] According to this argument, the Venetian constitution could no longer be regarded as in some general sense perfect; it was only perfect for the Venetians.

Paruta's rejection of generalization about political behavior is related to another major difference between himself and Machiavelli. As concerned as Machiavelli with the possibility of a calculated politics and with the interaction between human action and political events, he comes to different conclusions. At times, to be sure, he seems to have clung with a part of his mind to the hope that government could "operate with certain laws and not by chance, and be equally secure both from external dangers and from civil discords," [194] that men, in short, could master fortune. The Venetian constitution was positive evidence of what could be accomplished by human wisdom and resolution. But most of his observations on this important question tended to be negative. Even Venice, he confessed, had been overwhelmed by fortune, through no fault of her own, in 1509.[195] Furthermore the rationality of the policy of any state, he recognized, was limited by the irrationality of others. Princes, he wrote, were particularly

---

[190] Pp. 360 and 73, where Paruta takes some exception to the saying "che l'evento sia il maestro degli stolti."

[191] Pp. 25–26. Here he is evidently making use of Aristotle.

[192] P. 106.

[193] P. 210. Cf. p. 101, where he develops the idea that forms of government must correspond to the character of the society to be governed.

[194] P. 21.

[195] P. 263.

likely to deviate from reason; and where appetites ruled, it was impossible "to make any certain judgment of the operations then born from them." [196]

For Paruta, fortune, after nearly a century of foreign domination over Italy, appeared to rule not half but nearly all human life, and the relation between deliberate human action and fortune had properly to be conceived not as one of direct opposition but as a subtle interplay. Recognition of this fact he considered the essential condition of a prudent politics, which had to be based not on the vain expectation of controlling events but on a resourceful accommodation to circumstance. Failure to perceive this, he believed, would result only in a total enslavement to fortune.[197] "In our civil actions so subject to chance," Paruta wrote, "man must imitate the good gambler who, because he cannot always score high, tries to use well what falls to his lot." [198] This conviction led him to a number of relatively pessimistic reflections. Since civil prudence could not foresee everything, he remarked, it could never be certain of attaining its ends;[199] and since in politics man is incapable of insuring the success of an operation, he should be judged not by its outcome but by the considerations that impelled him to act.[200] Yet it should be equally clear that Paruta's doctrine was not altogether fatalistic. It did not exclude responsible human action but rather attempted to define its function realistically within the larger structure of events.

The Venetians of Paruta's generation were particularly attached, for obvious reasons, to the Renaissance doctrine of the occasion, which was essentially concerned with the problem of action in a world dominated by forces beyond control. Its meaning, as we have observed, is simple: that the mark of the statesman is an ability to wait patiently for the moment of action, to identify it precisely, and then to act with decision and vigor. We have noticed that the doctrine had long been a commonplace of political discussion, both in Venice and elsewhere; for the *giovani* it was particularly useful to explain and to justify the transition from the passivity of the previous decades to a more active role in Italian and European affairs. Donà had invoked it, for example, in attempting to persuade Spain to join Venice

[196] P. 244. Here, in defending Venice against charges of miscalculation in aiding Pisa at the end of the previous century, Paruta offers a kind of lament for the passing of the rational politics of the Renaissance.

[197] Cf. *Sopra la pace*, p. 442.

[198] *Ibid.*, p. 428.

[199] *Discorsi*, p. 346.

[200] P. 247.

against the Turks in 1571. He had argued against delay on the ground that "the occasion would be lost" and in favor of action "should the occasion permit." [201]

Paruta repeatedly employed the conception. In the past, he observed, the Greeks had been unable to take advantage of the occasion for recovering their liberty that had been presented by the death of Alexander; and then, "not knowing how to use the opportunity of the times," they had fallen under the power of Rome.[202] For Paruta, the skill of Fabius had largely consisted in his ability to exploit his opportunities;[203] the medieval church had been able to expand her temporal domain by making good use of her occasions;[204] Leo X had erred in his attempt to expel the foreigner from Italy (itself a laudable goal) because of his defective "judgment or temperament in recognizing and knowing how to choose the opportunity of the time and the occasions." [205] And the ability of Venice to act on favorable occasions had also played a major role in her history. She had sometimes neglected them,[206] but they had also been a major element in her success. Thus Paruta defended the Republic's separate peace with the Turks after the war of Cyprus, which had after all not proved a suitable occasion for victory. "It is proper to a republic, and to a well-ordered republic like ours," Paruta wrote, "to know and to wait for such occasions and to use them well when they are presented. Only by time and by knowing how to make use of occasions on its own behalf has this republic, as may be seen, risen to such dignity above the other Italian princes." Waiting for the occcasion he considered peculiarly suitable to republics because, continuing from generation to generation, they could afford, as individual princes could not, to pass up doubtful occasions and wait almost indefinitely.[207]

Convinced that no regular and universal patterns could be discerned in human affairs and persuaded that "philosophy" was therefore irrelevant to politics, Paruta and his associates turned increasingly to history. Their leader, Leonardo Donà, was particularly devoted to it. He especially venerated Guicciardini, from whose *Storia d'Italia* he copied out long passages.[208] But

[201] As quoted by Seneca, *Donà*, pp. 75–76.
[202] Pp. 191–192.
[203] P. 59.
[204] P. 347.
[205] P. 346.
[206] Thus (p. 242) Venice had passed up opportunities to expand on the mainland.
[207] *Sopra la pace*, p. 441.
[208] Seneca, *Donà*, pp. 31–32.

the historical skepticism released by Patrizi some decades earlier, and above all the tendency of the new generation to deny the existence of any regularity, stability, or predictability in the political world, raised questions about the value of history, which had long been conventionally justified as a source of general instruction. The Venetians, to be sure, had tended to emphasize the political rather than the ethical values of historical study. But if human experience through the ages revealed no dependable regularities, as Paruta's difference with Machiavelli seemed to imply, what uses could then be attributed to the past? How could it any longer be maintained that history teaches "civil prudence"? The *giovani* gave no direct answer to this question, and their particular interest in history may thus appear, on the surface, slightly paradoxical.

Paruta did not see the problem clearly, and he justified his official Venetian history in conventional and eclectic terms. History, he asserted, satisfied curiosity and gave pleasure; and his own work was specifically intended to glorify Venice and to nourish political wisdom by describing instances of both good and evil fortune in the past. He neither rejected nor emphasized the value of history as a repository of heroic examples.[209] He had learned enough from Guicciardini to compare the historian to a weaver,[210] and he showed considerable skill in the task of drawing various complex strands into a coherent political fabric. But his *Historia vinetiana* (with its sequel on the war of Cyprus) is little more than competent and conventional narrative, chiefly of diplomatic and military events; it gives no evidence of a shift in the Venetian attitude to history. In his discourses, however, Paruta could write more freely, and they are of considerable historiographical interest.

They reveal a substantial skepticism about the possibility of historical knowledge, particularly of the ancient past but with some bearing on more recent history. The questions that interested Paruta most were, he recognized, beyond any definite answer, both those of a more practical sort, such as whether Rome did right in declining the aid of Carthage against Pyrrhus,

[209] *Historia vinetiana*, pp. 2–4. Only occasionally (as in the case of Alviano, p. 116) did he treat an historical personage as an exemplary figure. For further discussion by Paruta about historiography, see the letter, given in the *Opere politiche*, II, 449–454, which advocates the use of the vernacular; and Antonio Favaro, "Lettere passate tra Antonio Riccobono et il Procuratore Paruta d'interno allo scrivere le historie venete," *AV*, Ser. 2, II (1891), 169–180. In this exchange Paruta is chiefly concerned to argue that recent history should only be written by men associated, like himself, with the government. For general evaluation of Paruta as historian, see also Cozzi, "Pubblica storiografia," pp. 256–278.

[210] *Historia vinetiana*, p. 4.

and those of a more speculative kind, such as whether Rome might have lasted longer had she remained a republic. In the former case, which he considered in this respect typical of many questions about the past, he remarked that we lack the kind of knowledge "by which alone our operations can be well regulated, especially civil and military, which are subject to so many alterations." [211] Of the latter question he observed that "it is very difficult to penetrate to the true causes of events so great and so remote from our memory." [212] The first objection to asserting the utility of history was thus the difficulty of knowing enough about the past.

A second and related objection was the difficulty of comparing a situation in the present with some alleged counterpart in the past. Paruta did not entirely reject the doctrine of imitation. In the matter of military virtue, for example, he was clear that the moderns would do well to follow ancient models.[213] He suggested, without hinting any disapproval, that the Venetian strategy against the League of Cambray had been a deliberate attempt to emulate the Romans, who had so successfully played for time against Hannibal.[214] But Paruta so hedged the doctrine of imitation with restrictions and special conditions that in practice it could scarcely be of much service to any modern statesman. The first task in the making of a political decision was, for Paruta, the detailed and particular analysis of one's immediate predicament.[215] Only after this had been completed could one seek a useful model in the past; but one also had to bear in mind the possibility of a mistake in the analogy. Paruta pointed out that Venice had found no Fabius Maximus to oppose the French Hannibal in 1509.[216]

The value of ancient example was even more fundamentally weakened by the fact that (as we have already remarked) the Venetians, and notably

---

[211] *Discorsi*, p. 56.

[212] P. 175.

[213] P. 308.

[214] P. 253.

[215] Cf. p. 109, in the course of comparing Cato and Caesar: "A voler, dunque, conoscere, in questa diversità di cose, a quale consiglio accostar si convenga, poichè quel credito che può darne l'autorità d'esse, quanto a ciò che ora si tratta, si può riputare o pari o quasi che pari, è necessario l'andar considerando, quale sia l'inclinazione naturale di chi ha da porsi innanzi questi esempi per imitarli; quale sia il più vero fine che egli si proponga; e appresso, di quale forma di governo ordinata sia quella repubblica, nella quale egli è nato, e alla quale serve: perciocchè, senza tali particolari considerazione, male potrà alcuno risolversi quale maniera di vita e di costumi abbia a seguire."

[216] P. 253.

Paruta, did not on the whole share the cyclical view of history, still so important to Machiavelli, that was related to the doctrine of imitation in politics. Paruta was at times ready to admit that, since all things are imperfect, every state must mature and die, and be replaced by others.[217] But he discerned no pattern in this tragic fact of life to justify the notion that one state could draw lessons from another because it occupied an identical place in the cycle through which all states had to pass. He tended to see every state, every situation, and every event as unique. All history, from this point of view, was not cyclical but linear.

Paruta's discourses thus carry farther a tendency already apparent in his earlier work. In them he presents Roman history as a long continuity in which one phase can be distinguished from another, but each must be understood as prerequisite to the next. In this light the question whether one age in the Roman past was superior to another only testified to the absence of historical understanding. The poverty of Cincinnatus, Paruta pointed out, suited a primitive stage in the past but was irrelevant to later stages when conditions had changed. Similarly it was pointless to praise the later achievements of Rome at the expense of earlier periods in her history.[218]

At the same time the traditional Venetian bias against Rome inclined Paruta to believe in the general advance of civilization; like earlier Venetians he tended to favor the moderns against the ancients.[219] He based the case for the present age primarily on the progress of technology and the arts. The advance of architecture, painting, sculpture, and all the other ornaments of civil life seemed to him obvious, so that it was "clumsy modesty or ignorance" to deprecate the present.[220] Every day, he declared, these arts and the

[217] For example, p. 162, where Paruta maintains that the downfall of the Roman Empire was inevitable because of "la vicissitudine, prima, delle cose umane; la quale non permette, per la naturale loro imperfezione, che possano in uno stato ed essere medesimo perpetuarsi, ma vuole che con moto continuo girando, quando innalzarsi, quando abbassarsi convengano. Oltre li Romani, hanno fiorito in altri tempi altri popoli ed altre nazioni, benchè con forze e grido alquanto minore; altre età hanno veduto altri grandi imperii, sicchè l'oriente dell'uno è stato l'occaso dell'altro: ed è verissima cosa, che le signorie e gli imperii, come fanno le vite degli uomini particolari, anzi come avviene d'ogni cosa nata, col tempo invecchiano; e camminando con i termini ordinari e naturali, hanno principio, accrescimento, stato, declinazione e interito." This interest in the fatal procession of states was common in the political discourse of the period. Cf. Curcio, *Dal Rinascimento alla Controriforma*, pp. 37–38.

[218] The point is expounded at some length, pp. 125–126.

[219] An exception (somewhat equivocal in the light of his pacifism) was his acceptance, pp. 307–308, of the inferiority of the moderns in war.

[220] Pp. 294–295.

techniques of building ships and houses and of curing the sick were growing more perfect, "experience being the teacher." [221] From this standpoint the present, as the product of a longer experience, would almost inevitably be superior to the past. For this reason too man could hope to learn little from history.

The paradox that so emphatic a repudiation of the "lessons of history" coincided in Paruta with a considerable devotion to historical study was the consequence of a shift, of which Paruta's generation was still hardly aware, of the basis for interest in the past, comparable in kind to the shift that had occurred in Florentine historiography between Machiavelli and Guicciardini. Paruta continued to hold, in spite of all he had suggested to the contrary, that the past could supply "teachings useful to foresee the consequences of the arduous and difficult decisions of great princes." [222] But the real value of historical study for his generation was increasingly of a far broader sort. It provided not so much particular lessons as a general perspective on human existence. Paruta suggested this in his justification for studying the history of Rome:

> The example of this most powerful and most famous republic, once its civil institutions and operations are well known to us and measured by the truest and most general rules, will well teach us how to discern many perfections or imperfections of modern states. And where such knowledge is not useful to correct errors already too entrenched by corrupt customs, it will at least be useful to know how much each state should be esteemed and how long it can reasonably be expected to last. At the same time one must hold as a rule truer than all rules of order that disorder is often introduced by various and unthought of accidents. [223]

The true satisfactions of historical study, then, would appear to be as much intellectual as practical. By enabling men to compare themselves with other men, it can reveal to them what they are themselves. But although such knowledge was satisfying in itself, it had also a special kind of practical value, however different from what had previously been attributed to the study of history. Historical study, as the most direct approach to human experience,

[221] P. 333.
[222] P. 75.
[223] P. 37.

falsified it least. It revealed the complex and even contradictory character of life, and thus it corresponded to the deepening perceptions of the Venetians themselves. It therefore imparted a special sophistication about the world, and fitted men for politics not as a facile and academic science but as an art of perpetual accommodation to the contingent and unpredictable. Above all, history reinforced and illustrated the dynamic model of reality which, among the Venetians, had perhaps now achieved a larger acceptance than ever before.

Paruta's emphasis on the particularity of situations and events had a counterpart in his attachment to the particularity of states. Both concerns nourished the sustained attack on ancient Rome which provides the central theme of his *Discorsi politici* and sets him most obviously in opposition to Machiavelli. For Paruta Rome had set an example to be avoided, not imitated; such lessons as she had to teach were mostly negative. The significant facts of Roman history were not her long existence or the size of her empire but that she had once been a republic, that she had lost her liberty in the course of terrorizing the world, and that she had eventually disappeared. His interest was directed not to her rise but to her decline.

He was not immune from those feelings of admiration at the greatness of Rome and terror at her fall that would one day inspire Gibbon. He too approached the subject with awe. "This stupendous apparatus, constructed over a long course of years through the great virtue and the many exertions of so many valorous men," he wrote, "had finally to run the course common to human things, that is to be dissolved and to fall to earth; and with its ruin it brought on the greatest revolutions in things. Henceforth many noble cities were ruined; others were founded that became most noble; entire regions, their old inhabitants expelled, were occupied by new; new customs, new laws, new languages, new garments were introduced; and Italy, which had been the seat of so great an empire, was subjected to greater changes and graver calamities than other provinces." So vast a catastrophe seemed, to Paruta, to cry out for explanation.[224] But he converted his explanation into an indictment which, at the same time, is a vindication of Venice.

His indictment is the most comprehensive and fundamental among the many expressions of Venetian anti-Romanism. For Paruta's sense of the linear continuity of history and the organic relation of its successive phases meant that the decline of Rome could not be treated alone; it had to be explained as the culmination of a long process whose essential tendencies had

[224] P. 128.

been at work from the beginning.[225] At the same time these tendencies were of a particular character. Paruta's curiosity could by no means be satisfied with the general consideration that all earthly things must pass away. He proposed to identify the specific circumstances that had brought about the collapse of the Roman world, and in this concrete sense "to penetrate to the truest causes of things." [226]

He began by assuming, in accordance with conventional emphasis on the "original institution" of a state and the indelible character of its people, that the fatal defects of Rome had been present from the beginning. Rome had never managed "to overcome certain bad qualities contracted from the first birth of the Republic," he observed. "Therefore, remaining always a kind of badly tempered body in which various evil humors were continuously being generated, it was almost always sick, troubled by numerous civil discords. And it came to the end of its life sooner than it should have done in view of its many other most noble characteristics." [227] His conviction of the perennial weaknesses of Rome was so great that his problem seems at times not so much to explain why Rome fell as, in view of the seriousness of her defects, how she managed to survive for so long.[228]

This view of the matter had the advantage, for a Venetian, of making it unnecessary to admire Rome in any period of her history, even during its republican phase. He did not doubt the superiority of republicanism. He reviewed at considerable length the arguments that Rome would have lasted longer as a republic,[229] and he agreed that the corruption of the Roman state would have been more difficult "if many citizens had been its custodians together, as they were in the Republic." [230] Although the seeds of decay had been present from the beginning, imperial government had hastened their germination.[231] But Paruta could not believe that imperial rule had by itself been responsible for the collapse of Rome.[232]

For Paruta two basic causes had destroyed Rome; both, as it happened, suggested the superiority of Venice. The more important, as he frequently

[225] The full curve of Roman history, seen as analogous to the ages of man, is described on p. 112.
[226] P. 128.
[227] P. 36.
[228] Cf. p. 130.
[229] Pp. 167–168.
[230] P. 175.
[231] Cf. pp. 112–113: ". . . anzi, per lo più, andò l'imperio in diverse parti e in diversi tempi declinando, fin tanto che più precipitosamente cominciò poi correre alla sua ruina."
[232] The point is developed on pp. 161ff., with conclusions on pp. 174–175.

insisted, was a set of internal weaknesses which a suitable constitution might have corrected: the disproportion, incompatibility, and disorder of the social elements composing the commonwealth.[233] Unable to coordinate the members of the body politic, the Roman government had repeatedly disintegrated in a chaos of competing, self-centered special interests.[234] From this circumstance Paruta drew a republican lesson: "The chief precepts for legislators who wish to establish a free city are that the magistrates should be conceded limited authority and for a short time, so that all the citizens can participate in the government but none dispose of it freely, lest they convert it to their own profit; and then that property should be reduced to some equality, or at least provision made that it should not be immoderately increased, so that no citizen should be envied or suspected by the others for excessive power."[235] The failure of Rome to apply these sound principles in her domestic life had ultimately also proved disastrous for the quality of Roman arms. For Paruta Rome had been conquered not by German valor but by internal decay, as the defects of her polity had spread into the army, producing "the corruption of customs, the loss of good discipline, the disagreements and degradation of the captains and soldiers of those times." [236] Exploits on the field of battle evidently had less to do with the course of history than political institutions and the general condition of society.

Yet he devoted more attention to the second basic defect of the Romans, which was moral and intellectual rather than political, though related to the weaknesses of the Roman constitution. Unable to comprehend Aristotle's teaching that happiness is the true end of political life, the Romans had employed all their energies and organized their government for war; obsessed by ambition, they had attempted to conquer the world. "And how," Paruta asked, "could a city be long preserved which puts its end in those things that are the means towards the end? How could it enjoy any true felicity, if it did not know or esteem it and indeed abhorred the peace and quiet in which it is born?" [237] From the failure of Rome to understand the proper end of politics had come other evils. Thus, "since the acquisition of a

[233] Thus, pp. 93–94, Paruta insists that the Roman Republic did not fall because of external circumstances (in this case the end of the danger from Carthage, long a stimulus of the political virtues) but through internal deficiencies. See also p. 13.

[234] Paruta took no sides. He condemns both nobles and plebes, pp. 13–14.

[235] P. 12.

[236] P. 141. Paruta's analysis (though he does not make the point) was equally applicable to the Italian disasters after 1494.

[237] Pp. 93–94.

great state is generally achieved with some injustice, so it is removed from the true end of good laws, which never depart from the good." [238] Conquest also brought neglect of the positive virtues of civic life; hence the expansion of Rome had bred incompetent and irresponsible citizens while, at the same time, vastly extending the tasks of political administration.[239] The collapse of Rome thus illustrated the principle that "governments devoted to empire are also generally destined for a short life." [240]

But although Paruta stressed the militarism of Rome, he could not bring himself to acknowledge that she had exhibited unusual military talents; he attributed her success chiefly to the absence of formidable rivals. The Romans, he noted, would have been no match for Alexander, or for any of the earlier world monarchies.[241] They had conquered Greece only because the Greeks had been divided.[242] The benefits of the *pax romana*, in his view, had been much exaggerated. Rome, he remarked, had been "mistress of the world, but not for very long, nor could she really enjoy such greatness and prosperity in tranquility." [243] If Paruta idealized any ancient polity, it was the small state of Sparta. Although her poverty and austerity appalled him, her mixed constitution, liberty, internal order, and long life foreshadowed Venice.[244]

At times explicit, and constantly implicit, in Paruta's discussion of Rome is comparison with Venice. A conviction that the two cities were comparable is, indeed, one of the most striking characteristics of Venetian political discussion. Venetians persistently refused to admire Rome and to admit that she was unique;[245] for Paruta Rome and Venice were simply parallel instances of the same phenomenon which had developed in contrary directions. Both were republics, founded by refugees, which had developed from humble origins to a notable greatness.[246] But Venice had recognized that civil felicity is the true end of government, the history of Venice had on the

---

[238] P. 22.

[239] Pp. 21–22. On militarism as an element in the destruction of the Republic, see p. 88. The notion that Rome had perished from excessive greatness, nourished by Polybius, was another commonplace of the time; cf. Curcio, p. 42.

[240] P. 22.

[241] Pp. 37ff., 224–226.

[242] P. 192.

[243] P. 232.

[244] Pp. 14–15, 92–93, 111, 134, 184–185.

[245] For an example in Paruta, see p. 162, where he insists that Rome was one of a class, obeying general historical laws.

[246] See p. 219, where this is explicit.

whole been peaceful, Venice had nourished a responsible citizenry,[247] and therefore—the essential point—Venice might hope to last far longer.

Indeed because the fall of Rome had made possible the rise of Venice, Paruta could hardly regard it as an unmitigated disaster. For one thing, little had been lost, for Venice had preserved such virtue as the ancient world still possessed; she had gathered in "the remains of the nobility of Italy." [248] But although Paruta emphasized the unfortunate continuities of Roman history, in the case of Venice (as Venetians now tended to do) he stressed development. "The Republic of Venice has obtained a very excellent government," he declared, "but not in such a way that it has been regulated from the beginning by the same laws with which it is governed today. Rather, divers occasions have opened the way for the prudence of many of her citizens, who, adding new ordinances to old, have brought her to such a height of perfection." [249]

But Paruta was now considerably more interested in the developing relations between Venice and the rest of the world than in describing those internal perfections so dear to earlier generations. On this subject, he aimed again to display the superiority of Venice to ancient Rome. He was by no means ready to admit the military inferiority of Venice. Her citizens, he argued, had as great a capacity for heroism as those of Rome;[250] and under different circumstances Venice too might have conquered a great empire.[251] But geography had given her a different destiny. Because seapower could not extend an empire beyond the coasts, she had not found the opportunity to control a huge domain.[252]

The argument suggests ambivalence, as though Paruta longed on behalf of Venice precisely for what he condemned in the case of Rome. Also, there is a hint of ambivalence in his attitude to the expansion of the Venetian maritime empire in the eastern Mediterranean. He saw it as a source of glory and profit, but at the same time it had reflected "a decline from the first customs and regulations of the city, which had been more disposed to peace and to commercial affairs than to arms." Nevertheless, he was quick to point out, the Venetian possessions in the Levant had not been exploited imperialistically as stepping stones for further acquisition, but to advance the commerce of the Republic. Similarly the wars with Genoa had not been, for Paruta,

[247] Cf. pp. 27, 232.
[248] P. 147.
[249] P. 27.
[250] P. 219.
[251] P. 224.
[252] P. 215.

imperialistic in any conventional sense. The two commercial republics had fought each other for trade, not for empire; and much of the Venetian effort had been defensive. There is thus, in the end, an apologetic note in Paruta's treatment of Venetian expansion even in the thirteenth and fourteenth centuries. Although it had made possible the "best years" of Venetian history, this period had to be seen as only a passing interlude in a long history of devotion to peace. And the rise of the Turks had quickly brought the brief expansion of Venice to a close.[253] Aside from its apologetic interest, this sketch is historiographically impressive. It reveals a remarkable grasp of the ebb and flow of Venetian power and its foundations in the world scene hardly imaginable in earlier periods of Venetian history.

The conquest of the *terraferma* presented Paruta with a different interpretive problem. He considered the location of Venice unsuited to an empire on land, and he emphasized how slow she had been to turn in this direction.[254] During the first centuries of her existence her expansion on the mainland had been blocked by barbarian powers which, he carefully pointed out, had been formidable enough to destroy the mature Roman Empire. Later, after the German emperors had withdrawn from Italy, Venice might have easily moved in this direction; but, busy elsewhere, the Venetians had "left to others that fruit which easily could have been theirs." [255] Venice had at last been forced to turn to Italy only "by the insolence of the Carraresi and by other circumstances of those times." [256] Although again he refused to concede that the lack of a landed empire signified any inferiority on the part of Venice, Paruta was apparently inclined to regard the *terraferma* as only incidental to the identity and the historic interests of Venice.

His general concern to deny the importance of Venetian imperialism either in Italy or overseas has its point, finally, in his deep attachment to the particularity of smaller powers, among which Venice was now clearly to be numbered. He was aware of the dangers of an uninhibited political individualism. The divided Greeks offered him an instructive example: his enthusiasm for Thucydides may be recalled in this connection. Although Paruta's emphasis on the inability of the Greeks to unite to conquer an empire is somewhat equivocal, he regarded the Peloponnesian War as a tragic illustration of the results of political disunity.[257] "Excessive desire

253 Pp. 222–223.
254 P. 214.
255 Pp. 220–221.
256 Pp. 217–218.
257 Pp. 176, 179.

for liberty," he wrote, "as a result of which it is more difficult for one people to be subjected to another, was exactly what abbreviated the time of its enjoyment." [258]

But his instincts were on the side of smaller states, their right to exist, and the human values which, in his view, they alone could realize. He argued the point in various ways. Thus it could be given an anthropological foundation: the limits of human nature imposed limits on political organization. "The imperfection of our humanity means that just as the virtue of man is not only finite and limited but fragile and weak," he declared, "so we must aim at things not only limited and finite but enclosed within certain not very broad limits. If one does otherwise, one will be lost in an ocean from which there is no known or possible salvation." The Roman Empire had violated this principle of limitation.[259] He also argued for a plurality of states on the grounds of geography. In his defense of fortifications (themselves a means of preserving the boundaries between states), he noted that nature herself had created mountains to separate one people from another for the protection of "nations in which diversity of climate had produced diverse affects and customs and, as a consequence, a kind of natural enmity." [260] There were also sound pragmatic reasons for particularity. The bigger a state, the harder it is to rule; the history of Rome had revealed (among its other lessons) that a world empire is beyond the political talents of even the ablest statesman.[261]

Particularly interesting in Paruta's discussion of this issue, in view of the tendency of much modern scholarship to associate the creativity of the Renaissance with the political fragmentation of Italy, is his recognition that the very people whose political divisions had provided the most awful evidence of the dangers of particularism had nourished the richest artistic and intellectual culture the world had yet known. Although the Greeks had been unable to unite, and in the long run to fend off Roman domination, they had perhaps done something greater:

> The Greeks did not devote themselves only to arms but to the doctrines and the exercises of various liberal arts, which were either born among them or at least well cultivated and flourished for a long while. Nor was the number of those who frequented the academies to become

---

[258] Pp. 179–180.
[259] Pp. 133–134.
[260] P. 325.
[261] Pp. 134–137.

philosophers smaller than of those who exercised themselves in the con-
tests and other games to make themselves good soldiers. And how many
were the professors of oratory and of poetry! In their arts they succeeded so well that from them was taken the norm and the rule
according to which those afterwards worked who aspired to win praise
in these studies. In Greece, similarly, how many excellent artificers of
the noblest arts, particularly in sculpture and painting, appeared!
From this origin, or at least perfection, we do not have knowledge of a
higher principle than of what there was in Greece, so that every age has
celebrated the names of Phidias, Policletes, Alcamene, Aglaophones;
of Polignotus, Parrasius, Zeuses, Apelles, and many others. Thus Greece
became more renowned and more famous for the excellence of doctrines and of liberal arts than for skill in arms.[262]

Greece, like Venice herself, had evidently been altogether different from
Rome—different in political structure, different in achievement, different
above all in values. But Greece and Rome were long since gone and Venice
alone remained, the only state in the history of the world that had managed
to combine civil felicity, possible only in small and peaceful states, with
long duration.

It should be apparent that Paruta was not so successful in avoiding general
views as he had aimed to be. His *Discorsi politici* still owe a good deal to
books, though substantially less than the *Perfezione della vita politica*; both
his pacifism and his love of small states seem to be inspired by Aristotle as
well as by the needs of Venetian policy. The limits imposed by Aristotle
may also account for the small attention in Paruta's discourses to the national
monarchies beyond the Alps, a formidable species of particular state with
which in fact he had had considerable practical experience; the real world
had not yet replaced the bookish conventions of political discourse. In this
respect Paruta lagged considerably behind Machiavelli, although his objections to Machiavelli were on the whole to the point. Paruta was aware that
there might be a distinction between political virtue and virtue in the
abstract,[263] and he recognized that princes must "have regard to nothing
except what is of benefit to their own state." [264] But he was incapable of

[262] Pp. 183–184.
[263] See his comparison of Caesar and Cato, pp. 107–108, and p. 207 where he distinguishes between true virtue and political virtue. Cf. the discussion of ostracism, pp.
195ff., esp. pp. 199–200.
[264] *Sopra la pace*, p. 443.

facing the consequences of his own political and intellectual particularism by a forthright acceptance of reason of state.[265] Nevertheless the complete naturalism of Paruta's political vision, the relativism and pragmatism released by his denial of order and regularity in the realm of politics, his opportunistic attitude to action, his historicism, and his attachment to small and particular states provide strong evidence of the accelerated participation of Venice in the political attitudes of the Renaissance. At the same time his peculiarly Venetian hostility to ancient secular Rome, which brought most of these attitudes into focus, was subtly related to the growing Venetian animus against modern ecclesiastical Rome, whose increasingly vigorous claims contributed a major practical stimulus to their development. Paruta was not the most radical Venetian of his generation, but even he in this way seems to point ahead to the great clash between Venice and Rome that developed in the interdict of 1606–1607.

Nevertheless, for more than two decades after the advent of the *giovani* no serious crisis troubled the chronically tense relations between Venice and the papacy. Still hopeful of a peaceful solution for their differences, and perhaps increasingly anxious over the growing Italian dominance of Spain, both Sixtus V and Clement VIII, more politic than their immediate predecessors, seemed reasonably friendly to the Republic.[266] The Venetian ambassadors were careful meanwhile to cultivate friendly relations with the pope. Paruta, during his years in Rome, was particularly conciliatory. At every opportunity he emphasized the purity of Venetian morals, the fervor of Venetian religion, the veneration of the Republic for the pope.[267] And in Venice the government tried in minor ways to demonstrate its respect for the Holy See. It conferred nobility on the nephews of Sixtus V and presented a palazzo to the pope for the residence of the nuncio.[268] In 1596 the nuncio noted with satisfaction that the doge and senators had received the papal benediction bare-headed and on their feet, a gesture "extraordinary and unaccustomed." [269] And in 1598 the Republic accepted the papal seizure of Ferrara without a protest, though resenting it. She even provided the galley

[265] Cf. his disapproval of reason of state, *Discorsi*, p. 239.

[266] Cf. Priuli, *Relazione*, Albèri, Ser. 2, IV, 302–303, 319–321; and Gritti, *Relazione, ibid.*, pp. 344–345. In 1596 two Venetians became cardinals (Pastor, XXIII, 248).

[267] See for example his dispatch of Dec. 18, 1593, *Legazione*, II, 141–144. Cf. Cozzi, "Paruta, Sarpi e Ceneda," esp. pp. 202–203.

[268] Pastor, XXII, 152–153.

[269] As quoted by Brunetti, "Schermaglie," p. 119.

that brought the pope from Ancona to take possession of his new territory, and her ambassador accompanied him into the city.[270]

But there was more calculation than devotion in these actions; they were intended not to satisfy the pope in any serious way but to preserve the traditional structure of the Venetian church. Thus Lorenzo Priuli noted, on the completion of his Roman embassy, that "when the popes are closely united with the Republic, the good bishoprics and abbeys are dispensed according to her wishes and to her gratification, and chiefly in favor of her nobility." [271] And Paruta's reflections on the value of good relations with the pope seem notably cynical. "Above all," he declared, "men esteem the support of friendship and good understanding with popes because this gives them much reputation with other princes and increases the obedience and reverence of their subjects in their own states, or at least lends a certain appearance which is often no less useful than the effect itself in covering and putting a good face on the operations of the prince, even when they might be motivated by selfish interest." His explanation suggests a considerable affinity with Machiavelli: "Since religious zeal generally has much power over the minds of men, princes are commonly eager to embrace and peoples favor the side and cause protected and supported by the authority of the popes." [272] Even the partial complaisance of Venice came from attitudes and values utterly at odds with those of the Counter Reformation, a fact doubtless well appreciated at the Curia. And it succeeded only in delaying a radical confrontation, which developments—in Rome as well as in Venice—were now bringing increasingly near.

[270] Pastor, XXIV, 382–415; Battistella, *Repubblica di Venezia*, pp. 616–617; Seneca, *Donà*, pp. 231–232.
[271] Albèri, Ser. 2, IV, 302.
[272] *Ibid.*, p. 364.

·VI·

The Roman Challenge: Catholic Reformation as Counter Renaissance

THE deep, almost instinctive reluctance of Venice to acknowledge the merits of ancient secular Rome was closely related to her profound suspicion of modern ecclesiastical Rome. Both represented a principle of universal authority which threatened the existence of states like herself. And as the Catholic Reformation gathered impetus during the last third of the sixteenth century, the political and cultural developments in Venice described in the earlier chapters of this book seemed to be bringing the Republic closer to some dramatic confrontation with the papacy. For precisely during the years when Venetians were growing more insistent on their right to an independent secular politics based on calculated interests of state, and when Venetian culture was increasingly oriented to the immediate concrete and historical world, Rome was reacting with particular vigor against the political and cultural tendencies of the previous centuries. To understand fully what was at stake in the great Venetian interdict of 1606–1607, it is therefore necessary to take a closer look at developments in Rome.

The preoccupation among historians of sixteenth-century Roman Catholicism with the impact of the Protestant challenge has in some respects inhibited evaluation of the Catholic Reformation, especially in Rome. It has tended to isolate religious movements from other historical phenomena; and discussion of Catholicism in this period has too often been limited to the inquiry whether its major developments were a response to Protestantism (i.e., a Counter Reformation), a spontaneous expression of Catholic tradition, or some complex combination of the two. In light of the growing recognition that Protestantism was itself the subtle expression of profound changes, social and political as well as cultural, in the general atmosphere of later medieval and Renaissance Europe,[1] this question can now only appear superficial. For behind the new heresies of Luther and Calvin lurked enemies potentially even more dangerous, of whose existence the Catholic authorities were well aware. And the Curia was in the long run probably less concerned to suppress Protestantism (a passing challenge) than to turn back the growing political particularism of the age, to centralize an ecclesiastical administration almost everywhere becoming increasingly federal and autonomous, to subordinate an assertive laity to clerical authority, to end the dangerous freedoms of artistic and intellectual culture, and to reassert the validity of the objective, hierarchical, and philosophical conception of reality that supported its claims to oversee the manifold activities of Christendom; in short, to bring to a halt all those processes that historians have come to associate with the age of the Renaissance. In an important sense, therefore, the familiar distinction between Catholic Reformation and Counter Reformation, between a resurgence of the values and energies of traditional Catholicism and measures deliberately contrived in response to Protestantism, obscures an essential point. Any "Catholic Reformation" was inevitably in some degree also a "Counter Reformation," but its primary adversaries are symbolized by Florence and Venice rather than by Wittenberg and Geneva.

Among its other claims to our attention, the mounting tension between Venice and Rome is useful because it dramatizes this fundamental conflict. In the course of the sixteenth century, as we have now seen, Venice had become an increasingly articulate representative of Renaissance attitudes and values; and she had staunchly resisted the efforts of the papacy to control or to influence her ecclesiastical, political, and cultural life. She had done this, furthermore, in Italy, which had traditionally seemed essential to the security of the papacy, which was the natural starting point for any reassertion of papal authority over the Christian world as a whole, and which otherwise appeared at last to show a commendable respect for the pope. Rome's deep grievances against Venice will thus take us to the heart of the Catholic Reformation and its vision of what generally ailed the modern world.

Christian universalism, as we have remarked, had survived the eclipse of papal power in the early fourteenth century. It had enjoyed a vigorous

---

[1] As in the influential essay of 1929 by Lucien Febvre, "Les origines de la réforme française et le problème des causes de la réforme," included in *Au coeur religieux du XVIe siècle*, pp. 3–70; and Joseph Lortz, *Die Reformation in Deutschland*, 3rd ed. (Freiburg, 1948), esp. I, 3ff.

revival in the later fifteenth century following the papal triumph over conciliarism; and its persistent claims, gathering urgency as the world deteriorated, had rapidly assumed a central position in the thought and the programs of Rome during the later sixteenth century. It is therefore a paradox that the Curia was now less "universal" than it had been earlier. The proportion of non-Italians at every level of the papal government steadily declined in the sixteenth century. The popes themselves, after Adrian VI, were without exception natives of Italy. But there were also, during the sixteenth century, both absolutely and relatively, fewer cardinals from outside the peninsula. At the beginning of the century the Sacred College numbered thirty-five, of whom twenty-one, a mere 60 per cent, were Italians. But by 1598, when the number of cardinals had risen to fifty-seven, forty-six, or more than 80 per cent, were from Italy. A similar reduction in the proportion of foreigners was also occurring at the lower levels of the curial bureaucracy.[2]

The increased Italian character of the Curia, in view of the general condition of Italy in the sixteenth century, probably intensified the antagonism of the papal church to the political and cultural movements of the Renaissance. For the ecclesiastics in Rome, like other Italians of the period, were the victims and heirs of the long series of disasters, extending far back into the previous century, that had humiliated the peoples of the peninsula and left them exhausted, disillusioned, and profoundly insecure. Disorder and collapse had in most places discredited the communal ideals of the earlier Renaissance. Native tyrants and foreign conquerors had destroyed popular institutions and deprived political life of its dignity. Some theoretical egalitarianism and considerable social mobility were giving way to an increasingly stratified and rigid social order collecting around courts. The whole political and historical world now seemed at once dangerous, incalculable, and beyond control. Furthermore, now that an effective political particularism was chiefly manifested in the powerful states beyond the Alps, it could be seen to threaten not only what little remained of Italian liberty but also the spiritual independence of the papacy, the only honor left to the peoples of Italy. Under these circumstances a monolithic and authoritarian political system appeared the best hope for protection and order. Thus the Italian catastrophe had contributed heavily to the reassertion of theocratic universalism.

The political tragedy of Italy had also a profound intellectual and spiritual

[2] Delumeau, *Vie économique et sociale de Rome*, I, 219.

counterpart in a widespread contraction of cultural life. The notoriously restrictive orthodoxies of sixteenth-century Italy have conventionally been blamed on the "Counter Reformation," but this is perhaps to take the symptom for the cause. Men living in constant and growing insecurity longed for certainty in every dimension of life; and the troubles of the sixteenth century accelerated a movement, already foreshadowed in the shifting values of Florence under Cosimo and Lorenzo, away from a fluid culture of particular insights and toward a culture consisting of reliably general truths, from engagement with the ever-changing world of daily experience to the contemplation of eternal verities, from the burdens of freedom to a regulated order. The cultural authoritarianism of the papacy was thus also, in an important sense, the natural response to a basic need of the age. And since absolute assurance can only be supplied by principles claiming a universal validity, the particular ordeal of Italy contributed, in this respect too, to the universalism of the Catholic Reformation.

The search for an unimpeachable orthodoxy may be discerned at every level of Italian culture during this age, from the most frivolous to the most sublime. It is evident in the code of etiquette so elegantly expounded in Giovanni Della Casa's *Galateo;* in the rhetorical doctrines propounded by literary men throughout Italy; in the post-Renaissance academies, which guaranteed truth in the sciences and propriety in the arts;[3] and notably in the authority increasingly attributed to Aristotle, who had so stimulated the political discussions of the earlier Renaissance and could still inspire creative thought among the Dominicans of Spain. But in Italy Aristotelianism tended to become a rigid system, and the authority of Aristotle a mechanical criterion of truth. At the Jesuit college in Rome where Aristotle ruled, a leading professor, Francesco Toledo (1532–1596), claimed for Aristotle's logic a perfection so complete "that scarcely anyone has surpassed him in any point." "Moreover," he had continued in a kind of warning, "it appears that he has been more received by the church then other philosophers, especially in the last millennium; and he has been used in the instruction of youth to the exclusion of all others." [4] The opponents of Aristotle were regarded with something of the horror reserved for religious heretics.[5]

This general concern to identify and rest on authority found its loftiest

[3] Cf. the remarks of Albertini, *Das florentinische Staatsbewusstsein*, pp. 283–284.

[4] Quoted by E. A. Ryan, *The Historical Scholarship of Saint Robert Bellarmine* (Louvain, 1936), p. 26.

[5] On the general point see Luigi Firpo, "Filosofia italiana e Controriforma," *Rivista di Filosofia*, XLI (1950), 150–173, 390–401; XLII (1951), 30–47.

expression in the theological formulas of the Counter Reformation. For the dogmatic decrees of Trent should not be understood simply as a response to Protestantism; they were required above all to meet the deepest needs of the Catholic world, as determined, however, chiefly by Italian ecclesiastics with their peculiar anxieties. Trent, it is true, did not provide certainty enough, as the sequel revealed; scholastic theologians of various persuasions sought after even more precise definitions of doctrinal truth, following various authorities. The majority of Franciscans continued to favor Scotus, though others (including, for two centuries, the Capuchins) followed Bonaventura.[6] But the widely accepted authority of Aristotle helped to make his disciple, Thomas Aquinas, the most popular guide to the meaning of the faith in the later sixteenth century. Named a doctor of the church in 1567, Thomas was considered the supreme authority in theology by the most influential Italian theologian of this period, Robert Bellarmine. Bellarmine's mind had been shaped by his youthful study of Aristotle,[7] and from Aristotle he had naturally moved to Thomas. In 1570, at the beginning of a set of lectures on the Trinity at Louvain, he promised his students: "I guarantee that any one among you will make more all-round progress in two months devoted to the *Summa* than in several months' independent study of the Bible and the Fathers." [8] The Jesuit *Ratio studiorum*, although permitting deviation from Thomism on particulars, prescribed dismissal for any professor who showed himself hostile to the system.[9] The task of theology under these circumstances was chiefly to systematize and to clarify, in the interest of stating the faith, conceived as a body of coherent intellectual propositions, with a maximum of certainty and finality. The articulation of Catholic belief, in this perspective, became almost an administrative problem, and Bellarmine himself an administrator of doctrines. He organized them into hierarchies and systems so that they might be directed, in their most unequivocal and effective form, against doubt and heresy. Indeed, to make confrontation clearer he systematized even the views of his opponents.[10]

This general mental temper is fundamental to understanding most of the specific policies and actions of the Catholic Reformation. It sought for an

---

[6] Léopold Willaert, *Après le concile de Trente: La Restauration catholique (1563–1648)* [*Histoire de l'Église*, XVIII] (Paris, 1960), I, 271–279.

[7] Ryan, pp. 24ff.; James Brodrick, *Robert Bellarmine, Saint and Scholar* (London, 1961), pp. 12–14.

[8] Quoted by Brodrick, pp. 28–29.

[9] Willaert, I, 282, n. 2.

[10] Cf. Ryan, pp. 125–126.

inner security in intellectual constructions that were presumed to reflect, with absolute validity, the structure of reality itself, and that were therefore beyond doubt or question except on the grounds of internal logic or consistency with even higher levels of truth. And reality and truth were assumed to be of a general character, orderly, coherent and thus apprehensible to the intellect, unchanging and therefore totally reliable. Conversely whatever could be seen to alter, whatever could not be subordinated to a general principle, fitted into a universal system, rationally described, was by definition defective. We have clearly entered again into a world of thought uncongenial to the flexible and empirical culture of the Renaissance.

Therefore, the attack by the Catholic Reformation on the various dimensions of Renaissance culture had deep psychological and intellectual roots; and when ecclesiastics charged the writers and artists of the previous age with immorality and paganism, they were giving expression to a profound and general anxiety. The underlying attitudes and assumptions of Renaissance culture troubled the Catholic Reformation even more than its specific content: it sought to be open and free, and thus it exposed men to every sort of danger. In this respect it was much like the sexual impulse, which also so disturbed the men of the Catholic Reformation. Thus the decision in 1564 to drape the nude figures in Michelangelo's Last Judgment may be taken to signify rather more than a fear of lustful thoughts. The loincloths of Daniele da Volterra symbolized a deep and comprehensive distrust of free expression and the stern resolve of the Counter Reformation to contain and render harmless the exuberant and therefore dangerous potentialities of man.

Thus the frequent association of both Renaissance culture and Protestant heresy with the erotic in the polemics of the Counter Reformation was neither accidental nor merely scurrilous. It was based on the perception that men, in their sexuality, express attitudes to existence as a whole. This is the serious meaning in Bellarmine's attack on Petrarch and Boccaccio as celebrants of lust and, in the same breath, his denunciation of Theodore Beza for having composed erotic lyrics in his youth.[11] The association between sexual freedom and a more general escape from conformity to systems is almost explicit in Giovanni Botero, the great popularizer and in many ways the most typical exponent of Counter Reformation values.[12] Botero described

[11] Brodrick, p. 137.
[12] On Botero as a spokesman for the Counter Reformation, cf. Luigi de Luca, *Stato e Chiesa nel pensiero politico di G. Botero* (Rome, 1946); for Botero in general see also Federico Chabod, *Giovanni Botero* (Rome, 1934).

poets as "never very useful to the faith and to Christian customs," and blamed them, along with rhetoricians and painters, as chiefly responsible for the spread of Lutheranism. Erotic license seems also to have been associated, in Botero's mind, with ridicule of the church. In the same passage he attributed "the corruption of the most noble province of Germany" to the satires of Erasmus, and elsewhere he blamed the subversion of France on Rabelais and Marot.[13] Major writers of the Renaissance, including Boccaccio, Castiglione, and Erasmus, were allowed to circulate in Italy after suitable expurgation,[14] but they were regarded with little favor. Meanwhile hostility to Renaissance values also found expression in gestures of contempt for antiquity. Thus Sixtus V removed ancient sculptures from the Vatican and demolished antique ruins to procure building materials for his own projects.[15] The designation of Thomas Aquinas and of Bonaventura in 1588 as doctors of the church also struck at the superior claims of antiquity. This honorable title had previously been reserved for a few ancient church fathers.[16]

The attack by the Counter Reformation on the political attitudes of the Renaissance, and notably on Machiavelli, should thus be viewed in a broad context. As early as Pole's *Apologia* of 1539,[17] the influence of Machiavelli was seen as a cause for the revolt against the Roman church; and Catholics frequently attributed Protestantism to the machinations of rulers who had not scrupled to place political interest ahead of faith.[18] But Machiavelli was only an isolated voice; and although his writings were prohibited by the first Roman Index of 1552 and regularly thereafter, the attack on Renaissance politics was for some time desultory. The secularization of politics began to seem a major problem in the Catholic world, however, after the emergence of the *Politiques* in France. This group was viewed in Rome as a whole party infected by Machiavelli, and especially dangerous because its doctrines threatened to corrupt others. Botero attacked the "*politici*" with vigor and a clear sense of the issue: "They profess to prefer temporal to ecclesiastical peace

[13] *Relationi universali*, pp. 385–386, 436. The traditional notion that Luther's revolt from the church was directly caused by his "concupiscence" (in the most narrow sense) is perhaps related to these early charges.

[14] See Firpo, "Filosofia e Controriforma" pp. 150–152.

[15] Pastor, XXII, 235–238.

[16] *Ibid.*, XVII, 200; XXI, 138.

[17] Fully discussed by Luigi Firpo, *Storia dell'antimacchiavellismo*, pp. 54–107. Firpo gives part of this work in translation in an appendix.

[18] Cf. de Luca, *Botero*, p. 13, on the tendency of Catholics to identify Protestantism and Machiavellianism. Pole attributed the Anglican schism to the influence of Machiavelli; cf. Firpo, *Storia dell'antimacchiavellismo*, p. 104.

and the political state to the kingdom of God, to exclude Christ our Lord and
his Holy Gospel from the councils of state, and finally to adapt their deliberations not to the law of God but to present occasions. This is the prudence of
this world, which Saint Paul calls the enemy of God . . . . And the earth is
full of this sort of men, and they have thrown Christendom into confusion
and ruin." [19] After Botero the term *politici* became, for Italy, generic. It
applied to Machiavelli, Bodin (increasingly read in Italy)[20] and all other
advocates and practitioners of a secular politics. The latter part of the century
saw a growing attack on the political attitudes of the Renaissance, as manifested both in Italy and in France. Possevino, for example, wrote (among
others) against both Machiavelli and Bodin.[21] Tommaso Bozio proved
against Machiavelli that the Christian religion made states stronger and their
subjects more serviceable to rulers.[22] Fabio Albergati refuted Bodin (whose
works had been recently condemned) by comparing his views at tedious
length with the infallible politics of Aristotle.[23]

But systematic treatises in Latin were hardly sufficient to influence opinions
and deeply rooted habits, and works like Albergati's suffered through remoteness from the problems of the day. It was hardly enough to demonstrate
academically that Bodin and Machiavelli had wandered from the paths of
truth when, as Lodovico Zuccolo was to testify in 1621, "not only the counsellors in the courts and the doctors in the schools, but even the barbers and
the most humble artisans in their shops and gathering places talk and dispute
about reason of state, and persuade themselves that they know what things

[19] *Relationi universali*, p. 442.
[20] Cf. Firpo, "Filosofia e Controriforma," pp. 155–156. Bodin's *République* appeared
in an Italian translation by L. Conti in Genoa in 1588.
[21] In his *Judicium* (Rome, 1592). According to Charles Bénoist, *Le machiavélisme*
(Paris, 1907–1936), III, 33–35, Possevino wrote against Machiavelli without ever having
read a line written by him.
[22] In four works: *De robore bellico diuturnis et amplis Catholicorum regnis liber unus adversus
Macchiavellum* (Rome, 1593); *De imperio virtutis sive imperia pendere a veris virtutibus non
simulatis, libro duo versus Macchiavellum* (Rome, 1593); *De Ruinis Gentium et Regnorum
adversos impios Politicos libri octo* (Rome, 1596); and *De antiquo et novo Italiae statu libri
quatuor adversus Macchiavellum* (Rome, 1596), all dedicated to Clement VIII. These are
surveyed in Generoso Calenzio, *La vita e gli scritti del Cardinale Cesare Baronio* (Rome
1907), pp. 409–413.
[23] *Discorsi politici, libri cinque nei quali viene ripresa la dottrina politica di G. Bodin, difesa
quella d'Aristotele* (Rome, 1602). For this and other attacks on Bodin, see Firpo, "Filosofia
e Controriforma," pp. 156–158.

are done for reason of state and what not."[24] The political doctrines of the Renaissance had taken deep root, partly because the understanding they reflected was in fact indispensable (as it had doubtless always been) to any self-conscious and practical politics. Accordingly it was necessary to deal with Machiavelli not so much by direct assault as by that special flexibility and accommodation so long characteristic of the Roman church in the presence of new social and intellectual movements.

Botero's *Ragion di stato* (Rome, 1589) owes its importance to its apparent success in adapting the political realism of the Renaissance to the ideals and needs of the Catholic Reformation. It did so primarily by expounding views remarkably like those of Machiavelli but attaching them instead to the name of Tacitus. This historian of post-republican Rome had much of interest to communicate to readers in sixteenth-century Italy.[25] He had studied a world much like their own and drawn useful conclusions; as Guicciardini remarked, "Cornelius Tacitus teaches those who live under tyrants how to live and act prudently, just as he teaches tyrants ways to secure their tyranny." [26] But unlike Machiavelli, whom Botero barely mentioned, or Guicciardini, whom he ignored altogether, Tacitus had been a pagan. Nothing better than political realism could therefore be expected of him, and his realistic insights could become the basis of a Christian politics much as Aristotle had been more generally employed for Christian philosophy. The observations of Tacitus needed only to be inserted into a religious framework and sanctioned by the church. With the aid of Tacitus Botero expounded a Christian reason of state distinguishable from that of Machiavelli mainly in its rather mechanical acknowledgment of the superior authority of the Catholic faith as a source of political strength.

The worldliness of Botero's wisdom is particularly striking precisely in that aspect of his thought which chiefly made it acceptable to the Counter Reformation: his insistence on the special utility of Catholicism for rulers of states. Machiavelli had emphasized the civic value of religion in general, but he implied that Catholicism had proved far less satisfactory (to say the least) as an instrument of statecraft than the paganism of antiquity. Botero

[24] *Della ragione di stato*, in *Politici e moralisti del Seicento*, ed. S. Caramella (Bari, 1930), p. 25.

[25] For the vogue of Tacitus see, in general, Toffanin, *Machiavelli e il tacitismo*.

[26] *Ricordi*, Ser. C, No. 18. Cf. No. 13: "If you want to know what the thoughts of tyrants are, read in Cornelius Tacitus the last conversations of the dying Augustus with Tiberius."

accepted Machiavelli's basic insight but corrected him on this point. In fact, he argued, Catholicism could contribute more to the strength and order of a state than any other religion:

> If religion is of any value for the government of peoples (and it is of the greatest value), the Christian religion has that advantage, in comparison with all sects and human laws, which the true has over the false. For since no assemblage of men, however barbarous and proud, however wicked and criminal, can be maintained without any shadow or semblance of religion, how important for the conservation of republics and of kingdoms must be the authority and the force of the true and holy religion! If Aristotle counselled the tyrant at least to pretend to be religious to maintain himself in the state, how useful must it be to a prince and to a legitimate king truly to venerate God, to revere sacred things, to observe the Gospel! .... But of what force will it not be to maintain subjects in their duty and obedience to unite them and to hold them subject with that law that binds not only the hands but also the passions, that restrains minds, that tempers desires, that regulates the thoughts of peoples? that subordinates them to empire, that commands them, that makes them obedient and tractable not only to reasonable and moderate princes but also to insolent and knavish ones, not so much through fear of punishment as through obligation of conscience?[27]

We have encountered similar doctrines both in Florence and Venice; the novelty here is less one of substance than of sponsorship.

The whole argument, with its apparent concern for political order, seems to assume the legitimacy, in principle, of reason of state. Botero is concerned not to denounce this motive but to assimilate it, and he does so by distinguishing between a false and ineffectual reason of state which disregards the special utility of Catholicism, and a true reason of state which acknowledges its political value. On this basis he gives fundamental advice to princes. They must, he submits, observe faithfully all their religious duties as the first condition of effective government, discuss all questions of state with their spiritual advisers before submitting them to secular deliberation, and pay a scrupulous respect to the pope and other clergy. The promotion of true religion, Botero promised, was the best reason of state. It would insure peace

---

[27] *Relationi universali*, pp. 792–793. See also *Ragion di stato*, Bk. II, Ch. 15.

The redecoration of the Great Council Chamber: the recovery of Padua by Andrea Gritti in 1509 (*Palma Giovane*).

Ceiling of the Great Council Chamber. Pietro Zeno killed by the Turks while hearing Mass (P. Lorenzo).

at home and victory abroad; its neglect, on the other hand, would sap the martial vigor of peoples and bring all things to ruin.[28]

Meanwhile, as Botero regularly suggests, the acceptance of the formal priority of religion hardly needed to interfere with the realistic adaptations to circumstance, often so full of moral ambiguity, recommended by the political writers of the Renaissance. For his work also includes a large body of practical, thoroughly secular, and even cynical counsel for rulers. He remarked, for example, that "novelty is always hated and any change in old customs arouses resentment"; on this point he cited Tiberius, clever enough (as Tacitus depicted him) always to appeal to ancient precedent even for his most criminal acts.[29] Botero was also strongly in favor of a prudent flexibility. "Deliberate carefully the enterprise that you are about to undertake," he urged, "but do not plan the details of its execution, for this must depend largely on circumstances and opportunities, which are continually changing. To prescribe the action to be taken too particularly will make the undertaking more difficult and may lead to failure." This emphasis was associated with a position that, in other men, might well have been condemned as unprincipled opportunism. Botero was devoted to the doctrine of the occasion when it was accompanied by a show of loyalty to the church. "Learn to recognize the critical moment in war and affairs and to seize opportunities as they appear," he wrote. "There is a certain point of time when a fortunate combination of circumstances favors some piece of business which both before and after that moment would be most difficult: this is opportunity, and it is of supreme importance . . . . Might and cunning are of little avail if they are not aided and guided by opportunity." [30]

Botero's intellectual talents were not up to any genuine synthesis of conflicting attitudes and values, and his inconsistencies are frequently glaring. At times he seems also to have recognized that such political inducements to respect the faith as he had advertised would be hardly to the point in a truly Christian perspective. Thus he once acknowledged that the reward of a Christian could only be claimed in heaven; Machiavelli and the Politiques had therefore been wrong to promise earthly prosperity to a devout prince.[31] Nevertheless he also maintained that piety brought lesser benefits on earth

---

[28] *Ragion di stato*, Bk. II, Chs. 14–15; Bk. IX, Ch. 8.

[29] Bk. II, Ch. 9. I quote from the translation of P. J. and D. P. Waley, *The Reason of State* (New Haven, 1956). Tacitus is cited often throughout the work.

[30] Bk. II, Ch. 6. The *Relationi universali*, p. 265, includes a whole section headed "Dell'occasione." Cf. Chabod, *Botero*, pp. 108–109.

[31] *Relationi universali*, p. 792.

and that conformity to the wishes of the church was a necessary condition of felicity in this world. This conviction, a nice illustration of the sentimentality Machiavelli had so detested and at the same time a calculated instrument of ecclesiastical control, was an important element in the orthodoxy of the Catholic Reformation.

The Counter Reformation also attacked the historicism of the Renaissance, partly by trying to suppress it, partly (as Botero treated Renaissance politics) by absorbing it. The Renaissance historians seemed dangerous to the church on several counts. They had given useful service to secular states, and they had generally treated the church and its hierarchy with disrespect. Machiavelli and Guicciardini in particular had attacked its policies and criticized its leadership. But above all historians had been generally inclined, like political writers, to regard their work as an autonomous science, to interpret all phenomena as a part of the natural order, and to insist that their conclusions should be based on some kind of evidence. The intellectual orientation of the historian was even more objectionable than his conclusions; and the appeal to history, like Renaissance literature, was generally associated with heresy.[32] The authorities of the Counter Reformation frequently sought simply to suppress historical writings deemed damaging to the interests of the church. Thus they were successful in deleting major passages from Guicciardini's *Storia d'Italia*. His full discussion of Alexander VI and his scathing essay on the temporal power were excised from all Italian editions of the work;[33] and Possevino meanwhile denounced Guicciardini for endangering faith and morals and above all for attributing events to fate or fortune rather than to Providence.[34] Possevino also urged the royal patron of Gianmichele Bruto not to permit the publication of his history of Hungary because of its unfavorable treatment of Clement VII.[35] De Thou's *Historiae sui temporis* went on the Index in 1607 because it was neither severe enough in denouncing Protestantism nor sufficiently enthusiastic about the Council of Trent.[36] The most

---

[32] Cf. Firpo, "Filosofia e Controriforma," p. 156, for detestation of Bodin's *Methodus*.

[33] Luciani, *Guicciardini and His European Reputation*, pp. 14ff., 193ff. The first complete edition was the French translation of 1568.

[34] *Ibid.*, p. 200, citing Possevino, *Bibliotheca selecta de ratione studiorum, ad disciplinas, & ad salutem omnium gentium procurandam* (1593).

[35] Veress, "Il veneziano Giovanni Michele Bruto," p. 161.

[36] Cf. Gaetano Cozzi, "Paolo Sarpi tra il cattolico Philippe Canaye de Fresnes e il calvinista Isaac Casaubon," *BSV*, I (1958), 75–76.

famous methodological treatise dealing with the new history, Bodin's *Methodus*, was condemned in 1590.[37]

But since interest in history had become too general to disregard altogether, expurgation and suppression were also accompanied by an effort to make historical literature in various ways more palatable to the church.[38] This was done partly by shifting the concern of the historian away from an autonomous research into the actual workings of the political world and back to rhetorical elegance, partly by reviving the notion of history as ancillary to ethics and above all to religion. The Counter Reformation demanded of the historian a general respect for orthodoxy and order; he was expected to follow the rules of his art and to inculcate respect, not only for virtue and the Catholic faith but also for the political and ecclesiastical establishment. These demands were formulated in various clerical treatises on the art of history which were to reach a climax with Sebastiano Macci's *De historia* (Venice, 1613) and Agostino Mascardi's *Dell'arte istorica* (Rome, 1636). Macci, a theologian from Urbino who dedicated his work to the pope's secretary of state, insisted that only a good Catholic could write history, based his general principles explicitly on Aristotle, and denounced Guicciardini; he emphasized the historian's style and had little to say about his method. Although Mascardi stressed the historian's obligation to truth, he criticized contemporary historiography primarily for its rhetorical defects and preached respect for authority both in church and state.[39]

The men of the Counter Reformation were particularly interested in the ways in which historiography, presumably so useful to secular states, might also be made to serve the interests of the church: to defend it against its critics, to bolster its claims, and to dramatize its sacred destiny. Botero, who was especially aware of the value of historical composition for the church, emphasized its utility to discipline behavior and deepen faith. Thus he denounced contemporary historians for their neglect of religion, which he interpreted as proof of a defective sense of values. "Caring only to write about affairs of state or military undertakings, matters more suited to feed curiosity than to regulate passion," he charged, "they make no mention of the successful and contrasting achievements of our holy faith, as though they

[37] See the introduction to Beatrice Reynolds' English translation (New York, 1954), p. xxviii.

[38] For what follows see, in general, Spini, "I trattatisti dell'arte storica," pp. 109–136.

[39] Cf. the passages quoted in A. Belloni, *Il Seicento* (Milan, 1929), pp. 445–448.

were a low matter and of little consequence." The time had come, he believed, to remedy this deficiency: "If ever writers had an occasion to take up
the work of narrating the successes of the Christian religion, they have it
most notably in our times. For [the faith] is on the one hand most grievously
afflicted both by the open weapons of the heretics and the secret arts of the
politici throughout Europe, and on the other marvelously spread through
countries unknown to antiquity and through innumerable islands of the
ocean." He aspired to be the Christian historian required by the times:

> Truly, I have addressed myself to the great venture of having under-
> taken the work. For since I have not devoted myself to the conversion
> of the gentiles or the reduction of the heretics to the evangelical
> light . . . it was suitable for me to have some part in this, at least by
> celebrating those who are busied in so glorious an operation, in keeping
> their memory and virtue alive. And perhaps he who reads in my Rela-
> tions about the labors of saintly personages in risking the thick darkness
> of the gentile world and in uprooting the poisonous dissensions of
> heresy and in diffusing the name of Jesus Christ with all their strength
> and making it famous, will feel his emotions aroused and his mind
> inflamed to imitate them. Thus my work, however weak and crude,
> will give birth to generous and notable results.[40]

Botero's aim, like that of earlier Renaissance historiography, was thus
clearly not to satisfy curiosity but to produce results by inciting the reader
to emulate the heroes of the past: not, however, the worthies of pagan antiquity but the saints and martyrs of the Christian past, including participants
in the recent struggles and triumphs of the church. History fulfills its highest
end, in this view, by assimilation into hagiography; and the accomplishment
of this task would seem to depend less (if at all) on competence in research
than on rhetorical talents, on vivid representation and the power of persuasion; Botero is interested in exploiting rather than studying the past.[41]
This conception of history would also seem to preclude attention to much
beyond the actions of individuals.[42]

But another way in which Botero exploited history suggests, at least on

---

[40] *Relationi universali*, p. 384.

[41] Cf. de Luca, *Botero*, p. 114.

[42] Chabod, *Botero*, pp. 64–65, has also noted the failure of Botero's political thought to
look beyond the acts of princes.

the surface, some concern with the actual structure of events. Through history, he declared in his *Ragion di stato*, "a man learns for himself at the expense of others";[43] and in this apparently Machiavellian sense he appealed to the past for instruction in civic prudence as well as for ethical and spiritual example. History, he believed, revealed the disastrous results of preferring false to true reason of state. Above all it proved that rulers who defied the pope regularly came to a bad end, for God wished to demonstrate by concrete events "that the earthly power is obligated to obey the spiritual, and that temporal punishments are ministers of the spiritual superior." Among his many examples (evidently chosen to enforce papal demands for the submission of France) were Philip the Fair, whose sons had all died childless and whose daughters-in-law had all been adulteresses; Louis XII, who had had no direct heir; and Henry III, who had been assassinated.[44] Briefly in France during 1585, Botero paid particular attention to the lessons of her history, which illustrated his general view of human destiny:

> The crown of France arrived at greater power than any other in Christendom by protecting the church, by wars against the infidels, by zeal for the Catholic religion, by ennobling the kingdom with the most magnificent temples and the clergy with the richest incomes. These are the ways that brought the house of France and the French to the peak of greatness. Now for those that have destroyed them: not heeding the Apostolic See except for interest of state; taking income from the clergy to give to the laity; conferring bishoprics and abbeys on soldiers, courtiers, and worse; making a league with the Turks and war on Christians, peace with heretics, enmity with Catholics; for reason of state protecting Geneva and Sedan, sinks of every impiety and wickedness. So, because we are like those with whom we converse, the purity of their faith declined through living with Turks and Huguenots; and, everything being reduced to foolish and bestial reason of state, the bond of souls and the union of peoples in faith was dissolved. Religion is a thing so necessary to the conservation of kingdoms that those who do

[43] Bk. II, Ch. 3.

[44] *Relationi universali*, pp. 381–382. It is instructive to compare Botero's treatment of the daughters-in-law of Philip the Fair with that by Villani, his probable source (Bk. IX, Ch. 66). Villani had written of the adulteries: "This misfortune, it was said, befell [Philip's sons] as a miracle by reason of the sin that prevailed in that house of taking their kinswomen to wife, not regarding degrees, or perchance because of the sin committed by their father in taking Pope Boniface." Villani is clearly far less categorical.

not have true religion and faith must find support in whatever superstition or sect they may live in. For to think of uniting Catholics and
heretics together is madness. For the Catholic faith is so pure and noble
that it does not tolerate anything contrary to its purity and immaculate-
ness.[45]

Utterly persuaded that historical truth must coincide with his dogmatic
preconceptions, Botero failed to see the danger in an appeal to the refractory
and frequently embarrassing world of fact. The Venetians, against whom the
same arguments were employed, would take advantage of this weakness in
the argument.

Although hardly more representative of the attitudes of the Catholic
Reformation than Botero, the vast historical enterprise of Cardinal Baronius
was destined for greater influence. The *Annales ecclesiastici* was immediately
designed to refute the Magdeburg *Centuries*, and it has generally been regarded chiefly as a massive repository for the sources of ecclesiastical history.
But, as its lofty sponsorship suggests, it was also far more. Baronius began
the work at the command of Philip Neri, head of the Oratory; and it was
promptly taken under papal patronage. Sixtus V praised it, and the early
volumes of the *Annales* were among the first to be printed by the new press
at the Vatican. Clement VIII regarded Baronius so highly that he made him
his confessor.[46] These marks of favor in the highest places indicate the importance attached to his work, which gave classic expression to the historical
vision of the sixteenth-century papacy.

Baronius was in important respects a responsible scholar. Although he did
not consider his ignorance of Greek and Hebrew an insuperable obstacle to
writing the history of the ancient church, he insisted on the importance of
documentary research, on an accurate chronology, and on the superior
authority of writers contemporary with the events they described.[47] Like his
close friend Bellarmine (and in opposition to others at the Curia), he doubted
the authenticity of the Donation of Constantine.[48] The conclusions of his

---

[45] *Relationi universali*, pp. 271–272.

[46] Calenzio, pp. 212–213, 227–233, 350–353, 838–839.

[47] See his little memorandum on method, quoted by Calenzio, pp. 151–152.

[48] See his letter of 1607 to Bellarmine, given in full by Calenzio, pp. 802–803. But
Baronius managed to sidestep the issue in the *Annales*. See his curiously brief treatment of
the matter in connection with the year 324, *Annales ecclesiastici* (Bar-le-Duc, 1864–1883),
IV, 88–89. In fact the historical question interested Baronius little; he preferred the
canonical argument that the pope possessed full temporal authority as heir to the universal
kingship of Christ.

work, nevertheless, were clearly not the product of his investigations but their antecedent. His purpose was to demonstrate, by the accumulation of as much evidence as possible, what Rome already knew dogmatically to be true. Against the charge of its enemies, Catholic as well as Protestant, that the church had deteriorated radically since antiquity, he developed the thesis that, on the contrary, it had never altered. "Just as successive links form a single chain," he declared at the beginning of his third volume, "so years joined to years by many cycles of years compose one same work, and reveal to you that the Church has been always one and the same. Thus, certainly, nothing can seem more pleasing to a pious mind which desires only the truth, nothing more delightful than to consider the Christian faith in which it believes to have been the same since the beginning of the church, as taught, spotlessly preserved, and guarded in sanctity through all the centuries." [49]

The *Annales ecclesiastici* was intended to reveal not so much the history of the church as, by historical evidence, its constant superiority to history. The work of Baronius, as an extended celebration of the triumph over time, thus gives expression to a conventional aspiration of the Renaissance. Furthermore Baronius chose to emphasize the timelessness precisely of those dimensions of the church that, for its critics, were most susceptible to change. Rejecting dogma as the proper concern of even a church historian,[50] he dealt almost entirely (and in this respect too much like a Renaissance historian) with the political and institutional dimensions of the church. He recounted the lives of the Fathers but ignored their beliefs. Baronius may therefore have replied less directly to the Centuriators, for whom doctrine was always at the center of ecclesiastical history, than to critics within the Roman communion, notably the Venetians.[51]

In the course of this undertaking Baronius gave the first extended development to one of the hardiest myths in European historiography: the conception of historical Christendom as a unified polity that not only had recognized the theoretical sovereignty of the pope but had also generally obeyed him in

[49] In the epistle to the reader included in earlier editions; I quote from that of Cologne, 1609: "Ut enim catenam unam conficiunt connexi annuli; ita annis anni coniuncti pluribus annorum circulis unum idemque opus perficiunt, atque unam tibi eamdemque semper existentem repraesentant Ecclesiam quo quidem piae menti, verique solummodo cupidae, nihil accidere gratius, nihilque potest esse iucundius, dum Christianam fidem, quam credit, eamdem ab ipso Ecclesiae exordio cunctis saeculis traditam, illibate servatam, sancteque custoditam considerat."

[50] See his letter to Talpa, Dec. 9, 1589, quoted by Calenzio, p. 255.

[51] Cf. Pontien Polman, *L'élément historique dans la controverse religieuse au XVIᵉ siècle* (Gembloux, 1932), pp. 531–537.

practice. The ideal was hardly novel, and, as we have seen, a few primitive historical arguments in favor of a universal papal monarchy had been advanced as early as the fourteenth century. But earlier writers had for the most part been satisfied to enunciate the ideal as an aspiration only; even *Unam sanctam* was clearly conceived as a protest that what should be was not. But Baronius now proposed to demonstrate, systematically and on the basis of massive scholarship, that whoever rejected papal leadership either in temporal or in spiritual things was guilty of rebellion against an established order whose traditional character could be traced to the very beginnings of the Christian era, often indeed to an origin in the Old Testament. Thus the life work of Baronius seems to be related to that of Bellarmine as part of a larger strategy, as though, while Bellarmine demonstrated rationally what ought to be true, Baronius was to prove historically that it always had been true.

The *Annales ecclesiastici* promptly became an armory of arguments, of which the numerous champions of Catholic orthodoxy made heavy use. But it also became a source of bitter controversy among Catholics. Two examples will illustrate this fact and display the general tendency of the work. The first was a controversy unleashed by the eleventh volume of the *Annales* (1604) over what was rather misleadingly described as the problem of the "Sicilian monarchy." [52] In 1097 Urban II, as the Spanish government claimed, had conceded to the ruler of the Two Sicilies the right to function personally in those states as the legate of the Holy See, and thereby to exclude any other papal legate. The Spanish crown therefore maintained a royal tribunal, styled the *Monarchia Sicula*, through which it performed all the functions of a legate. It judged ecclesiastical persons and cases, excommunicated and absolved laymen and clergy of every rank, and blocked appeals to Rome. Earlier efforts by the pope to end this distasteful arrangement having failed, Baronius attacked it by denying the validity of the document to which it appealed. He argued (as it turned out, erroneously) that the diploma of concession was a forgery. His position was taken as an affront by the Spanish ruler and widely interpreted as a sign of the aggressive mood of Rome toward all secular rulers. Baronius was generally believed to be aiming beyond the ecclesiastical autonomy of Sicily at the legitimacy of Spanish rule. Already out of favor in Spain for his attack on the legendary association of Saint James with Compostella, this new offense insured Spanish opposition to the otherwise promising

[52] The controversy is discussed in detail by F. Ruffini, *Perchè Cesare Baronio non fu papa* (Perugia, 1910). See also Calenzio, pp. 651–659.

candidacy of Baronius for the papacy in 1605. The controversy over this matter was also followed with interest by Catholics elsewhere, notably in Venice.[53]

Of a more obviously general bearing was Baronius' treatment of the coronation of Charlemagne, an event of central importance for the theocratic ideal. In dealing with the fourth century Baronius expressed his conviction that the Donation of Constantine had not been strictly necessary; he took the position favored by the canonists that the temporal authority of the pope was of divine foundation, not the gift of men. Therefore Leo III, in crowning Charlemagne and thus transferring the imperial office to the West, had merely exercised his God-given authority. Baronius also made the point that in creating an emperor the pope was only carrying on a function that God had originally entrusted to the Old Testament priesthood; Leo III was the direct heir not only of Christ, the king of kings, but also of Samuel, who had anointed Saul and later transferred his kingdom to David. There had been no innovation in the church, from this perspective, since the foundation of the world. Baronius on Charlemagne would be much cited by the more militant champions of the Counter Reformation.[54]

But the Counter Reformation, in spite of the labors of Botero and Baronius, was not entirely comfortable with argument from history. Discussion on this level had been largely provoked by Rome's enemies, and it had always the disadvantage that it might stimulate further research and contrary evidence; thus historical argument was potentially dangerous and was also likely to prolong (as it did) rather than to end debate. But the reserve of the Counter Reformation toward history was not merely tactical. It had deeper sources. The categories by which Catholic thinkers sought to comprehend all dimensions of reality were primarily systematic and rational; and discussions of the origins and development of phenomena had not only practical disadvantages but seemed fundamentally irrelevant to a world in which essential reality was assumed to be eternal and immutable. The dangers of historical investigation had to be warded off, but even a historiography safely under ecclesiastical control excited relatively little positive enthusiasm. Bellarmine, otherwise so learned, largely ignored the historical writings of

[53] See, for example, Sarpi's letter to Jacques Leschassier, Nov. 23, 1610, Ulianich, p. 96, and his letters to Jérôme Groslot de l'Isle, March 15 and 29, and May 10, 1611, *Lettere ai Protestanti*, ed. Manlio Busnelli (Bari, 1931), I, 164, 167, 172, hereafter cited as Busnelli.

[54] *Annales*, XIII, 347–350. Cf. Botero, *Relationi universali*, p. 382.

recent centuries; and so far as he required a historical framework, he depended on the traditional four monarchies and the conventional division of world history into three ages of two thousand years' duration.[55] The Jesuit *Ratio studiorum* allowed almost no place for historical study, which failed to develop wherever the Society of Jesus was influential.[56] And although the "positive theology" which the Counter Reformation inherited from the Erasmians was concerned to recover, authenticate, and study ancient documents, and to this extent required the techniques of historical research, its purpose became, under official auspices, not the preparation of an authentic historical record but the bolstering of a static orthodoxy. For the Counter Reformation the structure of reality took precedence over history, and truth was best apprehended not as development but as a rational structure of propositions.

Thus the political universalism so passionately advocated by the Counter Reformation was primarily supported by systematic and rational arguments based on the theocratic claims and hierarchical patterns of thought enunciated in earlier centuries. Leo X, for example, renewed the claims of *Unam sanctam* in the Fifth Lateran Council,[57] and that famous bull received repeated defense during the following century.[58] Meanwhile the radical papalism of Augustinus Triumphus was revived in Rome, particularly during the pontificate of Sixtus V. The *Summa de potestate ecclesiastica* of Augustinus was reprinted in 1582 and again during each of the next three years, and it became a standard repository of papalist arguments.[59] The pope, Augustinus had argued, has immediate power of jurisdiction over temporal as well as spiritual things; all earthly power, he maintained, is exercised by divine permission and only at the discretion of the pope. A large group of Italian theologians and jurists elaborated on these views during the later sixteenth century.[60] The degree to which the Catholic Reformation was in general reaction against the recent development of Europe is here particularly apparent.

---

[55] Ryan, pp. 33–34, 63ff.

[56] Ryan, p. 24; Polman, p. 500.

[57] The point is brought out by F. Heiler, *Altkirchliche Autonomie und päpstlicher Zentralismus* (Munich, 1941), p. 318.

[58] Joseph Lecler, "L'argument des deux glaives (Luc XXII, 38)," *Recherches de science religieuse*, XXII (1932,) 294–295. Bellarmine cited *Unam sanctam* and defended its authority. See *De potestate papae in rebus temporalibus*, Ch. 3, in his *Opera* (Venice, 1721–1728), V, 34.

[59] Wilks, *Sovereignty in the Later Middle Ages*, p. 11. See also J. de La Servière, *La théologie de Bellarmin* (Paris, 1909), p. 130, n. 1.

[60] See the names mentioned by Lecler, pp. 172–173, 288, 295.

The political aspirations of the Catholic Reformation were based on the firm conviction that a universal state is the only proper form of political organization; it insisted, in short, that Christendom must be an effective political reality.[61] All particular kingdoms and republics were still regarded by papal theorists as the subordinate members of an enduring world state; any genuine fragmentation of the social order was seen as intrinsically evil, the expression and consequence of sin. Every human government, in this view, also appeared to be subject to a single universal system of justice based ultimately on eternal and divine law; this conviction made it difficult for Rome to respect systems of customary law in the particular states of Europe.[62] Such a theory obviously made any acceptance of the legitimacy of pagan or non-Catholic governments difficult and perhaps impossible. It added a theoretical reason to the fear of heresy for objecting to the maintenance of diplomatic relations with Protestant states by such Catholic powers as Venice.

Botero translated this general position into a popular statement designed, like his discussions of reason of state, to appeal to a rather secular set of motives. "I believe that the human race would live most happily if the whole world were reduced under a single prince," he declared, "because in addition to the fact that a greatness and almost immense majesty approaching the divine would be seen in the world, this mode of government would be more durable, more practicable, and more enjoyable than any that exists." Rome too thus had its conception of utopia, but of a different kind from the particularistic utopia cherished and perhaps represented by Venice. In a universal state, Botero argued, all men could think of themselves as belonging to the same country, indeed to the same household. And its prince, with the resources of the world at his disposal, would have no reason to burden his subjects with immoderate taxes; accordingly "they would live happily in the greatest abundance of everything." A plurality of states seemed to Botero, on the other hand, an evil "like plague, like a storm," permitted by God only as punishment for sin. The conduct of international business through "counterbalancing the forces of the powers" struck him as thoroughly objectionable. He identified balance of power with "all the reason

[61] See, in general, Rodolfo de Mattei, "Contenuto ed origini dell'ideale universalista nel Seicento," *Rivista Internazionale di Filosofia del Diritto*, X (1930), 391–401; and Chabod, *Botero*, pp. 115–118.

[62] On the hierarchy of laws see, for example, Bellarmine, *De clericis*, Ch. 29, in *Opera*, II, 163–165. For Catholic attacks on the English common law on this basis, cf. Thomas H. Clancy, *Papist Pamphleteers. The Allen-Persons Party and the Political Thought of the Counter Reformation in England, 1572–1615* (Chicago, 1964), pp. 107–124.

of state of modern politicians" and remarked that "those who attach so much importance to balancing do not aim at all at the universal good, nor at that of Christendom, nor at that of the human race; but they have as their aim the particular good not of this or that state and people but only of this or that prince." To Botero any political unit less than the whole *respublica christiana* must inevitably be exploited and victimized by selfish rulers.[63]

The idea of any genuine separation between the spiritual and temporal components of the universal Christian state was emphatically rejected by the thinkers of the Catholic Reformation. They echoed their medieval predecessors in comparing the two powers to soul and body, and developed the familiar analogy at length. So Bellarmine: "The temporal and spiritual power in the church are not discrete and separate, like two political kingdoms, but are united so that they compose one body; or rather they are like body and soul in one man, the spiritual power being like the soul and the temporal like the body." [64] And the implications were clear: "Spirit is so related to flesh that although it should not impede its actions when they are good, spirit nevertheless rules and moderates, and sometimes restrains, sometimes stimulates flesh as it judges expedient for its own ends. On the other hand flesh has no empire over spirit and cannot direct, judge, or coerce it in any way. Therefore the ecclesiastical power, which is spiritual and thus naturally superior to the secular, can when necessary judge and coerce it." The earthly kingdom must be the obedient servant of the celestial kingdom.[65]

This meant in practice that the pope must be able to command all things, without interference from below. Botero insisted: "The pope has his greatness and superiority over the whole human race immediately from God, whence it cannot be restricted nor altered by anybody whatsoever." And

---

[63] *Relationi universali*, pp. 703–704. On p. 718 he shifts to the view that equilibrium is based on nature, but such inconsistencies are not uncommon in his thought.

[64] ". . . potestas temporalis & spiritualis in Ecclesia non sunt res disjunctae & separatae, ut duo regna politica, sed sunt conjunctae, ita ut unum corpus faciant; vel potiùs ita se habent, ut corpus & anima in uno homine, est enim potestas spiritualis quasi anima, & temporalis quasi corpus." (*De laicis*, Ch. 18, *Opera*, II, 272.)

[65] "Spiritus ita se habet ad carnem, ut quamvis non impediat actiones ejus, cùm bene se habent, eam tamen regat & moderetur, & aliquando cohibeat, aliquando excitet, prout ad finem suum expedire judicat. Contra verò, caro nullum habet imperium in spiritum, neque eum ulla in re dirigere, vel judicare, vel coercere potest. Sic igitur potestas ecclesiastica, quae spiritualis est, ac per hoc naturaliter saeculari superior, saecularem potestatem, cùm opus est, dirigere, judicare, ac coercere potest." (*De clericis*, Ch. 29, *Opera*, II, 165). See also *De potestate pontificis temporali*, Bk. V, Ch. 7, *Opera*, I, 440.

although (like Bellarmine) he admitted the theoretical possibility of some limitation on the temporal authority of the pope, he seems in practice to have regarded papal power as almost boundless. He began by attributing to the pope a direct temporal suzerainty over both Naples and England. But this, Botero continued, was "nothing in comparison with his spiritual greatness, which others call ecclesiastical." Sweeping over rivers and mountains, crossing the oceans, this spiritual authority gave the pope an unlimited right to intervene in politics, as he might see fit. As common father of mankind the pope had the authority to settle all differences among rulers, as he had shown by establishing the line of demarcation between Spain and Portugal. He could organize leagues against the infidel. No important decision could properly be taken anywhere in Christendom without his concurrence. Among those occasions when popes had exercised their general rights of supervision Botero pointedly mentioned both the triumphs of Julius II and the creation of the league that had defeated the Turks at Lepanto—events that evidently seemed as significant in Rome (though in a contrary sense) as they seemed in Venice.[66]

The converse of the superiority of the spiritual power was the inferiority of the temporal. Insistence on this point gave particular offense to the dignity that Venetians (and doubtless other lay statesmen) attributed to political responsibility. It implied that all temporal governments, dedicated to lower values and prone to sin, must be retained under a constant ecclesiastical tutelage. Bellarmine insisted: "The temporal kingdom not only is not accommodated to be the end, that is the highest good of man, but is also not to be the means for acquiring it." His practical conclusion from this was that the Christian prince should follow the counsel of his spiritual directors and "not receive as the true law of God, perchance, the laws of false prophets, such as those are who are now called *politici*." For, Bellarmine went on, the clergy are generally superior to the laity as, "in a sense, carried into heaven and, placed above human nature, exempted from our affections."[67] As he had declared in the first sermon after his ordination, priests should "think in their hearts a little and hear God's voice speaking to them: I have exalted thee and desired thee not to be an angel but a god among men."[68] But governments directed by mere laymen were all too human.

[66] *Relationi universali*, pp. 377–383.

[67] Quoted by Pompeati, "Le dottrine politiche di Paruta," pp. 344–345, from *De officio principis christiani libri III* (Rome, 1619), Bk. 1, Ch. 1.

[68] Quoted by Brodrick, pp. 26–27.

As a Thomist Bellarmine did, of course, propose (as has been widely remarked) that the pope's direct authority was limited to spiritual things and that his right to intervene in political affairs was merely indirect; it was permitted, that is to say, only when spiritual interests were threatened by the acts of temporal rulers.[69] Bellarmine was in this respect by no means the most radical member of the Curia; indeed his views were offensive to the majority when first published during the pontificate of Sixtus V. The pope himself was antagonized, and in 1590 the first volume of Bellarmine's *De controversiis* was put on the Index.[70] But Bellarmine's own moderation chiefly emphasizes the extreme views that generally prevailed in Rome. Indeed the significance of the limitation he attributed to papal authority should not be exaggerated. It still permitted the pope, since he alone could judge when the interests of the faith might be at stake, to intervene at will in temporal affairs. As a controversialist Bellarmine emphasized not the limits but the magnitude of papal authority; for example, it included, as he insisted, a right of intervention not only when rulers threatened the church but also when they failed to promote its interests.[71] In his later years, furthermore, he minimized the importance of his own distinction between the direct and indirect power of the pope in the temporal realm.[72]

The contribution of the Catholic Reformation to modern constitutionalism can be fully understood only in the light of the fundamental concern of the papacy to establish the superiority of the spiritual power over all temporal governments. The constitutional basis of political authority and constitutional restraints on rulers, it is true, occupied a considerable place in the political thought of men like Bellarmine. He argued that since all men are

---

[69] His position was essentially that of Innocent III: ". . . sententia media, & Catholicorum Theologorum communis, Pontificem ut Pontificem non habere directè & immediatè ullam temporalem potestatem, sed solùm spiritualem; tamen ratione spiritualis habere saltem indirectè potestatem quamdam, eamque summam, in temporalibus" (*De potestate pontificis temporali*, Bk. V, Ch. 1, Opera, I, 433). Nevertheless Bellarmine does not here absolutely exclude a more radical position, and his emphasis was rather on papal power than on its limitations. Cf. Ch. 6 in the same book (p. 439): "Pontificem ut Pontificem, etsi non habeat ullam merè temporalem potestatem, tamen habere in ordine ad bonum spirituale summam potestatem disponendi de temporalibus rebus omnium Christianorum."

[70] For the attack on Bellarmine in Rome, see Brodrick, pp. 105–110.

[71] *De potestate pontificis temporalis*, Bk. V, Ch. 6, Opera, I, 440: "Itaque spiritualis non se miscet temporalibus negotiis . . . dummodo non obsint fini spirituali, aut non sint necessaria ad eum consequendum. Si autem tale quid accidat, spiritualis potestas potest & debet coercere temporalem omni ratione ac via, quae ad id necessaria esse videbitur."

[72] See below, p. 429.

naturally equal, political authority must have a popular origin; and he drew an important conclusion: "Kingdoms are not immediately instituted by God but by men, and therefore they can be changed by men into other forms of rule." [73] He also admitted some natural right of resistance against the injustices committed by secular governments. [74] Botero too insisted that "all legitimate kingdoms have had their origin in election by the people; and therefore, in their coronation ceremonies, the kings swear to respect the privileges of the peoples and the peoples to be faithful to them." [75]

But it is difficult to suppose that the thinkers of the Catholic Reformation, whose essential concerns were of a different kind and whose prejudices were generally in favor of descending themes of authority, had much genuine interest in the rights of peoples, particularly in an age of growing contempt for the political competence of the masses. The constitutionalism of these men was chiefly intended not to glorify popular government but to attack the independent and unlimited authority claimed for royal government. [76] Above all it was directed against the claims of rulers to govern by divine right. The effect of the constitutionalist argument was to leave the pope as the only ruler in Christendom whose authority came directly from God. [77] Constitutionalism, decisively rejected in the struggle with conciliarism, was never considered applicable to the church.

Their rather abstract interest in constitutionalism was at any rate not sufficient to incline the men of the Curia to look benignly on such functioning constitutional governments as that of Venice. The leaders of the Catholic Reformation exhibited, in fact, a considerable bias, both practical and theoretical, against republicanism and in favor of monarchy. Part of the reason was a tendency to believe that only the strong authority of a prince could guarantee orthodoxy, and conversely to associate heresy with more broadly based governments. Botero noted that in Germany most free cities had turned Protestant while many princes had remained faithful to the pope, and he thought this no accident. "It is certainly important," he wrote, "to

[73] *De clericis*, Ch. 28, *Opera*, II, 162: "Regna non sunt immediatè à Deo instituta, sed ab hominibus, & ideo ab hominibus mutari possunt in alias regiminis formas."

[74] Cf. La Servière, p. 272.

[75] *Relationi universali*, p. 380, against the divine right theory of the *politiques*.

[76] Cf. Guenter Lewy, *Constitutionalism and Statecraft during the Golden Age of Spain: A Study of the Political Philosophy of Juan de Mariana, S.J.* (Geneva, 1960), p. 137.

[77] Cf. Bellarmine, *De clericis*, Ch. 7, *Opera*, II, 126: "... nos non negare, quin aliquando populus elegerit, sicut etiam nunc in quibusdam locis eligunt Reges, sed id juris habere eos, vel habuisse ex concessione Pontificum, non ex jure divino." See also p. 122.

understand how it happens that free cities embrace heresy more readily than princes. Perhaps the reason is that heresy brings with it liberty, both in opinion and in way of life; and the label *liberty*, though false, is capable of attracting the people, who are devoted to it, in any direction. This does not happen with princes, who, through their preeminence over their subjects, already enjoy complete liberty." [78] Urban communes, as Rome well knew, had for centuries been peculiarly susceptible to heresy. Botero associated the popular election of rulers with Calvinism.[79]

Rome also found republics exasperatingly difficult to deal with. Their cumbersome procedures, the need for public debate even on the most sensitive issues, the problems of gaining majority support, and conflict between administrative agencies made them unpredictable. "With you," Clement VII had said of the Venetians to Gasparo Contarini in 1529, "everything depends on a single ballot," as though this put all in doubt.[80] The critics of Venice regularly attacked the Senate (in the words of a nuncio late in the century) as "a body composed of such a great number of men and of so many different minds";[81] and nuncios frequently complained of the inconveniences of dealing with a "government which does not depend on a single will." [82] Thus the papal nuncio was particularly dismayed, in 1583, at the prospect of a more broadly based government in Venice. "In such a confusion of things," he reported in strong disapproval, the Republic had determined that "the Senate should take up henceforth all the negotiations that are daily carried on with Princes, and that it should deliberate and reply as necessary with the vote of the more than two hundred heads that make up this body. Hence we may expect many impertinences and infinite unpleasantness in addition to tedious delays, since not only has the entire authority of the Council of Ten been abolished, but that of the College much limited." [83]

The same defects made secrecy impossible, exposed authority to criticism, and interfered with the prompt obedience of inferior to superior. Although such improprieties might be viewed with a certain equanimity when

---

[78] *Relationi universali*, pp. 391–392.

[79] *Ibid.*, p. 434.

[80] Pastor, X, 37.

[81] Anton Maria Graziani in 1598, quoted by Brunetti, "Le istruzioni di un nunzio pontificio" p. 374.

[82] See, for example, the remarks of Alberto Bolognetti, nuncio in Venice between 1578 and 1581, in Stella, *Chiesa e Stato*, pp. 52–53.

[83] Dispatch of Lorenzo Campeggi to Rome, May 7, 1583, quoted by Stella, *Chiesa e Stato*, p. 67. Cf. Brunetti, "Istruzioni," p. 373.

confined to the secular dimensions of government, they became intolerable in dealings with the church. For republics, since they seemed to command a more complete loyalty from their subjects than princes, were also more likely to support their governments against the church.[84] They were inclined to be more aggressively anticlerical, more vigorous in asserting civil jurisdiction over the clergy. The Venetian government was in this respect only the most prominent example of a general phenomenon. In Milan the Senate remained more hostile to the demands of the Curia than the Spanish viceroy;[85] and the Senate of Lucca so resented the aggressive jurisdictionalism of its bishop that in 1605 it declared him an enemy of the state, and he found it advisable to absent himself for thirteen years in Rome.[86]

The thinkers of the Catholic Reformation also based their reservations about republics on more general considerations. Although Bellarmine later insisted that "no legitimate form of government" was repugnant to Christianity,[87] and although he professed some theoretical approval of the mixed constitution, he shared the general conviction of Thomists that monarchy is ideally the most perfect form of government. The monarchical constitution of the church attested to this fact, which was also confirmed by the clear preference of Scripture, by nature, and above all by reason.[88] For, in the most fundamental sense, monarchy alone could supply complete order:

That government is best which is most ordered; and it can be demonstrated that monarchy is more ordered than aristocracy or democracy. All order consists in this, that some should command and others should be subjugated. And order may be discerned not among equals but among those who are superior and inferior. Now, where there is monarchy, there all certainly have some order, since there is no one who is not subject to someone, with the single exception of him who has responsibility for all. For this reason there is the highest order in the Catholic church, where the people are subjected to the parish priests, the parish priests to the bishops, the bishops to the metropolitans, the

[84] Cf. the views of Bolognetti in Stella, *Chiesa e Stato*, p. 52.

[85] See Chabod, *Storia religiosa dello Stato di Milano*, pp. 73–82.

[86] Augusto Mancini, *Storia di Lucca* (Florence, 1950), pp. 259–263.

[87] In his *Risposta ad un libretto intitolato 'Trattato et resolutione sopra la validità delle scommuniche, di Gio. Gersone Theologo e Cancellier Parisino* (Rome, 1606). I cite from the edition in *Raccolta degli Scritti usciti fuori in istampa, e scritti a mano nella causa del P. Paolo V. co'signori venetiani* (Coira, 1607), I, 310. Henceforth cited as *Raccolta*.

[88] See in general *De potestate pontificis temporali*, Bk. I, Ch. 2, *Opera*, I, 251–254.

metropolitans to the primates, the primates to the pope, the pope to God. Where government is by an aristocracy, the people have a certain order, since they are subjected to the aristocrats; but the aristocrats have no order among themselves. Democracy lacks order to a much greater degree, since all the citizens of the same condition and authority participate in governing the republic.[89]

It is evident that Bellarmine's preference is based very little on how the various types of government can be observed to work in practice. The order with which he is chiefly concerned is not political but metaphysical: order is finally what corresponds to the hierarchical structure of ultimate reality. Botero, who shared his preference, was at least somewhat more concrete. In discoursing on "the excellence of monarchy," he argued that monarchy was best because it tended to be larger and to last longer. But there seems also some metaphysical (as opposed to a political) impulse even in this suggestion: monarchy was finally preferable to Botero because, being larger and more permanent, it approaches closer to universality and eternity.[90]

The same ultimately metaphysical biases appear to underly the particular criticisms directed by these writers against republics. For republicanism was patently based on the acceptance of conflict and division as a perennial condition of social existence, and its constitutional procedures were designed not to abolish but to coordinate and balance opposing interests. But for Bellarmine contradiction was to be conquered and eliminated, not acknowledged and manipulated. And he believed that, for this reason, republics could not be expected to function well; where responsibility was divided, every man would look after his private interests, and the common good would be

---

[89] Ibid., p. 253: "Eo siquidem melior gubernatio est, quo magis est ordinata: magis autem ordinatam Monarchiam esse, quàm Aristocratiam vel Dimocratiam, sic demonstrari potest. Omnis ordo in eo positus est, ut alii praesint, alii subjiciantur: nec enim inter pares, sed inter superiores & inferiores ordo dignoscitur. Ubi autem Monarchia est, ibi omnes omnino ordinem aliquem habent, cùm nemo sit qui non subjiciatur alicui, eo solùm excepto, qui curam omnium gerit. Hac ratione in Catholica Ecclesia summus est ordo, ubi plebes subjiciuntur Parochis, Parochi Episcopis, Episcopi Metripolitanis, Metripolitani Primatibus, Primates Pontifici maximo, Pontifex maximum Deo. Ubi verò gubernatio penes Optimates est, plebes quidem ordinem suum habent, cum subjiciantur Optimatibus, sed Optimates inter se ordinem nullum habent. Multò etiam magis Dimocratia ordine caret, cum omnes cives ejusdem conditionis, & auctoritatis in Republica censeantur."

[90] Relationi universali, pp. 700–702. Again Botero was not entirely consistent; in writing about Venice he praised republics above principates (pp. 763–766).

neglected.[91] Botero related this general problem to the religious question. "The dangers and inconveniences into which a state falls through a change in faith," he declared, "do not move the senators of a republic as they do a prince, because the senators let themselves be moved in great part by their private interests; but the interest of a prince is identical with the good of the state. In addition, to change religion can be of some use to an individual but contrary to the public welfare." [92] Republics were evidently subject to heresy not only because they allowed freer rein to the licentious preferences of the masses but through the intrinsic constitutional and even philosophical defects of republicanism.

Princes, then, were to be preferred to republics because they were more reliable from a religious standpoint and easier to work with, and because authority (though it might in certain cases be conceived as flowing in the other direction) moved more naturally from the one to the many, from superior to inferior. But the sense of hierarchy also meant the obligation of princes to perform specific duties for the church. They were required to give it the same protection they rendered to all else within their states; but they also owed it special services. Notable among these was the obligation to enforce true belief on all subjects. Bellarmine was clear on the point. "This liberty of believing everything is mortal for the church," he declared. "It destroys her unity, made up of unity in faith. Princes, therefore, if they wish to be faithful to their duty, must in no way concede this liberty . . . . Freedom of thought is nothing but freedom to err, and to err in a matter of particular danger." [93] The obligation to protect orthodoxy was naturally extended to include the suppression of heretical writings.[94]

But the state, inferior by nature, could do little of positive value for the church. It served her best by keeping out of the way, and most ecclesiastical pronouncements about the duties of princes were directed at preventing them from engaging in actions of various kinds. Above all they were to exercise no authority over the clergy or the property of the church. For Bellarmine all that had been offered and consecrated to God was, *ipso facto*,

---

[91] Cf. *De potestate pontificis temporali*, Bk. I, Ch. 2, *Opera*, I, 254.

[92] *Relationi universali*, p. 392. The case of Germany moved him to this general observation.

[93] *De laicis*, Ch. 18, *Opera*, II, 272: ". . . sed Ecclesiae exitialis est haec libertas; nam vinculum Ecclesiae est unius fidei confessio . . . & ideo dissensio in fide, Ecclesiae est dissolutio. Debent igitur Principes hanc libertatem nullo modo permittere, si fungi munere suo volunt."

[94] *De laicis*, Ch. 20, *Opera*, II, 274–276, is devoted to this problem.

beyond the jurisdiction of any secular authority.[95] In practice this meant the immunity of the church from taxation and of its clergy from prosecution in civil courts. Such immunities had considerable practical value, but they were also important to maintain the principle of hierarchy and the intrinsic superiority of the clergy to the laity. As Bellarmine remarked, to expose a priest on any matter to the judgment of a layman would be as absurd as putting a shepherd under the control of his sheep.[96]

Nor had the theorists in Rome any doubt about the proper course in the event that a ruler failed or refused to meet his obligations to the church: he was to be subjected to the full range of ecclesiastical censure, including excommunication and deposition by the pope. Bellarmine insisted that the pope had the authority even to "force the people themselves, under penalty of excommunication, not to serve an excommunicated king and instead to elect another for themselves." [97] He defended the authority of the pope to exclude Henry of Navarre from the throne of France.[98] And Botero proclaimed, before his more popular audience, what the pope might do in the case of "the scandal given by princes who either through malice pervert the public good and the administration of the church, or through negligence permit the ruin of religion in their states." "For either reason," he asserted, "the popes, if the evil is incorrigible, consider excommunication and interdict. And if these weapons have little effect, they declare the princes incapable of the stations and unworthy of the rank in which God has placed them. They absolve their subjects from the oath of fidelity and transfer their kingdoms and empires to others. The reason: that in the church of God the secular power is like the body and the spiritual like the soul, whence the former must obey and the latter command in everything that pertains to the public good of the church. Scandalous princes are like putrid members and scabbed

---

[95] *De clericis*, Ch. 29, *Opera*, II, 165: "Certè autem in ea, quae sunt oblata & consecrata Deo, & quasi propria ipsius Dei facta sunt, nullum jus habere possunt Principes saeculi."

[96] *Ibid.*, Ch. 28, p. 161: "Nam omnino absurdum est, ut ovis Pastorem suum quocumque modo judicare praesumat." This whole chapter is concerned with clerical immunities.

[97] *De potestate papae in rebus temporalibus*, Ch. 3, *Opera*, V, 34: ". . . potest summus Pontifex ligar Principes saeculares vinculo excommunicationis; potest per eandem solvere populos à juramento fidelitatis, & obedientiae; potest obligare eosdem populos sub excommunicationis poena, ut Regi excommunicato non pareant, atque ut alium sibi eligant Regem."

[98] In his *Responsio ad praecipua capita apologiae, quae falso catholica inscribitur, pro successione Henrici Navarreni in Francorum regnum, auctore Francisco Romulo* (Rome, 1586). "Francisco Romulo" was probably a pseudonym for Pierre de Belloy.

sheep, which must be cut off from the healthy parts and expelled from the flock."

To illustrate the right of the pope to censure and depose rulers, he listed instances—biblical, medieval, and recent—in which rulers had been so treated by ecclesiastical authority. But his examples are, in some cases, curious. Among others he listed the Hohenstaufen emperors, Louis XII of France, and both Henry VIII and Elizabeth of England.[99] That the disciplines of the church had in many of these cases no practical effect evidently did not trouble men like Botero. The validity of the pope's right to root up and pluck out kingdoms and empires had, for them, been sufficiently established by the simple fact that popes had asserted and continued to assert it; that princes themselves had rarely endorsed the claim was essentially irrelevant. The truth, and in a sense even historical truth, was limited, for these men, to what was systematically and rationally necessary; what had actually happened had almost no bearing on the matter.

The right of ecclesiastical authority to take extreme measures against intransigent princes found its logical culmination in an ecclesiastical doctrine of tyrannicide, from which several writers of the Catholic Reformation did not shrink.[100] They generally believed, though they did not always care to assert openly, that rulers whom the pope declared to be deposed, as well as all heretical princes, were automatically illegitimate, were therefore tyrants, and were to be removed from power—if necessary by assassination. The more circumspect Bellarmine avoided giving this position explicit support, though he accepted it by implication; but other Catholic theologians, particularly from the Society of Jesus, were fairly open on the matter. That the faithful were generally encouraged to regard the killing of refractory and heretical princes as acts of piety is suggested by Botero's report of the death of William of Orange. "He was slain in Middelburgh," Botero wrote, "by a certain Balthasar, who was moved by zeal for religion and for the public good as he showed in death, which he endured not only with patience but with marvelous gladness." [101]

Yet it would be rather misleading to understand this aspect of the Counter Reformation as primarily the affirmation of a set of ideals concerning the nature of reality and the structure of authority within the Christian society.

[99] Relationi universali, pp. 380–381.
[100] On this point see, in general, Lewy, pp. 133ff.
[101] Relationi universali, p. 447.

Before the ideology we have just described was an authoritarianism of attitude and of act. Rome, indeed, would doubtless have preferred to do without authoritarian doctrine, which was only required because authority had been questioned, and which exposed the claims of papal and spiritual authority to further discussion and to refutation. The genius of Rome had traditionally resided in administration and law, not in speculation and theology; and the Roman church had long tended to conceive of itself largely as a system of government.[102] From this standpoint even the heresies of the Protestants had from the beginning seemed less significant as error than as rebellion: as sins against authority rather than against truth, and therefore to be suppressed by force rather than dignified with reply. The men who dominated the Curia had long been, for the most part, not theologians concerned with questions of belief but lawyers interested in questions of government, as the Venetians had from time to time observed with mixed feelings. Thus the characteristic gestures of the Catholic Reformation in Italy were practical, not theoretical: the revision of Gratian promoted by Gregory XIII and brought to a culmination by Clement VIII, the collection of pontifical constitutions by Sixtus V, the reorganization of the Sacred College into a body of specialized and far more efficient congregations.[103]

And as a government bent on evolving more effective mechanisms of control over Catholic Christendom, the papacy of the Catholic Reformation was developing along characteristic lines. It became more than ever monarchical. And while Bellarmine and Botero reiterated papalist arguments against conciliarism, the popes were taking practical steps to check the tendency toward a religious federalism based on a system of autonomous local and national churches which had given ecclesiastical expression to the growing particularism of the contemporary world. This required, first of all, a transformation in the relations between the pope and the College of Cardinals, in which particular interests had traditionally been able to exert pressure in Rome. The tension between pope and cardinals, which went back at least to the conciliar period, had never been entirely resolved, although the popes had won a series of victories since the fifteenth century.[104] But in the later sixteenth century the superiority of the pope was made definitive.

---

[102] Cf. the interesting observations of Ullmann, *Government and Politics in the Middle Ages*, p. 51 and *passim*.

[103] On these actions see Pastor, XIX, 279–280; XXI, 223, 249; XXIV, 230.

[104] See Jedin, *Konzil von Trient*, I, 60–79.

This was accomplished in various ways. The sharp increase in the numbers of cardinals reduced the importance of individual figures as, in an aristocratic age, did the elevation of clergy with low social origins; the personal poverty of such men also helped to restrict their influence.[105] In 1583 the sudden appointment of nineteen new cardinals by Gregory XIII, without consultation or advance notice, particularly irritated those who already belonged to the Sacred College. But when its dean, Cardinal Farnese, protested, the pope added insult to injury by explaining that his action was designed to avoid long and wearisome discussion.[106] What the papacy found irritating in the constitutional procedures of the Venetian Republic was intolerable in the government of the Roman church.

Of particular significance was the reorganization of the Sacred College in 1588 by Sixtus V. By dividing it into fifteen smaller bodies which functioned separately and henceforth rarely assembled as a whole, the pope largely converted it from a quasi-constitutional agency into an appointive and specialized bureaucracy. The bull announcing this change also made clear that the pope was not to be considered *primus inter pares*. He was, it pointed out, the unique head of the church; the cardinals bore the same relationship to him as the Apostles to Christ (not, it may be noted, to Peter); and they existed to aid him with burdens which, properly speaking, belonged to him alone.[107] Henceforth the Venetian ambassadors described the government of the church much as they described the autocratic government of Tuscany. Paruta noted that Clement VIII reproved the cardinals for speaking "too freely and, as he said, boldly," and that the pope had threatened to discipline them. They must, Clement had declared, accept in silence whatever he had decided.[108] The views of the pope, Giovanni Dolfin reported in 1598, now counted for everything, the consistories for nothing.[109]

We have already observed the attempt of the papacy, as it affected Venice, to impose effective control over bishops. Sixtus V in 1585 required every bishop-elect to visit Rome before his consecration, and all Italian bishops to appear regularly every three years. He also called on bishops to provide regular reports to Rome on the fulfillment of their duties and the condition

[105] Giampiero Carocci, *Lo Stato della Chiesa nella seconda metà del secolo XVI* (Milan, 1961), p. 105.

[106] Pastor, XIX, 231.

[107] Pastor, XXI, 5, 245ff. Cf. Carocci, p. 104. The pope's explanation that he wished to use his cardinals as republics used their senators seems either disingenuous or to suggest a considerable ignorance of republics.

[108] Albèri, Ser. 2, IV, 414. Cf. his dispatch of Dec. 25, 1593, *Legazione*, II, 152–153.

[109] Albèri, Ser. 2, IV, 460.

of their dioceses.[110] Clement VIII added to these requirements, as we have seen, an examination in canon law and theology before confirmation for every new Italian bishop. The alliance between the pope and the monastic orders, especially those of recent foundation, gave the pope a further means of influence which alarmed local authorities. As Paruta observed: "What really makes the authority of the pope great is that he commands a huge number of men in the states of every prince, that is, the religious who are immediately subject to him." [111] Meanwhile the system of nunciatures, kept in touch with Rome by communication as regular as that of the Venetian ambassadors, provided another effective means of centralization.

These measures in behalf of papal authority were supplemented by an intensified clericalism, generally required by the hierarchical structure of reality but also needed to insure the effective functioning of the church as an instrument of government. The stubborn refusal of the Roman church to concede such nondogmatic points as communion in both kinds or the possibility of a married clergy should be understood as an expression of concern on this point. Concession, narrowly conceived, might have been politic in Germany, but it would have broken down the qualitative distinction between clergy and laity and thereby subverted the effectiveness of the church as an agency of discipline and control.

The clericalism of the Catholic Reformation found various expressions. Some were direct, such as the formal exclusion of laymen from the cardinalate in 1586.[112] But more important was the general atmosphere that now prevailed in Rome, to which laymen like Paruta were particularly sensitive. "One often sees, not only with wonder but also not without some scandal," he wrote, "how certain men, vested with some ecclesiastical dignity and for this alone esteemed and respected, have by some action, often of a highly impertinent sort, acquired the name (as they say in Rome) of good ecclesiastics, that is defenders of the interests of the church against the laity, even though otherwise they may often be persons whose customs deserve little praise. On the other hand it is a remarkable thing that it is held against any prelate if he is too favorable to the laity, as a thing odious and contrary to the thoughts and conceptions of the Curia. And in this connection I have certainly heard important personages sometimes speak as

[110] Pastor, XXI, 4–5, sees the centralization of the episcopate as one of the major achievements of this pontificate. See also pp. 134–135.
[111] Albèri, Ser. 2, IV, 361.
[112] Pastor, XXI, 228.

though the laity were not members of the same flock or in the same sheepfold with the clergy." [113] In Rome the clergy were assumed to be shepherds, not sheep.

Insistence on the qualitative distinction between clergy and laity seems to have been accompanied in Rome by some degree of contempt for the normal occupations of laymen. The attitude doubtless has a long lineage, and it perhaps owed as much during the Counter Reformation to the aristocratic bias of the age as to its clericalism. But the art of the Counter Reformation, as Delumeau has observed, differs markedly from that of the Middle Ages in its neglect of scenes depicting manual labor and lower class life. The ecclesiastical authorities in Rome chose to pour the capital of the church into monumental buildings and other forms of conspicuous consumption rather than into more permanently productive enterprises. Meanwhile heavy taxes drained capital away from private sectors of the economy. Undisciplined in the industrial arts, the Roman population, which might in this period have been directed into constructive occupations, grew increasingly parasitical. By the end of the century it numbered more beggars and (in spite of moralizing, legislating, and occasional arrests) more prostitutes than any other city in Italy. The attitudes of the Counter Reformation bear some responsibility for the fact that the *dolce vita* became a permanent feature of the Roman scene in the course of the sixteenth century.[114]

The reinvigoration of the church and the exaltation of its clergy were accompanied by practical efforts to impose ecclesiastical authority on temporal rulers. The general claims of the church were periodically expressed through the bull *In coena domini*.[115] Read annually from Catholic pulpits on Holy Thursday, the bull denounced heresy, and in addition it listed in some detail various actions prohibited to secular rulers. The origins of the bull are obscure. It seems to have been first promulgated in the later fourteenth century, but it was issued repeatedly in the fifteenth and sixteenth, successive editions being modified or amplified to fit changing needs. Julius II, who attached particular importance to the bull, formally gave it the force of law in 1511; but its most vigorous application began with the pontificate of Pius V. *In coena domini* regularly forbade rulers to receive or to correspond

[113] Albèri, Ser. 2, IV, 375.

[114] Delumeau, I, 365ff., 432, 515–516. His second volume, p. 521, describes this development as "la défaite du travail."

[115] For what follows see, in general, Raffaele Giura Longo, "La bolla *In Coena Domini* e le franchigie al clero meridionale," *Archivio Storico per la Calabria e la Luciana*, XXXII (1963), 275–280; and Cecchetti, *La Republica di Venezia e la Corte di Roma*, I, 445ff.

with non-Catholics. It prohibited any appeal to a council from the decisions of Rome. It forbade taxation of the clergy without the permission of the pope. It prohibited secular courts from exercising jurisdiction over members of the upper clergy, and it encouraged appeals from local courts, civil or ecclesiastical, to Rome.

The edition of the bull released in 1568 was unusually vigorous. In addition to the usual prohibitions, it forbade governments to condemn or to expel a papal nuncio, it prohibited any state from banishing a subject made a cardinal by the pope (an action of which Venice had recently been guilty), and it revoked any privileges of jurisdiction over clergy previously conceded by Rome. The Venetian ambassador interpreted the bull to mean that the pope claimed to rule the world temporally as well as spiritually, but Venice was not the only state to take offense. The Spanish viceroy in Naples confiscated every copy of the bull he could find, and threatened severe measures against any bishop who might publish or apply it. In Spain no bishop dared to promulgate the bull. Rome took a dark view of such defiance. The nuncio in Venice interpreted the refusal of the Republic to allow the publication of the bull as "something schismatic, and a first disposition to heresy." [116]

Meanwhile Rome also pressed its claims to the practical supervision of temporal affairs, even (whenever possible) against the great powers. Thus Sixtus V tried to bar Henry of Navarre from the throne of France. "In the fulness of power which the King of Kings and the Lord of Lords has conferred on us, by the authority of God almighty," he proclaimed, "we pronounce and declare Henry . . . of full right dispossessed and incapable of succeeding." [117] Nor were such gestures directed only against princes who were open heretics. In 1589 Sixtus, primarily offended by Henry III's alliance with Navarre, declared him excommunicated unless he released some distinguished prelates whom he had imprisoned and appeared in Rome, either personally or by proxy, within sixty days. Since the French king failed to comply with these conditions, he apparently died excommunicate.[118] And even the Habsburg states were not altogether immune from such treatment. Although they generally tried to avoid antagonizing Spain by making theoretical claims of large resonance, the popes of the later

[116] Pastor, XVIII, 35–36; Quazza, *Preponderanza spaqnuola*, pp. 266–268; Stella, *Chiesa e Stato*, pp. 46–47.
[117] Quoted by Willaert, I, 381.
[118] Pastor, XXI, 318–319.

sixteenth century firmly opposed the jurisdictional claims of the Spanish governments in Milan and Naples. Gregory XIII was particularly aggressive about these matters. Political realities considerably restricted what could be done, but the claims and intentions of Rome were clear enough.[119]

The revival of the crusading ideal by the popes of the Catholic Reformation gave further expression to the conception of the pope as effective head of a united Christendom. The organization of new crusades was as constant a preoccupation of Rome during this period as at any time in the Middle Ages, particularly after the encouragement provided by Lepanto. That great victory over the infidel caused Pius V to indulge in grandiose hopes. He dreamed of a decade of heavy fighting in which the enemies of the faith would at last be annihilated; and to realize this vision he proclaimed a plenary indulgence for all who would participate, the same inducement offered to the crusaders of earlier centuries. He also proposed that their property should be taken under the protection of the church during their absence; he declared a moratorium on any lawsuit in which they might be engaged; and he exempted them from all taxation—gestures doubtless of some interest from the standpoint of the secular authorities. Among its other prohibitions, the version of *In coena domini* issued in 1573 denounced any attempt to undermine the league against the Turks: this when the air was filled with rumors of peace between Venice and Constantinople.[120] Later popes, as we have seen, maintained the pressure for a renewal of the crusade. Nothing would have demonstrated more effectively the reality of papal leadership in the world.

After some centuries of exposure to the historicism released by the Renaissance, the universalism of the Counter Reformation is likely to appear curiously unrealistic. The particularism of Europe, for better or for worse, now seems, by the sixteenth century, to have been far too deeply established to be rooted out by such resources as were available to the papacy. European life had been too thoroughly secularized for the effort to impose an ecclesiastical tutelage to have any real hope of success; the autonomous culture of the modern age proved far more powerful than the forces

[119] Paolo Prodi, "San Carlo Borromeo e le trattative tra Gregorio XIII e Filippo II sulla giurisdizione ecclesiastica," *Rivista Storica della Chiesa in Italia*, XI (1957), 195–240; Pastor, XXIII, 202–206.

[120] Pastor, XVIII, 441; XIX, 323–331; XXII, 145–149; XXIII, 265. In 1598 Clement VIII expressed his hope that he might one day celebrate mass in Santa Sophia (XXIV, 401).

attacking it from Rome. But none of this seemed obvious in Italy during the later sixteenth century. This was partly, perhaps, because the sufferings, the fragmentation, and the weakness of Italy made the secular accomplishments of the new civilization appear singularly vulnerable. In Italy ecclesiastical authority might appear to triumph and a show of fidelity to the values of the Counter Reformation be maintained. But the aspirations of Rome were also based on a confidence in the ultimate course of history which came not from the scrutiny of conditions and events but from an ideal, and from what was taken to be a divine promise of its realization. For Rome what ought to be must eventually come about. Meanwhile she would do everything in her power to hasten its coming.

At the end of the sixteenth century her efforts intensified. Heartened by signs that the Turks could be beaten, encouraged by the pacification of France under a ruler who seemed eager to show his loyalty to the pope, supported by powerful new religious orders, served by a reorganized and effective curial bureaucracy, and with popular heresy in Italy firmly under control, the papacy could now mount a far more systematic campaign than ever before against the dangerous political and philosophical ideas of the Renaissance. The chronology of the papalist counteroffensive is thus significant. The last decade of the sixteenth century and the early years of the seventeenth produced a special wave of ideological assaults and condemnations. Although Machiavelli had long been on the Index, he was systematically refuted only after 1589; in that year Botero's *Ragion di stato* appeared, to be closely followed by the works of Possevino and Bozio, and by Ribadeneyra's *Principe cristiano*. The works of Bodin were condemned in 1593, and two years later his political doctrines were refuted by Albergati. The Platonism of Francesco Patrizi was denounced, and the old philosopher was forced to profess his total submission to the church in 1594. The works of Telesio, so subversive of the general ideal of hierarchy, were put on the Index in 1596, and his views were sweepingly condemned nine years later. During the same period Pomponazzi received a new condemnation, and the works of Charron, Campanella, and Bruno were prohibited.[121] The fate of the last is well known; it should be seen as the most savage action in a general campaign. Galileo's turn was soon to come.

The growing tension between Rome and Venice must be understood not

---

[121] For this major assault at the end of the century, see, in general, Firpo, "Filosofia e Controriforma." For the condemnation of fideist writings see also René Pintard, *Le libertinage érudit dans la première moitié du XVIIᵉ siècle* (Paris, 1943), I, 66.

only as a consequence of developments within Venice herself but also against the whole background of the attitudes and policies of the Catholic Reformation and in the light of this chronology. Rome had long seen Venice as a special problem. Although, as now seems likely, the indictment prepared by Carafa in 1532 was not primarily about Venice but described religious conditions within the Republic to illustrate more general problems,[122] the concern of Aleander shortly after was rather more specific. He detected among the Venetians "a perversion of consciences" which reflected the general decadence of Christian piety. "It is true," he wrote, "that through the fault of the sins of all Christians, the whole world is grown very cold in the things of the Christian religion; and it has above all become cruel against the name and property of ecclesiastics; and consequently these lords travel along with the rest."[123] But Venice was peculiarly important for the religion of Italy; and she worried him. He was anxious because of her proximity to regions where Protestantism was strong and because her government might not prove powerful enough to withstand an uprising by the people, whose orthodoxy was always likely to be shaky; Aleander too thought princely government more effective.[124] As early as 1534 he expressed his apprehension that Venice might follow England into schism.[125] "These Venetian gentlemen," he had written to the pope, "have certainly given, and daily give your Holiness cause to be badly content with them, so that they deserve some punishment when it might be possible."[126]

Several elements in Aleander's view of the Venetian problem are worth attention here. One was his reluctance to blame the unseemly policies of the Republic on Venice as a whole. They had been imposed, he asserted (in spite of his remarks about the general decline of Christian piety), by "four or five old men," among whom he probably included Gasparo Contarini;[127] the notion that the wickedness of Venice could be attributed to the malice of a tiny band of conspirators, and was therefore an accident, was to prove regularly attractive to Rome. It reflected the moralism of the Catholic Reformation, its emphasis on individual responsibility, and its persistent inability to comprehend large historical processes and collective traditions.

[122] This is the view of Gaeta, *Un nunzio pontificio a Venezia*, pp. 87–88. Cf. Pastor, X, 310–313, 421–423.
[123] Quoted by Gaeta, p. 67.
[124] Gaeta, pp. 123–124.
[125] *Ibid.*, p. 82.
[126] Quoted by Gaeta, p. 29.
[127] Gaeta, p. 121.

At the same time it minimized the seriousness of Venetian resistance to the wishes of the pope. In this sense it encouraged optimism; it suggested that the elimination of a handful of wicked men might solve the problem. We shall encounter this explanation of Venetian conduct again.[128]

On the other hand Aleander was convinced that, whatever the explanation for her policies might be, Venice deserved punishment; and this conviction too seems to have become habitual in sixteenth-century Rome, even though the chastisement of Venice did not head the Curia's list of priorities. Aleander was for the time being inclined to caution. Immediate action against Venice might do more harm than good, he suggested; it might drive her into alliance with the Protestants or the Turks. He therefore advised the pope to suppress his resentment for the moment and wait patiently for an appropriate occasion.[129] This recommendation, repeated half a century later by Alberto Bolognetti,[130] was largely followed. For the rest of the century Rome bided her time and concealed her resentments as well as she could, while the day of reckoning drew slowly closer.

Numerous issues, which we have already touched on from the Venetian side, kept Roman suspicions of Venice alive. Some were essentially secular, although the Curia was inclined to regard any resistance to demands connected with the specific interests of the Papal State as in some sense defiance of the spiritual power. Rome, for example, increasingly resented Venetian control of the Adriatic, the virtual blockade of Ancona, and constant Venetian interference with the movement of shipping out of the Po. At the end of the century the Curia was inclined to be more aggressive on these matters too. In 1593 the pope declared Ancona a free port in an effort to divert commerce from Venice,[131] and his possession of Ferrara was followed by a more vigorous defense of free shipping on the Po.[132] The Adriatic question, as the nuncio Graziani noted in 1596, "was a perennial source from which spring daily occasions for perpetual controversy." [133] And while Rome argued that the marriage to the sea with a ring provided by the pope meant that all Venetian rights in the Adriatic were a papal concession, the

---

[128] See below, pp. 363–367.

[129] *Nunziature di Venezia*, I (1533–1535), ed. Franco Gaeta (Rome, 1958), pp. 37, 168.

[130] See Stella, *Chiesa e Stato*, pp. 42–43, 53–55.

[131] Ludwig Beutin, "La décadence économique de Venise considérée du point de vue nord-européen," *Aspetti e cause della decadenza economica veneziana nel secolo XVII* (Venice, 1961), p. 98.

[132] Benvenuto Cessi, "Il taglio del Po a Porto Viro," *AV*, Ser. 3, XXX (1915), 339ff.

[133] Antonio Graziani, quoted by Cessi, *Storia di Venezia*, II, 144.

Venetians retorted that the ceremony (like the Donation of Constantine in the eyes of the canonists) "merely confirmed what they already possessed and conceded nothing they did not have."[134] Another bitter controversy broke out in 1592 when Venice took into her service an outlawed subject of the pope. That such problems could not remain altogether secular when they involved the pope was suggested by Clement VIII's threat on this occasion. If he tolerated this insult, he informed the Venetian ambassador, he would show himself ungrateful for the position God had given him. He added firmly: "We shall do what God may inspire us to do."[135] Unlike secular princes, the pope evidently ruled over his temporal state by divine right.

Meanwhile there were persistent ecclesiastical issues, and here too such complaints as Rome had made earlier in the century seemed to arouse increasing vehemence. Venice, Clement charged, was closing her eyes to the sale of heretical books, and he was concerned that her hospitality to the English might lead to the further spread of heresy.[136] His nuncio vigorously denounced Venetian policy toward the Turks as a scandal and a "grave sin in the sight of God."[137] Friction mounted over questions of jurisdiction which (together with the Adriatic question) the nuncio described as "those two hydras that constantly grow twice the number of members that are cut off."[138] There were general charges from Rome that the magistrates of Venice "showed no regard" for the decrees of Trent on jurisdictional questions,[139] and particular resentments over familiar sorts of encroachment on clerical privilege. Clement VIII was especially incensed at the Venetian treatment of bishops—worse, as he informed Paruta, "than under the dominion of the Turks."[140] Venice taxed the clergy for special purposes, and her rectors arrested members of episcopal households and then reprimanded bishops who complained to Rome.[141]

Clement VIII was inclined to take the offensive. He questioned Paruta closely about the way parish priests were chosen in Venice, with the evident,

---

[134] As reported by Graziani, quoted in Brunetti, "Istruzioni," p. 376.

[135] The incident is described in Seneca, Donà, pp. 207ff.

[136] Paruta's dispatches of Nov. 19, 1594, and Jul. 17, 1593, Legazione, II, 489, and I, 265–266. Cf. Pastor, XXIV, 214–215

[137] Brunetti, "Schermaglie veneto-pontificie," p. 121.

[138] Brunetti, "Istruzioni," p. 375, quoting Graziani.

[139] Cf. Stella, Chiesa e Stato, p. 49.

[140] Dispatch of March 26, 1594, Legazione, II, 252.

[141] See, for example, the dispatch of June 26, 1593, Legazione, I, 244–245.

purpose of putting a stop to the arrangement if he could;[142] and he pressed, with the threat of formal censure, for the required examination of the patriarch in Rome. The Senate thought it advisable to allow Matteo Zane, the patriarch-elect, to visit the pope in 1601, though it stipulated that nothing in the trip should be construed as compromising the traditional rights of the Republic. But although the pope did not dare to submit Zane to an examination by the regular committee of cardinals, he asked a few vague questions himself in the course of a personal interview. Afterwards the pope claimed that the prescribed examination of the patriarch had taken place and the precedent of Venetian compliance established.[143]

But papal distrust of Venice was also more fundamental. Precisely when it seemed advisable in Rome to deepen respect everywhere for the pope and his authority, the Venetians appeared more and more openly disrespectful. Priuli noted this feeling at the Curia in 1586. It troubled Rome, he remarked, that Venice regularly neglected to express any positive acknowledgment of the papal primacy, even in spiritual matters;[144] and a few years later an embassy recorded the pope's displeasure with some Venetians for saying "that the pope commands at Fermo and in his own household, but not among us." On the contrary, the pope had declared: "In the things of religion we can command the whole of Christendom." [145] Paruta too, during his years in Rome, was sensitive to the feeling that Venetians were exhibiting less reverence for the present pope than for his predecessors.[146]

But the Venetian position on the superiority of the pope in temporal matters was a particular grievance to the Curia. Venice, Priuli had maintained in Rome, was like other sovereign princes in recognizing no superior whatsoever in temporal things. But he had been informed that putting the matter so broadly was unacceptable. Not only was this position denounced as "prejudicial to papal authority in cases of heresy, where they claim a very extensive authority," Priuli had reported, but he had been reminded that papal authority covered "difficulties that might arise between sovereign lords which, having no earthly judge, can be dealt with by the pope, as many doctors hold, so that their differences might be compromised for the sake of public quiet and the welfare of peoples." Venice was positively

[142] Dispatch of Feb. 27, 1593, *Legazione*, I, 112–113.

[143] Benzoni, "La conferma del patriarca," pp. 132–133.

[144] Albèri, Ser. 2, IV, 300.

[145] In the joint report of Donà and Badoer, quoted by Raulich, "La contesa fra Sisto V e Venezia," p. 314.

[146] Albèri, Ser. 2, IV, 434–435.

obligated, he had been informed, to promote papal authority in temporal matters, "the world being in its present condition." [147]

Thus Rome did not hesitate either to protest particular actions of the Venetian government or to inform the Republic of what the church generally required of her. The pope, as the nuncio Cesare Costa told the doge in 1585, was ready to support Venice with his prayers and even with more material benefits. But, the nuncio went on, he required something in return. He expected "the filial love and zeal for religion which must not be measured by the rules of statecraft and prudence but must be accepted with the simple confidence and the sentiments of the true believer, which are always the same and cannot be altered by events or by the will of men. It is to its obedient submission to the Holy See and its faithful observance of the canonical precepts that your illustrious Republic, so small in its beginnings, owes its greatness, power and glory of today. Its close union with the Holy See is a guarantee of the maintenance of peace at home and of great importance to its good name in Italy." [148]

This statement is of considerable interest. It meant that, to satisfy the pope, Venice would have to abandon an independent, secular politics, and subordinate her own interests to the general needs of Christendom as interpreted by the pope. In addition it meant that Venice must accept an interpretation of her own history very different from that which she had long held. The orthodox historiography now being developed at the Curia was evidently not confined to the church. It also required that all secular history should illustrate Botero's doctrine that the true secret of worldly greatness consists of obedience to the pope. In this view the successes of Venice had been, as Agostino Valier argued, the effect not of any special wisdom and virtue on the part of her people but simply of her fidelity to the Roman faith. Botero made this point more concretely in his comment on the events of 1177. He accepted the traditional account that had made Venice appear so helpful to the pope, but he drew from it not the exceptional status of the Republic in the political universe but the substantial rewards of serving the church. As a result of this episode, he concluded, "the Venetians have had most of the ornaments of their doge from the Roman popes . . . and their superiority over the sea from Alexander III." [149] Other writers took an even less genial view of Venetian history. When Baronius came in his

[147] *Ibid.*, p. 300.
[148] Quoted by Pastor, XXII, 146–147.
[149] *Relationi universali*, p. 382.

Annales to the year 1177, he denied to Venice any special role at all in the settlement between pope and emperor.[150] Bellarmine, in the course of arguing that monarchies last longer than other forms of government, found Venice no exception to the rule. The Scythian and Assyrian monarchies and even that of the Franks, he pointed out, had lasted longer than she. He also denied that she possessed a genuine mixed constitution.[151]

Although these suggestions of refusal to accept what Venice claimed for herself were doubtless aggravating, they were less immediately dangerous than the hostility occasionally displayed toward her by the popes themselves. For in spite of the good advice of the more tactful nuncios in Venice, the popes of the later sixteenth century found it increasingly difficult to conceal their general impatience with her. Although Paruta liked to dwell on those occasions when Clement VIII expressed some affection for the Republic, he was forced to recognize the pope's fundamental hostility, which could not be altogether repressed. "Very often and for the smallest actions of your Serenity or of your ministers," Paruta reported, "[the pope] has shown himself so offended and has interpreted matters in so bad a sense, and also used threatening language, that there is just cause for wonder and doubt about the innermost feelings in his mind." [152] Only a general and profound irritation can explain a violence of language that Paruta found altogether disproportionate to its immediate occasion.[153]

Thus during the years when Venice, under the leadership of the *giovani*, was increasingly conscious of her heritage as a free republic, the papacy was

---

[150] *Annales ecclesiastici*, XIX, 421-431. For the indignant Venetian reaction see Sarpi's *Trattato circa le ragioni di Ceneda*, p. 210, in his *Opere* (Helmstadt-Verona, 1761-1766), VI: and the reply to Baronius by the jurist Cornelio Frangipane, also in Sarpi's *Opere*, IV, 381-430, under the title *Allegazione ovvero Consiglio in jure per la vittoria navale contra Federigo I Imperadore, ed atto di Papa Alessandro III.*

[151] *De potestate pontificis temporali*, Bk. I, Ch. 2, *Opera*, I, 254: "Objicient fortasse Rempublicam Venetorum, quae annos numerat supra mille & centum. At nec ipsa pervenit ad annos regni Scytharum, vel Assyriorum; immò ne Francorum quidem: & praeterea non est Respublica Venetorum Aristocratia admixta Politiae, quam formam Calvinus laudat, sed Aristocratia admixta Monarchiae: nec ullum in ea civitate locum habet Dimocratia."

[152] Albèri, Ser. 2, IV, 434.

[153] Cf. his dispatch of Jul. 15, 1595, *Legazione*, III, 209, reporting the pope's description of the embassy from Ceneda, whose cause was supported by Venice. The pope, Paruta wrote, had applied to the envoys "those names and titles that are given to Judas, betrayer of Christ, calling them sons of iniquity, forgetful of eternal salvation, led on by the spirit of the devil, and other similar words."

deepening its universalism and growing rapidly more articulate and aggressive in promoting its own authoritarian perspectives and values. The tension between the two powers was on the surface political and ecclesiastical, but underlying all their particular disagreements was the profound conflict between two antagonistic cultural worlds and two visions of reality. Even before they were actively pitted against each other in the great struggle initiated by the interdict of 1606, the fundamental character of their conflict found expression in an occasional dramatic confrontation.

One such confrontation came during an interview in 1581 between Leonardo Donà, then ambassador to Rome, and Gregory XIII. Donà had waited on the pope to discuss the delicate problem of Aquileia, over which Venice claimed rights that were contested by the patriarch of the place with support from Rome. Donà, on this occasion, explained to the pope that his instructions had been delayed because of prolonged consideration of the matter in Venice. But the implication that Venetian opinion was essential to settling the question evidently annoyed the pope, who reproved the ambassador. "It is not sufficient to *consider*, Signor Ambassador, as you put it," the pope declared. "It is necessary to consider *secundum iura*, and you in Venice are not doctors of law." Donà had replied with dignity, as he reported, "that, as his Holiness knew very well, we had in Venice, thank God, our own conception of legality and our own laws, with which we are governed; and that it could be said on this point that your Serenity had the most capable advisers." "Also, thank God," he had told the pope, "when your Serenity wanted any light on either [your own] communal laws or those of others, you did not lack the means of obtaining it nor the capacity to understand it, having always had as a particular goal to want only the truth and to proceed always in the company of duty."

Donà's point was that the Venetian lay state did not intend to surrender to alleged specialists in Rome the responsibility for deciding matters pertaining to its own interests, a response that failed to mollify the pope. Gregory had replied sarcastically: "Yes, we know that you are very intelligent, and also that many of you have a knowledge of philosophy beyond what is afforded by the light of nature, which is prior to laws and on which laws are based. But you are also accustomed to prolong decision excessively with your debates." Donà understood the issue. The pope, persuaded that truth and right are absolute and that they must therefore be imposed with an equally absolute authority, objected to the inconveniences and delays inherent in all free debate, which seems ultimately to depend on a different conception of truth and right. The Venetian ambassador replied to the pope directly. Truth, he declared, could only be achieved by an open clash between conflicting views, and "especially in a government by many like that of your Serenity." So the republican world of Venice challenged the authoritarian world of the Catholic Reformation.[154]

Equally illuminating was a similar confrontation, a little more than a decade later, between Paruta and Clement VIII. In 1593 Paruta visited the pope to discuss the reconciliation of Henry IV of France with the Roman church. The pope expressed considerable reluctance, as he had done before. "And how, please," he had asked Paruta, "can we make the decision to bless Navarre, which is the same as constituting him king, if the Sorbonne of France has already declared that this can by no means and under no circumstances be done, and in addition certain theologians here in Rome have written and confirmed it? And truly it is settled by the canons that a man who has once fallen into heresy and taken up arms against the church can no longer be raised to a dignity." But Paruta had chosen not to take the question as merely rhetorical. "Holy Father," he had replied, "the laws can never include or foresee all cases. Besides, great princes are above the laws; nor, with their persons and in the most serious and important cases, like that at issue here, should things be measured according to ordinary rules and methods. Indeed it sometimes happens, according to the common saying, that the best rule and the most useful advice is to observe no rule." [155] On this occasion the rigidity of the Catholic Reformation gave way before the flexibility of the Renaissance. But it would not always do so, particularly where it saw a real chance of having its way.

[154] The encounter is described in detail by Seneca, *Donà*, p. 141, n. 2.
[155] Dispatch of Aug. 21, 1593, *Legazione*, I, 307.

.

The Venetian Interdict:
Men and Events[1]

Do not start a quarrel with a powerful republic unless you are sure of victory and stand to gain much by it, for love of liberty is so strong and so deeply rooted in the hearts of those who have enjoyed it for a long time that to overcome it is difficult and to extirpate it is almost impossible. The schemes and opinions of princes die with them, the policies and deliberations of free cities are permanent. Do not start a quarrel with the Church, because it is unlikely that your cause will be just and in any case it will appear impious and will profit you nothing.—Botero, *Reason of State* (Waley tr.), p. 44.

ON Christmas Day in the year 1605, the papal nuncio in Venice, Orazio Mattei, appeared before the College to present a brief from Rome.[2] He had in fact received two briefs eight days earlier with instructions to deliver both to the Venetian government immediately; but, in his anxiety over this errand he had first delayed, and then he either forgot one of the briefs or deliberately disobeyed the order to convey both at once, an omission for which he was subsequently reprimanded.

His apprehension was well founded; the Venetian ambassador in Rome had already acquainted his government with the general substance of the pope's messages,[3] and the nuncio could hardly have expected a warm reception. The pope had instructed him to serve notice that unless the Venetian government promptly revoked several laws which his Holiness considered infringements on the rights and liberties of the church, he would excommunicate the Senate as a body and impose an interdict on all territories of the Republic.

[1] The best general introduction to the bibliography of the Venetian interdict is Carlo de Magistris, *Carlo Emanuele I e la contesa fra la Repubblica Veneta e Paolo V (1605–1607): documenti* (Venice, 1906), pp. xxv–lii; hereafter cited as Magistris. Among earlier narrative accounts, that of Battistella, *La Repubblica di Venezia*, pp. 613ff. is particularly well balanced.

[2] Cornet, p. 17 and n. 3. This compilation of diplomatic correspondence and transactions of agencies of the Venetian government supplies a basic documentary narrative of the interdict from the Venetian side; to it Cornet has added a rich body of notes.

[3] It may be useful for what follows to bear in mind that couriers normally took four or five days between Rome and Venice, but it was possible to make the trip in as little as forty-one hours (Delumeau, *Vie économique et sociale de Rome*, I, 50, 53).

The nuncio's task had been to present an ultimatum; and his clumsy choice of the festival honoring the birth of the Savior for the performance of this unpleasant duty seemed, in Venetian eyes, a gratuitous aggravation of what was in any event an act of brutal aggression.[4] Thus began a major ordeal which gave Venice one of the last opportunities in her history to win an impressive victory.

For Venice chose to defy the pope; and the interdict, duly imposed in the spring of the following year, proved to have an importance which neither side could have fully appreciated at the outset. Because the struggle between Rome and Venice had both political and religious reverberations in many directions, it heightened the general tension that was to be released, a little more than a decade later, in the Thirty Years' War. However forgotten today, the international importance of the interdict was fully grasped by contemporaries, and for more than a year the attention of thoughtful men and of governments all over Europe was fixed on the small Italian republic at the head of the Adriatic. At the same time the episode was a disaster for the Counter Reformation insofar as that ambitious movement aimed to realize medieval ideals for the social and political organization of Christendom. Among its other distinctions, the Venetian affair was the last in the series of major interdicts by which the papacy had attempted, since the high Middle Ages, to impose its political leadership on the Christian Republic.[5]

For Venice herself the interdict was the climax of the long political education traced in this book. As a direct challenge to her autonomy and to the survival of the whole system of values implicit in the complex ideal of Renaissance liberty, the crisis brought on by the papal attack compelled Venice to examine the meaning of her long existence and of her special mode of adjustment to the world. And because, in her defense of republican values, Venice expounded them to an attentive world, the episode gave her an opportunity to show that Renaissance ideals were still vital and to demonstrate, before the widest possible audience, the nature of the conflict between the Renaissance achievement and the medieval vision of the Counter Reformation. Finally the interdict pushed into prominence, as one of the major publicists of the Venetian cause, the keen, subtle, and controversial monk, Fra Paolo Sarpi.

[4] The Senate complained of the nuncio's tactlessness to the French ambassador the following April (Cornet, p. 51).

[5] Cf. Alban Haas, *Das Interdikt nach geltendem Recht, mit einem geschichtlichen Überblick* (Amsterdam, 1929), p. 13.

That the clash between Rome and Venice had been long in preparation should be obvious from the developments traced in earlier chapters, but its particular timing was the result of a combination of specific circumstances. Among these was the relative peace that had descended on Europe during the first decade of the seventeenth century,[6] for peace in remoter areas freed Rome for attention to more local problems while it made Venice feel less secure. There was some irony here, for Venice had calculated that the pacification of France and the reestablishment of effective government by Henry IV would serve her interests by restraining Spain. These developments in some measure served this purpose. Spain, already in financial difficulties, felt compelled to reduce her military commitments all over Europe; and within a few years she had concluded peace with France (1598) and England (1604), and begun negotiating a truce with her rebels in the Low Countries. But Spanish disengagement elsewhere opened up new possibilities of aggression in Italy; and Venetian danger was meanwhile enlarged by the negotiations after 1603 for an end to the war with the Turks which had so long distracted the Habsburgs of Central Europe. With her old enemies increasingly free to conspire against her, Venice moved into the new century in a mood of growing anxiety about her political position. Suspicious of the intentions of the powers around her, she was inclined to interpret any move on the part of Rome as a threat, inspired by Spain, to her political independence.

Even more serious for Venice were the economic consequences of general peace. Venetian prosperity was already deteriorating before the end of the sixteenth century. Ship construction, long a weak spot in the Venetian economy, declined further; and by 1605 Venice was buying more ships abroad than she built at home. Corsair activity, to which the cumbersome Venetian galleys were particularly vulnerable, had meanwhile been on the increase. Corsairs generally claimed some connection with a national or religious interest but in practice rarely paid much attention to the nationality or the faith of their victims, and Venice suffered from all directions. The cost of commercial insurance rose to prohibitive levels as a result.[7]

Now, under these already dubious conditions, general peace in the west freed the English, the French, and increasingly the Dutch for aggressive

[6] Braudel, *La Méditerranée et le monde méditerranéan*, pp. 546–548, needs some qualification for Venice on this point.

[7] See, in general, Tenenti, *Venezia e i corsari*, esp. pp. 119ff. Frederic C. Lane, "Recent Studies on the Economic History of Venice," *Journal of Economic History*, XXIII (1963), 330, suggests a relation between the European peace treaties and Venetian economic reverses.

commercial penetration of the Mediterranean. As a result Venice, already largely excluded from Atlantic trade by the disruptions of war and by English mercantilism, found her Mediterranean commerce in a rapid decline. Furthermore special circumstances at this time favored the Atlantic powers in the Levant. Devaluation of Turkish currency early in the new century gave specie unusual value in eastern markets; and the merchants from western Europe, adequately supplied with hard money, were able to buy at unusually low prices. But Venice was at this point short of money and preferred in any case to trade her own manufactured goods, with the result that other merchants bought up the silks and cottons Venice had been accustomed to transport from Syria or Asia Minor to Europe. Her imports of textiles from the Near East declined rapidly, above all between 1603 and 1605—precisely, that is to say, on the eve of the interdict. As if all this were not enough, the same years saw the successful development by the Dutch and English of the Cape route for spice trade with the Indies. Spices at last ceased almost entirely to flow through the Levant, and Venetian merchants had finally to abandon their traditional role as the suppliers of spices to Europe. By the second decade of the seventeenth century Venice was herself buying spices from the Atlantic powers.[8] The full extent of the disaster was not yet apparent at the time of the interdict, but that event clearly took place during a time of growing economic difficulty. Venice still possessed vast wealth and was well able to support a major struggle,[9] but her rulers must have already begun to suspect that her decline into provincial mediocrity was perhaps after all inevitable.

Under these circumstances it was natural that Venice felt irritable, particularly toward an old enemy whose pretensions seemed deliberately calculated to affront her increasingly precarious dignity; and the Venetian government treated Rome with particular harshness. During this period Venice decided to terminate the long-established practice by which the papal nuncio had been accustomed to imprison Venetian clergy without a license from any civil magistrate; henceforth specific authorization from the Council of Ten was required.[10] Venice also chose to make an issue again, this time

---

[8] Sella, *Commerci e industrie a Venezia*, pp. 7ff.

[9] On this point see Kellenbenz, "Le déclin de Venise," p. 116. After thirty-five years of peace the financial position of the government seemed particularly strong; see the letter of Canaye to Commartin, Aug., 1606, *Lettres et ambassade*, III, 161–162. After noting the huge reserves in the public treasury, Canaye added: ". . . mais leur principale richesse est, que quand ils veulent, toutes les bourses de leur subiects sont à leur commandement, parce qu'ils payent fort bien. Les richesses de cette ville sont tres-grandes."

[10] Savio, "Il nunzio a Venezia," pp. 86–87.

rather more belligerently, of Rome's insistence that the patriarch-elect visit the Holy City for examination before confirmation in his office. The Venetian ambassador suggested to the pope, in the fall of 1605, that if the examination were truly so important, it was a curious fact that the church should have endured for a thousand years without it; and the new patriarch, Francesco Vendramin, stayed home, unconfirmed by the pope.[11] Meanwhile, given the nature of the economic difficulties of Venice, persistent Roman objections to commerce with heretics or infidels must have seemed particularly aggravating.[12]

But the sudden deterioration of Venetian commerce had also, perhaps, a more direct and tangible bearing on the backgrounds of the interdict, since it increased the importance for Venice of economic alternatives to trade. Above all it helped to remind the Republic of the importance of agriculture. The general principle, however, that the land might be made to supply income which the sea could no longer provide pointed to a new area of conflict with the church. For if agriculture was to be of any help to Venice in her time of need, it had obviously to be controlled by the laity; but, as it appeared to the Venetian patriciate, in point of fact arable land was falling increasingly into the possession of the church. This impression seems to have had some basis. Throughout Italy ownership of land by the church had been expanding in the period of the Counter Reformation;[13] and special conditions had carried this tendency significantly farther in Venetian territory than elsewhere. Ecclesiastical corporations had participated enthusiastically with their special accumulations of capital in the great reclamation projects of the age,[14] and both the possessions and the income of the Venetian clergy were certainly great. During the interdict, when the subject was hotly debated, Bellarmine

[11] Filippo Nani Mocenigo, *Agostino, Battista e Giacomo Nani* (Venice, 1917), pp. 89ff. See also Cornet, p. 6, n. 1. For Vendramin in general, see Niero, *I patriarchi di Venezia*, pp. 109–117.

[12] Certain of the clerical "pretensions" listed by Paolo Sarpi, *Sulle pretensioni delli ecclesiastici*, in *Istoria dell'interdetto e altri scritti editi ed inediti*, ed. Giovanni Gambarin (Bari, 1940), II, 99, suggests this, esp. nos. 53–60, which deal with claims to control commercial and other relations with non-Catholics. This collection, with the exception of the *Istoria dell'Interdetto* itself, will hereafter be cited as *Scritti*.

[13] Cf. Carocci, *Lo Stato della Chiesa*, pp. 183–184.

[14] See Stella, "La proprietà ecclesiastica nella Repubblica di Venezia," esp. pp. 67–70, where some of these projects are described. The situation in the Veneto was thus rather different from that in the rest of northern Italy, as described by Carlo M. Cipolla, "Comment s'est perdue la propriété ecclésiastique dans l'Italie du Nord entre le XIe et le XVIe siècle," *Annales*, II (1947), 317–327. Stella finds the anxiety of the Venetian patriciate quite comprehensible.

himself admitted the Venetian charge that the church owned a quarter of the land in the state. Furthermore his suggestion that this was really a very modest acquisition considering the twelve hundred years the process had been going on could hardly have been reassuring to the Venetians; it implied the disposition of the church to acquire even more.[15] Venice was particularly disturbed that a large proportion of the revenue from ecclesiastical benefices went to Rome instead of remaining to nourish the domestic economy;[16] and Venetians noted too that the newer monastic groups, those most responsive to Roman direction and least reliable in their support of the Venetian state, above all the Jesuits and the Capuchins, had recently been making large acquisitions of land.[17]

These worries found expression in several measures which aimed to restrict the economic and political power of ecclesiastics in the Venetian state and which the Curia was to find particularly objectionable. The earliest of these in time, although not the first to come to the attention of the pope, was a law passed by the Senate in May of 1602 dealing with lands leased from the church by laymen on long-term emphyteusis contracts. On the pretext that the tenant in such cases had made substantial improvements, the effect of the law was to prohibit the resumption of such lands by their ecclesiastical proprietors.[18] The real motive of the law was to keep as much land as possible in the possession of laymen and as much landed income as possible within the Venetian state, but churchmen found it intolerable that the civil magistrate should presume to interfere with contracts negotiated by the spiritual power. The law was also particularly objectionable to the church because it suggested that ecclesiastical property was not necessarily inalienable.[19]

[15] Roberto Bellarmino, *Risposta alle oppositioni di Fra Paulo Servita contra la scrittura del Cardinale Bellarmino*, bound with Bellarmine's *Risposta al trattato dei sette teologi di Venetia* (Rome, 1606), p. 92. For a contemporary Venetian estimate of the amount of wealth controlled by ecclesiastics, see Antonio Querini, *Aviso delle ragioni della serenissima republica di Venetia, intorno alle difficoltà che le sono promosse dalla Santità di Papa Paolo V* (Venice, 1606), p. 16; I cite the edition in the *Raccolta*, I, 11–33.

[16] Stella, "Proprietà ecclesiastica," pp. 52, 72.

[17] This point was noted by the Venetian publicist Marc'Antonio Capello, *Delle controversie tra il sommo pontefice Paulo Quinto, et la serenissima republica di Venetia parere* (Venice, 1606), p. 120.

[18] The text of the decree is given in Cornet, p. 269, App. IV. It is analyzed from the papal point of view in Lelio Baglioni, *Apologia contro le considerazioni di F. Paolo* (Perugia, 1606), p. 46. The conditions normally governing contracts of this nature are discussed in the *Difesa delle censure pubblicate da N. S. Paolo Papa V nella causa de' Signori Venetiani fatta da alcuni teologi della religione de' Servi in risposta alle considerationi di F. Paolo da Venetia* (Perugia, 1607), pp. 207–208.

[19] This point is very clear from the *Difesa de' Servi*, pp. 209–210.

Two other pieces of Venetian legislation had been the specific cause of the first brief presented by the nuncio. The first of these was an act of the Senate early in 1603 prohibiting the construction of new churches anywhere in Venetian territory without the permission of the government.[20] Since this law merely extended to the entire Venetian state a regulation long applied in the city of Venice, the Venetians could claim that it was conservative in principle; but the motives behind regulation of land-usage in the island city were obviously different from those for its control in the *terraferma*, and the new law expressed an aggressive mood not entirely unfriendly to change. Furthermore, although the law identified no ecclesiastical group whose possession of a new church was regarded as especially undesirable, both sides seem to have been clear that the act was aimed primarily against the Jesuits. It was thus a particular challenge to the forces of the Counter Reformation. Venetian spokesmen were to argue that failure to establish regulations of this kind would encourage the free admission into the state, under the pretext of religion, of bodies of foreign clergy who, in the interests of some foreign power, would attempt to infiltrate the towns and fortresses of the Serenissima and captivate the minds and consciences of her subjects.[21] The measure also, of course, limited clerical property rights. From the standpoint of Rome, this law was a direct challenge to the desire of the Counter Reformation, as expressed in Loyola's *Rules for Thinking with the Church*, to multiply churches.[22] It also raised the issue of the priority of spiritual and secular values and of the relationship between the spiritual and secular authorities in society.

This issue was posed even more sharply by another law, enacted in the spring of 1605 and also a target of the papal brief, limiting the alienation of landed property to the church by laymen.[23] Again this measure simply extended to all Venetian territory a regulation previously applied only in Venice herself. The new law declared that laymen could transfer lands to the church for a period of no more than two years; at the end of this time the

[20] Text in Cornet, p. 268, App. III; analyzed in Baglioni, p. 57.

[21] For examples, Paolo Sarpi, *Considerazioni sopra le censure*, in *Scritti*, II, 199; Querini, *Aviso*, pp. 13, 20–21. Rome saw the measure as specifically directed against the Jesuits; cf. [Antonio Possevino], *Risposta di Teodoro Eugenio di Famagosta all'aviso mandato fuori dal sig. Antonio Quirino* (Bologna, 1607), pp. 23ff.

[22] See Rule 8 in the second part of the *Spiritual Exercises*.

[23] Text in Cornet, p. 265, App. I; analyzed in Baglioni, pp. 64–65. For the immediate circumstances of the law, see Stella, "Proprietà ecclesiastica," pp. 74–77; as with the other laws, it passed in the Senate by an overwhelming majority. See also the discussion by Cardinal Borghese, letter of Dec. 16, 1605, to the nuncio in Savoy, in Magistris, p. 6.

lands had to be sold to a layman, the price being then given to the church. The arrangement suggests that the Venetian government was less concerned with the wealth of the church as such than with the steady decline in the proportion of land owned by laymen.[24] Ecclesiastics, still attached to landed wealth as more "secure" than other forms of property, found this provision particularly offensive.[25] The advocates of Venice insisted that the true motive of the law was the need of the government for a secure and substantial income. It was unjust, they argued, for the burden of supporting the state to be borne by a steadily diminishing number of lay landholders, particularly in view of the increasingly threatening international situation. Venetians emphasized, in this connection, the need of a strong Venice to hold back the Turks as she had done at Lepanto;[26] but the major worry of the government, insofar as it was here concerned with military questions, was the menace of Spain and Austria.

The second papal brief, which the nuncio only brought himself to deliver toward the end of February, dealt with a different offense: Venice had asserted with conspicuous vigor, in two specific instances, her right to try clergy accused of major crimes in civil courts. One concerned a canon of Vicenza, Scipione Saraceno, who had been accused of tearing down, with manifestations of scorn, a public announcement bearing the seal of Saint Mark (a particularly reprehensible action), and of offenses against public decency incidental to general moral turpitude;[27] the other concerned an Abbot Brandolino of Nervesa, who was accused of sorcery, incest, and murder.[28] The Venetian government in these cases was asserting a traditional claim which she had long implemented in practice; but to do so at precisely this

[24] For some indication that the law was not entirely successful in achieving this purpose, see Woolf, "Venice and the Terraferma," p. 417.

[25] Cf. *Difesa de'Servi*, p. 110: "Ma chi non sà, ch'altro è il prezzo, & altro la cosa stabile? Il prezzo è soggetto a molti pericoli, come di perdita, e di furto; dove lo stabile è sicuro, ne si perde, ò perisce. Il prezzo non porta frutta, ne rendita alcuna; lo stabile porta utile, e guadagno."

[26] Querini, *Aviso*, pp. 14–15.

[27] Text of the decision by the Council of Ten to proceed against him in Cornet, pp. 266–277, App. II. Cornet has also collected additional documents on this case in "Paolo V e la Republica Veneta. Nuovo serie di documenti (MDCV-MDCVII). Tratti dalle deliberazioni secrete (Roma) del Consiglio dei Dieci," *AV*, Ser. 1, V (1873), 39–50; these suggest Saraceno's long record of misbehavior.

[28] Sarpi, *Istoria dell'Interdetto*, p. 14. Cornet, "Paolo V e la Republica," pp. 53–54, presents evidence that Brandolino expressed his willingness to be judged in a secular court.

time was a sign of resolution which, given the atmosphere of the Curia, could only have been interpreted as flagrant defiance. It dramatized in the clearest terms imaginable the problem of the relationship between the clergy and temporal authority.

Yet there is no evidence, however rash these measures may seem in retrospect, that Venice aimed at a rupture with Rome. In her sensitive state she was merely anxious to define her place in the modern world, lest passivity in the presence of the dangerous pressures she felt to surround her be taken as a sign of weakness and an invitation to aggression against cherished rights and values. Venice probably hoped that expressions of resolution would place her in a more favorable position for negotiating with Rome on all outstanding issues; she hoped for friendship with Rome, but on her own terms. She therefore reacted with proper respect to the election of Camillo Borghese as pope in the spring of 1605, choosing a delegation of her most respected senators to honor him. At the same time they were directed to discuss with the new pope the exemption of the patriarch from formal examination in Rome, a contribution from the Venetian clergy for the support of the state, and a variety of jurisdictional questions.[29] Venice evidently chose to behave as though the situation was entirely normal. In September, as a sign of friendship and a token of respect, she honored the pope's brothers and his nephew and Secretary of State, Scipione Borghese, by naming them patricians of the Republic. The pope expressed his satisfaction.[30]

The situation in Rome, nevertheless, was unfavorable to a peaceful settlement of the issues now coming to a head. It was true that the new pope had been opposed by the Spanish faction at the Curia and supported by the French,[31] so that his election was greeted in Venice with a measure of satisfaction even though there was some feeling that (like Pius V and Gregory XIII) he lacked political experience.[32] But he promptly gave an ominous hint of his true disposition by calling himself Paul V; and he soon revealed that he was very much a pope of the Counter Reformation who proposed to continue and even to intensify all those tendencies in Rome whose unfolding

[29] Cornet, pp. 5–6. Those originally selected were Leonardo Donà, Francesco Vendramin, Francesco Molin, and Giovanni Mocenigo; but Pietro Duodo and Francesco Contarini replaced Donà and Vendramin.

[30] Nani Mocenigo, *Nani*, p. 99. On Cardinal Borghese, see Pastor, XXV, 55ff.

[31] Pastor, XXV, 37–38; Cornet, p. v.

[32] Sarpi, *Istoria dell'Interdetto*, p. 44, where the doge is represented as charging the pope with ignorance of "how the world is governed." Cf. Cornet, p. vi.

Venice had observed with such alarm.[33] Within the Curia he intensified the trend toward personal rule, ignoring the views of the cardinals at least as much as his predecessors had done and paying even less attention to the decisions and advice of the various congregations.[34] His jealousy for the papal dignity was demonstrated by the execution in Rome in the fall of 1605 of a wretched man of letters for possessing a writing that compared Clement VIII with the tyrannical emperor Tiberius.[35] Paul V also founded the secret papal archives to preserve old documents recording past claims and victories of the papacy, an ominous sign for the future.[36] Eventually he was to be largely responsible for the sanctification of the Counter Reformation. His pontificate began the processes for the beatification and canonization of its major heroes: Carlo Borromeo, Philip Neri, and above all the Jesuit leaders Ignatius Loyola, Francis Xavier, and Aloysius Gonzaga.[37] His pontificate, in addition, was the first seriously to challenge the new science; it began the investigation of Galileo. In politics Paul V showed himself from the outset notably hostile to republics; before his engagement with Venice he had attempted to impose his will on Lucca and Genoa, whose governments had shown some disposition to interfere in what Rome regarded as ecclesiastical matters. Genoa had yielded to the threat of spiritual censures, a circumstance which presumably encouraged the pope to suppose that similar tactics would work against Venice.[38]

Political and jurisdictional authority occupied a particularly prominent place in Paul V's conception of the papal office; few modern popes have seen the church so narrowly as a species of government. At times he expressed himself as though he believed that the pope's only mission was to rule the church and to protect his authority as its governor. The fatal brief delivered to the College in December of 1605 is a typical expression of his conception of the papal office. The pope warned the Venetian government:

However much we are desirous of public peace and quiet and direct our thoughts to the end of governing the Christian Republic as quietly

[33] There is no recent study of Paul V; for older works see Magistris, p. xxxviii, n. 1. On his earlier initiatives in jurisdictional matters, see Sarpi, *Istoria dell'Interdetto*, pp. 4–8, and *Scrittura in materia della libertà ecclesiastica*, in *Scritti*, II, 140–142. Cf. Pastor, XXV, 115–118, 310ff.

[34] Pastor, XXV, 302, 316–318. All the separate congregations declined under Paul V, with the significant exception of the Congregation of the Index.

[35] *Ibid.*, pp. 78–79.

[36] *Ibid.*, pp. 99–102.

[37] *Ibid.*, pp. 255ff.

[38] *Ibid.*, p. 120; Sarpi, *Istoria dell'Interdetto*, pp. 7–8.

as we can solely in the service of God, and however much we desire the minds of all men, and especially of great princes, to be in conformity with our own, nevertheless if ever the dignity of the Apostolic See should be offended, if ecclesiastical liberty and immunity should be impugned, if the decretals and canons should be despised, and if the rights of the Church and the privileges of ecclesiastical persons should be violated, *which is the sum of our responsibility*, do not think that we will dissimulate in any way, or be lacking in our duty. Assuredly we wish you to be certain of this, that we are not moved by any human emotion, and that we seek nothing but the glory of the Lord God, and that we have no other end than to exercise perfectly, insofar as it is possible, the Apostolic government to which God, with his singular benignity, has called us in spite of our unequal abilities." [39]

Thus estimating the duty to which he had been summoned by God, Paul V was remarkably impatient with any opposition, particularly on such matters as the nature of the church, his own position in it, and the relations between the church and the temporal world. He took a broad view of papal infallibility, and the charge of heresy against those whose views differed from his own came easily to his lips. Thus, for Paul V, it was *heresy* to claim any absolute authority for lay governments over their subjects, *heresy* to deny the authority of the Inquisition over laymen, *heresy* to claim that rulers held their authority directly from God, *heresy* to deny to the pope the authority to depose kings, *heresy* to deny to him a comprehensive jurisdiction over temporal things whenever they touched on things of the spirit, "*quia aliter Christus omnium Dominus non satis providisset bono Ecclesiae regimini.*" [40] On none of these matters, in other words, was it legitimate or tolerable to differ from his own views. Venice had evidently to deal with a formidable opponent.[41]

The Curia had long been biding its time, quietly nourishing its numerous grievances against Venice, and, in accordance with the familiar Renaissance precept, waiting for the favorable occasion to impose its authority over this uncomfortably close and peculiarly refractory member of the Christian

[39] Text in Cornet, pp. 18–22: italics added.

[40] Texts collected in R. Taucci, *Intorno alle lettere di fra Paolo Sarpi ad Antonio Foscarini* (Florence, 1939), pp. 117–118. These come from a later period, but they seem representative of the pope's attitude during the interdict.

[41] The Venetians were not alone in their impression of the pope's unusual rigidity on jurisdictional matters. For similar Florentine impressions, cf. Achille de Rubertis, *Ferdinando I dei Medici e la contesa fra Paolo V e la Repubblica Veneta* (Venice, 1933), p. 8.

Republic.[42] Even before making an issue of the offending Venetian legislation, Paul V had taken up a number of older complaints with the Venetian ambassador. He had called again for Venetian assistance in the struggle with the Turks in Hungary, he had demanded navigation rights for his temporal subjects in waters controlled by Venice,[43] and he had insisted that the patriarch-elect present himself in Rome for the prescribed examination.[44]

After the interdict was imposed it also became clear that Rome, in addition to these and the immediate jurisdictional grievances, had a long series of other complaints against Venice. A pamphlet by the Jesuit Possevino recalled them at some length. Venice had given refuge to bandits fleeing the Papal State, the author reminded his readers. She had infringed on the rights of the patriarch of Aquileia. She had made a secret peace with the Turks: her abandonment of the Christian cause after Lepanto was still an important item on the papal bill of particulars. She gave protection to schismatic-heretical Greeks, of whom there were 14,000 in the city of Venice alone; and she tolerated the presence of Marranos, Turks, and every kind of heretic. While suppressing the spiritually reliable Jesuit *studio*, she encouraged the teaching of heretical ideas at Padua; indeed, a long series of wicked doctrines had been born there, stemming from Marsilio more than two centuries before, transmitted by "Pomponazzi and other similar pestilential authors," and contributing now, through hundreds of heretical German students, to the spiritual destruction of northern Europe: for all of this Venice was to blame. She had allowed the publication of obscenities while mutilating and altering such works of sound theology as issued from her presses. But perhaps worst of all she had regularly blocked the work of ecclesiastical reform, impeded the renewal of the religious orders, prevented the application of the decrees of Trent by the bishops of the *terraferma*, and obstructed implementation of the bull *In coena domini*.[45]

It was no doubt true, then, as Baronius was to charge, that the most recent actions of the Venetian government were simply an intolerable addition to a long accumulation of grievances. The patience of the papacy, Baronius

[42] Cf. Cozzi, *Contarini*, p. 101, which argues that the real motive behind the papal initiative was less the particular actions of the government than its general orientation. Cessi, *Storia della Repubblica di Venezia*, II, 144ff., conveniently assembles the various Roman complaints against Venice.

[43] Sarpi, *Istoria dell'Interdetto*, pp. 8–9.

[44] Cornet, pp. 5–6.

[45] Possevino, *Risposta di Teodoro Eugenio*, pp. 46–50.

indicated, had been at last strained beyond its breaking point.[46] But it is doubtful that patience, especially in a venerable and experienced institution like the papacy, has any absolute limit; and the decision of the pope for a direct confrontation with Venice at this time on issues which were, for the most part, of long standing certainly depended on a variety of additional considerations. One, ironically enough, was probably, as we have noted, that reconciliation with France which Venice had done so much to arrange. It had freed the papacy from its long dependence on the Habsburgs, suggested that the hostility of Venice would not necessarily throw the pope even more into the power of Spain, and allowed him a new freedom of action.[47] Indeed the international scene generally appeared more favorable for some decisive assertion of papal authority over Christendom. Henry IV was making friends with the Jesuits and otherwise giving every indication that he recognized the value of the pope's friendship. The new king of England was far different from the fierce Elizabeth; a pacifist in his foreign policy, he spoke (perhaps sincerely) of religious reconciliation. In Spain a strong king who had kept the church firmly subordinated to the policies of the royal government had given way to a weaker one. Meanwhile Catholicism was recovering ground in Germany and Poland, and the emergence of Arminianism suggested a more pacific and congenial atmosphere in the Netherlands. The tendencies of the modern world had long seemed distressingly unfavorable to the ideal, so ardently cherished by the leaders of the Counter Reformation, of a united Christendom directed to spiritual ends by the pope; but now, for a change, the auspices were encouraging. Under these conditions defiance of the pope in Italy, precisely that region in Europe which ought always to be most responsive to papal influence, was singularly intolerable. And the fact that, as it happened, the defiance came from so humble a quarter as Venice, which seemed increasingly less important in comparison with the great monarchies beyond the mountains, not only compounded the offense but also provided Rome with a remarkable opportunity.[48] It gave her a chance to attack directly, on

---

[46] *Presbyteri Card. tit. SS. Neri et Achillei Sedis Apostolicae bibliotecari PARAENESIS ad rempublicam venetam* (Rome, 1606), p. 116. I cite the edition in the *Raccolta*, I, 97–125.

[47] Cf. Pastor, XXV, 316 and 334, n. 4.

[48] The Venetians seem to have felt this strongly. Cf. Sarpi, *Istoria dell'Interdetto*, pp. 4 and 14, and *Libertà ecclesiastica*, in *Scritti*, II, 143, where (comparing the Venetian situation with that of Genoa) Sarpi reflects the conviction in Venice that the pope intended to reduce her to the same degraded level as the other petty republics of Italy. In his harangue to the Jesuit leaders on May 6, 1606, Leonardo Donà made the point that the pope should not think "he had to do with a republic like Genoa"; see the account of this

grounds of her own choosing and with a good prospect of success, the whole unfortunate political heritage of the Renaissance. By challenging Venice the papacy might hope to achieve a dramatic triumph over the conception of an independent secular politics determined by the selfish interests of particular states, and over the entire range of worldly values on which such a conception was based. The Roman attack on Venice during the course of the interdict was to constitute a kind of seventeenth-century *Syllabus of Errors*.

The first hint to Venice of serious trouble ahead had come in the course of an audience granted by Paul V to the Venetian ambassador, Agostino Nani.[49] In his youth, like so many of the *giovani*, Nani had been devoted to philosophy, and he had amused himself by editing a philosophical work of Agostino Valier. But he had soon entered into the active life and had served Venice in a series of responsible posts both at home and abroad before his appointment to the Holy See. As ambassador in Madrid he had been notably aggressive in protesting a violation of his official residence (and therefore of the honor of Venice) by local authorities pursuing a fugitive.[50] The choice of such a man as ambassador to the Holy See in 1603 was another indication of the Venetian government's intention to pursue a firm line with Rome.

On October 21, 1605, Nani waited on the pope, and it was on this occasion that Paul V gave the first sign of his anger at recent developments in Venice. During the early part of the interview the pope objected to the arrest and imprisonment of the canon of Vicenza, claiming that the spiritual power had thereby been injured by the temporal and insisting on his determination to retain entire jurisdiction over the clergy. He then went on to express his particular objection to the law passed by the Senate the previous spring limiting the right of laymen to give lands to the church. This law, the pope insisted,

---

speech by the Jesuit superior in Venice, in Pirri, p. 108. See also Antonio Querini's analysis of the pope's motives in *Historia dell'Escommunica*, pp. 258-259, major sections of which are printed in Carlo de Magistris, *Per la storia del componimento della contesa tra la Repubblica Veneta e Paolo V (1605-1607): documenti* (Turin, 1941). This collection will hereafter be cited as *Componimento;* unless otherwise indicated, references to Querini's *Historia* will be to this edition. For Querini the pope, misled by his advisers and inexperienced in the ways of the world, hoped to exploit the good will accompanying any new pontificate and to initiate his rule over the church with an easy and notable triumph. Cf., on the papalist side, Bellarmine's *Risposta a un libretto intitolato Risposta di un Dottore di Theologia* (Rome, 1606), p. 175; I cite from the *Raccolta*, I, 149-182.

[49] For Nani's career, in addition to Nani Mocenigo, see Cornet, p. 1, n. 1.

[50] This incident, in February of 1597, is described at length by Nani Mocenigo, pp. 35-50.

was scandalous, indefensible, and "full of disorder"—a phrase to whose meaning we shall return. It was also, he maintained, "contrary to the Council and to every imperial law"; it made the church inferior even to private persons; it did not deserve the name of a law; those responsible for it had exposed themselves to the gravest penalties. In addition the pope identified even at this point the ultimate grounds for his discontent, the real issue posed by the offensive legislation. He charged that the Venetians had been induced to enact it—the term had clearly acquired an offensive ring—*per ragion politica.*

Nani replied to the first point by emphasizing the gravity of the crimes committed by the canon and by an appeal to Venetian custom. The second point he first approached in general terms. He assured the pope that the law in question was undoubtedly based on justice and reason and that his Holiness would have no cause for complaint. As though suspecting that deeper complaints lurked beneath the surface here, he also reminded the pope that Venice had always been loyal to the faith and that Venetians had long been ready to die for it. He then went on to suggest the financial motive behind the law by complaining about the small contribution from property already acquired by the church to support the state. But most interesting of all was his acceptance of the pope's definition of the issue fundamental to the confrontation. He boldly defended Venetian policy by an appeal to *ragione di stato.*[51] So conflict was joined from the beginning at both the most specific and the most general levels.

This first encounter between Nani and the pope was typical of a whole series of negotiations extending over the next two months in both Venice and Rome. In Venice they were conducted by the nuncio Mattei, an ecclesiastic who, according to Sarpi, regarded every pious work as worthless unless accompanied by absolute devotion to clerical privilege and who was accustomed to silence all opposition with the words, "I am pope here, and I wish only obedience."[52] Mattei appeared regularly in the College to press the pope's demands. The Senate, in reply, professed to be hurt by any imputation

[51] Cornet, pp. 1–2. Cornet also gives the text of Nani's account of the interview to the Council of Ten in "Paolo V e la Republica Veneta," pp. 41–44. Leonardo Donà, by this time doge, was to appeal to the same principle in speaking to the nuncio on Feb. 10: "... et la ragione di stato non comporta, che si dia quello che può pregiudicare alla liberta et la reputatione della Republica per la speranza di haver altri maggiori beni" (Cornet, pp. 270–271, App. V). The Venetians displayed curiously little sense that such language might be antagonistic.

[52] *Istoria dell'Interdetto,* p. 5.

of Venetian hostility to the church and suggested that the pope must have been misinformed. The Venetian government, it pointed out, had contemplated nothing new; and besides, it blandly informed the nuncio, the law forbidding the transfer of land could not properly be described as discriminatory against ecclesiastics since it merely proscribed certain actions by laymen. The Venetian authorities also pointed out that vast properties had already been acquired by the church over the centuries, and they urged that the ability of the state to meet such public needs as defense against the Turks would be endangered if more property passed to the church. In regard to the other matter, it reminded the nuncio that the trial of criminal clergy in civil courts was customary in Venice and had in fact often been sanctioned by the Holy See. These points were to be made over and over again in the weeks ahead.[53]

In addition the Senate began to appeal to more general considerations. It reminded the pope that Venice had been "born and preserved always free by the grace of God," so that neither for reasons of conscience nor out of any other kind of obligation was she in the habit of rendering an account to any other power of actions undertaken for the benefit of her subjects which did no harm to others. By December the Senate was stating pointedly that in temporal matters such as those in question patently were the Republic acknowledged no superior but God.[54] In the middle of that month it selected its strongest advocate, Leonardo Donà, to go to Rome to assist Nani as ambassador extraordinary to the pope.[55]

Meanwhile the resolution of Paul V became even more firm. His charges against Venice grew; he was evidently requesting members of his staff to note further instances of Venetian encroachment on the rights of the church. Early in November the pope complained of Abbot Brandolino's imprisonment,[56] and before the end of the month he was attacking the law of 1603 controlling the construction of new churches.[57] His manner seemed to Nani increasingly severe and impatient. Speaking "with infinite ardor and incredible emotion," Nani reported, the pope had concluded one important interview by declaring "that he had been placed in that see by almighty God to maintain ecclesiastical jurisdiction"; and he threatened to take the case against Venice before his consistory if the offending measures were not withdrawn. Nani, in reply, pointed to precedents. He suggested that because the

[53] Cornet, pp. 3ff.
[54] Ibid., p. 5, n. 1; p. 10 and n. 2.
[55] Ibid., pp. 13–14.
[56] Ibid., p. 7.
[57] Ibid., p. 10, n. 1.

spiritual authority could forbid ecclesiastics to sell to laity, the temporal authority had a corresponding power over its subjects. He expressed fear that, uncontrolled, the church might absorb all the property in the state. He appealed to the authority of Augustine. He protested the loyalty of Venice to the Catholic faith. All was useless; the pope impatiently twisted a button on his amice, closed his right eye ("a natural sign of feeling for him," remarked the acute Nani), and smiled disdainfully to show that he "gave no consideration to the reasons adduced." The pope also appealed on this occasion to general principles. He maintained that all private property belongs absolutely to its individual owners and that no prince has the right to touch it. He also informed Nani: "We are above all things, and God has given us power over all, and we can depose kings and anything else, and we are in particular above those things *quae tendunt ad finem supranaturalem.*" [58] Opposition thus only strengthened the pope's resolution. On December 10 he prepared the briefs which his nuncio had been directed to present to the Venetian government, and two days later he expounded his grievances against Venice to the full consistory. He was notably explicit to his cardinals that the failure of Venice to make a complete submission would result in excommunication.[59]

When the nuncio at last performed his unwelcome mission, the incumbent doge, Marino Grimani, was dying;[60] and the College took advantage of this circumstance to delay reading the pope's communication until a new doge had been selected. In this situation the choice of a successor to Grimani was bound to have unusual significance, both practically and symbolically; and the patricians of Venice demonstrated their resolve to resist the pope by electing as the new doge, on January 10, 1606, the most vigorous representative of the values and jurisdictional rights of the Venetian Republic, Leonardo Donà.[61]

---

[58] *Ibid.*, pp. 7–11.

[59] The *Acta consistoralia* for Dec. 12, 1605, are printed in *Componimento*, pp. 1–5. See also the letter from Anastasio Germanio, a Turinese ecclesiastic at the Curia, to the Duke of Savoy, Dec. 13, 1605, in Magistris, pp. 3–5.

[60] He actually died on Dec. 26 (Cornet, p. 17 and n. 4).

[61] *Ibid.*, p. 18. For an account of this election from Florentine sources, see Rubertis, *Ferdinando I dei Medici*, pp. 18–19, n. 2. The story has often been told, as in A. Bianchi-Giovini, *Biografia di Fra Paolo Sarpi* (Zurich, 1836), I, 236, how, in a conversation in 1592 concerning jurisdictional matters between Donà and the future Paul V, then Cardinal Borghese, the latter had declared, "Se fossi papa, alla prima occasione vi scomunicherei." To this Donà is supposed to have replied, "Ed io se fossi doge, mi riderei della scomunica."

If the papal brief amounted to an official challenge from Rome to Venice and more broadly from the Counter Reformation to the values of the Renaissance, the election of Donà marked the formal acceptance of that challenge. The office of doge had for some time been above party and even above politics; recent doges had been for the most part old men not markedly identified with any particular program or faction whose selection had been mainly a reward for a life of distinguished service to the Republic. But Donà was no such neutral choice.[62] The English ambassador, Sir Henry Wotton, reporting that his election had been opposed chiefly on the ground that so much ability might push the government in the direction of monarchy, immediately saw it as evidence that, at a critical moment, Venice recognized the need for leadership.[63] Donà, he wrote a friend ten days after the election, was "a wise and beaten [experienced] man in the world, eloquent, resolute, provident; and of all this the State seemeth to have very much need, being fallen into terms of great contumacy with the Pope." [64] With Donà's election as doge a direct clash was inevitable; the choice proved that Venice was unwilling to make any significant concession, and it was now obvious that the *impasse* between Rome and Venice could only end with a major humiliation for one side or the other.

Since the papal brief attached, for the time being, no time limit on the compliance to which it summoned the Venetian government, negotiations continued in both Rome and Venice. Donà's selection as doge meant that he could no longer serve as special ambassador to the pope,[65] and he was replaced by Pietro Duodo, who, however, did not reach Rome till the end of March.[66] Meanwhile Mattei continued to visit the College, and Nani to argue with the pope. Late in February the nuncio at last presented the pope's second brief, the document he had neglected to transmit in December. The doge received it coldly. It expressed the pope's displeasure at the Venetian arrest of ecclesiastical persons, denied that the practice could be in any way justified, and ordered that the clergy whom the Venetians had so

[62] Cessi, *Storia di Venezia*, II, 145–146, emphasizes this point.

[63] Letter to the Earl of Salisbury, Feb. 18, 1606, in Smith, I, 344. Wotton's continuing admiration for Donà is indicated by his letter to Salisbury of June 23, 1606 (*ibid.*, I, 354). See also Sarpi, *Istoria dell'Interdetto*, p. 19.

[64] Letter to Sir Thomas Edmondes, Jan. 20, 1606, Smith, I, 340.

[65] Querini expressed the belief that Donà's election as doge was prejudicial to a settlement with the pope because Venice thereby lost his services as a negotiator (*Historia dell'Escomunica*, pp. 259–260).

[66] Cornet, p. 39.

presumptuously seized should be turned over to the nuncio immediately for proper disposition by their ecclesiastical superiors.[67]

But the resolve of Venice to resist the pope's demands grew steadily more firm. It was nourished by a set of fundamental convictions which became gradually more explicit, central among them the sense that Venice was the victim of an unprovoked aggression. From the Venetian standpoint the pope had wantonly undertaken to overturn a system that had proved eminently satisfactory to all concerned for centuries.[68] The judgment of clergy in secular courts, for example, as the Senate explained to the French ambassador, was "a laudable and immemorial custom of our ancestors," entrusted to them by God himself, "transmitted through them to us, and exercised by the Republic continuously without interruption until the present day with the greatest moderation." [69] Furthermore, as the Venetians had observed, the arrangements under attack in Venice seemed to prevail without challenge from Rome in other parts of Catholic Europe.[70] Thus Venice was not only disturbed by the challenge to that liberty "which the divine goodness has preserved inviolate for twelve hundred years through innumerable dangers." [71] Her self-esteem was also badly wounded by a kind of discrimination which implied contempt for her rank among the states of Europe. In addition, Venice, with the typical ecclesiological bias of the Renaissance republic, could not bring herself to acknowledge that the issue was genuinely *religious*. She interpreted the papal initiative as a brutal attempt to grasp at power in the secular world. Paul V appeared to her merely the successor, a century later, of Julius II. From this standpoint the Roman claim that a spiritual issue was at stake was, in the words of Fra Fulgenzio Micanzio, only a Medusa's head "to frighten the timid." [72] On these issues, as the Venetian leaders repeatedly protested, Venice was more Catholic than the pope.[73] Under such conditions it was impossible to make concessions to the Curia; and the Venetian government, while continuing conversations in Rome, prepared to resist.[74]

[67] *Ibid.*, pp. 33–35.
[68] This theme recurs repeatedly in Sarpi, *Istoria dell'Interdetto*.
[69] Cornet, pp. 50–51 (for April 12, 1606).
[70] Venetian publicists would repeatedly cite jurisdictional practice elsewhere, especially in France and the Iberian peninsula. See below, pp. 370, 474, for example.
[71] Sarpi, *Istoria dell'Interdetto*, p. 71.
[72] *Vita di Frate Paolo*, p. 159.
[73] For example the harangue of Donà to the Jesuit leaders, Pirri, p. 108. Cf. Sarpi, *Istoria dell'Interdetto*, p. 66.
[74] Cf. Wotton's observations, letter to Edmondes, Feb. 17, 1606, Smith, I, 341: "In this business there are two remedies, the one, to do that which the Pope desireth, the

Precedent for Venetian behavior in the face of ecclesiastical censure was available from the past. The Venetians deliberately recalled their earlier confrontations with the pope, and Venice behaved much as she had done during the Ferrarese war in 1482–1484 and again against Julius II in 1509–1510.[75] One of her first steps was to seek legal support, since the issue presented itself immediately as juridical. She therefore decided to submit the laws to which Rome had objected not only to her regular legal consultants but also to leading jurists at Padua, Pavia, and Vicenza. These men had no doubt been chosen for the task with some knowledge of their bias in matters of this kind, and it is hardly surprising that the lengthy opinions they produced were entirely favorable to Venice. The laws at issue, they held, in no way infringed on the legitimate rights of the church, and the right of Venice to enact them was· unquestionable. In addition the government engaged the services of particular specialists, first of all the famous jurist Menocchio.[76] Then, on January 28, after consulting him unofficially, the Senate took the fateful step of appointing, as official *consultore* in theology and canon law, the learned Venetian Servite, Fra Paolo Sarpi.[77]

Sarpi was then fifty-three, a man of mature years.[78] Born Pietro (he had taken the name Paolo on entering the monastery), he was the son of a merchant who had come into Venice from Friuli; but the father had died

---

other, to give him sufficient reason why they should not do it. They have resolved even from the beginning on the second. And I must needs tell your Lordship, not in sport, but in very good earnest, that this breach hath put many kinds of men into work. The politiques, how to find delays; the canonists, how to find distinctions; the divines, how to find a new religion; which last point they divided into two resolutions, either to force their Latin priests to say mass after the excommunication, or to pass to the Greek faith." See also the vigorous reaction to the threat of excommunication attributed by the Florentine resident Montauti to the doge's brother, in Rubertis, *Ferdinando I dei Medici*, p. 19.

[75] The Council of Ten ordered copies of documents pertaining to earlier censures to be prepared for the use of the College (Cornet, ''Paolo V e la Republica Veneta,'' p. 60). That these precedents were much on the minds of the Venetians may also be seen, for example, in the *Risposta data a Paolo V Sommo Pontefice sopra l'Interdetto da esso fulminato contro la Serenissima Repubblica di Venezia*, a work attributed (because of its florid style in my opinion falsely) to Sarpi and included in his *Opere*, VI, 149–160. The author remarks, pp. 154–155, referring to Clement V, Sixtus IV, and Julius II, ''. . . tre volte fuori d'ogni termine ragionevole furono da più Papi scomunicati.''

[76] Cozzi, ''Sarpi tra Canaye e Casaubon,'' p 53. See. also Cornet, p. 23 and n. 2.

[77] Cornet, p. 27 and n. 2. Text of the appointment is given in Clemente Maria Francescon, *Chiesa e Stato nei consulti di fra Paolo Sarpi* (Vicenza, 1942), pp. 11–12, n. 1. Francescon also discusses the history and duties of the office, pp. 5–8.

[78] All accounts of Sarpi's early life are based on the *Vita* written by his close associate and successor, Fulgenzio Micanzio. The most complete biography of Sarpi is still,

when Sarpi was a child. His mother was from a family of Venetian *cittadini*, and she may well have transmitted to her son some of the attachment of that class to public service. Sarpi's association with the ruling group began early, in any event, in a school kept by his maternal uncle, to whom his education was confided. The school was attended by many young nobles, including Andrea Morosini, with whom he formed friendly ties. Nicolò Contarini was also a friend of his youth.[79] At the age of twelve Sarpi was entrusted by his uncle to the instruction of a scholarly Servite from Cremona, Gian Maria Capella. A Scotist theologian and a mathematician, Capella transmitted many of his interests to the young Sarpi. It is also doubtless a measure of his influence that Sarpi, at the age of thirteen, put on the Servite habit.

Sarpi's precocity soon aroused the wonder of contemporaries. At fifteen he was carrying on public disputations, and at eighteen the bishop of Mantua made him a reader in canon law and positive theology.[80] Meanwhile his interests were steadily broadening, and he studied a wide range of subjects: Greek and Hebrew, the natural sciences and history, civil as well as church law, ancient along with scholastic philosophy.[81] He also began to learn about the world by experience in conducting its affairs. When he was twenty-seven he was elected provincial of his order; and a year later, in 1580, he was appointed to a committee to reform its constitutions, a duty which took him for the first time to Rome, where he spent seveal months. He was back in Rome again for three years to conduct the legal business of his order as its procurator-general between 1585 and 1588,[82] and during this period studied

unfortunately, that of Bianchi-Giovini cited in note 61 above; for older works see also Cicogna, *Saggio di bibliografia veneziana*, items 3757–3769. The best recent introduction is perhaps that of Chabod, *La politica di Paolo Sarpi*. For Sarpi as a problem in historical interpretation, see also Giovanni Getto, *Paolo Sarpi* (Rome, 1941), pp. 7–43; Gaetano Cozzi, "Paolo Sarpi: il suo problema storico, religioso e giuridico nella recente letteratura," *Il Diritto ecclesiastico*, LXIII (1952), 52–88; and Giovanni Gambarin, "Il Sarpi alla luce di studi recenti," *AV*, L–LI (1953), 78–105.

[79] Cf. his letter to Jacques Leschassier, Nov. 10, 1609, Ulianich, p. 61.

[80] Micanzio, *Vita*, pp. 1–8. Chabod, *Politica di Sarpi*, pp. 24–28, emphasizes the importance of the Mantuan phase of Sarpi's life, suggesting that during this time Sarpi developed his passionate interest in learning and first became concerned with the Council of Trent as a political phenomenon.

[81] Micanzio, *Vita*, pp. 8–15, 26–29, 69; Francesco Griselini, *Memorie anedote spettanti alla vita ed agli studi del sommo filosofo e giureconsulto F. Paolo Servita* (Lausanne, 1760), p. 11. The latter work is of particular interest for Sarpi's early attainments because the author had access to a mass of Sarpi's papers subsequently destroyed by fire.

[82] It is remarkable, in view of this early activity, that after the onset of the interdict Sarpi seems to have taken little interest in his order. When his Gallican correspondent Jacques Gillot requested information about its origins, Sarpi had little to say (letter of Dec. 8, 1609, Ulianich, pp. 142–143).

the institutional structure of the church and made friends with Bellarmine and other influential personages.[83] Meanwhile, when he could, he frequented cultivated circles in Venice. He taught philosophy and theology in the Servite convent there, attracting numerous students; he took a doctorate at Padua in 1578, making the acquaintance of scientists and other scholars; and after his return from Rome in 1588 he associated with the group that gathered at the house of Morosini.[84]

He exhibited a particular interest in the world outside Venice and associated as much as he could with foreigners.[85] Sarpi's vision, in spite of his devotion to his native city, was always remarkably broad, and it is significant for our understanding of Venetian leadership during the period of the *giovani* (so different from that of the previous generation, or from what it was to become in the future) that it should have chosen to rely on a man with such wide horizons. Sarpi found various opportunities for contact with other Europeans. He encountered them at Padua, in the *ridotto* Morosini, at the shops of foreign merchants. He took a particular interest in the French, in whose Gallicanism he must have recognized, from an early point, something akin to the attitudes of Venice.[86] He was friendly with Arnauld Du Ferrier and André Hurault de Maisse, French ambassadors between 1567 and 1596, both of whom had close ties with the cultivated Gallican magistracy. These men nourished, in Sarpi as well as in others of his circle, an interest in the French civil wars[87] and in French thought on a wide range of vital issues; and eventually Sarpi found himself corresponding with scholars like Peiresc and the jurist-historian de Thou, for whom he was asked to secure books.[88] In 1603 he obtained a copy of the Koran for Isaac Casaubon;[89] the nominal Protestantism of his foreign associates evidently made no difference to Sarpi. One of his closest friends was the Huguenot physician Jacques Asselineau,[90] and he met other

---

[83] Micanzio, *Vita*, pp. 30ff.; Bianchi-Giovini, *Biografia*, I, 48ff. For the relations between Sarpi and Bellarmine (of great interest because of their subsequent confrontation), see Micanzio, pp. 32, 130–131, 133. Micanzio also noted the friendship of Pope Urban VII for Sarpi (p. 31).

[84] Micanzio, *Vita*, pp. 68ff., represents these years as the calmest of Sarpi's life.

[85] Cf. Chabod, *Politica di Sarpi*, pp. 31–32; Getto, *Sarpi*, p. 56. The general importance of Sarpi's contact with foreigners for the development of his thought is a major theme of Gaetano Cozzi, "Fra Paolo Sarpi, l'anglicanesimo e la Historia del Concilio Tridentino," *RSI*, LXVIII (1956), 559–619.

[86] On the whole subject of Sarpi's relations with France, see now the introduction to Ulianich.

[87] Micanzio, *Vita*, p. 45.

[88] Ulianich, pp. xiii–xiv.

[89] Cozzi, "Sarpi tra Canaye e Casaubon," pp. 33–34.

[90] Micanzio, *Vita*, p. 29.

foreign Protestants at the shop of a Flemish merchant in Venice known as the Golden Ship.[91]

It can hardly seem surprising that, long before he was taken into the service of Venice, so free a spirit as Sarpi had aroused the suspicion of ecclesiastical authority. Charges against him began remarkably early in his career; they seem both a tribute to the strong impression he left on all who encountered him and a sign of the timidity and insecurity of Italy in the later sixteenth century. He was still in his early twenties when, briefly in Milan in the service of Carlo Borromeo, he was denounced to the Inquisition for having ventured an opinion that the Trinity could not be demonstrated out of the first chapter of Genesis.[92] Later he was reported to the authorities several times for other reasons: for dealings with Jews, for a facetious remark interpreted as denying the efficacy of the Holy Spirit, for communication with heretics, for wearing his beretta improperly and using the wrong kind of slippers, for failure to recite the Salve Regina at the end of the Mass.[93] None of these charges came to anything, but, in the very triviality of most of them, they suggest the degree to which Sarpi had been identified from an early point in his life as a man on whom the authorities would do well to keep an eye. In 1601 the papal nuncio in Venice, noting his influence in the city, described him as "a man who can believe anything he should not and disbelieve anything binding." The nuncio also reported a rumor that, with some others, he participated in "a little school full of errors":[94] presumably the *ridotto* Morosini. Nor was his reputation at Rome improved when, in a letter that found its way into the hands of the Cardinal Protector of the Servite Order, Sarpi allowed himself to speak of the dubious means by which men were accustomed to advance themselves at the Curia.[95] Twice before the interdict Sarpi was refused the bishopric which his friends in Venice sought to obtain for him.[96] His rejection may well have affected his attitude to the Curia.[97]

[91] See Gaetano Cozzi, "Una vicenda della Venezia barocca: Marco Trevisan e la sua 'eroica amicizia,'" *BSV*, II (1960), p. 114, on the importance of this establishment in Venetian intellectual life.

[92] Micanzio, *Vita*, pp. 17–18.

[93] *Ibid.*, pp. 52–54, 75.

[94] The full text of the dispatch, dated Nov. 10, 1601, is given in the anonymous "Come Paolo Sarpi non fu vescovo di Nona," *Civiltà Cattolica*, Quaderno 2073 (Nov. 7, 1936), 198.

[95] Micanzio, *Vita*, p. 34.

[96] One of these episodes is fully described in "Come Sarpi non fu vescovo," pp. 196–205. Sarpi wanted the bishopric chiefly to have greater leisure for his studies. The Venetian ambassador was informed in Rome that Sarpi had been rejected not because of his doctrines, which were considered satisfactory, but for other reasons not specified.

[97] Cf. Chabod, *Politica di Sarpi*, p. 33.

Yet, although Sarpi had associated familiarly with members of the ruling group for many years so that they must have been aware of his general abilities and of his particular competence in theology and canon law as well as of his devotion to his native city, there is little evidence that he had concerned himself actively with political matters, either ecclesiastical or secular, before Venice was threatened with the interdict.[98] He himself, at any rate, chose to interpret his entry into public affairs as an abrupt change, entered into only from a sense of necessity,[99] in a life that had previously been devoted mainly to the study of mathematics and the natural sciences, which he was now compelled to abandon. His formal appointment as *consultore teologico-canonico* was, as he saw it, a major turning point in his career. By it he had been converted, like other Venetians whose careers we have noticed, from a life of speculation to the *vita activa civile*.[100] Even if this version of the event was not strictly accurate, the sense it expresses of the essential alternatives for the conduct of life is evidence, again, of the attitudes prevailing in the ruling circles of Venice.

The human ideal which Sarpi's public appointment was taken to realize is given its fullest enunciation in the account of the great transformation in his life supplied by his faithful disciple, Fra Fulgenzio Micanzio, in words which also clearly reflect Sarpi's own civic values.

At this time [Fra Fulgenzio wrote], it can be said that his quiet studies ended along with his private life; and from this time to the end of his years, he entered another world, or rather the world, and it pleased God to call him to works to which he would never have thought of applying himself. But man is not born for himself alone, but principally for his country and for the common good. I leave it to others to discuss [in general terms] whether the wise man should apply himself to government. Our Padre [Sarpi] will give us a [practical] example of one who rejects neither labors nor dangers for the service of God and of country. [He shows] that the wise and good man is far from [accepting] the false doctrine invented by a rabble of seditious deceivers that nothing but evil should be said of secular politics, although it is

---

[98] His only recorded engagement with political issues was an opinion in 1596, probably given orally, on the proposed Index of Clement VIII (Chabod, *Politica di Sarpi*, p. 54).

[99] Cf. his letter to Gillot, Aug. 14, 1612, Ulianich, p. 154: "... neque ego unquam, nisi cogente necessitate, ad scribendum animum appulissem."

[100] See, for example, his letter to Groslot, July 22, 1608, Busnelli, I, 22. For a different interpretation of this transition, see Getto, *Sarpi*, p. 62.

instituted by God. [He also shows] that in politics the good man can serve the divine Majesty with a vocation so pious and excellent that nothing equals it, or at least nothing surpasses it.[101]

Sarpi entered public life with a sense of religious mission, and he evidently thrived on the change; his health, previously delicate, suddenly improved.[102] The words with which he concluded his first *consulto*, which he prepared even before the Senate had confirmed his appointment, may be taken, therefore, as more than perfunctory: "I have desired nothing more ardently in all my life than to be able in some way to serve your Serenity, my prince, under whom I was born in this glorious city." [103] On the other hand nothing also better illustrates the clash of values between Venice and the Counter Reformation papacy than the fact that Sarpi's entrance into the service of the Venetian state was bitterly condemned in Rome. He was warned to consider that he would be held to account in heaven for having "abandoned God for the world, the cloister for the court, and religion for politics." [104] For Sarpi such an interpretation of his action was simply perverse; he knew no better way to serve God than through action to benefit the community in which, by God's grace, he had been born.[105]

It is important to consider with some care the circumstances of Sarpi's entrance into public life, for this event raises a fundamental issue in regard to the meaning of the struggle between Rome and Venice. From the account so far presented, it would seem clear that this conflict had remote origins, that it had been long in preparation, and that Sarpi's active involvement came relatively late. In our reading, the crisis of 1605–1607 was a clash between historic communities which embodied antithetical attitudes and antagonistic forces of the most basic character. Such an interpretation is by no means intended to deny the importance of Sarpi, but it clearly assigns to him, and

[101] Micanzio, *Vita*, p. 76.

[102] *Ibid.*, p. 93. Fra Fulgenzio makes no explicit connection but again notes the correlation between Sarpi's health and his service to the state on p. 145.

[103] *Consiglio in difesa di due ordinazioni della Serenissima Republica*, in *Scritti*, II, 16. Cf. similar expressions in Sarpi's early *consulti* given in Francescon, p. 12, n. 1.

[104] This warning was made by Giovanni Antonio Bovio, *Risposta alle considerationi del P. Maestro Paolo de Venetia* (Rome, 1606), p. 41; I cite from the edition in the *Raccolta*, II, 19–87. Micanzio, *Vita*, p. 96, indicates that pressure was applied in Rome on the Servite general to forbid Sarpi and himself to accept Venetian service.

[105] Cf. Micanzio, *Vita*, pp. 151–152, explaining Sarpi's rejection of invitations to enter the service of other governments.

indeed to other individual personalities, chiefly a representative significance. It finds Sarpi's historical importance primarily in the degree to which he managed to embody and to express Venetian values and in the success with which he served Venetian interests.

This view is in direct conflict with an interpretation of the Venetian interdict and of Sarpi's role which has been dominant since the event itself. Sarpi has generally been represented not as the agent but the inspiration of Venice, as the prime mover behind the otherwise incomprehensible resistance of a community which would else have readily complied with the demands of the pope.[106] This interpretation is now clearly unacceptable. Even without the massive evidence of the traditional character of Venetian jealousy on all questions of ecclesiastical jurisdiction, it would be difficult to believe that the conservative and relatively rigid Venetian patriciate could have been manipulated for his own mysterious purposes by a monk of humble social origins, however intelligent and learned. Sarpi, in any case, lacked the dramatic talents of Savonarola.[107] This erroneous interpretation of Sarpi's role, nevertheless, was itself an element in the historical situation, and its origins are worth some attention.

The idea that Sarpi was primarily responsible for Venetian policy may now, perhaps, be most usefully seen as the particular form taken by a deeply rooted tendency in Rome to attribute the behavior of Venice to a conspiracy on the part of a small band of wicked men. As early as April 1606 the pope himself blamed the recalcitrance of Venice on "wicked spirits who counsel evil";[108] and this explanation of the situation was employed repeatedly in later papalist statements.[109] Venice, according to this view, was behaving badly because she had been deceived and led astray by false counselors. Various explanations were adduced to account for the behavior of these wicked men. According to one view, they had absorbed poisonous doctrines from the writings of the great medieval heretics: from Marsilio of Padua, from Ockham and Wyclif.[110] Another explanation, rather more penetrating,

---

[106] Cf. the works listed in note 78 above.

[107] Cf. Wotton's observation to the Earl of Salisbury, Sept. 13, 1607, Smith, I, 400: "His power of speech consisteth in the soundness of reason than in any other natural ability."

[108] Cornet, p. 53, n. 2.

[109] For example, Lelio Medici, *Discorso sopra i fondamenti e le ragioni delli ss. Veneziani* (Bologna, 1606), p. 199; I use the edition in the *Raccolta*, II, 183–210.

[110] Antonio Possevino under the pseudonym Paolo Anafesto, *Risposta all'avviso del sig. Antonio Quirino* (Bologna, 1607), pp. 6–7, 45, 49.

associated Venetian policy, as one writer declared, with "those infamous *politici* imitated by your false counsellors with such stupidity when, blaspheming politically, they dare to affirm with their wicked tongues that the prince ought to behave now like a wolf, now like a lion." [111] Although the charge of Machiavellism was in this period used indiscriminately against any enemy, Rome appears to have recognized promptly that in some sense Venice was acting in the political tradition of the Renaissance.

But although Sarpi's official appointment must have been known in Rome almost immediately, it was nevertheless several months before he began generally to be identified as a major culprit. The general account of the situation prepared late in the spring by the Jesuit superior in Venice, Bernardino Castorio, listed Sarpi among the advisers to the Venetian government but gave him no special attention; Castorio was convinced that the major fault lay with Leonardo Donà.[112] Other papalist writers also continued to identify Sarpi as no more than one among a group of evil advisers.[113] Only in midsummer of 1606 was Sarpi beginning to be regarded as "the sower of all the dissensions," [114] in the phrase of one of his enemies.

But the eventual insistence in Rome that Sarpi was chiefly to blame for the interdict seems to have been based not so much on his personal opinions[115] or his role as adviser to the Venetian government as on recollections of the

[111] Ventura Venturi, *Della maiestà pontificia* (Siena, 1607), p. 97.

[112] In Pirri, pp. 92–121. This report was composed between May and June of 1606, some three months after Sarpi's appointment. Castorio showed rather more interest, indeed, in another Venetian theologian, Giovanni Marsilio, perhaps because Marsilio was a former Jesuit.

[113] Medici, *Discorso*, p. 185, gave primary blame to Antonio Querini, author of the *Aviso delle ragione della serenissima republica di Venetia*: Possevino, in *Risposta di Teodoro Eugenio di Famagosta*, p. 6, identified Sarpi as merely one (with Marsilio) of several "nuovi Alchimisti," though elsewhere singling him out for special attention. See also the dispatch of Germonio to the Duke of Savoy, June 27, 1607, in "Fra Paolo Sarpi, documenti inediti dell'Archivio di Stato di Torino," ed. Alessandro Luzio, *Atti della R. Accademia delle Scienze di Torino*, LXIII (1927–1928), pp. 48–49, which suggests that as late as two months after the end of the interdict Sarpi was not yet clearly identified as individually responsible for the defiance of Venice; hereafter cited as Luzio.

[114] From a letter of unknown authorship to Rome, July 20, 1606, in Pietro Savio, "Per l'epistolario di Paolo Sarpi," *Aevum*, X (1936), 20, note; hereafter cited as *Aevum*. By the early months of the next year the leaders of his own order were hinting that the unhappy events in Venice had been entirely the work of "this sinister counselor" (*Difesa de' Servi*, Preface).

[115] Indeed, a Servite professed surprise at Sarpi's behavior during the interdict in view of his previous conduct: ". . . havendolo conosciuto sempre, in tutte le sue attioni molto riguardevole, e circospetto nel parlare, e massime mordacemente" (Baglioni, *Apologia*, p. 2).

nuncio Offredi's report, half a decade earlier, concerning Sarpi's participation in an "academy" devoted to spreading erroneous doctrine.[116] A pamphlet by Possevino recalled the nuncio's memorandum and also associated Sarpi with the view that Aristotle had not believed in the immortality of the soul.[117] The inference was then drawn that an entire generation of noble Venetian youths had been corrupted by contact with Sarpi's instruction; and from this it was a simple matter to conclude that Sarpi had been appointed not so much to advise the state as to supervise the conduct of its affairs by a ruling group, his erstwhile disciples, whom he had earlier seduced through his teachings.[118] In this interpretation Leonardo Donà, in spite of the fact that he was sixteen years Sarpi's senior, was seen as his most apt pupil.[119] In this general way every distressing tendency in Venice was finally traced to Sarpi. Soon after the interdict a papalist document described the entire body of advisers to the Venetian government and the whole leadership of the Venetian state as "disciples and academicians of that schoolmaster Paolo Servita, who is said publicly to have inherited the poison of Luther, the atheism of M. Spirone of Padua, and the impiety of Marsilio of Padua." [120] Cardinal Borghese described Sarpi in 1611 as one "whose impiety goes so far that he can be regarded not merely as a heretic but as a heresiarch," as one indeed who "aims at nothing less than infecting all that republic—if, however, anything still remains healthy." [121]

In view of what must now be clear about the backgrounds of the interdict as well as the absence of proof for the primary role assigned to Sarpi in this conspiratorial interpretation, these allegations may be safely dismissed. Yet once we have recognized their improbability, we may still find them of

[116] On the background of this charge, cf. also R. Amerio, *Il Sarpi dei pensieri filosofici inediti* (Turin, 1950), p. 17.

[117] *Risposta di Teodoro Eugenio*, pp. 5, 34.

[118] See the letter from Cardinal Perbenedetti to the pope, March 9, 1607, *Aevum*, X (1936), 12, which relays information about the existence in Venice of an "atheist company" dedicated to the introduction of "liberty of conscience" and headed by Sarpi and the doge.

[119] For a Venetian refutation of these charges, see Pandolfo Offman, *Avvertimento, et ammonitione catolica. Al Padre Antonio Possevino Giesuito* (Venice, 1607), pp. 100–102; I cite from the edition in the *Raccolta*, II, 97–109. Offman was particularly concerned to refute the charge that Donà had been a product of Sarpi's "Academy," but his contention that Donà had never spoken to Sarpi before his election as doge is almost certainly false. The pamphlet suggests, however, the sensitivity of the Venetian government to charges of Sarpi's responsibility.

[120] Quoted by Cozzi, *Contarini*, p. 104.

[121] Letter to the nuncio in France, March 18, 1611, *Aevum*, X (1936), 11–12, n. 3.

considerable interest for what they suggest incidentally about the mind of the Counter Reformation. Thus we may note how the ascription of Venetian resistance to the diabolical plot of a few wicked men, or more narrowly to the influence of a single, depraved individual, served the papal interest at the time. It implied that the Venetian position was not the reflection of policies and attitudes rooted in the history and structure of the community. It minimized the Venetian cause by denying its seriousness.

Yet the charge against Sarpi was also more than a cynical invention. It reflected those larger attitudes to political and historical phenomena which we have observed in the previous chapter, notably the concern to elevate into a quasi-dogmatic truth the notion of the papacy's constant and effective leadership over an obedient and united Christendom. The defiance of Venice, from this standpoint, could only be explained as a historical accident. At the same time the deficiency in this view of the political world is evident. It recalls the emphasis on individual initiative and the corresponding failure to perceive large historical forces characteristic of the early Renaissance. But the prominence of conspiracy theories in more recent historiographical disputes and their persistence in general discussions of social change should warn us that the tradition which the Renaissance first expressed and then sought to transcend was rooted in man's profound reluctance, particularly when crisis threatens the whole structure of his existence, to acknowledge that change is an inescapable dimension of life.

To recognize, meanwhile, that Sarpi acted as the instrument of the Venetian community rather than as its inspiration should be helpful not only to understand the interdict but also to put into some perspective a figure who has too often been taken out of his social and historical context, not only to be hissed as the villain of the piece but also (with equally unfortunate results for understanding the past) to be applauded as its hero. This is not to question either the importance of his contribution to Venice in the struggle with the papacy or his personal distinction, but simply to suggest that Sarpi should be understood as the creature of the interdict, not its creator. It was that event which drew him into public life and engaged him in the political and historiographical activities that were to make him famous throughout Europe.

The services for which Sarpi had been retained by the Venetian government were essentially those of a lawyer. His duty was to defend the interests of his corporate client with all the learning and sagacity at his command, not to express his private views on religious and political questions. Thus the originality of his compositions, whether in the form of official opinions addressed to the heads of state or as pamphlets addressed to a wider audience, should not be exaggerated.[122] What Sarpi brought to his task was less a specific point of view than vast reserves of legal and historical scholarship, impressive powers of organization, a singular talent for debate, and an unusual willingness to make explicit the ultimate implications of what Venetians had long maintained. His interdict writings are on the whole less impressive for their original substance than for the learning, the incisiveness, and the intellectual energy with which they are filled.

Sarpi's first assignment, performed even before he had entered officially on his new position, was to prepare a defense of the Venetian laws attacked in the first papal brief to be delivered by the nuncio. The *consulto* Sarpi submitted[123] was, on the whole, undistinguished. It argued (like other opinions solicited by the government) that the laws in question could not be properly considered antagonistic to the church since they dealt only with the conduct of laymen. In addition Sarpi made much of the many precedents of these laws and their long acceptability to previous popes; the appeal to custom, which made Rome the aggressor and allowed a conservative role to Venice, was central to the Venetian case. Sarpi's first *consulto* also gave vigorous expression to his devotion to Venice, revealed his strong sense of the sovereignty of the lay state, and refused to concede to the church, as a legal and institutional entity, any special position in the state. "Because the prince," Sarpi insisted, "can command that no one may build without a license, he can therefore command that no one may build churches without a license; and just as he can command that no one may alienate landed property, so he can command that no one may alienate it to the church." [124]

The opinions of Sarpi and other counselors were promptly employed to prepare the Senate's formal answer to the pope, which stressed the customary nature of Venetian practice. To alter it "would only pervert and totally confuse the foundations and the form of our government," the Senate declared. In addition, it pointed out, to accede to the pope's wishes would do violence to the deep ancestral piety of Venice; it would, in effect, brand as "violators of ecclesiastical liberty" those past generations responsible for Venetian practice, "men of the highest piety and religion, deserving well of the Apostolic See for infinite benefits conferred, who, we piously believe,

[122] As, I think, Chabod tended to do in *Politica di Sarpi*, pp. 54ff.

[123] The *Consiglio in difesa di due ordinazioni della Serenissima Repubblica*, in *Scritti*, II, 3–16. This is carefully analyzed by Chabod, *Politica di Sarpi*, pp. 55–63. But cf. Cozzi, "Sarpi tra Canaye e Casaubon," pp. 54–55.

[124] *Scritti*, II, 11.

enjoy blessedness in heaven." The document also adduced other arguments: the number and splendor of churches already existing in Venetian territory, the burden on the laity whose resources were constantly diminishing while the church grew richer, the fact that all issues in the present crisis were temporal so that the church was meddling in affairs that were none of its concern.[125] This answer, with its implication of the right of the laity to judge in such matters, naturally failed to impress the pope. When Nani presented it to him early in February, the pope read it gravely and then heatedly denounced it as a tissue of frivolities.[126]

With his second *consulto*, which dealt with the "force and validity of just and unjust excommunication" and with the measures Venice might employ against the impending censures, Sarpi began to display his real effectiveness as a controversialist.[127] His major advice to the Venetian government was that, since the penalties threatened by the pope were undeserved, they might properly be ignored and resisted as Venice had ignored and resisted such pressures in the past. Sarpi insisted that the laws to which Rome had taken exception constituted a "good and holy work, useful to your state, necessary to good government, and commanded by God." Failure to have enacted such laws would only have been to neglect "the good of the Republic and its subjects"; God himself would have been angry. Since the threatened censures could not be justified in any way, they ought to be neither received nor obeyed. The Venetian government might also bear in mind, Sarpi pointed out, that interdiction had no precedent in the primitive church but was of relatively recent origin; and from it was likely to flow a host of inconveniences including "harm to divine service, in devotion among peoples, damage to souls, proliferation of heresies." Interdiction ought therefore to be employed very sparingly. Fundamental to his argument was again the implication that the lay community had both a right and a duty to judge ecclesiastical pronouncements. Meanwhile Sarpi also insisted throughout, as he had done before, on the traditional, orthodox, and Catholic nature of these views.[128]

---

[125] Cornet, pp. 23–27.

[126] Knowledge of Sarpi's role in the preparation of this reply produced particular indignation in Rome, where a secret process against him was soon begun. See the letter from the Jesuit general in Rome to Possevino, April 1, 1606, intercepted by Wotton and turned over to the authorities in Venice, text in Cornet, App. VI, p. 274.

[127] *Scrittura sopra la forza e validità della scommunica giusta ed ingiusta, e sopra le remedii 'de iure' e 'de facto' da usare contro le censure ingiuste*, in *Scritti*, II, 17–40. Analyzed by Chabod, *Politica di Sarpi*, pp. 63–73.

[128] *Scritti*, II, 30, 34, 29, 16, 18, 20.

In subsequent *consulti* during the spring of 1606, Sarpi amplified and added to these arguments. He defended the right of Venice to try criminal clergy in civil courts, and he presented further arguments to prove the propriety of lay control over acquisitions of property by the church and over the construction of church buildings.[129] Meanwhile he studied the various papal grievances against Venice and began to review European precedents for Venetian practice, beginning with the period of the investiture struggles; in Venice, as in Rome, the present struggle was understood as a continuation of the long medieval conflict between *sacerdotium* and *magisterium*.[130] Sarpi also gave particular advice to the Venetian government. Thus, perhaps with the outcome of the Council of Trent already on his mind, he opposed an appeal to a general council, at least for the time being.[131] Finally, he advocated the suppression of writings in support of the papal position [132] and at the same time a deliberate effort to present the Venetian case to the rest of Europe.[133] Sarpi recognized the international context of the local crisis in which Venice was involved, and he saw that the cause of Venice could be represented as the cause of all sovereign states.[134] The papal arguments he dismissed as merely abstract and doctrinaire. They lacked force, he argued, through their failure to take into consideration the concrete actualities of the historical situation.[135]

In Rome, meanwhile, Nani had been making no progress with the pope, who awaited with impatience the arrival of the special ambassador.[136] In March the Senate replied to the papal protest against the arrest of ecclesiastics, again expressing regret at the evident desire of the pope to "weaken and destroy the institutions of our Republic, bequeathed to us through many generations by our ancestors and never attacked by anyone." Venice, the Senate claimed once more, had always judged clerical crimes. This power,

---

[129] *Ibid.*, pp. 40ff.

[130] For example in *Consulto sui remedii da opporsi ad una eventuale aggravazione della scommunica*, in *Scritti*, II, 161ff., he reviewed the measures taken by governments since the time of the emperor Henry IV to deal with ecclesiastical censures. The Jesuits in Venice had also been struck by the parallel with events during the pontificate of Gregory VII; cf. the relation of Castorio, Pirri, p. 116, which describes how the fathers read together at table in Baronius about matters "appropriate to what we are now experiencing."

[131] In the *Consulto sui remedii*, in *Scritti*, II, 155–170.

[132] *Ibid.*, p. 167.

[133] *Ibid.*, p. 168.

[134] As he represents it in *Considerazioni sopra le censure*, in *Scritti*, II, 252.

[135] Cf. *Scrittura in materia della libertà ecclesiastica*, in *Scritti*, II, 143.

[136] Cornet, p. 32.

on which the good order of the state depended, had been born with the Republic; it had never been a concession from the Holy See but was rather a direct commission from God himself. The pope listened to this response with disdain and made it clear that he was not interested in lengthy discussion; he demanded prompt satisfaction.[137] When the special ambassador Duodo at last arrived at the end of the month, therefore, his interview went badly. The pope was resolved on the immediate redress of his grievances, but Duodo had been delegated only to state once more why Venice felt compelled flatly to reject all the pope's demands. Duodo concluded his report of the encounter glumly: "What we can tell Your Serenity is this, that his Holiness claims to be so well informed about this business that he does not wish to enter into any controversy or discussion or debate about it." [138] The impasse appeared complete. The pope required immediate and total obedience; Venice sought to avoid it by negotiation and delay.

During the early part of the new year, the pope's resolve to make an example of Venice grew ever more firm. Noting the element of innovation in the offensive Venetian laws, he remarked to Nani that these were "not the times to broaden privileges"; and he denied the authenticity of the documents by which the Venetians proposed to demonstrate the traditional character of their position.[139] He remained convinced that the obligation to persist in his demands was central to his high office. He was evidently certain, as well, of his own triumph in the event of a direct confrontation. The Curia expected that Venice, convinced at heart that her policies were wrong, would quickly capitulate once the pressure of outraged public opinion was brought to bear on the government through the imposition of an interdict.[140] The pope had also received some encouragement to discipline Venice, along with vague assurances of support, from Spain.[141]

[137] *Ibid.*, pp. 36–38.

[138] *Ibid.*, pp. 39–43. *Componimento*, pp. 14–16, 19–29, also includes several dispatches from Nani and Duodo during this period.

[139] Cornet, pp. 29, 40. The only archives having any authority in ecclesiastical matters, the pope asserted, were those in Rome. He demanded, evidently to Duodo's chagrin, that the ambassador produce the originals of papal briefs alleged to support Venetian claims.

[140] Bellarmine, *Risposta a fra Paolo*, p. 93, for example, expressed the conviction that Venetians, whatever they might say, must really fear the censures. The *Difesa de' Servi*, p. 254, openly defended interdiction as a means of bringing public pressure to bear on governments.

[141] See the letters from the Count of Verrua, his ambassador in Rome, to the Duke of Savoy, Dec. 26, 1605, and July 10, 1606, in Magistris, pp. 8–9, 122. The Venetians tended throughout the period to regard the papacy as the tool of Spain; cf. Micanzio, *Vita*, p. 99, and Sarpi, *Istoria dell'Interdetto*, p. 76.

Many cardinals during this period were inclined to take a more political line than the pope. The pope claimed substantial support from his cardinals, but he was chiefly encouraged by those dependent on the Spanish crown.[142] Many cardinals were not particularly hostile to Venice. The Venetian cardinals, as was to be expected, did their best to soften the pope, arguing (as it turned out correctly) that "these spiritual weapons might be despised, and from that might follow consequences of a worse nature." The pope only replied that, both as cardinals and as Venetian gentlemen, they ought rather to persuade their own government to soften its position.[143] The French cardinals were cautious but expressed confidence in the wisdom of the Republic, and various Italian cardinals evidently dreaded a serious crisis in the peninsula on political grounds. Even Bellarmine and Baronius had grave reservations about the pope's tactics. When Nani and Duodo called together on Bellarmine, that cardinal admitted his inclination to take rather a broad view of the jurisdictional issue and his belief that it was less important than the problem of reform. After the interdict he informed the Venetian ambassador that, if he had been consulted, he would have opposed the censure. Baronius thought that Spain was a greater danger to papal authority in Italy than Venice.[144] But, as we have observed, the opinions of cardinals now counted for little in Rome. Decisions were made by the pope.

Paul V remained adamant; and at last, on April 17, he assembled his consistory and announced the excommunication of the doge and Senate and the interdiction of all territories under Venetian rule unless Venice submitted completely within twenty-four days. The cardinals, except only for the Venetian prelates and the French Cardinal Du Perron, who claimed to be sick,[145] quickly approved the action; and the pope's brief of excommunication

---

[142] Cornet, pp. 39, 90–91, n. 2.

[143] Ibid., pp. 53–54. For the efforts of the Venetian cardinals to make peace, App. XIX, pp. 322–337. Throughout the interdict Cardinal Delfino provided Venetian correspondents with news of developments in Rome (cf. Querini, *Historia dell' Escomunica*, p. 285).

[144] Cornet, pp. 45–48. Venetian sources give the impression of great caution on the part of most cardinals about committing themselves to firm views on the issues. Sarpi, *Istoria dell'Interdetto*, p. 35, was eager to suggest that few cardinals supported the pope out of conviction, and that they did so at last only through cowardice, interest, or ambition.

[145] See his letter to the French king, April 18, 1606, in Jacques Davy Du Perron, *Les ambassades et negotiations* (Paris, 1623), p. 465. In a further effort to remain impartial, he declined a papal invitation to write against the Venetians (letter of May 28, 1606, p. 479).

was duly issued.[146] Addressed to all clergy in the domains of Venice, it listed as grounds for spiritual censure the laws limiting bequests to the church and the construction of buildings, and the arrest of the two clergy by the Venetian authorities. In addition it mentioned for the first time the law of 1602 dealing with emphyteusis contracts. The brief declared all these actions null and void, forbade observance of the offending laws, and concluded with the sentences of excommunication and interdict.[147] Within a few days copies of the brief had been posted in Rome and distributed to the cardinals and to representatives of princes.[148]

As soon as news of the decision had reached Venice, Duodo was directed to return home. He paid a last call on the pope to protest the innocence of Venice, but the pope insisted again that the censures had been proposed "as a duty of his office and an obligation of conscience," that the case was "clear and decided," and that the sentence was a "remedy used in similar cases by his precedessors, a remedy not mortal but medicinal." [149] In Venice itself, meanwhile, the nuncio was making a last attempt to obtain satisfaction for his master; but his repeated demands only succeeded in antagonizing the doge. Donà informed him with some vehemence that "no prince, either great or small, could be pleased to hear what his Holiness had done." The doge seemed particularly annoyed at the pope's refusal to negotiate or even to discuss the Venetian position; such treatment, he insisted, should not be employed "with a free prince of the quality, by the grace of God, which we are." Venice, he complained, had been "denigrated and vituperated" by the pope "in the Theater of the World which is the Roman Curia." The nuncio could only reply that it was not for sons to oppose their father.[150] The exchange nicely epitomized the conflicting attitudes of the two sides.

A few days after the papal sentence had gone into effect the Senate informed the nuncio that it had been gravely offended by the action; that Venice, resolved to conserve her liberty and to submit to no man, would defend herself in whatever way might seem appropriate; and that it regarded

[146] Cornet, pp. 54–55. A record of the consistory is printed in Romanin, *Storia di Venezia*, VII, 561–568. It does not altogether bear out the Venetian charge of papal dictation (as in Sarpi, *Istoria dell'Interdetto*, p. 17). Each cardinal was permitted to give his opinion, and the tone of the proceedings seems to have been fairly matter-of-fact and businesslike.

[147] Latin text in *Raccolta*, I, 1–7.

[148] Cornet, pp. 62–63.

[149] *Ibid.*, pp. 64–66.

[150] *Ibid.*, pp. 66–67. A document describing the nuncio's last appearance in the College, May 8, 1606, is also printed in *Componimento*, pp. 44–46.

the sentence as unjust and therefore invalid and null. The next day, May 8, the nuncio announced his departure from Venice, and the Senate ordered Nani to leave Rome.[151]

The excommunication of the Venetian government and the interdiction of Venetian territory went into effect early in May of 1606 and continued until April 21, 1607. Rome had doubtless hoped in the beginning that Venice would capitulate promptly, after some searching of conscience on the part of the ruling group and a brief experience with the public effects of an interdict. But although the excommunication of the Senate certainly caused considerable anguish for some of its members, the solidarity of the patriciate was impressive. Although they varied in the degree of their hostility to the papacy,[152] nearly all Venetian nobles seem to have been convinced that the issues leading up to the censures were secular rather than spiritual, that Rome was therefore encroaching in an area where the church should not meddle, that Venice was in the right, and that the censures were unjust. Thus, throughout the period of the interdict, measures aimed at strengthening resistance to the pope passed the Senate by overwhelming majorities.[153] Rome had seriously underestimated the strength of Venetian sentiment for ecclesiastical autonomy.

Meanwhile the effect of the interdict in stirring up Venetian subjects against their government was frustrated by the energetic action of the Senate and doge. Anticipating the effort of Rome to publish in Venetian territory its "unjust and invalid" censures, the Senate on April 27 prohibited the transportation or reception of papal bulls; any bull that came to the attention of any Venetian subject was to be conveyed immediately to the public authorities on penalty of death.[154] A few days after the interdict had gone into effect, the doge addressed a letter to all ecclesiastics in lands ruled by Venice informing them that, since Venice recognized no superior in temporal things, the censures announced in Rome were to be regarded as "not only unjust and undeserved but also as null and of no value and thus invalid." The clergy

---

[151] Cornet, pp. 73–76; *Componimento*, pp. 42–44.

[152] Lists of more aggressive and more moderate Venetian leaders are given by Cozzi, *Contarini*, p. 103. The list of readers of subversive books supplied to Roman authorities by the renegade Fulgenzio Manfredi after the interdict (*Aevum*, X [1936], 31–35) may also be taken as a roster of anti-curial patricians.

[153] Publication of a formal protest against the papal brief of April 17 was approved in the Senate, for example, by a vote of 160 to 3 (Cornet, p. 73, n. 1).

[154] Cornet, p. 65.

were further advised of the government's expectation that they would continue the performance of their pastoral duties as before.[155] This suggestion was promptly translated into a decree requiring them to say mass as usual, to remain in the state, and to notify the government of any orders to the contrary from their superiors.[156] These measures were largely effective. A few copies of the interdict were eventually posted in churches and other public places, but they were quickly detected and torn down,[157] so that few Venetian subjects could study them.[158] The clergy, meanwhile, a good many no doubt sorely troubled, for the most part continued with their pastoral offices.

The Curia did all it could to apply pressure on Venice. Whether to aid study of the present situation or as a warning to the Republic, various documents connected with earlier censures of Venice by Clement V, Sixtus IV, and Julius II were assembled and printed together: bulls of excommunication, solemn warnings, absolutions.[159] Thus Rome, too, saw the new interdict against the background of earlier confrontations; the pope, hoping for a similar outcome in his own case, spoke frequently of Julius II.[160] We may observe that this attention to previous instances of Venetian defiance was markedly inconsistent with the contention that Venice was presently departing from a long pattern of faithful obedience to the Holy See.[161] Emphasis on the parallel in Rome is of some interest, nevertheless, because of the assumption behind it that Julius II, in 1509, had acted as far more than a temporal prince who was only incidentally the pope; it suggests the profound continuities of papal universalism even during the Renaissance. These reminiscences in Rome will also remind us that the Venetian interdict of 1606 was by no means unique.

Meanwhile efforts were made to penetrate the iron ring Venice had drawn around her territories. Hundreds of copies of the bull of interdiction were

[155] Text in *Raccolta*, I, 8.

[156] Cornet, p. 76.

[157] Canaye to Villeroy, May 3, 1606, III, 29–30.

[158] This was recognized even in Rome, as revealed in the anonymous diary described by Antonio Gadaleta, "Di un diario dell'interdetto di Venezia del secolo XVII," *ASI*, Ser. 5, XVIII (1896), 100.

[159] Preparation of this document is reported in letters of Abbot Gradenigo in Rome to his brother, Dec. 2 and 9, 1606, summarized in Cornet, App. XIX, p. 330.

[160] See the dispatch of Giovanni Magno, Mantuan representative in Rome, Aug. 26, 1606, reporting the pope's remark that Julius II had treated the Venetians as they deserved (*Componimento*, p. 358). The pope also suggested to the Florentine resident that the Venetians would do well to remember Julius II (Rubertis, *Ferdinando I dei Medici*, p. 23).

[161] But see too Possevino, *Risposta di Teodoro Eugenio*, p. 7.

printed in the vernacular and shipped to cities close to the boundaries of the Venetian state, to be smuggled in whenever possible.[162] Centers like Mantua and Bologna became bases for agitation against the Venetian government and for the dispatch of pamphlets and secret messages addressed to Venetian clergy.[163] Papalist writers pressed the Venetians to obey the pope, assuring ecclesiastics that the government would never carry out its threats.[164] The Carmelite Giovanni Antonio Bovio, for example, reminded them that they must be ready to man the walls of the City of God and, if necessary, to die like good soldiers in defense of its liberty.[165] They were confidently informed that revolt in Venice was imminent.[166] At the same time the exclusion of Venice from the benefits of full communion with the Roman church was dramatized in various ways. In June the pope proclaimed a jubilee but pointedly excluded interdicted peoples from participation,[167] and in Catholic courts abroad papal nuncios tried to bar Venetian ambassadors from religious services.[168]

The pope also contemplated more serious steps against the Venetian government. He had been antagonized by the doge's letter to the clergy within the Venetian state, and he considered citing him formally before the Holy Office in Rome for heresy. To his intimates he insisted that the issue was one of principle, and that to maintain it he was prepared to endure a multitude of practical inconveniences. Cardinal Del Monte reported to the Grand Duke of Tuscany (who was considerably perturbed by the idea that

[162] Rubertis, *Ferdinando I dei Medici*, p. 36, n. 1.

[163] A papal commissioner was dispatched to Mantua in June to direct measures against Venice (Cornet, pp. 112–113, n. 1). Many of the works written against Venice were printed in Bologna.

[164] For example, Bellarmine, *Risposta al trattato dei sette teologi*, pp. 19–20.

[165] *Risposta*, pp. 84–85.

[166] Venturi, *Maiestà pontificia*, p. 157, predicted that an outraged populace would revolt and convert the patrician republic into a democracy or a monarchy. Giovanni Marsilio, *Essame sopra tutte quelle scritture . . . contro la giustissima causa della Serenissima Repubblica di Venetia* (Venice, 1607), p. 32, expressed particular indignation at Roman efforts to exploit social division in Venice. See also the letter of Cardinal Spinola to Cardinal Borghese, April 18, 1607 (*Aevum*, X [1936], 5–7) expressing confidence that a split would develop between the government and its subjects and his eagerness to exploit it.

[167] Francesco Scaduto, *Stato e Chiesa secondo fra Paolo Sarpi e la coscienza pubblica durante l'interdetto di Venezia* (Florence, 1885), p. 36. Canaye reported Venetian resentment in his letter to Villeroy, July 11, 1606 (III, 118).

[168] Cornet, p. 97, notes the success this pressure had at the imperial court. See also the dispatch of the ambassador Francesco Soranzo from Prague, May 29, 1606, *Componimento*, pp. 64–65.

a prince should be so treated) the pope's declaration "that if he wished to consider this business according to human interests, there would be a good deal to say and many things to consider; but one who is a Christian and head of the Christian people like himself confides in God rather than in the things of this world. If God should wish to abase his Church, he will conform to the will of his Divine Majesty; and if the Arians and Diocletians should return and it becomes necessary to flee into the caves, he will do so willingly, and even more willingly he will lay down his life there, as so many martyrs have done." [169]

For the time being, however, this grim prospect seemed remote; and as it became increasingly evident that none of his measures had much effect on Venice, which instead only grew more defiant, the pope seemed less interested in the model of the ancient martyrs than in that suggested by Julius II. Even before the interdict had been announced, Cardinal Borghese, the pope's nephew and Secretary of State, had spoken darkly to the French ambassador—doubtless anticipating that his words would be reported in Venice, as indeed they were—about the possibility of supplementing spiritual weapons with temporal; and Venice soon began to hear reports of military preparations in the Papal State.[170] The bankers of Genoa, her ancient enemy, offered the pope a large loan to make war on Venice;[171] and a group of intransigents at the Curia began to draw up plans for a military alliance based on the Habsburg powers to bring Venice to her knees.[172] Pressure was also brought on Catholic powers supplying mercenaries to Venice to withdraw their subjects from her service.[173]

But the military preparations in the Papal State were also partly to guard against the possibility of assault by an unpredictable enemy and partly

[169] This letter is dated June 16, 1606; text in Rubertis, *Ferdinando I dei Medici*, p. 43 n. 1. For Venetian indignation at the proposal, see Canaye's letter to Henry IV, June 2, 1606 (III, 62).

[170] Cornet, p. 63 n. 4. See also documents in Cornet, "Paolo V e la Republica veneta," pp. 85–86.

[171] Delumeau, *Vie économique et sociale de Rome*, II, 845.

[172] Taucci, *Intorno alle lettere di fra Paolo Sarpi*, pp. 30 ff., has assembled the evidence. The pope himself talked of recourse to material arms; see the report of his remarks in the letter of Anastasio Germanio to the Duke of Savoy, Jan. 9, 1607, in Magistris, p. 282. The pope referred to offers of military support he had received from various princes. See also various documents in *Componimento*, pp. 150–254, 443–454.

[173] Cornet, p. xii. Querini noted the desertion of Florentine troops and of certain subjects of the pope himself (*Historia dell'Escommunica*, pp. 268–269, 282–283).

bluff.[174] Above all the papacy sought an ideological triumph, a victory for the principles of the Counter Reformation. Accordingly it embarked on a massive literary campaign against the defiant Republic.[175] The nuncios throughout Catholic Europe were directed to explain the pope's grievances against Venice.[176] In addition, pamphlets and books, often of considerable length, in Italian as well as Latin, poured from the presses of Rome, Bologna, and other cities in Italy; and the best minds among the ecclesiastics of the peninsula, as well as some of the dullest, were pressed into service. Often tedious, repetitious, and entirely devoid of intellectual distinction, frequently only hortatory or vituperative, the compositions prepared on behalf of the pope represent collectively, nevertheless, an impressive statement of the attitudes and convictions of the Counter Reformation and above all of its ideals for the constitution both of the church and of society as a whole. We shall examine at some length in the next chapter the substance and implications of these writings as the vehicle of an ideology and a state of mind. Here we shall be concerned only with their tactical role in the struggle to subdue Venice.

In one sense, of course, the resort to a broad discussion of issues, even when carried on in the most polemical and even scurrilous terms, was a concession to Venice. The basic issue between the two powers was the issue of authority; and authority is seriously compromised in principle whenever it is compelled to argue—to appeal, that is, to something beyond itself. The pope had from the beginning wanted mere obedience, not discussion; authority with a proper sense of its own dignity (a virtue abundant in the seventeenth century) scorns to bandy words with those who ought simply to submit. The dilemma here accounts for an undercurrent of frustration and rage which runs through

---

[174] See, for example, the proposal of Cardinal Borghese to the nuncio in Spain, May 29, 1606, *Componimento*, pp. 113–114, that the Venetians should be allowed to believe that Spanish troops actually headed for Flanders were bound for Italy. Cf. the letter of Cardinal Du Perron to the king, Jan. 9, 1607 (*Ambassades*, p. 550) surmising that news of a papal decision for war was only a ruse.

[175] The literary aspect of the struggle is reviewed bibliographically in Scaduto, *Stato e chiesa secondo fra Paolo Sarpi*, pp. 55–71. Other lists of interdict writings may be found in the appendix to Canaye, vol. III, and in Giovanni Soranzo, *Bibliografia veneziana* (Venice, 1885), pp. 89–97.

[176] See, for example, the various instructions in Magistris, p. 39 (for Savoy), and *Componimento*, pp. 47–49, 51–52, 55–58 (for the Empire). Cf. A. Cauchie, "Témoignages d'estime rendus en Belgique au Cardinal Baronius specialement à l'occasion du conflit de Paul V avec Venice," *Per Cesare Baronio* (Rome, 1911), pp. 20–22

many of the papalist writings stimulated by the Venetian interdict. By challenging the principle of authority, above all the supreme spiritual and paternal authority of the pope, Venice had from the Roman standpoint committed a kind of primal outrage. The Venetians heard of demands in Rome that the Republic should be required to send an ambassador with a halter around his neck to beg the pope's pardon.[177]

Among those for whom the notion of carrying on a debate with rebels and parricides was almost unendurably repugnant was Baronius, who had quickly abandoned his early reservations about the papal demands on Venice and now exerted all his influence in favor of the utmost intransigence.[178] His *Remonstrance to the Venetian Republic* suggests in both substance and tone something of Luther's savage reaction to the peasant revolt.[179] Particularly outraged by Venetian refusal to submit to appropriate discipline (since the sinner, if he is to be cleansed of his sin, must accept punishment),[180] Baronius' pamphlet is full of invocations of the wrath of God, fiery furnaces, threats and predictions of woe for the impious Republic. For Baronius, in addition, the behavior of Venice, and especially the Venetian appeal to an established historical tradition, must have seemed a practical refutation of his life's work, a denial of the thesis developed in the massive *Ecclesiastical Annals*. Indeed that work probably served the papal cause better than his pamphlet. Whereas the pamphlet succeeded only in embittering the Venetians further and in attracting numerous equally violent replies,[181] the *Annals* were exploited as a great arsenal to be drawn upon against the Venetians by other papalist writers.[182]

There were far more effective participants in the dispute on the Roman side, Bellarmine in particular, who composed several works against Venice

[177] Cornet, pp. 100–101, n. 2.

[178] *Ibid.*, pp. 54–55, esp. n. 2. On the intransigence of Baronius, cf. Ruffini, *Perchè Cesare Baronio non fu papa*, pp. 73–74.

[179] The *Paraenesis ad rempublicam venetam* (Rome, 1606), is reviewed in detail in Calenzio, *Baronio*, pp. 751–758. Calenzio notes, p. 762, that at this time Baronius also composed a short treatise demonstrating that all who presume to contest the rights of the church are heretics.

[180] *Paraenesis*, p. 101.

[181] See the letter of Antonio Provana, his agent in Venice, to the Duke of Savoy, Aug. 8, 1606, in Magistris, pp. 156–157. Provana thought the tract of Baronius a great tactical blunder. This judgment was shared by some in Rome, perhaps even the pope; cf. Cornet, pp. 326, 328.

[182] See, for example, the *Risposta* of Bovio, *passim*. Indeed the Venetians occasionally found support in Baronius; see the letter of Provana, June 27, 1606, in Magistris, p. 115.

and was identified by the Venetians as one of their most serious opponents.[183] Bellarmine generally maintained a more measured tone than Baronius, even though one Venetian writer complained of his uncivil use of the *tu* form in addressing his opponents, as though he considered them a trifle childish.[184] Sarpi expressed personal respect for him,[185] and Bellarmine's earlier writings were occasionally cited on the Venetian side.[186] A seasoned participant in ecclesiastical controversy, his contribution to the debate over the Venetian interdict constantly illuminates its substantive issues. The aged Jesuit Antonio Possevino, long a resident of Venice, was also an active participant in the literary battle, writing under various pseudonyms which deceived no one.[187] Sarpi thought his works particularly vicious.[188] Major contributions on the papal side were made, in addition, by the theologian Bovio, a member of the commission to investigate the controversy *de auxiliis* and a defender of Molina;[189] by the Sienese Olivetan Ventura Venturi, who particularly

[183] His interdict writings included: *Risposta ad un libretto intitolato 'Trattato et resolutione sopra la validità delle scommuniche, di Gio. Gersone Theologo e Cancellier Parisino'* (Rome, 1606); *Risposta al trattato dei sette teologi di Venetia, sopra l'Interdetto della Santità di Nostro Signore Papa Paolo Quinto* (Rome, 1606); *Risposta alle oppositioni di fra'Paulo servita contra la scrittura del cardinale Bellarmino* (Rome, 1606); *Risposta alla difesa delle otto propositioni di Giovan Marsilio Napolitano* (Rome, 1606); *Risposta a un libretto intitolato Risposta di un dottore di Theologia* (Rome, 1606); and, under the pseudonym Bellarmine also employed against James I of England, *Avviso alli sudditi del Dominio Veneto di Matteo Torti Sacerdote e Teologo di Pavia* (Rome and Ferrara, 1607). Some of these works also appeared in Latin.
[184] Marsilio, *Difesa*, p. 233.
[185] *Apologia per le opposizioni fatte dall'illustrissimo e reverendissimo signor cardinale Bellarminio alli trattati e risoluzioni di Giovanni Gersone sopra la validità delle scommuniche*, in *Scritti*, III, 46.
[186] As by Capello, *Delle controversie, passim*.
[187] *Risposta di Teodoro Eugenio di Famagosta* (cited note 21 above); *Risposta del Sig. Paolo Anafesto all'Avviso del Sig. Antonio Quirino* (n.p., n.d.); *Nuova risposta di Giovanni Filoteo di Asti* (Florence, 1606). For the authorship of the first, with criticism of its acerbity, see the letter of Acquaviva to Possevino, Nov. 25, 1606, in Pirri, p. 305; for the second and third see Canaye's letters to Commartin, Sept. 22, 1606, and Alincourt, May 19, 1607 (III, 218, 598). In addition a personal letter from Possevino to Capello was published by the latter, under the title *Lettera al maestro Marc'Antonio Cappello Minor Conventuale*, along with a reply (Venice, 1606). The last of these is included in the *Raccolta*, II, 235–246.
[188] *Scrittura in difesa delle opere scritte a favore della serenissima republica*, in *Scritti*, III, 249. Pirri, p. 39, suggests that resentment at Possevino's literary efforts contributed to the permanent exclusion of the Jesuits from Venice. Canaye was also critical of Possevino, with whom he had previously been friendly (letter to Welser, July 7, 1606, III, 109).
[189] In addition to the work cited in note 104 above, Bovio published a *Lettera . . . al R.P.M. Paolo Rocca . . . nella quale si discorre . . . sopra a due lettere del Doge e Senato di Vinetia*, etc. (Milan, 1606). Sarpi and Micanzio respected the first of these sufficiently to

concerned himself with the distinction between true and false *ragione di stato*;[190] by Giovanni Amato, once a Venetian subject, who argued that Venice had indeed abandoned a long tradition of devotion to the pope;[191] and by a group of Servite leaders anxious to demonstrate, in spite of Sarpi, the general reliability of the order.[192] Even Campanella was stimulated to write against Venice.[193] Several anonymous writings were also represented as the work of pious Venetians devoutly opposed to the policies of their government.[194]

Rome seemed eager to find spokesmen from as wide a variety of backgrounds as possible, as though to prove that detestation of the Venetian position was universal. But whatever their differences the purpose of these compositions was always the same: to demonstrate that the policy of Venice was erroneous, whether tested by history, by reason, or by the common witness of the church. This contention obviously depended on a positive conception of Catholic teaching on various matters which could hardly yet be said to have achieved formal definition; hence the controversy reveals, on the papalist side, an active effort at the development of dogma. For the time being we shall content ourselves, however, with Sarpi's summary of this effort, reasonably accurate if hostile. In his *History of the Interdict*, composed soon after the event, Sarpi described the Roman case elaborated in these numerous writings under four general headings. The papalist writers, he said, had maintained that the temporal power was properly subordinate and subject to the spiritual, that the pope had the right to dethrone rulers and to release subjects from obedience, that the clergy have no obligation to obey temporal rulers, and that the infallibility of the pope is to be interpreted in a very broad sense.[195] These were the issues of the struggle as it was understood in Rome.

---

compose an extended reply, *Confirmatione delle considerationi del P. M. Paulo di Venetia contra le oppositioni del R.P.M. Gio. Antonio Bovio* (Venice, 1606); see esp. pp. 41–42. Micanzio prepared the work with Sarpi's collaboration (p. 42); it appeared under the anagramatic pseudonym *Iteneu Ichanom Itnegluf.*

[190] *Della maiestà pontificia* (Siena, 1607).

[191] *Breve discorso del principio della Republica di Venetia* (n.p., n.d.).

[192] Cited in note 18 above.

[193] *Antiveneti*, recently edited by Luigi Firpo (Florence, 1944).

[194] In addition to Possevino's "Teodoro Eugenio," whose author posed as a refugee from Cyprus, the *Discorso, sotto nome di sentenza d'un clariss. senator Veneto* (n.p., n.d.). This is included in the *Raccolta*, II, 273–280.

[195] *Istoria dell'Interdetto*, pp. 108–109.

The dominant mood in Venice, meanwhile, was self-righteous as well as increasingly stern and determined. The French ambassador professed alarm, though perhaps chiefly to impress on the Curia the seriousness of the situation.[196] The Venetians were prepared to hint at the most alarming possibilities, if only as part of a war of nerves. The doge suggested, with manifestations of horror, that Venice might be provoked into open schism or even into heresy.[197] There were warnings that the course chosen by the pope might lead to the desolation of all Italy[198] and rumors that Venice was supporting bandits in the papal state or ready to declare war if the pope did not lift the interdict promptly.[199] But, although there was some sentiment in Venice for attacking the states of the church,[200] this militancy was largely verbal. It is significant that during the whole course of the interdict Venice made no move to weaken the pope's shaky and unpopular control over Ferrara, although urged to do so by the duke of Modena.[201]

The most serious among the immediate problems of Venice was to maintain the loyalty of all her subjects. The solution to this difficulty depended, as with previous interdicts, on rejecting the present interdict as unjust and invalid, as we have seen, and on preventing its observance. For this purpose steps were taken to prevent the circulation in Venetian territory of writings favorable to the papal position,[202] a prohibition (bitterly resented in Rome)[203] hardly consistent with the Venetian demand for a full discussion of issues; but the Republic was fighting for its life. It was of critical importance, too,

[196] Thus I am inclined to discount his description of the Senate as dominated by young men with "more warmth in the liver than prudence in the brain" (letter to Du Perron, Aug. 5, 1606, III, 152) as chiefly intended to shock Rome. Canaye's usual emphasis was quite different; see, for example, his letter to Alincourt, Sept. 15, 1606 (III, 204), where he writes, more typically, of "a Senate full of prudence."

[197] Cf. Chabod, *Politica di Sarpi*, pp. 102–103, 120; and Sarpi, *Trattato dell'Interdetto*, in *Scritti*, III, 14–15. Offman, p. 105, hinted broadly at what Rome might expect by noting that papal losses at the time of the Protestant revolt had been provoked by abuses less serious than those Venice was now resisting.

[198] *Ad Paulum V. Pontificem Maximum epistolae duorum clarissimorum iurisconsultorem, anno MDCVI*, p. 133, in the *Raccolta*, I, 127–135.

[199] Letters of Provana to the Duke of Savoy, May 6, 1606, and Jan. 13, 1607, in Magistris, pp. 53, 287.

[200] Cf. Querini, *Historia dell'Escommunica*, p. 264. It was suggested that Venice might recover territories lost to the pope in the previous century, or at the very least intimidate him into withdrawing the censures.

[201] Cornet, pp. ix–x. Nevertheless an attack on Ferrara was seriously discussed; see *ibid.*, pp. 73, 89, and 275–277, App. VII.

[202] *Ibid.*, p. 112, for example.

[203] See the attack in Possevino, *Risposta del Sig. Anafesto*, pp. 3–4.

for the government to maintain the full cooperation of the clergy. Not only were ecclesiastics particularly vulnerable to papalist arguments, but above all Venice could maintain that the interdict was without effect only if the clergy continued their duties as before. On their loyalty also largely depended the obedience of the laity, and the clergy were therefore objects of the government's particular concern and attention.

The government's effort to maintain the obedience of the clergy was generally successful. Throughout the period of the interdict, the state dealt vigorously with ecclesiastics. Even before the censures were imposed, the Senate had required all clergy in the state to pass along to the College unopened any communications received from Rome; the close relatives of Venetian bishops were summoned before the College and directed to advise their ecclesiastical kinsmen to obey and defend the government; and selected members of the clergy were directly admonished by the Council of Ten to convey to that body any messages concerning the impending censures they might receive.[204] As the record of one such session declares, "all replied promptly that they would obey." [205] The Ten also prohibited the clergy from preaching on political matters. They were advised "to contain themselves within those limits which are proper to their ministry, in spiritual preachings." [206] Meanwhile the Senate committed itself to protect, presumably against reprisals from Rome, all clergy who chose to obey the government.[207]

Recognizing clearly their historic role as instruments of papal control, the government paid particular attention to the religious orders. Their heads were among those called before the Council of Ten;[208] and the Senate made explicit its special concern with the obedience of the monks, warning that any who left the state would not be allowed to return and making provision against their absconding with property belonging to the church.[209] Later actions aimed to prevent their emigration and provided for the examination, as potential sources of disorder, of all friars who wished to enter the Venetian state. The new Capuchin and Theatine orders were given a special warning

[204] Cornet, p. 55 and n. 3; Cornet, "Paolo V e la Republica," pp. 55–58.

[205] Cornet, pp. 58–60.

[206] *Ibid.*, p. 51; the order was dated Jan 23, 1606.

[207] *Ibid.*, p. 68. All these measures are described by Querini, *Historia dell' Escomunica*, pp. 260–263, which also claims that many Venetians regarded the government's policies as too lenient.

[208] See the Jesuit report of this in Pirri, pp. 66–67.

[209] Cornet, p. 71.

to remain in the city of Venice and to celebrate all religious offices as before, with the doors of their churches open. Reliable patricians were appointed to keep an eye on particular monasteries in and near Venice.[210] Nicolò Contarini, for example, had charge of San Francesco della Vigna and San Domenico, where some support for the pope was suspected.[211]

Enforcement of the government's policy on the clergy of the *terraferma*, especially its remoter parts, was a matter of special concern. Rectors were everywhere directed to send inspectors to churches and monasteries, to exhort the clergy to obey the decrees of the state, and to discipline the stubborn. They were advised also to pay particular attention to the opinions and conduct of confessors.[212]

Many clergy, especially among the regulars, actually were disposed to obey the pope rather than the lay government of Venice.[213] The Venetian authorities encountered resistance in many places: from the Carmelites of Verona, whose prior was arrested and sent to Venice;[214] from monks and nuns on Murano;[215] from the clergy of Bergamo and other places near the Milanese border, spiritually subordinate to the archbishop of Milan, many of whom managed to flee;[216] from a group of Paduan canons.[217] Nor was resistance confined to lesser clergy without patrician connections; a number of bishops also gave the government cause for anxiety. Antonio Grimani, bishop of Torcello, was at the time nuncio in Florence and free to obey the pope; it is of some interest, therefore, that he refused even to receive the Venetian secretary in his house. The patriarch of Aquileia was reluctant to obey the order of the Senate against posting the notice of the interdict. The bishops of Treviso, Verona, and Brescia tried to resign their ministries and, when this was forbidden, continued at their posts only under pressure. The brothers of the bishop of Verona, for example, were threatened with the confiscation of all their goods unless they persuaded him to conform to the policy of the

[210] *Ibid.*, pp. 120, 93, 80, 93–94 and n. 3.

[211] His report to the Council of Ten, Nov. 24, 1606, is in Cornet, "Paolo V e la Republica," pp. 276–278.

[212] Cornet, pp. 216, n. 1, 141, n. 3, 217.

[213] On this point see Raffaello Putelli, "Il duca Vincenzo Gonzaga e l'interdetto di Paolo V a Venezia," *AV*, Ser. 3, XXII (1911), 127ff.

[214] Cornet, p. 88, n. 2.

[215] Provana to the Duke of Savoy, March 24, 1607, in Magistris, p. 443.

[216] Cornet, pp. 96, 133–134, 157, n. 1. Giovanni Marsilio admitted the problem in his condemnation of an anonymous attack against priests who had taken over vacant parishes, *Essame*, II, 7.

[217] Cornet, p. 94, n. 3.

government. The bishop of Zante managed to flee just before his arrest.[218]

Committed to obeying their ecclesiastical superiors and yet members of a society which had always insisted on a quasi-religious obligation to the state, many clergy must have felt deeply torn. Not all solved the problem so cunningly as the Benedictines of Venice, who, according to Wotton, put every letter they received into a box unopened, lest they inadvertently discover an order from their general to obey the pope; they thereby hoped, as Wotton put it, "to save their consciences by way of ignorance: which point of subtle discretion is likely to be imitated by other orders." [219] Typical for many must have been the anguish of the episcopal vicar of Padua, as reported by an old friend in a deposition before the Council of Ten: "He began to tell me something of the controversies going on with His Holiness and of the distress in which he, poor man, finds himself, through having from the one side orders directly opposed to those which come from the other. Therefore he remains greatly perplexed and doubtful, not knowing which side to take, and he indicated his resolve to depart in order to free himself from all anxiety." The vicar nevertheless seems to have been persuaded to stay.[220]

The government was prepared to take a severe line against the most intransigent supporters of the pope. Clergy brought before agencies of the state were exposed to menacing gestures and verbal threats;[221] and the authorities behaved on occasion with great brutality. A poignant case involved some communities of devout women on the island of Murano, some of them nuns, others laywomen living together, who were generally resolved to obey the interdict. The abbess of the Bernardine convent there had replied with courage to representatives of the Council of Ten who called to remonstrate with her. They described how she had replied "with great plainness and boldness that she would always obey in temporal things and would give her life for the service of her Prince, but that in spiritual things she wished to obey the Pope, head in the spiritual realm; and that she did not wish to give up her

---

[218] *Ibid.*, pp. 65, n. 1, 80–81, 91, n. 1, 94, 136, 140–141; Provana to the Duke of Savoy, Jan. 23, 1607, in Magistris, p. 298; A. Battistella, "Un'eco in Friuli della contesa dell'Interdetto," in *Paolo Sarpi ed i suoi tempi: studi storici* (Città di Castello, 1923), pp. 106ff.; Eugenio Bacchion, "Le vicende trivigiane dell'interdetto di Paolo V," *AV*, Ser. 5, XV (1934), 166. The last work gives a general picture of Venetian problems and policy at the local level.

[219] Letter to the Earl of Salisbury, May 26, 1606, Smith, I, 350.

[220] Deposition in Cornet, "Paolo V e la Republica," pp. 80–81.

[221] See the vivid account of the treatment of leaders of the clergy by the Council of Ten on April 19, 1606, in Castorio's *Relazione*, Pirri, pp. 93–94.

soul to anyone, but to take care of it herself, to give herself to God." All their attempts to conquer her "obstinate ignorance" had been in vain; and when her thirty-four nuns were interviewed privately, with a single exception they took the same position. Their conformity to the wishes of the government was finally obtained only by their total seclusion, with the doors and windows of the convent boarded up, until the nuns gave in.

The fate of the community of pious laywomen on the island was even more pitiable. When two officials called on them, inspected the premises, and invited them to submit, they first requested time to consider. The visitors then abandoned all pretense of courtesy and sternly required each member of the group to give her personal decision. When most indicated a wish to obey the pope, the officials pronounced the community dissolved and ordered the immediate expulsion of the women from the house. This agitated them deeply, their resistance collapsed, and they promised to obey the government; but, unprotected by any formal organization, they were expelled anyway.[222] The government was particularly worried about the loyalty of women who might have fallen under the influence of dubious confessors; elsewhere, too, nuns had showed themselves unresponsive to the claims of the Venetian state.[223]

But the government recognized at an early point that it could accomplish little with some categories of ecclesiastics. These it dealt with by expelling them from the state—some foreign priests, inquisitors, and above all the new religious orders of the Counter Reformation, with their shallow local roots and their particular attachment to Rome. The Jesuits were expelled first, and they were soon followed by the Capuchins and Theatines.[224] The expulsion of the Jesuits was followed by a decree banishing them permanently from the Republic and by prohibitions against communication with them abroad by any Venetian subject.[225] Such actions may be taken as a tribute to the peculiar effectiveness of the Society in promoting ideals which, in the eyes of

[222] Documents in Cornet, "Paolo V e la Republica," pp. 83ff.

[223] See in this collection, for example, the touching letter from the nun Tadea Cossaza, to her brother, a Venetian noble, from Padua, Dec. 21, 1606, describing the isolation of a handful of nuns loyal to Venice in a convent largely hostile to the government.

[224] Cornet, pp. 84, 110, 141, n. 1, 74ff., 277–279, App. VIII; Pirri, pp. 89–204; Gilberto Govi, "La partenza dei Gesuiti dal Dominio veneto," *Memorie della Classe di Scienze fisiche, matematiche e naturali della R. Accademia dei Lincei*, ser. 4, I (1884–1885), 622–640.

[225] Cornet, pp. 105–107, 130.

the ruling group, aimed to destroy the traditional freedoms of the republic.[226] The influence of the Jesuits over women had been an object of particular anxiety,[227] and it is likely that the government was pleased to have a pretext, in the Jesuit insistence on obeying the interdict, for accomplishing what was desired on more general grounds. At any rate the government continued to collect evidence against the Jesuits long after the interdict.[228]

But although individual clergy and several religious bodies gave the government trouble, its success in keeping the mass of clergy under control was remarkable. Most of the clergy submitted[229]—a few with enthusiasm, many no doubt with reservations, some out of indifference or cowardice. The patriarch of Venice himself showed the way to the inferior ranks in the Venetian hierarchy; not only did he celebrate mass, he also ordained to the priesthood while the interdict was in force[230] and wrote in defense of the government.[231] The behavior of the Venetian clergy during this difficult period invites comparison with the behavior of English clergy in the previous century.

With the clergy generally docile and ready to demonstrate the nullity of the censures by carrying on as usual, maintenance of loyalty among the laity was relatively simple. Some territories caused the state anxiety—Bergamo and Verona, for example, were not altogether satisfied with the government's

[226] For a general indictment of the Jesuits, see Giovanni Marsilio, *Difesa a favore della risposta dell'otto propositioni* (Venice, 1606), pp. 283–284; I cite the edition in the *Raccolta*, I, 183–291. See also Giovanni Simone Sardi (pseud. for G. B. Leoni), *Due discorsi sopra la libertà ecclesiastica* (Venice, 1606), which blames the interdict on Jesuit intrigues (also in the *Raccolta*, II, 211–227). For other attacks on the Society of Jesus, cf. Offman, pp. 102–103, who represents the Jesuits as teachers of rebellion in the interest of a universal papal monarchy; Gio. Battista Palmerio, *Lettera alli fedeli sudditi del Dominio venetiano* (n.p., 1606), pp. 4–5, which depicts the special Jesuit vow of obedience as a threat to rulers; and Sarpi, *Istoria dell'Interdetto*, pp. 71–73.

[227] On this influence see letters of Provana to the Duke of Savoy, May 13, 1606, Dec. 2, 1606, and April 7, 1607, in Magistris, pp. 61, 232, 481. See also the report of Canaye to Henry IV, May 18, 1606 (III, 34). Sarpi mentioned the problem, *Istoria dell'Interdetto*, p. 73. It was also a source of special anxiety to the enemies of the Jesuits in France; cf. LeJay, *Le Tocsin au roy* (Paris, 1610), pp. 47–48.

[228] Pirri, pp. 29–30.

[229] This is recognized by Pastor, XXV, 136–138; cf. Gadaleta, "Diario," p. 102.

[230] See "Dokumente zum Ausgleich zwischen Paul V und Venedig," p. 202, for a denunciation of his behavior by the papal nuncio, July 7, 1607.

[231] *Assertiones Hieronymi Vendrameni sacredotis theologi, ac Sancti Mauritii Venetiarum Plebani tuendae contra Venetae Reipublicae Detractores ac Maledicos* (Venice, 1606).

policy.[232] But, whether from affection for the Republic, or from a mixture of local sentiment and traditional anti-curialism, the lay population of the state generally supported the government;[233] and its loyalty was carefully encouraged. While an effective system of spies and secret agents identified dissident subjects,[234] the government made sure that its grounds for opposing Rome were fully known throughout its domains. A vigorous letter addressed to all subjects of the Serenissima in early May emphasized the divine foundation of human government, made the official case for those Venetian laws and practices that had offended the pope, and appealed to a complex of lay and local prejudices. It concluded by charging the pope with rigidity and calling on all to defend their "common and particular rights." [235] Support was also stimulated by a series of public meetings; in Padua such a gathering ended with pledges of support for Venice to the death and enthusiastic shouts of "Viva San Marco!" [236] Great public displays of the wealth of Venice emphasized her dignity and power; and traditional ceremonies, such as the marriage to the sea, were celebrated with unusual éclat.[237] Meanwhile the government encouraged preaching against papalist doctrine from Venetian pulpits;[238] reports of radical sermons in Venice reached Pierre de L'Estoile in Paris.[239] Doggerel verses and other works in the

[232] Querini was fairly open about this, *Historia dell'Escommunica*, pp. 278–279. See also the evidence in Putelli, "Gonzaga e l'interdetto," pp. 129–130; *Aevum*, X (1936), 32, n. 2; Cornet, "Paulo V e la Republica," pp. 60–61. A broadsheet, headed *La Città di Verona ai Lettori*, pointedly proclaimed (as though there were some need) the loyalty of the community to Venice.

[233] Canaye was early impressed by this; see his letters to Villeroy, May 18, 1606, and Commartin, May 19, 1606 (III, 40, 42). Cornet, pp. 279–285, App. IX, gives a long list of cities and individuals on the mainland offering to support the government. For other particulars see Battistella, "Eco in Friuli"; Federigo Odorici, "Paolo V e la città di terraferma. Note istoriche in appendice al Giornale pubblicato dal Cornet," *ASI*, Ser. 2, X (1859), 179–180; and Agostino Zanelli, "Di alcune controversie tra la Repubblica di Venezia e il S. Officio nei primi anni del pontificato di Urbano VIII," *AV*, Ser. 5, VI (1929), 192–193.

[234] Cf. Provana's letter to the Duke of Savoy, June 27, 1606, in Magistris, pp. 115–116.

[235] Pp. 9–10 of the text in the *Raccolta*, I.

[236] See the report from a priest in Padua, Pirri, p. 71.

[237] Provana's letters to the Duke of Savoy, May 6, 1606, and Feb. 10, 1607, in Magistris, pp. 52, 317.

[238] Provana to the Duke of Savoy, Dec. 27, 1606, Feb. 5, 1607, March 31, 1607, *ibid.*, pp. 262, 309–310, 466; Cornet, "Paolo V e la Republica," p. 280.

[239] *Mémoires-Journaux*, ed. J. Brunet (Paris, 1875–1896), VIII, 254: "Un homme d'honneur et de qualité m'a dit que madame de Rohan l'avoit asseuré d'avoir receu lettres de Venize, par les quelles on lui mandoit que pour le present on preschoit publiquement dans

common language of Venice were also composed against the pope and·circulated as broadsheets.[240]

At the same time the government felt it essential to insist that Venetian policy involved no breach with religion, indeed was the expression of profound religious conviction. In addition, it was necessary to demonstrate constantly the meaninglessness of the interdict by a great display of religiosity. Religious observances in Venice were accordingly multiplied and celebrated with unusual publicity and ostentation. Bellarmine charged bitterly that many Venetians who before had rarely attended mass now went daily, merely to show their contempt for the pope.[241] The Senate voted substantial sums for charitable works and prayers for the state,[242] and the usual festivities were prohibited after Christmas of 1606 lest Venice should expose herself to charges of scandal.[243]

The Corpus Christi procession of 1606, early in the course of the interdict, was converted into a particular demonstration of Venetian dedication to righteousness and proper understanding of the Christian faith; several observers were sufficiently impressed to record what they saw in some detail.[244] The procession itself was unusually rich and splendid, beyond anything that could be remembered from previous years. The sacred vessels were massive and costly; and numerous clergy were required to participate, although, as one observer noted, "some of the religious in less number" than on other occasions.[245] The most interesting element in the procession was a series of representations which dramatized the Venetian cause against the pope, among others Christ with two Pharisees and the motto "Render unto Caesar the things that are Caesar's, and unto God the things that are God's";

Venize que le Pape n'avoit aucune puissance sur le temporel, mais sur le spirituel seulement; et que sa jurisdiction ne s'estendoit plus avant que sur ce qui concernoit la spiritualité, et nullement sur la temporalité."

[240] For example the *Copia d'una lettera scritta da Pisanio di Pizzoni, pescaor da Buran de Mar, a Papa Paolo V*, included (with several similar pieces) in the *Raccolta*, I, 406–412. Remarkably violent and disrespectful, it represents the pope as a violent and senile madman. For Venetian treatments of the interdict in verse see Antonio Medin, *La storia della Repubblica di Venezia nella poesia* (Milan, 1904), pp. 291–314.

[241] *Risposta ai sette*, p. 23.

[242] Cornet, pp. 59, 174.

[243] Provana to the Duke of Savoy, Jan. 9 and Feb. 5, 1607, in Magistris, pp. 284, 309.

[244] Provana to the Duke of Savoy, May 30, 1606, in *ibid.*, p. 91; Wotton to the Earl of Salisbury, May 26, 1606, Smith, I, 350; and the anonymous *relazione* in Cozzi, "Sarpi tra Canaye e Casaubon," pp. 105–106.

[245] *Ibid.*, p. 105.

the doge of Venice, aided by Saint Francis and Saint Dominic, supporting the falling church; Leonardo Donà as a youth, blessed by Saint Mark; Venice herself, constant in the faith. Other slogans traditionally cited on behalf of states were also prominent: "All power is from God," "Let every man be subject to higher powers," "My kingdom is not of this world." Henry Wotton, who observed all this with special interest, was ready with an interpretation: "The reasons of this extraordinary solemnity were two, as I conceive it. First, to contain the people still in good order with super-stition, the foolish band of obedience. Secondly, to let the Pope know (who wanteth no intelligencers) that notwithstanding his interdict, they had friars enough and other clergymen to furnish out the day." [246]

All these efforts to consolidate public opinion behind the government were enough to prevent pressures from the papalist camp from having any large effect on the Venetian populace. All available evidence indicates that, as even a Jesuit was forced to recognize, "all the people, and perhaps also many Religious [were] of a firm opinion of the justice of the cause of the republic." [247] While patricians pledged money to support the state during the crisis,[248] Venetians of the lower classes argued the Venetian cause with strangers in foreign inns. In Modena, when a priest informed two humble fishermen that they and all their countrymen were excommunicated, they took strong issue with him, claiming that Venetians were better Christians than the subjects of the pope.[249] The Venetian interdict was a failure largely because the Venetian masses were generally indifferent to it,[250] much as Venetians had been indifferent to earlier interdicts. In spite of the Counter Reformation, the secular government remained in Venice the final judge of the proper boundary between things spiritual and temporal.

Meanwhile Venice by no means neglected the possibility of military attack She began immediately after the papal brief of April to strengthen her defenses; and, according to the normal pattern in the Mediterranean world, she devoted the fall and winter of 1606/07 to preparations for war in the

[246] *Smith*, I, 350.

[247] From a memorandum in the hand of Castorio, Pirri, p. 75; cf. Canaye's letter to Commartin, April,28, 1606 (III, 17–18). Sarpi naturally emphasized popular support for Venice, *Istoria dell'Interdetto*, pp. 42, 53.

[248] Cf. Provana to the Duke of Savoy, Jan. 27, 1607, in Magistris, p. 303.

[249] This episode is described in a deposition by one of those involved before the Council of Ten, in Cornet, "Paolo V e la Republica," pp. 82–83.

[250] This is also the conclusion of Bacchion, "Vicende trivigiane," pp. 172–173, from the study of the reaction in a particular area; the people and clergy alike generally agreed with the government that the issue was political rather than religious.

spring. The Senate authorized increases in the size of the army, strengthened fortifications on the mainland, and ordered its governors overseas to look to the defenses of the islands. Troops were enlisted in Albania as well as in the *terraferma* cities, and negotiations were begun to raise more in Switzerland, Lorraine, and Germany. The fleet was prepared for action, the work being pressed forward even on holidays; and representatives of the government in foreign ports were instructed to urge Venetian sailors everywhere to return home.[251] In addition plans were made to deprive the pope of the means of financing a war by borrowing for Venice all available specie in Italy.[252]

Some Venetian maneuvers during the period of the interdict seem to have been a kind of blackmail. The government refused Turkish proposals of an alliance against Spain and the pope, although it made sure that its agent in Constantinople was in a position to give a full account of the situation to the authorities there.[253] But Venice made a considerable point of reminding Rome that previous abuses on the part of the papacy had driven faithful Catholics into heresy; Sarpi suggested broadly that Protestantism had been caused by the injudicious application of ecclesiastical censures.[254] The threat this implied was clearly recognized in Rome, where the affinities between Venetian arguments and the views of Lutherans and Calvinists received considerable emphasis.[255]

The threat was all the easier for Venice to make because of the profound interest the interdict aroused in Protestant countries, where serious division among Catholics in Italy was seen as an opportunity for the expansion of Protestantism.[256] The Estates General of the Low Countries, no doubt discerning a potential ally against Spain, promptly offered such help to Venice as it could render; and Maurice of Nassau personally tendered his services to the Republic.[257] In France various Huguenot nobles volunteered to

---

[251] Cornet, pp. 59–60, 79–80, 101, 118, 120–122, 135, 140, 161, 185, 191, 192–193, 197, 202–203, 212–213, 228; *Aevum*, X (1936), 3–6, n. 3; Provana to the Duke of Savoy, Jan. 9, 1607, in Magistris, pp. 283–284. See also the long report of Jan. 1607, prepared by Benedetto Moro for the Senate, on the military condition of the *terraferma*, in *Componimento*, pp. 362–436; and Enrico Celani, "Documenti per la storia del dissidio tra la Repubblica di Venezia a Paolo V," *AV*, Ser. 2, XVII (1899), 243–267.

[252] So Canaye reported to Henry IV, Feb. 2, 1607 (III, 460).

[253] Cornet, pp. 138, 141, 152, 211–212. See also the documents pertaining to Venetian-Turkish discussions in *Componimento*, pp. 134–149.

[254] *Apologia*, in *Scritti*, III, 88.

[255] See below, pp. 480–481.

[256] Cf. Nürnberger, "Paul V und das Interdikt," p. 208.

[257] Cornet, pp. 96, 101. Venetian replies (*ibid.*, p. 111) were grateful but noncommittal.

fight for Venice,[258] and at least one Calvinist theologian in Sedan replied to Baronius on behalf of Venice.[259] But the Protestant who interested himself most actively in the Venetian affair was the English ambassador to Venice, Sir Henry Wotton, through whom James I also followed the situation closely, characteristically attracted as much by its theoretical as by its political implications. The king professed to see in the situation an opportunity for the reunion of divided Christendom and for the comprehensive reform of the church through a general council in which England, as well, presumably, as other nations no longer in communion with Rome, would participate on equal terms. He also used the occasion to continue his personal (although hardly private) controversies with Bellarmine; and he gave a vague promise of support for Venice in the event that Spain should give military assistance to the pope.[260]

Wotton himself discerned major possibilities for both England and Protestantism in the situation. Violently antipapal, as became an Anglican diplomat, he rejoiced, as he wrote the Earl of Salisbury at the start of the interdict, "to have lived to see a Pope notoriously despised by a neighbor state." [261] He praised the "wisdom and magnanimity" with which Venice had handled the affair, and he expressed his hope for true religion in Italy as a result. "I hope God hath appointed the re-entrance of His truth by such a beginning into this goodly country, which hath so long slept in error and ease," he wrote; "and as his Majesty shall have the honour, so I will have my part in the comfort, that this poor family [i.e., the ambassador's household] hath given them the first example (and I hope without any notorious scandal to our profession) of God's incorrupted service on this side of the mountains, since the Goths and Vandals did pass them, and confounded the marks and limits both of State and of religion." [262] Frequently in the College to encourage the Venetians to persevere "in so good a cause," [263] his enthusiastic offers of service finally went far beyond his instructions. He was particularly ardent in the promotion of a league of states, to include Venice

---

[258] *Ibid.*, p. 115, n. 2.

[259] L'Estoile, VIII, 271, for Jan. 1607. L'Estoile thought it worthless. This is probably the same work whose publication, according to Canaye, offended the Venetian Senate, which wanted no association with Protestants (letter to Commartin, Nov. 3, 1606, III, 263).

[260] Cornet, pp. 108–109, 125, 152–153. Cf. Sarpi, *Istoria dell'Interdetto*, pp. 60–61, 95.

[261] April 28, 1606, Smith, I, 346.

[262] May 19, 1606, *ibid.*, I, 349.

[263] As he reported to Salisbury, Feb. 2, 1607, *ibid.*, I, 374.

but for the most part Protestant, which would bring the pope and Spain to their knees and, in general, protect the rights of sovereigns against the pretensions of the papacy.[264] The Venetians responded politely but refused the service of English volunteers and made no commitments.[265] Although, as Fra Fulgenzio Micanzio explained many years later, the predicament of Venice required her to listen to all those with whom she might have a common interest,[266] she was not at all sympathetic to proposals for action that might disturb the peace of Italy, and her foreign policy had long been opposed to entangling alliances. It was perhaps enough for her purposes that the frequent visits of the English ambassador to the College should be known in Rome.

In fact, although Venice had no objection to frightening Rome (while insisting on her complete loyalty to the Catholic faith) with the possibility that she might make common cause with the Protestants, her major appeal for support abroad had a different basis. She aimed to convince the rest of the world that the Venetian cause was in principle the cause of all sovereign states, and that through Venice the pope was striking at every independent prince and at the political liberties and the dignity of the entire secular world.[267] Her essential case was not that of the Reformation but of the Renaissance.[268]

To make this case foreign diplomats in Venice were kept informed of the situation as it developed, and Venetian envoys everywhere were from the beginning instructed to give full accounts of the course of events and of the Venetian position to the governments to which they had been posted. As early as December 1605, the ambassadors in Vienna, Paris, and Madrid were provided with an official explanation of the Venetian position which emphasized the traditional character of Venetian claims and pointed to similar practices elsewhere. Spain was by no means excluded from this effort; in April the Spanish ambassador in Venice was informed by the doge that the real aims of the pope were "to command absolutely in temporal

[264] Smith makes this point, I, 75ff.; cf. Cornet, pp. 87–88, 120, 146–148, 189, 191, 194, 206–207.

[265] Provana to the Duke of Savoy, Nov. 15, 1606, in Magistris, pp. 216–217; Cornet, p. 140.

[266] *Vita di Fra Paolo*, pp. 157–158.

[267] Sarpi made the point repeatedly in the *Istoria dell'Interdetto*.

[268] The Venetians were at some pains to refute imputations of Protestant sympathy. See Donà's rejection of the charge of Calvinism to Castro, Nov. 17, 1606, in Cornet, pp. 295–296, App. XII. See also Micanzio's discussion of this issue, *Vita di Fra Paolo*, pp. 156ff

things, and to subordinate all princes to his power even in lay matters." [269]
Such tactics on the part of Venice naturally caused indignation and anxiety
in Rome.[270] From the Venetian standpoint, to assert that the cause of
Venice was the cause of all sovereign states was not only immediately
useful to gain sympathy elsewhere in Europe; it was also a way of asserting
the equality of the Republic in an important qualitative sense with the big
powers. In addition, to insist that an Italian republic was the same sort of
entity as the great states beyond the Alps emphasized the universal application
of the political teachings of the Italian Renaissance.

But Venice was not content to state her case merely through official
diplomatic exchanges, which could provide only a limited forum for
publicizing an elaborate and complex position with the broadest possible
ramifications. The Venetian position was also elaborated by a large-scale
literary effort, both in Italy and abroad, which aimed to meet the papal
challenge at every point, to state as strongly as possible the case for Venice,
and to point out the consequences of a papal victory for the whole of
European Christendom. This effort had the particular advantage over formal
pronouncements by the government that it could be advanced by statements
which were often technically no more than expressions of individual
opinion. They could be prepared rapidly and with a minimum of care, they
could range freely over the issues, they could exploit a variety of rhetorical
devices, they could hint and insinuate what might be unwise to state openly,
and if they went too far they could be disowned by the government.[271]
By the same token, because of the freedom with which they were composed,
the numerous books and pamphlets written on behalf of Venice are often
more revealing about Venetian attitudes and Venetian claims than any
official statement.

The Venetians began to consider literary justification of their position in
reaction to news that theologians were taking up their pens in Rome. Early
in April the government directed Nani and Duodo to remind the pope that
two could play at this game. They were to tell him that Venice had numerous
formidable authorities on her side, all eager to defend her; and a month
later the Senate set aside four hundred ducats to "recognize the labors" of

[269] Cornet, pp. 15–16, 52, 57–58, 60–61, 68.
[270] Cardinal Borghese expressed anxiety over this development as early as April 29,
1606, in a letter to the nuncio in Turin, in Magistris, p. 36.
[271] Sarpi also recommended unofficial statements of the Venetian position because it
was inconsistent with the government's dignity to justify its acts publicly (*Consulto su i
remedii da opporsi ad una eventuale aggravazione della scommunica*, in *Scritti*, II, 168).

those busy writing about "present matters." [272] For the time being, nevertheless, Venice moved cautiously, no doubt hopeful that, if she behaved with sufficient determination at the outset and avoided provoking her adversary excessively, the pope might still back down. The first compositions prepared in defense of Venice were therefore, for the most part, not immediately printed but held in reserve.[273]

But there was one fateful exception to this cautious policy. During the spring an anonymous editor (actually Paolo Sarpi) published a vernacular version of a short work by Jean Gerson on the validity of excommunication, accompanying it with a short prefatory letter, falsely dated from Paris, in praise of that author.[274] The offense which this action gave in Rome was extreme.[275] Gerson's argument was bad enough; he had been concerned to describe theoretical situations in which ecclesiastical censures represented an abuse of the power of the keys and were therefore invalid, and his suggestion that it might be meritorious to resist an improper excommunication implied some right of private judgment against the authority of prelates. But even more was involved. The appeal to Gerson was clearly intended to recall the existence of a medieval tradition regarding ecclesiastical government which the papacy now wanted forgotten, and also to secure Gallican support for an opponent with which the Curia had hoped to deal in isolation.[276] In addition publication of such a work in Italian deliberately took the discussion out of the hands of professional theologians and invited the participation of the laity, a precedent that struck Rome as full of danger.[277] The Venetian argument that the papal condemnation of Venice had to be

[272] Cornet, pp. 47–48, 82.

[273] Cozzi, "Sarpi tra Canaye e Casaubon," pp, 59–60. Querini's *Aviso* and Sarpi's *Considerazioni sopra le censure* were not immediately printed; Marsilio's *Risposta d'un dottore in theologie* was withdrawn from circulation after criticism. Cf. Canaye's letter to Alincourt, June 3, 1606 (III, 68). On the apprehension created by the prospect of Venetian publication in Rome, see Cardinal Borghese's letter to the nuncio in Savoy, April 29, 1606, Magistris, p. 36.

[274] *Trattato e resoluzione sopra la validità delle scommuniche di Giovanni Gersone*, in *Scritti*, II, 171–184.

[275] See Cozzi, "Sarpi tra Canaye e Casaubon," p. 58; cf. Cornet, p. 89, n. 1.

[276] For the popularity of Gerson in France at this time, see Delaruelle et al., *L'Église au temps du Grand Schisme*, II. 862.

[277] Bellarmine, *Risposta a fra'Paolo*, p. 116, specifically attacked vernacular publication. Bovio, *Lettera . . . al R. P. M. Paolo Rocca*, A3ᵛ–A4, had been particularly concerned about this issue. It would have been a better proof of their interest in the truth, he reminded the Venetians after publication of the letters of the doge to the clergy and people of Venice, had they published in Latin for the learned, instead of seeking to deceive and seduce the simple.

answered in the language in which it had been disseminated[278] hardly met
the objection. For Rome ecclesiastical authority alone should properly deal
with such matters. But Pandora's box had been opened; and, both sides
needing now to persuade the same lay audience, much of the exchange that
followed was conducted in the vernacular. Late in the summer Bellarmine
replied to Sarpi-Gerson in Italian;[279] and he was soon joined, though first
in Latin, by Baronius. From this point the literary battle grew increasingly
heated. Venice, indignant at the onslaught of the two most famous
writers in Rome, now began to publish numerous works in her own
defense.[280]

Much of the discussion was carried on anonymously or pseudonymously,
a tactic that Rome occasionally professed to find (when adopted by Venice)
outrageous.[281] It may be that the cause of her anger went rather deeper
than a natural frustration at the obstacle this presented to identifying and
denouncing the guilty. To publish anonymously was also a means of
evading the surveillance of authority; anonymity created an area of individual liberty, and therefore it raised a serious issue of principle.

The more important of those who wrote for Venice, however, were
generally known, not only because they signed their names at least to some
of their works, but also because they formed a kind of theological council
to supervise the literary campaign.[282] The names of seven of them were
attached to a general defense of the Venetian position, issued during the
summer, whose systematic and general character suggests that it was directed
above all to the Venetian clergy. The seven were also given regular pensions
by the government.[283] In addition other theologians associated themselves

---

[278] Offered by Marsilio, *Essame*, II, 2.

[279] With the *Risposta ad un libretto di Gio. Gersone*.

[280] On the effect of the works of Bellarmine and Baronius in stimulating the Venetian
literary campaign, see the letter of Canaye to Du Perron, Aug. 25, 1606 (III, 191). He
had foreseen this result and had tried to prevent the Roman publications (letters to Alincourt and Villeroy, June 14 and July 15, 1606, pp. 76, 124, 126). Sarpi himself, conveniently forgetting his edition of Gerson, represented August as the beginning of the
literary war, "offensive on the side of the pope, defensive on the side of the republic"
(*Istoria dell'Interdetto*, p. 102). Many Venetian writings issued from the presses of Roberto
Meietti; on him see Dennis E. Rhodes, "Roberto Meietti e alcuni documenti della
controversia fra Papa Paolo V e Venezia," *Studi secenteschi*, I (1960), 165–174,

[281] See, for example, Bellarmine's attack on the printing of anonymous works in
Risposta alla Risposta, p. 151.

[282] Cornet, p. 123.

[283] This work was the *Trattato dell'Interdetto*, included in the *Scritti*, III, 1–41. For the
pensions of its authors, see Cornet, p. 142, n. 1.

with the Venetian cause. The most prominent of the Venetian theologians was Sarpi himself, the author of the most vigorous and incisively argued of the many works in favor of Venice.[284] The degree to which he dominated the campaign, like his influence on the government, has nevertheless been exaggerated: he was by no means the only man of ability on the Venetian side. His *Considerazioni sopra le censure* was an unusually careful presentation of the Venetian case; its preparation, commissioned by the government late in the winter, took Sarpi several months.[285] He followed it with an elaborate reply to Bellarmine's attack on the arguments of Gerson.[286] Sarpi's services were highly regarded; at the end of September the Senate doubled his stipend.[287]

The closest to Sarpi personally among his collaborators was the younger Servite monk, Fra Fulgenzio Micanzio, whose devotion to Sarpi has tended somewhat to obscure his own real abilities.[288] Born near Brescia in 1570,[289] Micanzio, unlike some of his theological colleagues, was a subject of the Republic, and he was destined to show a loyalty to Venice equal to Sarpi's. He had been in Venice during the last decade of the sixteenth century, when he frequented the *ridotto* Morosini with Sarpi; and, a teacher of theology at Bologna on the eve of the interdict, he returned to Venice to assist Sarpi on the occasion of the latter's appointment as *consultore* to the Republic. When Sarpi died, Micanzio succeeded him in this office. After he joined Sarpi, it was remembered to Micanzio's discredit that he had suggested the possibility of salvation for Greek Christians;[290] but he was invaluable to Sarpi, who recognized his devotion and relied on him heavily.[291] Micanzio, for example, went systematically through the *Annals* of Baronius, taking

[284] This was widely recognized at the time, for example by L'Estoile, VIII, 245. Not long after the interdict, nevertheless, Sarpi was critical of his own contribution to the discussion at that time. See his letter to Gillot, March 18, 1608, Ulianich, p. 127, in which he explains that it had been defective through the need to write very quickly and to appeal to a general audience.

[285] See the remarks of Gambarin, *Scritti*, III, 282–283.

[286] These works appeared at the end of the summer; cf. Canaye's letters to Commartin, Aug. 25 and Sept. 22, 1606 (III, 188, 218).

[287] Cornet, p. 142, n. 1.

[288] Cf. Cozzi, "Sarpi, l'anglicanesimo e la Historia," p. 593, n. 1.

[289] For his biography see Antonio Favaro, "Fra Fulgenzio Micanzio e Galileo Galilei," *AV*, Ser. 3, XIII (1907), 35ff.

[290] See the letter from an unidentified writer presumably known to the pope, July 20, 1606, *Aevum*, X (1936), 20n.

[291] Cf. Sarpi's remarks as reported by Christoph von Dohna, July 28, 1608, *Briefe und Akten*, II, 79.

careful notes;[292] and, working with Sarpi, he prepared a long reply to various papalist attacks on his master.[293]

Others who argued the Venetian cause, some with considerable learning and intellectual force, were not native Venetians. About their motives in offering themselves to Venetian service one can only speculate. Some were doubtless merely representative of that restless and shadowy literary under-world, the degenerate heritage of the rhetorical tradition of the Renaissance, which could always produce brains and pens for sale to any buyer, but others may have shared in some degree the convictions they were paid to defend. Among these foreigners the most effective was probably Giovanni Marsilio, a Neapolitan and a former Jesuit.[294] A theologian of considerable learning, his mental constitution particularly qualified him for discourse with ' men of his own kind; and his manner of expression, in contrast to Sarpi's usual style of discourse, was often strikingly scholastic.[295] He com-posed vigorous replies to both Bellarmine and Baronius.[296] He was eventually accused of seeking to establish an "academy" for teaching subversive doctrine,[297] a charge that testifies to his personal influence. The Franciscan theologian Marc'Antonio Capello, it may also be observed, previously a friend of Possevino, exhibited a similar cast of mind in his reply to Bellarmine.[298] Although Capello was a native Venetian, ecclesiastical pressures were eventually stronger in his case than patriotism, and just before the interdict was lifted he fled to Rome.[299]

But the literary defense of Venice was not left only to clerical theologians.

[292] This work was called to my attention by Professor Delio Cantimori. It is now in the Biblioteca Marciana, Ms. It., Classe XI, Cod. 174.

[293] The work described in note 189 above, which in passing replied to others besides Bovio. Early in it Micanzio stated that he was writing out of devotion to Sarpi as well as to Venice (p. 5).

[294] See the attack on him in Possevino's *Risposta di Teodoro Eugenio*, p. 6. Provana de-scribed him as a mere pedant in his dispatch of Aug. 8, 1606, to the Duke of Savoy, in Magistris, p. 156.

[295] As in his *Risposta d'un dottore in theologia* (n.p., n.d.), for the most part a systematic list of propositions, each supported by a massive anthology of authorities.

[296] His *Votum pro republica veneta* (Venice, 1606) is directed against Baronius; his *Difesa a favore della risposta* is in reply to Bellarmine.

[297] The Roman deposition by the now renegade Fulgenzio Manfredi (in Savio, *Aevum*, X (1936), 21) made this charge. Certain dispatches of the nuncio after the interdict also suggest Marsilio's importance (*ibid.*, p. 25, n. 1).

[298] *Delle controversie tra il sommo pontefice Paulo Quinto, et la serenissima republica di Venetia* (Venice, 1606).

[299] Provana to the Duke of Savoy, March 31, 1607, in Magistris, p. 466. See also the instruction of the Council of Ten that he be apprehended if possible, in Cornet, "Paolo V e la Republica," pp. 111–112.

Among the numerous minor pamphlets were replies to Possevino framed by foreign writers who claimed to have known him as students.[300] But the most prominent layman to serve Venice with his pen was Antonio Querini, a patrician of some importance in the government, whose *Aviso delle ragioni della Serenissima Republica di Venetia* made a typically Venetian demand for a more purely spiritual church. Above all, however, this work offered a vigorous defense of the Venetian position on political grounds; its emphasis on the necessities of the state and the duties of governments to meet them made it seem particularly appropriate for dissemination abroad. The Senate although it delayed domestic publication of the work, ordered it sent to all representatives of Venice at foreign courts.[301] Rome took an especially dark view of Querini and his malignant influence on the highest councils of the state.[302]

The government also made a major effort to recruit French writers on behalf of Venice.[303] The Venetian ambassador in Paris, Pietro Priuli, was supplied with substantial sums of money for this purpose. Although he found the theologians at the Sorbonne reluctant to come out openly against the pope, one of them supplied him with a list of older works whose republication might serve as an oblique defense of the traditional character of the Venetian position, among them the *De potestate regia et papali* of John of Paris and writings by Ockham, Pierre d'Ailly, Almain, and John Major. Priuli was more successful in enlisting the services of laymen. The Gallican jurists Louis Servin and Jacques Leschassier both composed short tracts in defense of Venice which sought to establish the identity of French and Venetian interests against Rome.[304] The Huguenot scholar Isaac Casaubon was also persuaded to begin, although he did not finish, a work in favor of Venice.[305]

For Venice to discuss issues and to justify her conduct was itself an act of

---

[300] So Offman's *Avvertimento, et ammonitione catolica* and *Condoglienza di Stanislas Przvovski Lublinense studente in Padova* (n.p., n.d.), in the *Raccolta*, II, 228–233, which particularly assailed the Jesuits for meddling in the politics of eastern Europe.

[301] Cornet, p. 110, n. 2. See the discussion of this in Cozzi, "Sarpi tra Canaye e Casaubon," pp. 59–60.

[302] See the *Relatione* in Odorici, "Paolo V e le città," p. 174.

[303] For what follows, see Ulianich, pp. xxviiff.

[304] Louis Servin was the author of *Pro libertate status et reipublicae venetorum Gallofranci ad Philenetum epistola* (Paris, 1607), Leschassier of *Consultatio Parisii cujusdam de controversia inter sanctitatem Pauli V et Serenis. Rempublicam Venetam, ad virum clariss. Venetum* (Paris, 1606).

[305] Entitled *De libertate ecclesiastica liber singularis ad viros politicos qui de controversia inter Paulum V Pontificem Maximum et Rempublicam Venetam edoceri cupiunt.*

defiance against an ecclesiastical authority which demanded immediate and simple obedience, and various compositions defending Venice had also to devote some attention to justifying their own existence. One early pamphlet offered the excuse, dressed up as a legal opinion, that self-defense was a right of nature to which even the pope must defer. It also defended in general terms the right of free speech.[306] Sarpi himself was later to explain that the writings composed on behalf of Venice merely spelled out in words the meanings implicit in the actions of the Venetian government; if the latter could be justified, then obviously the former could be justified as well. For this reason, he argued, Venice could never repudiate the doctrines advanced in her behalf.[307] He neatly summarized the essential arguments in this huge body of literature as he had summarized the position of the other side: that God had instituted two powers in the world, presumably parallel; that divine law does not exempt the clergy from that obedience to the secular authority required of all men; and that, since infallibility belongs to God alone, it is altogether proper to admit the possibility of papal error in a given instance.[308] As with the writings from the papal side, detailed analysis of the various contentions offered in behalf of Venice will be presented in the next chapter; their general bearing should nevertheless be kept in mind at this point because it explains the violent reaction they produced in Rome.

Rome expressed its displeasure at the Venetian literary campaign by the most furious denunciations, both of the tactic itself and of those who took part in it, and by making every effort to stop it. The pope himself spoke of the Venetian compositions as "pernicious little books" containing "manifest heresies."[309] Bellarmine was fairly restrained. He suggested that the Venetian writers were hardly among "the most reformed Religious"; they had not come, he continued with conscious understatement, from the ranks of "the best Priests, or the most famous Theologians in the Church"; they rather resembled those who had misled Germany.[310] In September and October the works of Sarpi and other Venetian theologians were examined by the Holy Office and found to contain numerous "temeritous, calumnious,

---

[306] *Ad Paulum V. pontificem maximum epistolae duorum clarissimorum Italiae iurisconsultorum* (Venice, 1606); in *Raccolta*, I, 127–135.

[307] *Scrittura in difesa delle opere scritte a favore della serenissima republica nella controversia col sommo pontefice*, in *Scritti*, III, 234–257, a work of 1608; the passage cited is on p. 234.

[308] *Ibid.*, pp. 237ff. See also his summary, *Istoria dell'Interdetto*, pp. 106–108.

[309] See the passages collected in Taucci, *Intorno alle lettere*, pp. 118–119; and the letter of Cardinal Du Perron to Henry IV, Sept. 4, 1606 (*Ambassades*, pp. 508–509).

[310] *Risposta a fra'Paolo*, p. 135.

scandalous, seditious, erroneous, and heretical propositions"; and those whom Rome now identified as the three leading Venetian publicists, Sarpi, Giovanni Marsilio, and the Franciscan Fulgenzio Manfredi, who had been preaching the Venetian case in various churches,[311] were directed to appear personally before the tribunal of the Inquisition in Rome, under penalty of excommunication.[312] The three preferred to remain in Venice, where, indeed, they compounded their offenses by publishing formal replies to the citations against them,[313] and their excommunications followed as a matter of course.[314] Meanwhile other efforts were made to detach the theologians from Venetian service. Possevino, for example, hinted to Capello that his abandonment of Venice would find some material reward.[315] Sarpi maintained that the whole papalist attempt to put an end to public defense of the Venetian position was only a dreary confession of the weakness of the case for the pope; he insisted that it had been so interpreted by the world at large.[316]

The world at large was, at any rate, remarkably interested in the whole affair; and in this respect, at least, the Venetian effort to open up the issues behind the struggle to general discussion was a considerable success. One of the most interesting (and, no doubt, from the standpoint of ecclesiastical authority, alarming) elements in the situation was the eagerness of many observers to study both sides of the question in order, presumably, to make up their own minds. This interest is attested by the existence of anthologies of writings on the interdict, printed in 1607 in Latin, Italian, and French, which assembled side by side the major tracts emanating from both Rome and

[311] The author of *Degnità procuratoria di S. Marco* (Venice, 1602), he was well regarded in Venice before the interdict. A flattering notice concerning him appears in Giovanni Stringa's 1604 edition of Francesco Sansovino's *Venetia città nobilissima*, sig. PPPPPlv. But he may have had trouble before with the ecclesiastical authorities; see *Aevum*, XI (1937), 316–317 n. Never given official appointment by the government (as Sarpi insisted to Groslot, Nov. 11, 1608, Busnelli, I, 43), his sermons, as they were reported in Rome, were considered particularly offensive (correspondence of the Duke of Mantua with Ercole Udine and Giovanni Magno, Aug. 1606, in *Componimento*, pp. 351–362).

[312] Taucci, *Intorno alle lettere*, p. 70. For the particular passages censured in Sarpi's writing, see *ibid.*, pp. 119ff.

[313] *Theologorum venetorum Jo. Marsilii, Paulo veneti et fr. Fulgentii ad excommunicationis, citationis et monitionis romanae sententiam in ipsos latam responsio* (Venice, 1607); in *Raccolta*, II, 257–271.

[314] Text of Sarpi's excommunication, Jan. 5, 1607, in Vincenzo M. Buffon, *Chiesa di Cristo e Chiesa romana nelle opere e nelle lettere di fra Paolo Sarpi* (Louvain, 1941), p. 7n.

[315] In the *Lettera* cited above, n. 187, p. 238, in the *Raccolta*.

[316] *Apologia*, in *Scritti*, III, 114. L'Estoile commented on the futility of papal efforts to suppress Venetian writings (*Mémoires*, VIII, 245).

Venice;[317] Venice, as a mark of confidence in her cause, took some initiative in publishing these collections. Other collections favored one side or another. A volume of Venetian compositions in German translation, for example, appeared at Frankfurt am Main.[318] Numerous works also circulated individually: Venetian writings sent to Paris as soon as they appeared, some of them published there in clandestine editions;[319] papalist works sold at the Frankfurt fair.[320] Interested persons, like the scholar Casaubon, also wrote letters on the subject to their friends.[321] The world clearly had plenty of opportunity to study what was involved in the case.

Insofar as it reacted to the issues themselves, its response was on the whole favorable to Venice: it seemed clear enough that Venice did represent against the pope the interests of all sovereign governments. James of England, as was to be expected, had no compunction about admitting as much to the Venetian ambassador.[322] But even the most staunchly Catholic among the ruling groups of Europe gave signs of sympathy for the Venetian cause, among them several petty princelings of Italy. The Duke of Savoy refused to allow the censures against Venice to be promulgated, and prohibited his archbishop from publishing a general condemnation of Venetian writings.[323] In Poland the Diet disapproved of the interdict against Venice, and the Polish king forbade its publication; the archbishop of Warsaw was sympathetic to Venice, and the bishop of Cracow gave instructions that Venetians should be allowed to attend all religious services.[324] Indeed, signs of approval for Venice, at least in principle, were not lacking even in

[317] *Controversiae memorabiles inter Paulum V Pontificem Max. et Venetos; De excommunicatione contra eosdem Venetos Romae promulgata XVII. Aprilis anno MDCVI. Acta et scripta varia controversiae inter Paulum V et Venetos* (Vicenza, 1607); the *Raccolta* cited above, Ch. VI, n. 87, which is somewhat fuller; and *Pieces du memorable proces esmeu l'an M.DC.VI. entre le pape Paul V et les seigneurs de Venise* (Saint Vincent, 1607).

[318] *Excommunication oder Bannbrieff Pauli V Röm Bapsts wider den Durchleutigen Hertzog Rath und gantze Gemein zu Venedig*, listed in Richard Krebs, *Die politische Publizistik der Jesuiten und ihrer Gegner in den letzten Jahrzehnten vor Ausbruch des dreissigjährigen Krieges* (Halle, 1890), p. 138.

[319] Ulianich, p. xxviii; L'Estoile, *Mémoires*, VIII, 254.

[320] L'Estoile, VIII, 295, listed several papalist works he had acquired from this source.

[321] Casaubon wrote on the subject to Petau and Scaliger (Ulianich, p. xxviii).

[322] Cornet, pp. 152–153, for the ambassador's report of the king's words.

[323] Magistris, p. 69, n. 1; Cardinal Borghese to the nuncio in Turin, July 25, 1606, in *ibid.*, pp. 147–148, reporting the pope's displeasure and ordering a protest. The court of Mantua, on the other hand, was hostile to Venice (Putelli, "Gonzaga e l'interdetto," pp. 204ff.).

[324] Cornet, pp. 114–115; Pastor, XXV, 166.

Habsburg lands. The Venetian ambassador to the imperial court reported his clear impression that the ministers with whom he conferred found the Venetian case entirely compelling, and they were strongly inclined to criticize the pope.[325] Venetian residents in the Spanish dependencies in Italy also reported support for Venice: Venetian writings were eagerly read in Milan; in Naples pamphlets attacking Venice were suppressed, and the viceroy agreed that the rights of all lay princes were at stake in the affair; important personages in Palermo secretly praised those Venetian laws relating to ecclesiastical affairs that had so angered the pope.[326] In Turin the Spanish ambassador expressed his personal approval of the Venetian cause,[327] and influential members of the Spanish clergy favored the admission of the Venetian ambassador to divine services in Madrid.[328]

The most enthusiastic foreign partisans of Venice were the Gallican magistrates of Paris, where Latin epigrams circulated against the pope and his supporters.[329] Servin and Leschassier, as we have noted, had been persuaded to write in behalf of Venice. Both men of dignity, their participation in the struggle suggests how easily Gallican circles saw the Venetian position as their own. Pierre de L'Estoile, another member of this group, carefully recorded in his journal the course of events in Italy, collected the writings of both sides, and systematically set down a series of reactions wholly favorable to Venice.[330] He noted the particular interest of France in the expulsion of the Jesuits from the territories of the Republic, an event which evoked the publication of verses in Paris.[331] The writings of Sarpi, he reported, were "seen in Paris and much praised and collected by all good and learned men." Sarpi's life, he noted, was proving even more persuasive on behalf of Venice than his arguments; it had caused him first of all to be "admired and revered in Venice as a saint," and it had given "great weight and authority to his books." L'Estoile so esteemed Sarpi that he bought a duplicate of the *Considerazioni sopra le censure* (in its French translation) to circulate among his friends.[332] At the same time, the writings of Bellarmine

[325] Cornet, pp. 70–71, and nn. 1–2.

[326] *Ibid.*, pp. xv, 155, n. 2, 78, 110.

[327] Pietro Contarini, the Venetian ambassador, to the doge, May 6, 1606, in Magistris, pp. 51–52.

[328] Cornet, pp. 113–114, n. 1.

[329] L'Estoile, VIII, 275, 292–293.

[330] *Ibid.*, pp. 198–199ff. By early summer of 1607 he had accumulated fifty-three compositions defending and attacking the interdict (p. 310).

[331] *Ibid.*, p. 222.

[332] *Ibid.*, p. 255. L'Estoile also thought well of Querini's *Aviso*, though he did not regard it so highly as Sarpi's work (p. 261).

and Baronius filled him with distaste.[333] Nor, indeed, did such interest as L'Estoile displayed in the resistance of Venice to the pope decline quickly. Jacques de Thou was eager to include an account of it in the *Historiae sui temporis*,[334] and the whole episode was still vivid enough seven years later to require extensive treatment in the first volume of the *Mercure François*.[335] The papal nuncio, on the other hand, was much distressed by the degree of French interest in the Venetian cause and by the indifference of the French government to the dangers it presented.[336] His concern was obviously a further tribute to the success of Venice in stimulating attention to the issues implicit in the situation.

At the same time it is also clear that no power, however attractive it may have found the Venetian case, was willing to support the Republic merely out of a general and rather theoretical sympathy. To some extent the failure of the secular powers to side openly with Venice reflected their appraisal of the practical significance of the papal offensive. They saw in it little danger to themselves, and their nonchalance was perhaps a more devastating comment on the ambitions of the Counter Reformation than their active support for the beleaguered Republic might have been. At the same time they were concerned to prevent the Venetian crisis, so petty in itself however freighted with theoretical significance for the contenders,[337] from turning into a general European war. The Habsburg powers and France feared each other far more than they feared the pope, even a pope victorious over Venice. The Venetian interdict therefore became an occasion for further jockeying between France, Spain, and the Empire. For this reason it distantly continued the earlier Habsburg-Valois struggles over Italy (as, indeed, contemporaries were inclined to recognize)[338] as well as being one of the earliest among the crises leading to the Thirty Years' War.

[333] *Ibid.*, pp. 270, 281.

[334] This seems to have provided the initial impetus for Sarpi's *Istoria dell'Interdetto*. See Gambarin on the background of this work in the edition cited, pp. 245ff.

[335] *Le Mercure François*, I (Paris, 1614), 48a–70a, 89b–104b, 120a–128a. The treatment, detached in tone, incorporates many documents from both sides.

[336] Letter of June 9, 1609, *Aevum*, X (1936), 70.

[337] In his letter to Henry IV, May 18, 1606 (III, 33), Canaye paraphrased the king's view of the behavior of both sides: "... an Iliad of inconveniences for a Helen of so little merit that all past history reveals no example of Christendom being troubled for a thing so trifling."

[338] The Duke of Savoy, whose position between the great powers gave him some grounds for anxiety, saw in the Venetian crisis a threat of the resumption of the Italian wars of the previous century. For this echo of Renaissance politics, see the very interesting letter of Pietro Contarini to the doge, March 30, 1607, in Magistris, p. 460.

In addition to their common attitudes toward the struggle, each side had particular interests to protect or to prosecute. The states of Europe failed to aid Venice because each was primarily concerned to promote its own advantage. They were much less interested in the principles both sides invited them to support than in such possibilities as the situation might offer for the extension of influence in Italy or the enlargement of national or dynastic prestige. The election of Paul V, as we have noted, had been interpreted as a victory for France, and to protect his advantage at the Curia Henry IV had now to avoid being carried away by such sympathies as the Venetian cause might naturally have aroused in him. At the same time he hoped somehow to retain the friendship of Venice, which might still be useful in the event of war.[339] Spain, on the other hand, regardless of her sensitivity to the general interests of princes, saw in the situation an opportunity to weaken an old obstacle to her Italian hegemony and to recover her position as the most reliable arm of the church. But both powers were disposed to behave with great caution, playing on Roman fear of Venice or Venetian fear of Rome chiefly to induce greater reliance on themselves, and meanwhile protesting friendship and offering service to both sides.

Venice hoped above all for the support of France, partly because assistance from a Catholic power would not compromise her claim to respect the traditional faith, partly because alliance with Spain was obviously out of the question.[340] A close understanding with Savoy would also have been desirable; but Savoy was under pressure to declare for the pope[341] and, without a firm commitment from France, was too weak for anything but neutrality. It suited France to be regarded as the major protector of Venice, at least up to the point at which any real action might have been required; and the French ambassador, Canaye de Fresnes, personally favorable to

[339] Cf. his letter to the Venetian government, Feb. 15, 1606 (*Lettres*, VI, 580), in which he refers to "la parfaicte amitie que les Roys nos predecesseurs ont entretenue de tous les temps avec vostre honorable republique. A quoy nous correspondrons tousjours par tous vrais et sinceres effects."

[340] Venice took great care to keep France fully informed of developments in Italy, especially involving Spain; cf. Cornet, pp. 30–31, 48–52, 59, 98–100, 119, 154, 187–188. See also Querini, *Historia dell'Escomunica*, pp. 265–266, which speaks of balancing Spanish support for the pope with aid from both France and England.

[341] Cornet, p. 211, n. 3. That the Duke of Savoy was personally sympathetic to Venice is suggested by his attendance, with his sons, at a carnival celebration at the house of the Venetian ambassador (Contarini to the doge, Feb. 24, 1607, in Magistris, p. 334). But Florence was generally hostile to Venice; see Querini, *Historia dell'Escomunica*, pp. 268–269, 272–273.

Venice, promoted the idea of a close Franco-Venetian alliance. He was inclined to see the Venetian interdict as a major turning point both for the evolution of Catholicism and for the European position of France. He tended to identify the two: the predominance of France in Europe would promote, in his view, healthier tendencies in the church.[342]

But while Canaye hoped personally that France would try to settle the affair on Venetian terms, other French statesmen had rather different purposes. Although the French king professed displeasure at papal tactics[343] and refused to bar the Venetian ambassador from religious services in Paris,[344] he was evidently alarmed by the provocative behavior of the Venetians, concerned lest Venice misinterpret the benevolence of France and reject reasonable terms of accommodation with the pope, and irritated by Venetian intransigence.[345] His real aim, in which he was supported by Villeroy and Cardinal Du Perron, was to play peacemaker in Italy, a role calculated to increase his influence in both Venice and Rome and to reduce the influence of Spain. This role required encouragement of Venice within limits (lest there be no crisis to exploit in his own interest), but above all the preservation of his own reputation for neutrality.[346] It is hardly surprising, therefore, that Venice eventually grew increasingly suspicious of the good faith of France.[347]

The policy of Spain was determined by similar considerations. She encouraged the pope to take a firm line,[348] but her vague promises of military support in the event of war were based on a strong conviction that war was unlikely.[349] Meanwhile her ambassador in Venice, Francisco de

[342] His activities and aims are discussed in Cozzi, "Sarpi tra Canaye e Casaubon," pp. 20 ff. For Rome's displeasure with him, see Nürnberger, p. 511, n. 1. Canaye generally described the issues behind the interdict in a way favorable to Venice, identifying the Venetian position with his own Gallican views; for examples see his letters to Henry IV, April 19, 1606; to Villeroy, Oct. 5, 1606; and to Alincourt, April 15, 1606 (III, 5–10, 229, 2–3). He admired both the doge and Sarpi (letters to Commartin, July 18 and Aug. 25, 1606, ibid., pp. 143, 162, 188). As a diplomat he nevertheless attempted to maintain a proper reserve; cf. his letter to the king, May 3, 1606 (ibid., p. 26).

[343] Cornet, pp. 30–31, 36, 92.

[344] Sarpi, Storia dell'Interdetto, p. 60.

[345] Cornet, pp. 128–130. See his letter to Canaye, July 18, 1606. (Lettres, VI, 637–638).

[346] Cornet, pp. 78–79, 120, 122–123, 155–156, 164–165, 204–205, 207. For Du Perron see Cozzi, "Sarpi tra Canaye e Casaubon," p. 38.

[347] Cornet, p. 197 n.

[348] The text of Philip III's very general pledge of support is given in Cornet, App. X, p. 285.

[349] Priuli reported from Madrid that Spain would fight for the pope only in the event of a Venetian attack (Cornet, p. 119, n. 1).

Castro, Lerma's nephew, whose continuance in Venice reflected Spain's practical refusal to honor the interdict, sought to persuade the Republic of the good intentions of his prince[350] and to bring about a settlement on terms as favorable as possible to the pope; the Spaniards suggested tactfully that Venice should make up by her own wisdom for the folly shown by the pope.[351] In Madrid and in Venice, if not in Rome, the representatives of Spain were cautious.[352] Spain, like France, wished to have it both ways.

Meanwhile every major Catholic prince, and the minor princes of Italy as well, devoted themselves to the pious work of making peace between Venice and the pope. Their eagerness to have some part in arranging a settlement was, no doubt, partly the result of a general anxiety over the possibility of a war that would probably involve them all; but it was to an even greater degree a reflection of their common desire to win the kind of prestige that Venice herself had long claimed in connection with the event of 1177. Evidently such prestige (with its patronizing overtones that must have produced shudders in Rome) was highly prized, for the various powers pleaded with Venice to make some concession merely as a mark of honor to themselves, vied with each other to discuss terms, sought to exclude each other from any part in the settlement, or attempted pitifully to be associated in any fashion at all with the effort.[353] Ambassadors, regular and special, jealously keeping an eye on each other's comings and goings, followed one another at the Roman Curia and in the Venetian College.

The intervention of the duke of Savoy, designated to represent the emperor

[350] Canaye reported that the Spanish representatives in Venice claimed to disapprove of the interdict (letters to Villeroy, April 20, 1606; to Commartin, April 28, 1606; and to Henry IV, May 3, 1606, III, 15, 17, 26).

[351] Cornet, p. 93.

[352] See, for example, the reply of the Spanish government to the Venetian ambassador Francesco Priuli, May 13, 1606 (Cornet, p. 84; cf. pp. 94, 105); and the dispatches of Priuli in *Componimento*, pp. 6–13, 17–19, 29–31. The Spanish government managed to avoid excluding the Venetian ambassador from religious services at court by giving them up (letter of Roncas to the Duke of Savoy, Aug. 6, 1606, in Magistris, pp. 153–154).

[353] For examples see Sarpi, *Istoria dell'Interdetto*, p. 203. The distinction that the role of mediator was thought to convey is suggested in a dispatch from Pietro Priuli in Paris to the doge, March 28, 1607, in Magistris, p. 455. Pressing on Villeroy the advantages of French mediation, Priuli suggested that the French king "would be recognized by all princes as true and only mediator of these differences." Various documents connected with efforts at mediation by the Hapsburg powers are given in *Componimento*, pp. 47–133. For the efforts of the Grand Duke of Tuscany, see Rubertis, *Ferdinando I dei Medici*, *passim*.

late in the proceedings, was a particular annoyance to all other powers.[354] Genuinely concerned about the possibility of war as well as ambitious for his own "honor" in the situation, the duke proposed to pay personal visits to both Rome and Venice. But his visits (although protocol forbade direct objections, and indeed required protestations of obligation and gratitude) were deplored by everyone. France and Spain objected because they wanted the "honor" of the settlement for themselves. Venice and Rome were both embarrassed, partly by the need to deal with still another delicate problem of honor,[355] partly by the difficulty and expense of supporting a visiting ruler with a large entourage; in Rome it was rumored that the duke would travel with a retinue of eight hundred persons.[356] All parties, with the exception of the transparently eager Savoyards, opposed the duke's plan as likely to introduce complications and new difficulties just when some sort of composition appeared imminent. The frivolity of the external mediators makes a nice contrast with the deadly seriousness over questions of principle displayed by the protagonists themselves.

For months both sides appeared totally intransigent, each requiring of the other not merely the first step toward a settlement but absolute capitulation. Rome demanded that Venice withdraw her laws, while Venice required Rome to lift the censures. But as the impasse continued and the Roman expectation of a quick Venetian collapse seemed increasingly unlikely, the pope began to show signs of softening. By October 1606 he had proposed that the issues be resolved by a commission which would include theologians favorable to Venice, though he required Venice first to withdraw its protests against the interdict, to turn over its clerical prisoners to the ecclesiastical authorities, and to agree in advance to accept the decisions of the commission. Six weeks later he also offered to revoke his censures simultaneously with Venetian withdrawal of the protests against them. He still insisted, however, that Venice in some way admit the validity of the interdict and readmit the religious she had expelled.[357] By January he proposed that if Venice would suspend her laws, papal bulls of similar substance would be issued to replace them. Thus Venice could retain such practical arrangements as she felt necessary, while authority would remain

---

[354] Cornet, pp. 180ff.; many documents in Magistris, pp. 324ff.
[355] For Venetian opposition and attitudes in Rome, see *ibid.*, pp. 455, 430.
[356] Magno to the Duke of Mantua, March 24, 1607, *ibid.*, p. 447.
[357] Cornet, pp. 143–145.

with the pope.[358] Such proposals indicated the pope's growing realization that he could not expect total victory.

Meanwhile there were occasional signs of hesitation among some elements in Venice itself, particularly over tactics. A few senators had been profoundly disturbed by the situation almost from the beginning and thought the policy of their government a radical departure from the traditional prudence of the Republic. One of these, Angelo Badoer, in June 1606 pleaded with his colleagues to abandon their defiance of the pope; his feelings about the actual weakness of the Venetian state both within and without are in sharp contrast to the optimistic and aggressive mood of the *giovani*. He attacked the pride and luxury of his contemporaries, "so different from our ancestors," and saw in the unbridled Venetian exploitation of the *terraferma* grounds to doubt the loyalty of the subject populations; his speech is interesting among other reasons as a piece of social criticism. He was doubtful that Venice could find allies in the event of a military attack, and he feared a repetition of the catastrophe of 1509. The present plight of Venice, he insisted, called for the conservation of Venetian liberty by the arts of peace, not its belligerent extension. The Senate should remember, he declared, that "lordships and powers, like all things of the world, have their increase, their moment of achievement, and their decline." Badoer had clearly lost faith in the eternal destiny of his native city, and he feared any initiative that might precipitate its decline. Venice, he argued, should not only avoid antagonizing the pope with hostile writings (now evidently under consideration) but, recognizing that union with the pope was her only security, should immediately humble herself before him as, he tactlessly suggested, she had done before Julius II: "The miseries of that time, so similar to this, I should like to see as our constant mirror and rule in present affairs." [359] But the reaction to his plea was harsh. Badoer was accused of aspiring to a bishopric as a means of recouping his recent bankruptcy (an experience that might well have made him gloomy), and of deficient patriotism. The French ambassador was sure that he had ruined his career.[360] There was, Canaye observed in a letter to the French ambassador in Rome, no division in the Senate except on the best way to resist the pope.[361]

[358] *Ibid.*, p. 196.

[359] Full text of the speech is given in *Componimento*, pp. 326–351, and in Cornet, App. XVI, pp. 307–315. Badoer's criticism of Venetian society is much like that of Possevino, *Risposta di Teodoro Eugenio*, p. 14.

[360] Letter to Villeroy, June 30, 1606 (III, 103–104).

[361] Letter to Alincourt, June 24, 1606 (III, 83).

Division on this issue from time to time emerged. Among the more flexible senators was Andrea Morosini, who may have been dubious about the wisdom of the literary campaign[362] and who favored a French proposal that the two criminal clergy might be turned over to France for eventual assignment (if the French king pleased) to the pope. Morosini argued against insisting on a settlement excessively humiliating to the papacy, and advocated at least minor concessions as an alternative to war. But although the proposed concession appeared small and Morosini's advocacy was clearly, unlike Badoer's, merely prudential, it also aroused strenuous opposition. Morosini was answered by Antonio Querini, who attacked any satisfaction to a pope so utterly in the wrong. Even Querini favored turning over one of the clergy to France since retaining the other protected the general principle of Venetian jurisdiction, but he insisted that any general concession would merely invite further aggression.[363] The intransigent group in Venice relied on the standard arguments against appeasement.

Serious disagreements over policy began to develop during the fall and winter of 1606/07, when at least some elements in the patriciate were apparently at last convinced that continued resistance might well bring on a war in which Venice would face Spain and the pope without allies. At this point a majority in the College, with Donà himself as their chief spokesman, advocated suspension (though not revocation) of the laws to which the pope had objected. Yet, although his former confidence was reduced, Donà sounded in his defense of this recommendation more like a Renaissance *politico* than before. Thus he excused himself for having changed his mind; he had altered, he said, because circumstances were different:

Let us not deem it the duty of a prudent man always to have the same opinion, but that which the accidents and rather variable conjunctures of human affairs counsel. And certainly, since the principles and accidents of things vary, it is essential for the deliberations based on them also to vary. Thus he who otherwise might pretend to the

---

[362] Cf. his official *Historia veneta*, VII, 348, where he noted (though perhaps only for tactical reasons appropriate to the period after the interdict) that many Venetians at the time doubted the wisdom of the literary campaign.

[363] These speeches are included in Querini's *Historia dell'Escomunica* and reproduced by Cornet, pp. 286–294, as App. XI. Their authenticity is made the more likely by the moderate tone of Morosini's later writings (see below, ch. X) and by the fact that Querini, who later developed strong reservations about the intransigent position, here represents himself as a spokesman for the radicals.

title of consistency and constancy in his opinions should rather deserve
a reputation for imprudent pertinacity and unconsidered obstinacy,
since everyone, even of superficial intelligence in things of state,
knows that civil matters are variable and subject like the sea to the
diversity of the winds, to the violence and diversity of accidents. For
this reason man should regulate his opinions exactly as on a sea voyage,
according to the quality of the winds. Nor is he obliged always to have
the same opinion, but rather the same end: the good and safety of the
Republic.

Thus, Donà reminded the Senate, a prudent flexibility rather than rigid
adherence to principle was the key to political survival. This, he remarked,
Venetians had always understood, and, "accommodating their decisions
to necessity," had chosen courses "which, if indeed they were not entirely
good, freed us nevertheless from greater evils" and for centuries secured
the state. In expressing his apprehension that war might bring foreigners
into Italy, Donà also pointed generally to the lessons of history, perhaps
more specifically to his study of Guicciardini. "Ancient and modern
histories," he declared, "are full of the ruinous consequences which auxiliary
and foreign troops have brought even on those who have called them to
their aid."

But even Donà's great influence was not enough to win support yet for
a more conciliatory course. In the Senate Alvise Zorzi answered him in a
speech that minimized the likelihood of war and denounced the proposed
concessions as a humiliation extorted by violence. Nicolò Contarini was
even more forceful. He argued that the right of Venice to make her own
laws was the essential condition of her liberty, and that, since one concession
leads to another, surrender on one point would eventually mean the loss of
everything for which the Republic stood. Above all Venice would lose
"that reputation and dignity which is truly the soul of states" and the
actual principle of political conservation.[364] The doge was also, according
to Querini, severely criticized throughout the city.[365] Thus the recommendations of the College were rejected; and the intransigents, for the time being,
remained in control. But, as we shall see in Chapter IX, the position of
Donà at this point foreshadowed the policy of the Republic once the crisis
of the interdict was past. The tension between a relatively opportunistic

[364] This debate, from Querini, is printed in Cornet, pp. 297–305, as App. XIII.
[365] *Historia dell'Escomunica*, pp. 280–281.

adaptation to circumstance and stern adherence to republican principle, the twin legacy of Renaissance politics, also pointed to the later predicament of Fra Paolo Sarpi.[366]

For the time being, therefore, Venice rejected the various proposals so hopefully conveyed from Rome by assorted foreign envoys. Each was firmly reminded that Venice, peacefully going about her own affairs in her legitimate and traditional ways, had been brutally and wantonly attacked by a power bent on the destruction of her liberty. She could therefore make no concessions; to do so would only encourage further aggressions. Whatever his private doubts, the doge was compelled to state repeatedly that Venice would engage in serious discussion of outstanding issues only if the pope lifted his censures and both sides returned to the situation before the interdict. Venice would do nothing under coercion.[367]

All the same, most Venetians wanted peace as well as victory. Whatever needed to be said in public, divided counsels, the restiveness of some elements in the populace, the absence of firm external support, and diplomatic pressures for a settlement were gradually producing some effect. And as the pope showed growing signs of giving way, it began to seem increasingly possible for the Republic to offer at least a token concession. The French proposal earlier defended by Morosini slowly won increasing acceptance; and Venice consented at last to negotiate on this basis.[368] If the censures were lifted, the government agreed, it would withdraw its protest and surrender the two criminal clergy to the king of France, who might then, on his own responsibility, turn them over to the pope. The gesture, it was made clear, was not to prejudice the general right of the Venetian authorities to deal with the clergy as they dealt with their other subjects; and Venice steadfastly refused to beg the pope formally to end the interdict (thereby implying its validity), to suspend any of her laws, or to allow the banished monks to return. But she was ready, by early spring in 1607, to make some effort to resolve the general impasse.

This small gesture proved sufficient. In February 1607 Canaye finally persuaded the Senate to accept mediation by the Cardinal de Joyeuse, and a settlement was finally concluded under French auspices. Joyeuse proved

---

[366] See below, Ch. IX.

[367] Examples in Cornet, pp. 80, 81–82, 111–112, 114, 130–131, 150, 159–160, 168–170, 171–172, 184, 205–206.

[368] For all these negotiations, *ibid.*, esp. pp. 207ff.

particularly satisfactory because he apparently saw himself as representing the French king rather than the Curia. He was enthusiastically received in Venice,[369] where he promptly emphasized to his hosts that his royal master expected nothing from Venice prejudicial to her dignity and honor. He was content to warn the government of the damage all powers might expect from a war.[370] When the Republic, taking him at his word, refused further concessions, he remonstrated only mildly before traveling to Rome to report that a settlement chiefly depended now on surrender by the pope. His first reception at the Curia was understandably cool, but Joyeuse was persuasive. It was in any case apparent that there was no practical alternative. The pope did insist that Joyeuse try to secure readmission for the Jesuits but admitted that even this was no absolute condition for peace.[371] On April 2 Canaye was able to report in Venice that Joyeuse was on his way with a brief revoking the interdict, and soon afterwards the Cardinal arrived in Venice to report the terms of the settlement. The interdict and its accompanying excommunications were formally revoked on April 21, 1607, the prisoners were then turned over to the French authorities as a favor to their king, and the Venetian protest against the censures was withdrawn. On the same day numbers of clergy who had insisted on observing the interdict were freed by the Venetian government.[372] Joyeuse made only a slight effort on behalf of the Jesuits before giving up the issue. Nothing was said about the Venetian laws that had precipitated the struggle. Thus Venice seemed to have won almost a complete victory in her long and arduous confrontation with Rome.[373]

The settlement, nevertheless, had left many details unspecified, and disagreements over its meaning, symptomatic of major tensions that no paper agreement could resolve, promptly broke out. One of these had to do with the manner in which the lifting of the interdict should be recognized; in an age in which ceremony was a serious and almost sacramental expression of fundamental realities, the point was substantial. Whereas Joyeuse proposed to celebrate the event with an ostentatious mass, the Venetian government,

[369] Querini, *Historia dell'Escomunica*, p. 287.

[370] Cornet, pp. 214–215.

[371] Querini, *Historia dell'Escomunica*, pp. 289–290, is particularly interesting on the course of the discussions in Rome.

[372] *Ibid.*, p. 295.

[373] Cornet, 229ff.; see also the documents in "Dokumente zum Ausgleich." Venice announced the end of the interdict with a broadsheet addressed to all the clergy in her domains.

ignoring the interdict to the end, saw no need for such open recognition of what had never been legitimately in effect. It prohibited public demonstrations of joy[374] and attempted to prevent the celebration, over which Joyeuse nevertheless presided, from being widely attended.[375] Above all, following an opinion on which Sarpi had been emphatic,[376] it wanted no act of absolution which might be interpreted to mean that Venice admitted some fault and a need for forgiveness. The government opposed even a benediction, because it might be misunderstood as a sign of contrition.[377] Joyeuse, immediately frustrated in his eagerness to absolve the refractory Venetians publicly, gave private absolution to ten priests and authorized them to absolve others; but the government put a stop to this effort.[378] Later, to the indignation of the Venetian authorities,[379] the Cardinal addressed a formal letter of absolution to the clergy in Venetian territory;[380] and Rome chose to insist that some kind of absolution had been given and received in spite of vehement denials in Venice.[381] The question was destined for future debate and was a continuing source of bitterness on both sides.[382]

An even more serious problem was caused by Venetian doctrine, still circulating in a mass of polemical writings which the Curia wanted at all costs to suppress, but whose validity the Venetians felt to have been only confirmed by the lifting of the interdict. For Venice proper principles had triumphed, and the notion that they ought now to be disowned by those

[374] Querini, *Historia dell'Escomunica*, p. 292; Provana to the Duke of Savoy, April 28, 1607, in Magistris, p. 499.

[375] Querini, *Historia dell'Escomunica*, p. 294. For differing reports on the government's success, see *Componimento*, p. 295, n. 1.

[376] In his *Parere come metter fine al monitorio*, in *Scritti*, III, 201–206.

[377] Cornet, p. 237, n. 1.

[378] Cardinal Spinola to Cardinal Borghese, April 28, 1607, in *Aevum*, X (1936), 8; Provana to the Duke of Savoy, April 28, 1607, in Magistris, pp. 499–500. For the pope's displeasure with Joyeuse's lack of firmness on the matter of absolution, see the letter from Borghese to Cardinal Barberini, May 15, 1607, quoted by Nürnberger, p. 511.

[379] Querini, *Historia dell'Escomunica*, p. 297.

[380] The text, dated May 2, is given in Cornet, App. XV, p. 307.

[381] Letter of the nuncio in Venice to Borghese, July 28, 1607, in *Aevum*, X (1936), 6–7, n. 1.

[382] Thus Sarpi was called on to compose a "true account" of what had actually occurred in the settlement of the interdict (*Informazione particolare dell'accommodamento*, in *Scritti*, III, 222–233) in reply to a contrary interpretation promptly printed in Bologna in 1607. Sarpi insisted that there had been no absolution, since Venice acknowledged no fault, and that the clerical prisoners had been turned over to France without prejudice to Venetian jurisdiction over the clergy.

whom they had so well served was absurd. Joyeuse claimed to have left Venice with the understanding that, as he wrote to Cardinal Borghese, "the writings published in favor of their cause were to perish, and those in favor of the Holy See to remain alive, since the pope is judge of good and bad writings, a point on which no Christian prince can contradict or oppose him." [383] But this claim, given the mood of Venice, only suggests (if Joyeuse was sincere) his failure to understand the situation. In fact Venice was in no hurry even to cease the publication of antipapal tracts. During the last week in April two more vigorous compositions were issued in defense of Venice, and the government showed further signs of its appreciation of the theologians in Venetian service.[384] Nearly a year later Sarpi was requested, in his official capacity, to give his opinion on whether the government should repudiate (obviously since it had never done so) what had been written in its defense. He urged, as might have been expected, that since the writings in question had been no more than the expression of Catholic truth and the defense of Venetian interests, their repudiation would mean the surrender of all that had been so strenuously won.[385]

The real issues, therefore, remained unsettled. Venice had won a battle, but the adversary was as hostile and implacable as ever. Many at the Curia were intensely displeased by the terms of the settlement,[386] and the pope accepted them (as Sarpi also seems to have recognized)[387] only because the alternative would have been worse: the total dependence of the papacy on Spain and the growth of antipapal sentiment elsewhere. Indeed, so reluctant was Rome to accept defeat that some followers of the pope tried to persuade themselves that the struggle against Venice, except in a few trivial details, had been a great victory for the papacy.[388]

The difficulty was, of course, that, in a manner which the Renaissance

[383] This letter, Aug. 19, 1607, is in *Aevum*, XI (1937), 46–47, n. 1.

[384] Provana to the Duke of Savoy, April 28, 1607, in Magistris, p. 499.

[385] This *consulto* (*Scrittura in difesa delle opere scritte a favore della serenissima republica nella controversia col sommo pontefice*, in *Scritti*, III, 234–257) was presented to the College on Feb. 25, 1608.

[386] Letter of Pietro Contarini to the doge, June 16, 1607, reporting on conversations with the ambassador of Savoy, who was just back from Rome, in Magistris, p. 511, n. 1.

[387] See the report of Christoph von Dohna, in *Briefe und Akten*, II, 85.

[388] This was the claim of the anonymous diarist, presented in Gadaleta, who felt (p. 107) that the pope had won on every point but the return of the Jesuits. Thus the pope had been correct (as the diarist reported) in informing a consistory on April 30 following the settlement "that the Church and ecclesiastical dignity have lost nothing but gained much." Italy had been preserved from ruin, and only "certain things of little moment" had been sacrificed.

would clearly have appreciated, practical considerations of power had imposed their own immediate and practical demands on an ideological problem and produced a resolution of their own. But this outcome was finally irrelevant to the issues themselves; the problem remained, in its own terms, essentially unsolved. Two cultural worlds had confronted each other in a dialogue in which a good deal needed to be said. The next chapter will examine more carefully the substance of their discourse.

·VIII·

The Venetian Interdict:
The Confrontation of Ideals

AS a particular clash of interest between two political forces, the Venetian interdict of the early seventeenth century hardly seems important enough to have justified the risks on either side; and so it appeared to many Europeans at the time. Rome risked, and was eventually compelled to endure, a bitter humiliation. But even if her calculations had been right, even if Venice had been forced to submit, the effort would still very likely have compelled the papacy to concentrate the best minds in the church for months against a local power of declining importance, at a time when apparently far graver problems were demanding solution. Yet the behavior of Venice appeared to many contemporaries even more foolish. The intransigence of a small state surrounded by hostile neighbors and without reliable allies seemed curiously rash for a government with a long record of prudent realism. Venetian willingness to risk annihilation in defense of the right to bring an occasional criminal priest to trial and to maintain a few laws, mostly of recent origin, appeared an ironically impolitic way of defending the *polis*.

But underlying the immediate issues in this conflict were profound differences both in principle and in attitude toward all aspects of human experience. These differences, more tentatively expressed by previous generations on both sides, have been reviewed in earlier chapters of this book. It was the function of the interdict, assisted by the growing inclination of Europeans in this period to deal in rigid absolutes, to clarify, systematize, and at last bring fully to the surface the antithesis between the political and cultural achievements of the Italian Renaissance and the ideals of medieval Catholicism, now reinvigorated by the Counter Reformation. Each side in the bitter struggle over the interdict was persuaded that the outcome was crucial for all that it held most dear.

This was particularly true for Venice. Rome took a longer view of things, and that she finally gave in may be attributed partly to her greater perspective. Confident that she would endure as long as the world itself, certain that she would prevail in the end, the papacy could afford to wait. But Venice, increasingly aware of the threatening tendency of events, no longer had any such assurance, no matter how confident her spokesmen tried to appear. Defeat in this struggle, her leaders were convinced, would put an end to everything in which Venice had so long found satisfaction. She would lose, in general, the specific identity that depended on her independence, and in addition numerous particular blessings she had long prized. As Possevino had indicated, a papal victory would mean the end of Venetian contact with the non-Catholic world (a prospect equally ominous for Venetian commerce and Venetian culture), rigid control over Venetian intellectual life, an end to the subversive liberty at the University of Padua, and vigorous censorship of the press.[1] If Venice should be forced to submit, it seemed obvious that the whole quality of Venetian life would be altered for the worse.

But the massive debate accompanying the political maneuvers described in the last chapter was more than a clash between explicit arguments. Much of the difference between the two sides depended on antithetical attitudes and assumptions too deep and intimate for conscious recognition. Proceeding from different premises, the writers on both sides often give an impression of discoursing in different languages that perversely insist on using the same vocabulary. As a result each group triumphantly scored points against the other, chalked up favorable marks on its private boards, and felt righteous indignation when its opponents refused to admit defeat. Charges of dishonesty accumulated, bad feeling mounted, and each side was increasingly inclined angrily to dismiss the arguments of the other. For Rome Venice was moved only by an impious greed compounded by rebellion. For Venice the lofty pretensions of the papacy simply masked the lust for power.

One of the major obstacles to genuine communication was a profound difference in intellectual constitution. Papalist discourse tended to be systematic and rational in the familiar style of the medieval schools, while

---

[1] In the *Risposta di Teodoro Eugenio* he obliquely attacked Paduan philosophical discussion (p. 5), Venetian military alliances with Swiss Protestants (p. 9), the luxurious lives of the Venetian nobility (p. 14), the free discussions of the Venetian *ridotti* (p. 34), the presence in Venice of schismatic Greeks (p. 46), the printing of obscene, heretical, and "mutilated" theological books in Venice (pp. 49–50), and the exclusion of the clergy from politics (pp. 52–53). The implicit (and at times explicit) thesis of the work is that the pope has a responsibility, and must have complete freedom, to correct all these delinquencies.

Venice generally preferred the concrete and flexible style congenial to Renaissance republicanism. Thus Bellarmine and his colleagues attacked the Venetians as bad logicians,[2] inundated the discussion with masses of authorities,[3] and accumulated classifications and subtle distinctions. Bellarmine, for example, did not care to discuss *liberty* without distinguishing half a dozen senses of the term.[4] The mental world of these men was fixed and certain, and they conceived of intellectual discourse as the task of revealing its firm, clear outlines.

But the works of Sarpi and his associates (though they frequently felt the need to reply in kind) usually display quite a different spirit. Sarpi ridiculed Bellarmine's distinctions as pedantic,[5] and his own compositions are permeated with a sense of the relativity of human practice "to what the variety of the times may bring." [6] As he remarked to his government at an early point in the struggle, he was convinced that "examples move more than reasons." [7] He constantly preferred facts to speculation;[8] he observed in his first *consulto* that "it is not suitable to proceed in these cases by conjectures, deductions, or syllogisms, but by explicit laws." [9] By the same token the Venetian theologians were critical of their opponents' habit of pressing Scripture into a rigid, dogmatic framework. "One ought not take refuge in allegory but stick to the proper and literal sense," Marsilio loftily informed Bellarmine;[10] and Sarpi constantly insisted that a proper interpretation of

[2] Thus in his *Risposta alla difesa delle otto propositioni di Giovan Marsilio Napolitano*, p. 142, Bellarmine ridiculed Marsilio as one whom Aristotle would have excluded from his school for incompetence in logic.

[3] Bovio, for example, in his *Lettera al R. P. M. Paolo Rocca*, sig. Bl^r, insisted, against the Venetian citation of Gerson, that a proposition can stand only if supported by many authorities. The *Difesa de' Servi* (*passim* an application of the general principle that truth depends on the consent of numbers) triumphantly concludes a section (p. 26) by asking: "Now what will the adversary say to so many authorities of doctors, of sacred letters, of Fathers, of canons, and of councils? He will not be able to deny them if he professes to be Catholic."

[4] *Risposta ad un libretto di Gersone*, p. 310. Bovio was disdainful of Sarpi's failure to "divide" his argument with this kind of clarity; his own method reduced chaos to order by divisions and lists (*Risposta alle considerationi del P. Maestro Paolo*, pp. 21–22).

[5] See his *Apologia*, in *Scritti*, III, 50, where he speaks ironically of Bellarmine's "apparatus of six liberties."

[6] This typical phrase appears in the *Considerazioni sulle censure*, in *Scritti*, II, 221, in connection with the varieties of secular jurisdiction over the clergy.

[7] *Sopra la forza e validità della scommunica*, in *Scritti*, II, 39.

[8] Cf. his ridicule of Bellarmine's "airy" hypotheses (*Apologia*, in *Scritti*, III, 178–179).

[9] *Difesa di due ordinazioni*, in *Scritti*, II, 6.

[10] *Difesa a favore della risposta dell'otto propositioni*, p. 203.

Scripture always required a sense of context. "Sacred Scripture should be read as a whole, not in passages," he advised the most distinguished of the Roman theologians.[11] Such minds were also little impressed by the familiar medieval arguments from analogy, to which their adversaries still constantly referred. "Propositions that are to be established as dogmas should not be based on similitudes of similitudes," Sarpi observed stiffly in reference to the association of Peter with the rock;[12] and Capello was not at all persuaded that the relationship between body and soul had a bearing on the relations between Venice and the pope.[13] Roman theologians appealed to historical precedent, and Venetians cited canons or exploited syllogisms when they seemed useful. But neither side was entirely comfortable with the weapons of the other.

But although issues could not always be joined directly, the basic character of the conflict is clear; and it emerges nowhere more sharply than in the utterly different meanings the two sides assigned to the conception of *order*. On its deepest level the Venetian interdict may be seen as nothing less than a struggle over the nature of order in the entire structure of reality. For the Roman theologians order meant conformity to the principles governing the universe, natural and supernatural, in all its aspects, which united its discrete elements into a general system and supplied harmony and meaning to the whole. For the Venetians order had a limited and practical significance. Order was simply the necessary condition of social existence, and any attempt to fill it with a more sublime content would only subvert that true order relevant to the human condition.

Lelio Medici, the Inquisitor-General in Florence, offered an unusually full account of the papalist vision of order. "Now it is very clear and a conclusion approved by all the theologians," he declared in a typical piece of exegesis, "that all the works of God have order in themselves." Thus in the story of the Creation the fact that "God saw all the things that he had made and they were very good" (Genesis 1:31) meant clearly that they were ordered. It could not be otherwise, Medici argued, "because if they were not ordered, there would necessarily be confusion among them, which would mean imperfection in all things and especially in God." It was equally clear

---

[11] *Apologia*, in *Scritti*, III, 87. In various places in this work Sarpi insists that Scripture be interpreted in context; cf. pp. 100, 106–107, 132, 133.

[12] *Ibid.*, pp. 129–130. Cf. p. 132, where he objects to carrying too far the figure of Christians as sheep.

[13] *Delle controversie*, p. 94.

to this writer that order had a specific and identifiable character. Its essential principle was hierarchy, the distinction between higher things and lower, above all the due subordination of inferior to superior. "Order," Medici continued, "carries with it this condition, that lower things, being less perfect and noble, should be subordinated to higher, to the more perfect and noble, a point on which there is no difficulty." [14] Possevino was both more specific and more complex:

> In the world there are the elements and the higher spheres; but because the whole remains in order, they are conserved together. In man there are a soul and body of diverse natures, and God found a way to join them together. Nor, because the heart, the brain, the liver administer motion, heat, and life to the body, do they suffice to keep man alive, because the intellectual soul is necessary, without which, as without its proper form, the whole would remain a cadaver. . . . In heaven there are, equally, various hierarchies, nor does one prejudice another because, each power being subordinated to higher powers, they preserve that admirable union from which all stability and joy derive.[15]

This general conception of order was central to the papalist view of all social organization. "The order that shines through in all the works of God," the Servite leaders wrote against Sarpi, "is also found in every human congregation. For because order cannot exist without chief and head, since the principle of order consists in this, it happens that in every multitude gathered together, insofar as order exists, there is a chief and head on which the ordered multitude depends. This appears in families, in armies, and in all other regulated assemblies." Inherent in nature, the same principle of order also applied inevitably to the church: "In the same way most beauteous order appears in this holy congregation of the faithful, which is the Christian church, as in the family, or an army, or even, as Saint Paul suggests, a human body." Thus it was clearly necessary "that there should be one head and chief, and in consequence levels of authority and subjection. Because in every ordered assembly it is necessary that some should rule and others should be subject; some should command and others obey; some should give laws and others observe them, and with their observance direct and conduct themselves to the destined end." [16]

[14] *Discorso, sopra i fondamenti e le ragioni delli ss. Veneziani*, p. 191.
[15] *Risposta di Teodoro Eugenio*, p. 39.
[16] *Difesa de' Servi*, p. 42.

Ventura Venturi made the system, as a political conception, particularly neat. All powers, he observed, had places in the hierarchical order of things. "Nor are temporal princes, or senators, disunited from this hierarchy," he wrote, "but a part and principal member of it. For just as [the celestial hierarchy] consists of angels and archangels, thrones, principates, powers, dominions, so in the human hierarchy there correspond the thrones of empires, kingdoms, princes, governments, republics, and all other powers, which therefore, with just and harmonious proportion, are successively ordered by, disposed by, and finally depend on the supreme hierarch, the pope." Measured by this ideal, a world of fragmented political units was utterly unacceptable; unity was essential to the system, though for practical as well as theoretical reasons. Quite properly, for Venturi, the most venerable authorities in philosophy and politics had celebrated a single, all-inclusive principate "because the multitude of princes without order, connection, or any dependence on each other mostly results in discord, or is less respected or less vigorous. Virtue is greater, more effective, more respected, more feared, in the degree to which it is kept united and gathered in a single lord."

But the principle of subordination inherent in the entire system was above all intended to subject the whole political order to spiritual direction. "All temporal things serve, are ordered by, depend with ordered dependence, on spiritual things," Venturi declared. "And since the Christian Republic is composed of both political and spiritual governments, it is necessary for the political end to be directed finally to the spiritual end, in which the true and entire felicity of man consists, and that political and temporal powers should depend on and be ordered by spiritual." The notion of an independent prince was literally damnable. There was also, therefore, no place in this system for an autonomous "civil felicity." [17]

The Roman case against Venice was based on this conception of universal order which, in both its spiritual and social dimensions, Venice had flagrantly violated. The Republic had in the final analysis been guilty of rebellion against the principle of order implicit in the very nature of reality. Baronius saw this clearly. Venice, belonging to a lower level in the universal hierarchy, had dared to touch what belonged to a higher. Her offense proceeded finally from the fact that "the hierarchical order is overthrown" [18] when a lower part of the universal system usurps what belongs to a higher. And from defiance of the universal principle of order, descent into more concrete forms of order seemed, to the Roman theologians, entirely predictable. Bellarmine

[17] *Della maiestà pontificia*, pp. 28–33, 73–74.
[18] *Paraenesis*, p. 104.

moved easily from condemnation of the more general rebellion of Venice to predictions of a multitude of specific disorders; for men of his stamp, any compartmentalization of experience seemed impossible; the slightest movement was likely to set off reverberations in the entire system of Catholic practice. "He who begins to despise the orders of the Head of the Church," Bellarmine argued, "will have no scruples against despising any other order. With the same artifice Martin Luther persuaded many that Christian liberty consists in a broad conscience and in being unafraid of defying all the orders of Holy Church; and thus we have seen so many monks and nuns unscrupulously leaving their monasteries, throwing away the sacred habit, and taking husbands or wives; and so many peoples throwing down the sacred images, ignoring vigils and fasts, and no longer knowing what Lent, Confessions, Vespers, and masses are. Finally we see how, from this beginning of not fearing the power of the Vicar of Christ on earth, some provinces have lost every vestige of Christian Religion." [19] For Bellarmine a proper recognition of the objective order of the universe should find practical expression in obedience to an order of the pope.

The Venetian theologians made little effort to refute the papal conception of order directly. Indeed their indifference to this abstract challenge on its own sublime level is one of the clearest indications of the distance between the two antagonists. For Venice order posed a practical, not a speculative, problem. True order was precisely what her own admirable constitution had so effectively created, and the Venetian constitution required no sanction beyond its own perfection and success. Thus the real Venetian reply to the Roman conception of order was not direct refutation but insistence on the familiar Renaissance conception of the liberty of states; the grievance of Venice against the pope consisted above all in the fact that he treated her, in politics, as a subordinate rather than an equal.[20] The order of Venice depended not on her participation, as a subordinate member, in a monolithic and hierarchical system but on her detachment and independence from all systems. It was because Venice was free, because no alien power had the right to interfere with her genial political processes, that her government had become a model of stability for the rest of Europe.

A second basic issue between the two sides, closely related to their utterly different conceptions of order, was thus posed by contrasting views of liberty,

---

[19] *Risposta ad un libretto di Gersone*, p. 313. See also Amato, *Breve discorso*, p. 3, which denounces the Venetians for believing "that no one can be above them."

[20] Cf. Sarpi, *Istoria dell'Interdetto*, p. 8, where Sarpi complains of the pope's demand, as though to an inferior, that Venice contribute to the war against the Turks in Hungary.

to which both professed attachment. The kind of liberty the papalists considered valid was a function of universal order. Campanella informed the erring Venetians that "liberty consists in living according to eternal reason." [21] True liberty thus meant the freedom of higher things from control by lower, and of lower things to obey higher. In practice this meant the maintenance of clerical privilege. The Servite theologians faced this squarely. "The adversary," they wrote against Sarpi, "little understood that word *liberty*, for if he knew that liberty in this discussion is a privilege given to the church by God, or by the pope, or by emperors, as the doctors teach, he would not introduce that new term of secular liberty, attributing it to the laity." [22] Bovio made the point even more emphatically:

> It is appropriate for the church to have ecclesiastical liberty, because its power is supreme and exempt from every other; but to the secular power, which according to all the doctors (I speak of the Catholics) is subject to the ecclesiastical, secular liberty in this sense does not belong . . . laymen being mortal [but] churches perpetual, the cause of religion being more favored even among the barbarians than that of the world, and finally (which is most important) the two powers by which these laws are made not being equal but the ecclesiastical superior. [23]

True liberty was thus the exclusive possession of the church. Concretely this meant that criminal priests must not be punished by the civil power and that the right of the church to withdraw wealth indefinitely from the lay economy was absolute. The church could take such "liberties" as it chose. [24]

Thus one conception of order and liberty opposed another. Just as the Venetian ideal of liberty violated the papal sense of order, so that of Rome challenged the Venetian understanding of order. As Sarpi observed, the ecclesiastical definition of liberty seemed calculated only to throw the actual life of society into confusion. [25] But we may also discern here the familiar

[21] *Antiveneti*, p. 7.

[22] *Difesa de' Servi*, p. 139.

[23] *Risposta alle considerationi*, p. 42. Cf. Bellarmine, *Risposta a fra Paulo*, p. 75.

[24] Cf. Possevino, *Risposta di Teodoro Eugenio*, pp. 46, 49–50.

[25] Sarpi made the point in his *Trattato dell'Interdetto*, in *Scritti*, III, 7–8. Cf. his *Scrittura della libertà ecclesiastica*, in *ibid.*, II, esp. 139–140, where he interprets "ecclesiastical liberty" as a mere demand for license; and *Considerazioni sopra le censure*, in *ibid.*, II, 194ff., where he describes the demand for such liberty as a novelty and notes that Saint Paul spoke only of Christian liberty. See also Querini, *Aviso*, p. 25, and Micanzio, *Confirmazione*, p. 65, which defines the true liberty of the church as simply freedom from sin.

Renaissance antithesis between the contemplative and the active visions of human experience, now raised to a highly practical level. The interdict provided the papalist theologians with an opportunity to impose the abstract conclusions of systematic thought on a significant representative of the mis-guided modern world. Venice, on the other hand, was defending the practical values and necessities of social existence. This is the meaning of what was perceived, in Rome, as the righteous opposition of principle to politics.

Against this background Venetian assertion of the right of private judg-ment to concern itself with the pronouncements of ecclesiastical authority takes on its full seriousness. Not only did this claim incorporate a conception of human dignity long embedded in Renaissance republicanism; it was also an affront to the abstract principle of order. Bellarmine, to be sure, was relatively mild on this point. He did not consider every act of private judg-ment as necessarily sinful, although in general he thought obedience more pleasing to God. But even he saw subversive implications in the Venetian doctrine that private judgment was a duty. It would, he observed, damage "the discipline of every well-ordered congregation, both spiritual and temporal";[26] and he pointed out that, generally speaking, freedom of con-science simply meant freedom to err.[27] The Florentine Servite Lelio Baglioni was more emphatic. Insisting on every man's duty of obedience to his legitimate superiors, he pointed out that the claim to private judgment would result in "the total dissolution of the ecclesiastical hierarchy"; he warned that the pretensions of Venice in this regard would produce general confusion in the world.[28] Bovio made a similar effort to persuade those responsible for the tranquility of states that the Venetian position was in essence seditious. It was subversive to every form of authority, he declared, "not only of holy Church, but of every other government, political or do-mestic, public or private." Venice, in espousing such doctrines, was in Bovio's view striking at all good order, including her own. "This pernicious doc-trine," he declared, "apt to raise all subjects in rebellion, ought no less to displease the Venetian Republic itself and every other prince in the world, as well as holy Church, although directed against her alone, since in effect it impugns every legitimate power and is likely to cause every evil in every place and time."[29]

[26] *Risposta ai sette,* p. 33.
[27] *Risposta ad un libretto di Gersone,* p. 311.
[28] *Apologia,* II, 52, 5, 39–41.
[29] *Risposta alle considerationi,* pp. 83–84.

Here too the Venetians had no wish to espouse general positions with unlimited implications. They were only asserting the right of laymen to determine for themselves the justice of ecclesiastical sentences and the propriety of obedience. They did not at all believe in the right of subjects to measure the justice in decrees of secular governments. The distinction, under the circumstances, was convenient, but it was not merely cynical. It was rooted in the religious traditions of Venice and indeed of Renaissance republicanism in general. Sarpi took the position that, where the soul is at stake, each man has an individual responsibility which hardly applies, is indeed forbidden, in temporal things, where "the public good must take precedence over the private." Hence each man must consider for himself whether the decrees of the church are just, but he is obligated simply to obey the commands of his prince.[30] This contrast between the individualism permitted in spiritual matters and the conformity required in politics also corresponds to the typically Venetian balance between freedom in private life and the acceptance of social responsibility. The tension here may have exposed the spokesmen of Venice to charges of inconsistency, but the Venetian way seemed to have worked well in practice.

In the Venetian insistence on the right of private judgment in religious matters there was also a positive evaluation of the autonomy of individual experience. In the Venetian perspective, the value of human individuality (and by implication of other sorts) did not depend on its retention within a larger system, whether metaphysical or social, whose objective validity was guaranteed by a body of experts. Even Venice existed, as Paruta had made clear, for the Venetians, not the Venetians for Venice. Thus for the Venetian theologians each man was directly and individually responsible to God by his very nature. His difference from the animals distinguished him from the rest of God's creation, whose patterns of order (whatever they might be) were irrelevant to his peculiar status. Capello stated the position in very general terms; but although he wrote of man in the abstract, his intention was to defend the right of each individual to judge what was most important for himself: "The irrational animals alone know good and evil things without reflection, through nature; but man cannot know them without discourse and without judgment, and to this end he was endowed by God with reason." [31] Marsilio made the point with special authority, adding to it the dimension of action. He saw in the native instinct or light of every individual

---

[30] *Apologia*, in *Scritti*, III, 166–167.
[31] *Delle controversie*, p. 15. See also *Epistolae duorum iurisconsultorum*, p. 134, which sees freedom of speech, because essential to self-preservation, as based on natural law.

a sufficient guide for the conduct of life; thus clerical direction was useful only in doubtful cases. Disregard of the promptings of private judgment was, for Marsilio, merely irresponsible.[32] Sarpi too emphasized the obligation of the individual to exert himself to the utmost before shifting the burdens of decision onto superior authority. He was particularly confident in the ability of the layman to perceive "what is pious and Catholic doctrine" in the conflict with the pope.[33] He also suggested, ostensibly summarizing the official position of Venice rather than presenting his personal views, that blind dependence on the judgment of superior authority "removes the essence of virtue, which is to act through certain knowledge and choice." [34] Venice, then, was defending against Rome the dignity of free and responsible human action; and her position on this issue also helps to explain her antipathy to the Society of Jesus, with its special dedication to obedience.[35] Obedience to man, as Sarpi insisted, might well mean disobedience to God.[36] The peculiar seriousness of religious decisions was thus taken to impose a special obligation on every believer to think for himself.

Antagonistic conceptions of order were even more clearly basic to the conflict between the two sides over the relationship between the spiritual and temporal authorities. Both, as we have seen, belonged for Rome to a single system, a point essential to the argument that one was superior to the other. Bellarmine, disclaiming now any preference for one form of political organization over another, saw all types of earthly government as included in "the City of God, which is the Church Universal." [37] This principle converted princes as well as popes into religious ministers, as Bellarmine recognized, "but popes are occupied in a more eminent ministry than kings." [38] Bovio stated the relationship of the two powers with particular clarity and fullness:

> Politics and religion cannot rule in distinct countries separated by mountains, rivers, or other boundaries; because every community of

---

[32] *Difesa a favore della risposta*, p. 277.

[33] *Apologia*, in *Scritti*, III, 110; *Difesa delle opere scritte*, in *ibid.*, III, 237.

[34] *Istoria dell'Interdetto*, p. 107.

[35] Sarpi charged that the doctrine of blind obedience despoils "the human creature of the reason God gave him as a light to follow always" (*Difesa delle opere scritte*, in *Scritti*, III, 241–242). See also the attacks on blind obedience in Sarpi's *Trattato dell'Interdetto*, in *Scritti*, III, 21ff.; and Capello, *Delle controversie*, pp. 150–152.

[36] *Apologia*, in *Scritti*, III, 161.

[37] *Risposta ad un libretto di Gersone*, p. 310. On the inclusion of both powers in the church see also Bellarmine, *Risposta alla risposta*, p. 158; and Baglioni, *Apologia*, p. 15.

[38] *Risposta a Marsilio*, p. 168.

men, like every man in himself, being made by God and subject to him, must have within itself religion, with which it renders to God due tribute of worship and adoration. Since, therefore, politics and religion must exist together in the same republic, they must not co-exist as equals, lest differences and discords be interminable. Hence one had to be subordinated to the other, since where there is no order there is confusion, and where all powers are not subordinated to one supreme power there cannot be good government. . . . Now we see which of the two must be subordinated and subject to the other. Politics undertakes to procure the felicity of this earthly life, religion that of celestial life. Politics ordains the whole body of the republic under an earthly prince, religion orders both the entire republic and its head under the supreme Head and Lord God. Politics rules and governs earthly things, religion directs them to the eternal. Politics is occupied for the most part with what pertains to the body and to corporal things, religion with that which concerns the salvation of souls. Who does not see clearly, therefore, that just as man is subject to God and the body to the soul, and just as this life is ordained as the way to the heavenly fatherland and these earthly things as a stairway to celestial, so politics is subject and subordinate to religion, and the prince and temporal government to the head of religion and of the church?[39]

Other papalist writers made the same general case repeatedly, drawing on all the conventional medieval authorities and images.[40]

This position obviously recognized some difference between the duties of the two powers, but its essential point was their arrangement in hierarchy, the subordination of politics to religion and of princes to the pope. Possevino, here more Augustinian than Thomist, made clear that such an arrangement was required because secular government owed its institution to sin, which it existed to discipline.[41] Amato emphasized that only the spiritual power came directly from God.[42] The Servite theologians insisted on the subordination of means to ends.[43] Venturi appealed to the principle of subordination inherent in nature.[44] But whichever standard argument was invoked, the

[39] *Lettera al R. P. M. Paolo Rocca*, sig. B2ᵛ-B3.
[40] They are collected in *Difesa de' Servi*, pp. 43–48.
[41] *Nuova risposta di Giovanni Filoteo di Asti*, p. 4.
[42] *Breve discorso*, p. 4.
[43] *Difesa de' Servi*, p. 154.
[44] *Maiestà pontificia*, p. 72.

conclusion was always the same. In Bovio's words, "all the Catholic doctors agree that the church, the spiritual, has power over the temporal." [45] Both swords, as Bellarmine insisted, appealing to Bernard and *Unam Sanctam*, were properly at the disposition of the church.[46] He took the occasion afforded by the interdict, indeed, to minimize the importance of his earlier objections to the direct temporal power of the pope. The important point was that the pope ultimately possessed supreme authority over temporal as over spiritual things.[47]

The papalist writers by no means limited themselves to claiming for the pope the right and duty to intervene in temporal affairs when secular rulers were guilty of sin or when their policies threatened spiritual interests. Bellarmine was, perhaps, inclined to be satisfied with this much, saying that "who does not believe this is not Catholic";[48] but some of his colleagues were inclined to be more explicit. Possevino, Venturi, and the Servites, differing sharply with contemporary Dominican thought, were at one in denying the legitimacy of any government whose ruler did not recognize the supremacy of the pope. The last argued in addition that even a Catholic ruler who fell into heresy was *ipso iure* deprived of his office.[49] Baglioni, himself a Florentine, pointed to the role of the pope in creating the Grand Duchy of Tuscany as proof that all political power was transmitted through the Holy See.[50] Papalist writings also claimed for the pope, as ultimate sovereign in temporal affairs, the right to build churches on private property without the consent of the owner,[51] and such legislative authority as might be appropriate to the "prince of the whole Christian republic to govern it directly in faith and customs." [52]

We have already observed that the papalist position denied the separate identities as well as the full sovereignty of particular governments. Each

[45] *Lettera al R. P. M. Paolo Rocca*, sig. B2^v.

[46] *Risposta alla risposta*, p. 161.

[47] *Ibid.*, pp. 164–165. See also Bovio, *Lettera al R. P. M. Paolo Rocca*, sig. B2^v.

[48] *Risposta ad un libretto di Gersone*, p. 310 bis; cf. his *Risposta a Marsilio*, p. 155, where he recognizes that a Christian prince is subject to the pope not as a prince but as a Christian.

[49] Possevino, *Nuova risposta di Giovanni Filoteo di Asti*, p. 5, found Turkish rule illegitimate on this ground. See also Venturi, *Maiestà pontificia*, pp. 22–23; and *Difesa de'Servi*, p. 54, which argues that the authority of a prince is legitimate only if confirmed by an oath to the Holy See.

[50] *Apologia*, pp. 44–45.

[51] *Difesa de'Servi*, p. 86.

[52] *Ibid.*, p. 32.

state, in this conception, was once again a member of the Christian republic rather than a discrete political unit determining its particular course on the basis of its own needs. Bellarmine was clear that his own thought was posited on the reality of Christendom, not merely as a cultural and religious but as a political entity. "If Christians, as Christians, are members of Christ," he wrote, "certainly properly, and as the theologians say formally, Christ is head of Christendom, of all Christians, and of the Christian states and kingdoms."[53] Other Roman theologians were less loftily logical in describing the political order as a universal empire. The Servites, although hardly able to deny the existence of other temporal rulers, assigned political authority "above all" to the emperor.[54] Possevino, less respectful of the temporal power, pointed out that "if the true empire is vested in the master of Rome, I do not see how the pope, created by God in the person of Saint Peter, [and] lord of Rome, together with his successor through the free cession of Constantine, should not have the imperial authority."[55]

The Venetian response to all of this was partly direct. It flatly rejected the hierarchy of the two powers in favor of their distinction and separation; Marsilio cited, in this regard, the famous text of Gelasius.[56] For Venice the spiritual and temporal magistrates, pope and ruler, were parallel and, in the words of Capello, more like "the two arms of the Christian republic," which ought to aid each other, than like soul and body.[57] Marsilio compared them to gold and lead, different in kind as well as value.[58] Insistence on the separation and parallelism of the two powers was also accompanied by an attack on the political conception of Christendom. Sarpi distinguished between the Christian church, of which the pope was in some sense head, and Christendom as the collectivity of Christian kingdoms and states, of which he was assuredly not;[59] and Marsilio insisted on the legitimacy of non-Christian governments as an argument that the lay power cannot in principle be subject to the pope.[60]

[53] *Risposta a fra Paulo*, p. 83.

[54] *Difesa de' Servi*, pp. 42–43.

[55] *Nuova risposta di Giovanni Filoteo di Asti*, p. 20.

[56] *Difesa a favore della risposta*, p. 239.

[57] *Delle controversie*, pp. 34–35.

[58] *Difesa a favore della risposta*, p. 249; see also *Epistolae duorum iurisconsultorum*, p. 129. Not all the defenders of Venice were so clear on this point, however; cf. Fulgentio Tomaselli, *La mentite Filoteane, overo Invettiva di Giovanni Filoteo d'asti contra la Republica Serenissima di Venetia confutata* (Padua, 1607), p. 397, in the edition in the *Raccolta*, I, 389–405.

[59] *Apologia*, in *Scritti*, III, 64–65.

[60] *Difesa a favore della risposta*, p. 198.

The Venetians also tended to dismiss papalist theory as the transparent rationalization of a huge lust for power. For Sarpi the pope's true aim was the establishment of world monarchy, not in a spiritual but in a vulgarly political sense;[61] for Giovan Simone Sardi the religious arguments merely veiled crude temporal ambition.[62] One Venetian pamphleteer went so far as to suggest that the recent improvement in morals at the Curia was a cynical calculation to facilitate the temporal conquest of the world.[63] The danger to the secular state, as Sarpi endeavored to show, was great. Even the old claim of the right of the spiritual power to intervene in temporal affairs *ratione peccati*, as he saw, meant in practice an unlimited intervention, since every human action raises moral and spiritual issues. It would mean, for politics, the pope's right "to examine all laws, all edicts, all pacts, all successions, all the transactions of princes." It would give the pope an unlimited right to intervene in the private life of every individual, and it would authorize interference with every commercial transaction:[64] Sarpi was concerned both for the dignity of individual existence and for the Venetian economy. Thus not only the good order of Venice but the essential values of Venetian life depended on the rejection of what was, for Rome, the order both of Christendom and of the universe.

The radical difference between the two sides over the nature of order emerges even more distinctly in the Venetian conception of the state developed in these writings. Venetian statism confronts us again with the paradox that a society which appeared to encourage freedom in matters of the spirit should insist on rigorous obedience to government. But although Venetian writers deliberately presented their case in general terms to attract the support of rulers in every kind of state, it should be kept in mind that they were thinking concretely of the Venetian government and its peculiar structure. If they were statists, they were thus also constitutionalists; the prince whose dignity they defended and whose authority they sought to confirm was the elected doge who represented (but did not rule) the sovereign state of Venice, a state which responded (particularly under the *giovani*) to a control at least as broadly based as in most republics previously known to history, and which was in theory devoted to the common welfare. Venetian

---

[61] See the opening lines of the *Istoria dell'Interdetto*, pp. 3–4; cf. *Epistolae duorum iurisconsultorum*, p. 132.

[62] *Libertà ecclesiastica*, p. 213.

[63] Offman, *Avvertimento, et ammonitione catolica*, p. 105.

[64] *Apologia*, in *Scritti*, III, 65–66.

statism should be somewhat distinguished from the vulgar adulation of personal despotism common elsewhere.

It must be recognized, nevertheless, that, against the extreme claims of the papacy to organize and control Christendom, the Venetian writers pressed extreme claims for the right of the state to direct, in the public interest, every aspect of life in society. They entirely rejected in politics the private judgment they advocated in matters of the spirit. Sarpi was perfectly clear on this point. Writing particularly of the clergy but generally of the obligation of all citizens, he declared: ". . . it belongs to the prince to judge of the law and also to revoke it, and God commands them to obey it without examination." [65]

Venetian statism was based on the idea that, just as individual believers are directly responsible to God in spiritual things, so particular states, having been instituted by God for the governance of peoples, are directly responsible to him in temporal things. Political life therefore, like personal life, does not derive its sanctions from a systematic hierarchy of authorities but is, in this world, autonomous, and otherwise answerable only to God. That this argument was employed to defend a seventeenth-century republic will remind us that the association of divine right with kings was incidental; its essence concerned the nature of government in general, regardless of form. Since the form of government is irrelevant to the argument, furthermore, the theory seems to admit the ascending theme of authority and even to leave open the possibility of popular sovereignty.

The Venetian position was still sometimes eclectic. Occasionally it combined the argument from divine institution with the idea that political organization is directly required by the nature of man, but either position tended to exclude the church from a supervisory role in political life. Capello joined the two arguments in a characteristic pronouncement. "The political power," he wrote, "is a faculty immediately given by God to human nature, with which all men must necessarily be governed in order to live good and blessed lives in society, in conformity with natural reasons." [66] There are overtones here of Paruta's concern with "civil felicity."

More frequently now, however, the appeal to the divine right of government appears without any naturalistic admixture, for the supernatural claims

---

[65] *Sul giudicar le colpe di persone ecclesiastiche*, in *Scritti*, II, 53.

[66] *Delle controversie*, p. 34. Capello saw secular government as essential to the very preservation of life. Human nature, he argued, can exist without the ecclesiastical but not without the political power. For man's political needs are rooted in his nature as a civil being, whereas he is capable of eternal blessedness (the concern of the church) only through grace (*ibid.*, p. 39).

of the papacy had to be met on their own ground. Marsilio's first pamphlet maintains at the outset, for example, that the power of all secular princes, without exception, "is conceded to them immediately by God." [67] Sarpi demonstrated the same proposition from Scripture as well as from earlier ecclesiastical authorities.[68] He also emphasized the special responsibility, imposed on any government because of the divine source of its authority, to defend its position against any challenger, naturally including the pope. Sarpi's statement of the point is typical of the Venetian case in substance but (as on other matters) distinguished by its intellectual force and precision: "Because the civil being of every republic or kingdom comes from God and is directed to his glory," he declared, "therefore it is not permissible, without sin and offense to God, that its proper liberty, which is the civil being of every principate, should be taken away and usurped. Nor ought there to be any doubt that negligence in its defense is a grave offense against God, and most grave when it is voluntarily allowed to be usurped." [69] Venice, therefore, had to stand her ground because her sovereignty was a religious trust. Capello described the temporal magistrate as "political pastor of the laity";[70] and a lesser pamphleteer insisted that, albeit in a separate sphere, a prince was as much a vicar of Christ as the pope.[71]

Because of his religious character the prince, according to Sarpi, also had particular obligations to virtue and piety. Sarpi's sketch of the ideal prince might, indeed, usefully be compared with the character of Leonardo Donà. "The prince," Sarpi wrote, "is more obligated than the private man to be fearful of God, zealous for the holy faith, reverent to the prelates who hold the place of Christ. But he is also more obligated to flee hypocrisy and superstition, to conserve his dignity, to retain his state in the exercises of holy religion, and to prevent from happening to his people what happened to the Hebrews, who, thinking themselves deprived of the true God because of the long absence of Moses, made themselves one of gold. If this thing were well considered, the world would not be in the evil straits in which it now finds itself." [72] One of the first responsibilities of the prince, then, as a minister of God, was to prevent the establishment of idolatry; specifically this meant that it was sinful for a prince to obey an unjust interdict.[73] The ministerial

[67] *Risposta d'un Dottore in theologia*, p. 138.
[68] *Sopra la forza e validità della scommunica*, in *Scritti*, II, 38–39.
[69] *Considerazioni sulle censure*, in *Scritti*, II, 251.
[70] *Delle controversie*, p. 48.
[71] Tomaselli, *Le mentite Filoteane*, p. 398.
[72] *Considerazioni sopra le censure*, in *Scritti*, II. 249.
[73] *Trattato dell'Interdetto*, in *Scritti*, III, 36.

conception of the state which the Venetian theologians derived from the idea of its divine institution can hardly be described as Machiavellian. But, from the standpoint of the papacy, it was probably something far more sinister.

Papal theologians had for some time taken issue with the idea of divine right, and they promptly objected to it again. Bellarmine insisted that no temporal ruler acquired his authority directly from God. He received it instead, Bellarmine maintained, only indirectly, through inheritance, as in France, or by election, as in Venice herself.[74] But the unfamiliar constitutional structure of a republic gave Bellarmine, with his monarchical bias, some trouble. His comparison between the supreme magistrates of Venice and France implied that the doge was the effective head of the Venetian government. Yet he knew that the doge was not a true ruler, and on this score he found Venetian claims to an extensive princely authority based on divine commission absurd. So he attacked Marsilio's insistence on the princely authority of Venice in a passage which also hinted that forces subversive of the Republic lay behind resistance to the pope. Marsilio, he claimed, had depicted the Venetian prince

as if he were an absolute monarch, saying that he is natural lord of his state. If this is so, the republic of Venice has lost its liberty, nor can it truly be called a republic, since it has a lord and a natural lord. A lord is one who can do what he wishes with his own, being able to give, to sell, to pawn, to trade. And he is a natural lord who has dominion through heredity, through succession of blood, through birth, rather than through election or donation. Whether it is proper for the doge of Venice to be natural lord of the state of Venice, I submit to the judgment of everyone who knows the things of that republic. This author says in addition that the prince of Venice knows no superior in temporal things except God. And what is this but making him absolute lord, like kings, to whom the republic has transferred all its power? But if the republic is a true republic, and free, as she claims, she has not transferred all power to the prince, but has communicated to him that part which is shared with him; and she can increase it, decrease it, and remove it entirely, and also punish the prince if he wishes to make himself master with penalty of death, as she once did in the case of Marino Falier. Consequently the doge must recognize as superior in

74 *Risposta alla risposta*, p. 153.

temporal things not only God but also the republic, by which we mean the Great Council.[75]

There is at least a hint here that Bellarmine discerned in a republic no sovereign power comparable to that of a king, a circumstance which made the Venetian claim to divine right appear, in his eyes, particularly ridiculous. Venetian correction of his mistake was easy to provide, and it came promptly. Querini had already explained that princely authority in Venice resided not in any person but in the Republic itself, which was, collectively, a "free and independent prince." It could not be denied, he wrote, "that the republic-prince, including this one of such greatness and dignity," had all the powers properly exercised over their subjects by kings.[76] Marsilio now informed Bellarmine that "the doge is only head of the republic, which is the true prince"; and he went on to point out that "the word *prince* is generic to signify emperors and kings as well as republics." [77] He had also the impudence to suggest that if election precluded rule by divine right, the pope could hardly claim that his own authority to govern the church came directly from God.[78] The point reminds us again of the general tendency in Renaissance thought to conceive of the church as a constitutional structure analogous in form and development to the structures of secular government. If the analogy was permissible, Bellarmine's reasoning implied that supreme authority in the church resided in the College of Cardinals.

The basic issue here was clearly over the nature of sovereignty; and the Venetian interdict invites our attention, among its other features, as one of the earliest in the long series of seventeenth-century disputes over sovereignty. But in the form in which we encounter this issue here, it is clearly also an extension of the Renaissance preoccupation with liberty in the first sense noted in this book: as the absence of any political superior.[79] The Venetians

[75] *Ibid.*, pp. 175–176.
[76] *Aviso*, p. 26.
[77] *Difesa a favore della risposta*, pp. 271–272.
[78] *Ibid.*, p. 220. In fact the conception of Venice as a collective principate was clearly recognized in Rome soon after the interdict. See the letter of the nuncio Ubaldini in Paris to Cardinal Borghese, Nov. 11, 1608, *Aevum*, XI (1937), 17, n.; and the *Relatione* given by Odorici, "Paolo V e le città," p. 174, both of which describe the Senate as prince of Venice.
[79] On this view of sovereignty in Italian political thought generally, cf. Rodolfo de Mattei, "La concezione monocratica negli scrittori politici italiani del Seicento," *Studi storici in onore di Giocchino Volpe* (Florence, 1958), I, 336ff.

saw the point and spoke frequently of their devotion to liberty in this meaning. Sarpi remarked that the Republic "had always been ready to do everything it could [to satisfy the pope], saving only the sacrifice of liberty, which
she cannot allow to be diminished without most gravely offending the
divine Majesty";[80] and he reported the insistence of the Venetian government to the Spanish ambassador that it would rather "risk every adverse
fortune than bow its neck to the yoke." [81] Rome, on the other hand, recognized with equal clarity that sovereignty in this meaning was a direct challenge to the principle of order, which depended on submission to superior
powers. For the papacy, with its sense of hierarchy, there could be no sovereign in this world but the pope.

It was precisely their own very different conception of order which also
led the Venetians to a clear awareness that the issue of sovereignty was
central to the conflict with the pope. Sovereignty, in their sense of the term,
was the only guarantee of order. In his first *consulto* Sarpi had offered a careful
definition of sovereignty; his discussion of the point came close to providing
the basic argument of this work:

> No one will deny to the prince the power over the area, the surface,
> and the land of his whole empire, and over the private persons who
> possess it, because this is *de iure divino*, as is manifest in sacred scripture
> and as the doctors attest. This power of the prince, which they call
> *majesty* or *sovereignty*, is distinct from the dominion which the private
> person possesses, as Seneca noted; and it is so superior to it that the
> prince can take away dominion from the private person, but the private
> person cannot in any respect prejudice the power of the prince. This
> kind of sovereignty, in a well ordered republic, requires that the prince
> can dispose of any thing and person according to the necessity and
> utility of the public good. On the other hand the private person cannot
> do anything against the prohibition of the prince.[82]

We may note in this description of sovereignty the emphatic priority it
assigns to public over private interests and its lack of concern for individual
rights of any kind. Sarpi was in full agreement, as he put it, with the "common doctrine that the prince, for the public good, can take away the rights

---

[80] *Istoria dell'Interdetto*, p. 115.
[81] *Ibid.*, p. 145.
[82] *Difesa di due ordinazioni della serenissima republica*, in *Scritti*, II, 12.

of private persons"; and he defended this principle as "not repugnant to natural equity." [83] He did not, however, leave the definition of the public good entirely to the discretion of governments. More than once Sarpi made clear that the duty of the prince included vigorous defense of "the life, honor, and property" of his subjects;[84] on this point he happily suggests Locke as much as Machiavelli. In other writings he listed further attributes of sovereignty. It was, for example, necessarily unified. "The well ordered republic being one," he declared, "it is necessary that it should be governed by one supreme power, to which everything should be subject." [85] Sovereignty was also inalienable. When property is transferred from a layman to the church, therefore, the prince retained his authority over it.[86]

But the fundamental attribute of sovereignty, for Sarpi, was its adequacy. The power which the state exercised by divine right had necessarily to be sufficient to accomplish the primary purpose for which God had instituted government, namely the maintenance of that practical order which was the necessary condition of "civil felicity." Sarpi was emphatic on this point. "Nature," he wrote, "when it gives an end, also provides all those powers which are necessary to obtain it." Would God, he inquired rhetorically, do less?[87] He had answered the question before: "God, on whom the prince who is responsible for the public tranquility immediately depends, has also given him power to impede and to remedy all the things that disturb it." [88] By the same token the defense of princely power was not only a religious obligation; it also went to the essence of the state. The issue was therefore a matter of fundamental principle, a question not of the size but of the quality of a state. So Sarpi concluded an early *consulto*: "I cannot refrain from saying that no injury penetrates more deeply into a principate than when its majesty, that is to say sovereignty, is limited and subjected to the laws of another. A prince who possesses a small part of the world is equal in this respect to one who possesses much; Romulus was no less a prince than Trajan, nor is your Serenity now greater than your forebears when their empire had not

---

[83] *Sulla alienazione di beni laici alli ecclesiastici*, in *Scritti*, II, 126, 128. Cf. *Epistolae duorum iurisconsultorum*, p. 130: ". . . haec omnia sunt introducta ob publicum interesse; & ius publicum praefertur iuri Ecclesiastico, ex Peritorum, & Pontificummet sententia."

[84] He repeated the formula several times, as in the *Considerazioni sulle censure*, in *Scritti*, II, 229, 248, 251.

[85] *Sul giudicar le colpe di persone ecclesiastiche*, in *Scritti*, II, 46.

[86] *Difesa di due ordinazioni della serenissima republica*, in *Scritti*, II, 14–15.

[87] *Considerazioni sulle censure*, in *Scritti*, II, 212.

[88] *Sopra l'esenzione delle persone ecclesiastiche*, in *Scritti*, II, 131.

extended beyond the lagoons. He who takes away a part of his state from a prince makes him a lesser prince but leaves him a prince; he who imposes laws and obligations on him deprives him of the essence of a prince, even if he possessed the whole of Asia." [89] The limited power of Venice in the world was thus irrelevant to its sovereign status. Sarpi's arguments recall Bartolus: having discussed ancient and medieval imperial practice, he remarked that "this republic, if indeed it is a very small prince in comparison with those emperors" had nevertheless the same power in its tiny state as they in their vast empires.[90] Accordingly he advised his government to "be serene in conscience, and do what is necessary and opportune to maintain your sovereignty without any scruple." [91]

As Sarpi's references to law will have already suggested, the Venetians, like Bodin, regarded full legislative authority, the key to the maintenance of political order, as the heart of sovereignty; the right to do "anything needful" meant above all the right to make and to enforce laws. By claiming a comprehensive right to interfere with the laws of Venice the pope thus touched on the most sensitive nerve of the body politic. Princes, the Senate had reminded the French ambassador, "are necessarily deprived of sovereignty when they are subjected to the censures of popes, who can compel them with excommunications to adjust the laws in their way." [92] The Venetian government had seen this issue clearly. At an early point it had insisted to the pope on its right to make laws, a right which "God gave to the first men who established the republic, and through them transmitted to the present and continuously exercised with moderation, never exceeding legitimate limits." [93] Each of the particular Roman complaints was an attack on some aspect of the legislative authority of the Venetian state.

Notable in the Venetian conception of sovereignty was its refusal to exclude private property from the sphere into which government could properly intrude—a reflection perhaps of the happy fact that Venice had been uniformly controlled by the property-owning class itself and had never in her memory been subjected to personal despotism. Querini, therefore, did not hesitate to describe the authority of the prince in spatial terms which suggest a general proprietorship. The legal authorities were in agreement, he remarked, "that the prince is patron of all the space and, as they say, of all the area contained in his dominion, whence it is not legal for anyone to

[89] *Sopra la forza e validità della scommunica*, in *Scritti*, II, 40.
[90] *Sul giudicar le colpe di persone ecclesiastiche*, in *Scritti*, II, 49.
[91] *Sopra la forza e validità della scommunica*, in *Scritti*, II, 40.
[92] Sarpi, *Istoria dell'Interdetto*, p. 115.
[93] *Ibid.*, p. 24.

enter it without his consent . . . and they add that if it cannot be justifiable to enter the house or the property of any private person to build churches there . . . much less can such violence be done to the prince, who has a more absolute dominion over the lands possessed by him than the private or particular person." [94] For Venetian theorists, therefore, princely dominion included the right to dispose of all property in the state. The prince, Capello argued, "has greater dominion over their goods than the subjects have." [95] Sarpi was even more precise: "The prince has ordinary and extraordinary rights of tribute over lay property, and in addition the personal services of the possessor; furthermore goods, while they belong to the laity, are subject to confiscation." [96]

It was on this ground that the Venetian government claimed the right to limit bequests and to restrict the building of churches. In addition, Sarpi, at any rate, urged openly that the intervention of the state was required because the clergy were growing too rich. He emphasized the danger to society when they held property far out of proportion to their numbers, particularly when they employed their wealth for themselves rather than for the common good. He also noted the uneven distribution of clerical wealth.[97] Sarpi's position implied not only the right of the laity to intervene in the administration of ecclesiastical property, but even more broadly the right of princes to concern themselves with the distribution of wealth among their subjects. The reverberations of the position, which the Venetian theorists spelled out with so little hesitation, were therefore remarkably wide; and it is also useful to recall, here as in other connections, the wide circulation of Venetian writings abroad.

Nor was the papacy reluctant to broaden discussion of the issue of state power over private property. Roman theorists returned to the question again and again, as though the Venetian extension of dominion to include a broad authority over private wealth constituted some particular outrage. Rome, from this standpoint, posed as the champion of personal freedom, casting the Venetian government in the role of tyrant.[98] The Servite writers distinguished carefully between the rights of the prince over private land and

---

[94] *Aviso*, pp. 19–20.

[95] *Delle controversie*, p. 111.

[96] *Sopra l'esenzione delle persone ecclesiastiche*, in *Scritti*, II, 135.

[97] *Sulla alienazione di beni laici alli ecclesiastici*, in *Scritti*, II, 101–120; *Considerazioni sopra le censure*, in *Scritti*, II, 204, 208. Querini, *Aviso*, p. 16, also expressed concern at the maldistribution of ecclesiastical wealth, as though this problem was a proper concern of the secular government.

[98] Sarpi noted this charge, *Istoria dell'Interdetto*, p. 12.

those of its owner: "The private person has proprietary power over it; the prince has jurisdictional power. For this reason the private person can dispose of it as he pleases; the prince cannot, except for the common good and public utility." [99] Nor was the exception admitted here intended to give any comfort to the Venetian case, as should be evident in the tone with which Baglioni expressed his agreement: "No one will concede that princes, however just and good they may be, can dispose freely and at will of the goods of subjects, taking from one and giving to another. This would be too much; and everyone has this saying on his lips: that he wishes to do with his own as he pleases. And just princes have never believed they could do this, nor have they ever exercised such authority, which is directly contrary to the law of nature." [100] Papalist theory, in its concern to protect the church from state encroachment, aimed, like nineteenth-century liberalism, to confine secular government as narrowly as possible.

In presenting these arguments, Rome was trying to identify the interests of the church with the common interests of society, but this was not where her major concern lay. The essential point for the papacy was not what the church had in common with other interests in European society but the ways in which she was special. The real outrage was not that Venice presumed to interfere with private property in general, but that she dared to interfere with the property of the church. Baronius warned the Venetians solemnly that laymen are forbidden to lay hands on the things of God.[101] This concern with the special character of the church emerged with particular clarity in connection with another dimension of the struggle over sovereignty: the dispute over the legitimacy of bringing accused clergy to trial in secular courts, a practice which raised the issue of the equal authority of the prince over all persons resident in the state.

The Venetian position was simple: no distinctions of quality could be made among the members of human society before the law; the needs of social order required that the law be equally applied to every man. Querini was emphatic: "The Republic, as free and independent prince, has, by the nature of its principate, authority over all its subjects indifferently." [102] For Sarpi the survival of the state depended on the maintenance of this

[99] *Difesa de' Servi*, p. 86. See also Possevino, *Risposta del sig. Paolo Anafesto*, pp. 40–41; Baglioni, *Apologia*, pp. 34, 60; Bovio, *Risposta alle considerationi*, pp. 33, 39.
[100] *Apologia*, p. 50.
[101] *Paraenesis*, p. 109.
[102] *Aviso*, p. 26.

principle. "A natural body could not endure which had within itself one part not destined to belong to the whole," he wrote; "even less can a civil body endure which has in its midst a man who recognizes others than the prince [as his superior] in human and temporal things." [103] For the Venetians, the authority of the Venetian state to punish criminals of every description was an inevitable consequence of the purpose for which the state had been divinely instituted; and that the clergy should be exempted from an obligation which was not only common to all men but also finally of religious foundation appeared to them particularly unseemly. History, too, was invoked to support the Venetian position. The Venetians observed that Venetian practice was a "custom never interrupted for more than a thousand years." [104] Ecclesiastical courts, they insisted, nowhere functioned except by concession from the secular power.[105] Sarpi also suggested that the trial of criminal clergy in Venetian courts was of "marvelous utility to the ecclesiastical order and useful in maintaining its dignity, which had been in a considerable decline on account of the negligence of the authority which ought to provide for it." [106] The scandals of the Renaissance papacy were still well remembered in Venice; the inability of the church, at least during some periods, to discipline its own officers thus became another argument in favor of civil jurisdiction over the clergy. Civil jurisdiction was seen as an instrument for the reform of a corrupt church.

Behind Venetian practice and the arguments by which it was defended also lay the conviction that a priest, whatever else he might be in addition, was first a civil being, that he shared the common needs of men as citizens, and that he ought therefore to have a share in the obligations of citizenship.[107] Querini, again, had been clear on this point: "It suffices to say that a

[103] *Considerazioni sopra le censure*, in *Scritti*, II, 222. For his full argument, see *Sopra l'esenzione delle persone ecclesiastiche*, in *Scritti*, II, 130–138. Sarpi was emphatic that jurisdiction over all subjects was essential to sovereignty; cf. *Considerazioni sopra le censure*, in *Scritti*, II, 222.

[104] Sarpi, *Istoria dell'Interdetto*, p. 12. See also his *Risposta al breve circa li prigioni*, in *Scritti*, II, 71, where he insists that Venice at her very beginnings had received the right from God to punish criminals. Cf. also Capello, *Delle controversie*, p. 91.

[105] Sarpi, *Apologia*, in *Scritti*, III, 71, where he bases his argument on the inalienability of sovereignty, including its jurisdictional authority. See also his *Consiglio sul giudicar le colpe di persone ecclesiastiche*, in *Scritti*, II, 41–70; cf. Marsilio, *Difesa a favore della risposta*, pp. 210–211, for the origin of ecclesiastical courts in antiquity, and *Risposta d'un Dottore in theologia*, p. 144, on the general point.

[106] *Risposta al breve circa li prigioni*, in *Scritti*, II, 72.

[107] Sarpi evidently saw the performance of civic duties as good works in a religious sense; cf. *Sopra la forza e validità della scommunica*, in *Scritti*, II, 21.

city is composed of citizens, and that citizens are those who enjoy the benefit of civil life through being preserved in peace among themselves, through being defended from foreigners, through experiencing the good care of their resources and possessions, and finally through enjoying those blessings and felicities to which the whole body of citizens has been directed. This is not possible to obtain without community in the laws and good public ordinances, and without common judges. This is natural order, and essential to be observed in all cities." [108] By Querini's definition the clergy in any state were citizens like other men, a point on which Sarpi agreed, drawing the appropriate practical conclusion: "Ecclesiastics are citizens and parts of the republic; but the republic is governed with the laws of the prince. Therefore they are subject to him, so that, resisting, they sin before God no less than laymen." [109] From the Venetian standpoint this conception of ecclesiastical persons as citizens hardly reduced their dignity. On the contrary, it opened up to the clergy an area of virtuous activity from which they would otherwise have been excluded; as Capello noted, it recognized their capacity for "civil felicity." [110] In this perspective that "liberty" from the normal responsibilities of political life which Rome demanded for the clergy would actually have denied them the benefits of the only kind of order relevant to the human condition. The kind of privilege Rome called *liberty* was, for Sarpi, mere *license*.[111]

Rome took the position that the clergy composed a separate and superior order, and their submission to lay jurisdiction, by subordinating higher to lower, represented another intolerable challenge to the basic principle of order. The papacy saw the clergy not as citizens of any earthly city but only of the City of God. For Possevino, therefore, it was simply "monstrous," in a very exact sense, "for ecclesiastics to obey laymen," as the Venetians proposed, "just as it is monstrous that the head should be subject to the feet, the greater to the less, those who are consecrated to the divine cult to profane men." [112] Bellarmine also set about, in his more measured way, to prove to the Venetians that princes have no authority over ecclesiastics. Priests, he

---

[108] *Aviso*, p. 26.

[109] *Sul giudicar le colpe di persone ecclesiastiche*, in *Scritti*, II, 50. See also Nicolò Crasso, *Antiparaenesis ad Cesarem Baronium Cardinalem, pro Sereniss. Veneta Republica* (Padua, 1606), in the *Raccolta*, II, 281–320, p. 288, on the priest as citizen of the secular state.

[110] *Delle controversie*, pp. 44–45.

[111] *Istoria dell'Interdetto*, p. 4, where Sarpi makes the terms synonymous.

[112] *Nuova risposta di Giovanni Filoteo di Asti*, p. 18.

declared, must not be judged by other men because, in relation to the laity, the clergy are gods. A man who despises a prelate despises God himself, and it is far worse for a layman to disobey a prelate than for a prelate to injure a layman.[113] Pursuing the same line of thought, he pointed out the superiority of holy orders, as a sacrament, to baptism; he argued on this basis too that the clergy should not be subject to the laity.[114] Bellarmine also traced separate ecclesiastical courts back to the primitive church, denying that they had come into existence as concessions from the emperors.[115] Possevino carried the historical argument even farther, invoking the thesis of Baronius that in these important matters nothing had ever changed.[116] The Servite writers agreed that clerical immunities were based on divine law rather than human privilege. They also shared Bellarmine's view that although the clergy in any state normally behave in conformity with civil law, they do so not out of any obligation to obedience but voluntarily, according to the precepts of reason and nature.[117] The papal theologians thus appear to assign to the clergy the same right of private judgment respecting the civil power that the Venetians attributed to the laity respecting the ecclesiastical power.

As these sentiments may suggest, the theologians who wrote against Venice at times give the impression of regarding Christianity as a philosophy of order instead of the gospel of salvation, and its primary mission as the enforcement of hierarchy rather than the saving of souls. Thus Baronius argued that the laity should keep silent even when accusations against ecclesiastics happened to be true.[118] Several clerical writers on the papalist side suggest, indeed, such radical contempt for ranks in the social scale lower than their own that, from a different direction, they too appear unwittingly to subvert the principle of hierarchy; they give the impression of wishing the lower to be absorbed into the higher, of tending to a kind of social monophysism. Against the Venetian effort to restrict the building of churches the Servite theologians argued that there could never be enough churches to honor the Deity: "If all the world were full of temples, and all creatures were continuously praising God with tongue and spirit in these temples, they would not give sufficient praises and convenient honor to his greatness and

---

[113] *Risposta alla risposta*, pp. 152ff.; *Risposta a fra Paulo*, pp. 100–102.

[114] *Avviso di Matteo Torti*, p. 128.

[115] *Risposta alla risposta*, pp. 155–157.

[116] *Nuova risposta di Giovanni Fileteo di Asti*, p. 28.

[117] *Difesa de'Servi*, pp. 20–22.

[118] *Paraenesis*, p. 119. He cited the example of the sons of Noah, who covered their father's shame.

uncreated majesty." [119] The point for these men was not (as with François de Sales) that every human activity could be converted into an act of worship, but that deliberate acts of worship should properly preclude and replace all other activity. Their attitude to government was comparable. They did not, in fact, show much respect for the civil power even when it confined its action to the sphere they thought suitable to it, and their remarks occasionally suggest that they could be finally satisfied only with a comprehensive theocracy. The Servites argued that the clergy, though distinct from the body politic, were nevertheless its soul and principle of life. "As the soul rules and governs the natural body," they wrote, "so the ecclesiastic maintains and conserves the Republic." [120] Possevino was more explicit about the implication of this suggestion; Venice, he declared, ought to include members of the clergy in its various governing bodies.[121]

With their utterly different evaluations of the political order, the two sides took opposite positions on how it should be preserved. The Venetians, looking at the actual workings of the world around them, recognized that the various states of Europe did not compose any discernible unity; and their view of international relations began with the assumption that the survival of any state depended on the effectiveness with which it looked after its own interests. Sarpi, in reply to Roman complaints that Venetian commercial regulations injured the subjects of the pope, represented as the collective position of Venice that "every prince commands to his subjects what serves the convenience of his own state, without regard to what follows in others." [122] Capello had insisted that "the prince, for the public welfare, is master of the lives, and much more of the property of all his subjects";[123] and Sarpi cited with approval an opinion of the French ambassador that "the republic put its liberty above every other consideration, because *salus populi suprema lex esto*." [124] His own penal philosophy was based not on the guilt of the offender but on the utility of his punishment for society.[125] Querini was inclined to see the stability of Venetian government as an

[119] *Difesa de' Servi*, p. 80.
[120] *Ibid.*, p. 79.
[121] *Risposta di Teodoro Eugenio*, pp. 52–53. He pointed as appropriate models to the French *parlements* and the imperial college of electors.
[122] *Istoria dell'Interdetto*, p. 9.
[123] *Delle controversie*, p. 132; see also the longer statement, p. 126.
[124] *Istoria dell'Interdetto*, p. 31.
[125] See for example his remarks in *Considerazioni sopra le censure*, in *Scritti*, II, 227ff.

argument in favor of its traditional legal structure;[126] the end in this case evidently justified the means. He also regarded the republican constitution of Venice as a guarantee of the propriety of its acts, as though a republic ought particularly to be immune from interference by the pope in the name of morality or religion.[127] All governments, in this view, may be autonomous, but republics should be more autonomous than others. Such an argument was particularly unlikely to impress favorably the theologians at the Curia.

Each side accused the other of Machiavellism. Sarpi himself attributed to the pope the doctrine that the end justifies the means, the end in this case being "the conservation and increase of the temporal authority which they claim"; hence the efforts of Rome to incite subjects to rebellion.[128] But the charge of preferring politics to principle was more frequently directed by Rome against Venice; Rome, with good reason, recognized that its true enemy was the political mentality of the Renaissance. Again and again Venice was accused (as though the criminality of this were self-evident) of basing her policy on *ragione di stato*, which Bovio did not hesitate to label as heresy. It was, he wrote, a "heretical concept of certain impious men who believe that reason of state dispenses from all laws, human and divine, and legitimizes every injustice and impiety, so that anything which favors the preservation and increase of the state is held incapable of harming the soul." [129] Bellarmine sentimentally contrasted the behavior of Venice in this respect with that of the "many pious and religious princes in the Church of God," [130] while other writers described the Venetian theologians as disciples of Machiavelli, Bodin, and other "atheists" too abominable to merit reply.[131] Her leaders seemed in Rome mere *politici*.[132]

The Spanish Franciscan Francesco di Sosa, replying to a work by Marsilio, carefully distinguished various "political" attitudes, finding them all simultaneously in his opponent. The first type of *politico*, he said, was openly dedicated to self-preservation and self-aggrandizement in this life. Men of this kind reduced all government to "laws of state which they constantly

---

[126] *Aviso*, pp. 26–27.

[127] *Ibid.*, pp. 17–18.

[128] *Sui remedii da opporsi ad una eventuale aggravazione della scommunica*, in *Scritti*, II, 159.

[129] *Risposta alle considerationi*, p. 79.

[130] *Risposta alla risposta*, p. 174.

[131] So Amato, *Discorso*, p. 19.

[132] Venturi uses the term *politici* repeatedly in *Maiestà pontificia*. See Pastor, XXV, 113, for contemporary charges that Venice had given birth to the *politique* movement.

change according to changing circumstances" and which they regularly adapted to suit their own convenience. Their primary offense was thus an unprincipled flexibility, with the most abominable consequences for religion. Contemptuous of truth, such men readily shifted from one profession of faith to another. This, Sosa observed, "was the way and the intention of Machiavelli and of the author of the accursed book *De tribus impostoribus mundi*"; one may assume that he was also afraid of Venetian discussions with Protestants such as Wotton. The second political type, Sosa went on, acknowledged the truth of religion and chose to stick with fixed forms of belief but preferred one to another because of its political utility and its incompatibility with Catholicism; this type had been responsible for the recent proliferation of "lying sects." The third type was not essentially different but, for reasons of selfish and worldly interest, chose to conform externally to the Catholic religion.[133] Behind this attack on Venice one can also still discern, perhaps, Spanish hostility to the king of France.

But the basic objection to an autonomous politics of the Renaissance sort was that it subverted spiritual order. It gave a controlling position to the lower aims of politics, whereas political ends should give way, in every instance, to spiritual. The Servite writers made the point with particular clarity. They admitted that the purpose of law was the utility of the community. Nevertheless, they insisted in connection with the aberrant Venetian legislation, it was essential to bear in mind "that there is another higher end and a greater and more excellent good, which is the spiritual good and the end of the ecclesiastical power, from which the political end cannot derogate . . . every reason of state must yield to the spiritual end." [134] A valid appreciation of the order of ends should make evident, as Venturi remarks, that "reason of state certainly depends originally on religion, not religion on it; and therefore the principate ought to serve religion, not religion the principate." The prince's obligations to the faith took precedence, therefore, over all his other duties for Venturi, who sought also to incorporate the Renaissance preoccupation with individual glory into a Christian framework by suggesting that true glory consists in piety and obedience to the pope.[135] True glory, according to this view, was not properly the attribute of an individual; it came rather from due participation in the pattern of universal order.

[133] *Discorso contro due trattati stampati senza nome d'auttore intorno le censure che N. Signore Papa Paolo V pronuntiò contro la republica di Venetia*, trans. Ambrosio Cordova (Naples, 1607), pp. 59–61.

[134] *Difesa de' Servi*, pp. 63–64.

[135] *Maiestà pontificia*, pp. 115, 110, 90ff.

But although this consideration provided the primary argument on the papal side, the Roman theologians did not hesitate in addition to exploit fully the baptized Machiavellism of such publicists as Botero. Venturi, for example, almost seems to have written against Venice with Botero's *Ragion di stato* open before him. His discussion of the issue was particularly direct. He began with a clear distinction between two kinds of reason of state, which he designated as "accursed reason" and "blessed reason." Reason was blessed when it took its vigor from true religion, remained united with it, conformed to its demands; it was accursed when "on any point separated from it, daring to rebel, and deliberately contravening divine or natural law." Where a prince violated the laws of God or nature, Venturi declared, "the state will become a confusion, the government a tyranny. The prince will have an unjust dominion, and his rule ought then to be described as conforming rather to his own unreasonable pleasure and particular interest than to reason of state." [136]

But virtue was not left by the papal theologians to be simply its own reward. They also promised, like Botero, the most concrete political benefits from conformity to true reason of state. The practical advantages of respect for the faith were based, for Venturi, on the fundamental connection between religion and society. Without religion, he held, it would be impossible to sustain any form of social organization, any government, any valid justice. Religion was "the foundation of cities and of kingdoms, the principle of all laws, the nerve of civil conversation." All founders of governments, he pointed out, had recognized the need for religion by providing for worship and its necessary institutional framework.[137]

This general principle naturally found its most effective application, for Venturi, in the political value to any Christian government of communion with the pope. As the supreme representative on earth of the principle of unity and of all other eternal values, the pope alone could, in his view, offer to governments effective assistance in the common struggle of all sublunary things against division, alteration, and decay. Acceptance of universal order was the most dependable guarantor of political order. "Without Christ, without him who is his vicar on earth," Venturi maintained, the state would be deprived of its "securest base" and its "most vigorous support"; it would be exposed "to various dangerous mutations"; "order would be disordered"; all regard for laws and justice would collapse; anyone who sought "to

---

[136] *Ibid.*, pp. 109ff.
[137] *Ibid.*, pp. 37–38. He developed the point at some length in connection with antiquity, pp. 38–40.

convert ancient liberty into a principate" would find support (a particular threat for Venice); such civil discords as had in the past caused republics to degenerate into kingdoms and empires to fall under the sway of single princes would multiply. All the unhappy tendencies in the political history of Renaissance Italy, by this interpretation, proceeded from Renaissance infidelity. Fidelity and obedience to the pope, on the other hand, could be counted on to bring great political rewards. The obedience of the ruler to the pope set the best possible example of obedience to his subjects; unity in the Catholic faith provided the essential foundation for unity and peace in secular society; military victories could be expected to accompany pious union with the pope.[138] The rewards of fidelity to the church could be expected, indeed, to continue beyond death even in this world; historians would glorify the faithful ruler.[139]

False reason of state, on the other hand, turned out to be false not only because it violated general principles but also because it eventually turned out badly in practice. Disobedience to the pope invariably produced internal disorder and led rulers to bad ends. Girolamo Del Bene, among many others, cited the wretched fates of medieval emperors who had defied the pope.[140] Venturi, among others, noted the close relation between Protestantism and political revolt; nothing, he remarked, inflamed men against each other more bitterly than religious difference. "There will never be peace, or faith, or love, or true friendship," he declared, "between those who believe differently." [141] Men who refused to obey the pope would also be unable to lead virtuous and orderly lives. "What else," Venturi asked, "signifies, in impious language, independence from the Vicar of Christ, than to wish to be free in all ugly and wicked actions? than to wish to live without restraint, unbridled, without religion? than to recognize no principle of moderation, but only to be dominated by appetite? than to let oneself be guided, like a beast, by sensual appetites and carnal pleasures? than to make licit whatever one pleases, and to subjugate to sense, indeed to oppress and to overthrow, reason, spirit, truth, justice, God himself?" [142] It is clear enough why Rome had to represent Venice as a singularly immoral place; logic required it. And these general principles of Christian reason of state received specific application to Venice.

[138] Ibid., pp. 144ff., 129ff., 153.

[139] The point was made by Possevino, *Risposta di Teodoro Eugenio*, p. 19. Enemies of the church, he pointed out, are regularly condemned by historians.

[140] *Risposta alla domanda fattagli circa l'esito di ciò che passa tra Paolo V e la Repubblica di Venezia* (Bologna, 1606), pp. 8–10.

[141] *Maiestà pontificia*, pp. 139–140, 142.

[142] Ibid., p. 125.

Possevino recorded the admonition of earlier popes who had felt the need to remind Venice "that the Republic did not have from God that privilege which, through the mouth of Christ, had been conceded to the Apostolic See, to endure with him even until the consummation of the world." [143] But if Venice piously submitted to the pope, she might hope to postpone, for at least a while, her own destruction.[144]

Since the ostensible causes of the interdict were legal and jurisdictional, the dispute also concerned itself with the nature of law, a subject that touched on the attitudes of the two sides toward government. Rome charged again and again that the Venetian legislation to which it took objection was in some fundamental sense illegal, while Venice insisted that, on the contrary, the Roman position was an assault on the law. Behind this clash lay, again, the contrast between two conceptions of external reality and of human experience.

For Rome law was embedded in the structure of the universe. Law was first of all an eternal principle of universal application; and particular laws, notably including the legislation of particular societies, were legitimate only when they reflected and conformed to the general principle of law. Furthermore law partook of the general order of things; it too had its hierarchies. Some authorities, some kinds of law were inevitably closer to the general source of law, reflected its substance more accurately, and therefore ought properly to take precedence, when differences appeared, over other authorities and other kinds of law. These principles meant that princes were never free to legislate arbitrarily or simply on the basis of local needs and conditions. Responsible only for an inferior level of the Christian Republic, itself a vast commonwealth in which local needs had always to be subordinated to universal interests, not only were princes required to adapt their enactments to the principles of divine and natural law, but their laws were also subject to review by ecclesiastical authority. By the same token canon law, in every state, had always to take precedence over civil law.[145]

The most practical consequence of the Roman position proceeded, however, from its implications for the place of custom, the basis of the Venetian

[143] *Risposta di Teodoro Eugenio*, p. 11. Baronius specifically predicted that Venice would lose her cherished republican government (*Paraenesis*, p. 121).

[144] The practical advantages of Venetian collaboration with the pope are central to the anonymous *Discorso, sotto nome di sentenza d'un clariss. senator Veneto*.

[145] Baglioni, *Apologia*, pp. 48–49; *Difesa de' Servi*, pp. 37, 120; Medici, *Discorso*, p. 200. For the papal claim to superiority over all laws in all places, cf. Sarpi, *Sulle pretensioni delli ecclesiastici*, in *Scritti*, II, 100.

legal system, in the structure of law. On this point the papal theologians repeatedly exposed the potential radicalism of the Counter Reformation. They insisted repeatedly on the impotence of custom, as a legal principle, against the superior authority of canon law, of papal decrees, and above all of abstract justice, with which they claimed a special familiarity. No subject evoked a louder chorus of agreement among them than this, on which the Servite theologians offered a particularly comprehensive statement:

> If it is a question of divine or natural law, on which the immunity [of the clergy from civil jurisdiction] depends, no custom can repeal it. Nor, if a human papal law is at issue, can either civil law or custom prejudice it, as has been shown so many times, since papal law derives from a higher source and is of greater authority than human law, or custom founded on evil, like this . . . even if custom in that republic should presume (as it does not) to judge ecclesiastics and every papal law concerning immunity, the pope, nevertheless, with his authority, can make laws which annul every custom, as it is seen that he truly does, expressing himself in the bull *in Coena Domini,* and in papal constitutions, *Non obstantibus quibuscunque; consuetudinibus,* etc.[146]

At the same time we may observe that this contempt for custom is oddly at cross-purposes with the thesis, developed in the masterwork of Baronius, that the proper organization of Christendom was rooted in historical actuality, a position which it would appear to make irrelevant. This relative contempt for custom suggests again that history was, after all, of very limited interest for the mind of the Counter Reformation.

The Venetians naturally did not argue that custom, to which they constantly appealed, should take precedence over divine or natural law. Sarpi readily admitted its inferiority to both.[147] He was also prepared to appeal to these higher laws on behalf of Venice. He insisted, for example, on the natural right of the prince to defend his "civil being" even against the pope.[148] He also recognized that some kinds of actions might be intrinsically contrary to natural law—for example homicide or adultery.[149] But most

---

[146] *Difesa de'Servi,* p. 186. See similar statements in Bovio, *Risposta alle considerationi,* p. 73; Baglioni, *Apologia,* pp. 52, 55; Bellarmine, *Risposta ai sette,* p. 63, and *Risposta alla risposta,* p. 177. Sarpi, *Istoria dell'Interdetto,* p. 12, represented Paul V as rejecting the Venetian appeal to custom "perchè era tanto peggiore, quanto piu vecchia."

[147] *Considerazioni sopra le censure,* in *Scritti,* II, 223.

[148] *Sopra la forza e validità della scommunica,* in *Scritti,* II, 38–39.

[149] *Sulla alienazione di beni laici alli ecclesiastici,* in *Scritti,* II, 105.

human acts and situations could not, in Sarpi's view, be treated in this categorical way. Most matters, he argued, were by nature neither just nor unjust but raised issues merely of convenience; these were, in his view, precisely the concern of the civil law, which has therefore to respond not to ultimate principles but to immediate conditions.[150] Sarpi largely denied that civil law was based on nature and reason, and thus he rejected for it any relationship to larger patterns of order in the universe. On the other hand he did not mean that the civil law was merely arbitrary. Its criterion, however, should be the interest of the immediate community.

In addition, as no one was now better aware than the Venetians, communities differ and times change; and this also had to be reflected in law. As Sarpi pointed out, "all nations do not have the same laws, which indeed are sometimes contrary to each other, because of the fact that different purposes require different ordinances."[151] "Every prince in his own state," he remarked again, "can in such matters [as the regulation of clerical wealth] establish whatever the conditions of the times and places require, and also change things once constituted if changing conditions demand it."[152] Capello put the issue even more generally: "Laws are to behavior like medicine to illnesses; and therefore, just as a different illness requires a different medicine, so different times, different customs, different conditions, require various, diverse, and sometimes contrary laws."[153]

This remarkable emphasis on the flexibility of law, or more precisely of laws, was somewhat balanced by the Venetian respect for custom, about whose authority on legal questions Rome had such strong reservations. In one of its many aspects the struggle between the papacy and the republic was thus a conflict between systematic law, enunciated by superior authority on the basis of general principles, and established custom. Capello offered a resounding affirmation of the authority of custom: "Long established customs which are not contrary to divine law, to the sacred scriptures, or to the traditions of the fathers, have force to abrogate all positive law, and ought to be observed by all as most holy laws; and whoever does not observe them sins no less than if he had transgressed against [any other] just law."[154] It should be recognized, however, that for the Venetians with their skepticism about abstractions, custom was not so much a rigid system of precedents

[150] *Sul giudicar le colpe di persone ecclesiastiche*, in *Scritti*, II, 52–53.
[151] *Ibid.*, p. 53.
[152] *Sulla alienazione di beni laici alli ecclesiastici*, in *Scritti*, II, 105.
[153] *Delle controversie*, p. 125.
[154] *Ibid.*, p. 105.

as a means of transmitting the experience of the community from generation to generation. This was Sarpi's point when he maintained that "customs have the force of laws and ought to be continued and observed in the places where they are in use and vigor." For him, unwritten law had precisely the advantage over fixed written codes that it was constantly validated by experience.[155]

But political and legal questions did not pose the only fundamental issues behind the struggle over the interdict. As in the earlier phases of the Renaissance, serious ecclesiological questions were lurking just below the surface of political debate, and occasionally they rose at least partly into view. In fact, the Venetian challenge to the Roman conception of the church probably worried the papacy far more directly than the political questions we have so far examined. The difficulty for Rome, furthermore, was not limited to the fact that particular actions of the Venetian government had implications for the status of the clergy and the role of the laity in the church which had to be rejected out of hand. Beyond this, in the course of defending these acts the theologians of Venice developed, more explicitly and radically than ever before, those tendencies in Italian Evangelism, long kept alive in Venice, which had so frightened the leaders of the early Counter Reformation some seven decades earlier. The resurgence of this religious tradition helps further to explain the urgency in Rome's need to discipline Venice. Far more than jurisdictional questions were at stake.

The Roman position on the nature of the church and its constitution was definite, although by no means fully accepted in all parts of the Roman communion. Roman theologians were clear that the church was a visible institution (rather than "a nothing," as Possevino described the alternative),[156] of which the clergy, as Bovio expressed it, constituted "the more important and worthy part," so that it was proper to limit the term *church* merely to its clerical members.[157] In the church the laity rightly had no authority whatsoever; and it was essential, as Possevino insisted, to resist the perverse impulse of laymen to reform the church: one should ask them: "*Et quis constituit vos iudices?*" [158] The right of the church to own property was also patent; it was entitled to operate in the world by whatever instruments seemed useful.[159]

[155] *Sul giudicar le colpe di persone ecclesiastiche*, in *Scritti*, II, 62–64.
[156] *Risposta di Teodoro Eugenio*, p. 44.
[157] *Risposta alle considerationi*, p. 31.
[158] *Risposta di Teodoro Eugenio*, p. 15.
[159] *Difesa de' Servi*, pp. 100ff.

Since the Venetian Senate had defied the pope on what were considered in Rome ecclesiastical questions, the papalist writers also emphasized the monarchical structure of the church and glorified its ruler. Campanella called the pope *Deus Deorum*.[160] Bellarmine emphasized that the conciliar question was settled; for him only a heretic could still concern himself with the issue.[161] The pope was now clearly the absolute head of the church; Bellarmine made the point sharply to Sarpi: "The pope does not have a limited power, like other prelates, but absolute power to pronounce, to ordain, and to command whatever is necessary for the governance of the church, and power to prohibit, to absolve, to dispense, in all things the necessity of souls requires .... Finally ... Christ has communicated to his vicar the fullest power, not absolutely, but insofar as it is communicable to a mortal man." [162] Papal power, stemming immediately from God,[163] obviously could not be affected by the desires or actions of men.[164] It was also universal: papal decrees applied everywhere, regardless of the views of local authorities.[165] The pope's authority, furthermore, extended both to the spiritual life of the church and its institutional direction; it included power to do anything necessary to rule the church and promote its purposes.[166] The papal theologians did not, on the whole, go beyond the limited conception of papal infallibility finally accepted as dogma,[167] but they objected strenuously to any emphasis on those areas in which the pope might be considered subject to error.[168] At the same time they attributed to him a broad disciplinary authority. Baronius proclaimed a double ministry for Peter: *pascere* but also *occidere*, to nourish spiritually but also to destroy physically.[169] Rome, he declared, was the root, and detachment from her brought spiritual death; to maintain his connection with the source of all spiritual life, every Christian had the duty of simple and immediate obedience to the pope, without argument or discussion.[170] Bellarmine admitted that it might be possible to exalt the pope too extravagantly, but he was tolerant of such

[160] *Antiveneti*, p. 18.
[161] *Risposta ai sette*, pp. 27–29.
[162] *Risposta a fra Paulo*, pp. 126–127.
[163] *Risposta a Marsilio*, pp. 148–150, contrasting papal authority in this respect with that of temporal princes.
[164] *Risposta a fra Paulo*, p. 125.
[165] *Risposta ai sette*, p. 7.
[166] *Risposta alla risposta*, p. 168.
[167] Cf. Baglioni, *Apologia*, I, 42, and II, 45ff.
[168] Cf. Bellarmine, *Avviso di Matteo Torti*, p. 124.
[169] *Sententia super excommunicatione Venetorum*, in the *Raccolta*, p. 135.
[170] *Paraensis*, pp. 103, 113–114.

excesses. The error of seeing the pope as God wielding all power in heaven and earth was a weakness more pleasing to the Deity, he suggested, than the boldness of those who sought to abase the pope's authority.[171] He equated Venetian defiance of the pope with the sin of Eve.[172]

The Venetian theologians admitted an element of truth in these doctrines but thought it seriously compromised by exaggeration. Sarpi regarded many papal formulations as heretical, according to his own careful definition of *heresy*. "This word," he declared, "not only signifies a pertinacity in denying certain articles of the faith but also in forming opinions of one's own not truly contained in the faith, in wishing to force others to believe them as if they did belong to the faith, and in separating oneself from those who hold to an unadulterated Christian faith without any addition of what one happened [privately] to like. It is popularly but also truly said that a man can be a heretic either for believing too little or too much, for denying any article of faith and for wanting as an article what is not." [173]

The Venetians, with their long tradition of lay participation in ecclesiastical administration, took particular exception to the clerical conception of the church favored in Rome. Sarpi regarded the identification of the church with its clergy as a usurpation.[174] The clergy, Querini insisted, are not the whole of the church but only that part chosen to serve the rest.[175] Since every Catholic Christian is a member of the church, Fulgenzio Tomaselli argued, he is equally entitled to call himself an *ecclesiastic*.[176] A proper definition of the church, these men insisted, must take into account its lay majority; the church, Sarpi maintained more than once, "is the congregation of the faithful diffused throughout the whole world." [177] If only on the level of words, this definition of the church was a neat way to dispose of the papal demand for "ecclesiastical liberty." *True* ecclesiastical liberty, as Querini pointed out, was the freedom of all members of the church to follow and to teach the precepts of Christ and the Apostles, not the special privilege of a minority.[178]

The Venetian claim that all Christians were ecclesiastics, although it did

---

[171] *Risposta ad un libretto di Gersone*, p. 320 bis.

[172] *Avviso*, p. 123.

[173] *Difesa delle opere scritte a favore della serenissima republica*, in *Scritti*, III, 248.

[174] *In materia della libertà ecclesiastica*, in *Scritti*, II, 139.

[175] *Aviso*, p. 28.

[176] *Le mentite Filoteane*, p. 397.

[177] *In materia della libertà ecclesiastica*, in *Scritti*, II, 139. See also his *Apologia*, in *Scritti*, III, 69–70; and Capello, *Delle controversie*, p. 120.

[178] *Aviso*, p. 28.

not obliterate every difference, also tended to reduce the importance of the qualitative distinction, so strenuously maintained by Rome, between clergy and laity. The lay bias of the Venetian writers occasionally took extreme forms. Sarpi himself hinted that the special training of clerical theologians was irrelevant to salvation;[179] and a German defender of Venice, Pandolfus Offman of Breslau, suggested that the corrupt lives of contemporary clergy made their salvation (in contrast to that of the devout rulers of Venice) particularly dubious.[180] But the Venetians preferred, on the whole, to direct their attack against the special claims of the pope, on which, both in the theory of their opponents and as a serious practical danger, the special authority of the clergy appeared to depend.

The Venetian writers did not deny the pope any authority in the church. Marsilio made a special point of the fact that the doge recognized the pope's superiority *in spiritualibus*.[181] But the admission served only to emphasize the limits of papal authority, and the Venetians concentrated on defining the pope's powers as narrowly as possible. Above all they opposed the notion that the pope could define them for himself. As Sarpi stated their general position: "The power of the supreme pontiff to command Christians is not unlimited, nor does it extend to all matters and modes, but it is restricted to the end of the public utility of the church and has divine law for its rule." [182] The pope, Sarpi argued ambiguously, wielded only Christ's human powers, not his divine; papal jurisdiction covered spiritual matters only and could be exercised only for edification; the pope had no authority whatsoever over those who were not members of the church.[183] In expounding the views of Gerson, Sarpi also emphasized the ministerial role of the pope and noted that "the minister is a servant" and that a servant can hardly claim an unlimited right to rule.[184] He rejected the specific identification of *the rock*, in the familiar text, with the person of Peter, noting too an inconsistency between the conceptions of Peter as foundation and as head;[185] and he suggested that *the keys* properly represented not so much the authority to bind and to loose as, in the one case, power and, in the other, the wisdom and discretion that

---

[179] By maintaining that the true Gospel, which teaches imitation of the suffering Christ, is equally known to the ignorant (*Considerazioni sopra le censure*, in *Scritti*, II, 215).

[180] *Avvertimento, et ammonitione catolica*, p. 101.

[181] *Difesa a favore della risposta*, p. 218.

[182] *Trattato dell'Interdetto*, in *Scritti*, III, 15.

[183] *Ibid.*, pp. 15–17, 20.

[184] *Apologia*, in *Scritti*, III, 151.

[185] *Ibid.*, p. 129.

should regulate it.[186] Nor did Sarpi stand alone in these sentiments. Capello, as though the eventuality were likely, proposed as a general principle that, when the two authorities appeared to conflict, men should obey God rather than the pope.[187] Offman claimed to have heard ordinary Venetians say aloud, "I wish to be Catholic and Christian in spite of Rome," and others declare, "If the pope cannot put me in heaven without my consent, even less can he condemn me to hell; because he is not God but the minister of God, who saves all that trust in him." [188] Men of this sort found the broad papalist claims monstrous. Sarpi accused canonists who equated the pope with God of blasphemy;[189] he also declared that "to ascribe to the pope an exorbitant and enormous authority without limit, without law, and without rule, is a false opinion, alien from scripture and from the holy Fathers; but to assert further that it is necessary to the faith to believe it is heresy." [190]

Nor did the Venetians absolutely reject papal infallibility. Even Sarpi indicated that there was a narrow sense, in matters "where God had promised his assistance," in which the principle had always been acceptable in the church.[191] But, given the circumstances, the Venetian writers naturally emphasized the existence of a far wider area in which the pope was not only fallible but possibly more fallible than other men. It is difficult to imagine, indeed, in what sphere Sarpi might have recognized the pope as infallible. "It is enough," he wrote, "for all to agree that the pope can err in particular judgments; and we have many examples of errors committed by the highest pontiffs. In the sacred canons it is assumed not only that the pope can err, but also that he can become a heretic." [192] Marsilio, too, noting that "the vicar of God is not God but man, and his will is not eternal law but mutable," reminded his readers how frequently popes had erred in the past and noted occasions when popes had reversed the acts of their predecessors.[193] Such sentiments were peculiarly distasteful to Rome. The Servite theologians associated Sarpi's views on papal infallibility with the heretical Magdeburg

[186] *Considerazioni sopra le censure*, in *Scritti*, II, 254. This interpretation of the keys did not originate with Sarpi; cf. Jedin, *Seripando*, p. 667 for Cajetan's version of it.
[187] *Delle controversie*, pp. 9–10.
[188] *Avvertimento, et ammonitione catolica*, p. 107.
[189] *Sopra la forza e validità della scommunica*, in *Scritti*, II, 26.
[190] *Difesa delle opere scritte a favore della serenissima republica*, in *Scritti*, III, 248–249.
[191] *Ibid.*, p. 240.
[192] *Trattato dell'Interdetto*, in *Scritti*, III, 4. The Holy Spirit, Sarpi asserted, guides the pope only in a few special cases (*ibid.*, p. 24). See also his *Considerazioni sopra le censure*, in *Scritti*, II, 246ff.
[193] *Essame*, I, 46–48.

Centuries.[194] For Lelio Medici the Venetian view of papal authority was the equivalent of "wanting to destroy and annihilate the Christian religion and to take away from it everything firm and stable and certain." [195]

Venetian reservations both about the special status of the clergy and about papal authority also reflected those deeper impulses in Venetian ecclesiology at work during the earlier Renaissance. The Venetians were unenthusiastic about the official directors of the institutional church because they tended to view the church as essentially a spiritual body. An emphatic dualism lies back of the views of Sarpi and his associates, a sense that the spiritual and temporal belong to distinct realms of experience, that they must be attended to in different ways. Venetian theologians saw the work of salvation as largely spiritual and invisible, and they were inclined to minimize or even to reject the relevance to it of any visible or institutional agent. As Sarpi put the point to Bellarmine, salvation depends more on "the interior motions of the soul" than on any means at the disposal of the pope.[196] Such a position is fundamental also to the Venetian feeling that ecclesiastical censures might be ignored with impunity. Sarpi assured his countrymen that only their own spiritual deficiences could really exclude them from the church. "The theologians give as a certain and infallible rule," he declared, "that when a man is certain in his own conscience that he has not sinned mortally in the matter for which he is excommunicated, he can be secure in his conscience that he has suffered no hurt to his soul and is not excommunicated with God nor deprived of the benefits of the church." [197] God, according to this view, could be properly glorified only by the invisible work of the spirit, not by those external actions which belong to the temporal order. For Sarpi the Christian Gospel was, on this point, unequivocal:

We see from the divine Scriptures that the glory of God consists in the propagation of the Gospel and in the good life of Christians, and in sum,

---

[194] *Difesa de' Servi*, p. 298.
[195] *Discorso*, p. 205.
[196] *Apologia*, in *Scritti*, III, 171.
[197] *Sopra la forza e validità della scommunica*, in *Scritti* II, 21. See also his *Apologia*, in *Scritti*, III, 96, which distinguishes communion with God from community with other men in the church militant; *Consulto sui rimedii*, in *Scritti*, II, 155–156, where he argues that excommunication is no more than a declaration of spiritual death already incurred through sin and is itself without real effects; and *Sopra la forza e validità della scommunica*, in *Scritti*, II, 17ff., where he contrasts ancient and modern conceptions of excommunication.

as Saint Paul says, in the mortification of the outer man and the life of the inner, and in the exercise of works of love. But if the glory of God consisted in the abundance of temporal goods, we should have to fear for ourselves, because Christ has promised to his own nothing but poverty, persecutions, inconveniences. And finally, as even the ordinary man knows, travail and suffering are the marks and proofs of the friends of God, and no one, the Gospel says, follows Christ without taking his own cross on his shoulders.[198]

His conviction that the true Christian Gospel is that of the inner man and that the Christian life consists in imitating the suffering Christ is all the more remarkable because it appears in a *consulto* in which Sarpi was appealing to attitudes that he assumed his patrician readers would share.

Some kind of ideal for the clergy follows inevitably from this conception of the nature and activity of the church: they should be limited to invisible and spiritual things. The highest duty of a priest (again Sarpi was appealing to the assumptions of his fellow Venetians) consisted in "preaching the Gospel, holy admonitions and instructions about Christian customs, the ministry of the most holy sacraments, the care of the poor, the correction of crimes which exclude from the kingdom of God." [199] Notably absent from his conception are the accumulation and administration of property of any kind, the exercise of any sort of jurisdiction, the management of institutional agencies large or small, and governing authority over other men of any quality or degree. The ideal is in sharp contrast with the papal view of the clergy as brain and skeleton of a visible and institutional body. "The prelates should not dominate nor command with authority [*imperio*]," Sarpi declared, "but with examples and corrections of piety and of charity";[200] the church could properly claim no external, coercive authority. The pastoral charge consisted exclusively of love and peace, Marsilio replied directly to Baronius; the notion that it also included a duty to kill was, he observed, deeply repugnant.[201] Sarpi took a moderate position on clerical property, although he

---

[198] *Considerazioni sulle censure*, in *Scritti*, II, 214–215.

[199] *Ibid.*, p. 214. Cf. *Sul giudicar le colpe di persone ecclesiastiche*, in *Scritti*, II, 50 "Ecclesiastical authority pertains only to eternal salvation, and it is not allowed to have any temporal thing as end."

[200] *Considerazioni sulle censure*, in *Scritti*, II, 253; *Apologia*, in *Scritti*, III, 168; and *Della potestà coattiva*, in *Scritti*, III, 216–221. The last was not written until 1608 but clearly continues the arguments of the interdict.

[201] *Votum pro Serenissima Republica Veneta*, p. 249.

noted the example of the Apostles;[202] but Nicolò Crasso recommended that the clergy should live on the offerings of the faithful.[203]

The long tradition favoring a poor church clearly coincided with the interests of Venetian society and was a useful ally of Venetian policy. Yet it would be wrong to conclude that Sarpi and his friends were merely exploiting cynically a serious religious motive for reasons of state. Sarpi's own writings, at least, given the impression of long saturation in that complex of religious concerns which had found expression for centuries in demands for a more spiritual church, and back of Sarpi are the complaints and pleas of generations of reformers. Some of the fervor on the Venetian side was due to a sincere belief that the Venetian program was not only essential to the state but would also save a church that had long been degenerating through an excessive concern with external and institutional matters inappropriate to its essential nature and destructive of its sacred mission. The Venetians obviously did not regard wealth, institutions, and politics as evil in themselves. But they did believe that the papal church had allowed itself to be diverted from its proper responsibilities into matters with which it properly had no concern. The interdiction of Venice seemed a clear case in point.[204] As Sarpi remarked, the result had been a tragic decay:

> Popes, instituted by Christ to attend to the salvation of souls and to nourish them by preaching the word of God and by administering the most holy sacraments, left this responsibility to the friars and to humble priests, and devoted themselves diligently to increasing the exemption of the clergy and to broadening their immunity, with notable damage to the common and public welfare of cities and dominions. This has proceeded so far that, meriting the name rather of license than of liberty, it has now been converted into an exemption from all Christian works . . . . Christian perfection no longer consists in the exercise of the virtues, in piety and mercy, but in broadening and widening this liberty with which the earth is now being acquired and (we are given to understand) heaven will be acquired in the life to come.[205]

To the insistence of the pope, in his first brief against the Venetians, that the essence of his duty was to protect his authority to govern the church, Sarpi

---

[202] *Sopra l'esenzione delle persone ecclesiastiche*, in *Scritti*, II, 137; *Considerazioni sulle censure*, in *Scritti*, II, 206.

[203] *Antiparaenesis*, p. 291.

[204] Sarpi noted pointedly that the devil could accomplish his purposes even through the church (*Apologia*, in *Scritti*, III, 90).

[205] *Della libertà ecclesiastica*, in *Scritti*, II, 139–140.

had replied immediately: "Thus he has renounced all the offices that Christ gave to Saint Peter: to preach, to teach, to minister the sacraments, to feed the flock of Christ; and he has transformed this pastoral office into a fiscality, etc., as though the glory of God did not consist in the salvation of souls and internal goodness, but only in these external things." [206]

The Venetians recognized the value of institutions and administrative skills in carrying on the world's work. But they made a sharp distinction between what was appropriate on the one hand to the business of the world and, on the other, the spiritual and invisible operations of the church. Thus, like some medieval thinkers and also (incidentally) like Luther, they assigned all institutional direction and jurisdiction, not excluding what was necessary for the mission of the church, to the lay power. And Sarpi spelled out to the Venetian government what he represented, and what he presumably imagined it would accept, as sound and traditional Catholic doctrine:

The Catholic doctrine is that Christ our Lord gave to his ministers power to teach the truth of his holy doctrine and what are good and evil works, and to admonish and to reprehend delinquents that they might amend their ways, and if they are incorrigible also to denounce them to their masters and superiors and magistrates, exhorting these to correct them with the temporal power which God has given them to punish the wicked and reward the good. The ministers are also to proclaim to these magistrates their duty and the wrath of God if they should fail in it, referring also to higher magistrates for the correction of lower.[207]

The clergy, then, were to act as teachers and advisers but nothing more; and they did so, in a sense, as employees rather than masters of their congregations.[208] It was not for them to impose disciplines. This does not mean that there was no coercive power at the disposal of the church, or even (in a sense) that it was totally absent from the church. It was present, however, in the laity, who were also, in Venetian eyes, important members of the

[206] Nullità nelli brevi del pontefice, in Scritti, II, 90. Cf. Marsilio, Risposta d'un Dottore in theologia, pp. 141, 143, which argues that since Christ had exercised no temporal authority, he could have transmitted none to Peter. Papal authority could thus be only spiritual.

[207] Della potestà coattiva, in Scritti, III, 218–219.

[208] Trattato dell'Interdetto, in Scritti, III, 38. Sarpi seems to have seen this relationship as essentially contractual, which suggested that clerical enforcement of the interdict was in effect a breach of contract.

church. We have returned, therefore, to the sense of the value and dignity of the lay condition that we have so often encountered before in the Renaissance republics.

Sarpi assigned to the lay power or prince a broad authority in ecclesiastical government, though we should note again that although the Venetians presented the argument in general terms, their actual point of reference was Venice herself. When they spoke of the prince in relation to the church, they meant the prince in the Venetian sense, as representative of the community, speaking and acting in its name. At the same time, in performing his religious function, the prince was understood to act not in his political role but as agent of the lay element in the church, whose duty included an obligation to spare the clergy tasks inappropriate to spiritual office.[209] The civil magistrate, therefore, had not only to oppose the church when it encroached on the political sphere, that is, for *ragione di stato*. As an important personage within the church, as in an important sense an *ecclesiastic*, he had also to act for *ragione di chiesa*. He was obliged by natural law, as Sarpi remarked, "to defend the church from tyranny, from the abuse of the papal power." [210] He also had a duty to recall the church, when it seemed excessively distracted by temporal concerns, to its spiritual responsibilities.[211]

A further important implication of this position emerges from the fact that the Venetians attributed this large administrative authority in the church not to a universal emperor but to the prince as sovereign of a particular state who, given, the rights and realities of modern politics, recognized no superior. Since there were many princes of this description, the argument (although the Venetians did not care to make much of the point themselves) evidently conceives of the church as a unity only in some remote spiritual sense. The visible, institutional church, in this view, was at best a confederation of particular churches, each based on a particular political community and administered by its own lay government.[212] Such a view seems to underlie the Venetian contention that the interdict was not valid because it had never been regularly published in Venice, or again Sarpi's argument that the decrees

[209] Cf. Sarpi, *Sul giudicar le colpe di persone ecclesiastiche*, in *Scritti*, II, 49.

[210] *Sopra la forza e validità della scommunica*, in *Scritti*, II, 37.

[211] *Ibid.*, p. 39. It was "for the service of the churches of his state" that the prince was obligated to resist ecclesiastical encroachments on the temporal sphere. But Sarpi did not attribute authority to the prince over the clergy in religious matters; cf. *Sul giudicar le colpe di persone ecclesiastiche*, in *Scritti*, II, 43.

[212] This view seems to lie behind Venetian omission of the adjective *Roman* in references to the church, a point on which papalist writers were sensitive. Cf. Bellarmine, *Risposta a fra Paolo*, p. 138; and Possevino, *Risposta di Paolo Anafesto*, pp. 11–12.

of Trent were not binding anywhere without the consent of local political authorities.[213] He was quite open in his opinion that religion depended on a covenant between God and a particular people. "When a city, kingdom, or people receives the Christian religion," he declared, "it receives at the same time a *ius* that divine worship and the ministry of the holy sacraments should be exercised in its lands; and there results from this a kind of pact or contract between God and the people that it should be the people of God, and he should be God of the people." [214] The notion of a series of individual covenants of this kind hardly leaves much room for a universal church as a visible institution; and already during the period of the interdict Sarpi displayed much interest in the liberties of the Gallican church[215] and spoke as though he did not regard the Anglican church as outside Christendom.[216] The·substantial autonomy of the Spanish church also suggests how widespread were the assumptions which the Venetians now made explicit.

The notion of the church universal as a federation of particular churches based on the actual political divisions of Christendom explains the persistent, albeit largely theoretical, attraction of conciliarism for the Venetians, since the general council was (among other things) a device for giving such community to the various churches as would be consistent with their actual autonomy. Sarpi insisted that, in point of fact, whether the pope or the council was superior was still an open question in the church, and he indicated his own preference for conciliar supremacy.[217] Marsilio was persuaded that God would be pleased if Christian princes joined in calling a council to reduce the papacy to conformity with primitive models,[218] and Capello noted that the emperor had convened councils in antiquity.[219] But there were now serious practical objections to any Venetian appeal to a council, as Sarpi recognized. He believed that such an appeal would further antagonize the pope while promising little benefit;[220] he must already have come to regard the most recent general council of the church as a major triumph for Rome.

[213] *Trattato dell'Interdetto*, in *Scritti*, III, 5–6.

[214] *Ibid.*, p. 37.

[215] As in *ibid.*, pp. 184–189. Canaye noted Venetian admiration for the Gallican liberties at this time (letter to Hotman de Villiers, Oct. 12, 1606, in *Lettres*, III, 233).

[216] *Apologia*, in *Scritti*, III, 184ff.; *L'appellazione al concilio*, in *Scritti*, II, 79.

[217] *Trattato dell'Interdetto*, in *Scritti*, III, 17–18; *Apologia*, in *Scritti*, III, 117ff.; *L'appellazione al concilio*, in *Scritti*, II, 74–85.

[218] *Essame*, II, 6.

[219] *Delle controversie*, pp. 67ff.

[220] *La forza e validità della scommunica*, in *Scritti*, II, 33.

For the time being he was also more concerned to maintain the independence of particular churches than to promote their unity.

The republican consciousness of Venice also affected the Venetian attitude toward the internal structure of the church. The Venetians had long been persuaded that a republican constitution like their own was the ideal form of government; and naturally, in view of the common tendency of the age to view the church as a kind of government, they had already tended to criticize the *ecclesia* for its failure to conform more closely to this ideal. Now, under the provocation of the interdict, this tendency became more explicit. Marsilio maintained that God operated in the church through constitutional procedures working as secondary causes and that in this respect popes were in the same position as secular rulers.[221] Sarpi represented the church as originally and ideally a republic that had been gradually subverted by papal tyranny. Both objected to the notion that its monarchical structure had been instituted by God. Marsilio, though judiciously leaving the question open, gave favorable consideration to the possibility that sovereignty in the church was the legitimate possession of the whole community.[222] Sarpi, taking the election of the pope to indicate his proper subordination to the church as a whole, insisted on the right of the ecclesiastical community (like any other) to judge its head.[223] He also attributed a substantial role to the college of cardinals, the analogue of the Venetian Senate in the government of the church.[224]

Bellarmine's indignant repudiation of these views nicely illustrates how controversy made Venetian doctrine more radical and explicit. For Bellarmine, here showing a clearer understanding of Venetian policy, had discerned at an early point where the Venetian arguments were tending. He insisted that ecclesiastical government was in no way comparable to secular:

> The holy church is not similar to the republic of Venice, or of Genoa, or of any other city, which gives such power to its doge as it pleases and can therefore say that the republic is above the prince. Similarly it is not like an earthly kingdom, in which the peoples transfer their authority to the monarchy and in certain cases can free themselves from the royal dominion and submit themselves to the government of

[221] *Difesa a favore della risposta*, pp. 204–205.

[222] *Ibid.*, p. 199.

[223] *Apologia*, in *Scritti*, III, 131–132. Cf. *Sopra la forza e validità della scommunica*, in *Scritti*, II, 35, 37, for discussion of the pope as tyrant.

[224] *Istoria dell'Interdetto*, p. 17; *Della libertà ecclesiastica*, in *Scritti*, II, 145.

lesser magistrates, as the Romans did when they passed from the royal dominion to consular government. For the church of Christ is a most perfect kingdom and an absolute monarchy which does not depend on the people nor have its origin from them, but depends only on the divine will.[225]

Bellarmine insisted that the Venetian position practically denied the primacy of Peter, and he shrewdly accused the Venetians of looking, in the church, for the image of Venice; he represented the Venetian position, indeed, with some accuracy, though he doubtless intended no more than a *reductionem ad absurdum*:

> If Christ established the church from the beginning in the form of a republic, the church has erred and abandoned the form given by God by changing into a monarchy. If monarchy is better than a republic and therefore the church changed, then Christ erred in giving it the form of a republic. Indeed, it would follow [from the Venetian position] that Christ would not be monarch of the church but head of the republic, like the doge of Venice; because the same people has never been seen to compose both a republic and a kingdom, nor has a kingdom ever had the form of a republic. If Christ is king and the pope is his general vicar, then the church is not governed like a republic but like a kingdom; and the pope is not a magistrate dependent on the church, but a vicar dependent only on his master Christ.[226]

Marsilio did not hesitate to take up this challenge; he replied to it by comparing the internal development of the papacy with that of Venice, answering dogma with history in a characteristically Venetian way. He denied Bellarmine's identification of Christ with his ministers; the monarchy of the former, he maintained, could by no means be attributed to the latter. He also insisted openly on the comparability, and from this on the contrast, between pope and doge; the church had degenerated from republic to principate, while Venice had retained her original excellence. "Whether Saint Peter has had such a primacy till now as the doge of Venice, who indeed, although he has a great preeminence is nevertheless subject to the whole republic," Marsilio wrote, "I leave to those whom it touches. This

---

[225] *Risposta ad un libretto di Gersone*, p. 322.
[226] *Risposta a Marsilio*, p. 165.

suffices for my point, that the edicts which were issued in the primitive church in the name of the republic are now made in the name of one only. I will leave to him who denies it so say whether this signifies change." The tempered government of Venice herself, a constitutional republic, is indeed Marsilio's model for the church. Just as the prince, he declared, "must regulate his absolute power by his councils and the laws of his state, so the pope must regulate his according to the council of disinterested and dispassionate cardinals who desire his welfare and that of the church, according to the canons, according to the councils." [227] The constitutional analogy between the Sacred College and the Venetian Senate was now out in the open.

The exchange illustrated the central place in the conflict of antithetical visions of the development of Christian Europe. Each side accused the other of novelty[228] and gave at least lip service to the authority of a tradition capable of betrayal. They defined this tradition in different ways and elaborated contrasting views of the past. But it is also clear that they did not finally attach equal importance to argument from history. While Venice had come gradually to understand the world, including increasingly herself, as a product of history, whose actual structure had therefore to be taken into account, Rome, with her confidence in abstract thought, possessed what she considered a superior access to truth. Thus, although the Roman theologians cited texts from Scripture, appealed to the canons of ancient councils, quoted the opinions of the Fathers, and found relevant examples in the past, they did so, in the manner of Baronius, chiefly to bolster a rigid dogmatic structure. The Venetians had a historical mythology of their own, and their excursions into history were heavily partisan. But they were disposed to attach more real importance to historical evidence than their opponents, and they were far more inclined to appeal to historical argument.

A major element in the Venetian vision of the past was the familiar ideal of the perfection of the primitive church which, however alien from a genuine historical consciousness, provided the Venetians, as it had done for others, with some perspective about the church in later ages. The

---

[227] *Difesa a favore della risposta*, p. 201.

[228] This emerges with particular force in Canaye's remarks before the College on March 30, 1606. When the Venetians pointed out that they were merely defending established practice, Canaye referred to papal charges circulated in France "that your Serenity makes novelty and is the occasion of clamors and rumors; and from what I understand through the things your Serenity has deigned to tell me, I know, as I have always believed, that the novelties come from Rome" (Cornet, p. 45).

Venetians supplied a description, satisfying at least to themselves, of many aspects of the early church and called on Rome once again to conform to ancient models. Sarpi explicitly associated piety with reverence for antiquity;[229] and Marsilio was emphatic about the authority of the primitive church, whose practice he contrasted with "what has been preached by human avidity, human interests, and human traditions, after those first golden times of our holy church." The original leaders of the church, he noted, had been "poor and ignorant fishermen" who had never said, "Embrace our preaching, else we will come with an army to destroy your city, else we will declare you excommunicated and abominable, we will condemn you to death." [230]

On many points the Venetians found in Roman claims or practice some deviation from the primitive church: on papal infallibility, on the kind of liberty proper for a Christian, on apostolic poverty, on the excommunication of corporate bodies like the Venetian Senate, on blind obedience.[231] Sarpi made a special point of the different roles assigned to laymen in the ancient past and the present. "Truly," he wrote, "there is a great difference in belief and practice between the ancients and those of the present time about whether those of the faithful who are called laity ought to have any part in ecclesiastical government, or whether it belongs solely to the clergy. It is certain that in antiquity all the faithful participated in the elections of bishops and clergy and in the governance of churches; but now the entire government is done by the ecclesiastics alone." [232] Above all the Venetians appealed to primitive practice as a precedent for relations with the pope. Sarpi found in Paul's rebuke to Peter a model for Venetian resistance to Rome,[233] and he also proposed Peter as a model for modern popes: "Do we wish to determine whether the excommunication of a pope is valid? Let us see whether Saint Peter would have delivered it; and if we find it remote from apostolic love and modesty, we should not believe that it has the force of apostolic authority." [234]

Venetian insistence on ancient practice as a rigid norm by which the church

[229] As in the *Istoria dell'Interdetto*, p. 119.

[230] *Essame*, I, 6, 40.

[231] Sarpi, *Considerazioni sulle censure*, in *Scritti*, II, 209, 252–253; *Sopra la forza e validità della scommunica*, in *Scritti*, II, 19–20; *Istoria dell'Interdetto*, p. 107. See also Querini, *Aviso*, p. 28; and Micanzio, *Confirmatione delle considerationi*, pp. 64–65.

[232] *Sul giudicar le colpe di persone ecclesiastiche*, in *Scritti*, II, 48.

[233] *Considerazioni sopra le censure*, in *Scritti*, II, 253.

[234] *Sopra la forza e validità della scommunica*, in *Scritti*, II, 26.

is to be judged in every subsequent age obviously means that the church should be immune to all change. It is thus closely related to the tendency in Venetian ecclesiology to spiritualize the church, to distinguish it from the visible and institutional order which *is* vulnerable to history. In this way, therefore, Venetian idealization of the primitive church seems to exclude rather than to reflect a sense of history. But in another way it makes possible a genuinely historical vision of the church. For by insisting on the rigidity of apostolic practice, Sarpi and his associates were establishing an objective standard by which change could be recognized and measured. Whereas Baronius had aimed to show the consistency of modern and ancient practice and therefore read into the past the essential absence of change, the Venetians discerned marked contrasts. So Sarpi answered an attempt to equate a modern papal pronouncement with the words of Saint Paul: "Certainly a comparison of anyone of this century with Saint Paul, and a decree of any person with a canonical scripture will hardly appear very reasonable to pious consciences." [235] Micanzio defended, against Bovio, the general propriety of distinguishing different periods in the history of the church;[236] and Sarpi, concerned to locate the beginning of the church's deviation from its original excellence, found it in the eleventh century, above all in the investiture struggles.[237] The Venetians were thus now applying the Renaissance sense of discontinuity with the ancient past more and more systematically to the history of the church. Like the historians and theologians at the Curia, they too saw what they wanted to see, and their vision was full of distortions of a different kind. But, by admitting the possibility of discontinuity, they were taking a long step toward the liberation of history from dogma. The fruitfulness of all of this would be finally revealed in Sarpi's *Istoria del Concilio Tridentino*.

The benefits of the new perspective are apparent above all in Venetian treatment of the Middle Ages. For the medieval past the Roman theologians were consistently faithful to the vision of Baronius, which recognized no break with the church of antiquity or even with the protochurch of the

---

[235] *Apologia*, in *Scritti*, III, 101; cf. *ibid.*, p. 57.

[236] *Confirmatione delle considerationi*, p. 65, in connection with Bovio's insistence that "ecclesiastical liberty" had always existed.

[237] More specifically in connection with the origins of politically motivated ecclesiastical censures in *Consulto sui remedii da opporsi ad una eventuale aggravazione della scommunica*, in *Scritti*, II, 157, and *Trattato dell'Interdetto*, in *Scritti*, III, 39–40; more generally in *Difesa delle opere scritte a favore della serenissima republica*, in *Scritti*, III, 239–240.

Hebrews, but only an organic development, the gradual unfolding of the original deposit of faith, the progressive fulfillment of the divine commission to the church. What was of primary importance here, however, was not the process of development but the substance of what was developed; and their ability to identify this also determined the historical method of the Roman writers. They used the past chiefly as a repository of examples of what they proposed to establish, picking and choosing, neglecting differences in context, lifting episodes out of the stream of time to prove a point; in this way conflict between history and systematic thought was impossible. The papalist theologians dealt in this way with later Roman and medieval history to demonstrate, against Venice, that the authority of the pope had consistently been accepted in temporal things as well as spiritual, and that only an occasional wicked ruler had ever presumed to defy it, always to his sorrow. There was no recognition among these writers of the complex realities of medieval history, no sense of the constant tension and struggle between rival positions on both sides strong, respectable, and venerable, no notice of the many centuries when the papacy had in fact been subordinated to civil authority. They agreed with their opponents that any practice or belief in the church was valid only in the degree to which it could be proved unchanged and unchanging. But, for obvious reasons, they were unwilling to entertain the possibility that change had, in fact, occurred.

They concentrated on demonstrating the theocratic character of medieval society and indeed of Hebrew history from the beginning. Lelio Medici, describing Abel as the first priest, maintained that the chosen people had been ruled by priests for many generations and had only lost this privilege at the time of Saul as a punishment for insolence.[238] Venturi extended a similar claim into the gentile world. He argued that all peoples everywhere had venerated their clergy and given them privileged status, and he devoted particular attention to the religious zeal of ancient Rome, a virtue he depicted (like Machiavelli) as largely responsible for Roman military success.[239] The point received its most enthusiastic demonstration, however, in the events of the Christian era. Baglioni maintained that Christian rulers had always recognized the primacy of the pope, although his use of the emperor Frederick II as an illustration seems equivocal.[240] The Servite

[238] *Discorso*, pp. 189–191.

[239] *Maiestà pontificia*, pp. 39–40, 47ff., and *passim*. On clerical privilege in the pagan world, see also *Difesa de' Servi*, pp. 13–17.

[240] *Apologia*, p. 10. He also represented the ancient Christian emperors as having submitted legislation affecting ecclesiastical liberty for papal approval before promulgation.

theologians vigorously defended the donation of Constantine.[241] Bellarmine himself traced the principle of papal intervention in temporal affairs *ratione peccati* back through *Unam sanctam* and Innocent III to Gregory the Great. "Whoever does not believe this," he declared, "is not Catholic." [242]

The essential proposition which these men sought to demonstrate was that most rulers during the Middle Ages had, unlike the Venetians, readily obeyed the dictates of the pope. In the words of Medici, "These canons and decrees, and innumerable others of the supreme pontiffs, have been received with the greatest reverence and observed by all faithful and Catholic emperors and kings as oracles issuing from the mouth of God." [243] Nor should the qualification "faithful and Catholic" be taken as an oblique admission that perhaps only a few medieval rulers, after all, had really obeyed the pope. The Roman theologians accumulated examples to prove that popes had actually exercised supreme authority in the political world and that the obedience of rulers had truly been general. In their reading of medieval history the Carolingian rulers were converted into the loyal servants of popes who, recognizing Carolingian piety, had first conferred France on Pepin and later transferred the empire to Charlemagne. In the next century a further demonstration of papal authority could be discerned in John XII's transfer of the empire once more from the French to the Germans. Venturi transformed the humiliation of Henry IV at Canossa into an instance of laudable imperial humility; thus even that bitter foe of papal claims was converted into a witness of their acceptability.[244] Bellarmine did not go quite so far, but he cited the depositions of Henry, of Otto IV, and of Frederick II as evidence that the pope had always possessed the right to deprive rulers of their thrones.[245] The conception was also extended into modern European history. Bovio claimed that the Habsburg rulers of the sixteenth century, Charles V and Philip II of Spain, had always respected the claims of the church.[246] Baglioni, it is true, acknowledged that a few rulers had dared to oppose the pope; but their histories only proved to him that such men invariably came to bad ends. Among others he pointed to the miserable fate of Frederick II and his line, of the Byzantine emperor in

[241] *Difesa de' Servi*, p. 198, citing numerous authorities including both Baronius and Bellarmine.

[242] *Risposta ad un libretto di Gersone*, p. 310 bis.

[243] *Discorso*, p. 200. For the general scheme see also Sosa, *Discorso*, pp. 15ff.; *Difesa de' Servi*, pp. 49ff.; Venturi, *Maiestà pontificia*, pp. 83ff.; Baronius, *Paraenesis*, pp. 104–105.

[244] *Maiestà pontificia*, pp. 106–107.

[245] *Risposta alla risposta*, p. 171.

[246] *Risposta alle considerationi*, p. 43.

1453, and of the English king Henry VIII, whose house saw "strange events" and whose family was eventually extinguished.[247]

All this being true, Venetian objection to ecclesiastical censure as a modern innovation was of minor importance, but the Roman writers also found remote precedents for the measures the pope had taken against Venice. Baglioni found a direct reference to interdiction in a writing of pope Nicholas I and indirect evidence of its existence even earlier.[248] Bellarmine traced the discipline back through actions of Alexander III and Gregory VII to Augustine. He also thought there were grounds for seeing the first interdict in the expulsion of Adam and Eve from Paradise, Eden being a figure of the church and the fruit from the tree of life signifying the sacraments.[249]

But in fact papalist writers appealed to history with distaste and largely because the Venetians had to be met on their own ground. Francesco di Sosa expressed indignation at the Venetian appeal to history as a common trick of heretics.[250] On one occasion, too, Bellarmine heaped scorn on Sarpi for his display of historical erudition and then withdrew from discourse of this unworthy kind, preferring to take refuge in authority. The incident is illuminating. Sarpi had discussed the general right of popes to censure rulers; according to Bellarmine he had recounted "many histories of wars between the kings of France and of England to show off his erudition and to swell the volume," and he had objected to the decretal Bellarmine relied on by claiming "that it cannot be defended when understood as universally as the words mean." Sarpi, that is to say, rejected the general significance of a specific and local pronouncement. Bellarmine did not care to argue in these terms: "To these things I will not reply, because Innocent III is well enough defended by the greatness of his authority, goodness, and science, especially since his decretal is in the *Corpus Canonicus*, of which no one can speak badly unless he wishes to declare himself alien from Holy Church."[251]

Nor was this an isolated case; Bovio was equally revealing. Reproving Sarpi for maintaining that the modern Roman conception of ecclesiastical

---

[247] *Apologia*, pp. 94–96.

[248] *Ibid.*, II, 63.

[249] *Risposta ai sette*, pp. 66–67.

[250] *Discorso*, p. 46.

[251] *Risposta a fra Paulo*, p. 81. Bellarmine was here referring to Sarpi's review of the specific meaning of Innocent III's censure against John of England (in *Apologia*, in *Scritti*, III, 59).

privilege had not existed in the ancient church, he declared that this seemed to him no proper way to speak and no conception for a Catholic to hold: "The Catholic believes that the Apostolic Roman Church is Catholic, which means universal, in all places and in all times the same. Therefore if, in ancient times, the councils and the popes defined the truth and decreed justly, it cannot be said that the more modern councils and popes during the past four hundred years have not had the same assistance from the Holy Spirit in defining and decreeing. This would be as much as to say that since then we have been without the true visible church." [252] A Catholic, then, was compelled to deny the possibility of innovation or discontinuity in the history of the church, even on such matters as the authority of the spiritual power over rulers and the social status of the clergy. From such a position the distance was short to denouncing any deviation from the papalist reconstruction of the past as heresy. Bellarmine crossed it when Marsilio expressed disbelief that Charlemagne had actually received his imperial title from the pope. Marsilio's opinion, Bellarmine declared, "can be called heresy in history and temerity in theology, because it is repugnant to all the histories and to the sacred canons." [253]

The Venetians reacted vigorously in defense of the autonomy of historical investigation. To the charge of heresy in history Marsilio replied directly: "There cannot be heresy in history which is profane and not from sacred Scripture . . . [on the coronation of Charlemagne] the historians are not in agreement, but one historian attributes it to one cause, another to another." [254] The real issue was whether any circumstance impinging on the history of the visible church could properly be described as profane. Behind this disagreement over history lay basic differences in ecclesiology.

The Venetians also stressed particular deficiencies in historical practice to which the Roman concern with dogma had presumably led. Sarpi lamented the deletion of passages favorable to the authority of princes from new editions of "good authors," [255] and various Venetian writers attacked Baronius, whose *Annals* Sardi represented as a device to promote the universal monarchy of the pope.[256] When Bellarmine appealed to the

[252] *Risposta alle considerationi*, pp. 27–28.
[253] *Risposta alla risposta*, pp. 166–167, in reaction to Marsilio, *Risposta d'un Dottore in theologia*, p. 143.
[254] *Difesa a favore della risposta*, p. 243.
[255] *Difesa delle opere scritte a favore della serenissima republica*, in *Scritti*, III, 247–248.
[256] *Discorsi*, p. 215.

authority of Baronius in connection with the deposition of John XII, Marsilio remarked:

> Of Cardinal Baronius, I will only say that he is a historian still alive whose works are suspect on the question of immunity. Indeed, it must be said that he rejects all the old historians; and if he admits any, takes the words in an improper sense; and those which are contrary to his case he says have been inserted into that historian. He does precisely this in this history, in which he denies the authority of Liutprand, approved in the church for the space of seven hundred years, and of other writers of those times. Therefore, since his *Annals* do not have in the world that respect which they are believed to enjoy, and since a book ought soon to be published entitled *Errores Cardinalis Baronii*, where in particular are exposed more than twenty errors he has made in denying that very old history of Pope John, one should not speak of his authority.[257]

Sarpi, too, although he did not boggle at citing Baronius himself on occasion,[258] attacked his work for imprecision, the suppression of unfavorable evidence, and gratuitous additions to the record.[259] He also hinted at more fundamental objections to the Roman vision of history by questioning the relevance of Old Testament precedent to the modern church. In defending Gerson he slyly noted the failure of one of his scholarly authorities "to understand how, so many years before there was a pope, he should have been spoken of in the book of Kings." [260]

In opposition to the Roman vision of a unified medieval Christendom ultimately responsive in all things to the direction of the pope, the Venetians presented their own version of the past, and above all of the historical position of the papacy in relation to Christendom. None of the Venetian writers was yet ready to offer a coherent account of the matter, but the general direction of their thought is apparent. They believed that the church had suffered a considerable decline from its primitive purity, that institutional interests had tended increasingly to replace spiritual concerns, and that the papacy had periodically attempted to impose a temporal monarchy over the

---

[257] *Difesa a favore della risposta*, p. 262.
[258] *Apologia*, in *Scritti*, III, 138, against Bellarmine.
[259] *Ibid.*, pp. 135ff., 145–146.
[260] *Ibid.*, p. 148.

whole of Christendom. They made these points, however, without insisting on any general pattern in events such as, with another kind of mind, might have had eschatological overtones. Sarpi contented himself with the observation that it would be hard to say whether there had been more good or more bad popes since the Carolingians.[261] Marsilio was somewhat more general but in the manner of the Florentine historians, blaming the major woes of Italy, past and present, on the political ambitions of the papacy "with its diabolical policy of divide and conquer." "Who can contain his tears," he lamented, contemplating the result of papal intrigue, "remembering the shameful and grievous tragedies which unhappy Italy has witnessed for many centuries: tragedies happening between those two most evil factions of Guelfs and Ghibellines, of whites and blacks? . . . Through these factions the liberty, the beauty, the greatness of many parts of Italy has been extinguished." [262] But the Venetian writers also noted instances, during the Middle Ages, when the position of the church in Christian society had been worthy of emulation. Charlemagne's relations with the clergy were, for Sarpi, an admirable precedent,[263] and another Venetian writer, recalling the old story, exhorted Paul V to follow the example of Alexander III, who had known so well how to deal with Venice, seeking her aid rather than ordering her compliance.[264]

The Venetian writers were not disposed to deny that some episodes in the medieval past appeared to support papal claims; they merely insisted on denying that medieval history could in general be interpreted in this way. Thus Sardi maintained that Gregory VII and Boniface VIII had been exceptional rather than typical. They had misrepresented what was really an attempt to introduce major novelties into Christendom as the recovery of a lost superiority and dominion, but most popes had respected the traditional authority of princes.[265] Sarpi went to the heart of the matter by observing that the claims of the medieval papacy to jurisdiction could not by themselves legally establish it. They had also to be freely accepted by those affected,[266] and there had been numerous examples of rulers

[261] Ibid., p. 154. On the other hand he recommended to the pope the imitation of ancient rather than medieval models (Nullità nelli brevi del pontefice, in Scritti, II, 88–89).
[262] Essame, I, 33.
[263] Sul giudicar le colpe di persone ecclesiastiche, in Scritti, II, 44, 49, 51, 57.
[264] The author of the anonymous Risposta a Paolo V (in Sarpi's Opere, VI), p. 153.
[265] Discorsi, p. 219.
[266] Apologia, in Scritti, III, 59, in connection with Innocent III's censure of John of England.

who had resisted the pope: among others the emperors Henry IV, Henry V, Frederick II, and Ludwig of Bavaria, John of England, and Philip the Fair.[267] The strength of contemporary Gallicanism was undoubtedly responsible for the particular interest with which he examined the independence that had characterized French relations with the papacy.[268]

From his general examination of the past Sarpi concluded that the medieval effort to impose the political leadership of the pope had been a failure. "For the most part, indeed ordinarily," he wrote, "princes attacked by [popes] have been protected by God, and their subjects have not believed that any man could ever free and absolve the soul from the oath and obligation it has to their prince. And therefore they have continued in due obedience." [269] Marsilio made the point, in reply to the Machiavellian sentimentalism of Rome, that in fact some rulers who had defied the pope had come to rather good ends, notably Philip the Fair and Louis XII of France, whereas Boniface VIII, who had presumed to censure princes, had met a most unpleasant fate; but Marsilio made clear that he did not regard any examples of this kind as significant.[270] He did insist, however, on the relevance of the calamities the church had regularly suffered whenever it had aggressed against the rights of secular governments.[271] Medieval history in general, then, could not properly be made to support the claims of the Curia.

Similarly the two sides gave alternative interpretations to the history of Venice. The Venetians, whose essential case was that Venice in the present crisis had acted only to conserve practices hallowed by time and sanctioned

[267] *Sui remedii da opporsi ad una eventuale aggravazione della scommunica*, in *Scritti*, II, 157ff.

[268] As early as *Sopra la forza e validità della scommunica*, in *Scritti*, II, 31–32, 40, he saw parallels between the situations of Venice and of France under Boniface VIII. See also *Trattato dell'Interdetto*, in *Scritti*, III, 41; and *Apologia*, in *Scritti*, III, 62, 80–81, which provocatively defends French learning and piety in the age of Gerson. Sarpi was not the only Venetian writer who looked to France; see also the *Epistolae duorum iurisconsultorum*, p. 132. On the other side Baglioni, *Apologia*, p. 54, directly attacked Venetian appeal to French precedent; and Bellarmine also denied any parallel between the Gallican liberties and the claims of Venice (*Risposta ad un libretto di Gersone*, p. 323).

[269] *Sui remedii da opporsi ad una eventuale aggravazione della scommunica*, in *Scritti*, II, 161.

[270] *Difesa a favore della risposta*, p. 287.

[271] *Ibid.*, p. 214, for a list of examples.

by success,[272] insisted that Rome was encroaching on temporal affairs; and they drew on all the clichés of official Venetian historiography in their defense of the cherished freedom of the Republic. They urged that, since her foundation early in the fifth century, Venice had never recognized a political superior; thus submission to the pope would break the long continuity of her history.[273] Sarpi pointed out the independence of Venice from Roman law at the outset. "The republic of Venice," he wrote, "born in the time of the empire of Honorius and Theodosius by the grace of God free, not subject to any prince in its laws, was in its beginnings governed rather with its own good customary laws than with written law." [274] Among other expressions of her liberty were, of course, those practices to which Rome now took exception and which, Sarpi insisted, earlier popes had found unexceptionable.[275] For Marsilio the Venetians were men with a long record of freedom defending themselves against enslavement;[276] and Tomaselli was carried away by his vision of Venice as the embodiment of antique republican virtue:

> Maintainer and conservator of her liberty from her beginning until our time, she both kept and increased her empire during the great troubles and disasters of Christendom against the fury of the barbarians. Lover of internal and external peace, she has with her own authority balanced and counter-weighted the power and authority of other princes. She has reconciled the greatest princes to the church of God. In her councils are new Hortensii, new Demosthenes, new Ciceros. In her political governance, an aristocracy of the best has always prevailed, with the love and approval of the subject peoples. With her prudence and good government, she has represented in human eyes a model of the ancient Roman republic. She has always been the ornament and splendor of our Italy. Today we see still preserved so

[272] In addition to the evidence presented in the previous chapter, see Sarpi, *Istoria dell'Interdetto*, pp. 75, 191; and *Apologia*, in *Scritti*, III, 93. See also Marsilio, *Essame*, p. 17; and Querini, *Aviso*, pp. 18ff.

[273] Thus Capello, *Delle controversie*, p. 91.

[274] *Sul giudicar le colpe di persone ecclesiastiche*, in *Scritti*, II, 64. Cf. *Istoria dell'Interdetto*, pp. 15–16; *Risposta al breve circa li prigioni*, in *Scritti*, II, 71; *Considerazioni sopra le censure*, in *Scritti*, II, 217ff.; and Marsilio, *Difesa a favore della risposta*, p. 265.

[275] *Considerazioni sopra le censure*, in *Scritti*, II, 245.

[276] *Essame*, I, 14.

noble a treasure in this city, emporium of all the nations of the world.[277]

We may also observe that for Sarpi the liberty of this noble republic did not make her unique among the governments of Europe. Like Machiavelli, he was aware that Christendom had not been a political unity during the Middle Ages. With the decline of the ancient Roman world, he wrote, "the Christian republic was divided into many kingdoms and principates, until our century." He dated this development at the year 800,[278] a date that gave to Venice the distinction of a longer history of freedom than other states.

Each side was more effective in attacking the historical myths of its opponents than in presenting its own history; and the reply from Rome began with a firm denial that Venice had been originally free in the sense claimed. The Roman writers pointed out that the territory on which the first Venetians had settled was then a part of the Roman Empire and had later belonged to the Greeks.[279] Obviously, then, the original liberty of Venice was a fiction: she had always had a political superior. Amato argued that Venice could only have been relieved of subjection to the emperor by an authority greater than he: namely the pope. The liberty of Venice had therefore originated, he maintained, when the pope, excommunicating the eastern emperors, had relieved them of their dominions.[280] Thus, citing Bernardo Giustiniani, the papalist writers pointed out that the election of the first doge had been sanctioned by the pope, on whom the legitimacy of Venetian government therefore depended.[281] They also pointed to various marks and ceremonies of Venetian dominion traditionally associated with the pope, including the marriage to the Adriatic with a papal ring and the symbols of authority which the Venetians had associated with the peace of 1177.[282] They concluded that any Venetian jurisdiction over the church could only be a revocable concession from Rome.[283]

For the most part the Roman writers represented the history of Venice,

[277] *Le mentite Filoteane*, p. 392.
[278] *Sul giudicar le colpe di persone ecclesiastiche*, in *Scritti*, II, 44.
[279] Baglioni, *Apologia*, pp. 26–27, 32; Bellarmine, *Risposta a Marsilio*, p. 163. Cf. Amato, *Discorso*, pp. 6–9; and Venturi, *Maiestà pontificia*, pp. 85–88.
[280] Amato, *Discorso*, pp. 5–6; Possevino, *Risposta del sig. Paolo Anafesto*, p. 29.
[281] Amato, *Discorso*, p. 13; *Difesa de' Servi*, p. 56.
[282] *Difesa de' Servi*, pp. 56–57; Baglioni, *Apologia*, pp. 30–31.
[283] Bovio, *Risposta alle considerationi*, pp. 24–25; Baglioni, *Apologia*, pp. 26–27.

from these laudable beginnings, as a long career in piety only recently interrupted. Earlier Venetians, they claimed, had recognized the superiority of the spiritual power. They had accepted the clergy as their natural leaders; they had collaborated closely with medieval popes in the crusades and against emperors; and when they had offended the church, they had humbly sought forgiveness.[284] Venturi, at least accepting the events of 1177 as a fact, imagined the extravagantly papal sentiments the Venetians must have employed to bring about the submission of Frederick I, and he invoked as a more recent example of Venetian dedication to the Holy See the assistance he imagined Venice to have given to Paul IV against Spain.[285] So pious a history, these men argued, had been the major cause for the long prosperity of the Venetian state. She had, until her recent descent into false *ragione di stato*, been a most successful practitioner of the true;[286] disaster had recently come upon her because she had forgotten the secret of her long happiness. So Possevino:

> While this republic maintained true piety, for eight hundred years, and was subordinate to divine law, and left due jurisdiction entirely to the church which Christ had given her, she flourished and increased; and in your squares there were never any dealings with heretics, with schismatics, with Turks, with Marranos. Men came from Constantinople and Alexandria, and the bodies of saints arrived from the East to find refuge among you, as to a safe port. But when, become fat and swollen, the republic began to grow stubborn, behold what a swarm of nations, of heresies, of schisms, and worse trample through and desecrate your squares and your own houses. So you have lost the cities in the Levant, the islands in the sea, Coron and Modon and other approaches on the mainland, and most recently your kingdom of Cyprus.[287]

---

[284] Amato, *Discorso*, pp. 9–12, 20; Possevino (as Paolo Anafesto), *Risposta all'avviso*, pp. 9–11; Baronius, *Paraenesis*, pp. 105–107, 122–123; Venturi, *Maiestà pontificia*, pp. 41–44; Campanella, *Antiveneti*, p. 17. On the ground that they had been so well reared in a long tradition of piety, Venturi insisted (pp. 15–16) that the Venetians could not truly believe what they were now saying, and urged them to express what was really in their hearts.

[285] *Maiestà pontificia*, pp. 23–24, 121–122. Cf. Campanella, *Antiveneti*, p. 17.

[286] Amato, *Discorso*, pp. 4ff.

[287] Possevino, *Risposta di Teodoro Eugenio*, pp. 39–40. Cf. Amato, *Discorso*, p. 3, describing Venetian practice as "innovations of these modern Senators."

Venturi was tactless enough to apply this lesson to the events of 1509–1510. Venice, he pointed out, had lost her possessions on the mainland when she had defied Julius II but had recovered them again once she had humbled herself;[288] the point might also have been taken as a threat. Nor could Venturi have seemed more ingratiating when he described the recent history of Venice as a decline from pious youth into blasphemous senility;[289] the biological image touched on another sensitive nerve.

The Venetians could hardly have been more favorably impressed by the Roman use of Florence as a model of piety for Venice to emulate. Bellarmine cited two cases in which Saint Antonino had excommunicated the magistrates of the Florentine republic: once for daring, even in a mild way, to lay hands on a pair of disorderly priests, and again for holding a papal envoy as a hostage even with "some color of justice." But the rulers of Florence had at last humbly submitted, and Bellarmine drew a moral which suggests a rather peculiar vision of Florentine history: "So the constancy of the ecclesiatical prelate and the piety of the temporal lords easily found a remedy for every disorder." [290] Baglioni and Lelio Medici, both writing from Florence, noted that in 1516, faced with the problem of excessive property passing to the church, Florence had properly sought relief from Leo X and graciously obtained it. Venice, they urged, should follow her pious example rather than impiously laying secular hands on the possessions of the church.[291] But Possevino, recalling the fact that republics had in fact regularly defied ecclesiastical censure, made a sterner use of the comparison. Venice, he wrote, should take no comfort from previous instances of republican defiance. Florence and Pisa, once flourishing republics that had dared to resist papal interdiction, "finally lost their liberty, which

---

[288] *Maiestà pontificia*, pp. 122–123. Papalist writers reminded the Venetians again and again during this interdict of what had befallen them when they had defied Julius II and of their broken promises to him. See Possevino, *Risposta di Teodoro Eugenio*, p. 42; Bovio, *Risposta alle considerationi*, p. 42; Baglioni, *Apologia*, p. 79; *Difesa de'Servi*, p. 167; Bellarmine (as Matteo Torti), *Avviso*, p. 127; the *Discorso* of the anonymous senator, pp. 277–288; Campanella, *Antiveneti*, p. 18. Capello responded (*Delle controversie*, p. 158), by denouncing references to "oaths of peace with Julius II which have never been seen;" and Marsilio (*Essame*, I, 37) found it peculiarly revolting that Rome had not hesitated "to recall the very pernicious example of Julius II."

[289] *Maiestà pontificia*, p. 45.

[290] *Risposta ai sette*, pp. 24–25. Sosa, *Discorso*, p. 70, also cited the good example of Florence in the time of St. Antonino.

[291] Baglioni, *Apologia*, p. 69; Medici, *Discorso*, p. 209.

they have never recovered."[292] The lesson and the threat were again obvious.[293]

While the Roman writers were giving this treatment to Renaissance republicanism, Venetian writers found the occasion ripe for discussing the causes of the Protestant Reformation, which they chose to represent as a warning to Rome. Sarpi made the point as part of his protest against Bellarmine's patronizing attitude to the writers of Gerson's time. He observed that "the unhappiness of those times and the length of the schism in the Roman church cannot be denied, just as a far greater unhappiness cannot be denied in these times, when so many kingdoms have made a total separation from the same church."[294] The Venetians predictably blamed the Reformation entirely on those forces in the church against which they themselves were struggling, characteristically ignoring all doctrinal questions. Querini pointed to the excessive wealth of the church as a source of scandal to the laity and a cause of the Protestant revolt,[295] while Sarpi attributed it in more general language to the illegitimate ambition of the hierarchy: "It is now manifest to the whole world, and histories are full of the fact, that the separation which happened a hundred years ago in Germany did not originate in the disobedience of the subjects but in the abuse of power in the prelates." Sarpi mentioned in particular extortionate demands for money, "extravagant modes of conceding indulgences," and the temporal ambitions of popes. He also proposed, against the background of the Reformation, an interpretation of more recent developments in the Roman communion. Having lost control over so many kingdoms, he suggested, some men in Rome desired "to make up intensively, in those few regions which remain, for what has been lost in extension."[296]

Such treatment of the Reformation was not only a way of mitigating and apologizing for heresy; it also suggested some affinity between the

[292] *Risposta di Teodoro Eugenio*, p. 40.

[293] Genoa was also cited, in the fictitious *Lettera della Repubblica di Genova alla Repubblica di Venezia* (Milan, 1606), as a model for her old enemy to follow. This work pointed out that the recent Genoese surrender to the pope on jurisdictional issues had turned out to the advantage of Genoa.

[294] *Apologia*, in *Scritti*, III, 80.

[295] *Aviso*, p. 16.

[296] *Apologia*, in *Scritti*, III, 83, 173, 80. See also Offman, *Avvertimento, et ammonitione catolica*, p. 105, on abuses (smaller than at present) as cause of the Protestant revolt.

plight of Venice and the participants in the Protestant revolt and it was probably intended as a warning: Venice, pushed too far, could go the way of Germany. The suggestion doubtless contributed to suspicions at the Curia about the intentions of Venice. Sosa openly proposed that heretics were behind the unhappy business in Venice,[297] Bellarmine charged that heretical books were circulating there,[298] and it was reported that books en route from Germany to Venice had been seized and burned in Trent.[299] Roman theologians also associated the Venetians indiscriminately with a long list of heretics, both medieval and modern: the Waldensians, Marsilio of Padua and other supporters of Ludwig of Bavaria, and Wyclif, among those before the emergence of Protestantism.[300] Among more recent figures, the Servites pointed to the influence in Venice of Erasmus, whom they branded a heretic; and Bellarmine compared Sarpi with Luther and Calvin for using "the word of God against God." [301] He implied also that Sarpi shared Protestant views on the mass, clerical celibacy, monastic vows, fasting, invocation of the saints, prayers for the dead, and the veneration of images.[302] Bovio associated Sarpi specifically with Luther on Christian liberty;[303] and Sarpi was also associated with Melanchthon, Peter Martyr, and the Magdeburg *Centuries*.[304] The Roman leaders appeared particularly concerned that Venice might follow the example of England; Bellarmine accusingly noted the applause for Venice there.[305] Such charges reflected, again, the

[297] *Discorso*, p. 5.

[298] *Risposta a Marsilio*, p. 145.

[299] Provana to the Duke of Savoy, Nov. 15, 1606, in Magistris, p. 217.

[300] Bovio, *Lettera al R. P. M. Paolo Rocca*, *passim*; Possevino, *Risposta di Teodoro Eugenio*, pp. 5–6; *Difesa de'Servi*, p. 19; Bellarmine, *Risposta a fra Paulo*, p. 120.

[301] *Risposta ad un libretto di Gersone*, p. 313. See also his *Risposta a fra Paulo*, p. 79, where Sarpi's position on the relations between popes and emperors in antiquity is identified with Calvin's, and p. 100, where Sarpi's limited view of clerical office is associated with Luther.

[302] *Risposta a fra Paulo*, pp. 135–136.

[303] *Lettera al R. P. M. Paolo Rocca*, sig. A2ᵛ.

[304] Bellarmine, *Risposta a fra Paulo*, p. 120; Bovio, *Risposta alle considerationi*, pp. 66, 81.

[305] *Risposta ai sette*, pp. 23–24. For concern about English influence (naturally heightened by the presence of the articulate Wotton in Venice), see also Bellarmine's comparison of Venetian with Anglican doctrine on the relation of ruler to clergy in *Risposta alla risposta*, p. 80; Baronius, *Paraenesis*, p. 119; and Provana to the Duke of Savoy, Aug. 8, 1606, in Magistris, p. 155. Sarpi made the point that English support for Venice was political, not ideological, in *Istoria dell'Interdetto*, pp. 95–96, 124. But cf. Arturo Carlo Jemolo, *Stato e chiesa negli scrittori politici italiani del seicento e del settecento* (Turin, 1914), pp. 18ff., for the general importance of Anglicanism in Italian juris-dictional thought in the seventeenth century.

reluctance of Rome to recognize the deep local roots of Venetian resistance. They were another version of the theory that Venetian resistance was the work of a small band of conspirators badly disposed to the Catholic faith.

That the resistance of Venice ever posed serious danger from this standpoint now seems unlikely. Venice did not object to heightening Rome's anxiety over the possibility of her conversion to Protestantism, and Rome exaggerated the Protestant leanings of the Republic to stimulate support for the papacy throughout the Catholic world. But the Venetians protested their loyalty to the traditional faith, which included for them some acknowledgement of the spiritual supremacy of the pope.[306] Marsilio in particular undertook to defend Venice against charges of heresy. He distinguished the Venetian position from that of those Protestants who believed "that the temporal prince is also head *in spiritualibus*," he ridiculed the Roman fear of heresy by noting that a radical antisacramentalism was the only serious deviation from orthodoxy in Italy, and he suggested that the real heretics of the peninsula were to be found in Rome rather than Venice. But he also pointed out that a man who is a heretic in one respect may speak the truth in many others; a doctrine was not necessarily reprehensible because it was shared by a heretic.[307] Venetians were quite willing to admit their substantial agreement with many Protestants.

At the same time, although the likelihood of Venetian adherence to Protestantism was slight, Rome had, from her own standpoint, substantial grounds for worry; the essential elements in the Catholic vision of reality were at stake in the debate occasioned by the interdict. The fundamental issue in that debate was whether the universe in all its dimensions, spiritual, metaphysical, moral, social, political, and physical, possessed a fixed, objective, and hierarchical order accessible to the human understanding, by which man, individually and collectively, could know exactly what he was and where he stood, and by which he could determine clearly his course through life. Venice had denied, in effect, the existence of such an order, provoking the deepest anxieties among its adherents, and in this way had aligned herself with the major tendencies of the modern world which Rome was resolved to annihilate. These tendencies had appeared most dramatically in the republican cultures of Renaissance Italy; but other recent developments, perhaps as important as the Renaissance, were displaying comparable

---

[306] On this point I am in complete agreement with Chabod, *Politica di Sarpi*, pp. 117ff.
[307] *Difesa a favore della risposta*, pp. 285, 191, 274, 188; *Essame*, I, 21.

tendencies. Thus Protestantism, at least initially, with its rejection of mediation, its spiritual egalitarianism, and its acceptance of political particularity, had represented a similar challenge to the traditional ideal of order; and Rome was hardly mistaken in its association of Renaissance and Reformation. Nor was it an accident that the papacy was so soon to take up the challenge presented by the new science; Galileo too, by attacking the accepted order of the physical universe, had assaulted the order of reality itself. Venice, in this light, seems to have been only the occasion for a struggle over the whole direction of European cultural history.

Venice after the Interdict: The Decline of the Republic and the Isolation of Paolo Sarpi

THE lifting of the interdict in April of 1607 appeared, on the surface, a great victory for Venice. She had defied Rome, and on every significant issue the pope had backed down. But although damage to the papal cause was severe, it also became increasingly apparent that Venice was in some trouble, both because of the interdict and for more general reasons. Within a few years she was showing signs of moral and material exhaustion. The Republic was entering at last into her long and now irreversible decline.

Although her defiance of Rome had apparently ended well, its spiritual cost had been heavy. The Curia had not been altogether wrong in reckoning on the traditional piety of the Republic, which had at least respected the spiritual leadership of the pope; and the more intense piety of the previous century had made consciences generally more sensitive. Thus, although Venetian resistance to ecclesiastical censures might seem proper to men like Sarpi, Donà, and Nicolò Contarini, it imposed a considerable burden on the minds of many Venetians who could not so easily interpret the pope's every gesture as an expression of the *libido dominandi* and who increasingly longed for genuine reconciliation with the Holy See. A delayed reaction to the spiritual strain of the interdict was probably an important element in a slow weakening of the Venetian republican consciousness during the period that followed.

Meanwhile the effect of her spiritual wounds was accelerated by a further deterioration in the worldly position of Venice. Unrelenting external pressures against which no secure support could be found made the bold posture in international affairs advocated by the *giovani* seem increasingly unwise. In addition, the growing economic disasters of this period tended to restore to power a social group traditionally more conservative on religious questions, more closely involved with the church through the possession of major benefices, clerical in sympathy, and (for Venetians) unusually respectful of papal authority. The result of all these circumstances was a steady movement away from the political and religious ideals that had dominated the Republic for a generation. By 1610 Sarpi was reporting sadly to his correspondents in France that the papists were in control.[1] The last phase in the history of the Republic had now begun, and Sarpi's relation to Venice gradually altered.

The interdict was followed by several years of wary readjustment; and that changes were under way was not immediately apparent. Sarpi described the chronic tension that succeeded the direct confrontation between Venice and the pope:

> It was universally believed that the controversies had been actually extinguished, since the soldiers were presumably dismissed and the apostolic nuncio was residing in Venice, just as the Venetian ambassador was resident in Rome. But the prudent saw clearly that the fire was covered over but not extinct, since the omission of certain particulars in the settlement only concealed new tumults. It was well said by the learned physician that the unpurged residues of diseases customarily bring about relapses. The outcome in the present business will show the truth of this maxim in civil things. The controversies never reach the point of a break because the Republic has been and is resolved, for its part, not to interrupt the public quiet; and the pope has learned through experience that his spiritual weapons have no edge and his temporal weapons are extremely weak, as well as that Spanish auxiliaries are readier in the service of their own government than in satisfying the appetites of others. Nevertheless the event has shown that the pope has not accomplished greater novelty rather through lack of power than lack of will.[2]

He compared the new situation to a body of water recently disturbed by winds: "these having ceased, it still moves." Both sides, he reported, simulated friendship and maintained all the diplomatic proprieties, "but at

[1] Letter to Jerôme Groslot de l'Isle, April 27, 1610, Busnelli, I, 119.
[2] From the fragmentary continuation of his history of the interdict, *Istoria dell'Interdetto*, p. 225. Since Sarpi wrote this to make sure that the full meaning of the interdict should not be lost, the work itself testifies that the struggle had not ended.

times signs of deep anger break out."[3] Suppressed hostility, the steady refusal of either side to acknowledge validity in the position of the other, mutual hurt, and constant suspicion combined to create an atmosphere in which rumor flourished and any enormity seemed possible.[4]

In this new situation the papacy faced a serious dilemma. The stern convictions and purposes of Rome had only been strengthened by Venetian resistance, a fact soon to be dramatized by the beatification of Ignatius Loyola in 1609 and the first attacks on Galileo a few years later; his associations with Sarpi were not the least of the charges against him.[5] But it could hardly be denied that the desire of the pope to assert his authority in the Catholic world had received a serious setback at the hands of a relatively minor power. Rome obviously could not hope now to obtain any immediate satisfaction on the jurisdictional issues that had provoked the interdict, and worse still Venice could not be forced to admit the validity of the censures imposed on her. Rome might claim that absolution had been given, but the claim was worth little if the Venetians refused to be absolved. And they acknowledged no guilt.[6]

Furthermore, Venice was still militant, and fresh action against her seemed for the moment unpromising and even dangerous. Her doge still appeared to Rome "more political than Catholic";[7] her theologians were held in high honor, and their perilous doctrines still dominated the minds of her rulers;[8] she persisted in maintaining friendly relations with Protestant states; she still restricted the Inquisition. Rome was also apprehensive that worse might lie ahead. Roberto Ubaldini, the nuncio in Paris, reported (as though this were news) that the Venetian government aspired to control ecclesiastical benefices and their incomes in the manner of France and Spain, and he warned the king that it hoped, for reason of state, to introduce liberty

[3] Letter to Groslot, Sep. 4, 1607, Busnelli, I, 3.

[4] See, in general, Taucci, *Intorno alle lettere di Sarpi*, pp. 68ff.; Chabod, *Politica di Sarpi*, pp. 128–129; and Federico Seneca, *La politica veneziana dopo l'Interdetto* (Padua, 1957), pp. 2–3.

[5] Pastor, XXV, 284–285, 293. For Rome's persistent bitterness toward Venice, see also Rubertis, *Ferdinando I dei Medici*, pp. 355–356, and Stella, *Chiesa e Stato*, pp. 73–74.

[6] Cf. the letter of Cardinal Spinola to Cardinal Borghese, Apr. 28, 1607, *Aevum*, X (1936), 8.

[7] These words appear in the *Relatione dello stato, costumi, disordini et rimedi di Venetia*, a Roman document composed a few years after the interdict, given in part in Odorici, "Paolo V e le città di terraferma," p. 174.

[8] Cf. the letter of Borghese to the nuncio in Spain, Feb. 19, 1609, in Savio, "Il nunzio a Venezia," p. 92, n. 1.

of conscience.[9] Rome above all feared a schism of the Greek sort.[10] Overt pressure, jurisdictional or political, seemed likely to drive Venice to some desperate extreme. The nuncio in Venice, Berlinghiero Gessi, warned in the fall of 1607 that new censures might even lead to another breach with Rome and the election of Sarpi as patriarch of the Republic.[11]

Roman policy toward Venice was immediately, therefore, extremely cautious. The day after the lifting of the interdict, the Venetian inquisitor advised the papal secretary of state to avoid any general condemnations for the future and instead to denounce only individuals;[12] and the nuncio who was dispatched to Venice a month later was officially instructed to make issues only when he was sure of success, "since it is perhaps a lesser evil not to contend than to lose; in summary, in all this matter your lordship must use his prudence." [13] The nuncio, in turn, recommended to Cardinal Borghese as a "good and useful thing that, when the inquisitors are to come into these territories, they should receive a good admonition to proceed modestly and within appropriate limits with the rectors of places." [14] The problem of the patriarch's examination remained unsettled, though a vague accommodation was reached on the same lines as before. Vendramin presented himself at the Curia in 1608, and the pope confirmed his nomination after a few rudimentary questions in the course of an apparently informal discussion. The same procedure was followed with his successors.[15] The Curia by no means abandoned its claims, but it hoped, in the nuncio's words, that "the benefit of time" would produce a change in the composition of the government.[16]

But if Rome was for the time being quiet about particular issues, she did not relax her ideological pressure. The Curia tried to score a general point by obtaining the suppression of the writings and doctrines with which Venice had defended herself, by efforts to persuade the theologians of Venice to repudiate individually the positions they had taken and to quit the

---

[9] Ulianich, p. cxxxvi. See also the letter of Ubaldini to Borghese, June 9, 1609, in Taucci, p. 229.

[10] Cozzi, *Contarini*, pp. 119–120; Ubaldini to Borghese, May 1609, *Aevum*, X (1936), 13, n. 2.

[11] Gessi to Borghese, Nov. 24, 1607, *Aevum*, X (1936), 18, n. 1.

[12] Letter of April 29, 1607, in Savio, pp. 56–57, n. 2.

[13] Instruction dated June 4, 1607, Luzio, p. 30.

[14] April 26, 1608, in Savio, p. 65.

[15] Niero, *I patriarchi di Venezia*, p. 16; Rubertis, pp. 382–386.

[16] Gessi to Borghese, July 14, 1607, *Aevum*, X (1936), 48–49, n. 4.

Republic, and by attacks on those who remained firm. Venice might be the city of the devil[17] and rotten with "peccant humors," to use the phrase of Cardinal Borghese in an angry letter to the nuncio;[18] but at least her condition might be clearly identified as morbid, and perhaps the disease could be prevented from spreading. The pope's secretary of state insisted that a remedy would be found to counteract the influence of "those false theologians." [19] Rome persisted in blaming a few pernicious individuals for the policies of Venice.

Some effort was made, through clergy in Venice who were sympathetic to Rome, to secure the repudiation of Venetian doctrine on its home ground. Vendramin himself was persuaded to repeat in Venice the criticism of Venetian doctrine he had heard in Rome, but the College promptly summoned the unfortunate prelate to appear before it and expressed "amazement and disgust" at his behavior; and the doge, in a harsh reprimand, informed the wretched patriarch "that all were obligated to defend their country, and that the books of [the Venetian] writers contained many things good and useful for the liberty of princes, and that therefore he was not to say the contrary, especially since, because of his rank, his words mattered greatly." [20]

The confessional was also more than once employed to fight Venetian principles, but it did not prove much more useful. When, in September of 1608, a senator reported to the authorities that he had been refused absolution because he refused to give up his copy of Querini's *Aviso*, the priest involved was promptly expelled from the state. The nuncio's protest, on the ground that the government had violated the sanctity of the confessional, was firmly rejected. The nuncio also took this occasion to argue that the works composed on behalf of Venice had been justly banned for heresy; and when the College defended their orthodoxy, he reminded the senators that they were not theologians. But he sadly admitted to Rome that there seemed to be no remedy for the attachment of Venetians to their interdict writings.[21] The

[17] Cf. the *Relatione* in Odorici, p. 177: "Si può dire che il demonio qui tenga il suo seggio; poichè come una bocca internale, da questa città escono tutte le scelleraggini."
[18] Nov. 21, 1609, *Aevum*, XI (1937), 305, n. 1.
[19] Borghese to the nuncio in Turin, May 5, 1607, Magistris, p. 506.
[20] See Gessi's report of this incident to Borghese, Feb. 7, 1609, *Aevum*, X (1936), 51–52, n.
[21] Sarpi to Groslot, Sept. 30 and Dec. 9, 1608, Busnelli, I, 37, 51; Sarpi to Antonio Foscarini, Sept. 30, 1608, *Aevum*, XI (1937), 43. For Gessi's account, *ibid.*, pp. 43–47; see also Taucci, pp. 93–94, and Savio, p. 84.

Venetian authorities also blocked, as directed against themselves, the publication of an old bull of Pius V denouncing defenders of heretics.[22]

Meanwhile Rome continued the attempt, already successful in the case of Capello, to detach the theologians from the service of the Republic. Shortly after the lifting of the interdict, Monsignor Gessi began to consider how they might conveniently be spirited away. He suggested to Cardinal Borghese in August that if one could be seized and transported to the papal state, the others might flee. Fulgenzio Manfredi struck him as the easiest to take, since he generally went out by night and "the woman whom he frequents is known." Such a procedure seemed to him justified since the theologians had been summoned to Rome by the Holy Office, and too much time had already passed without a trial.[23] The point is of some interest because it makes clear that some conception of legality, transcending all local arrangements, lay back of the Roman attitude to these men. What the ecclesiastics contemplated was not mere kidnapping, but in some sense the apprehension of fugitives from justice: the legal enforcement of true order by the supreme authority in the Christian Republic.

But less radical measures were successful in several cases. In August of 1608 Manfredi, whose vehement pulpit tirades against the pope had begun to disquiet even Sarpi,[24] suddenly fled to Rome, having been promised both money and personal safety.[25] His defection was followed, in December, by the more shocking flight of Pietro Antonio Ribetti, recently patriarchal vicar of Venice, one of the seven official theologians during the interdict and a man of presumed reliability as well as high status.[26] A few days later the jurist Menino, who had also written for the Republic, left for Rome.[27] These blows were serious. Although Sarpi minimized the abilities of the fugitives, he did not conceal his dismay at the effect of their desertion on public

[22] Antonio Provana to the Duke of Savoy, Aug. 7, 1607, Luzio, p. 33.

[23] Aug. 4, 1607, *Aevum*, X (1936), 49, n.

[24] Cf. Sarpi's remarks to Christoph von Dohna, according to the latter's reports of July 28 and Aug. 4, 1608, *Briefe und Akten*, II, 79, 82.

[25] Sarpi reported this event and Manfredi's subsequent career in Rome in a series of letters to Groslot, Aug. 26, Sept. 30, and Nov. 11, 1608; Feb. 17, 1609; Feb. 16, June 8, and Aug. 3, 1610, Busnelli, I, 29–30, 37–38, 43, 66, 112, 125, 130–132. See also *Aevum*, XI (1937), 35–40; and the vivid letter of William Bedell to Adam Newton, Jan. 1, 1609, in *Two Biographies*, pp. 245–247.

[26] Various documents connected with this event in *Aevum*, XI (1937), 49–51. See also letters of Sarpi to Groslot in Busnelli, I, 52, 58, 66, 158, 160. The fact that Ribetti had recently been removed as patriarchal vicar (Rubertis, pp. 383–384) may have influenced his defection.

[27] Sarpi to Groslot, Dec. 23, 1608, Busnelli, I, 55.

opinion. The subjects of the Republic would feel, he wrote, that they had been misled by men who had not themselves believed in what they were saying.[28] This was precisely the effect at which Rome had been aiming, and the Venetian government responded by imprisoning two priests who had encouraged the flights[29] and by increasing the stipends of the theologians who remained.[30] But the damage had been done.

Although Ribetti and Capello appear to have settled quietly in Rome, the less stable Manfredi was persuaded to provide information about the religious climate in Venice well calculated to deepen anxiety in the Curia. He exaggerated, but his report had some basis in fact. He claimed that the rulers of Venice aimed at a general withdrawal of obedience from Rome. They proposed, he asserted, to establish a more spiritual church whose doctrine would be based on Scripture alone. Its sacrament would be administered in both kinds, fasting would be reduced, services would be conducted in the vernacular, and the Bible would be made available in Italian. Manfredi also declared that Calvinism was openly disseminated in Venice with the approval of the government, a charge that even the nuncio branded as false.[31] But Manfredi's report did him little good and was perhaps a measure of desperation. Less than two years after his flight from Venice he was convicted as a relapsed heretic and executed, though possibly less for his guilt than because his death, as the nuncio believed, might have a salutary effect in Venice.[32]

In spite of the nuncio's hopes, Giovanni Marsilio could not be tempted to quit Venice. Esteemed by the doge and other members of the ruling group, he died there in 1612, refusing to the last to retract what he had written against the pope.[33] Sarpi was also beyond temptation, as the nuncio recognized from an early point; he noted generally that those theologians who were native Venetians could probably not be induced to leave for Rome both

[28] Letter to Foscarini, Dec. 9, 1608, *Aevum*, XI (1937), 52.

[29] Gessi to Borghese, Jan. 17 and 31, 1609, *Aevum*, X (1936), 50, n.

[30] Sarpi to Groslot, Jan. 20, 1609, Busnelli, I, 62, noting his own refusal of the increase; Gessi to Borghese, Jan. 24, 1609, *Aevum*, XI (1937), 53, n. 1.

[31] Manfredi's deposition is given in *Aevum*, X (1936), 18ff., 45–48. For Gessi's reaction, see *ibid.*, p. 22, n. 2, and pp. 48–54.

[32] Various dispatches dealing with his fate in *Aevum*, XIV (1940), 55–57. These suggest that Manfredi may have retained a considerable personal following in Venice.

[33] For Marsilio's situation in Venice, *Aevum*, X (1936), 46, 48, 52, 60, and XI (1937), 41, 304. Sarpi reported his death, speculating on the possibility of poison, to Groslot, Feb. 14, 1612, Busnelli, I, 217; and to Jacques Leschassier, Feb. 14, 1612, Ulianich, p. 103. See also Orazio Pauli to Savoy, Feb. 14, 1612, Luzio, p. 42.

for patriotic reasons and out of fear of which might happen to their families.[34] Under these conditions Rome was reduced to maintaining close surveillance over their activities and accumulating further evidence in the hope of some future occasion to strike.

The attention of the Curia was particularly fastened on Sarpi, not so much because of his role during the interdict as because, alone among the Venetian theologians, Sarpi and his *alter ego* Fra Fulgenzio constituted a lively present danger as well as a reminder of past humiliation. This was in part because of his remarkable popularity. The nuncio reported that he was "esteemed and revered more than is credible," not only for his abilities but also because of his reputation for sanctity.[35] But the danger Sarpi posed came also from his official position as canonical and theological adviser to the government and the influence he was presumed to wield over its policies. He clearly hoped to assist in further resistance to the pope. Once the crisis of the interdict was past, Sarpi carefully defined the duties of his position in a manner which emphasized again the claims of the government to exercise broad authority over ecclesiastical matters and opened up for himself opportunities for substantial influence. The canonist of the Republic, he suggested, in a *consulto* which described the duties he had performed for several years, "can serve where ecclesiastical discipline is involved, coordinating the two jurisdictions, spiritual and temporal, so that one does not interfere with the other." More specifically the canonist might be useful in connection with the publication of "bulls, edicts, or other new ecclesiastical precepts," taxation of the clergy, rights of presentation to benefices and of asylum in churches, questions of clerical immunity of every kind, appeals against "censures or other precepts" imposed by the hierarchy, and disputes over the possession of ecclesiastical benefices. In all these matters, Sarpi concluded, "the canonist who serves the prince does not have to advise on the merit of the case but simply on the competence of the court; and if the case pertains to the temporal court, its merit is then judged by the prince or magistrate according to his conscience." [36] His essential task was thus to determine the boundary between

[34] Letter to Borghese, July 12, 1608, *Aevum*, XI (1937), 39–40, n. 2.

[35] See Gessi's dispatches to Borghese during 1607 and 1608 as collected by Taucci, pp. 86–87, and his letter of July 31, 1610, *Aevum*, X (1936), 59–60. Pastor's contention, XXV, 215, that Sarpi was "detested, in his last years, by the nobility and shunned by the people," seems to me to have little basis in fact, although it is true that his political influence declined.

[36] In Francescon, *Chiesa e stato*, pp. 7–8, n.4, from an opinion of 1611. See the similar statement in Sarpi's *Scrittura sopra l'offizio del canonista*, in *Opere*, Suppl. II, 130.

spiritual and temporal authority in every case where the issue was of practical importance for the subjects of the Republic. Rome was particularly offended because Sarpi aimed to perform this task as a delegate not of the church but of the civil power.

His definition of the duties of the official theologian of Venice, an office also intrinsically repugnant to Rome, had implications possibly even more striking. The task here, he wrote, was to advise the government "in cases of religion and of conscience." The Republic might need such counsel, he explained, "when the inquisitors try to draw to that tribunal cases which do not pertain to it," whenever a new prohibition of books was proposed, and "when Greek subjects might have recourse to the prince against their prelates in spiritual cases which, according to the ancient practice of the Greek Church, have always been judged by the princes, and which is with reason continued to the present." [37] Sarpi did not propose that Venice should in general follow the Greek model, but his favorable impression of it may be assumed. It is clear at any rate that he proposed to assist the Venetian government in exercising considerable influence over matters which the authorities in Rome regarded as exclusively their own.

His popularity and his position gave to Sarpi, in the opinion of the nuncio, a remarkable authority in the conduct of Venetian affairs. Reviewing Sarpi's career since the interdict, Gessi reported in 1611 that "the mind and the actions of Fra Paolo the Servite are . . . the worst, nor do they tend to anything less than to separate these lords from Rome, persuading them in every case to the usurpation of ecclesiastical jurisdiction, which I believe they hope to reduce to the terms of the monarchy of Sicily. And Fra Paolo will persuade them to still worse if he can, since unfortunately he acquires greater credit every day with his hypocrisy and astuteness." [38] It was now widely believed in Rome that the leading figures in the Venetian government were little more than disciples of Sarpi; in the words of one observer, "They have made their master the theologian of the Signoria—he and his *accademici* infect and seduce that poor republic." [39] Sarpi was accordingly blamed for a series of particular actions of the Venetian state: for the refusal of the government to condemn the compositions of the interdict years, for its prohibition against the sale of a work by Bellarmine on papal authority in temporal affairs, for

[37] *Consulto* of 1611 in Francescon, p. 7, n. 3; see also Sarpi, *Scrittura sopra l'offizio del teologo*, in *Opere*, Suppl. II, 130.

[38] Letter to Borghese, Oct. 8, 1611, *Aevum*, XIII (1939), 612 n. 3.

[39] From the *Relatione* in Odorici, p. 175.

the government's resistance to the acquisition of a major benefice in the Veneto by the pope's nephew.[40] In one way or another Sarpi had to be put out of the way.

An early effort to remove this dangerous figure from the Venetian scene miscarried badly. On the evening of October 5, 1607, as he was returning to his convent from the Palazzo Ducale, Sarpi was attacked by three assassins, who stabbed him several times in the head and neck and then fled. The ultimate source of this attack has never been established; but Sarpi, in a wry pun, professed to recognize in a dagger removed from one of his wounds "il stilo romano," and it was noted that his assailants took refuge in the Papal State. His injuries proved superficial, however, and the chief result of the attack was to confirm his popularity and to release a wave of popular indignation against his enemies.[41] William Bedell, chaplain to the English ambassador, sent home a vivid description of the Venetian reaction:

But to have seen how this matter was taken was admirable. The whole city was in a broile; the Councell often called in the night; the chiefest of the senate flock'd to the monastery, where the wounded Father lay; the next day the people every where in clumps and clusters talking of this matter; the professor of Anatomy and Chirurgery, Aquapendente, a man of great age, learning, and experience, sent for by publick counsell to Padua, and joyned with other physicians to cure the wounds; an edict published against the cut throats, with a strange tally sett on their heads; and which is specially to be marked therein, they are expressly stiled the ministers of this conspiracy, as if others were the authors and contrivers.[42]

Savoy's agent in Venice, by no means one of Sarpi's admirers, reported how, following the attack, Sarpi was everywhere hailed as a saint. "In short," he wrote, "such demonstrations have been made towards this *frate*, that greater would perhaps not have occurred if the person of the Prince himself

---

[40] Gessi to Borghese, Feb. 14, 1609, in Savio, p. 83, and Oct. 16, 1610, *Aevum*, XIV (1940), 69–70, n. 16; Pauli to Savoy, July 23, 1611, Luzio, p. 39.

[41] For a full account of the attempt, see Fulgenzio Micanzio *Vita del Padre Paolo* (n.p., 1658), pp. 102ff. Sarpi described it himself to Groslot, Dec. 11, 1607, Busnelli, I, 6. See also the documents in *Aevum*, XIII (1939), 589–590; and the letter of Provana to Savoy, Oct. 6, 1607, Luzio, p. 37; and Rubertis, pp. 356–363, for an account from Florentine sources as well as a good discussion of Roman involvement.

[42] Letter to Adam Newton, Jan. 1, 1608, *Two Biographies*, pp. 236–237.

had been attacked." [43] Nor were the effects of the attempt limited to Venice. Henry IV informed the nuncio in Paris that the attack on Sarpi's life had done much harm to the Catholic cause,[44] and the veneration in which he was held abroad considerably increased.[45]

Although the nuncio in Venice was wise enough to realize that any further efforts of this kind would seriously endanger his own mission,[46] the assassination of Sarpi continued to be discussed from time to time in Rome; and other attempts on his life, all abortive, were made.[47] Sarpi professed to care little about his own survival, but the government compelled him to take precautions and insisted warmly on its eagerness to give him every protection. The nuncio reported a speech of Donà in the College which had proclaimed "with the greatest affection that the Republic was deeply satisfied with him and that they loved him so much that for his sake, if it should be necessary, they would go to war with any prince whatsoever . . . . Other senators said the same." [48]

Frustrated in its efforts to lure Sarpi to Rome and unable to dispose of him by violence, the Curia was reduced to burning his writings in the *Campo dei Fiori*.[49] But the nuncio in Venice advised against burning him in effigy, "although such execution would be holy and just," because it would be too great a scandal that "a declared heretic burned in effigy should here be not only favored and salaried but principal adviser in ecclesiastical things, and in particular reviser of all the bulls and directives of Rome." [50] Rome could only keep a close watch over Sarpi's activities, gather evidence of his heresy, and denigrate him whenever and wherever possible. The nuncio kept him under careful surveillance, reporting in detail on his way of life. So he described it in 1609:

> Fra Paolo, the Servite, attempts in all his actions to present a good and exemplary appearance to the people and frequently celebrates mass. For some time, however, he has left off going into the choir and does not

[43] Provana to Savoy, Oct. 16, 1607, Luzio, pp. 37–38.

[44] Ubaldini to Borghese, April 12, 1609, *Aevum*, X (1936), 67–69, n. 1. Cf. the outrage felt by Villeroy at the attempt, *ibid.*, pp. 68–69.

[45] Cf. Ulianich, p. xxxvii.

[46] Letter to Borghese, July 26, 1608, *Aevum*, XIII (1939), 590, n. 6.

[47] Sarpi to Groslot, May 27, 1608, and Jan. 6, 1609, Busnelli, I, 14, 59; Micanzio, *Vita*, p. 123.

[48] Letter to Borghese, Nov. 26, 1611, cited in Taucci, p. 88.

[49] Taucci, pp. 76–77.

[50] Letter to Borghese, Oct. 8, 1611, *Aevum*, XIII (1939), 612, n. 3.

confess in church but confesses in the room of one of his friends. He has also left off going to the common table and eats alone or with Fra Fulgenzio. He studies much and, it is said, is writing a book about the authority of the supreme Roman pontiff with the idea of having it printed abroad. He goes often into the College, as consultore of the most Serene Republic, on the business on which they consult with him, in which these lords credit him more than I can say. He converses almost every day for a long time in the shop of certain Flemish merchants named Cecchinelli, at the *ponte di Berettari in merciaria*, and talks with many foreigners, who have bad opinions in the things of religion, and similarly with nobles who are badly affected towards the Apostolic See. When he goes through Venice, he wears chain mail, gauntlets and probably other armor, and three well armed *frati* also walk behind.[51]

But the nuncio's efforts to obtain evidence of Sarpi's specific wrongdoing were a failure.

His enemies were somewhat more successful in their attempts to lay hands on samples of Sarpi's extensive correspondence abroad, on which they kept a careful and anxious eye. Spies and couriers were offered money to supply copies of his letters, and eventually Ubaldini in Paris succeeded in obtaining Sarpi's letters to the indiscreet Protestant Francesco Castrino. The nuncio also arranged for the transcription and transmission to Rome, by a dissatisfied secretary, of Sarpi's letters to Antonio Foscarini, the Venetian ambassador in France. This feat seemed so important that the pope himself studied the letters carefully for proof of Sarpi's heresy. He annotated them marginally and came to know Sarpi's hand well.[52] But the evidence obtained in this way was inconclusive, and the efforts of papal representatives in Venice and Paris to impress statesmen with Sarpi's guilt were unavailing. Gessi admitted that all his warnings against Sarpi's plots to introduce Calvinism into Italy were regarded in Venice as papalist inventions animated by passion and hatred;[53] and to Ubaldini's insistence on the gravity of Sarpi's errors, Villeroy had replied dryly "that the world does not believe there are heresies in the writings of Fra Paolo." He advanced his own opinion "that they contain nothing but the defense of the temporal authority of princes."[54]

[51] Letter to Borghese Nov. 7, 1609, *Aevum*, X, (1936) 60, n. 1. See also *ibid.*, p. 30, n. 1.
[52] Taucci, pp. 2–3, 253ff.; and *Aevum*, X (1936), 84, n. 3, and 87–88; XI (1937), 295, n.
[53] Letter to Borghese, Dec. 8, 1611, *Aevum*, X (1936), 41, n.
[54] Ubaldini to Borghese, April 28, 1609, Taucci, p. 115.

Portrait bust of the Doge Nicolò da Ponte *(Vittoria)*.

Portrait of the Doge Leonardo Donà.

Rome was hopeful that the death of Leonardo Donà in 1612 would at last make it possible to discredit Sarpi with his government, and a complicated scheme was proposed to coordinate French allegations of Sarpi's heresy with the disappearance from the scene of his chief protector. But this project also failed, primarily because the French government refused to cooperate;[55] and the Curia at last gave up its long effort to destroy Sarpi. Eventually it made a brief attempt to secure him by gentler tactics; there was talk of making him a cardinal in return for his full submission.[56] Nothing came of the idea, but it marked the end of the period of his greatest danger; and the last decade of Sarpi's life, although he still felt the need to behave with great caution, was relatively more calm. But Rome had by no means forgotten his offenses. After Sarpi's death in 1623 the nuncio in Venice demanded that his body be disinterred and submitted to trial for heresy.[57]

This prolonged and intense concern in Rome with the activities of Sarpi is of interest not only as an index to the bitterness against him at the Curia and to its fear of the damage he might still be capable of inflicting on the Roman church. It also suggests again Rome's persistent refusal to admit that she had to deal with the deeply rooted sentiment of a substantial community. The Curia continued to attribute the resistance of Venice to a wicked minority and perhaps chiefly to Sarpi; it seemed nearly persuaded that with his elimination all would be well. Sarpi was Rome's favorite scapegoat, but he also enabled the Curia to maintain the hope that political and social existence could be brought into stable conformity with its ideals.[58]

Venice was for some time after the interdict in a bitter, resolute, and defiant mood, resolved to protect her theologians and to defend their doctrines.[59] Papalist writings, including works of Bellarmine, were banned in the city;[60]

[55] *Aevum*, X (1936), 75ff.

[56] Gaetano Cozzi, "Traiano Boccalini, il Cardinale Borghese e la Spagna, secondo le riferte di un confidente degli Inquisitori di Stato," *RSI*, LXVIII (1956), 239–240.

[57] Letter of Sismondo d'Este to Savoy, Oct. 14, 1623, Luzio, p. 53.

[58] Cf. Gessi's letter to Borghese, July 31, 1610, *Aevum*, X (1936), 59, on the wisdom of bringing formal charges of heresy against Sarpi and his associates: ". . . veramente è non meno difficile il farne giudicio che il trattarne, poiche non si governano questi signori in simili materie con la ragione, ma con li loro affetti, e quelli che dominano et hanno lingua sono li politici et poco amici di Roma."

[59] Provana to Savoy, April 14, 1607, Magistris, p. 486. On the Venetian mood in general, see the documents in Magistris, pp. 302–325.

[60] Sarpi to Castrino, May 12, 1609, *Aevum*, XIII (1939), 579; to Groslot, Sept. 28, 1610, Busnelli, I, 142; to Leschassier, Nov. 23, 1610, Ulianich, p. 96.

Gaspare Scioppio, passing through, was arrested because he had a copy of Campanella's *Antiveneti*.[61] A monk who called the doge a heretic was banished,[62] and the clergy were admonished "to preach the gospel and not to enter into matters of state." [63] The exclusion of the Jesuits was vigorously maintained,[64] and French attacks on the Society of Jesus, though officially prohibited, circulated widely.[65] The position of the nuncio in Venice was particularly uneasy. Venetian clergy were warned to keep away from him, bishops refused to assist him,[66] and his activities were spied on; even his gondolier was a government spy who reported on his movements every four or five days.[67] The doge deliberately humiliated him by bringing him into contact with the government's official theologians.[68] He also informed the nuncio belligerently that there were as good Catholics in Venice as in Rome.[69] More than three years after the interdict the nuncio reported that he was still without the least influence in the Republic. On every issue he attempted to discuss with the government, whether the business of the Inquisition, surveillance over the printing industry, or jurisdiction over the clergy, he encountered complete intransigence.[70]

Venetian agressiveness toward the church took various forms. Soon after the interdict, the government made a point of trying criminal clergy in civil courts to show that the surrender of the two accused clerics constituted no precedent;[71] and during the next few years several priests were tried and executed,[72] in one case without the formal degradation intended to protect

---

[61] Mario d'Addio, *Il pensiero politico di Gaspare Scioppio e il Machiavellismo del Seicento* (Milan, 1962), pp. 66–67.

[62] Pauli to Savoy, Nov. 19, 1611, Luzio, pp. 41–42.

[63] Gessi to Borghese, Feb. 14, 1609, *Aevum*, X (1936), 53, n. 1. See also reply of Borghese, Feb. 28, Savio, p. 93, n. 1.

[64] It was officially renewed in 1612 (Pauli to Savoy, March 17, 1612, Luzio, p. 43).

[65] Gessi to Borghese, Dec. 4, 1610, *Aevum*, XIV (1940), 67; Sarpi to Leschassier, Jan. 4, 1611, Ulianich, p. 99.

[66] Savio, p. 56. See also Rubertis, p. 367, on the fate of a patrician whose meetings with the nuncio came to the attention of the authorities.

[67] Cozzi, "Boccalini, Borghese, e Spagna," pp. 230–231.

[68] An incident of this kind is described in a letter from Provana to Savoy, Oct. 16 1607, Luzio, pp. 38–39.

[69] Provana to Savoy, Aug. 21, 1607, Luzio, pp. 33–34. cf. Magistris, p. 317.

[70] Letter to Borghese, Aug. 3, 1610, *Aevum*, XI (1937), 307 n. This is the central point in Savio.

[71] Provana to Savoy, Aug. 21, 1607, Luzio, p. 33.

[72] Sarpi counted thirty-six clergy condemned to various punishments (letter to Groslot, Dec. 9, 1608, Busnelli, I, 51). For particular cases, see his letters to Castrino, Oct. 13, 1609, Busnelli II, 57; to Foscarini, Oct. 10 and 22, 1609, and Jan. 5, 1610, *Aevum*, XI (1937), 312–313, 299, 289–290, n.

clerical dignity.[73] Rome could only protest helplessly. The nuncio reported bitterly, after the government had refused him the right to arrest members of the clergy on his own initiative, "that in this, and all similar cases, they do not have the slightest intention of giving up their pretensions, that is to supervise [*conoscere*] the cases of ecclesiastics." [74]

The government interfered with ecclesiastical matters in other ways as well. Alleging the need to protect public morals, it ordered that churches should be closed in the evening; Sarpi interpreted the pope's protest at this infringement on ecclesiastical liberty as evidence that he put power above purity.[75] The Inquisition continued to be closely regulated, and the Senate reminded its lay members that they had been appointed exclusively to serve the government.[76] Efforts were also made to prevent Venetian benefices from falling into the possession of clergy attached to the Curia; for Sarpi this was central to maintaining the independence of the Venetian church.[77] Meanwhile the jurisdictional claims of Venice were extended by formal legislation. A law of 1613 forbade secular magistrates to obey ecclesiastical tribunals outside the state and specified that the obedience of clergy to decrees emanating from abroad required permission from the secular magistrate.[78] In addition, clergy were excluded by a law of 1614 from the administration of property belonging to pious associations of laity.[79] Venice was resolved to maintain the traditional autonomy of her church and the role of laymen in its administration.

The Evangelical mood so strong among the *giovani* grew possibly even more fervent during the years immediately following the interdict, an event which proved to some Venetians both the depravity of Roman religion and the holiness of their own. Leonardo Donà replied to the nuncio's protests against Protestant activity in Venice by informing him dryly that "the Republic lived in as Catholic a manner as Rome, and more." [80]

What the ruling group understood by Catholicism during these years may be studied in a series of Lenten sermons preached by Fulgenzio Micanzio during the spring of 1609. No text of the sermons appears to have survived,

[73] Gessi to Borghese, Dec. 19, 1609, *Aevum*, XI (1937), 299–300, n.

[74] Quoted by Savio, p. 88, from a dispatch of 1608.

[75] Letter to Leschassier, Jan. 6, 1609, Ulianich, pp. 35–36.

[76] Sarpi, *Sopra l'officio dell'inquisizione, SG*, pp. 121, 126–128.

[77] Letters to Leschassier, July 8, 1608, and April 27 and June 8, 1610, Ulianich, pp. 18, 81, 84.

[78] Sarpi mentioned this in *Scrittura sopra l'autorità della nunziatura per la licenza de' brevi*, in *Opere*, Suppl. II, 128.

[79] Stella, "Proprietà ecclesiastica," p. 76.

[80] Quoted by Cozzi, *Contarini*, p. 111.

but contemporary accounts indicate their general content and the excitement they produced.[81] Fra Fulgenzio was evidently more forthright than Sarpi in expressing his religious views; perhaps he was more fervently committed to an Evangelical faith. He defended the position Venice had taken during the interdict, he insisted on the obligation of princes to discipline the clergy, and he attacked the concern of the church with temporal power. But the peculiar interest of his preaching derives from his attempt to place these matters in the positive context of a religion of grace based on Scripture rather than human tradition. The hostile account of the nuncio agrees, in this respect with Sarpi's own references to the sermons:

> [Fra Fulgenzio] says frequently that Christ is the only head of the church, or that we have no other head than Christ. He exaggerates in saying that one ought to study and to attend only to Holy Scripture, without so many interpreters. He preaches and greatly exalts contrition, so that he seems to exclude confession, although sometimes he mentions it rather coldly. He greatly exalts faith in the blood of Christ and the grace of God for our salvation, and leaves out or rarely refers to works. He exhorts to the exact observance of divine precepts, minimizing the authority of those of men, which he wishes to be examined. He says that secular princes should have a care for religion, and that only Christ should be adored as God. And as for ecclesiastical censures, he preached on Wednesday what he has also put into print.[82]

The nuncio was profoundly interested in Micanzio's sermons. Certain that Micanzio was a heretic and hopeful to discover evidence of specific heresies, he arranged to be informed in detail about the monk's words. He received reports from spies of his own, and in addition (at his request) the Holy Office in Rome ordered that "two or three learned and intelligent but above all faithful persons" should be sent to Venice to listen to the sermons.[83]

[81] The fullest account is supplied in Gessi's dispatches to Rome as assembled by Taucci, pp. 219ff. See also Wotton's letter to James I, March 20, 1609, in Smith, I, 447–449, and the letters of Sarpi cited below.

[82] Letter to Borghese, April 4, 1609, *Aevum*, XI (1937), 67–68, n. Cf. letters of Sarpi to Castrino, April 28, 1609, *Aevum*, XIII (1939), 573–574; to Christoph von Dohna on the same day, Busnelli, II, 148; to Jean Hotman de Villiers on the same day, Ulianich, p. 185; to Groslot, April 28 and May 12, 1609, Busnelli, I, 76, 80; to Leschassier, May 12, 1609, Ulianich, p. 43; and to Foscarini on the same day, *Aevum*, XI (1937), 66–68. See too, on Micanzio's devotion to the Bible, Favaro, "Micanzio e Galileo," pp. 63–64. Lenten preaching had from the beginning been a favorite vehicle of Evangelism.

[83] Cardinal Arigoni, secretary to the Holy Office, to Cardinal Spinola, legate in Ferrara, March 21, 1609, quoted by Taucci, pp. 223–224.

But these efforts to trap Micanzio were in vain. The doctrinal content of his pronouncements was evidently too vague—as it had traditionally been in Italian Evangelism—to justify particular charges. The inquisitor of Treviso, who had come to hear Fra Fulgenzio preach at the nuncio's request, left Venice without even bothering to communicate with that prelate;[84] and the nuncio himself confessed his frustration. The monk, he complained, had expressed "concepts so equivocal and mutilated that they can be understood in several ways." [85] Micanzio was more circumspect in his later sermons than at the outset;[86] he was careful to support confession in principle and to describe as heresy the belief that man can be saved without works by good intentions alone. But the assumption that the imprecision in his treatment of doctrine concealed a secret attachment to a rigidly dogmatic Protestantism may reveal more about the nuncio himself than about the preacher.

This possibility is borne out by the firm support given Micanzio's doctrines by the rulers of Venice. The nuncio protested violently against the sermons, claiming that they were attended only by Protestants and Greeks; but the doge replied (as though formally to identify the sentiments of the preacher with the Venetian community) that the nuncio had been badly informed, "because most of his listeners were nobles of this city." [87] Sarpi reported that the chief effect of the protest had been to stimulate the attendance of still more of the nobility.[88] But more than hostility to Rome lay behind the government's insistence that (in the doge's words) the Servite "was preaching good and Catholic doctrine," [89] and the formal statement of the Venetian ambassador in Rome that the sermons were doctrinally unexceptionable.[90] Venice recognized in Micanzio's sermons the traditional religious preferences of the Republic. At the same time Sarpi admitted that Micanzio found critics; Venetian Evangelism was also clearly under attack.[91]

Protestant enthusiasm for these sermons, reports of which circulated widely, no doubt increased the anxiety they aroused in Rome;[92] and vague charges that Sarpi and his friends were engaged in a conspiracy to convert

[84] Gessi to Borghese, April 4, 1609, *Aevum*, XIII (1939), 577–578.

[85] Gessi to Borghese, March 14, 1609, *Aevum*, XI (1937), 66–67.

[86] Cf. the French ambassador's report, April 14, 1609, quoted in Taucci, p. 228.

[87] Letters of Pierre Asselineau to Castrino, March 16 and s.d., 1609, *Aevum*, X (1936), 24–25. See also "Nuovi documenti su fra Paolo Sarpi e Fulgenzio Micanzio," ed. Achille de Rubertis, *Civiltà moderna*, XI (1939), 383–385.

[88] Letter to Groslot, March 17, 1609, Busnelli, I, 71.

[89] Gessi to Borghese, March 14 and 21, 1609, Taucci, pp. 222–223.

[90] Borghese to Gessi, March 21, 1609, *Aevum*, XIII (1939), 575–576, n. 3.

[91] Letter to Castrino, April 28, 1609, *Aevum*, X (1936), 19, n. 1.

[92] See the references assembled in Taucci, p. 226, n. 1.

the Republic to Calvinism were made from time to time.[93] But the likelihood of such an event was certainly no greater than before, and indeed Venice, having defied the pope on the grounds of her superior Catholicity, had in these years an even greater stake in maintaining her reputation for orthodoxy. Even the nuncio, in his calmer moments, saw that there was little inclination to heresy among the rulers of the Republic. A few months after Fra Fulgenzio's sermons, he was reporting to Rome "that these lords have no inclination to change Christian doctrine . . . at present I believe that there is no danger of change." [94] Sarpi himself, who chose to impress Protestants with his sympathy for their views, gave little encouragement to their hopes. He acknowledged that three-fourths of the nobility were openly hostile to the pope, "but of these scarcely thirty of the religion." [95]

Micanzio's relaxed attitude to the definition of doctrine seemed as dangerous to Rome as what it suspected of his doctrines themselves. This tendency in Venetian piety, which was related to a more general permissiveness in matters of belief and conduct, was a general source of concern to the nuncio. He was particularly distressed at his inability to control the sale of books and the reading of the nobility, reporting sadly that there was for the time being no remedy "for the great liberty these lords wish in this and also in other things." [96] Even the laymen delegated to serve with the Venetian Holy Office demanded that the heretical content of any work, albeit prohibited in Rome, be demonstrated (presumably to themselves) before it could be banned in the Republic;[97] and in a situation where the authorities were at least as suspicious of Rome as of Geneva and other Protestant centers, the charge that obviously heretical books circulated widely[98] was very likely true. The list of books read by the *"grandi et litterati"* of Venice supplied by Manfredi to the Roman authorities is of particular interest. It includes Calvin's *Institutes* and several treatises by English divines, the latter probably a consequence of Wotton's missionary zeal. But Manfredi also suggested that the Venetians were ranging widely through the literature of the Italian

---

[93] See the report attributed to a renegade Venetian, *Aevum*, X (1936), 54–56, n. 4, and the accusations against a Paduan jurist discussed by Savio, pp. 62–65.

[94] Letter to Borghese, Oct. 24, 1609, *Aevum*, X (1936), 25, n. 1. See also the dispatch of Aug. 25, 1607, *ibid.*, p. 23, n. 2. The issue is well discussed by Chabod, *Politica di Sarpi*, pp. 125ff. The deep Catholic piety of Venice in the seventeenth century is also recognized by Giuseppe de Luca, "Della pietà veneziana nel Seicento," pp. 215–234.

[95] In his conversation with Dohna, Aug. 7, 1608, Busnelli, II, 125.

[96] Letter to Borghese, Feb. 14, 1609, *Aevum*, X (1936), 28, n.

[97] Savio, p. 73.

[98] *Ibid.*, p. 81.

Renaissance. He noted their interest in an anthology that combined the anti-papal compositions of Petrarch and other critics of the Curia with the anti-papal sections cut out of Guicciardini's *Storia d'Italia*, and he asserted that most of the nobility owned works of Machiavelli.[99] Gallican writings, almost equally detested in Rome, also circulated freely in Venice, among them the banned history of de Thou, which was widely available in the bookshops, and some years later Richer's radical *De ecclesiastica et politica potestate*.[100]

Nor was the free atmosphere of Venice solely a matter of books. The Venetians stubbornly defended the right of Cremonini to interpret Aristotle on the soul as he saw fit;[101] and Galileo's friends, who had deplored his departure from Padua and warned him of dangers ahead, offered him sanctuary in Venetian territory when his tragic prosecution loomed.[102] And the release by the Venetian authorities in 1611 of the relapsed heretic Giacomo Castelvetro, arrested by the Inquisition as he passed through the state,[103] suggests a remarkably relaxed attitude to Protestantism. The nuncio in Paris, conversing with the king (and perhaps forgetting Henry IV's responsibility for the Edict of Nantes) accused the Venetians of believing in the utility of liberty of conscience "for the conservation and propagation of a state."[104] Not many years later the Spanish ambassador to Venice, stressing the licentiousness of the Republic, drew out the obvious corollary to freedom of belief. "The whole city," he reported, "is dedicated to Venus."[105]

Rome was cautious and Venice defensive, and this was enough to preserve an uneasy peace between them. But they were not friendly, and periodic crises disturbed their relations. These especially arose as the international situation altered, for it was clear to both sides that any resumption of their struggle depended on the pope's ability to find willing allies. The preservation of Venetian liberty, in a cultural as well as a political sense, thus depended on

[99] The list in *Aevum*, X (1936), 26–27.

[100] Sarpi to Castrino, March 16, 1610, *Aevum*, XIII (1939), 619; to Groslot, April 10, 1612, Busnelli, I, 228.

[101] Savio, pp. 67–71; Spini, *Libertini*, pp. 146–147.

[102] A. Favaro, "Giovan Francesco Sagredo e la vita scientifica in Venezia al principio del sec. XVII," *AV*, Ser. 3, IV (1902), 371; Giorgio de Santillana, *The Crime of Galileo* (Chicago, 1955), p. 208.

[103] Pauli to Savoy, Sept. 13 and 17, 1611, Luzio, p. 40.

[104] Ubaldini to Borghese, June 9, 1609, *Aevum*, X (1936), 66.

[105] Bedmar, "Relazione," p. 23. This document is not dated but was probably composed in 1618 or 1619.

the international scene. The truce of 1609 in the Low Countries was a source of particular anxiety to Venice, for it promised to free Spain for action in Italy. The nuncio in France noted the consternation of the Venetian ambassador in Paris at this event,[106] and Sarpi was profoundly worried by it.[107] There was good reason for their anxiety. In Madrid, well before the truce was arranged, the Duke of Lerma had spoken of it as a prerequisite to Italian action.[108] And a year after the truce the danger to Venice was gravely compounded by the assassination of the French king. Venetian apprehension on these matters will also remind us that the hostility of Rome was not the Republic's only problem during these years. Related pressures along other fronts were helping to sap the energies of the patriciate.

"Venice," Sarpi declared to Christoph von Dohna in June of 1613, "desires quiet, but she puts above it the liberty of Italy." [109] Although her concern for Italian independence suggested that Venice might still be willing to make war on the peninsula, Sarpi's words also hint at why, in the years after the interdict, she was increasingly forced on the defensive and compelled to content herself once again with maintaining her influence in the Adriatic and her dominions on the mainland. Her dealings with the rest of Europe were intended not to give her a role in the general international situation but only to protect her position. Thus it is notable that although the conflict over the interdict was one of the complex preliminaries to the Thirty Years' War, Venice took no part in that great struggle.[110]

The central problem of Venetian foreign policy was still, as for several decades, to hold the surrounding Habsburg powers at bay by the threat of joining an anti-Habsburg league, but at the same time to avoid any real entanglement in the general pattern of European conflict. Spain and Austria remained the primary dangers to her existence. The power of Spain was waning, but in one respect this only increased the peril to Venice. Spanish viceroys in Italy, less firmly controlled from Madrid, acted increasingly like independent princes and made threatening gestures on their own against the

[106] Ubaldini to Borghese, March 17, 1609, *Aevum*, X (1936), 66, n.

[107] See, for example, his letters to Groslot, Sept. 16 and 30, 1608, Busnelli, I, 35, 39.

[108] The nuncio in Madrid to Borghese, Aug. 20, 1608, *Aevum*, XI (1937), 33, n. 1. Cf. Seneca, pp. 23–24.

[109] Busnelli, II, 175.

[110] On the defensive character of Venetian foreign policy after the interdict, see Sestan, "La politica veneziana del Seicento," esp. pp. 47–48; and, in greater detail, Seneca, *Politica veneziana, passim*.

remaining independent states in Italy, particularly against Venice. In 1617, for example, a fleet from Naples alarmed her by invading the Adriatic.[111] Meanwhile the Habsburgs of Central Europe, supported by the pope, continued to press for some modification of Venetian claims to control that lifeline of her existence; and the seventeenth century saw an intensification of the dispute over dominion on the sea. Habsburg encouragement of the Uskok sea raiders finally drove the Republic to a declaration of war in 1615, but two years of conflict proved nothing except the inability of Venice now to support a major military effort.[112]

The struggle between Venice and the Habsburgs also found ideological expression. Against Spain the Venetians flaunted the values of civic liberty. One Venetian pamphleteer described the proud titles of the Spanish grandees as "simple appearances and encumbrances" and "names without essence." He contrasted them with his own free birth "in a free city, metropolis of a great republic, which is patron of kingdoms and of provinces, glorious for illustrious and lofty deeds, whose honors, even including the majesty of the principate, I can attain by reason of participation. You, on the contrary, were born liege and dependent, slaves to the will of another, on whom as if by a thread your life and all your fortunes depend." [113] Spain, on the other hand, repeated the charge that the Venetians were impiously devoted to reason of state. Bedmar included the accusation in his *Relation:* "They hold anything legitimate which promotes the security of ruling, and they applaud losses of Your Majesty. Out of self-interest they consider your profit to be the destruction and ruin of their things; and for reason of state they embrace and destroy at one blow all piety and fear of God, maintaining intelligence with enemies of God and of the Roman Church, having dealings with various perverse princes. And under the pretext of conserving the Republic, they cause the ruin of plans for the increase of the holy faith, consulting, discussing and deciding everything according to their habitual way of political government." [114]

[111] Smith, I, 148.

[112] Cozzi, *Contarini*, p. 167.

[113] This anonymous pamphlet bore the title *Risposta alla lettera scritta contro la Serenissima Republica di Venetia dal sig. Duca d'Ossuna vicerè di Napoli alla S.ta di nostro sig. Papa Paulo V*. It is reviewed and quoted in A. d'Ancona, "Saggi di polemica e di poesia politica del sec. XVII (da una Miscellanea veneta)," *AV*, Ser. 1, III (1872), 409.

[114] Bedmar, p. 21.

The most serious ideological attack on Venice was an anonymous work whose concern with fundamentals was immediately announced in its title: *Scrutiny of Venetian Liberty*.[115] Inspired by Austrian opposition to Venetian claims in the Adriatic and published at Mirandola in 1612, this critical "scrutiny" subjected the major dimensions of the vaunted liberty of the Republic to the most scathing historical analysis. It first refuted the myth of perpetual freedom. Venice had by no means been "free" from the start, the work insisted; she had been established within the ancient Empire and had therefore been originally subject to Rome. Later, it argued, the Republic had belonged to the Gothic kingdom of Theodoric and to the empires of both Justinian and Charlemagne; and in subsequent centuries she had been subject to the German emperors. Furthermore her subjection had been formally acknowledged by the Venetian ambassador to Vienna in 1509.

After dealing with the first dimension of Renaissance liberty, the author turned to the second. Venice was not free, nor had she ever been, he asserted, in the sense that she had been governed by her own citizens. Her first doges had been absolute and arbitrary rulers; such internal freedom as her people had obtained was the product of gradual development; and the freezing of her Great Council had reversed that process and begun the enslavement of the vast majority of Venetians, for whose wretched plight the author professed outrage and sympathy. The whole argument was supported by massive references to the works of Venetian historians, with which the author was evidently familiar. This devastating attack, which went through at least five editions before the end of the century and was widely read, produced much indignation in Venice but, although Sarpi himself considered an answer,[116] no major systematic reply from a Venetian. Perhaps it came too close to the truth; the illusions it attacked no longer carried the conviction they had possessed for earlier generations.

Various European states presented themselves to Venice as possible counterweights to the Habsburg powers, but none proved altogether satisfactory. This was true even of France which, indifferent to the local problems of Venice and the dangers of her position in Italy, solicited her participation in a

---

[115] *Squitinio della libertà veneta nel quale si adducono anche le raggioni dell'Impero Romano sopra la Città & Signoria di Venetia* (Mirandola, 1612). For discussion of this work and its authorship, and an attribution to Gaspare Scioppio, see Gaeta, "Mito di Venezia," p. 74.

[116] Griselini reported having seen the materials Sarpi had collected for this purpose in the library of the Servite monastry in Venice (*Memorie e aneddote*, p. 198).

general anti-Spanish alliance that would have exposed her territory to Habsburg conquest.[117] Henry IV, with his eagerness to retain the goodwill of the pope, was also thoroughly unreliable, even though in principle, as neither the king nor Villeroy boggled at informing the nuncio, France was on the side of Venice.[118]

But the French king was notoriously careless of principle in the practical conduct of his government, and in 1609 Henry IV was party to an action that seriously embarrassed and weakened the most staunchly antipapalist elements in the Venetian government. A letter, supposedly from the Protestant pastor Giovanni Diodati in Geneva to a French correspondent, had fallen into the hands of the nuncio in Paris; and after strategic editing by Ubaldini, Coton, and perhaps the king himself, it was transmitted to the government in Venice by the French ambassador. This communication purported to describe a recent visit to Venice undertaken to promote the religious subversion of the Republic. The letter expressed optimism that, through further preaching by Fra Fulgenzio, God would "plant his candlestick in that place." "Knowledge there commences to be very great," it continued; "liberty there is almost like ours and the reading of our books is open, and not only are life and customs condemned, but many speak of doctrine publicly and in the presence of anyone . . . . The greater part of the Venetian nobility is either won over or secured. The doge is wholly on the right side; this is known from his frequent and diligent assiduousness at the sermons of the good father. The pope gnashes his teeth and no longer knows what to do; he is afraid to return to thunderbolts. His lamentations move the Venetians to laughter and make them all the more stubborn, and God daily raises up new matters of shame and confusion in Rome and of just indignation and revenge in Venice." The French ambassador also confided to the nuncio that, besides transmitting the fatal letter, he had "rather exaggerated these dangers and emphasized the zeal of his king for the good of the most Serene Republic, and particularly that it should remain Catholic." [119]

The consequences of this revelation in Venice were serious, though possibly less because of its substance than because the episode indicated the limits beyond which Venetian freedom could not be pushed without jeopardizing the international position of the Republic. Sarpi had already

[117] Seneca, *Politica veneziana*, esp. pp. 4ff., 13, 30–35.

[118] Ubaldini to Borghese, Jan. 22, 1608, and June 9, 1609, *Aevum*, X (1936), 67, 73, n. 1.

[119] Text of the altered letter in *Aevum*, XI (1937), 282–283, n.; for the ambassador's admission, see *ibid.*, X (1936), 23, n. Taucci, pp. 233–240, discusses the plot in general.

begun to doubt the reliability of French support. In one of the rare expressions of open passion in his correspondence, he had recently exploded: "I conclude that the French are insupportable, full of arts, selfish, uncivil; and if there is any other bad quality, they are not without that." [120] Of the supposed Genevan letter he wrote to Foscarini in Paris: "It is not evident that the intention is good, but certainly the effects are not good." [121] There were no dramatic changes in the Venetian scene as a result of the French disclosures, but they appear to have accelerated a general alteration in the atmosphere of the Republic. The year 1609 was a good one for the papal cause in Venice, as Sarpi and the nuncio agreed. During this period Nicolò Contarini was excluded from the College.[122]

But Venice could not get along without support from a strong French monarchy; and although Sarpi's personal reaction to the assassination of the French king was reserved, the event filled him with apprehension,[123] as it did his compatriots. The nuncio reported to Rome the general dismay of the Venetians, "since it appears to them that the most Serene Republic has lost a great friend and that the balance he provided to the actions and power of Spain has ended. It appeared here that he was very useful for the peace of Christendom." The government, he continued, had dispatched special couriers with the condolences of the Republic and had appointed extraordinary ambassadors to support the French government in its grief and readjustment.[124] For a brief moment, with the balance of power evidently destroyed, Venice and Rome seemed likely to be driven into each other's arms. The Venetians rejoiced at reports of the pope's concern for the future of France (on which his own independence also depended), and they expressed willingness to join him in a military alliance to preserve the French state from destruction.[125]

Besides France, the only other allies Venice might have found were Protestant; and although there were serious obstacles to alliance with heretics, including strong opposition within the Republic, the government for some time kept open the possibility of joining the kind of league that eventually

[120] Letter to Foscarini, Sept. 10, 1609, *Aevum*, XI (1937), 281.

[121] Sept. 29, 1609, *ibid.*, pp. 282–283. Cf. Sarpi's letter to Groslot, June 22, 1610, Busnelli, I, 127.

[122] Cozzi, *Contarini*, p. 128.

[123] Letters to Jacques Gillot, June 8 and Oct. 12, 1610, Ulianich, pp. 123–125, 145, and to Castrino, July 6, 1610, Busnelli, II, 91.

[124] Letter to Borghese, May 29, 1610, *Aevum*, XIV (1940), 39–40.

[125] Gessi to Borghese, May 29, 1610, *ibid.*, 33.

was aligned against the Habsburgs in the Thirty Years' War. Sarpi probably corresponded with Protestants and encouraged Protestant hopes about the religious future of Venice with this possibility in mind, and the nuncio in Paris complained that the Venetian ambassador there seemed to prefer the company of Huguenots and the agents of Protestant princes.[126]

Venice, as we have noticed, had been encouraged by Wotton to hope for aid from England during the interdict, and the English ambassador continued to nourish this hope in the years that followed. Donà himself may have depended on English help. Sarpi reported his description of England as "the best friend we have" because she shared Venetian antipathy to the pope and because of her ability to give assistance by sea.[127] But Venice was increasingly disillusioned about the meaning of the vague encouragements offered by the English king, who talked a great deal and took little action. Sarpi was frequently witty at the expense of a ruler who preferred academic discourse to statesmanship,[128] and the failure of James I to succor the Dutch, who were far closer to England than was Venice, did not escape Venetian notice.[129] Venice kept open the channels of communication with England and received the polemical compositions of its ruler with courtesy (before prohibiting their sale),[130] but her respect for England steadily declined. When Wotton returned to Venice for his third embassy in 1621, he was received with little ceremony.[131]

Anglican retention of episcopacy may well have made England seem to Venice a more congenial confederate than other Protestant powers. But although her relations with the Protestant states of Germany were slight, she also made some gestures, especially after the truce of 1609, toward establishing closer relations with the Dutch. In the fall an exchange of ambassadors took place between the two commercial powers, and the Dutch envoy was received with some pomp.[132] But the permanent diplomatic

---

[126] Ubaldini to Borghese, Nov. 11, 1608, and March 3, 1609, *Aevum*, XI (1937), 17, n., 71–72, n.

[127] According to Christoph von Dohna, letter of Aug. 23, 1608, *Briefe und Akten*, II, 87.

[128] See below, pp. 526–527.

[129] It was pointed out to them by the French ambassador during the interdict. See Cornet, p. 211, n. 1.

[130] Sarpi to Castrino, Aug. 18, 1609, Busnelli, II, 47. Thomas Coryat reported seeing the portrait of James I publicly exhibited in the Piazzetta in 1608 along with portraits of Henry IV and Philip II (*Crudities* [Glasgow, 1905], I, 424).

[131] Smith, I, 176–177.

[132] Sarpi to Foscarini, Oct. 22 and Dec. 9, 1609, *Aevum*, XI (1937), 298–299, 304–309, and to Groslot, Dec. 9, 1609, Busnelli, I, 101.

exchange feared in Rome was not established; Sarpi several times noted the strength of the opposition to it in Venice.[133] Dutch troops nevertheless served Venice in the war against Austria in 1615–1617.[134]

The Venetian position in Europe thus remained acutely insecure. Venice found no reliable ally whose assistance would not have brought her more danger than relief, and her survival during the tense years after the interdict was perhaps chiefly due to the disarray of her enemies and their involvement with even weightier problems than the defiance of the Venetian Republic. Meanwhile Venice had to confront a growing economic crisis more serious than any she had yet faced.[135]

Much as Spain kept her reputation as a formidable military power during the seventeenth century, Venice preserved hers as a wealthy commercial metropolis.[136] But the economic difficulties already apparent before the interdict were growing in magnitude. They were no easier to face after the enormous expense of resisting the pope, and subsequent events aggravated the Venetian predicament. Depredations by the Uskoks and other corsairs continued,[137] and commercial insurance rates rose steadily higher.[138] But above all the commercial rivalry of the English and the Dutch, the latter after 1609 no longer at war with Spain, now became unbearable. By 1620 Venice had been almost completely excluded from the markets of the Levant.[139] And, as if to complete her commercial disaster, the Thirty Years' War, which destroyed the prosperity of Germany, seriously reduced the demand for Venetian commodities in the last market where her position had remained strong.[140]

A more resourceful society might have adapted more successfully even

[133] Letters to Groslot, Nov. 20 and Dec. 4, 1612, and Jan. 29, 1613, Busnelli, I, 251, 253, 261. For the nuncio reaction, Gessi to Borghese, Nov. 28 and Dec. 5, 1609, *Aevum*, XI (1937), 309–311.

[134] Cozzi, *Contarini*, p. 163.

[135] See, in general, Cozzi, "Una vicenda della Venezia barocca," pp. 96–99; and Woolf, "Venice and the Terraferma," p. 417.

[136] Sella, *Commerci e industrie*, pp. 69ff., collects many examples of European opinion on this point.

[137] Sarpi mentioned them several times in his letters, as to Christoph von Dohna. May 26, 1609 (?), and to Groslot, Sept. 11 and 25, 1612, Busnelli, I, 241, 244–245, II, 150,

[138] Cf. Braudel, *La Méditerranée et le monde méditerranéen*, p. 708; the cost of insurance in the Levantine trade rose to 20 per cent in 1611 and to 25 per cent in 1612.

[139] *Ibid.*, pp. 500–502; Braudel, et al., "Le déclin de Venise," p. 37, and Kellenbenz, "Le déclin de Venise," p. 117 and *passim*.

[140] Sella, *Commerci e industrie*, pp. 51–53.

to the unpromising situation in which Venice now found herself, and members of the *giovani* were still resilient enough in 1610 to propose to revive Venetian prosperity by converting Venice into a free port. They evidently envisaged a future in which Venice would remain a wealthy emporium for the goods of all nations, even if the ships in which those goods arrived were chiefly foreign. The proposal came close to acceptance, but in the end it was defeated, partly because the restrictive traditions of the Republic (and indeed of nearly all Europe) were against it, partly because of the strenuous objections of the nuncio, who feared that Dutch and English merchants might import Calvinism into Venice among their other commodities.[141] Instead Venice chose to meet the crisis by applying a vigorous protectionism which only accelerated her commercial decline.[142]

These disasters doomed to failure the hopes of the *giovani* to maintain the prosperity of the Republic through commercial renewal; and the social base of their government, consisting largely of lesser nobles dependent on commerce, began to disintegrate. The Great Council, through which this large group had exercised control, became less and less stable and manageable as the lesser nobles grew increasingly impoverished, demoralized, disaffected, and hopeless.[143] The coincidence of such conditions at home with pressures from abroad made the government understandably jittery. Indeed, the supposedly secret and ruthless movements of the Council of Ten, the spies, the unheralded suppression of conspiracy, the corpses mysteriously dangling in the Piazza, seem to have been little more than symptoms of nervousness and insecurity among the rulers of the Republic. Even the famous Spanish plot of 1618 now appears to have been only a figment of their anxious imaginations.[144] Similar fears also brought about the sudden execution in 1622 of Sarpi's old friend and collaborator Antonio Foscarini for treason, on grounds later discovered to be false.[145]

The old group of *antipapalisti* remained generally in control at least until the death of Leonardo Donà in 1612, and the choice of Nicolò Contarini as

---

[141] Cozzi, *Contarini*, pp. 18–20, 139–147. For the nuncio's position, Gessi to Borghese, Aug. 7, 1610, *Aevum*, XI (1937), 307–308, n.

[142] Beutin, "La décadence économique de Venise," p. 100.

[143] This development reached a climax with the movement of Renier Zeno after 1623, well described in Cozzi, *Contarini*, pp. 229–283, 198–199.

[144] Giorgio Spini, "La congiura degli spagnoli contra Venezia del 1618," *ASI*, CVII (1949), 17–53, CVIII (1950), 159–174.

[145] Foscarini's tragic fate is described in the dispatches of G. Giacomo Piscina to Savoy, April 9 and 23, 1622, Luzio, pp. 50–52.

doge in 1630 shows that its influence persisted spasmodically for many years. The papal nuncios continued to complain of the hostility they encountered in the ruling circles of the Republic; as late as 1624 the nuncio thought them still dominated by "the false doctrines of Fra Paolo." [146] But the domestic scene was clearly changing as power in the government shifted again, perceptibly if not steadily, to the great nobles whose estates on the mainland were now apparently destined to be the major source of Venetian wealth. By the fall of 1609 Sarpi was speaking anxiously of dangerous adversaries in the Senate and above all the College,[147] and three years later the envoy from Savoy interpreted the election of Marcantonio Memo to succeed Donà not only as a victory for the old patrician families so long excluded from power but also for the friends of Rome.[148] The victory was temporary, but an era was drawing to a close.

Part of the change was the result of reluctance, in a dangerous time, to offend clerical interests, and the printers and booksellers of Venice were now compelled to operate more cautiously. Two years after the interdict Sarpi had to recognize that the freedom of discussion permitted by that event was exceptional. Nothing could now be printed, he wrote in the summer of 1609, without the approval of the Inquisition; the only difference between Venice and the rest of Italy was that not everything was printed that pleased the Holy Office.[149] The *Historia* of Jacques de Thou, condemned in Rome, could not be printed in Venice; James I's reply to Bellarmine, denounced by the nuncio, was prohibited.[150] Particularly striking was the government's hesitation in releasing Sarpi's quasi-official history of the interdict itself. Originally composed for incorporation into the vast work of de Thou and finished in the spring of 1610, it had been repeatedly scrutinized and emended by patricians close to the inner circles of the government, which finally decided not to send the work off at all.[151]

But the change went deeper, as Sarpi also realized. A year after the interdict he was lamenting the strength of Jesuit influence among the parish priests, and of papalist doctrine among scholars at Padua who ought to have known

---

[146] Cozzi, *Contarini*, pp. 237–238.

[147] Letters to Foscarini, Sept. 29 and Oct. 14, 1609, *Aevum*, XI (1937), 287–293.

[148] Pauli to Savoy, July 28, 1612, Luzio, pp. 44–45. For Sarpi's judgment of Memo as a good man but weak, see his letters of July 31 and Oct. 23, 1612, to Groslot, Busnelli, I, 235, 247.

[149] Letter to Castrino, Aug. 18, 1609, Busnelli, II, 46.

[150] *Aevum*, XI (1937), 284–285.

[151] Sarpi mentioned the problem several times to Groslot, Oct. 13, 1608, April 27, 1610, Sep. 25, 1612, Busnelli, I, 42, 120, 243–244.

better.[152] One year later he complained of the reluctance of Venetian clergy to resist the jurisdictional claims of the pope, and in 1610 he noted the steady increase of curialism in the Republic. Nor was the change limited to members of the clergy.[153] The laity of Venice, including many close to the government, responded enthusiastically to the papal jubilee proclaimed for 1608,[154] and there were public demonstrations against Leonardo Donà four years later at that venerable doge's funeral.[155] The change also found striking expression in the pattern of nomination to the patriarchate of Venice. On the death of Vendramin in 1619 the Republic, which had long chosen laymen for its supreme ecclesiastical office, selected Giovanni Tiepolo, an ecclesiastic, from a group of candidates most of whom were also ecclesiastics. Meanwhile Venice was beginning to taste the rewards for her general change of heart. Vendramin, the first Venetian so honored in many years, was in 1615 made a cardinal.[156]

The change was major, though perhaps less fundamental than Sarpi feared. Its actual character may be judged from the second thoughts of Antonio Querini, who had so vigorously argued the Venetian case during the interdict. In retrospect the behavior of the Republic, both before and during the altercation with the pope, seemed to him a vast, though instructive, mistake; his inclination to extract lessons from the experience reveals, however, that the habits of Renaissance politics were by no means dead. Renaissance attitudes are also conspicuous in his particular observations. The interdict, he believed, had been the work of extremists on both sides; Venice had then taken a deplorably rigid position that had made negotiation impossible; she had miscalculated the entire situation from beginning to end, especially the resolution of the pope and the likelihood of support from the other secular powers.[157]

He could not entirely suppress his sense that the interdict, in spite of its

[152] Letters to Leschassier, May 13 and Aug. 26, 1608, Ulianich, pp. 12, 20. In 1611 the Paduan jurists were forbidden to discuss juridical questions; cf. Melchiorre Roberti, "Il collegio padovano dei dottori giuristi," *Rivista Italiana per le Scienze Giuridiche*, XXV (1903), 186.

[153] Letters to Leschassier, Sep. 29, 1609, and March 2, 1610, Ulianich, pp. 56, 72.

[154] Various documents, including an ironic letter of Sarpi to Foscarini, Sep. 30, 1608, *Aevum*, XI (1937), 42–43.

[155] Pauli to Savoy, July 28, 1612, Luzio, p. 44.

[156] Niero, pp. 116–117. De Luca, "Pietà veneziana," p. 227, describes the spread of pious practices among the populace during Vendramin's patriarchate.

[157] From his *Historia dell'Escommunica, Componimento*, pp. 257–260, and Cornet, pp. 338–339, App. XX.

cost in money and reputation, had been a victory for Venice. But it had chiefly proved the enormous danger of religious strife and of enmity with the pope, and Querini insisted that Venice must not count on such successes in the future. Venice, he declared, must not generalize from the past: "There is no more perilous decision than that which is based on example." But although Querini here sounded like Guicciardini, he could find a more general instructiveness in the Republic's recent ordeal: the necessity, for the survival of Venice, of good relations with Rome. "Nothing can put public liberty in greater danger," he declared, "than not having good intelligence with the pope. This teaching was well understood by our ancestors, who had always on their lips, and much more in their hearts and their actions, these precepts: not to irritate the Turk, to stand well with the pope, to reward the good, to punish the bad. They saw these as the four wheels that carry the chariot of our government safely on its way. Our ancestors well knew that the ship of the Republic was safe when it was anchored on good intelligence with the Church." Prudence, not militance, he concluded, was now the best policy for Venice; "great actions" were evidently no longer for her. Venice, in his view, had clearly passed into that senescence foreshadowed by Gasparo Contarini's biological image; henceforth, as befitted old age, she should employ her brain rather than her hands "and conquer, as they say, sitting down." In an important respect, therefore, Querini suggests a remarkable deterioration in Venetian morale; and indeed the inclination to take risks that had character-ized some *giovani* had been chastened and subdued by recent events. Venice would henceforth behave more conservatively, as she had done before 1583. But at no point did Querini's reflections hint that Venice had not, in principle, been in the right. His objections to recent Venetian policy were entirely political.[158]

Sarpi's position in Venice, as these changes developed, was ambiguous. He symbolized a glorious moment in the recent past of the Republic, and Venice (whatever happened) was by no means prepared to repudiate the triumphant defense of her liberties. She could still admit officially to no fault. Sarpi had therefore to be protected, and he kept his office. Furthermore he continued to enjoy considerable popular veneration; and the nuncio, as we have seen, remained afraid of his influence. But although his professional acumen was still valued and his opinions continued to be solicited on par-ticular jurisdictional questions, Sarpi's durable militancy was inappropriate

[158] Cornet, pp. 337–339, App. XX.

to the new mood of the Republic, and it was increasingly apparent as the interdict faded into the past that he no longer enjoyed the full confidence of the government. As early as 1608 he was reporting difficulty in obtaining books from abroad, not merely because packets destined for Venice were likely to be opened in such places as Trent but also because his imports were under surveillance in Venice itself.[159] Although he was able for some time to carry on a frank and extensive correspondence with foreigners, including many Protestants, this too eventually had to be suspended as the friendly ambassadors who were pleased to transmit his letters were replaced by others less obliging. By 1613 his direct communication with the outside world had almost ceased; it was possible now only occasionally and under special conditions.

In 1611 the government took deliberate steps to dissociate itself from him. "To give satisfaction and to appease the pope," as the envoy of Savoy reported, the College determined to exclude him from such general contact with the affairs and correspondence of the Republic as he had previously enjoyed, although to spare his feelings the decision was expressed as a general prohibition against access to official secrets, and he was offered an increase in salary.[160] The purpose of the regulation was nevertheless clear to all, and the attitude behind it was underlined when Memo, the new doge, refused soon after his election the next year to grant Sarpi a private audience.[161] During this period, too, Sarpi's advice on official appointments was disregarded; men he had opposed were in 1611 chosen to fill the important post of patriarchal vicar and the chair of canon law at Padua.[162] The shift in his fortunes hardly surprised him. Early in 1610 he had written to Foscarini: "It is so ordinary a thing for republics, when the need is past, to forget the deserving, that there is nothing marvelous about how now, when some consider themselves safe, the most important and meritorious subjects have been forgotten, *et factos praetores qui fecere mirantur.* But things have their cycle, and the valorous will overcome fortune in the end." [163] As the political situation deteriorated, Sarpi sounded increasingly Florentine.

---

[159] Letter to Groslot, June 12, 1608, Busnelli, I, 16; Coryat, I, 380, reported that Sarpi had been forbidden contact with Protestants in Venice.

[160] Pauli to Savoy, Oct. 29, 1611, Luzio, p. 41. See also Gessi's letters to Borghese, Oct. 15 and 22, Nov. 19, and Dec. 3, 1611, *Aevum*, X (1936), 42–44.

[161] Pauli to Savoy, Aug. 14, 1612, Luzio, p. 45.

[162] Pauli to Savoy, Oct. 8, 1611, Luzio, p. 41; Cozzi, *Contarini*, pp. 130–131. Nevertheless one of Sarpi's friends was appointed to the less sensitive chair of medicine.

[163] Feb. 16, 1610, *Aevum*, XI (1937), 314.

But the growing separation between Sarpi and the government he ostensibly continued to serve was not only the consequence of his association with policies the patriciate was now inclined to find embarrassing. It was the result also of qualities in Sarpi himself which considerably limited his usefulness to Venice. For although he had taken deep satisfaction in his transition to the active life of politics, it should not be forgotten that he was already a man of mature years at the time of the interdict and that his youthful formation had been monastic and in some measure scholastic. He had already devoted himself for many years to the service of his order and to a variety of contemplative pursuits. He was not, therefore, a typical Venetian, in spite of his long association with the patriciate and his interest in Venetian affairs, but a complicated mixture of attitudes from two different worlds. Indeed the contribution of ecclesiastical culture to his intellectual formation had been an important element in his usefulness to the Venetian state. He had served Venice during the interdict as a scholar and thinker as well as an advocate: a man skilled in research as well as in assembling evidence and marshalling arguments, and adept in drawing out the full implications of general principles. And Sarpi had hardly become a full-fledged statesman simply through shifting a mind largely formed in a quite different arena to politics and history. He retained some limitations in his dealings with the world (however much he believed in action on principle), and these doubtless contributed to his exclusion from political responsibility.

The incompleteness of his transition to the *vita activa* is apparent in two tendencies which became increasingly evident in the years after the interdict. One was a mixture of instability in the presence of unfavorable events and indecision which, although we know it chiefly through the complaints of his Protestant associates, must also have reduced the government's confidence in his judgment. His attitude toward the shifting political scene oscillated wildly; he may have recognized that change ruled the world, but he found considerable difficulty in accepting its inconvenient dominion. At one moment he seemed to fear war, at another to be sure of peace; one day he was regretting the failure of his friends to deliver a blow at the enemy, another day he seemed to long only for peace and quiet. Though he studied the political world, he could never fully define his own attitude to it or decide what should be done in it. Even Micanzio recognized this flaw in his hero: "Although he was quick and ready in speculation, he seemed extremely irresolute in deciding on action. He thought and thought again but never seemed fully satisfied, and this fluctuation constantly increased." Micanzio accounted for this by suggesting that Sarpi suffered from an excess of prudence accompanied by an extraordinary knowledge of history, qualities which customarily make men timid and inert.[164] Bedell deplored his caution,[165] and Wotton thought him "as in countenance so in spirit, liker to Philip Melanchthon than to Luther, and peradventure a fitter instrument to overthrow the falsehood by degrees than on a sudden; which accordeth with a frequent saying of his own, that in these operations *non bisogna far salti*."[166] The mood of Venice was also cautious, out of a sound awareness of danger. But Sarpi's caution seems rather to have originated in a constitutional inability to take the leap from an intellectual comprehension of events to action.

But paradoxically of even greater significance in limiting his usefulness to Venice after the interdict was perhaps the rigidity of his very attachment to Venetian principles.[167] For, while other Venetians, true *politiques*, recognized the necessity of accommodation to the world in the interest of attaining limited and practical ends, Sarpi remained intransigent. While they saw the necessity for compromise (compromise itself being an essential principle of politics), Sarpi tended increasingly to elevate the needs of Venice into a set of absolutes with universal application. He became, in his own way, the proponent of a system; and although Venice did not cease to hold a primary place in his affections, a general program for world order, at once political and ecclesiological, increasingly occupied his mind. He saw himself no longer merely defending Venice but engaged in a mortal struggle between good and evil, between a few lonely champions of virtue and piety and a handful of wicked men at the Curia, with the fate of the world hanging in the balance. By treating the political values of the Renaissance in this way, Sarpi falsified even as he championed them. A product of the Counter Reformation himself, he was not ultimately political enough to serve the needs of Venice.

Yet habits of mind inappropriate to the contemporary world of action were singularly well adapted to articulate the assumptions and convictions of Venetian political life. Through the very intellectuality which reduced his

---

[164] *Vita*, p. 175.
[165] Letter to Dr. Samuel Ward, 1607, *Two Biographies*, p. 225.
[166] Letter to the Earl of Salisbury, Sept. 13, 1607, Smith, I, 400.
[167] Cf. Chabod, *Politica di Sarpi*, pp. 89ff.

usefulness to the state, Sarpi, with all the fervor of a recent convert, gave to his new political and religious ideals an increasingly elaborate and sophisticated expression. He proceeded, between the interdict and his death in 1623, to express the old civic values once again, to relate them to new conditions, and to transmute them into new forms. By setting them in the largest possible frame of reference, he also brought them (in more than one sense) to a culmination. For with Sarpi we have come to the final stage in the evolution of the Venetian republican consciousness. It was now clearly in decline, no longer intimately related to the experience of a community, but surviving largely within an increasingly isolated individual. Just as Venice during the later sixteenth century had preserved, somewhat anachronistically, the civic spirit of the Italian Renaissance, so Sarpi now preserved, a little anachronistically, that of the Venetian Republic. But since Sarpi happened to be a man of genius, he was able to breathe some of his own intellectual vitality into a dying tradition and even to extend its effect, through his reputation and his writings, into other parts of western Europe. In the rest of this chapter we shall therefore be concerned with the mental world of Paolo Sarpi.

As had been true with so many earlier representatives of Renaissance thought, Sarpi's convictions and attitudes proceeded from a deep pessimism which found confirmation in the general conditions of his age and received expression in particular views about the helplessness of man and the limitations of the human intellect. In him the darker side of Renaissance culture continued to operate.

The world for Sarpi, in the absence of divine intervention, was hopelessly sick with a disease of long standing. He often used medical language for it, giving to traditional organic imagery a vividness which perhaps reflects his long association with the scientific community of Padua. "Christendom is a body so full of bad humors," he wrote in 1609 when he was particularly depressed by what seemed to him French betrayal, "that although its external parts are strong enough to contain them, so that for the present no abscess is flowing, it will not long be able to maintain this appearance of health. Indeed, I am afraid that the longer it delays bursting out in some evil issue, the worse it must produce." [168] The interdict, according to his diagnosis, had proved no more than a short crisis when, for a brief time, there had been hopes of a

---

[168] Letter to Hotman de Villiers, Sept. 12, 1609, Ulianich, p. 287.

fundamental cure. But the doctors had contented themselves by treating the ailing patient "with good foods but no medicine, forgetting the warning of Hippocrates that the more sickly bodies are nourished, the worse they get." The lamentable result had been that now, "in the parts which were already infirm the disease has taken such hold that it has passed into nature, the neutral members are sickened, and the good weakened. As the comedian said, 'Health itself cannot save this body.' " [169] On another occasion Sarpi, truly a man of several cultures, perceived recent events as a kind of Greek tragedy in which, helpless to avert catastrophe, he could do no more than act as the chorus.[170]

From time to time he diagnosed the sickness of the age in a specific way which suggested that it was, in principle, remediable. Thus he attacked the times for their peculiar dishonesty, their refusal to acknowledge the realities of experience, above all in political life, the abuse of Counter Reformation idealism to disguise the lust for power. There is a suggestion of Machiavellian indignation in his denunciation of hypocrisy as the primary evil of the age. "Everything is covered with the mask of religion," he wrote. "In other centuries hypocrisy has had some currency, but in this alone it is dominant and excludes all true piety. God have mercy on us!" [171] But, like Machiavelli, Sarpi evidently supposed that some remedy might be found for this ailment; and he was therefore willing, as we shall see, to exert himself in a remarkable effort at tearing away masks which, in his view, damaged religion and politics alike.

But although his gloom was nourished by the particular experiences of his generation, doubtless including the declining prosperity and influence of Venice, it also received more general expression. The philosophical outlook on the world which he had developed long before his entrance into public life had given it deep anthropological and even cosmological roots. One of his early *pensieri* insisted on the instability of all things (although he rejected traditional physics) as a kind of universal law;[172] and the uncertainty of the physical universe had its human counterpart for him in the imperfection and malice of men. He shared Montaigne's view of man as the most imperfect

---

[169] Letter to Groslot, April 1, 1608, Busnelli, I, 11.
[170] Letter to Groslot, March 28, 1617, Busnelli, I, 279.
[171] Letter to Groslot, May 26, 1609, Busnelli, I, 82–83.
[172] No. 99 in *Scritti filosofici e teologici*, ed. Romano Amerio (Bari, 1951). For what follows see, in general, Romano Amerio, *Il Sarpi dei pensieri filosofici inediti* (Turin, 1950). For the early date of the *pensieri*, cf. Micanzio, *Vita*, p. 43. See also Giovanni da Pozzo, "Per il testo dei 'Pensieri' del Sarpi," *BSV*, III (1961), 139–176.

of animals.[173] He insisted on the insatiability of human appetites,[174] above all of the *libido dominandi*, which must inevitably corrupt the best of men.[175] Hence, he remarked: "It happens with everything good and well instituted that human malice progressively devises methods of operating abusively and of rendering insupportable what was established to a good end and with the highest principles." [176] He could define happiness only negatively. It was that human condition in which nothing was lacking; and since this required stasis in an unstable universe, happiness was patently impossible.[177] He was occasionally tempted by the possibility of Stoic withdrawal and indifference,[178] but that too struck him as a vain hope;[179] and, as we have seen, he chose a different mode of accommodation to the imperfections of human existence. It found expression, perhaps, in another of his *pensieri* which conceives of happiness dynamically, as an ideal never to be fully realized but always to be striven for: "We are always acquiring happiness, we have never acquired it nor ever will." [180] Thus Sarpi, for whom restless motion was an inescapable condition of man's life in this world, has in effect converted the physical law of inertia into a theoretical foundation for the *vita activa*. Man, born into a world of movement and change of which his life is a part, can never in the nature of things attain the peace of the contemplative ideal but must struggle actively until the moment of his death.

Nowhere does Sarpi's sense of human limitation emerge more clearly then when he deals with the problems of knowledge, with the limits of human rationality, and with the nature of external reality so far as it is accessible to the human understanding. In these matters too the relationship is close between the mental constitution revealed by his early speculations and his later activity in the service of the Venetian state. The former often seems to provide an intellectual basis for the latter by making more explicit than ever before the attitudes underlying those conceptions of man's position in the universe which we have associated earlier with the politics of the Renaissance. Sarpi, like his Florentine predecessors, was an empiricist, skeptical

---

[173] *Pensieri* 404, 551. Montaigne was well known to Sarpi's circle; cf. Micanzio, *Vita*, p. 169.

[174] *Pensiero* 277.

[175] Cf. *Sopra l'officio dell'inquisizione*, SG, p. 145.

[176] *Su le immunità delle chiese*, SG, p. 293.

[177] *Pensiero* 250.

[178] As in *Pensiero* 399.

[179] As in *Pensieri* 250–252.

[180] *Pensiero* 250.

about all speculative thought, concerned with the utility and the merely human meaning of what can be known, and hostile to the construction of rational systems. At the same time it should be obvious how much further he has moved in this direction than the circle of Paolo Paruta. Where Paruta's friends were still given to lofty flights of rhetoric and still needed to relate their values to large abstract systems, Sarpi is terse, ironical, concrete. He evidently found abstract discourse chiefly useful to attack large systems, turning philosophy against itself. It is no accident that his most general pronouncements are merely fragments, scattered insights never developed into a coherent intellectual scheme.

Some of the *pensieri* seem nevertheless to have a direct bearing on his particular convictions about the conduct of life and the organization of human society, above all those dealing with the operations of the human mind. Although it is probably impossible to demonstrate that the order in which they have come down to us has either biographical or systematic significance, it is at least appropriate that the first of the *pensieri* ranks the modes of human knowledge in a descending order of excellence, beginning with the knowledge acquired through action. Sarpi maintains that we know both the essence and the cause of the things we do; we know the essence but not the cause of the things we observe; but of those things we know only through conjecture, we may know what is possible but not necessarily what is true.[181] The reflection was a product of his scientific activity and referred to the relative methodological value of contrived experiment, passive observation, and speculation, but its implications go beyond the cosmological and mathematical problems out of which it arose. Behind it lies that profound concern with actuality which we have encountered before in other contexts, among other places in Machiavelli. It reflects Sarpi's general antipathy to speculation as an avenue to truth, his constant preference for the direct encounter with all aspects of reality which he was later to apply to political life. The importance of the sentiment is indicated by his need to repeat it, to develop the thought in a slightly different way:

> There are four modes of philosophizing: the first with reason alone, the second with sense alone, the third with reason first and then sense, the fourth beginning with sense and ending with reason. The first is the worst, because from it we know what we would like to be, not what is. The third is bad because we many times distort what is into what we

[181] *Pensiero* 1.

would like, rather than adjusting what we would like to what is. The second is true but crude, permitting us to know little and that rather of things than of their causes. The fourth is the best we can have in this miserable life.[182]

Thus, if Sarpi hardly appears exuberant about the possibilities of human knowledge, he recognizes that some kinds of knowledge are within human power. Human knowledge is possible, however, only when certain requirements are met.

One of the essential conditions of valid knowledge, for Sarpi, is that it should be based on direct experience, a principle for which he invoked the authority of Socrates,[183] one of the few ancients who generally commanded his respect. More narrowly Sarpi meant by *experience* the perception of physical objects by the senses, preferably one's own,[184] for (in the Paduan tradition) he was inclined to doubt the existence, at least as an object of knowledge, of anything lacking a body.[185] He also denied the real existence of universals; "essence and universality," he wrote, "are works of the mind." [186] Yet he also admitted that the dependence of knowledge on sense, since it came through the variable sense organs of the subject, deprived it of any absolute validity; knowledge was relative and man the measure of all things.[187] In addition to his rather skeptical empiricism, therefore, he required mathematics, since "qualities are nothing but quantities."[188]

But since only a limited aspect of human concern is susceptible to measurement, Sarpi's relativism chiefly pointed in other directions. It meant that most of the knowledge man could command was merely tentative; like happiness, knowledge thus became for Sarpi an aspiration rather than a possession. This conception was reflected in his pedagogical method, which appears to have been designed not so much to transmit a body of propositions as to initiate a process in the mind of the student. Fra Fulgenzio reported

[182] *Pensiero* 146.

[183] Letter to Groslot, Jan. 6, 1609, Busnelli, I, 58.

[184] *Pensiero* 4; cf. letter to Groslot, May 12, 1609, Busnelli, I, 79.

[185] *Pensieri* 111, 114.

[186] *Pensiero* 371. On the problem of universals, see also 351, 369, 370, 373, 374, 376.

[187] *Pensiero* 190; see also 2, 45, 157, 424, 468. In the last two Sarpi applies his relativism to conceptions of beauty in the manner of Montaigne, specifically to allegations of beauty in the style of Cicero.

[188] *Pensiero* 459.

of his master that he did not teach "with ordinary lectures, which he considered a method more pompous than fruitful, but in the Socratic and obstetrical way," assigning readings, distinguishing in them between the true and the false, and thus shaping the intellect. It was "a way truly as singular and excellent for starting on the road to knowledge," Sarpi's disciple concluded, "as it is unused because of its unsuitability to pomp and ostentation." [189]

Conversely Sarpi held that the methods of speculative philosophy, its demonstrations and its transmission of allegedly definitive truths from master to student, should be sedulously avoided. Like his Renaissance predecessors he objected to abstract discourse on several grounds, first of all its irrelevance to human needs and even its tendency to interfere with their satisfaction. Philosophy, Sarpi observed, was worse than useless to console man's misery,[190] and general propositions (unlike the concrete examples supplied, for example, by history) were ineffectual in moving men to act.[191] They were likely to destroy man's instinctive ability to meet concrete needs in particular situations, each of which was finally unique: abstract discussion muddied the clear waters of truth, leaving men bewildered in the face of difficulties whose solution ought to be simple and obvious.[192] Rational philosophy, therefore, far from representing the spark of divinity in human nature, was for Sarpi both cause and symptom of its corruption, and a constant source of error; God, he remarked, "acts without discourse." [193]

Like the humanists of the earlier Renaissance, he also found scholastic philosophy morally repugnant because too often it appeared to serve only as a vehicle of human presumption and malice. Asked by a French correspondent to give his opinion on the matter, he attacked dominant tendencies in

---

[189] *Vita*, p. 79. A method of this kind seemed all the more important to him, no doubt, because of his observation that the "authorities" were diverse and contradictory, as in his letter to Leschassier, Dec. 11, 1607, Ulianich, p. 5. In *Pensiero* 247 he noted that reliance on authority caused men to ignore the evidence of their own senses.

[190] *Pensiero* 528.

[191] *Sulla instituzione, progresso ed abusi delle commende*, SG, p. 6.

[192] In *Pensiero* 504 he attributes all error in moral questions to "philosophizing with reason." For related passages see *Trattato delle materie beneficiarie*, SG, p. 112, where he argues that particular human problems are easily solved, whereas discourse concerning universals is merely baffling; *Su le immunità delle chiese*, SG, pp. 259–260, where he again rejects abstract speculation; and *Pensiero* 246, where he notes that error enters the syllogism not through the senses that establish its premises but through the reason as it operates on them.

[193] *Pensiero* 270.

the scholasticism of the day. It was essential, he wrote, "to guard against those who resolve things too magisterially, with a *respondeo dicendum*, as if they were arbiters"; and on this ground he was particularly critical of the growing influence of Thomas Aquinas, "regarded among the Jesuits and prelates as a very facile writer who does not entangle the mind in doubt but settles far too much for the reader." The Thomistic certainties were inappropriate, in Sarpi's view, to the human condition; it was better to read those philosophers who gave their opinions with more reserve and refused to "pedantize over other men in matters not settled." Among these he was much impressed by Ockham, whose skepticism and eventual conversion from academic speculation to a concern with large public issues strikingly paralleled his own. Ockham, Sarpi wrote, if only his works had been free of barbarism, would have been "a most judicious writer." [194] It would be a mistake, nevertheless, to take Sarpi's praise of Ockham as the announcement of his adherence to a school. What appealed to him was chiefly Ockham's recognition of the limits of philosophy and his critical spirit; Sarpi's remarks should be taken simply as his recognition of a kindred soul.

Sarpi's attitude to general ideas, especially of the kind evoked by the struggles of his time, was therefore complex. On the one hand he denied their intellectual value, insisting that they served merely to disguise motives too crude for public admission. As we have already observed, he regarded hypocrisy as the primary vice of the age; "I believe" generally turned out, particularly in the mouths of one's enemies, to be little more than a complicated and misleading form of "I want." As Sarpi wrote in his first *consulto* when the interdict was impending: "Interest many times hides the truth." [195] One result, as he saw, was to complicate human communication. The eagerness of men to believe only in what corresponded to their interests prevented them from seeing in ancient documents more than they wished to see;[196] it

[194] Letter to François Hotman, July 22, 1608, Ulianich, p. 73. Sarpi also declared here that "Gerson treats well what he touches but did not aim to treat everything." He had praised Occam in *Pensiero* 553 as well. In view of these sentiments it is of some interest that he found Mariana, a "rhetorician," less dangerous than Suarez the schoolman (letter to Leschassier, Aug. 3, 1610, Ulianich, p. 88). He blamed the degradation of intellectual discourse on the doctors of the mid-thirteenth century "when men began to treat things more subtly" (*Trattato delle materie beneficiarie*, SG, p. 110). *Subtlety*, for Sarpi, was pejorative.

[195] *Consiglio in difesa di due ordinazioni della Serenissima Republica*, in *Scritti*, II, 11.

[196] Letter to François Hotman, July 22, 1608, Ulianich, p. 174; cf. his observation, during the interview with the Prince de Condé in 1622, that a reader never understands the meaning intended by the author (in Cecchetti, *Venezia e la Corte di Roma*, I, 9–10).

meant too that exposure to truth generally did no more than strengthen attachment to falsehood.[197] In addition, the close connection between interest and belief caused doctrine to shift as interests changed. This was Sarpi's explanation for the decline from apostolic Christianity: "As Saint Cyprian lamented with great feeling, it is one of man's imperfections that whereas customs ought to conform to good doctrines and laws, on the contrary the doctrines of interested men are accommodated to their customs." [198] Human affairs "are so full of ambiguities," he wrote, that a plausible case can be made for any action or policy.[199]

But although Sarpi's position implies great skepticism about the truth of doctrines, he was by no means inclined to deny their importance in human affairs. On the contrary, he recognized all too well their practical and instrumental value. Committed to a struggle between concrete political forces in which the major weapons on both sides were ideas, Sarpi developed a keen perception of the social role of ideology in nearly the modern sense. "The matter of the books seems a thing of little moment," he advised his government in connection with the Roman effort to regulate publication, "because it is entirely a question of words; but from those words opinions come into the world which cause partialities, seditions, and finally wars." [200] He did not regard all religious belief as, in this sense, ideological. For him the church had been entrusted with an original deposit of genuine truth, independent of human interest and particular circumstance, which it was the church's mission to preserve immaculate and to propagate. The offence came from the ideological exploitation of truth, its adaptation for merely human ends to the contingent realm of politics in which it properly had no place. But, as a fact of political life, the practical value of ideology had to be recognized by statesmen. It was too useful a tool to neglect.

A number of Sarpi's *pensieri* reveal that, well before his involvement in politics, he had absorbed the Venetian habit of estimating knowledge primarily for its utility.[201] "Hence," he wrote, "we despise knowledge of things of which we have no need;" he interpreted useless knowledge as a kind of infirmity.[202] This utilitarianism was closely connected with his indifference

---

[197] Letter to Groslot, Nov. 23, 1610, Busnelli, I, 153.
[198] *Trattato delle materie beneficiarie, SG,* p. 50. Cf. p. 98: "Cosi le mutazioni degl'interessi portano seco mutazione e contrarietà di dottrina!"
[199] *Sulla publicazione di scritture malediche contra il governo, SG,* p. 229.
[200] *Sopra l'officio dell'inquisizione, SG,* p. 190.
[201] Cf. above, pp. 86–87.
[202] *Pensiero* 289.

to metaphysics and his relativism. Thus valid conceptions of order and dis-order, the source of so many grand pronouncements about the proper structure of society, could not be derived, in his view, from the abstract pat-tern of reality; they could only express what seemed useful or appropriate within a given frame of reference. "Therefore," he declared, "the republics, the buildings, the politics of the Tartars and the Indians are different." [203] These words were written well before he undertook to defend the right of Venice to conduct her own affairs without interference from Rome, an enter-prise to which they seem relevant.

But the usefulness of ideas struck him more directly after the interdict. Venice, as we have remarked, had long been impressed with the value of religion to preserve order in society, and Sarpi now developed the point into an argument for impressing subjects with the divine right of government. In 1613 he instructed the Venetian government "that the prince, especially when he rules with the arts of peace, clearly has *as principal instrument* that the people should hold this truth firmly, namely that the prince is established by God and rules with divine authority, and the subject is in conscience obligated to obey him, and offends God in not doing so." There is no reason to doubt Sarpi's sincerity in insisting that the proposition was true as well as useful, but the point seems almost an afterthought.[204]

His sense of the practical importance of ideas also caused him to emphasize the social value of education. "It cannot be expressed in writing," he advised his government, "how important the principles conceived by the young are to governments, both of families and of cities. Everyone knows by experience that every man acts according to the principles he believes; and he believes those things that have been instilled into his mind by educators, which, once they have taken root, it is impossible to detach. Hence nothing is more likely to change the governance of a family or city than education contrary to it." [205] But Sarpi also recognized clearly that, since (as he saw) societies differed and education was necessarily relative to concrete needs, discussion of the subject in general terms was futile. Thus he objected to the common view that the Jesuits had "no equal as educators," a position he found equivocal. "Educa-tion," he wrote, " is not an absolute thing which has grades of perfection, of which the Jesuit Fathers have attained the highest, but education is relative

---

[203] *Pensiero* 159.
[204] *Sopra l'officio dell'inquisizione*, SG, p. 191; italics mine.
[205] *Scrittura in materia dell'Collegio de'Greci di Roma*, in *Opere*, VI, 145–146. Sarpi was arguing that Jesuit education endangered the whole fabric of Venetian society.

to government. Therefore youth is educated in such a way that what is good and useful for one government is harmful for another, and education receives variety according to the variety of governments. What is useful for a military state, which is maintained and increased with violence, is pernicious to a peaceful, which is conserved through the observance of laws." Jesuit education, he insisted, by detaching human affection from other objects and directing it to spiritual ends alone, was effective in promoting the ecclesiastical ideal of government but evidently subversive in other contexts. A proper education for Venetians, as for any society "where the end is liberty and true virtue, and which the ecclesiastics do not hold subject," had to begin by inculcating a sense of familial obligation and obedience to the state.[206] Sarpi found both in the Gospel, and he seems to have been confident that they would also be reinforced by the study of history. The neglect of historical studies at Padua troubled him for this reason; it opened the way to the dubious ideology of the papalists.[207]

Intellectual formulations were thus chiefly important to Sarpi because of their instrumental role in politics and society, which he had come through the interdict to consider the proper focus of human life on earth. He felt that direct engagement in the *vita activa* was more, indeed, than a social duty; it became for him the most solemn of religious obligations. He urged the point in connection with Casaubon's duty, as he saw it, to press Polybius into the sacred cause of human liberty by means of his new edition which could counter the exploitation of Tacitus on behalf of tyrants.[208] Even a scholar could make a valid contribution to the practical needs of the age; so, in this connection, he wrote to his friend Leschassier: "The pious man must not abstain from politics; for since the enemies of public causes and of liberty force their deadly precepts on us under color of religion, so we must oppose them." [209] The sentiment was equally applicable to himself, and he evidently thought a good deal about his own conversion to the active life. He noted how the interdict (however indecisive in other respects) had proved the great turning point in his own career; it had stimulated him to consider seriously, as he wrote to a French correspondent, the "true liberty of the

---

[206] *Ibid.*, p. 145. Cf. his letter to Castrino, March 16, 1609, Busnelli, II, 27.
[207] Letter to Leschassier, May 13, 1608, Ulianich, p. 11.
[208] Letter to Leschassier, Feb. 16, 1610, Ulianich, p. 69.
[209] Letter to Leschassier, June 8, 1610, Ulianich, p. 84.

church," to the recovery of which he proposed henceforth to dedicate his life.[210]

Sarpi's insistence on the priority of action emerges with particular color in his wry and acidulous reactions to the literary pursuits of James of England, a ruler from whom (especially after the presumed defection of France) he would otherwise have expected significant aid. "If the king of England were not a doctor," he wrote in 1612, "we might hope for some good";[211] but, he noted, instead of arms and money James contributed nothing to the cause of political liberty but books and words.[212] His generation was in a sad way, he declared on another occasion, when it could only expect words from those who were able and ought to perform deeds.[213] News that James had established a college with a dozen theologians and two historians to defend the faith drew from him the ironical prediction that "we shall have books in great number." [214] James's war of words he found more wearisome than a war of steel.[215]

The trouble for Sarpi lay in James's failure to recognize the nature of kingship and its obligations, which were to action, not to theory. "It is one thing to be a clever theologian," he wrote, "quite another to be a valorous king." [216] Again he exclaimed: "What a misfortune is this, that everyone wishes to demonstrate excellence in an art not his own!" [217] Clearly Sarpi was not objecting only to the fact that James was, as he believed, an inept theologian. His basic objection was directed to the king's inversion of values, his preference of theory to deeds, particularly when the times called for action from those whose office was to act. The same indignation appears in the letters of Micanzio (letters in which Sarpi probably had a hand and to which he was almost certainly privy) to Sir William Cavendish during the early years of the Thirty Years' War. At first Micanzio evidently nourished

[210] Letter to Leschassier, Sept. 4, 1607, Ulianich, p. 3. Cf. the letter of Oct. 13, 1608, Ulianich, p. 27: "Bene ais, expressa semper nocent, praxis est utilissima, dissertatio et disputatio obest: id a tribus annis cogitavi et praedicavi."

[211] Letter to Groslot, May 22, 1612, Busnelli, I, 231. For what follows see also John L. Lievsay, "Paolo Sarpi's Appraisal of James I," *Essays in History and Literature Presented to Stanley Pargellis* (Chicago, 1965), pp. 109–117.

[212] Letter to Simone Contarini, Sept. 19, 1615, in *Lettere inedite di fra Paolo Sarpi a Simone Contarini ambasciatore veneto in Roma, 1615*, ed. C. Castellani (Venice, 1892), p. 49.

[213] Letter to Castrino, May 26, 1609, Busnelli, II, 37.

[214] Letter to Foscarini, Oct. 10, 1609, *Aevum*, XI (1937), 289.

[215] Letter to Castrino, Sept. 15, 1609, Busnelli, II, 52.

[216] Letter to S. Contarini, Dec. 13, 1615, Castellani, p. 61.

[217] Letter to Castrino, July 7, 1609, Busnelli, II, 44.

REMPVBLICAM BELLO
INVICTA VIRTVTE
RVM EVOLAVIT

NICOLAVS CONTARENVS
VEXATAM
PESTE FAME
SISTINENS AD

Portrait of the Doge Nicolò Contarini.

PAVLVS SARPIVS VENET^{VS}
CONCILII TRIDENTINI
EVISCERATOR

Portrait of Fra Paolo Sarpi.

some slight hope, though contrary to all experience with him, that James might act. So he wrote in 1619: "If he move not to the acquist of that which destiny seems to present him withall, we must needs acknowledge Gods great wrath against our sins. Speremus meliora. Truly God has given that king so much understanding and his studies so much learning that if in this occasion he had a will conformable he would obscure the glory of all his antecessors for many ages." [218] But the continuing inaction of the king led first to bewilderment and finally to total disillusionment and indignant denunciation. Fifteen months later Micanzio wrote: "To stand looking on for the doubtfulness of right and let him that is mighty grow still more mighty and be able to undermine all free states and the rest to make himself master of, some by fear some by corruption: if these reasons be good either in matter of conscience or of State, let your Lordship be judge .... If from England there come not some helpful resolutions and that well accompanied with deeds actum est: the Spaniards are conquerors of Germany and have Italy at their discretion, to proceed after as far as they can." [219] In their judgment of James I, Sarpi and Micanzio appear to be applying to the larger international community the same insistence on active engagement, and something of the same distaste for a passive and neutral contemplation of the world, that had been first enunciated so much earlier in the civic atmosphere of Renaissance Italy.

Meanwhile Sarpi (although given to abrupt changes in mood) from time to time applied the same concern for action to affairs at home, only qualifying his demand for commitment by insisting that it conform to the occasions presented by Providence. But even on this score he discerned danger in excessive caution. Nothing, he wrote to Groslot, is more dangerous than too much eagerness to avoid danger, and too much prudence ends in imprudence.[220] Again he resorted to medical imagery to make the point that political troubles often called for radical measures: "Everyone will certify that with civil disorders, just as with natural diseases, soothing remedies, although apparently effective for the moment, nevertheless aggravate the sickness and make it more fierce and atrocious for the future." [221] Hence he condemned his fellow Italians for an habitual caution that had frequently

---

[218] Letter of Dec. 27, 1619, as translated by Thomas Hobbes, in V. Gabrielli, "Bacone, la riforma e Roma nella versione hobbesiana d'un carteggio di Fulgenzio Micanzio," *English Miscellany*, VIII (1957), 220–221.

[219] Letter of March 21, 1621, *ibid.*, p. 221.

[220] Letter of Nov. 25, 1608, Busnelli, I, 48.

[221] *Aggiunta alla Storia degli Uscocchi*, in *Opere*, IV, 263–264.

lost "good occasions";[222] and he lamented the growing pacifism of Venice: "This republic desires peace and avoids war as a sick man avoids medicine." [223] In his conviction, so reminiscent of Machiavelli, that the vices of the age included passivity as well as hypocrisy, Sarpi not only suggested a private restlessness but also translated his theoretical attachment to the *vita activa* into a demand for bolder policies. Although he was unable to sustain the activist mood, it remained one of his fundamental ideals.

As had been the case with several of their Renaissance predecessors, an Augustinian religion of grace accompanied Sarpi's commitment to social duty, and perhaps even more that of the younger Micanzio.[224] This much is clear, even though Sarpi's religious position has in other respects been a matter of some disagreement. The problem has arisen primarily, I think, from his refusal to express systematic views, in theology as in philosophy; Sarpi exposed his position in fragments, somewhat like Pascal, or obliquely. In an age when few men were reluctant to dogmatize, such reticence has seemed puzzling. Some historians have supposed that he must have chosen to protect himself from persecution by hiding his real beliefs, while others have searched for evidence to prove that he was a sound Catholic or at heart a solid Protestant. To grasp Sarpi's position it should be recognized that he saw little need either to articulate his views on every point or to make clear choices among the various confessional alternatives. He remained, in the confessional age, still committed to the attitudes of Venetian Evangelism, in which it had always been easier to discern tendencies than dogmas.

In addition, the political needs of Venice required friendly relations with the Protestant powers and provided a practical motive for vagueness about doctrine. Sarpi could thus be both politic and sincere in speaking very generally with Protestants of their common interest in "the religion" and its reform; and they, perhaps understanding him even less than did his enemies in Rome, interpreted his position variously. The enthusiastic Wotton, hardly pausing to ponder the paradox, was certain that in Sarpi he beheld "a sound

[222] Letter to Groslot, Oct. 13, 1609, Busnelli, I, 98.

[223] Letter to Leschassier, May 9, 1610, Ulianich, p. 83. Cf. the remarks of Gaetano Cozzi in his edition (with Luisa Cozzi) of Paolo Sarpi, *La Repubblica di Venezia, la casa d'Austria e gli Uscocchi* (Bari, 1965), pp. 425–426.

[224] Micanzio, *Vita*, p. 73, noted his intensive study of Augustine's theology of grace. For what follows see also Boris Ulianich, "Appunti e documenti: Sarpiana: la lettera del Sarpi allo Heinsius," *RSI*, LXVIII (1956), 425–446.

Protestant, as yet in the habit of a friar." [225] The Calvinist Diodati, on the other hand, was less sure. He acknowledged that Sarpi and Micanzio had made much progress, but he doubted that they would ever arrive at "the full goodness and perfect beauty of the Gospel in its express form . . . so rooted is monkery in those who have never left it." [226]

Sarpi's personal religion appears to have been essentially that propounded in the famous Lenten sermons of Micanzio, in which, as we have remarked, the Venetian government found nothing exceptionable and the ecclesiastical authorities, with the best will in the world, could discover no evidence of heresy. Underlying it was that deep sense of personal responsibility in spiritual matters that had emerged so forcefully in the controversy over the interdict. In other respects Sarpi's position was rather a matter of tendencies and preferences which, while they may explain his relaxed attitude to some aspects of Protestantism, were generally consistent with Catholic orthodoxy.

Fundamental to Sarpi's religious vision was a sense of the utter transcendence of God together with its corollary, the absolute dependence of human affairs on the divine will.[227] But God's transcendence also meant that his ways were mysterious and that his purposes in any particular situation could never be assessed with assurance. The importance of such views for Sarpi's interpretation of the European scene is obvious, and he typically gave expression to them through his reactions to concrete events rather than in dogmatic pronouncements; Sarpi's theology was not an independent compartment of his mind but an essential dimension of his engagement with politics. He watched developments at home and abroad during the years after the interdict, and from a human standpoint he was in despair; but then he found consolation and recovered his perspective with Christian reflections.

The oscillation appears frequently in his letters. Soon after the settlement of the interdict his mood was gloomy: "It seems to me that nothing can be foreseen by reason; and having seen the things that have gone on here, I am

[225] Letter to the Earl of Salisbury, Sept. 13, 1607, Smith, I, 399. Cf. Bedell's view (letter to Adam Newton, Jan. 1, 1608, *Two Biographies*, p. 231): "These two I know (as haveing practic'd with them) to desire nothing in the world soe much as the reformation of the Church: and in a word, for the substance of religion they are wholly ours."

[226] Letter to Philippe Duplessis de Mornay, Jan. 8, 1608, in *Mémoires et correspondance de Duplessis-Mornay*, ed. A. D. de La Fontenelle de Vaudoré and P. R. Auguis (Paris, 1824-1825), X, 272. Cf. Diodati's letter to Christian von Anhalt, Nov. 22, 1608, *Briefe und Akten*, II, 131.

[227] See, in general, Luigi Salvatorelli, "Le idee religiose di fra Paolo Sarpi," *Atti della Accademia Nazionale dei Lincei: Classe di scienze morali, storiche e filologiche: memorie*, Ser. 8, V (1953), 311-360.

stupefied and become a kind of skeptic in human things." [228] But skepticism in human things opened the way to confidence in the divine conduct of events; it only meant that men could not trust in their own efforts but must discipline their expectations with humility and patience, confiding in God's power to convert immediate disaster into ultimate benefit.[229] When events were going badly for Venice, such convictions were a source of strength; and occasionally there is even a suggestion of relish in Sarpi's sense of the unpredictability of human affairs. "No divine work is advanced by human means," he wrote to Groslot de l'Isle in 1613, giving a Christian turn to a familiar Renaissance motif; "it may be that when a man believes himself at the top of the wheel, he will find himself at the bottom." [230] Providence, he wrote repeatedly, constantly converts human designs to unforeseeable ends of its own, and God regularly makes foolish the wisdom of the world.[231]

At times these sentiments seem merely calculated to justify his own temperamental reluctance to act, a quality so often galling to his friends. If all things expressed the will of God in some mysterious way, man's duty was to resign himself to whatever might transpire. Thus, persuaded at one point that it must be God's will for men to live "under the yoke," Sarpi wrote that, "if such is his glory, we must conform ourselves to his will and render thanks." [232] He felt the need frequently, in his later years, to insist on his own resignation to the course of events. But, at least in principle, passivity did not appear to him always appropriate; it corresponded to one kind of historical situation only, and the situation was bound to change. "That I am inactive," he once declared, "does not proceed from negligence; it is because to act unseasonably could destroy the means of acting opportunely." [233]

Sarpi's recognition of the need for resignation was thus simply the obverse of the familiar Renaissance doctrine of the occasion, and through it he was able to reconcile action with acceptance. The occasion, in this view, was a gift of Providence, the opportunity which God provides to men of good will for the accomplishment of his purposes. Without it action was indeed useless or worse: "Nothing is accomplished through human efforts except in the

[228] Letter to Groslot, Dec. 11, 1607, Busnelli, I, 7.
[229] Cf. letter to Groslot, Jan. 20, 1609, Busnelli, I, 61–62.
[230] March 26, 1613, Busnelli, I, 271.
[231] Letter to Groslot, Aug. 26, 1608, Busnelli, I, 29. See also the letters of April 1, 1608 (p. 9), Oct. 13, 1608 (p. 42), Jan. 6, 1609 (p. 59), April 28, 1609 (p. 78), and *passim* in Sarpi's correspondence.
[232] Letter to Groslot, Oct. 12, 1610, Busnelli, I, 143.
[233] Letter to Groslot, May 27, 1608, Busnelli, I, 14.

time of the divine consent; only attempts matured by occasions can generally bear fruit." [234] "In all things the occasion is the principal point," he wrote again; "without it everything turns out not only unfruitfully but also with loss. When God shows us the opportunity, we must believe it is his will that we should seize it; if he does not, we must wait in silence for the time of his good pleasure." [235] The interdict, it was true, had disappointed him. Contrary to his expectation, it had proved no more than a short interval of wakefulness during a long night, and Rome had managed to lull the world back to sleep.[236] But, however unpromising the present moment, there would be another occasion. The doctrine was clearly appropriate to the plight of Venice in a world dominated by great powers that, if she took a single false step, could easily crush her. It also helped Sarpi to reconcile the two sides of his own nature, and Christian Evangelism with Renaissance politics.

Sarpi's sense of the impotence of the natural man, so brutally confirmed by the history of Italy during the previous century as well as by more recent events, had a counterpart in his low opinion of human virtue. He applied it first of all to himself. "In the whole course of history," Micanzio wrote, "no one perhaps has penetrated so deeply into the nothingness of human nature (I may use such language because the Padre spoke so), and he esteemed himself a nothing." Like other followers of Augustine, he kept careful written account of his own defects.[237] The redemption of sinful man through grace was accordingly, for him, the center of the Christian religion; without it, he declared, the church could not exist. Compared with the issue in the controversy de auxiliis, he admitted, the jurisdictional controversies between Venice and Rome were inconsequential; however these turned out the church would survive, "but without the grace of God there would be no Christian." [238] The renegade Manfredi's account of Sarpi's instruction to the preachers of Venice is in this respect consistent with other evidence. Sarpi had exhorted them, Manfredi reported, "to commend, to celebrate, and to

---

[234] Letter to Hotman de Villiers, April 14, 1609, Ulianich, p. 183.

[235] Letter to Groslot, Nov. 25, 1608, Busnelli, I, 50.

[236] Letter to Leschassier, Sept. 4, 1607, Ulianich, p. 3.

[237] Vita, pp. 173, 70–71.

[238] Scrittura in difesa delle opere scritte a favore della serenissima republica nella controversia col sommo pontefice, in Scritti, III, 254–255. For Sarpi's study of the controversy de auxiliis, see Micanzio, Vita, pp. 72–74. In writing on the issues at stake, Sarpi took a clearly Augustinian position; see his advice in the Scritti filosofici, pp. 145–154. He saw Roman theology, on the other hand, as overburdened with articles of faith about the pope (letter to Leschassier, March 13, 1612, Ulianich, p. 108).

magnify faith and faithfulness in Christ, our lord and head, and the merits of his blood shed for our salvation, which he alone gives and no one else can give or impede, exalting and exaggerating the grace and mercy of God, which saves us, and not our works, which are worth little or nothing." [239] Such an emphasis, as much as the political implications of that event, helps to explain the sympathetic vibrations set off in Sarpi and Micanzio by the Synod of Dort.[240]

Divine grace seems also to have operated, for Sarpi, with a minimum of assistance from the visible church; he evidently preferred to derive both nourishment for the Christian life and the assurance of salvation directly from the Scriptures. He was a devoted student of the Bible, above all the New Testament which, scorning the assistance offered by the long exegetical tradition of the church, he studied "without any expositor but only with the Greek and Latin texts." [241] He was cool to many of the external expressions of Catholic piety, which (rather in the manner of Erasmus) he considered little but superstitious substitutes for a genuine religion of the heart. This was his view of both monasticism and the cult of the saints.[242]

For much the same reason he was indifferent and even hostile to a highly articulated theology. His Christianity was a kind of fundamentalism and finally a matter rather of personal experience than of speculation, a function of the *vita activa* rather than the *vita contemplativa*. For that reason (a point on which he would have agreed with Ockham), it seemed to him more readily accessible to simple men than to minds likely to become entangled in their own pretentious complexities. "To multiply articles of faith and to specify as its subject things not specific is to fall into past abuses," he wrote (to, of all men, a Calvinist); "why not be content to leave ambiguous what has been

[239] *Aevum*, X (1936), 21–22. In a letter to Leschassier, Sept. 14, 1610 (Ulianich, p. 93), Sarpi also protested against attributing any doctrine of salvation by works to Paul.

[240] See Micanzio's letters to Sir Dudley Carleton, June 7, 1619, in Cozzi, "Sarpi, l'anglicanesimo e la *Historia*, pp. 608–611; and to Sir William Cavendish, as quoted by Gabrielli, p. 227, n. 41. Cozzi, *Contarini*, p. 224, notes that Cornelius Jansen was also pleased by the decisions of Dort.

[241] Micanzio, *Vita*, pp. 71–72. Cf. the letter of Pauli to Savoy, Feb. 25, 1612 (Luzio, p. 43), in which the point is made that Sarpi and Micanzio believed in the explication of the Gospel "*ad litteram*, and not according to the commentaries."

[242] For a suggestion of his attitude to monasticism, see *Trattato delle materie beneficiarie*, SG, pp. 24–25. On the saints see his letter to Groslot, Jan. 3, 1612, Busnelli, I, 210. For his attitude to external observances in general, cf. Micanzio, *Vita*, p. 134, and Sarpi's letter to Gillot, Dec. 3, 1608 (Ulianich, p. 130), in which he attacks "superstition as" worse than impiety because, although impiety is ugly, it is also open and deceives no one, while superstition is contagious.

so up to now?" Dogmatic elaboration, he feared, would only result in new divisions among Christians, new forms of sectarianism.[243] He ridiculed the notion that men could be persuaded to change religion because a verb was "present and not preterit," as he once described the argument of a contemporary theologian.[244] Sarpi's disapproval of the enunciation of dogma was to be a major element, as we shall see, in his attack on the Council of Trent.

Since it suggests his inclination to tolerate a considerable range of individual variation, the attitude is also related to his general approval of the substantial intellectual and cultural freedom long characteristic of Venice. The severe Roman decrees against heresy, another expression of the dogmatic mentality to which he objected, were, as he noted, inconsistent with "the mild government of this state." [245] Sarpi did not favor absolute freedom of belief. Although he probably disapproved of the death penalty for it,[246] he was not opposed in principle to the prosecution of heresy; and he clearly regarded surveillance over books and ideas as a political necessity. "The regulation of printing is a matter worthy to be considered and reformed," he advised his government, "since any kind of doctrine, both profitable and pernicious, is easily disseminated through the presses from which are born consequences of the greatest moment . . . . Therefore it is necessary to see that books of bad doctrine, or contrary to the holy religion, or prejudicial to the authority of princes, or which introduce or foment wicked customs should not be printed." [247] The politically subversive doctrines propagated by the Curia particularly concerned him. It should be remarked, nevertheless, that the restrictions on free discussion favored by Sarpi were intended to protect the survival of the state which he regarded, in other respects, as the champion of freedom. He favored the suppression of ideas emanating from Rome because they aimed to deprive Venetians of their freedom of speech and action, and ultimately to control the thoughts and souls of all mankind. [248]

His positive attitude toward intellectual liberty sometimes has an almost Miltonic ring. A book to which no one takes exception is without value, he

[243] Letter to Groslot, Feb. 17, 1609, Busnelli, I, 65–66.
[244] Letter to Castrino, June 8 or 9, 1609, Busnelli, II, 40–41.
[245] Sopra l'officio dell'inquisizione, SG, pp. 185–186.
[246] Ibid., p. 132.
[247] Regolatione delle stampe, quoted in Francescon, p. 236, n. 1.
[248] Cf. letter to Gillot, March 18, 1608, Ulianich, p. 128; and Del vietare la stampa di libri perniciosi al buon governo, SG, p. 14.

wrote, "this being a sign that it contains nothing but vulgar opinions." [249]
He was also concerned to protect the autonomy of culture. On this ground
he offered an eloquent argument against the confessional oath Rome
proposed to impose on all students at Padua. "To confer a doctorate in
philosophy and medicine is to testify that the scholar is a good philosopher
and physician, and that he can be admitted to the practice of that art. To
say that a heretic is a good physician does not prejudice the Catholic faith;
it would prejudice it rather to say that he was a good theologian. The whole
world says that Hippocrates and Galen, infidels, are most excellent physicians,
and that there is not their equal among Catholics; yet our faith receives no
injury from this." [250]

Sarpi's sense of a connection between political and intellectual freedom
and the cultural achievements of the Renaissance is striking. The relationship
was particularly important to him because he considered the recovery of
ancient literature and legal studies based on the new philological scholarship
as the foundation of "good and sound doctrine." He noted that the papal
monarchy had originated and grown during the age of barbarism but was
shaken to its roots by "the restoration of polite literature." Conversely the
recovery of papal authority in his own time, as he bitterly remarked, had
meant the decline of learning in Italy and Spain. It could flourish now, he
wrote in 1608, only in the relatively freer atmosphere of France and Germany.
Sarpi had observed that the great centers of philological scholarship were no
longer in Italy as they had been a century before, and the explanation appeared
to him clear.[251] His identification of freedom as the necessary condition of
learning was general; he also attributed the ignorance of contemporary
Greece to "the servitude in which it finds itself." [252]

Liberty, in the various meanings that term had included for the Renaissance,
was much on Sarpi's mind. Man, he observed, has a natural aspiration to

[249] Letter to Castrino, Jan. 6, 1609, *Aevum*, XIII (1939), 560. He also remarked that
banning books only made them more desired (letters to Groslot, Feb. 17, 1609, and
Feb. 16, 1610, Busnelli, I, 65, 111). In addition, resident in a great center of printing,
he noted that the immoderate prohibition of books was bad for business (*Sopra l'officio
dell'inquisizione*, SG, 205).

[250] From a *consulto* of 1616, cited by Cecchetti, I, 49–50. See also Francescon, pp.
233–235.

[251] Letters to Leschassier, Dec. 23, 1608, and Nov. 23, 1610, Ulianich, pp. 34, 95.
See also his letter to Castrino, Jan. 6, 1609, *Aevum*, XIII (1939), 561, where he describes
the "good letters in the beginning of the last century" as a major cause of damage to
blind papalism.

[252] *Collegio de'Greci*, in *Opere*, VI, 146.

liberty, however obscured; and those who possess liberty must still defend it whole-heartedly.[253] Liberty, as the previous paragraphs have indicated, meant for him a large degree of autonomy for the spiritual and cultural activity of individual men; but this in turn depended on political freedom as the independence of particular states. That the Dutch were fighting for liberty in this sense from Spain was an element in his sympathy for their cause.[254] On the other hand it had been precisely because Venice "alone sustains the dignity and the true purposes of an independent prince" that the pope had turned against her.[255] Although he recognized that republican government had inherent weaknesses in dealing with crises,[256] his attachment to it remained profound.

But Sarpi seems most clearly to represent the political mentality of the Renaissance in his practical and relativistic attitude to questions of law and public policy. What mattered to him was not abstract right but the effectiveness of any measure to deal with concrete situations. On this score he marveled at the tactics of the Curia, which was apparently unable to learn from experience. "I cannot understand that Roman prudence, which commands without knowing if it will be obeyed," he exclaimed. "Every day they receive affronts because of this, and still they cannot accommodate themselves to what is due and timely." [257] He had long been convinced that standards of human conduct, lacking any ultimate foundation, differed widely from place to place;[258] and like others in the Renaissance tradition, who had often found support in Aristotle, he was convinced that the political institutions appropriate for one people might work badly for another.[259] Similarly, although for tactical reasons he occasionally appealed to natural law, he was inclined to believe that justice was itself derived rather from convention than from nature.[260] Only religious truths were eternal, he wrote to Leschassier, whereas laws are children of circumstance.[261]

[253] Letters to Leschassier, April 27, 1610, and March 13, 1612, Ulianich, pp. 78, 104. In the second of these Sarpi cites Livy.

[254] Letter to Castrino, Nov. 11, 1608, Busnelli, II, 6.

[255] Istoria dell'Interdetto, in Scritti, I, 4.

[256] Letters to Leschassier, Jan. 6, 1609, Ulianich, p. 35, and Foscarini, Jan. 5, 1610, Aevum, XI (1937), 313.

[257] Letter to Christoph von Dohna, April 28, 1609, Busnelli, II, 149.

[258] Pensieri 260, 471.

[259] Pensiero 414; cf. letter to Gillot, May 12, 1609, Ulianich, pp. 131-132, on the relativity of custom to the differing needs of states.

[260] Pensiero 420.

[261] April 27, 1610, Ulianich, p. 77.

Here Sarpi was concerned with the nature of his own profession as canonist. The problem of the lawyer, whatever law he practiced, was not so much to learn what the schools had to tell him (a relatively simple matter) as to grasp particular situations in their infinite variety. "As those who understand human affairs know," he declared, "actions are all singular, nor can two ever be entirely similar, and consequently each one needs its own rule. But law expressed as a universal rule for all things, necessarily defective through its universality, either includes cases which ought to be excepted or excepts those which merit inclusion." [262] In this perspective law itself became a subtle form of political activity, a delicate art of adjustment and improvisation directed to the balancing of interests and the maintenance of order.

The problem of distinguishing between major and minor crimes, arising from the need to define precisely the right of asylum, provides a nice illustration of Sarpi's approach to legal questions. The distinction, he argued, could not be based on the general definition of crimes themselves (for example murder, theft, arson, and so on), but had always to respond to all the particular circumstances attendant on the commission of each offense; "and because the accidents and circumstances of this sort are infinite, so that it is not possible to comprehend them all with rules, it is submitted to the good conscience and prudence of the judge to give judgment, all the characteristics of the case being well examined." [263] We may detect here an affinity between Sarpi's legal philosophy and his attraction to a religion which put faith above the works of the law.

Nevertheless Sarpi's rejection of any ultimate foundation in the nature of things for the actions and legislation of government by no means inclined him to regard political authority lightly. On the contrary: the absence of rational sanctions, given the weakness of human nature, made the authority of government seem to him peculiarly indispensable. On this point Sarpi broke radically with the naturalism of Paruta to adopt a thoroughly Augustinian politics. Government had come into existence, for him, not to supply the needs of man's essential nature, but to compensate for the defects of his fallen nature. If men were perfect, he had declared in his *pensieri*, they would be best off in a state of anarchy; but since they are not, they require government, which serves a kind of medicinal function. Like all medicines, government should seek the happy mean; it should be neither

[262] *Su le immunità delle chiese, SG*, p. 268.
[263] *Ibid.*, p. 281.

too weak (an invitation to license) nor too strong (tyranny).[264] The argument may suggest the superiority of an aristocratic republic.

But whatever the form of government, for Sarpi its primary instrument, given the refractory nature of man, must be fear: the fear of temporal punishment incurred by disobedience to human laws, the fear of eternal punishment incurred through disobedience to the will of God.[265] Sarpi's conviction on this point was related to a mechanistic conception of human behavior like that of Hobbes. It applies to individual conduct those physical principles which, in Renaissance thought, governed both the internal operations and the external relations of states. The problem of social control, here too, was to balance contrary forces; the centrifugal force of human appetite had to be countered by the centripetal force of coercion through fear.[266] In this light legislation was a branch of dynamics rather than of morality; laws were to be evaluated according to their ability to turn men in desired directions. Furthermore the force wielded by the government, to produce its desired effects, should be kinetic and not merely potential; hence laws had to be severely enforced.[267] Nor was Sarpi, in principle, opposed to judicial torture.[268]

At the same time he believed that the coercive resources of human government were not, in every concrete situation, adequate for the tasks of social discipline. He noted that the fear of earthly punishment had been supplemented, in some societies, by the threat of religious sanctions. Governments had frequently appealed, he observed, to what he called "the Torah," by which he seems to have meant not only the specific prescriptions of Jewish law (though he presumably included them in the conception) but also every ordinance regarded as derived from a supernatural source. Sarpi did not deny that "the Torah" in this general sense reflected the divine will or that it was a legitimate tool of politics. He suggested its legitimacy by calling it a "property of the republic." But he saw it *in concreto* as a human construction, assuming various forms according to the various circumstances of its origin, and "sensibly altering as happens to all earthly things." It was useful, but clearly distinct from the Gospel. Nor, at least before the interdict,

---

[264] *Pensieri* 403, 405.

[265] *Pensieri* 378–379. Cf. *Considerazioni sopra le censure*, in *Scritti*, II, 228–229.

[266] *Pensieri* 143, 257.

[267] *Pensiero* 379.

[268] This seems clear from his regret that Ravaillac had been executed without being made to confess the names of his instigators (letter to Groslot, June 22, 1610, Busnelli, I, 126).

did he consider it indispensable. Governments, he declared, in particular those of cities and republics in northern and western Europe, might well substitute other devices, among them the sense of honor, although "a false opinion." Sarpi's view of "the Torah" as "not so useful as some believe" suggests some repudiation, perhaps reflecting the Evangelism of his age, of the political Averroism so deeply rooted in the Venetian political mentality.[269]

It is remarkable, therefore, that his position after the interdict, at least in his public writings, was rather different. It may be that political experience convinced him, like earlier Venetians, that Venice could not dispense with "the Torah." When the theologians of the Curia argued that papal authority alone came directly from God, Sarpi responded that such views were calculated to make government impossible, since a sense of religious obligation was essential to maintain the obedience of a large proportion of mankind, even among the subjects of the Republic. "Few persons in the world act out of love of the good," he wrote; "most of the others are divided in two groups: some who act well through fear of spiritual punishments, some through fear of temporal punishments. When the spiritual fear is taken away, the obedience is lost of all those who think to be secret or to avoid punishment with favors or other means, and of those also who disregard it; all together these make a great number. On the other hand we see how easily some men render obedience through spiritual fear." [270] He insisted therefore that obedience to government was an obligation of conscience, not, as the curialists maintained, merely a response to force.[271] And although he held that the obligation was equally binding on the subjects of wicked princes,[272] he was also aware that in practice the reputation of a government for piety was essential to its authority.[273] Hence papalist denigration of Venice was profoundly dangerous.

Nevertheless, although Sarpi doubtless continued to believe in that divine right of all political authority to which Venetian theorists had so regularly appealed at the time of the interdict, he preferred in later years to discuss the state in legal rather than in theological terms. His comprehensive description of sovereignty suggests, perhaps, that he saw no conflict between the two. "It is also natural that everything situated within

---

[269] His conception of "the Torah" is developed in *Pensieri* 403, 405, 407, 413, 414, 423.
[270] *Sopra l'officio dell'inquisizione*, SG, p. 204.
[271] *Ibid.*, p. 203.
[272] *Scrittura in difesa delle opere*, in *Scritti*, III, 238.
[273] *Sulla publicazione di scritture malediche contra il governo*, SG, p. 221.

the boundaries of a State should be under the universal jurisdiction of the prince," he declared. "And this is not servitude but the liberty ordained by God and by nature, nothing being more abhorrent to both than anarchy and license. Hence the law that the prince should be recognized as superior in everything is always presupposed." The essence of sovereignty, he continued, consisted in the fact that no other independent jurisdiction could exist; nothing could be exempted or excepted from its operation.[274] "The prince," he wrote on another occasion, "is the source from which every jurisdiction issues and returns, just as the ocean is that from which all waters issue and where they return, so that it is an absurdity to speak of a jurisdiction which does not derive from the concession of the prince and does not return to him through recognition of the jurist." [275] What was on Sarpi's mind was less the theoretical basis of the state than the actual mode of its operation; it was from this that he had derived his sense of its actual nature.

The needs of government required, as Sarpi believed, that the authority of the state should be unlimited, although prudence dictated that its application should ordinarily be moderate and reasonable. Authority restricted, he argued, was not so much diminished as made more durable.[276] Restriction, however, should be self-imposed by the duly constituted magistrate, not imposed from below. For this reason Sarpi disapproved of the dissemination by government of any public defense of policy, a practice which implied the right of subjects to judge their rulers. Subjects, he advised, should be kept in ignorance of public affairs; otherwise, studying its daily operations, they might lose respect for government.[277] The admission suggests, perhaps, reservations of his own about the methods of politics as well as doubts about the political competence of the lower classes. At the same time we must observe again that such precepts had a somewhat different meaning for an aristocratic republic than for a princely despotism. As Chabod has remarked, Sarpi looked at all public issues from the standpoint of the state and its interests,[278] but the doge could never say "L'État c'est moi." The Venetian government remained a collective polity regulated by traditional and constitutional procedures.

Sarpi's conception of the church must be understood against the double background of his Evangelical religion of grace and his insistence on the

[274] From a *consulto* of 1612, cited by Francescon, p. 115, n. 1.
[275] From a *consulto* of 1619, cited by Francescon, p. 121, n. 1.
[276] *Sopra l'officio dell'inquisizione, SG,* p. 168.
[277] *Sulla publicazione di scritture malediche contra il governo, SG,* p. 230.
[278] *Politica di Sarpi,* p. 84.

need for strong and effective government. Each of these elements in his thought had, as we have seen, a long Venetian background. But, a more self-conscious intellectual than the typical Venetian statesman, Sarpi was prepared to face, directly and on a theoretical level, the ecclesiological issues implicit in them which previous generations of Venetians had on the whole managed in their practical way to evade.[279]

Sarpi required a conception of the church and its relation to the world which would safeguard the spiritual mission of the priesthood but leave intact the authority of rulers. Each needed, in short, to be protected from encroachments by the other. Sarpi's ecclesiology begins therefore with an emphatic insistence on the total separation of the spiritual and earthly regiments:

> God has instituted two governments in the world, one spiritual and the other temporal, each of them supreme and independent from the other. One of these is the ecclesiastical ministry, the other is the political governance. He has given the spiritual to the care of the prelates, the temporal to the princes; thus it was well said by the ancients that the ecclesiastics are vicars of Christ in spiritual things, and the princes vicars of God in temporal things. Therefore where the salvation of souls is involved all men, including princes, are subject to the ecclesiastics; but where public tranquility and civil life are involved all men, including ecclesiastics, are subject to the prince.[280]

But the clarity and balance of the statement are somewhat misleading; in actual experience, as Sarpi had sufficient grounds to know, human existence could not be so easily compartmentalized. On various occasions he was compelled to elaborate his fundamental position. The result is that a comprehensive ecclesiology can be pieced together from a long series of fragmentary pronouncements.

Formally stated, Sarpi's position was hardly original. He took, generally speaking, the way of Marsilio of Padua and other theorists of the later Middle Ages whom ecclesiastical authority now considered heretics. What gives Sarpi's views particular interest is not so much their novelty of content

---

[279] For general discussion of Sarpi's ecclesiology, see Buffon, *Chiesa di Cristo e Chiesa romana*, and the more cautious work of Boris Ulianich, "Considerazioni e documenti per una ecclesiologia di Paolo Sarpi," *Festgabe Joseph Lortz* (Baden-Baden, 1957), II, 363–444.

[280] From a *consulto* of 1608, cited by Francescon, pp. 110–111.

as their manner of development. Not content to present them in abstract terms, he pressed into service the attitudes and the scholarly resources of the Renaissance and based them on history. He argued that ecclesiological tendencies rejected with special urgency by the theorists of the Counter Reformation in fact represented the original and authentic form of Catholic orthodoxy, and he found support for this view in the concrete institutions and traditional practices of Venice and France, two of the Catholic powers least responsive to curial pressure. The major vehicle for Sarpi's argument was his massive *Istoria del Concilio Tridentino*, in many ways the last great monument to the historical mentality of the Italian Renaissance, which will be a major concern of the next chapter. Sarpi's historical thought will be more readily understood, however, in the light of other ecclesiological pronouncements, many of them contemporary with the composition of the *Istoria*. His ecclesiology assumed, during the years after the interdict, an increasingly central place in his thought, bringing into focus the whole range of his concerns, secular and religious, local and universal, and providing a kind of final distillation of the values and convictions implicit in Renaissance politics.

Sarpi's conception of the church, intended both to protect the transcendence of the spiritual and to guard the authority of rulers, was somewhat like Luther's in its distinction (not always carefully stated) between the ideal and invisible community of true believers and the complex of institutions through which the work of Christ is accomplished in the world. The distinction allowed him both to retain a lofty ideal of the church in which many of its traditional attributes could still find a place, and at the same time to accommodate himself to the limitations and contingencies of earthly experience.

He described the ideal church in various ways which seem intended to distinguish it from the visible institution of common experience. He saw it as emphatically not the clerical establishment; his church is the whole congregation of the faithful, headed by Christ and requiring no other chief; hierarchy and distinction of status have no place in his ideal. Including all believers everywhere, the church on this plane is, for Sarpi, universal. Teaching no doctrine but Christ's, it is also infallible. Above all, Sarpi's ideal church is spiritual; it is the kingdom of heaven, found in this world only in the hearts of men, to which (it may be added) excommunications and interdictions are irrelevant. Finally, as a spiritual body, its attributes are eternal, subject to no shadow of turning, immune to the accidents of history, beyond any development. By the same token, having no visible existence in this world, it can in the nature of things never come into conflict with earthly governments. Its only foe is Satan.[281]

Although in this transcendent form the church, for Sarpi, will be perfected only in heaven, and the church militant is a rather different kind of agency, the ideal was nevertheless relevant in various ways to his conception of the church's operation on earth. Above all it meant that in this world the functions of the church should be severely limited to "spiritual things, that is administration of the Sacraments, indulgences, masses, divine offices, and burials," as he once defined the tasks of the clergy.[282] He gave special emphasis to "the office of preaching and teaching the word of God and the doctrine of the Gospel." [283] These tasks the clergy were to perform "not with rules and worldly interests but with wholly spiritual ordinances." [284] Nor was the church to be tainted by any admixture of legalism, which for Sarpi was antithetical to the faith. Christianity, as he understood it, was essentially a body of general principles, above all that of love, whose practical application through legislation, a thoroughly human and nonspiritual activity, was no proper concern of the church.[285] He remarked of the canonists, with some scorn, that it was not "their profession to understand the mysteries of the Christian religion." [286] He also denied to the clergy any coercive authority through "the threats and impositions of temporal punishments" which are "abuses and nullifications and corruptions of the institution of Christ." [287] Finally, he considered the ownership of property generally inconsistent with the spiritual character of the church.[288]

Sarpi's ideal for the church was also reflected in his attitude to the clergy, to whom he denied special status, authority, or privileges.[289] They were for

[281] On all these points see the important ecclesiological discussions in Sarpi's letters to Gillot, Sept. 29 and Dec. 8, 1609, Ulianich, pp. 136–143. Buffon has collected various additional references, pp. 42ff.

[282] In a consulto of 1615, cited by Francescon, p. 161, n. 2.

[283] *Trattato delle materie beneficarie*, SG, p. 15.

[284] From an unpublished *consulto* on ecclesiastical liberty, quoted by Buffon, p. 42 n. 44.

[285] Cf. letter to Hotman de Villiers, April 14, 1609, Ulianich, p. 183. See also Sarpi's general comment on Old Testament law, *Trattato delle materie beneficiarie*, SG, pp. 31–32.

[286] *Trattato delle materie beneficiarie*, SG, p. 45.

[287] In a *consulto*, s.d., quoted by Francescon, p. 130, n. 1.

[288] Cf. *Trattato delle materie beneficiarie*, SG, *passim*.

[289] See the references on this matter assembled in Buffon, pp. 70–73. Hence, perhaps, the small importance Sarpi attached to the degradation of a criminal priest before execution in the letter to Foscarini, Oct. 22, 1609. *Aevum*, XI (1937), 300–301, and *Scrittura sopra la degradazione*, in *Opere*, Suppl. II, 137–139.

him different from other members of the church chiefly in their specialized duties, which he conceived simply as services performed on behalf of the whole community of the faithful. The clergy, for example, were merely administrators, under law, of the properties of the church, the possession of the entire Christian community.[290] Sarpi was particularly offended, as we have seen, by contemporary efforts to define the church as the clergy alone; and it is not unlikely that he doubted the sacramental character of holy orders.[291] Meanwhile he emphasized the obligation of the clergy to obey the civil authority, a matter on which he regarded them as in no way different from other men.[292] Their participation in the common responsibilities of political life notably included, for Sarpi, the duty to pay taxes. "The republic has a natural authority to tithe the clergy," he wrote, objecting on principle to the "concession" of the tithe from Rome;[293] and he remarked how in the cities of Italy, where the clergy had never been distinguished from other social groups as a separate estate, all classes contributed together for the support of government "under a single heading, which is the community." [294]

On the basis of his concern with the whole community of Christians Sarpi worked out a conception of ecclesiastical polity which at once provided a larger context for his denial of special status to the clergy and at the same time reflected something of the republican and constitutional perspective of Renaissance Venice. For Sarpi the church itself was originally a democratic republic, in whose major deliberations all the faithful had participated. It had then passed historically through the classic cycle of constitutional forms. As the church grew (and thus for purely political reasons), it was necessary to elect officers to conduct its business; thus its polity became aristocratic.[295] Against this background Sarpi's treatment of popes, sometimes explicitly, as *tyrants*, takes on new meaning;[296] he meant more than general abuse. The aspirations of Rome, now nearly realized, marked for him the culmination of the standard process of political decay so often regarded by the theorists of the age (except for a while in Venice) as inevitable.

[290] *Trattato delle materie beneficiarie*, SG, 105–106.
[291] This is the tentative conclusion of Ulianich, "Ecclesiologia," pp. 375–376.
[292] As in *Sopra l'officio dell'inquisizione*, SG, 150, where Sarpi neatly defines the mutual relations of priest and magistrate.
[293] Letter to Foscarini, Oct. 22, 1609, *Aevum*, XI (1937), 301–302.
[294] *Sopra le contribuzioni di ecclesiastici alle publiche gravezze*, SG, p. 255.
[295] *Trattato delle materie beneficiarie*, SG, p. 38. Cf. Buffon, pp. 51–52.
[296] As in his letter to Leschassier, Jan. 6, 1609, Ulianich, p. 35

Several elements in this position are worth attention. One is its reversal of Jesuit theory, of which it presents a kind of mirror image. Bellarmine, Mariana, and their colleagues had seen the pope's authority as divine but that of rulers as human; governments, in this view, had originated in election, and rulers were obligated to represent the interests of their peoples. Sarpi, on the contrary, ascribed divine authority to princes and a representative function to the ecclesiastical hierarchy. Ecclesiastical authority had for him resided originally in the community, and properly belonged to it still. This meant among other things the continuing right and duty of the laity to intervene in ecclesiastical affairs, above all to remedy abuses caused by the clergy.[297]

It also suggests that for Sarpi the particular form of ecclesiastical government depended on particular circumstances and could presumably be altered as circumstances changed; even the Venetian political system, as his generation had begun to recognize, could not be made to work everywhere. His belief that the original form of the church had been democratic may not have meant, therefore, that he insisted on democracy at all times and under every condition. On the contrary, as a Venetian he very likely considered a constitutionally balanced aristocracy on the whole best for any civilized community, including the church: Venetian indignation at papal reduction in the authority of the Sacred College is worth recalling on this point. But no particular form of polity had for Sarpi an absolute value. He was not, for example, against bishops, but he was not on the other hand in any religious sense an episcopalian.[298] But what is above all notable here is Sarpi's general understanding of the church as a constitutional order, subject in its visible form to historical change and open to manipulation and experiment. In this he appears to continue, but also to go far beyond, the tendencies of the earlier Renaissance.

As his attention to the mutability of its internal structure indicates, what chiefly impressed Sarpi about the church as it actually existed in the world were thus the ways in which it evidently differed from the ideal church, and in which indeed it had to accommodate itself to imperfection. "The fabric of the church of God, although formed by so great an artificer," he wrote to Groslot, "has always had and will always have imperfections

---

[297] As in *Sulla instituzione, progresso ed abusi delle commende*, SG, pp. 3, 5, 6, 14.

[298] Cf. the apprehensions about Anglican bishops in his letter to Leschassier, Feb. 3, 1609, Ulianich, p. 37. On another occasion he expressed approval of Calvinist polity (letter to Groslot, Feb. 17, 1609, Busnelli, I, 65). He also regarded any mixture of monarchy and aristocracy in the government of the church as impossible (letter to Groslot, April 9, 1613, Busnelli, I, 272).

because of defects in the material. But since the foundation remains, we must endure the deficiencies and let them pass, as human." [299] Micanzio noted Sarpi's recognition that every age in the history of the church, including the first, had been imperfect; Sarpi had always taught "that perfection and total purity are the end toward which the faithful man, and Holy Church itself, strive, not the way through which they labor." [300] The church militant was, in Sarpi's eyes, far different from the church triumphant; and it seemed to him essential to avoid the sentimentality—so common in Rome—that tended to confuse them.

A major difference between the two churches was structural: the church triumphant was doubtless one body in Christ, but the church militant was distinctly not. On this point Sarpi represented, against the ecclesiastical centralism of the Counter Reformation, the position of earlier Renaissance thinkers for whom the ideal of formal Christian unity had seemed an unrealistic and even a dangerous illusion. Indeed, visible unity held no attraction for Sarpi. We have already noted his identification of the church with the community of believers. Translated into those concrete and particular terms which to Sarpi were alone relevant to the human condition on earth, this meant the identification of churches with actual human communities: with urban republics like Venice, for example, or national monarchies like France and England. It also meant a wide range of local variation. Sarpi held, as we have seen, that only the general principles of Christian teaching had been divinely ordained; their detailed application might properly vary according to local need, which naturally could only be determined locally.[301] "What is useful to one state is not useful to another," he wrote, with particular application to religious matters. "The safety of this domain requires that religion should be kept inviolate in all its parts, avoiding every change and novelty of any kind whatsoever." [302]

As canonist of the Venetian government, he accordingly devoted himself to defending the local administration so long characteristic of the Venetian church, but with a clearer awareness than earlier generations of its larger implications. He waged the struggle on various levels, first of all on the issue of papal authority in the local church. Thus he denied (as during the interdict) that papal bulls could be published locally without the consent of the government, and he rejected the notion that the pope could authorize his nuncio to

[299] Letter to Groslot, Aug. 4, 1609, Busnelli, I, 88.
[300] *Vita*, pp. 160–161.
[301] *Trattato delle materie beneficiarie*, SG, p. 46.
[302] *Sopra l'officio dell'inquisizione*, SG, p. 188.

assume responsibilities over the church in the state to which he was assigned. On both matters Venetian practice was immediately at stake, but Sarpi pointed to precedents in other Catholic states; his ultimate appeal was thus to the traditional structure of the church universal.[303] He also fought on particular questions. He objected to the drain of ecclesiastical income from the local community to Rome;[304] he was concerned to prevent appeals to ecclesiastical courts outside the state;[305] he insisted that the Venetian Inquisition was a local agency not subject to Roman direction, that its officers should be natives, and that local heretics should not be sent to Rome for trial.[306] Above all he resisted Roman appointments to Venetian benefices, a practice deeply subversive of his conception of the church as a local institution.[307] His failure to obtain adequate Venetian support on this issue troubled him acutely.[308]

For Sarpi the church universal, so far as it existed at all in this world, was thus simply a federation of local churches which properly varied considerably from each other. Among these churches he obviously included those of Venice, France, and Spain. But although he certainly did not deny some primacy of honor (though not of jurisdiction) to the Roman church, it is by no means clear that he regarded communion with Rome as the test of membership in the church universal. His close relations with the English suggest that he considered the Anglican communion a part of the true church, and it seems likely that he accepted in the same fashion, as true churches, every Protestant group that was, according to his conception, identifiable with a political community or, like the Huguenots, accepted such identification in principle: all Protestantism, that is, except radical sectarianism. It appears to me incorrect, therefore, to attribute his interest in Protestantism only to the political needs of Venice, although these undoubtedly were a large factor in it. Developments among Protestants, as members of the true church, were entirely relevant to his own concerns and predilections as a Christian. He followed Protestant debates over theological issues, like those

---

[303] *Scrittura sopra l'autorità della nunziatura*, in *Opere*, Suppl. II, 127–129.

[304] *Trattato delle materie beneficiarie*, SG, pp. 84–85.

[305] *Considerazioni sopra la elezione di D. Ottavio Salvioni alla Pieve di S. Giuliano di Venezia, il quale era stato riprovato dal Patriarca, ed aveva appellato al Nunzio Apostolico*, in *Opere*, Suppl. II, 174–178.

[306] This is the central thesis of *Sopra l'officio dell'inquisizione*, SG, pp. 119–212

[307] *Trattato delle materie beneficiarie*, SG, p. 105; letters to Leschassier, Oct. 14 and Dec. 22, 1609, and April 27, 1610, Ulianich, pp. 58–59, 62, 76.

[308] Letters to Leschassier, Sept. 29 and Oct. 14, 1609, Ulianich, pp. 56–58.

raised by Arminianism, because of his own interest in a religion of grace; and he condemned some Protestant disputation not only as a source of political division but also because it recalled to him the irrelevant speculation and word-mongering of the schoolmen.[309]

He was even more deeply concerned with the larger issues Protestantism raised for the nature of the church. From this standpoint Protestantism seemed a hopeful development. As reaction against papal tyranny, it represented the decentralization and pluralism he considered appropriate to the human condition and the church militant.[310] This is probably why, although he supported the political unity of the Protestant world against Spain and the pope, he displayed little interest in the ecumenical impulses of the age. Indeed, he was probably antagonistic to contemporary movements toward religious unity and reconciliation with Rome, which in any case his practical sense considered unrealistic. The reconciliation of the Protestant world to Rome would only have reversed what he considered the most salutary development of the age.

Sarpi's conception of a spiritual church based on the political community also solved for him the problem of the relations between the two powers. At times, it is true, he wrote as though he considered them not only separate but parallel, like the pilot and captain of a warship.[311] But his more considered view was rather different and indeed closely resembled that of his opponents. As he declared in the course of stating the nature of his disagreement with Gallican theorists, a parallel relationship opened the way to conflict. To prevent this, a single supreme authority was necessary in every state; the sovereign prince must make all decisions affecting his subjects, including those concerned with the operation of the church. But the prince's administration of the church did not compromise its independence, in Sarpi's view, because the spirituality of the church placed it, in the nature of things, beyond the reach of the temporal power. The external machinery of the church was not to be confused with the spiritual community of believers.[312]

The visible instruments which the church, itself a spiritual body, wielded

---

[309] Cf. Cozzi, "Sarpi tra Canaye e Casaubon," pp. 97–99.

[310] Cf. letter to Groslot, July 22, 1608, Busnelli, I, 23: ". . . forse Dio in questo secolo vuole, con un mezzo più dolce del tentato nel secolo passato, estinguere la tirannide." In a letter to Gillot, May 12, 1609, Ulianich, p. 131, Sarpi remarked that, Germany and other nations having thrown off the papal yoke in the previous century, the whole weight of oppression was now directed against Venice.

[311] As in the *consulto* of 1608, quoted by Francescon, pp. 111–112, n. 3.

[312] Letters to Gillot, Sept. 29 and Dec. 8, 1609, Ulianich, pp. 137–142.

in individual states were thus, in Sarpi's view, the particular responsibility of the princes who otherwise governed their people. All ecclesiastical property (clearly not in itself spiritual) he considered a part of the temporal order and therefore the responsibility of its supreme authority.[313] All matters having to do with the external actions of men regardless of status were similarly within the province of the prince;[314] and this meant not only his exclusive jurisdiction over all subjects but also his duty to protect the interests of the local church against all who might injure it: among these not only laymen but also clergy, including external assailants in the Curia.[315] Sarpi was thus eager to vest final authority for ecclesiastical discipline in the secular magistrate.

He was sometimes explicit that the authority of the prince in ecclesiastical affairs was a dimension of political obligation. Thus he observed that the ruler's power to discipline the clergy was to be exercised not for the church but for the state, since ecclesiastical abuses bring with them deleterious political effects, or that princes were obligated to oppose religious novelty because of the disorders it customarily produced.[316] But Sarpi seems also to have favored an active role for the prince in the church on another ground—as the representative of the community which, in its spiritual dimension, constituted the church. Many of Sarpi's pronouncements appear therefore to be based on the assumption that the prince is an ecclesiastical as well as a political functionary, the supreme administrator of the church as well as of the state. Thus, he wrote, it was a mistake to suppose "that the particular care for religion is the property of the ministers of the church, just as temporal government belongs to the magistrate. It is not suitable for the prince to exercise either the one or the other: he should rather direct both, see that no one fails in his duty, and remedy the defects of the ministers. This is the responsibility of the prince, in the matter of religion as in every other part of the government." [317] There was a sense, of course, in which no prince, any more than any other man ecclesiastical or lay, could affect

---

[313] *Consulti* of 1609, quoted by Francescon, pp. 145, n. 3, and 146, n. 1. See also Sarpi, *Scrittura sopra un caso di truffa*, in *Opere*, Suppl. II, 126. For the magistrate's responsibility over church buildings, see Francescon, p. 248, n. 3.

[314] Thus in his letter to Gillot, Sept. 29, 1609, Ulianich, p. 137, Sarpi argued that insofar as the church was identified with the clergy, it was "part of the earthly republic" and subject to its rulers. See also various *consulti* quoted by Francescon, pp. 139–140, n. 2, 153, 177–178, n. 2, 229, n. 1, 230, n. 1.

[315] *Scrittura sopra l'offizio dell'inquisizione*, in *Opere*, Suppl. II, 108.

[316] Letter to Gillot, Sept. 15, 1609, Ulianich, p. 135; *Sopra l'officio dell'inquisizione*, SG, pp. 153–154.

[317] *Sopra l'officio dell'inquisizione*, SG, p. 154.

the church either for better or for worse. The ideal church, wholly spiritual, remained invulnerable to his actions. But in the church militant as in politics, although he might be advised on general principles by the ecclesiastical ministry, the prince remained the supreme magistrate because all governance, of the earth earthy, based rather on law than on love, belonged to him.

Sarpi thought that several peoples had managed to realize this ideal in some degree, notably the Greeks. Unlike the clergy of the Latin West, he observed, the Greeks had fully accepted the Pauline obligation of temporal obedience to the prince.[318] They had also accepted his administrative authority "even in what pertains to ecclesiastical discipline." [319] On the essential issue of ecclesiastical organization and authority which continued to divide East and West and which he considered still unresolved,[320] Sarpi clearly preferred the Greek position; and he disapproved of the insistence of Rome on acting as judge in its own cause.[321] As *consultore* to his government he generally defended the rights of its Greek subjects to religious independence from Rome.

In the West he also discerned in the Gallican church many characteristics of an authentic ecclesiastical polity. Alone among churches in communion with Rome, he wrote, that of France retained "some vestige of ancient liberty"; its cause was that of the church universal; the pattern in France, he suggested, might be the means God had devised (less radical than Protestantism in the previous century) "to extinguish tyranny" in his own time.[322] France for Sarpi signified genuine freedom; she had been the sole champion of liberty in Europe for centuries; her *parlement* was a "seminary of sound doctrine"; her concordats, the resumption of traditional rights, suggested that she was advancing while the rest of the Catholic world had been losing ground.[323] Accordingly Sarpi studied Gallican treatises eagerly (though not always agreeing with them) in hopes that they might be useful to Venice,[324] and he frequently appealed to the French church for precedents supporting Venetian claims.[325]

---

[318] *Ibid.*, p. 177.

[319] *Scrittura sopra le cause de'Greci*, in *Opere*, Suppl. II, 142.

[320] *Sopra l'officio dell'inquisizione*, *SG*, pp. 177–178.

[321] *Scrittura sopra le cause de'Greci*, in *Opere*, Suppl. II, 143ff.

[322] Letters to Groslot, July 22 and Sept. 16, 1608, and Feb. 17, 1609, Busnelli, I, 34, 36, 56.

[323] Letters to Gillot, Dec. 3, 1608, and to Leschassier, Sept. 4, 1607, and May 13, 1608, Ulianich, pp. 129, 3, 12.

[324] Cf. his letter to Foscarini, Oct. 13, 1610, *Aevum*, XI (1937), 320. Ulianich, p. xlii, redates this letter 1608.

[325] As in *Delle contribuzioni de'chierici*, *SG*, p. 243.

But Venice was the firing line on which God had immediately stationed Sarpi; and the cause of Venice remained not only that of all sovereign states but also of the universal church. As we have seen, he was frequently dismayed after the interdict by the failure of Venice to defend with sufficient vigilance and resolution the ideal pattern which had been evolved through her long history. Gasparo Contarini had merely hinted at doubts about the future; and if Paruta was thrown on the defensive, he had still been ready to reiterate the myth of an ideal polity. But Sarpi's faith in the timeless perfections of the Republic had clearly disintegrated. No state, he felt compelled to advise his government, was immune from the most serious defects, including even the kingdoms of Cyrus and Alexander, of the most heroic rulers of antiquity, and of Saint Louis, the holiest king of the Christian era; nor was it proper "to assume that the Republic is exempt from the conditions of human existence." [326]

Nevertheless Venice, although subject to decay and now seriously threatened with extinction, continued to represent Sarpi's ideal both politically and ecclesiastically; and, whatever his disappointment on various occasions, he remained devoted to her. Her civic perfection was for him the basis of her religious excellence. Every Venetian retained his general devotion to liberty, even though some might be less wise than others on how best to preserve it, as he once noted.[327] The stability of her political institutions (a point on which Venice was much superior to France)[328] was a constant source of strength and a cause for hope. It meant that the fate of Venice did not depend on the accidents of leadership, and even the death of Leonardo Donà in 1612, though a serious loss, made no fundamental difference. "The republic is so well ordered," Sarpi wrote, that "the same governance continues, the same ends, the same conceptions." [329] Meanwhile the unique stability of Venetian society was supported by a profound antipathy to change. The "natural instinct" of the Republic, he remarked, was "to retain old and tried things"; and this instinct was now the essential source of resistance to Rome.[330] Sarpi's confidence from time to time

[326] *Sulla publicazione di scritture malediche contra il governo, SG*, p. 223.
[327] Letter to Leschassier, Nov. 25, 1608, Ulianich, p. 31.
[328] Letter to Leschassier, Dec. 23, 1608, Ulianich, p. 33.
[329] Letter to Achatius von Dohna, Oct. 19, 1612, Busnelli, II, 197; cf. letter to Groslot, Oct. 23, 1612, Busnelli, I, 247.
[330] *Sopra l'officio dell'inquisizione, SG*, p. 139. Cf. conversation with Dohna, July 28, 1608, Busnelli, II, 123.

wavered, but Venice continued to represent not only his political but, like France and the Greeks, his ecclesiastical ideal.

It is against the background of these conceptions that we must understand Sarpi's profound disapproval of the Counter Reformation, which had for him not only failed to accomplish genuine reform but was fundamentally subversive of true religion. In his view, true reform depended on the retention of the clergy in their original, spiritual responsibilities, not the effort to assume authority in the temporal realm; on the maintenance of the essential bond between the church and the particular human communities of which it was the spiritual expression; on local autonomy rather than centralization; on the submission of pope and Curia to the same canonical restraints they proposed to impose on others; on the limitation, not the extension, of power. The pope, in this view, must be made to rule the church according to its earliest traditions and under law, in much the same way that the doge ruled Venice, as the constitutional monarch of a spiritual society in which sovereignty was delegated from below.

But the Counter Reformation seemed to Sarpi to have taken a different path. Profoundly contemptuous of tradition, it ignored the time-honored customs of local communities. In its insistence on the unlimited authority of the pope, it was fundamentally lawless. Above all it was driven by an unbounded ambition to rule the world. Sarpi appears to have discerned in it, indeed, no genuine spiritual concern. The centralizing policies of the Curia he explained simply as an instance of "the natural inclination of all men to command as much as they can" and to expand a limited into a universal jurisdiction.[331] In the concern of Rome to limit Christian trade with the infidel he perceived not honest zeal for the faith but an eagerness "to dominate and to subjugate the secular power, and to make some good profit." [332] The papacy, in his view, was merely attempting to repeat the ancient Roman conquest of the civilized world; it proposed, like the antique emperors, to combine political with spiritual dominion. And in this dubious interest it was prepared to exploit charges of heresy, excommunication, the disciplines of the confessional, appeals, and masses of dishonest scholarship— the whole arsenal of the Counter Reformation was dedicated to the same discreditable end. Fundamental to the entire enterprise was its corrupt

---

[331] *Sopra l'officio dell'inquisizione*, SG, pp. 167, 206. Cf. *Sopra le patenti dell'inquisitore*, in *Opere*, Suppl. II, 103.

[332] *Sopra l'officio dell'inquisizione*, SG, p. 181.

ecclesiology based on a deliberate confusion of realms. In the words of Micanzio: "The court of Rome neither thinks nor will think on religion further than as a secret of state and dominion and as wholly having respect thereunto." [333] This, then, was what the medieval conception of the church as government had finally come to.

Sarpi was inclined to deny that Rome had made much progress even in the reform of obvious abuses, for example nepotism, a practice by which Venetians had regularly professed to be shocked. Paul V, he wrote, "expects to enrich his family, and this is the main point of his administration." [334] He attributed the mediocrity of recent appointments in the Sacred College to financial motives: the Curia would get large sums for offices vacated by the new cardinals.[335] Annates he denounced as mere simony in disguise.[336] Meanwhile, as long as the Curia preferred "art" to "reformation," [337] politics to religion, the genuine needs of the church went unsatisfied. In 1608 Sarpi noted that conditions in the church had been far happier half a century earlier, that is, before the Counter Reformation had begun to gather force.[338] That whole movement had evidently resulted only in the precipitate decline of true religion: "The things that have occurred have rather caused dissolution than reformation." [339] Papal tactics, he observed, had turned out to be "a way not to make Catholics but only to cause one religion to be eliminated and none introduced." [340] Thus the Counter Reformation was for Sarpi not merely a danger to political life. It was also, and in part because it imperiled the liberty of states, profoundly subversive of the Christian faith.

For a combination of reasons, therefore, Sarpi dedicated his life after the interdict to fighting against the Counter Reformation. Positively he was fighting, in the first place, for Venice, for her rights as a free republic and the values she incorporated. In this sense Sarpi continued to represent the

---

[333] Letter to Sir William Cavendish, Feb. 1622, quoted by Gabrielli, pp. 228–229.

[334] Letter to Groslot, Sept. 1, 1609, Busnelli, I, 93. See also the letters of June 23 and Sept. 12, 1609, to Hotman de Villiers, Ulianich, pp. 186–187, and to Castrino, Oct. 13, 1608, and June 23, 1609, Busnelli, II, 5, 41.

[335] Letter to Castrino, Dec. 9, 1608, Busnelli, II, 14.

[336] *Trattato delle materie beneficiarie*, SG, p. 83.

[337] Letter to Leschassier, Dec. 22, 1609, Ulianich, p. 62: "Ita est, ut dicis: ars est, non reformatio."

[338] Letter to Leschassier, Oct. 13, 1608, Ulianich, pp. 26–27.

[339] Letter to Groslot, Sept. 27, 1611, Busnelli, I, 195.

[340] Letter to Groslot, Jan. 20, 1609, Busnelli, I, 61.

long tradition of civic politics championed by the great Renaissance republics. But he fought also as the advocate of what he considered the true conception of the church and its mission, consistent with the political ideals of the Renaissance, against the false as represented by Rome. In this respect Sarpi may also properly be taken as an instance of the mentality of the religious wars. He shared in the militancy, the single-mindedness, and the ungenerous spirit regularly provoked by ideological conflict, qualities not altogether consistent with the mentality of the Renaissance. At the same time the two dimensions of his concern reinforced each other in many ways.

They may both be seen in his approach to his more immediate field of action against the enemy, international politics. Here, against the universalist and religious preoccupations of the Counter Reformation, which seemed to him a disguise for the interests of Spain and the worldly ambitions of the papacy, he asserted the particularistic and political (though not necessarily unreligious) conceptions of the Renaissance. What he dreaded above all was the imposition, through Spanish arms, of what he significantly described as "an Octavian peace"; the imperial *pax romana*, the nostalgic ideal so dear to Europeans since the fall of Rome, meant for him precisely the most dreadful of political arrangements, a monolith in which all the achievements of such particular communities as Venice must surely perish.[341]

At the same time he was fully aware that no state could survive if it ignored developments elsewhere. Although he abominated any conception of Europe as a unified polity, he fully recognized that the Continent was a system of states whose actions profoundly concerned one another; and his understanding of this system continued to be determined by the familiar Renaissance conception of balance. Its order was not to be preserved through the application of those universal principles dear to the Spanish Dominicans and to his own contemporary Grotius, but by the manipulation of forces. Sarpi's political world, like Machiavelli's, is ruled by power, not by law.

The problem of Venice, as he clearly saw, arose primarily from the absence of any adequate counterweight to Spain.[342] Spain could thus hold the initiative in European affairs. Sarpi ruefully noted the "great Spanish felicity, that [Spain] not only freely wills war and peace, but also holds every one in suspense, forced to await the good pleasure of their declarations." [343] The aim of Venetian policy, he felt, was to find allies and so to

[341] See his letters to Castrino, March 31 and April 28, 1609, Busnelli, II, 28, 31.
[342] As in his letter to Castrino, June 8, 1610, Busnelli, II, 88.
[343] Letter to S. Contarini, May 30, 1615, Castellani, p. 34.

restore the balance of power: if the French were unreliable, then the English, the Dutch, the Germans, the Swiss, even the Turks.[344] Papal prohibitions against Catholic alliance with heretics he repudiated as another recent innovation based on the political ambitions of Rome.[345] But if the notion of an equilibrium suggests the attitudes of the Renaissance, at other times Sarpi favored quite a different conception. He wrote frequently, to Gallicans as well as Huguenots, of what might be hoped for from a great crusade in which, through an invasion of Italy, all antipapal forces, Protestant as well as Catholic, would finally put an end to the temporal ambitions of Rome.[346] The prospect of war did not altogether please him,[347] but there is perhaps more than resignation in his suggestion that, if a general European conflict should turn out to be "for the increase of [God's] glory and the advancement of the church of God, or at least the purgation of the world, we should not complain." [348] The multitude desires peace, he wrote on another occasion, "but the wise would like war." [349] Such words also suggest a reason for the decline of his influence in Venice.

Unable to procure so drastic a remedy for the sickly world, yet confident that God in his own good time must restore it to health, Sarpi was compelled to bide his time and meanwhile in some measure to conceal his hopes. Some of his letters during this period are remarkable for their candor, and concealment did not come easily for him. As he confided to Jacques Gillot, survival in Italy now required every man to wear a mask; although he naturally loved openness, gaiety, and freedom, he had to admit that he was no exception, and he compared himself to a chameleon.[350] To Christoph von Dohna he confided, "I never speak falsehoods, but I do not speak the truth to everyone";[351] and in a letter to Leschassier he made the

[344] Letters to Groslot, Sept. 25, 1612, and April 28, 1609, Busnelli, I, 244, 78. See also his letter to Foscarini, June 23, 1609, *Aevum*, XI (1937), 278–279, where he compares the reliability of various possible allies.

[345] In *Che sia lecito*, in *Opere*, Suppl. II, 117–119, Sarpi noted the employment of Turkish forces by Julius II and of Protestants by Paul IV.

[346] For examples see letters to Groslot, April 27, 1610, and Oct. 23, 1612 (Busnelli, I, 120, 248) and to Leschassier, Sept. 14, 1610 (Ulianich, p. 92).

[347] Thus he saw it as a catastrophe for Italy in his letter to Leschassier, March 2, 1610, Ulianich, p. 72.

[348] Letter to Groslot, May 12, 1609, Busnelli, I, 80.

[349] Letter to Groslot, Nov. 9, 1610, Busnelli, I, 151.

[350] May 12, 1609, Ulianich, p. 133.

[351] Conversation of July 28, 1608, Busnelli, II, 123.

point that the amount of truth appropriate for disclosure depended on circumstances.[352]

But although action against the enemies of Venice and the church was immediately impracticable, Sarpi was by no means wasting his time. "I do not rest from making myself every day both more ready and more fit, in case the occasion for action should present itself," he remarked. "I am like the artificer who, in a time unsuitable for his work, furnishes himself with materials for the opportunity; if it should not come, the accumulation can serve someone else." [353] Thus, while he refrained from disclosing his real thoughts and carefully scrutinized the times for some divinely sent occasion, he stored up such resources for future action as his professional position permitted. With Gallican and Huguenot magistrates and scholars he exchanged legal opinions, books, and information about the contemporary scene; doubtless their accounts of events in the outside world were increasingly useful to him as his access to official sources of information in Venice grew more restricted. He was constantly deepening his legal and historical researches, collecting precedents, gathering evidence for future use.[354] Although often discouraged and at times convinced that he would not himself live to see the final victory,[355] he continued to feel useful. On this ground he declined a royal invitation to take refuge in England. To have fled from Venice would have been an admission of defeat, of the futility of continuing the struggle; and Sarpi remained a man of faith.[356] Meanwhile, as a gesture of confidence in the future, he was composing the *Istoria del Concilio Tridentino.*

[352] April 10, 1612, Ulianich, p. 109.
[353] Letter to Groslot, Nov. 11, 1608, Busnelli, I, 45.
[354] Cf. letter to Leschassier, Jan. 6, 1609, Ulianich, p. 35.
[355] Cf. letter to Castrino, March 31, 1609, Busnelli, II, 28–29.
[356] Cozzi, "Sarpi, l'anglicanesimo, e la *Historia*," p. 573.

·X·

Renaissance Liberty and the Uses of the Past: Sarpi's History of the Council of Trent

The idea in Rome is to have us all one by one, and they let it be understood that they will have me dead. But this will not be done without God, and perhaps I will do them more harm dead than alive.

SARPI TO GROSLOT DE L'ISLE, August 26, 1608

ALTHOUGH, under repeated blows and constant pressure, the republican morale of Venice was now irretrievably declining, it was still to find expression in one of the great masterpieces of European historiography: Paolo Sarpi's *Istoria del Concilio Tridentino*. For this vast work was far more than the polemical venture into ecclesiastical history it is now generally considered. It drew on the whole range of political attitudes and historiographical advances so apparent in the compositions of the great Florentines and more recently attractive to the *giovani* of Venice, and its enormous popularity enabled it to transmit the values of Renaissance politics to later generations in transalpine Europe. Furthermore, under the stimulus of recent events it applied the historical perspective of the Renaissance deliberately and systematically to the church, the one area of investigation where free historical examination was most likely to be resisted. In this way Sarpi significantly extended the scope of the European historical consciousness.

During the last decades of the sixteenth century, as we have seen, the political culture of the Venetian patriciate had grown increasingly empirical and historical. The old myth of an eternal and essentially unchanging Venice, which in principle denied the absolute sovereignty of change in all things human, was never attacked directly; but it received less and less attention as Venetians addressed themselves to the task of understanding the constantly shifting political scene. The historicization of Venetian culture had been nourished from various directions, among them a conventional desire to display the virtues of those who had gone before for the emulation of young Venetians and the need to glorify and strengthen the state in time of danger. But, following views publicized by Patrizi, Venetian historiography had tended to throw off the rhetorical and ethical preoccupations of the earlier part of the century. It demanded truth rather than a hortatory style, and it aimed less at the inculcation of individual and civic virtue than at the formation of a political prudence through the vicarious experience of affairs.

These tendencies were to be fully realized in the work of Sarpi, but his accomplishment as a historian can be fully appreciated only against the more general background of the growing Venetian preoccupation with history. This had found expression in the resuscitation, with the appointment of Paruta as historian of the Republic, of a moribund official historiography. The government was henceforth careful to keep the post of official historian actively filled. Paruta was immediately succeeded, on his death in 1598, by Andrea Morosini; and then, in 1620, by Nicolò Contarini. Both, it will be noted, had been prominently identified with the *giovani*, and their appointments signified the importance with which the government continued to regard the composition of Venetian history. Both men also wrote voluminously; and in various ways their works supply some perspective for Sarpi's great history, which was written at the same time as much of Morosini's work and followed closely by that of Contarini.

Morosini's *Historia veneta*, which carries the history of the Republic to 1615, resembles Paruta's history in a number of ways. Based on much careful research, it pays some attention to internal affairs. Thus it records the foundation of the public bank in 1587 and the rebuilding in 1591 of the Rialto bridge in stone.[1] Morosini's particular praise for Leonardo Donà suggests a persistent loyalty to the ideals of his generation;[2] and in a brief tribute to the Venetian constitution he noted that the opportunity for public service was open to any virtuous man who loved his country.[3] He also hinted at Venetian sympathy, and his own, for the tragic fate of the Florentine Republic.[4] And his sense of the European context of Venetian history remained strong. He

---

[1] VII, 61, 144–145. Cf. V, 2–3, where he recognizes the need to describe internal affairs.

[2] VI, 681; VII, 465. He also composed a life of Donà, *Leonardi Donati, Venetiarum Principis, vita* (Venice, 1628).

[3] VII, 6.

[4] Cf. his treatment of the events of 1529–1530, V, 341, 348–349.

gave considerable attention to developments in France; and he was much impressed by Elizabeth of England, under whom, as he recognized, that nation had become a great commercial power.[5]

Morosini also shared the reservations of the *giovani* toward the political and institutional dimensions of the papacy. Like Paruta he saw Leo X as dominated by pride, ambition, and an abiding hatred of Venice.[6] He attacked Paul IV as a nepotist and warmonger, though admitting the sanctity of his early pontificate;[7] and he criticized Gregory XIV for obstinacy, severity in asserting his jurisdictional claims, and a general inclination "to balance everything not by the measure of the public good but with the subtlety of the legal ordinances of which he was a master." [8] He described in detail the gross political manipulations preceding the election of Clement VIII, after which his conclusion appears ironical rather than pious: "In the middle of this tempest of human passions, the omnipotent divine light shone forth which, as it is our duty to believe, sheds its ray on the elections of the highest pontiffs." [9] He emphasized the fearful and suspicious nature of Paul V and his deficient grasp of politics.[10] Because the opposite had patently occurred, he remarked that a pope "should undertake nothing with pride, but should behave toward other potentates with prudence joined to love, and should nourish their zeal and respect for the Holy See with an obliging behavior." [11] He defended the refusal of Venice to participate in a general crusade against the Protestants;[12] though moderate and discreet, he told the story of the interdict from the Venetian point of view and represented its outcome as a triumph both for "liberty and the dignity of the principate";[13] and he even included guarded praise of Sarpi.[14] The Curia was anxious to block publication of Morosini's work, although in this it was unsuccessful.[15]

---

[5] VII, 276–277.
[6] V, 6, 24–27.
[7] VI, 74ff.
[8] VII, 39.
[9] VII, 149–150.
[10] VII, 307–308.
[11] VI, 668, in connection with the disputes between Venice and Gregory XIV.
[12] As V, 358–359.
[13] VII, 398. Morosini's account of the interdict is, however, a rather superficial and essentially diplomatic narrative.
[14] VII, 347.
[15] F. Stefani, "Andrea Morosini," *AV*, Ser. 1, II (1871), 220–222. It was, however, put on the Index.

In other respects, nevertheless, Morosini's *Historia veneta* suggests the changing mood of the Republic during the period after the interdict, and even some reversal in the tendencies of Venetian historiography. Morosini made a point of attributing the long survival of the Republic in the first place to divine protection and only secondarily to her excellent institutions;[16] and although he did not in practice revert to providential explanation, he exhibited a sensitivity, such as we have not previously much encountered among Venetian writers, to the religious importance of recent developments in Rome. He was aware that major reforms were in progress, and he generally approved of them. He represented the reform decrees of Paul IV, though too severe, as the response to a genuine need;[17] and he applauded Pius V for humility, sanctity of life, and solicitude for the church's improvement.[18] His reservations about Gregory XIV were balanced by a recognition of how that pontiff "had applied himself with the greatest fervor to the propagation and decorum of Christian belief, making provision not only to nourish good seeds where they flourished but also to propagate them in distant lands, and in some also that had been attacked by the heretical infestation." Thus, Morosini noted, Gregory had established colleges in Rome "for the education of youth, to instill them with correct doctrine and religion"; and such establishments had spread, he noted with evident approval, not only into Germany, Poland, and other Italian cities, but also into Venice and her domains. Morosini evidently did not share Sarpi's antipathy to the educational agencies of the Counter Reformation.[19] His treatment of Protestantism was also notably harsh, though as much because it was a source of political disorder as for its erroneous doctrines.[20]

The attitude Morosini chose to express toward the Council of Trent is also quite different from Sarpi's and thus gives some further indication of the latter's growing isolation. Morosini presented the Council, on the whole, as a religious event, to which he attributed considerable importance. He expressed particular satisfaction with the concluding session, which, he reported, had convened "at the petition of the Christian princes with incredible and universal joy." [21] It had finally decreed "many things relating

[16] VII, 6. For Morosini as historian see also Cozzi, "Pubblica storiografia," pp. 278–292.
[17] Cf. VI, 150–151.
[18] VI, 218, 518.
[19] VII, 39.
[20] Cf. his treatment of the Huguenots, for example VI, 154, 172–173; VII, 173–175.
[21] VI, 175–176.

to the repair of the decayed discipline of the church," and it had done so—
for Morosini apparently a measure of its success—"without making any
mention at all of papal authority." [22] Furthermore he took some pains to
associate Venice at every point with the success of the Council. He reported
her demands for its final convocation, her pressure for its continuation when
even the pope wanted it suspended, her support for its decrees, and most
remarkably her staunch defense of papal authority against the attacks of
foreign prelates.[23] Morosini, or at least the government on whose behalf
he wrote, seems now to have been prepared to accept papal leadership with
an appearance of enthusiasm long alien to the Venetian patriciate.

Of equal interest are Morosini's attitudes to the writing of history. He
seems to have viewed his task far more rhetorically than had been usual in the
previous generation. He wrote in Latin, and he insisted that the historian
needed "not only practical experience and the knowledge of affairs, but also
an inexpressible abundance and strength of eloquence." His views on the
purpose of history resembled those of early sixteenth-century Venetians
rather than of Patrizi's disciples. His own aim, as he declared at the beginning
of his work, was to enhance "the advantage and the splendor of the fatherland
by reviving fleeting memory, and to recall from oblivion the famous deeds
of our most worthy forefathers." [24] The sentiment apparently reflected his
own position, for it also infused an account he composed privately of
Venetian participation in the Crusades, another expression of his piety. Men
go to much expense to recover fragments of statues from ancient ruins, he
observed in that work. "Why," he asked, "should one not do the same in
investigating the great actions that have been performed in past centuries in
the theater of this world? For from these not only is matter for delight
offered to the eyes and curiosity satisfied, but by virtue the minds of citizens
are excited and efficaciously persuaded to embrace every glorious enterprise." [25] Morosini's rhetorical bent had advantages for his history. His
dramatic sense, for example, was more highly developed than Paruta's.
A number of his sections are carefully arranged to end with great climactic
events such as the sack of Rome or the settlement of the interdict. Morosini's *Historia veneta* thus seems a much grander and more polished work than
Paruta's *Historia vinetiana*. Yet it also lacks the sense, apparent from time to

[22] VI, 201.
[23] VI, 156, 199, 205–206, 188–189.
[24] V, 2–3.
[25] *L'imprese et espeditioni di Terra Santa, et l'acquisto fatto dell'Imperio di Constantinopoli dalla Serenissima Republica di Venetia* (Venice, 1627), p. 3.

time in Paruta, of causal relationships and the general movement of events. There is, therefore, a discernible weakening of historical consciousness and republican militancy in Morosini, which was partly personal but was perhaps also related to the declining militancy of Venice in these years. Although the government insisted on publishing the *Historia veneta* in 1623 over the protests of the nuncio, it disregarded the advice of Fulgenzio Micanzio, Sarpi's successor as canonist of Venice, that Morosini's work should be published along with Sarpi's *Istoria dell'Interdetto*.[26]

But the *Historie venetiane* of Nicolò Contarini, composed during the next decade, vigorously reasserted *giovani* attitudes[27] and suggests that Sarpi was not alone in his views, even though fewer men now shared them. The anticurialism of the work, its highly personal quality, and its lack of polish no doubt all figured in the failure of the government to publish it, although it was well known and highly regarded in some circles.[28]

Contarini was even more concerned than Paruta with the truthfulness of history, a preoccupation of the Venetian school at least since Patrizi; and he commiserated with contemporary historians, reduced, as he put it, to a wretched slavery by the universal demand of the powerful for adulation.[29] His concern for truth was also accompanied by an insistence on the particularity of the historial realm which, as he recognized, was at odds with the demand for formal elegance and other qualities calculated to please readers. But the truthfulness and utility of history had to come first for Contarini. "Since in many things I shall descend to particulars which neither convey greatness to the writing nor delight the minds of readers," he wrote, "I will declare that I do not wish to avoid criticism. For I am persuaded of this truth: that whereas specious generalities give a useless pleasure, and sententious maxims can easily be formulated by men who lack knowledge and have had little experience, particular information dictated by experience and long attention, though disagreeable to some, is what solidly teaches the precepts of life." [30] With Contarini we have returned to the mental world of the great Florentine historians, toward which the Venetians had slowly been moving. Sarpi took much the same position.

Contarini's history is not altogether different from those of his official

[26] See Cozzi, *Contarini*, pp. 225–226.
[27] In what follows I have relied on Cozzi's thorough analysis of this work, pp. 197–227. My references are to the sections printed in his Appendix, pp. 305–380.
[28] Cozzi, *Contarini*, pp. 200ff.; cf. Foscarini, *Della letteratura veneziana*, p. 277.
[29] *Historie venetiane*, in Cozzi, Appendix, pp. 310–311.
[30] *Ibid.*, p. 311.

predecessors. Like Paruta and Morosini he paid close attention to the European context of Venetian history.[31] He shared Morosini's admiration for Elizabeth of England; at the same time he was also far more openly hostile to Spain. Possibly for this reason he expressed considerable interest in the Dutch, possible allies whose liberty he praised. Like Paruta he emphasized the importance of commerce to his own Republic, though he was compelled to recognize not only the depredations of corsairs but also the damage now done by foreign competition. He was aware too of the contribution of industry to Venetian prosperity, and he mentioned the drainage projects expanding agricultural production on the mainland.[32] He shared the common detestation of Protestantism, like Morosini stressing its contribution to political disorder.[33]

In other respects Contarini was rather different. Although he continued to take satisfaction in the independence of Venice,[34] he could no longer feel that tranquility about her future still generally possible for Paruta and even for Morosini. Long experience had taught him that civil life was like "the tempests of the sea," [35] and the imperfections of human nature, its vulnerability to the temptations of indolence, pleasure, and luxury, made all human institutions seem to him precarious and the felicitous intervals of human history inevitably transitory. A fundamental pessimism about man had altogether destroyed, for Contarini, the dream of social perfection that had inspired so many generations of his countrymen.[36] Here too he resembled Sarpi.

His vision of the recent history of Catholicism was also at odds with that of Morosini. Almost nothing about the contemporary Roman church pleased him; he attacked not only its political role and its jurisdictional claims but also the spirit of its institutions and the quality of its piety.[37] The history of the church presented itself to him as little more than a long decline from primitive holiness into temporal ambition and worldliness which had reached its climax and become definitive in the Council of Trent. Proposed by pious men to renovate the church and reconcile Christians, the Council had

[31] Cf. pp. 309–310, where he insists on the necessity for this. See also Cozzi's remarks, pp. 205–207.

[32] Pp. 311–312, 363–364.

[33] See Cozzi, pp. 212–214.

[34] Cf. p. 317, where he represents Venice as the only independent state left in Italy.

[35] P. 309.

[36] Cf. p. 311.

[37] Cf. Cozzi, pp. 218–224.

accomplished largely the opposite for Contarini as for Sarpi. Contarini admitted that it appeared to have done much. It had "not only refuted all the dogmas of Luther and those of Zwingli or Calvin, which are called reformed, but it gave great vigor to the Inquisition and a strong commission to prelates, undertook to reform all the practices of the Roman Church, and confirmed the authority of popes above all past Councils." But "this attempt produced the same result as throwing many logs on the fire. And many, either persuaded by the preaching of innovators, who were everywhere very numerous in these times, or through self-interest, passed to the new religions." [38]

In addition to these official histories of Venice, Venetians contemporary with Sarpi also composed histories of other states, notable among them a widely read account of the Wars of the Roses by Gian Francesco Biondi, once secretary to Pietro Priuli in Paris and later a religious refugee in England, from whence he maintained a correspondence with his old friend Micanzio.[39] But the most popular of the Venetian secular histories of this period was the *Istoria delle querre civili di Francia* by Enrico Davila, published in Venice in 1630 but begun much earlier, perhaps before the interdict. A brief examination of various aspects of this work will also be useful to establish the political and historiographical context of Sarpi's masterpiece.

Davila composed his account of the French civil wars from a close personal experience.[40] He was born near Padua in 1576 but, when his father entered the service of Catherine de'Medici, he was taken as a child to France and brought up at the French court. As a young man he fought in the army of Henry IV, first against the Catholic League and later against Spain. Returning to Venice in 1599, he found military employment with the Republic during the interdict, and later he held various important posts, including the governorship of Zara and Brescia. In Venice he associated intimately with *giovani* leaders. Andrea Morosini described him as "equally dear to Mars and Minerva," and Davila dedicated his history to Domenico Molino. Its subject

---

[38] Quoted by Cozzi, pp. 219–220.

[39] See Gabrielli, "Bacone, la riforma e Roma," p. 237. For Sarpi's interest in Biondi, see his letters to Hotman de Villiers, Apr. 14, 1609, Ulianich, p. 183, and to Christoph von Dohna, Mar. 16 and Aug. 4, 1609, Busnelli, II, 144, 155. Cf. Wotton's letter introducing Biondi to James I, Jan. 16, 1609, Smith, I, 446–447; this indicates that Biondi bore messages from Sarpi to the English king. Biondi's history was entitled *L'Istoria delle querre civili d'Inghilterra tra le due Case di Lancastro, e Iorc* (Venice, 1637).

[40] For what follows see the preface to the six-volume edition of Milan, 1807, which I cite. This preface reproduces a short biography by Apostolo Zeno. I have attempted here only a brief introduction to certain themes in Davila's work.

particularly interested this group, and it reflects many of their attitudes and values.

Davila has occasionally been compared with Guicciardini,[41] and his work exhibits a high degree of historiographical sophistication. Thus, although it conventionally discerns in the French civil wars "great actions and notable enterprises that are marvelously adapted to give salutary lessons to whoever maturely considers them," it recognizes at the same time the difficulties in intellectual mastery of complex political phenomena. Davila admitted that he had to deal with a "true revolution so confused and tangled that the causes of many movements do not appear, the counsels behind many deliberations are not understood, and an infinity of things is unknown." It is evident that for Davila the didactic value of knowledge depended on both a strenuous investigation of events and, as he put it, their "orderly recollection and exposition." Although he made a good deal of the advantage deriving from his personal engagement in French affairs, which had enabled him to know much at first hand and "to penetrate to the first root of the most ancient and remote causes," he was also sensitive to the problem of bias. He was himself, he claimed, "far removed from those attachments that are accustomed to lead the pens of writers astray." He hoped, he wrote, "to be able to come close to the proper order and the natural explanation of those things which, through many years of practice in the chambers of kings and constant exposure in the front ranks of armies, I have myself learned by experience and action." [42] He tried to be critical of his sources. On one occasion, for example, he refused to accept the truth of a report that members of the nobility had conspired to murder the French king in 1559. Although, if true, this would have confirmed his distrust of aristocratic factions, he was forced to disregard it. "I cannot bring myself to affirm it," he declared, "only on the frequently false reports of rumor, which is often raised and infinitely exaggerated, sometimes by fear, sometimes by the artifice of men." [43] His purpose was to supply a responsible and orderly narrative that might, precisely because of its truth, be instructive about the actual workings of history.

But his narrative was far more than a bare chronicle of events: Davila was profoundly interested in causes, both immediate and remote. Like Guicciardini and other historians in his own generation, he regarded human egotism as the primary motive in political history, constantly destroying order and

[41] As by Fueter, *Historiographie moderne*, pp. 153–155.
[42] *Guerre civili di Francia*, I, 3–5.
[43] I, 76.

impelling change. And his concern with the subversion of domestic peace by aristocratic conspirators makes of his work a kind of national analogue to Machiavelli's analysis of Florentine history. The problems of France had all arisen, in his view, from the "emulations and enmities among the great, ready to break out upon any least occasion into open dissensions." [44] He described these with considerable skill, laying the stage for the major action that began when the death of Henry II and the minority of Francis II opened the path to disorder. In this entire section Davila's sense of the disparity between the professed and actual motives of men is keen.[45] Meanwhile his distaste for the nobility is balanced by his admiration for the prudent Catherine, with her flexibility and her fine Italian sense of the occasion,[46] and for the finesse of Henry IV.[47]

Davila's account of the French past is thus held together by the kinds of political insight we have encountered repeatedly both in Florence and in Venice. He makes few generalizations, but those that appear have a familiar ring. Thus his observation about the failure of the conspiracy of Amboise sounds like Machiavelli or Paruta: "Conspiracies entrusted to few persons of proven discretion and the most certain faith are often easily exposed before being carried out." [48] He also suggests some bias against political universalism. The Roman conquest of the world impressed him as the imposition of a general slavery, and in considering the remote European past his sympathy lay with those nations not absorbed into the ancient empire. Conversely he suggests some joy in the variety of peoples that emerged with the breakup of the Roman world.[49]

An unusually significant element in Davila's historical vision was his conviction that, in order properly to understand the civil wars in France, it was necessary not only to have a realistic grasp of human nature in general, but also to probe into the remote past of the French nation, especially its early institutions. Since the wars had arisen over the succession to the crown, this meant that Davila had to begin with the Franks, who had agreed "to

[44] I, 38.
[45] See, for example, the account of Condé's attempt to rally opposition to the Guises, I, 62–66, in which Davila places Condé's true and his professed motives side by side without comment.
[46] For example, I, 58, and above all the assessment in connection with her death, III, 316–319, in which Davila reveals some pride in Catherine as an Italian.
[47] For example, III, 447–448.
[48] I, 80.
[49] I, 5–7.

establish the form of their future government by universal consent." Recognizing that monarchy was best for "expansion of dominion and great acquisitions," they had decided on a king, chosen through heredity for the sake of order and stability.[50] We may discern here something of the reconstruction of the past recently performed by the Gallican antiquaries, but the idea of a government constitutionally limited from the beginning must also have been attractive to Venetians anxiously looking to France for alliance. Davila's friends were no doubt equally impressed by his insistence (somewhat at odds with the description of a nation torn by civil strife) that "after a course of twelve hundred years, the French people continues to the present in the uncorrupted manner of government which was established from its first beginnings with a legitimate and natural form . . . . In all ages, the first forms of government have been justly observed with religious veneration; neither the power of command nor the authority of the laws has lost anything of its first observance and ancient splendor in so long a course of time." [51] France was thus in some respects like Venice, and Davila's conception of the French constitution suggests again the tendency now to see Venice as less special than earlier generations had considered her.

His work is also remarkable for the absence, at once *politique* and Venetian, of confessional bias. Davila's treatment of Calvinism was cool, but at the same time he seems to have recognized its intrinsic force as a religious position. Calvin himself he introduced as "a man of great but unquiet intelligence, wonderfully eloquent and widely erudite, who had departed from the faith held and observed for so many ages by our ancestors," [52] the last point, however, hardly a recommendation for a Venetian. Calvinism, he believed, had begun as a frivolity which later turned serious:

> The French, who are naturally curious and fond of inventions and novelties, began at first, rather for amusement than any real preference, to read [Calvin's] writings and attend his sermons. But as it happens, in this world, that things beginning in jest often end quite otherwise, these opinions were so widely disseminated in the church of God that they were eagerly embraced and obstinately believed by great numbers of people of every class; so that Calvin, who was at first looked upon as a man of little understanding and of a seditious, turbulent spirit, was

[50] I, 9–10.
[51] I, 7, 12–13.
[52] I, 69.

in a short time reverenced by many and was esteemed as a new and miraculous interpreter of Scripture and as an almost certain and in-fallible teacher of the true faith.[53]

Davila objected to Protestantism primarily (like others of the *giovani*) because, as novelty, it was inevitably seditious. On the whole he approved the effort of Henry II to expel this "peccant humor out of the bowels of France," and believed that only a series of accidents prevented its success.[54]

But the potential dangers of religious innovation had only become actual, Davila believed, when the seditious nobility chose, at the instigation of Coligny, cynically to exploit it. In contrast to Condé, who had rashly proposed to his colleagues an immediate resort to force, Coligny "thought it necessary to have recourse to industry and to art where there was such an evident lack of strength, and to arrange secretly, without revealing them-selves, that the undertaking should have the desired end with the ministry of other persons." Coligny pointed out to the other disaffected nobles "that there were multitudes of people all over the kingdom who had embraced the religious opinions recently introduced by Calvin." Persecuted, desperate, ready for any risks to defend themselves, the Calvinist masses needed only leadership and encouragement. Thus Coligny had argued that

> it would be highly expedient to make use of this means to give courage and form to this ready multitude, and to push it on secretly in a proper manner and with an opportune occasion to the destruction of the lords of Lorraine. In this way the princes of the blood and other lords of their party would secure themselves from danger, increase their strength by a great number of followers, gain the alliance of the Protestant princes in Germany and Queen Elizabeth of England who openly favored and protected their belief, put a better face upon the cause, lay the burden of so bold an attempt on others and make it believed for the future, by all the world, that the civil wars were first kindled and provoked not in the interest of the princes and of their pretensions to govern but by dissen-sions and controversies in matters of religion.

The argument seemed cogent but, as Davila's generation knew, human cal-culations are generally likely to go awry, if not to turn out directly contrary to man's intentions. Coligny's proposal, wrote Davila, "was a counsel and

[53] I, 69–70.
[54] I, 71–72.

resolution so pernicious and ruinous that it opened the door to all those miseries and calamities which, in an extraordinary way, have for so long afflicted and torn that kingdom. And it brought to a miserable end both the author of the proposal and all those who, led by their own passions or immediate interests, consented to it." But Davila notably avoided any suggestion that the hand of God had been responsible for the frustration of Coligny's designs and his bloody end.[55]

This analysis of the French civil wars, and above all its treatment of religious motivation, variously suggest the political perspectives of the Renaissance. Thus Davila clearly shared Machiavelli's sense of the importance of popular religious energies. They constituted for him a reservoir of power to be exploited by clever political leaders, potentially dangerous but presumably also (though Davila does not say as much) valuable if properly controlled. This seems evident even though Davila also shared the common belief of his age in the incalculable and unmanageable quality of events, a belief maintained in uneasy tension with the rather different view that their study might be useful. But the religious convictions of the upper classes seem to Davila a different matter. Although he admitted that some of the nobles who accepted Coligny's counsel were already secretly inclined to Calvinism,[56] Davila appears generally to have regarded the Calvinist professions of the aristocracy as a disguise for worldly ambition. He seems to have assumed that genuine piety was improbable among ruling groups and the religiosity of princes largely a political expedient.

Sarpi's *Istoria del Concilio Tridentino* was the mature fruit of the long evolution in attitudes and beliefs, both political and religious, described in the earlier chapters of this book. At the same time it must be seen in relation to contemporary Venetian historical writing, to which it exhibits both deep similarities and important contrasts. Like Morosini and Contarini, though without official sponsorship, Sarpi aimed, in addition to larger purposes, to serve Venice; and his work is peculiarly animated by the traditional anticurialism generally so prominent a feature of the Venetian state histories. He took much the same attitude to the nature of historical thought as Contarini and Davila, and like them he treated ecclesiastical history essentially as politics.

At the same time his project was novel. Its unofficial character allowed him an unwonted freedom; he was under no obligation to consider immediate

---

[55] I, 66–69.
[56] I, 68.

political necessities or to respect contemporary sensibilities. And since he was not writing about wars and princes, at least on the surface, he could disregard the conventions of political history which required a historian to concentrate on great deeds or to serve obvious didactic purposes. Because he was dealing with a society other than his own, he could also relinquish the assumption of a perennial identity underlying all historical accidents, and expose fundamental change. On the other hand the Council of Trent raised issues far closer to the experience and the interests of Venice than the histories of foreign states; Venice had become agressively self-conscious largely through the growing challenge of the Roman church. It would thus be difficult to imagine a historiographical enterprise more intimately related to republican sentiment than an account of what was now coming to seem the major episode in the formation of the Counter Reformation.

Venice, as we have seen, had not immediately discerned in the Council of Trent any serious danger to herself. Paruta's dialogues on civil life had hinted at some connection between the ecclesiasticism of Trent and hostility to the values of the Republic, and the growing militancy of Rome after the Council had ended was a matter of concern in Venice; but for some decades Venetians had paid little attention to the practical significance of the Council. This insouciance was violently shattered by the interdict. During that struggle Rome repeatedly cited Trent against the defiant Venetians, reminding them also that Venice had formally accepted and officially promulgated the decrees of Trent throughout her domains.[57] As Canaye reported in the fall of 1606, the Republic had already begun to regret that she had received the Council "so lightly, without regarding the consequences." [58]

Several times before the interdict was lifted, Venetian theologians had recognized the problem posed by Trent. Capello insisted on the right of any temporal ruler to reject decrees infringing on his own authority,[59] and Marsilio went much farther. He expressed doubt that any conciliar action could be valid in the absence of the French and against the opposition of the Spanish delegates; he attributed the general decisions of the Council of Trent, which he contrasted with the councils of antiquity, to "the misfortune of our times"; and he questioned Bellarmine's accuracy regarding the Council's position on clerical immunity, thus suggesting the desirability of a more reliable

---

[57] For examples, Baglioni, *Apologia*, pp. 8–9, 22, 35–36, 54; Bellarmine, *Risposta alla risposta*, p. 169; Bovio, *Risposta*, p. 60; *Difesa de' Servi*, pp. 30, 38, 215; Medici, *Discorso*, p. 204.
[58] Letter to Hotman de Villiers, Oct. 12, *Lettres et ambassade*, III, 233.
[59] *Delle controversie*, p. 91.

account.[60] Sarpi's general view of Trent had, therefore, a good deal of precedent in Venice.

His interest in the Council of Trent probably began early, though at first as simple curiosity and without the intention of writing its history. He had various opportunities to learn what had occurred when the Council still seemed a recent event and memories were fresh. As a young man in Mantua he had discussed it with Camillo Olivo, a secretary to Cardinal Gonzaga, papal legate during the last sessions.[61] Olivo knew a good deal about the political manipulation behind the scenes; and, no longer friendly to the Curia, he may have accustomed the young Sarpi to a somewhat unspiritual vision of the Council. Conversations with Gallican ambassadors in Venice, including Arnauld Du Ferrier who had been at Trent, doubtless furnished him with further information from a similar perspective. Sarpi must also have had various opportunities to satisfy his curiosity during his years in Rome.[62]

In addition the interdict, otherwise so important a turning point in Sarpi's career, confronted him, as it had other Venetians, with the problem of the authority of the Council. For the time being he did not write about it at any length; but he took issue with Bellarmine's interpretation of various decrees of the Council, pointed out its failure to settle many important matters, and hinted darkly that a full knowledge of its proceedings might lead to a view of its significance rather different from that promoted in Rome.[63] A few years later he minimized the meaning of Venetian acceptance of the decrees of Trent.[64] Thus the needs of Venice, and eventually the larger needs of Christendom and the church which the Venetian ordeal had led him to consider, naturally impelled Sarpi to investigate what had occurred at Trent.

Within a year after the interdict, Sarpi was systematically collecting information about the Council. Recognizing that the Gallican attitude toward

[60] *Difesa*, p. 258.

[61] See Micanzio, *Vita*, pp. 9–10. Sarpi mentions his youthful interest in the Council in a letter to Leschassier, Sept. 29, 1609, Ulianich p. 56. On the nature of Olivo's interest, cf. Chabod, *Politica di Sarpi*, pp. 27–28.

[62] For Sarpi's early sources of information, see in general Hubert Jedin, *Das Konzil von Trient, ein Überblick über die Erforschung seiner Geschichte* (Rome, 1948), pp. 83–89.

[63] As in his *Apologia*, in *Scritti*, III, 76–79. Here (p. 77) Sarpi indicated his interest in the publication of the acts of the Council, which, he seems to imply, had been deliberately suppressed by Rome.

[64] Letter to Leschassier, Sept. 1, 1609, Ulianich, pp. 53–54: "An respublica iuraverit in omnia verba concilii rogas. Dicam: tunc quando concilium publicatum fuit, pontifice petente, princeps scripsit omnibus magistratibus ut praelatis publicantibus et exequentibus decreta concilii, auxilio essent et contradictores compescerent, nihilque aliud princeps, vel dixit vel edixit de hoc concilio."

Trent resembled his own and doubtless stimulated by it, he was studying Jacques Gillot's version of the *Acta* of the Council only a few months after its publication in 1607;[65] and Bedell supplied him, before the end of 1608, with a copy of the Lutheran Chemnitz's *Examinis Concilii Tridentini*, a work, he may have seen earlier.[66] Both books, deeply critical of the Council, could only have confirmed his prejudices against it. And as early as 1612 it was known in England that Sarpi was writing a history of the Council of Trent.[67]

During the same period he was also busy with other historical works which, by describing both what followed and what had preceded, reveal his understanding of the Council of Trent as a crucial moment in the whole earthly career of the church. The first to be completed, the *Istoria dell'Interdetto*, not only met the need of Venice for an authoritative account of recent events from her own point of view.[68] It also revealed Sarpi's conception of the *terminus ad quem* of ecclesiastical history; such episodes as the Venetian interdict were, in his mind, the inevitable consequence of what had been accomplished at Trent. Largely a diplomatic history, this work leaves the impression that "negotiations" motivated by papal greed and worldly ambition had become the central activity of the church in the modern age.[69]

Next, Sarpi dealt with the previous history of the church in his *Trattato delle materie beneficiarie*, an account, far more general in its implications than the title might suggest, of the development of the church since antiquity from a purely institutional and material perspective.[70] That such an approach to

---

[65] Letter to Gillot, March 18, 1608, Ulianich, p. 127. Sarpi says in this letter that he has been collecting materials about the Council, a difficult task because the Jesuits had managed to suppress all but a few relevant documents.

[66] See Bedell's letter to Adam Newton, Jan. 1, 1609, *Two Lives*, p. 244.

[67] See the correspondence printed by Cozzi in "Sarpi, l'anglicanesimo e la *Historia*," pp. 595–602.

[68] For an account of the circumstances of its preparation, see the edition of Busnelli and Gambarin, pp. 245–256.

[69] Sarpi himself speaks of "il filo delle negoziazioni, che è la principal materia di questa istoria" (*Istoria dell'Interdetto*, p. 81).

[70] For the backgrounds of this work see the remarks of Gambarin, *SG*, pp. 303–311. Cf. Delaruelle et al, *L'Église au temps du Grand Schisme*, I, vii, for what may be taken as a tribute to Sarpi's acumen in focusing on this issue: "C'est lui, au vrai, qui definit cette Église médiévale, comme d'ailleurs l'Église d'Ancien Régime, et qui y commande tous les mécanismes juridiques, administratifs, pastoraux, psychologiques. Parler du bénéfice c'est parler de la *curia animarum*, c'est parler de la résidence, du cumul, de la carrière ecclésiastique; mais c'est aussi parler des réserves pontificales ou de la *nominatio* regia; et du même coup évoquer les immixtions des princes dans la vie ecclésiastique et la monarchie administrative romaine." See also, in the same work, pp. 297–298 and 295–313.

church history could even be possible was, for Sarpi, doubtless a sufficient indictment of the papal church; and it placed the Council of Trent in a long chronological perspective. It is also remarkable historiographically because it represented the slow degradation of the church not only as the work of corrupt and ambitious prelates but also as a product of general historical conditions.

Sarpi's major historical work should therefore not be interpreted as an isolated statement but in the context of his general vision of church history. The *Istoria del Concilio Tridentino* was intended to expose the most critical episode in the recent development of the church, significant, for Sarpi, because it linked the medieval deterioration of the church with the recent assault of the papacy on the Venetian Republic. The Council of Trent was important, in this view, because it had confirmed deeply-rooted tendencies inherited from the past which it should have reversed. Trent represented to Sarpi not the initiation of a general reform but its repudiation and failure.

In support of this general thesis, Sarpi often appealed to antiquity to show how sadly the modern Roman church had fallen away. But his actual point of departure was a somewhat idealized vision of the decentralized, lay-directed Venetian church animated by the characteristic piety of Italian Evangelism. Sarpi, in short, was defending not only or even primarily the practices of the apostolic age, but also and above all the typical preferences of Renaissance republicanism. In doing so he drew on many elements in the republican vision of man, society, and the nature of reality that had first found expression in Florence and later, with increasing vigor, in some elements of the Venetian patriciate. Sarpi's account of the Council of Trent is thus one of the last major expressions of the republican culture of the Italian Renaissance.

His debt to the Renaissance past is in the first place one of form and method. Instead of committing himself by making explicit judgments on events, he frequently preferred to express his views through a variety of indirect, often insidious rhetorical devices; his account of the Council of Trent is an immensely complex Renaissance dialogue. Instead of distributing blame or (more rarely) praise, he liked to allow an interpretation to emerge dramatically, through a confrontation between antithetical positions, which he skillfully manipulated to reveal the venality, hypocrisy, irresponsibility, irrationality, or mere folly of one side or the other—and at times of both. This technique was peculiarly suited to the history of a council, a deliberative assembly operating by debate. It had the additional advantages of complying with current objections to *discorsi* in histories and of relieving Sarpi of the responsibility of committing himself personally on various delicate questions. It also left the reader with a powerful impression of bitter antagonisms and disagreements at the Council. It was thus calculated to leave some doubt in the reader's mind that the deliberations at Trent had been guided throughout by the Holy Spirit.

Dialogues composed by Renaissance rhetoricians often have the disadvantage of leaving the personal views of an author in doubt. But this is rarely a problem with Sarpi, partly because his beliefs can be determined from other sources, partly because the essential bias of his account is obvious. The devices with which he clothed and at the same time promoted this bias nevertheless reveal considerable ingenuity. At times his dry and neutral tone seems intended to convey reservations about all sides in a debate, and he often allows opposing groups to discredit each other without comment. On other occasions he expresses his own opinion as the verdict of "the world" in general or the judgment of "sensible" or "pious" men. He is also inclined to indicate his view of a position not by an overt attack on its substance but by assigning disreputable or interested motives to its supporters; thus his sensitivity to the use of ideas as masks for interest finds frequent expression in a kind of *argumentum ad hominem.* Conversely he may suggest approval by his failure to attribute an argument to ulterior motives. He may also indicate personal sympathy by describing a position with care and later revealing it as the unpopular view of a minority or as unacceptable to the papal legates.

An early illustration of Sarpi's indirect manner is his presentation of the formal discourse with which the bishop of Bitonto opened the first session of the Council. Having noted the great interest in how the Council had begun, Sarpi summarized this address in a relatively direct and objective tone. It had emphasized the accomplishments of past councils, the awful responsibility of the present assembly, and the vastness of papal authority. But Sarpi then described the reaction of the bishop's listeners and contrasted it with their reaction to the opening remarks of the legates:

> The admonition of the legates was esteemed pious, Christian, and modest, and worthy of the cardinals; but the sermon of the bishop was judged very different, and its vanity and ostentatious eloquence were noted by all. Intelligent men compared those ingenuous and most true words of the legates with the very different speech of the bishop as a holy with an impious pronouncement . . . . It was esteemed arrogance

to affirm that the whole church would be in error if these few prelates erred, as if other councils of seven hundred bishops had not erred and the church had not refused to receive their doctrine. Others added that this was not in conformity with the doctrine of the popes, who do not concede infallibility except to the pope, and concede it to the council only by virtue of papal confirmation.[71]

In these few lines Sarpi has managed to reveal the antagonism between papalism and conciliarism, and by doing so to hint at fundamental doubts about the authority and seriousness of the Council itself. And he has done so without appearing to express any view of his own. Such subtleties, employed throughout the work, contributed enormously to its polemical force.

But Sarpi's debt to the Renaissance went far beyond rhetorical techniques. Basic to his work is, in the first place, the familiar insistence of Renaissance political discussion on the imperfection of man in every dimension of his existence; for Sarpi human nature is at once morally flawed and intellectually incompetent. Writing when darkness seemed to have closed over Italy and Venice was under political and cultural siege, he took an unusually pessimistic view of the human condition; in this respect he appears closer to Guicciardini than to Machiavelli. He often seems to exploit the Council, *because* of its claims to moral and spiritual authority, as an illustration, at once ironic and singularly compelling, of the inescapable folly and depravity of man. Again and again Sarpi appears to discern in the deliberations of the Council only the complicated interplay of passion and self-interest. Thus he described how the Council dealt with the question of episcopal residence; in this case he abandoned the pose of neutral observer: "Ambition or the obligation to follow the position convenient to their patrons prevailed among the curialists. Others were moved by envy. Lacking the art to rise to the heights to which [the curialists] had arrived or at which they aimed, and unable to achieve equality by advancing themselves, they wanted to pull them down to their own condition and so to make all equal. On this matter all wearied themselves according to their passions." [72] The same issue provoked Sarpi to note the power of human emotions, "which do not allow men to perceive contradictions." [73]

[71] *Concilio di Trento*, I, 209–210.
[72] II, 352–353.
[73] II, 358.

Sarpi was thus particularly sensitive to the ways in which the moral deficiencies of man cloud his intellect. But his distrust of human intellectuality, as the previous chapter will have suggested, was even more fundamental than this; nowhere does Sarpi resemble his Renaissance predecessors more closely than in his conviction of the intrinsic weakness of the human understanding, above all on such ultimate questions as those with which the Council was concerned. The Council, in his view, had been a failure for many reasons but notably because of its intellectual presumption, its insistence on pretending to understand and define matters beyond human comprehension, its doctrinaire rigidity on points that should only be approached with flexibility and a sense of mystery, its universal pronouncements on matters that admit of settlement only on the basis of varying local needs and individual preferences and insights. Adrian VI provided him with an opportunity to suggest his own views. This venerable figure, he noted, "had been nourished, reared, and habituated from childhood in the study of scholastic theology, and thus held those opinions as so clear and evident that he did not believe the contrary could enter the mind of any reasonable man." But the consequence of his rigidity had been a complete failure to understand Lutheranism or to credit its seriousness, with the result that all his countermeasures had proved superficial and ineffective.[74]

Among Sarpi's chief villains at the Council were therefore the scholastic theologians, who—he typically represented this judgment as a "German" criticism of the early decrees of Trent—"had made the philosophy of Aristotle the foundation of Christian doctrine, ignored Scripture, and put all in doubt, even to raising the question whether God exists and disputing on both sides." [75] But Sarpi's objection to scholasticism was not only directed against its method, so inappropriate to Christian faith. He also held it in contempt, like his Renaissance predecessors, for moral reasons. He believed that the impulse to articulate and systematize religious belief was basically neither spiritual nor intellectual but chiefly expressed only pride and malice. He regarded theological controversy, because it degraded spiritual realities to the weak and corrupted level of man, as a peculiarly offensive manifestation of human egotism; it seemed even worse than political ambition because it was mean and trivial. Sarpi therefore devoted himself with particular zest and skill to displaying its ugliness and fatuity, occasionally by attacking it more

[74] I, 32. In the following pages, nevertheless, Sarpi gives full credit to Adrian's sincerity as a reformer.
[75] I, 298–299. Cf. I, 251.

or less openly, often by describing theological discussion with an irony hardly equaled again before Gibbon.[76]

Sarpi's hostility to scholasticism and to the dogmatic temperament in general provides one of the constant motives in his treatment of the Council. He adopted Augustine as his own theological model, observing that "the modesty of that saint was not imitated by the scholastics," who exhibited "so much wilful vanity" that many of their tortuous arguments were not worthy of description.[77] "The prolixity with which the arguments were expounded by both sides was great, and no less the acrimony," he remarked of the debate over the sacraments between Franciscan and Dominican theologians; and he noted that even the papal legate had felt compelled to plead for "treatment with modesty and charity, and not with so much sectarian passion." [78] The scholastic mind, Sarpi observed, was generally a closed mind. Only a few theologians at Trent had sufficient mental dexterity "to suspend judgment until the arguments were weighed," and hence they too had failed to understand Luther.[79] But there was no sympathy for Protestantism in this position. Sarpi played no favorites, and he also blamed Luther for his combative dogmatism.[80] The *furor theologicus*, as Sarpi recognized, might contaminate any party.

Yet he was also aware, as in other connections, that the dogmatism displayed at Trent was not merely frivolous. The relationship, as exhibited in the Council, between what men professed to believe and the interests they were actually concerned to promote particularly fascinated Sarpi; and he frequently undertook to reveal the sordid purposes that protestations of high principle were designed to *mask*—a figure which appears more than once in the course of his work.[81] He noted that the attitudes of bishops toward accepting payment for ordinations to the priesthood seemed to depend on how rich they were. Thus, he observed, wealthy prelates readily condemned the practice as simony; but poor ones saw it as an opportunity (for others) to

[76] Cf. his description of the effort, by the faculty of the Sorbonne, to make France appear more Catholic than the emperor (I, 167–168): ". . . li teologi parisini a suono di tromba, congregato il populo, pubblicarono li capi della dottrina cristiana, venticinque in numero, proponendo le conclusioni e determinazioni nude, senza aggiongerva ragioni, persuasioni o fondamenti, ma solo prescrivendo, come per imperio, quello che volevano che fosse creduto."

[77] I, 276, 283–284, in connection with original sin.

[78] I, 380–381.

[79] I, 308.

[80] I, 397–398.

[81] For example, I, 237; III, 105.

display Christian charity.[82] Again, he reported, the apparent zeal that had induced Granvelle and the cardinal of Lorraine to agree on joint measures for the extirpation of heresy had actually stemmed, as everyone knew, from "ambition and the design to enrich themselves with the spoils of the condemned." [83] But Sarpi once more played no favorites; like Davila he also regarded religious innovation as often a disguise for secular ambition.[84] And his perception that men like to conceal interest under idealism found expression in neat and general aphorisms. "How differently," Sarpi exclaimed, "do men judge in what concerns their own interest from how they judge the affairs of another!" [85] "So it happens not only in human things but also in those of religion," he observed, "that when interests change, credulity changes." [86]

It was remarkable, however, that the unedifying and cynical game of fine words, at the Council and in episodes related to it, appeared to engage all sides equally and to deceive almost no one. Sarpi noted that although the emperor "gave many signs of grief" on hearing the news of the sack of Rome, "the world, seeing the pope remain a prisoner for another six months, perceived how much difference there was between the truth and the appearance." [87] When the Elector of Brandenburg offered his submission to the Council, men generally recognized the family interests that had "moved him to do so for the sake of a good appearance." [88] The Spanish ambassador had addressed the bishops subject to his king, directing them first to serve God and the pope and then reminding them that their royal master would take particular account of how they conformed to his wishes; but in doing so "he spoke in

[82] II, 363–364.

[83] II, 234–235.

[84] Cf. his account, in connection with the peace of Cateau-Cambrésis, of why the French and Habsburg rulers were concerned with the spread of Protestant teachings: ". . . facevano grandissimi progressi, ed erano prontamente udite e ricevute dagli uomini conscienziati. E quel che più agli re importava, li mal contenti e desiderosi di novità s'appigliavano a quella parte, e sotto pretesto di religione intraprendevano quotidianamente qualche tentativi, cosi nelli Paesi Bassi come nella Francia, essendo li popoli molti amatori della libertà, e avendo per la prossimità alla Germania gran commercio con quella" (II, 233–234).

[85] II, 225, in connection with the curious fact that Paul IV, who had complained that Henry II was too lenient towards Protestantism, nevertheless described his own Protestant mercenaries as angels sent by God.

[86] III, 367, in connection with the French change of mind about whether the final assembly at Trent should be considered a new council or a continuation of the old.

[87] I, 70. Cf. I, 65, where Sarpi suggests that the emperor's gestures of respect toward the pope were "un'arte di governo, coperta di manto della religione."

[88] II, 120.

such a way that each one understood the last words to be said seriously but the first for ceremony." [89] The cardinal of Lorraine had perhaps managed to carry the game a step farther by speaking with great eloquence, but at the same time in such a fashion that no one could tell where he actually stood.[90] Sarpi often seems impelled to tear away the draperies of an empty ceremony not so much because the world was in any doubt about what they concealed as out of a deep loathing for hypocrisy and that urgent craving for truth, as much moral as practical, increasingly exhibited by his generation. His impulse suggests, too, a middle-class revulsion against the decadence of an aristocratic and ecclesiastical formalism which still sought to translate into political relations a pattern of order that no longer carried conviction. In so chaotic a social world such deference to hierarchical obligation seemed ridiculous.

In such a world, indeed, all universal, hierarchically articulated, authoritative systems, whether of thought or of political and ecclesiastical organization, could only appear intellectually absurd, morally suspect, or politically sinister. Sarpi's understanding of the human function of such constructions would have made him suspicious of them from the outset. And, like his Renaissance predecessors, he combined a profound skepticism about claims to understand general and abstract truth with views about the nature of the church. These too fundamentally affected his treatment of the Council of Trent.

His very Venetian concern with the spiritual dignity of the laity and the rights of laymen in the administration of the church caused him to give major attention to the clerical bias of the Council, an important reason for his hostility to it. Trent, in his view, had become an instrument for the glorification of ecclesiastics. He noted (without comment) the contention of a bishop at the Council that laymen were "most improperly" understood as "the church," since canonically they had "no authority to command but only the obligation to obey . . . they must humbly receive whatever doctrine of the faith is given them by the church [i.e., by the clergy], and not dispute about it nor even think further about it." [91] The triumph of such attitudes at Trent presumably explained, for Sarpi, the scandalous censure recently

[89] III, 188.

[90] III, 89, 102. Sarpi is here, to be sure, characteristically ambiguous; it is not entirely clear whether he wishes to depict this figure as remarkably clever or remarkably obtuse.

[91] I, 224, in connection with the delicate question whether the Council should be officially described as "representing the church universal," a phrase suggesting the need for laymen at the council.

imposed on Venice. But, as he observed in another place, "learned and pious persons" thought it "absurd and impious" to hold "that laymen are incapable of spiritual things." For, these men had pointed out, laymen "are taken in adoption by the heavenly Father, called sons of God, brothers of Christ, participants in the heavenly kingdom, made worthy by the divine grace of baptism, of the communion, of the body of Christ, and what other spiritual things are there beyond these?" [92]

But this was clearly an unpopular position, and for the most part Sarpi could only record various gestures by the Council designed to elevate the clergy and degrade the laity. He remarked on the refusal of the fathers even to discuss the priesthood of all believers;[93] and he described their refusal to concede the chalice to laymen as an expression of the same impulse. As the Spanish prelates had pointed out in this connection (though opposed by "the wisest" present), "it was more than ever necessary to differentiate priests from others" in view of the Protestant idea of the clergy; "all those rites that can give them reputation" had to be strictly conserved.[94] Sarpi also seems to have reacted sympathetically to the proposal for a married clergy advanced by some German theologians. He not only presented their position with force but he also suggested, in reviewing objections to it, its affinities to the values and needs of Venice. The legates, he observed, had been bitterly criticized for allowing the matter to be discussed "as dangerous, since it was clear that by introducing the marriage of priests, they would all turn their affection and love to their wives and children, and consequently to family and country; and thence the close dependence of the clerical order on the Apostolic See would cease. To concede marriage to priests would be the same as destroying the ecclesiastical hierarchy and reducing the pope to no more than bishop of Rome." [95] Sarpi could only have regarded such an outcome as highly desirable.

Sarpi's conviction that the health of the church required the active participation of secular governments in its administration emerges repeatedly in his historical works. In his *Trattato delle materie beneficiarie* he emphasized the happy results of imperial church reform during the Middle Ages;[96] and in

[92] II, 105.

[93] III, 17–18: ". . . non furono trattati con discussione, ma con declamazione contra li luterani."

[94] II, 412. Many of "the wisest" prelates, on the other hand, favored this concession (II, 470). See also II, 474–475.

[95] III, 163.

[96] In *SG*, pp. 51–52. Cf. his letter to Gillot, Sept. 15, 1609, Ulianich, p. 135.

dealing with Trent he praised the reforms of Charles V[97] and gave extended treatment to the Gallican position on the rights of lay rulers over the church. The French ambassador to the Council had argued that "the authority of the kings of France over ecclesiastical persons and property was not based on the Pragmatic or on concordats and privileges granted by the pope, but on natural law itself, on Holy Scripture, the ancient councils and the laws of Christian emperors." The pope and the whole body of prelates, Sarpi reported, had been profoundly irritated by this claim; and some had gone so far as to charge the ambassador with heresy.[98] On the other hand the pope had been well pleased by the "arrogance" of a Spanish Jesuit who had denounced Catherine de'Medici for daring to intervene in spiritual matters; the pope had compared this bold figure to an ancient saint.[99] The clergy, as Sarpi observed in connection with the Augsburg Interim, could not abide the notion "that a temporal prince in a secular assembly should put his hand to religion." [100]

But for Sarpi the exclusion of secular influence from the Council was precisely one of its most serious defects; it was this that had largely prevented the adoption of a genuine program of reform. For true reform would have meant primarily the reform of the clergy, the restoration of its ancient discipline, an end to its arrogance and worldliness, its reduction to proper obedience and respect for secular authority; and these things could hardly be left to the clergy themselves. The princes of Christendom, who had in the past shown their concern for the church and their ability to reform it, could alone be trusted to effect a true program of reform at Trent. And Sarpi contrasted their hopes for the Council with the purposes of pope and prelates. Genuinely interested in reconciliation, they had wanted a free council that could address itself with vigor to the needs of the church, not an assembly managed and manipulated in her own interests by Rome. And caring little about the definition of doctrine (an enterprise Sarpi himself thought neither necessary nor desirable), they had correctly identified the essential problem as the renovation of the ecclesiastical institution.[101] Sarpi's laicism thus inclined him to view the Council as a bitter struggle for power between the secular

---

[97] *Concilio di Trento*, II, 40.

[98] III, 316–317.

[99] II, 304–305.

[100] II, 35.

[101] Sarpi emphasized the conflicting attitudes of emperor and pope, as in II, 4–24, 65–69, and the contrast between clerical and lay attitudes in France, II, 274–276. See also, more generally, I, 29, and III, 21–22.

princes and the clerical hierarchy; and the triumph of the latter was one of the major grounds for his indictment of it.

His vision of the Council was also deeply influenced by his distrust of universalism, both political and ecclesiastical. For Sarpi, universality had never been more than a fantasy. He denied not only that there had ever been a visible universal church but even a universal council or a universal empire. The emperors of antiquity, he noted, in spite of the universal titles given them by courtesy, had ruled scarcely a tenth of the world. And the so-called general councils of antiquity had represented only the Christians of the Empire, by no means the whole body of believers. The point was cleverly made. It managed simultaneously to diminish the achievement of ancient Rome, to emphasize the historic diversity of Christianity, and by denying the universality of even the venerated councils of antiquity to cast doubt on the traditional authority of a general council lately invoked on behalf of Trent.[102]

Against this background the universal authority attributed to more recent councils of the Latin church appeared to Sarpi even more absurd. They had devoted themselves, under papal direction, "not principally to calm religious disagreements as previously, but either (in truth) to make war in the Holy Land, or to assuage schisms and divisions in the Roman church, or also (in truth) to deal with controversies between the popes and Christian princes." They had, in other words, become essentially political, and even more local than earlier councils.[103] But they were still not local enough for Sarpi. Convinced that even ecclesiastical problems differed from region to region and that only men intimately acquainted with local conditions were competent to deal with them, he believed that questions of reform could only be solved effectively by national rather than general councils. Both the regional synods of antiquity and the ecclesiastical assemblies of mid-sixteenth century Germany proved, in his view, the falsity of the papal contention "that the things of religion cannot be treated in a national council." He seems to have been persuaded that Germany might have been pacified if only Rome had not interfered,[104] and his vigorous presentation of French arguments along the same lines indicates a strong belief in the possibility of a national solution for France. Thus the French chancellor, in opening the Colloquy of Poissy, had pointed out that the decisions of any general council must necessarily be

[102] I, 5.
[103] I, 6.
[104] Cf. II, 47.

made by "men who, as foreigners, do not know the needs of France and are required to follow the wishes of the pope. But the prelates present here, wise in the needs of the kingdom and united by blood, are better qualified to execute this good work . . . . The error of a general council has often been corrected by a national." [105] As the bishop of Valence piquantly observed, "It would be a great absurdity to watch Paris burn when the Seine and Marne are full of water, in the belief that it was necessary to wait to put out the fire for water from the Tiber." [106] But underlying Sarpi's hostility to universalism was always his profound belief that the lofty principle it appeared to embody was in reality only an instrument for the perennial imperialism of Rome. As he remarked, many men had approved the emperor's efforts, condemned at the Curia, to conciliate the Protestants, "because the issue was whether the various Christian regions should be governed according to their need and utility, or whether they should be made servants of a single city, in whose interests the others must spend themselves and even be desolated." [107] Thus Sarpi's Venetian particularism inclined him to emphasize a second bitter struggle at Trent: the conflict between papal universalism and local or regional interests.

At the Council itself this conflict had found expression in the disputes over the nature of episcopal authority. And although Sarpi's laicism somewhat prejudiced him against bishops, who at times evidently had "no other aim except to conserve their authority," [108] his sympathies were generally with them in their struggle against the pope. He certainly believed that episcopal authority depended in no way on papal approval;[109] the *giovani*, it will be recalled, had collided with Rome on this issue. Viewing reform as primarily a local problem, he regarded an essentially episcopal church as necessary for its solution.[110] And he gave extended treatment to the episcopal position at the Council which, as he remarked, the pope feared because it would have "reduced the papacy to nothing." [111] The bishop of Paris, he reported, had reacted against the papalist arguments so forcefully presented by Lainez with the charge that "in place of the heavenly kingdom, as the church is called,

[105] II, 300. Sarpi also remarked that the pope "riprendeva l'arenga del cancelliero come eretica in molte parti, minacciando anco di farlo citar all'inquisizione" (p. 305).

[106] II, 250.

[107] I, 101.

[108] I, 58, in connection with the bishops of Germany.

[109] Cf. his treatment of the advocates of an independent episcopate, III, 26–28, 38–40, 89–90.

[110] Cf. III, 45, where, by describing the objections of the legates, Sarpi suggests how fundamental an independent episcopate was to his own ideal for reform.

[111] I, 414.

he makes not a kingdom but a temporal tyranny . . . he takes from the church the title of Bride of Christ and makes her a slave and prostitute to one man." [112] But the dispute on this issue also served Sarpi's purposes by demonstrating once more that the Council had developed into little more than an angry and occasionally tumultuous struggle for power.[113] In addition, since the sequel proved that the authority of bishops had not been enhanced, the conflict also helped to show that the Council had been, from the standpoint of genuine reform, a failure.[114]

The polemical vigor of the *Istoria del Concilio Tridentino* should not be allowed to obscure the positive convictions on which Sarpi's attack on the Council was based. He was against clericalism because of his respect for the dignity of the lay magistrate, and against universalism because of his attachment to Venice and his conviction that particular states incorporated important values, not the least among them the ability to govern effectively. Similarly he detested what seemed to him the merely formal, dogmatic and authoritarian piety of the Counter Reformation because of his own attachment to the religious attitudes incorporated in Renaissance Evangelism. Indeed he recognized the existence of this movement, and indicated his sympathy for it. In the Italian background of the Council he remarked on the growth of an "evangelical" reform movement, distinct from Lutheranism, following the sack of Rome, a calamity which, he reported, had seemed at the time "a divine judgment against that government." [115] And he described the recommendations of Contarini's reform commission as so valuable that, but for their length, he would have reproduced them in his own work word for word.[116] They represented for him, clearly, a desirable model of reform that had not been adopted. There are also occasional suggestions in the history that he attached more importance to the effects of grace in the work of salvation than did the majority at Trent.[117]

[112] III, 53–54.

[113] Cf. II, 136, in connection with the problem of episcopal jurisdiction: "Nel che la mira dei vescovi non era altra che accrescer l'autorità propria, recuperando quello che la corte romana s'aveva assonto spettante a loro; e il fine delli presidenti non era altro che di concederli quanto manco fosse possibile: ma con destrezza procedevano l'una e l'altra parte, mostrando tutti d'aver una stessa mira al servizio di Dio, e la restituzione dell'antica disciplina ecclesiastica."

[114] See, on this point, Sarpi's letter to Leschassier, Feb. 16, 1610, Ulianich, p. 70.

[115] *Concilio di Trento*, I, 72.

[116] I, 133–134. For Sarpi's general view of Contarini, see I, 150.

[117] Cf. I, 326–330 (where he presents Pauline arguments with what seems to me some sympathy), 338, 364.

Sarpi's affinities with Renaissance Evangelism are particularly apparent in his hints of sympathy for the new positive theology espoused by a few of the fathers at Trent against the majority, consisting of scholastics and canonists. The subject gave him, to be sure, a further opportunity to expose disagreement within the Council and, once again, the defeat of the better cause by the worse. And since the positive method directed attention to the sacred texts in historical context and to other documents recording the teachings and practices of the early church, it was helpful to demonstrate the extent of her subsequent deviation. But it is hard to avoid the impression that Sarpi was also personally committed to biblical humanism as an alternative to the scholastic theology he despised. If Christian faith required only the Bible, the long technical training of a theologian lost most of its value; and the beliefs of a layman might have as much authority as those of the highest ecclesiastic. Sarpi noted, as particularly striking, the inclusion of Erasmus' annotations on the New Testament in the Index of Paul IV;[118] and he gave a full account of the arguments of those theologians who favored the freest and most direct study of the Scriptures.[119] But Sarpi's views emerge, for the most part, obliquely. Thus he reported, in the most objective tone imaginable, the remarkable claim of a Franciscan theologian that the faith had been "now so elucidated by the scholastics" that it was no longer necessary to study the Scriptures. Where previously the Scriptures had indeed required careful elucidation during church services for the instruction of the people, they could henceforth be used merely for embellishment, "like orations, so to speak"; formal veneration for them, perhaps like that given to relics, would now suffice.[120] It may be assumed that Sarpi thought superfluous any explicit attack on so scandalous an opinion.

A dramatic confrontation between the old theology of the schoolmen and the new theology of the "grammarians" thus provides another of the many subplots in Sarpi's complex account of the Council; and the outcome of this minor drama, like that of the larger drama which it advances, is tragic. Yet for a while, as Sarpi tells the story, the prospects for a happy ending, at least on this point, had seemed bright. There had been, from time to time, some impatience among the fathers at Trent with the interminable discussions of the schoolmen. Even the papal legates, eager to expedite matters for reasons of their own, thought it "contrary to the service of the Apostolic See to

[118] II, 330–331.
[119] I, 245–247.
[120] I, 251.

listen to the impertinence of the theologians, men accustomed only to books of speculation and, for the most part, to vain subtleties, which they consider (and which truly are) chimeras, and which cannot be proved because they do not agree among themselves." [121] In addition many bishops were often baffled by scholastic discourse. They were both annoyed by the intricacy and irritated at the fruitlessness of a debate in which "both sides so defended their own opinion, which they affirmed to be plain, clear, and intelligible to all, and on the other hand insisted on the infinity of absurdities that would follow from the contrary." [122]

A real effort was accordingly made in connection with discussions on the eucharist, Sarpi reported, to draw up rules of procedure which would restrict scholastic disputation. Henceforth, it was decided, "the theologians should confirm their opinions with sacred Scripture, the traditions of the Apostles, sacred and approved councils, and the constitutions and authority of the holy Fathers." The discussants were also directed "to use brevity and to avoid superfluous and useless questions and arrogant contentions." But the result had been chiefly to provoke a violent reaction from the schoolmen:

> They said that it was a novelty and a condemnation of scholastic theology, which in all difficulties made use of reason. And why was it improper to treat like Saint Thomas, Saint Bonaventura, and other famous men? The other doctrine, which is called *positive*, and which consists in collecting the words of the Scriptures and Fathers, was only a faculty of memory or really a labor of writing. It was old but known to be insufficient and of little use by the doctors, who have defended the church during the last three hundred and fifty years. This would give the victory to the Lutherans; because when it came to variety of reading and memory, they always triumphed through the knowledge of languages and wide reading of authors. A man who wanted to become a good theologian did not have time for such things since it was necessary for him to exercise his intellect and train himself to ponder things, not to enumerate them.

[121] II, 432.

[122] II, 98–99. Cf. III, 19: "Li prelati che stavano ad udire erano pieni di tedio, sentendo tante difficoltà, e prestavano l'orecchia grata a quelli che dicevano doversi tralasciare e parlar in termini universali: non senza mormorazione delli frati, che si stomacarono, udendo e vedendo in loro disposizione pel difinire articoli e prononciar anatemi senza intender le materie e aborrendo che gliele esplicava."

Mostly Italians, the scholastic theologians also appealed to national sentiment by asserting that any recourse to a positive method would favor German Catholics, who were adept in it.[123] And again, apparently without a word of his own, Sarpi has indicted his spiritual adversaries. He has displayed their arrogance and obscurantism; he has implied that the Council ignorantly repudiated the contributions of responsible modern scholarship; and he has implicated the scholastic disciplines favored by the church with the decadence of Italian scholarship increasingly apparent in the later sixteenth century.

This restriction on disputation had pleased most of the fathers and considerably speeded the work of the Council, and it was briefly maintained. But, as Sarpi made clear, the scholastic theologians soon recovered their former importance. They argued, successfully, that the decrees of the Council could not stand by themselves but required a species of explanation they alone could supply; and scholastic discussion therefore continued. Their contention that all things would be thrown into confusion should "the new grammarians" be accepted as the judges and arbiters of the faith[124] proved persuasive.[125] On this ground the traditional Vulgate text, in spite of its numerous defects, had also been retained.[126]

A number of impulses evidently nourished Sarpi's antagonism to scholastic method and his preference for a religion based on the Bible and other ancient sources of the faith. One, clearly, was his pessimistic evaluation of the formal rationality on which scholasticism depended. But his position also depended more positively on the conviction that faith is essentially a matter of personal experience rather than dogma, that it is best nourished by open and direct exposure to divine inspiration, and that it is likely to find different modes of expression in diverse individuals and diverse places. Dogma, like the administration of the church, had also in a sense to be decentralized. Thus, for religious as well as practical reasons, Sarpi favored considerable latitude in matters of belief. All these considerations heavily influenced his attitude to Protestantism in the *Istoria del Concilio Tridentino*, and also (because it chose to take so different a position) his attitude toward the Council itself.

Taking so dim a view of the detailed articulation of religious doctrine, he could not regard the religious differences presented by Protestantism as a

---

[123] II, 91. The references here to memory may recall the extended demonstration of the importance of this question for the Renaissance by Frances A. Yates, *The Art of Memory* (Chicago, 1966).

[124] I, 247.

[125] II, 94–98.

[126] I, 245–252, for Sarpi's discussion of this issue.

serious danger to the faith. The chief Christian princes, as he noted, had seemed to take much the same view. He observed that even at the Curia, although some had condemned the emperor's attempts to conciliate the Protestants, others had commended his prudence and piety, since "the Protestants were still Christians, albeit somewhat different from others in certain particular rites: a tolerable difference." [127] And the French chancellor whose insistence on local solutions to local problems he applauded, had also spoken of the Protestants as "brothers regenerated in the same baptism, worshipers of the same Christ." [128] Sarpi also remarked both on the ignorance at Trent of what Protestants actually believed and the rejection by the majority of the fathers of pleas for a charitable construction of Protestant views.[129]

His own treatment of Protestantism was in general neutral and objective, though with occasional hints of sympathy. He neither deplored nor rejoiced at the spread of the Protestant revolt,[130] and he presented such Protestant leaders as Luther and Beza with both respect and a cool eye to their moments of weakness.[131] Although he displayed as little interest in the dogmatic differences among Protestants as among Catholics,[132] he evidently found various Protestant attitudes congenial. He seems to have been favorably impressed by Luther's attack on indulgences,[133] and he persistently depicted the issue between Lutherans and Catholics as an opposition between Scripture and the authority of the schoolmen and the pope.[134] He noted Luther's charge that the pope had imposed a tyranny over the church, perverted Christian doctrine, and usurped the power of lay magistrates;[135] the coincidence of such views with his own could hardly have escaped him.

At the same time his detestation of religious persecution is from time to time apparent; on this matter Sarpi's position seems close to that of Erasmus. Without suggesting sympathy for their doctrines, which he described as "imperfect and crude," he represented the slaughter of the Waldensians (instigated, he noted pointedly, by the pope) as a wanton attack against a

[127] I, 100.

[128] II, 301.

[129] I, 308, 341.

[130] Cf. the neutral tone of I, 71, 135.

[131] For Luther, I, 21–26, for example; for Beza, II, 301.

[132] Cf. his treatment of the Marburg Colloquy (I, 77), as ridiculous for Sarpi as the theological debates at Trent.

[133] Cf. I, 111, and III, 396–397.

[134] As I, 13, 28–29, 89, 105, 308.

[135] I, 20. Note too how well Luther is made to appear in the exchange with Vergerio (I, 121–122).

harmless and simple people who had "begged for compassion without making any defense." [136] He noted that persecution had failed to halt the spread of heresy in the Low Countries,[137] that the burning of heretics had been profoundly unpopular in England and in France had provoked the "indignation of honest persons," [138] and that the brave death of Antoine Du Bourg had only increased conversions to Protestantism.[139] But he also reported the "contemporary" shock at Calvin's execution of Servetus, and above all at Calvin's defense of "putting the hand in blood for the sake of religion." Men had pointed out that Calvin's doctrine, "as the term heretic is taken in a more restricted or a broader sense, might one day harm him who has used it on another." [140] Sarpi was clearly on the side of latitude and flexibility on all religious questions, and of charity and open discussion rather than force in dealing with error. Thus, as he noted, critics of the Tridentine decrees on the Eucharist had protested that "if there were so many legitimate positions, it was necessary to express them, and not force men to believe by terror but with persuasion." But the Council had chosen to make the faith into "a despotism such as Saint Paul so much detests." [141]

Also a part of Sarpi's opposition to an authoritarian and persecuting faith was his steady conviction that it disguised the worldly ambitions of the clergy. His tolerance is therefore related to his concern with the rights and dignity of secular rulers and the autonomy of the Renaissance state. He reported the dismay in Milan at a proposal to introduce the Inquisition into that city, since in Spain the Holy Office "had not always operated to cure the conscience but very often to empty the purse and for other worldly ends." [142] And he made his case against the proscription of heretical books by means of a historical sketch which revealed that the practice had been unknown in the early church, had been invented by the papacy no earlier than the ninth century in conjunction with its growing political ambitions, and had only recently become common and systematic. The Index had been chiefly devised, he suggested, to promote a general ecclesiastical assault on the lay world; that of 1559 had "under color of faith and religion" condemned works defending the authority of rulers. "A lovelier mystery has never been

[136] I, 189–190; cf. II, 247.
[137] II, 234.
[138] II, 192.
[139] II, 242.
[140] II, 192–193.
[141] II, 438.
[142] III, 291.

discovered," Sarpi's sketch concluded, "to use religion to make men stupid." [143]

One of the major sources of Sarpi's hostility to the Council of Trent was its contempt for princes and the legitimate needs of political life, and he incorporated into his history various passages in defense of an autonomous secular politics which at the same time hint at the characteristic ecclesiological bias of the Renaissance. For example he pointedly recorded German objections that the Council had emphasized the Christian duty of obedience to the church but had been silent on the obligation to obey rulers, a matter which the Scriptures had stressed. The German critics had also remarked that "as regards the church, one finds an express obligation to listen to it, but obeying it is not so clear." [144] This had been, as Sarpi well knew, the position of Venice in 1606.

More than once he also exhibited the folly of objections, often heard at the Council, to political accommodation between religious antagonists. Anything but a fight to the death against Protestantism in France, the majority of the fathers had argued, would "elevate worldly things above those of God, and indeed ruin both together; because once a state was deprived of its religious foundation, it would also fall into temporal desolation." [145] The history of France during the half century since had presumably been a sufficient refutation of this simple contention, and Sarpi felt no need to attack it. But he allowed to the German supporters of the emperor's conciliatory policies an explicit reply to this kind of religious absolutism. They had observed that, as a general principle, "kingdoms and principalities should not be governed by the laws and interests of priests, who are more than other men interested in their own greatness and convenience, but according to the demands of the public good, which sometimes calls for the toleration of some defect . . . when a vice cannot be extirpated without ruining the state, it was pleasing to the divine Majesty that it should be permitted." [146] The French chancellor had taken much the same position at Saint Germain in 1563, Sarpi noted. Religion, the chancellor remarked, could be left to the prelates, "but where it is a matter of the tranquility of the kingdom and retaining subjects in obedience to the king, that cannot pertain to the ecclesiastics but to the royal counsellors." Cicero, he continued, was a better

[143] II, 328–331.
[144] I, 365.
[145] III, 191–192.
[146] I, 100–101.

model than Cato, "severe and rigid as a senator of Plato's republic," for "laws should seek to accommodate themselves to the time and the persons, like the stocking to the foot." The problem for the present was not "to dispute which religion was better, since it was not a question of forming a religion but of setting a kingdom in order. It was not absurd to say that many might be good citizens but not good Christians, and it was possible for those who did not have sacred things in common to live in peace." [147]

The proposed "reform of the princes" during the last session of the Council seemed of particular importance to Sarpi, for the decrees that finally emerged from the discussion of this matter, although modified to meet the objections of the major Catholic rulers, were fundamental to the Roman effort to discipline Venice during the interdict. "The substance of it was," Sarpi wrote, "that the Council, in addition to its decrees about ecclesiastical persons, determined to correct other abuses introduced by secular persons against the immunity of the church, confident that the princes would be content and cause due obedience to be rendered to the clergy. Therefore it admonished them, in addition to other things, that they should require from their magistrates, officials, and other temporal lords the same obedience required of the princes themselves to the supreme pontiff and the conciliar constitutions." [148] In its original form this proposal had been accompanied by the usual anathemas, which in this case pointed to the excommunication of rulers; and it had evoked strenuous protests, among others from the emperor. The French ambassador had objected that "excommunicating and anathematizing princes had no example in the ancient church and opened a wide door to rebellion;" he charged that the proposal aimed "to take away the liberty of the Gallican church and to offend the majesty and authority of the most Christian king." Following the example of Constantine, Justinian, Charlemagne, and Saint Louis, the ambassador maintained, his royal master had made "many ecclesiastical laws" that had greatly benefited the church.[149] Meeting with so much opposition, the legates had bowed to necessity and dropped the offensive anathemas; but the decree still embodied the principle that rulers are generally obligated to obey ecclesiastics.[150] This, as much as anything, required Sarpi to attack the general authority of the Council of

[147] II, 326–327.
[148] III, 309–310.
[149] III, 314.
[150] See Sarpi's summary, III, 379.

Trent, which, through the "reform of the princes," had aimed deliberately to abolish the autonomy of the political world.

In a rather different sense too Sarpi may be seen to have joined hands with his Renaissance predecessors. Since he viewed the apparently religious decisions of the Council as in reality an expression of sinister political interests and the papacy itself as an essentially political agency, a full understanding of what had transpired at Trent required him to provide an extended account of the political events leading up to the first session. Thus, chronologically as well as thematically, Sarpi's *Istoria del Concilio Tridentino* is in some degree a continuation of Guicciardini's *Storia d'Italia*. Among its other uses the Council of Trent allowed Sarpi to deal with the next phase in the continuing crisis of Italy that had so preoccupied Machiavelli and Guicciardini in their rather different moods. But now the Italian powers may be seen to count for even less than in the earlier phases of the crisis. The duke of Florence is no more than a presence, and even Venice is hardly mentioned. Only France, Spain, and the emperor can significantly affect events; and although the major action in Italy now is chiefly focused in Trent, it can only be explained by an even larger attention to developments abroad than had been necessary for Guicciardini.

And like the Florentines Sarpi found occasion to blame the pope for contributing to the decline of Italian liberty. Thus, echoing Paruta and Morosini, he criticized Paul III for joining the emperor in 1546 to crush the Lutherans of Germany. If the pope had had any regard for the needs of Italy, Sarpi wrote (though he characteristically attributed this judgment to "the powers of Italy"), he would have kept the war at a distance "and the ultramontane princes in an equilibrium of forces"; for "if the emperor had subjugated Germany, Italy would have been at his mercy and France would not have sufficed to oppose such power." But "if the emperor had been defeated, the eagerness of the [Lutheran] Germans to invade Italy was manifest." Since either outcome of the war would have brought disaster to the peninsula, the pope obviously should have tried to keep the peace. The passage, it may be observed, combines the ideal of balance in international relations, a sense of the folly of subordinating politics to religion, and an awareness of Italy's dependence on events abroad.[151]

Sarpi also exhibited a persistent anxiety about the precarious future of republics in a world dominated by great princes and the machinations of

[151] I, 321.

the pope. This concern emerged for the most part obliquely by way of his interest in the changing constitution of the church; but it is also apparent elsewhere, notably in hints of sympathy for the fate of Florence, which he seems to have taken as a particular warning to his own generation. He found it remarkable that after the sack of Rome the pope had been less interested in revenge on the emperor than in the recovery of Florence, and he described the pope's effort to lull the Florentines by pretending to have given up "all thought of temporal things." The fall of the last Florentine Republic seemed also to point another moral. "It was certain," Sarpi wrote, "that if the king of France and the Venetians had remained superior in Italy," Florence would have kept her liberty.[152] Venice and France apparently struck him as natural allies, not only against the Habsburgs but also against Rome. Meanwhile he seems to have detected a certain animus against republics at Trent. They ranked too low in the political hierarchy of Europe to secure recognition of their rights of ecclesiastical patronage; and Venice had only been able to retain her traditional prerogatives by passing as a special type of principate.[153]

The passivity forced on Italy and the general weakness of republics raised, for a reformer like Sarpi, the general problem of the possibility of action. From his standpoint, as we have observed, the world appeared both dangerous and largely incalculable. So "imbecile" were all human affairs that the most terrible damage might come tomorrow precisely from what had seemed most beneficial today,[154] and human plans were likely to produce results precisely opposite to those intended. The Council itself had illustrated this truth. Demanded by reformers and resisted by the Curia, it had turned out "wholly contrary to the design of those who procured it" and to the apprehensions of those who had feared it. The Council was therefore a weighty argument for trust in God rather than in "human prudence." [155] A considerable change has evidently taken place since the grave discussions of Paruta's youth in which prudence had been exalted as queen of the virtues.

Yet the change was not total, and Sarpi still found, in the idea of the occasion, a means of accommodation between prudence and the unpredictability of human affairs. He invoked the conception from time to time in the *Istoria del Concilio Tridentino*, as in his other writings of this period. Early in the work he restated it: "Many times occasions are born sufficient to produce

[152] I, 72–73.
[153] III, 356.
[154] I, 111.
[155] I, 4. Cf. III, 303, for another instance.

notable results, and they are lost in the absence of men who do not know how to make use of them. But, more important, in order to accomplish anything the time must come when it pleases God to correct human delinquencies." [156] If Sarpi's confidence in political calculation is substantially less than Machiavelli's it is perhaps greater, through its attachment to the ideal of Providence, than had been possible for Guicciardini. The Council of Trent, according to this principle, had failed, possibly because God had not chosen to provide an occasion for genuine reform but certainly because prudent men who wanted it had been lacking. So, Sarpi observed in one of his most ironical and ambiguous moments, Clement VII, "considering that any time is pleasing to God when it is a question of holy things," had chosen to call the Council without waiting for the approval of the princes. The whole outcome of the assembly seems foreshadowed by this decision, whether it is interpreted as evidence of the pope's neglect of the essential condition for successful action, or on the contrary (in view of the pope's fear of the Council) its most cunning application.[157]

But the most direct expression of Sarpi's debt to the political culture of the Renaissance is the sophisticated historical vision that permeates his account of the Council of Trent. Three general principles underlay his conception of the nature and purposes of historical composition, including his own work. He conceived of historical study, first of all, as a kind of empirical investigation designed to tell the truth about the past. He also regarded historical truth, no matter what its subject, as autonomous, governed by nothing beyond the internal structure of events and illuminated by the historian's general understanding of human nature and human affairs. Finally, he considered knowledge of history potentially useful and occasionally urgent; historical composition was to be judged above all by its utility for the purposes of men.

He conceived of historical method as the laborious accumulation of particular detail derived, as far as possible, from contemporary sources. Apparently anxious that his account of the Council might seem tedious, he paused occasionally to explain what he was about. "To some in reading this

---

[156] I, 8–9, in connection with the first appearance of Protestantism. Sarpi also attributed the initial failure of the emperor's efforts to secure a general council to the fact that the time was not yet ripe (I, 66): "Ma sì come li semi, quantonque fertilissimi, gettati in terra fuori di stagione non producono, così li gran tentativi fuori dell'opportunità riescono vani."

[157] I, 161–162.

relation," he wrote in the course of developing the complicated background of the first session, "its petty facts and reasonings may appear superfluous; but the writer of the history, having a contrary opinion, has deemed it necessary to show what tiny rivulets produced a great lake that covered Europe." [158] Back of this apology was Sarpi's recognition that his procedure violated the demand of contemporary rhetoricians that historians eschew an "imprudent pedantry" in favor of large effects. The rules suggested that Sarpi had erred by failing to distinguish between history, the representation of great actions in stirring form, and mere annals. On one occasion he defended his own practice by citing Homer, who had incorporated "frequent replies and minute narrations," and Xenophon, who "more delights the mind, and teaches more, by recounting the serious and jocular discussions of soldiers than the actions and councils of princes." [159] Sarpi thought of himself, with some reason, as an innovator.

But his major defense was not rhetorical; he argued that the obligation of the historian to tell the whole truth took precedence over all considerations of form, that the subject of a history should in fact determine its form, and that the novelty of his own work excused him from all expository coventions. He intended—as he explained with at least a hint of sarcasm—to follow the way of nature and so to accommodate "the form to the matter, not, as the schools prescribe, the matter to the form." His work would thus stand or fall "not so much through defect of form as through the nature of the matter," a suggestion with metaphysical as well as historiographical overtones. And the importance of the matter required the closest attention to minute detail, which most men would find both "benefit and pleasure in understanding." He was therefore resolved "at times to narrate certain particulars which, I am certain, many will esteem unworthy of mention." [160] Even though he might occasionally share such reservations, he wrote, he had been compelled to recognize that whatever he had been able to discover about the Council had been considered, by someone, important enough to record. And although the significance of a detail might elude himself, "some acute intelligence will perhaps discern there something worthy of observation." Any reader, he pointed out, could skim quickly over whatever failed to interest him.[161]

[158] I, 187.
[159] II, 3–4.
[160] III, 4–5.
[161] III, 85.

But Sarpi's estimate of his own method, though it reflects general convictions about the discrete and particular character of all reality, was somewhat disingenuous. He was by no means content, as this passage suggests, to hold up a mirror to his sources. He obviously took a highly active role in the selection and arrangement of his evidence. For although the lake engulfing Europe may have been fed by innumerable tiny rivulets, Sarpi was interested not in measuring its sources drop by drop but in describing, as it appeared to him, the formation and effect of the whole. And from time to time he openly proclaimed his decision to omit information that struck him as too trivial for inclusion. "Following my original plan," he wrote as he approached the debates at the Council on holy orders, "I will narrate only those opinions notable for their singularity or for the opposition between them." [162] His treatment of certain matters, he announced early in the work, would be fuller than that of others simply because some were worthier of attention. He compared himself to a harvester who found some fields more productive than others. Furthermore, he remarked, no reaper ever managed to gather in everything.[163]

Sarpi's understanding of the nature of historical truth was also utterly naturalistic, although not wholly irreligious. It was based on the absolute distinction, which had also shaped his ecclesiology, between the spiritual and temporal. History belonged entirely to the temporal realm; and, both to protect spiritual reality and to insure a valid grasp of this world, it had to be scrupulously distinguished from the unchanging, unconditioned, and eternally reliable truths of faith. Historical truth, Sarpi insisted more than once, was a matter not of authority but of fact; and authority, as he noted in connection with a decree of Trent which cited ancient precedent against the communion of children, "cannot alter things already done." [164] Shortly after Sarpi's death his faithful Micanzio echoed the master's sentiments in response to a curious claim that Catholics must believe, as an article of faith, that popes had always thirsted for the salvation of souls and never for anything less sublime. "I believe," Micanzio wrote dryly of the advocate of this proposition, "that he bases this on the goodness and sanctity of the present Highest Pontiff, disregarding the many histories of the lives of the popes,

[162] III, 9.

[163] I, 4–5; cf. II, 353, 449, 504. Sarpi also discusses the historian's problem of selection in his *Aggionta e supplimento all'istoria degli Uscocchi*, in *La Repubblica di Venezia, la Casa di Austria e gli Uscocchi*, pp. 12–13.

[164] *Concilio di Trento*, II, 437. See also the concluding words of his *consulto, Sopra le patenti dell'inquisitore*, in *Opere*, Suppl. II, 105.

some by contemporaries who would swear that popes can have some other kind of thirst." "This," he concluded sternly, "is to make an article of faith out of a matter of fact, which cannot be certain." [165] The distinction between the two orders of truth, the contingent and chronological order of history and the eternal and systematic order of faith, freed Sarpi, even more clearly than most of his Renaissance predecessors, to depict the earthly career of the church as an illustration (though a peculiarly significant one) of the general effects of passion and circumstance in human affairs.

He did not deny the ultimate responsibility of Providence for all historical occurrences, but his sense of the inscrutability of God's purposes prevented him from considering the conception useful to a historian. He invoked it himself only when events had turned out differently from what men had expected, for example when the Council convened for its final sessions in spite of a succession of accidents that seemed likely to suspend it permanently; and in view of his dark estimate of what had then transpired, this may well have been ironical.[166] He had remarked in an early *pensiero:* "When we see the connection between terms, we know naturally; but when we do not see it, because the intermediate causes are hidden, we have recourse to the non-natural." The more ignorant men were, he concluded, the more likely they were to regard things as "not natural." [167] He therefore mocked as willful obscurantism the joy of Rome in discerning a happy providential significance in such routine events as the death of Luther at an advanced age (to Sarpi scarcely a miracle),[168] or the demise of Henry VIII leaving only a minor heir. The latter event, Sarpi observed, had hardly proved a cause for satisfaction, since the reign of Edward VI compounded mere schism with a change in religion.[169] Similar celebrations over the deaths of Zwingli and Oecolampadius prompted him to comment: "It is certainly a pious and religious thought to attribute the disposition of every event to divine Providence, but to determine for what purpose events are directed by that highest wisdom is little more than presumption." He noted again that, after the deaths of these leaders, Protestantism made even greater progress among the Swiss.[170]

---

[165] Quoted by Cecchetti, *Venezia e la Corte di Roma*, II, 246 from a *consulto* of Apr. 6, 1623.

[166] *Concilio di Trento*, II, 185.

[167] *Pensiero* 265. Cf. *Pensiero* 308, which explains away the "heavenly voices" heard by peasants.

[168] *Concilio di Trento*, I, 236.

[169] I, 418.

[170] I, 95–96.

But in spite of his general reservations about the human mind, Sarpi believed that man could in some measure understand the pattern of causal relationships connecting events, and thus write history. Another of his early *pensieri* had cautiously but firmly reduced the mysteries of time to a neat formula which may have some relevance to his subsequent work as a historian. "The past and the future are not," he had written, "and yet it cannot be said that they are nothing, because they exist in a certain way: first since their material exists, either all together or in diverse places; and then because there are certain effects of the past, and certain causes of the future. It follows from this that the relationship exists; and since it exists, *something can be said.*" [171] He also applied the imagery of physics to historical causation. In discussing the failure of the Colloquy of Ratisbon, he remarked dryly: "It is not difficult, when the operators are known, to discern immediately from whence the motion has its beginning." [172] And his account of the Council of Trent is no mere narrative but an extended and complex essay in historical explanation. He justified his lengthy discussion of the various conferences and colloquies preceding it, for example, by pointing out that each had contributed to the convening of the Council and then to its character.[173]

Yet Sarpi's conviction that the structure of human affairs is theoretically explicable was also balanced by his skepticism; and one of his early observations about the physical universe seems equally applicable to history. No motion is irregular, he had written, even though a pattern of regular motions may appear irregular to one who does not understand the whole. And although a total understanding might be possible in theory, no man could expect to comprehend every simple motion; such knowledge belonged to God alone.[174] Knowledge that the natural order (of which history is a part) is rigidly deterministic might thus be of little use to the historian. *Something* could be said, but not everything, and perhaps sometimes very little; as Sarpi had written during the interdict: "In human things the truth is often so hidden that it is impossible to discover." [175] The confidence with which he

---

[171] *Pensiero* 145: "Il passato e il futuro non sono, ma non perciò si può dir che non siano, come il niente, imperciocchè son eglino in qualche modo: prima, per esservi la lor materia, o tutta insieme o in diversi luoghi; poi, perchè del passato v'ha qualcuno degli effetti, ed alcuna delle cause del futuro. Da questo segue che la relazione puro nulla non sia, perchè, sendo eglino relazione, non pare che nulla affatto dir si possano." The italics in my translation are added.

[172] *Concilio di Trento*, I, 237.

[173] I, 145.

[174] *Pensiero* 136.

[175] *Considerazione sulle censure, Scritti*, II, 249-250.

depicted what had taken place at Trent nevertheless appears somewhat to belie Sarpi's skepticism.

He was at any rate sufficiently persuaded of both the accessibility and the intelligibility of historical knowledge to be certain of the usefulness of writing history. For Sarpi, this was its primary justification. He attached little value to a disinterested knowledge of the past, although he admitted that among his motives for writing a history of Trent had been a general "taste for things human" and a "great curiosity to know the whole," presumably for its own sake.[176] But, as Micanzio reported, Sarpi had first been interested in history through observing its utility for politics at the court of Mantua;[177] and his utilitarianism persisted. When Groslot requested his opinion on the delicate matter of Pope Joan, Sarpi reported that he found no solid evidence either for or against her existence and personally doubted it; but he then declared: "I should not care to trouble myself to prove something that, once proved, would be of no further use to me."[178] History was for Sarpi not a matter for idle contemplation but an instrument of the active life. And he wrote the history of Trent for thoroughly practical motives. His purpose, he declared, was to expose what had been diligently concealed "by a great number of highly perspicacious persons," and thereby to prevent damage to the general interests of Christendom.[179]

History, in this view, served man simply by telling the truth, that is by being itself. The truth, Sarpi was convinced, would set men free, and history was thus on the side of Venice and of right. This conviction grew in him after the interdict. Nothing was more necessary, he wrote Groslot, since the adversaries of Venice were spreading lies, "than to manifest to the world the truth about the past."[180] He also attacked them for unscrupulously altering ancient texts; they rejected, in short, the autonomy of history.[181] To Leschassier he wrote that even the blind could see how the facts supported Venice and the Gallicans against Rome.[182] But although he shared Nicolò Contarini's detestation of histories composed for adulation, his objection was practical rather than moral. "What the world desires from history in the first place,"

---

[176] *Concilio di Trento*, I, 3–4.

[177] *Vita*, p. 8.

[178] Feb. 28, 1612, Busnelli, I, 219.

[179] *Concilio di Trento*, III, 4.

[180] May 27, 1608, Busnelli, I, 14.

[181] *Trattato delle materie beneficiarie*, SG, p. 32; *Su le immunitá delle chiese*, SG, p. 267, for examples.

[182] Feb. 14, 1612, Ulianich, p. 102.

he declared, "is the truth, and abhorrence of adulation. The writer who wishes to appear truthful must narrate both the good and the bad; he who tells only the good is not believed, since everyone knows the mixture in human things." Guicciardini, he observed, had done Venice good precisely because he represented her at times unfavorably; when he spoke well of her he had therefore been credited. Certain that truth was generally on the side of the Republic, Sarpi advised his government to publicize vigorously what had recently occurred.[183]

But Sarpi was also increasingly interested in the utility of truth for the larger cause of general ecclesiastical reform. For he was more and more deeply convinced that a responsible investigation of the past would show the flimsiness of the historical arguments for the universal claims of the papacy. Thus he argued against the alleged universality of the right of asylum:

> Some men, presupposing that the honor of immunity has been given to churches and holy places among all peoples in every period, have concluded that it is a natural thing in human society and, like all other obligations of natural law, should be observed in all cases simply and without any interpretation, and cannot be changed by custom, and so much the more among Christians as true religion is superior to false. And others, presupposing that in the Old Testament God commanded immunity first for his altar and then for the temple, have drawn the conclusion that it is *de iure divino* and therefore superior to every human power. It is a stupendous thing what edifices have been built on these presupposed foundations for the oppression of justice and the protection of wickedness, under the cover of zeal for the divine honor. But these constructions will fall immediately when the insubstantiality of the foundations is clearly revealed by the truth of history.[184]

But history could do far more than refute the falsehoods propagated by Rome. Sarpi shared the common Renaissance view of reform as the return to an original perfection, and he saw in historical study the essential means not only to reveal the outlines of that lost ideal but also to show the path men must retrace, back through the ages, to recover it once again:

> It is very necessary that just as we have arrived by stages at this profundity of misery, so we must ascend through the same stages to return

[183] *Scritture malediche contra il governo, SG,* pp. 227–228.
[184] *Su le immunitá delle chiese, SG,* p. 289.

to that summit of perfection on which the holy church once existed. This cannot be done without knowing what the administration of temporal things was in the beginning, and how that good governance was lost. Hence it is above all necessary to describe point by point how the church from time to time acquired temporal riches, and how with each change it appointed ministers to dispense and possess them. This will reveal to us the impediments which in these times block a good reformation, and will also show the ways to overcome them.

This remarkable passage appears in Sarpi's *Trattato delle materie beneficiarie*,[185] but its general vision both of church history and the manner in which the church must be reformed also underlies his *Istoria del Concilio Tridentino*.

It should be clear that Sarpi's understanding of church history is radically opposed to that which informs the *Annales ecclesiastici* of Baronius, and it may be that Sarpi thought of his historical work as a refutation of Baronius. Baronius was much on his mind after the interdict, and Micanzio's extensive notes on the *Annales* indicate the care with which the work was studied in Sarpi's immediate circle.[186] Baronius' only purpose, Sarpi insisted, had been to promote the temporal power of the pope. "That cardinal has not omitted to explain and to amplify in their place all the Roman pretensions over kingdoms, cities, places, and territories," he declared. It is a wonderful thing how he particularizes every least thing, and how he supports whatever favors the Curia, even doubtful and false things." [187] "Aiming to persuade us that the whole world has, once and always, been administered in such a way," Sarpi wrote to Leschassier, "he has perverted everything." [188] He noted the extreme sensitivity of the Roman authorities to any attack on Baronius,[189] he was pleased with Casaubon for undertaking to refute him,[190] and he expressed hope that historians in England might "attend to

---

[185] In *SG*, pp. 12–13.

[186] See above, p. 397.

[187] *Ragioni di Ceneda*, in *Opere*, Suppl. II, 210. See also Sarpi's *Trattato delle materie beneficiarie*, SG, p. 64.

[188] Mar. 18, 1608, Ulianich, p. 9.

[189] Letters to Groslot, Apr. 1 and Nov. 25, 1608, Busnelli, I, 12, 49; to Leschassier, Dec. 22, 1609, and Nov. 23, 1610, Ulianich, pp. 62, 96; and to Gillot, Mar. 2, 1610, Ulianich, p. 145.

[190] Letter to Groslot, May 8, 1612, Busnelli, I, 229. But to Casaubon himself Sarpi described Baronius as an unworthy antagonist (June 8, 1612, Busnelli, II, 219–220).

Baronius." [191] Much of his own historical investigation consisted of "attending to Baronius."

That historical scholarship was, for Sarpi, a formidable weapon in a great political and spiritual struggle only increased his sense of scholarly responsibility. Indifference to historical truth was appropriate, it seemed to him, only for the enemy, who either ignored the facts or, if this proved impossible, tried to suppress or distort them. He derided the historical ignorance of the theologians at the Council,[192] attacked the canonists for indifference to facts that belied their decretals and for citing forged documents,[193] and condemned Jesuit resistance (though claiming to understand it only too well) to the study of ancient texts.[194] The enemy was so resolved to prevent any independent appeal to facts, as he wrote Leschassier, that direct reference to Saint Paul or the early canons of the church was likely to provoke charges of heresy.[195] Truth, on the other hand, seemed to him to lie wholly with his own side, and the importance of the cause demanded the most scrupulous effort to reconstruct the past. This meant the need for caution in the weighing of evidence.[196] It also meant sensitivity to such matters as the changing sense of words, and Sarpi notably exemplifies the contribution of philological study in the later Renaissance to the modern historical consciousness as well as to demands for reform. As he remarked to Leschassier, the most important terms employed in discussing the church could be found in ancient documents. But the meanings of *pope, cardinal, deacon, ecclesia, catholic, heretic, martyr* had altered; "and although we profess to adduce the monuments of the ancients, we produce our own." [197]

Much of his historical study was directed to reconstructing the actual practice of the ancient church, partly because he took it in some respects as a model, but partly also to show (in spite of Baronius) that the modern Roman church was different.[198] Occasionally the facile appeals to antiquity by

[191] Letter to Castrino, Oct. 26, 1609, Busnelli, II, 58.

[192] Cf. *Concilio di Trento*, II, 426.

[193] *Trattato delle materie beneficiarie, SG*, pp. 69, 79.

[194] Letter to Leschassier, Mar.18, 1608, Ulianich, p. 9: ". . . sciunt quantum antiquitatis cognitio illorum conatibus obsit. Credi volunt, quod hodie servatur, perpetuum fuisse."

[195] Dec. 11, 1607, Ulianich, p. 5.

[196] Cf. his cautionary remarks to Leschassier, Aug. 26, 1608, Ulianich, pp. 21–22.

[197] Sept. 14, 1610, Ulianich, p. 93. Cf. *Pensiero* 409, which remarks on the changes and development of language.

[198] There are many echoes of this study in his letters to Leschassier. Cf., for example, Ulianich, pp. 3, 8, 10, 14, 15–16.

ignorant papalists provoked his irony. He represented even Cajetan, whom he otherwise treated with respect, as proposing the restoration of strict penances on the ground that "the golden age of the primitive church will then return, in which the prelates had absolute governance over the faithful." [199] Others at the Council, he reported, had so insisted on the antiquity of penance that "one who heard these doctors speak could only conclude that the apostles and ancient bishops had never done anything but stay on their knees to be confessed or to hear others confess." [200]

But Sarpi was considerably more impressed by what he took to be the Council's general indifference and even contempt toward antiquity. The French ambassador had reminded the fathers that the world expected from them a thorough restoration of ancient purity,[201] and the bishop of Arras had proclaimed that "they should consider the apostles and martyrs and the ancient church, and make her the model from which to take the lineaments of the offspring that was to be born; and since doctrine, religion, and discipline have all degenerated in these times, it is necessary to restore them according to antiquity." [202] But Rome had taken a different view of the problem of reform. Thus Lainez charged those who demanded that the Curia return to the ways of the primitive church with a failure "to distinguish times, and what things are suitable to these and what were suitable for those." [203] Rome preferred to argue not that the modern church was identical with the ancient but that it had considerably improved on the past. Not only did new conditions require different practices, but the truth was now better known. As a Bolognese curialist proclaimed: "Olden times should not be so much praised as to make it seem that something could not be done better in later centuries." [204] The response of the fathers to such presumption had not been altogether favorable. As Sarpi observed: "Some properly warned that one should speak of antiquity with greater reverence and not say that it lacked knowledge of the truth";[205] his own disapproval of such sentiments is apparent.[206] But such passages suggest his awareness that the historical

[199] *Concilio di Trento*, I, 34.
[200] II, 126.
[201] III, 82.
[202] III, 332.
[203] III, 230–231.
[204] II, 108.
[205] II, 416.
[206] Cf. II, 501, where Sarpi remarks of the papalist theory of progressive development: "Le qual cose chi ben osserverà, vederà chiaro quali fossero le antiche instituzioni incorrotte, e come, duranti ancora quelle, è stato aperto l'adito per rispetti mondani

arguments developed by Baronius were finally less congenial tools for the Counter Reformation than the systematic and rational arguments advanced by the canonists and theologians.

Nevertheless Sarpi himself did not entirely idealize the ancient church. His own ecclesiological ideal was spiritual and therefore timeless; and he admired the church in antiquity only in the degree to which it had kept aloof from the world and from change, left all problems of external organization, administration, property, and discipline to rulers, and for the rest (since the Spirit works only in the hearts of individual believers) remained essentially localized, free, and democratic. The ancient church, he hinted, could not serve as a model in questions of detail because its own practice had by no means been uniform, even on such important matters as baptism and the form of the mass.[207] But beyond this the church, Sarpi believed, had from its very origin been exposed to the world and was altered and corrupted by it. The apostles had accepted gifts from the faithful, entrusting them to Judas; and the ultimate treachery had ensued. Sarpi concluded from the case of Judas that the misuse and corruption of holy things could not be ascribed "to the particular misery of our own or of any times but to divine permission for the exercise of good men, considering that the origin of the nascent church was subject to the same imperfections." [208] He frequently referred to the apostolic church, but less as a model of actual practice than because it suggested an abstract and rather general norm by which to measure the imperfections of concrete actuality.[209] But reform, like happiness and knowledge, was for Sarpi always process and struggle; it could never be fully consummated, never finally achieved. Perfection had no place in his conception of earthly reality, and his tragic vision made no exception of the church.

He had nevertheless, during the years after the interdict, increasingly committed himself to the struggle for perfection; and this required identifying the particular modes of ecclesiastical corruption and trying to explain them so that they might be corrected. He thus attacked numerous specific abuses,

---

alle corruttele; e per quali interessi parimente; poichè indebolito il buon uso, l'abuso ha preso piedi, voltato l'ordine, e posto il cielo sotto terra: le buone instituzioni sono pubblicate per corruttele e dall'antichità solo tollerate; e li abusi introdotti dopo, sono canonizzati per correzioni perfette."

[207] I, 388–389; II, 453, where the point is made by a Dominican theologian.

[208] *Trattato delle materie beneficiarie*, SG, pp. 13–15.

[209] Cf. *Concilio di Trento*, III, 55, and his letter to Leschassier, Dec. 11, 1607, Ulianich, p. 5.

chiefly institutional, such as the commendam, the inalienability of ecclesiastical property, the right of asylum, payments for ordination, compulsory tithing, and coercion in matters solely of belief.[210] But these, as he saw, were only incidental expressions of a deeper evil, particular manifestations of the church's general inability to preserve its spirituality. As Luther had charged against the papacy, the church had resorted to "human reasons as if it were a temporal state" and to "that sort of wisdom which Saint Paul says is considered madness with God." [211] The church had been corrupted from the beginning by concerning itself with possessions and power. It had thus identified itself with those things that inevitably change and decay, and it had naturally changed and decayed in the process.

But although Sarpi considered ecclesiastical decay a perennial problem, like the deficiencies of human nature fundamental to it, he also attributed corruption to particular circumstances. These had allowed the possibility of decline, always present in this world, to become actual. The problem of explanation was thus historical as well as anthropological, and Sarpi located another set of causes in the political developments of the medieval centuries. His central thesis, developed systematically in the *Trattato delle materie beneficiarie* but underlying his other writings, was that the decay of political authority begun in the period of the barbarian invasions had gradually loosened all restraints on the clergy and left them a prey to their own most worldly impulses.

Thus, in proving against Rome the vulnerability of the church to the forces of general historical change, Sarpi resorted to an essentially political conception of causation in ecclesiastical history. The political disorders of Italy had spread into the governance of the church, where all was thrown into confusion;[212] and although Charlemagne (whose ecclesiastical policies Sarpi both understood and applauded) had briefly restored order, his death had opened the way to a general deterioration. Thus, Sarpi wrote in connection with the expanding claims of the upper clergy to a direct political

---

[210] *Concilio di Trento*, II, 361–362, 375–376; *Sulla instituzione delle commende*, SG, pp. 1–2; *Trattato delle materie beneficiarie*, SG, pp. 31, 80–82; *Sopra l'officio dell'inquisizione*. SG, p. 131; *Su le immunità delle chiese*, SG, pp. 260ff.

[211] *Concilio di Trento*, I, 122.

[212] *Trattato delle materie beneficiarie*, SG, p. 50: "La confusione che fu in Italia nelle cose politiche, per tanti che furono in quei tempi fatti re e imperatori, causò anco nelle altre città estremo disordine nelle cose ecclesiastiche, essendo li vescovi e li abbati ora fatti dalli principi, ora intrusi dalla potenza propria; e li altri ministri ecclesiastici similmente fatti ora da quelli che dominavano nelle città e ora dalli vescovi, e alcune volte li benefizi anco occupati da chi aveva potenza o favor popolare."

authority, "the posterity of Charles degenerating so that it was finally lost in obscurity, the bishops thought it better for them no longer to recognize that authority came from the prince, but rather to attribute it to themselves alone, and to exercise it as proper to the bishopric, and to call it ecclesiastical jurisdiction; and such was the beginning of what we now see always contested with princes and what at times throws civil government into some confusion." [213] But Sarpi was also concerned with the confusion that had resulted over the function of the clergy; its seizure of worldly power had begun a long decline in the church which had proceeded step by step through the centuries, aided by the blindness of European rulers. By the time of Gregory VII it had become clear that "the aim of the prelates was not the salvation of souls but support from the faithful for their own pretensions";[214] and little more than a century later Boniface VIII, the first pope to do so, "openly declared that he claimed temporal authority over princes." [215] Thus Sarpi saw the defects of the contemporary Roman church as deeply rooted in the past.[216]

Both Sarpi's personal ideal and his understanding of the long process of ecclesiastical decay may be seen more clearly in his application of this general thesis to a number of particular developments. Thus one of the earliest symptoms of the church's decline, he believed, had been a growing materialism. The Christian community, as he noted, had from the beginning received gifts, which were used partly to support its apostolic leadership, partly for the poor. But its income had grown rapidly, and even before the barbarian invasions there were hints of decline in the administration of this wealth. The clergy began to live more comfortably, and bishops began to keep a part of what had previously gone to charity. In the fifth century the income of the church began to be regularly divided into four parts, not necessarily equal: one for the bishop, a second for the other clergy, a third for ecclesiastical buildings, a fourth for the poor. At about the same time the wealth of the church, previously liquid, began to take the form of fixed benefices yielding a regular income, and it became increasingly attractive to ambitious

[213] *Ibid.*, pp. 39–40.

[214] These words are from the *Consulto sui remedii, Scritti*, II, 157. For the investiture controversies, see also the *Trattato delle materie beneficiarie, SG*, pp. 53–56.

[215] *Delle contribuzioni de'chierici, SG*, pp. 240–241.

[216] Fulgenzio Micanzio included a remarkable sketch of ecclesiastical history along these same lines in a *consulto* of April 6, 1623, printed by Cecchetti, II, 244–246. This traces the temporal and ecclesiastical claims of the papacy from Gregory VII through the canonists to Bellarmine.

men, both for its own sake and as the basis of political power. Rivals began to contend for it, often so violently that at last princes were compelled to intervene, both to protect the church and to preserve public order. But with the decline of princely authority and the rise of ecclesiastical power, benefices came altogether under the control of the clergy. There was thus a powerful economic motive in the investiture controversy promoted by Gregory VII.[217] Sarpi also noted a substantial economic motive in the sponsorship of the crusades.[218]

The growing materialism of the medieval church had also been abetted by clericalism: the claim by the clergy of an exclusive right to control (as in the case of the wealth of the church) what had originally belonged to the whole body of believers. For the church had begun as a democracy. "The word church," Sarpi wrote, "first meant only the congregation of all those who believed in Christ, who called each other brothers or disciples." [219] In this situation the clergy of every rank had been elected by the whole body of the faithful; and clerical offices had been true ministries, not "dignities, preeminences, prizes, or indeed honors." [220] But the clergy, chiefly moved by greed, had succeeded in excluding the laity "from the name of the church" [221] and from all authority in it. They ended the system of election[222] and henceforth chose their own members; and they also elevated themselves above other Christians by securing various privileges, financial, legal, and political.[223] Their claims to superiority had finally culminated in the assertion that even the authority of rulers was a concession from the pope.[224] In this way clerical office had been transformed from humble service into lofty status. And increasing numbers of men were naturally attracted to it, not (as originally) to minister to particular needs but to enjoy the various benefits of superior rank. One result, as it appeared to Sarpi, was that eventually

[217] Sarpi first outlined the general process at the time of the interdict in his *Considerazioni sopra le censure, Scritti*, II, 209. He described it again much more fully in the *Trattato delle materie beneficiarie*, and also referred to it in *Concilio di Trento*, I, 400–401, and II, 502.

[218] *Trattato delle materie beneficiarie, SG*, pp. 61–62.

[219] From an autograph fragment quoted by Francescon, *Chiesa e stato*, p. 174 n.

[220] *Concilio di Trento*, I, 345.

[221] I, 401.

[222] On the original election of all ecclesiastical officers and the subversion of this practice, see *Trattato delle materie beneficiarie, SG*, pp. 15–16, 23, 27.

[223] Sarpi traced the financial immunities of the clergy historically in two *consulti*: *Delle contribuzioni de'chierici, SG*, pp. 233–247, and *Sopra le contribuzioni di ecclesiastici, SG*, pp. 249–257. For jurisdictional and political privileges, see below.

[224] *Trattato delle materie beneficiarie, SG*, p. 58.

there were too many clergy, to the general detriment of political and social order.[225]

Related to these developments was the establishment of church courts with a broad disciplinary and administrative jurisdiction; and Sarpi revealed, against those who attributed the judicial powers of the clergy to divine law, how this situation too had been a natural product of historical circumstances. When Christians disagreed, he reported, since they were forbidden to go to law against each other, they had submitted their differences for settlement by the bishops, at first with the aid of the priests and deacons and in the presence of the full congregation. But gradually what had thus been still an act of the whole community was left to the bishops alone; and their judicial authority had eventually been given legal force and extended by a series of misguided imperial decrees. In this way the bishop was converted into a functionary of the state, and the distinction between religion and politics was fatefully obliterated. "By these steps," Sarpi wrote, "the charitable correction instituted by Christ degenerated into a domination and caused Christians to lose their ancient reverence and obedience." And increasingly rulers also relied on bishops as political counselors, thereby making them both more worldly and more powerful. The bishops had steadily enlarged their authority over clergy and laity alike; eventually they claimed it as a concession from Christ.[226]

All of this was scandalous enough for Sarpi, but it was not the root of the matter. He took an even more serious view of the changes in the constitutional structure of the church which had both accompanied and supported its growing materialism and clericalism. In his view the church, by assuming the attitudes and asserting the claims of an earthly government, had inevitably exposed itself to those transformations which all polities, as agencies of this world, are destined to endure. As we have seen, he believed that the church had originated as a kind of free and spiritual republic; but then, taking on an increasingly formal organization and more and more openly political responsibilities and attitudes, it had passed step by step through the same constitutional evolution as secular states, whose cycle of forms had been described long ago by the ancients and more recently by Machiavelli. Sarpi's analysis of the historical development of the church, and similarly his conception of reform, were profoundly influenced by the constitutional

[225] *Ibid.*, p. 34. The very idea of too many clergy may appear bold. Cf. *Concilio di Trento*, II, 358–359.
[226] *Ibid.*, II, 101–106.

speculation of the Renaissance. His basic questions are thus familiar: how does a republic degenerate into a principate? is such a transformation to be avoided or desired? can it be reversed? what is a tyrant and how does he behave? can he be restrained? The novelty of Sarpi's thought lies in the fact that he puts these questions to the church.

The subversion of the ecclesiastical constitution consisted generally, in Sarpi's vision, of a slow process of centralization that had proceeded step by step, first within particular churches and then within the church as a whole. The process had been set in motion by the clerical usurpation of authority. For a while, according to Sarpi, churches had been ruled by the "common council of the presbytery," which composed a local ecclesiastical aristocracy. But because priests often disagreed about the governance of local churches, a monarchical episcopate had seemed expedient; for Sarpi, it seems clear, bishops had not been instituted by Christ but had appeared in the natural course of events to solve immediate practical problems. Similarly some bishops had enjoyed greater authority than others for reasons of convenience. The bishops of a neighborhood began to meet in local synods to discuss common problems, and the bishop of the chief city in the locality would be accepted as leader "by custom alone" and "to facilitate the government." This system, Sarpi noted, still prevailed in the Greek church. But in the West the process of centralization had been completed under the bishop of Rome. He had appropriated for himself the titles of *pope* and *pontiff* once applied to the whole episcopate; and popes had steadily undermined the authority of their fellow bishops, above all by sponsoring successive monastic orders active everywhere, exempt from local episcopal authority, and subject only to themselves. Thus the western church had, in the course of the centuries, passed through the whole sequence of constitutional forms and in the usual order, from democracy through aristocracy to monarchy. And the papal monarchy had been converted into an open tyranny by the claim of the pope to stand above the canons that regulated the universal community of Christians.[227]

From a religious standpoint Sarpi obviously deplored this whole process, and as a reformer he was actively concerned that it should be reversed. Yet there is another side to his attitude. Like Machiavelli he was fascinated as well as appalled by power, and he could not suppress altogether his admiration

[227] The whole process is most succinctly traced in *Concilio di Trento*, I, 350–352. See also III, 54, and *Trattato delle materie beneficiarie*, SG, pp. 31, 41; and, for the papal subversion of law, *Sopra l'officio dell'inquisizione*, SG, pp. 176–177.

at its effective use, even in the church. Precisely because the popes had become both Italian princes and tyrants over the *respublica christiana*, they exposed themselves to the political evaluations made familiar by Machiavelli. At times, therefore, Sarpi seems to attack the actions or policies of popes not so much as morally or spiritually objectionable but simply as, from a political standpoint, imprudent or ineffectual. He hinted, for example, that the failures of Adrian VI had resulted from defects of intelligence and decision;[228] and he blamed the English schism on the pope "for having proceeded rather with wrath and emotion than with the prudence necessary to great enterprises." [229] In such cases, it would appear, Sarpi believed that the papacy might have done better to follow the example of Machiavelli's prince.[230] Precisely because the church had been converted into a tyrannical government, the most successful and dangerous the world had yet seen, Sarpi's analysis of its exploits could call into play the realistic political understanding stimulated by the whole Renaissance experience.

His general view of ecclesiastical development is fundamental to Sarpi's historical explanation of Protestantism, a subject on which, though he gave it only passing attention, he reveals a remarkable sensitivity to complex historical relationships. None of the simpler explanations of the time satisfied him. He quickly dismissed, for example, the notion that the Protestant revolt had been the achievement of one man, inspired (according to Catholics) by the devil. Luther, he declared, "was only one of the means, and the causes were more potent and recondite." [231] In the light of his longer perspective, the common view that particular abuses were to blame, though a partial truth which from time to time he recorded,[232] must also have appeared to him superficial. Similarly it was true and worthy of note that immediate tactical errors by the Curia had forced Luther into a more radical position, but this too had hardly been fundamental.[233] Nor was he convinced that Protestantism could be fully explained as a cloak for political ambition,

[228] *Concilio di Trento*, I, 35–38, 49.

[229] I, 107–108.

[230] Paul III seems to have come off better in this respect; cf. I, 115ff., for example, in which Sarpi reveals this pontiff as a master of dissimulation and manipulation.

[231] I, 236.

[232] As I, 28: "Veniva considerato che le novità non avevano avuto altra origine se non dagli abusi introdotti dal tempo e dalla negligenza delli pastori; e però non essere possibile rimediare alle confusioni nate se non rimediando agli abusi che n'avevano dato causa." See also II, 79–80.

[233] I, 121. Cf. p. 16, where Leo X is represented as regretting the measures he had taken against Luther.

although he recognized like Davila that powerful men had exploited it in their own interest.[234] He was fully aware that it had attracted numerous converts, particularly among the common people, who had been moved by religion.[235]

For Sarpi all these matters were relevant to the issue, but the essential cause of the Protestant revolt had been the steady subversion of the ecclesiastical constitution by the papacy, the conversion of the church from a republic into a tyranny, and the transformation of the faith from a religion of freedom and grace into a religion of authority. In this perspective *ecclesiastical* and *religious* history could not be readily distinguished; the profound corruption of the former had resulted in the corruption of the latter. And Sarpi identified the rise of heresy in western Europe with that moment in the history of the church, the investiture controversy, when the papacy had first asserted its authority over princes and decisively transformed the church into a system of government.[236] The ultimate abuse, it had inevitably exposed the church to all other abuses, both of belief and of practice. With Sarpi, therefore, the question whether the causes of the Reformation were primarily institutional or theological was basically meaningless. Both the protest against abuses and the doctrinal challenge had been directed against a more fundamental evil. Although Sarpi was sympathetic to both, he refused to identify himself finally with either. His target was the ultimate abomination.

Sarpi's conception of the general history of the church is particularly relevant to his view of the Council of Trent. The development of church councils he regarded as an epitome of what had happened to the church in general, with Trent as its climax. He believed that the earliest councils, following the precedent of Jerusalem, had been conducted in absolute simplicity, "without ceremonies or formulas" and with love as their only principle of operation. They had been headed solely by Christ and the Holy Spirit, and all their human participants had been equal, a situation which had also prevailed for some time after the rise of the episcopate. But eventually some spiritual decline became apparent, and as a result a more formal organization was needed. Thus "the chief among those assembled in the

[234] Cf. II, 45 (for England) and 248 (for France).

[235] Cf. II, 230. He also pointed to the importance of the preachers sent out from Geneva in disseminating Protestantism in France (II, 249).

[236] *Sopra l'officio dell'inquisizione*, SG, p. 133.

council, either for doctrine or the greatness of his city or church or for some other sort of eminence, undertook to guide the proceedings and to collect its judgments." Still later, as internal decay grew and external difficulties increased, it became necessary for the emperor to assume these tasks. But the separation of western Europe from the eastern Empire eventually made it possible to exclude secular princes from ecclesiastical councils, and the pope was thus able, step by step, to assume the authority previously wielded by the supreme temporal power. The pope had first dispatched his legate to any local council that came to his attention, and then had gradually claimed the exclusive right to convene, to preside over, and to guide the action of every general council. Thus the history of church councils had reached the same despotic stage as the rest of church history.[237]

The Council of Trent therefore served Sarpi as a striking illustration of the general politicization of the church and its tragic conversion into tyranny, and he gave some emphasis to the authoritarianism there of spokesmen for the pope. He was particularly interested in an address by Lainez, in October of 1562, which had starkly enunciated the papalist doctrine by making a sharp distinction between civil governments, whose rulers are responsible to the community, and the divinely appointed monarchical government of the church. Considered as a community, Lainez had proclaimed, the church "is born in servitude, without any sort of liberty, power, or jurisdiction, but subject in all and for all." Christ during his earthly life had "governed the church with an absolute and monarchical government; and on leaving this world, he left the same arrangement behind, appointing his vicar Saint Peter, and his successors, to administer it as he himself had done, giving them full and total power and jurisdiction, and subjecting the church to them precisely as it was subjected to him." This meant, Lainez had concluded, that the Council of Trent was utterly dependent in all its operations on the pope. Sarpi's own feelings about these sentiments were doubtless the same as those of one of the fathers present who, after listening to Lainez, expressed his amazement "that Christian ears should hear that the whole power of Christ might be communicated to another person." [238]

The consequences of the church's transformation into a government, and especially into the sort of government of which Lainez had boasted, were variously reflected, for Sarpi, by the proceedings at Trent. He was particularly struck by the absence of the love which presumably rules genuinely

[237] *Concilio di Trento*, I, 214–217.
[238] III, 47–53, 232.

spiritual bodies, such as the earliest councils had been. Instead, as an inevitable result of the change in the character of the church, the Council of Trent had patently exhibited, as we have already remarked, the same animosities and conflicts of interest manifested in all political life. Sarpi took considerable pains to emphasize, in his account of its history, tensions, disagreements, divisions, and confusion of every kind. He shows the representatives of princes, including the Venetians, constantly quarreling over precedence.[239] Spanish conceit displeases the other ambassadors,[240] and even the Habsburg princes are unable to agree.[241] The pope and the emperor are constantly at cross-purposes; bishops disagree with other bishops, and dispute the superior authority of the archbishops and patriarchs; the secular clergy contend with the regulars, and Dominicans with Franciscans; canonists oppose theologians, the schoolmen attack the grammarians, and even the papal legates are occasionally at odds. Sarpi repeatedly makes the point: "Words of some acerbity were born, and the rest of the congregation went on to discuss the matter, not without much confusion." [242] "Everything that might have pleased the ambassadors would have been either injurious to the Curia or distasteful to the bishops; nor could anything have been welcome to the bishops that would not have been prejudicial either to Rome or to the princes." [243] "The usual contradictions and contentions were excited anew." [244] A less edifying spectacle, Sarpi appears to be insisting, can hardly be imagined; and he reported the belief of many Protestants that the papists were far more profoundly divided than themselves.[245] It may also be observed that Sarpi's emphasis on this point is intended to suggest the absurdity of expecting reform and the reconciliation of Christendom from so divided an assembly.

The conversion of the church first into a polity and then a tyranny had also a second major consequence for the Council. It had deprived the fathers at Trent of that freedom of discussion and decision which alone might have produced some genuine spiritual accomplishment. The authoritarian papacy, as Sarpi emphasized, from the beginning had been opposed to a council as a

[239] As II, 385, 386, 419; III, 88–89, 208–210, 240, 257–258.

[240] III, 210–212.

[241] III, 176. Sarpi observes, with a kind of satisfaction, "Non però questi principi erano in tutto concordi."

[242] II, 369.

[243] III, 30.

[244] II, 491.

[245] II, 278.

threat to its authority. Clement VII, for example, being "well versed in the affairs of state," had persistently maintained for this reason "that in the occurrences of these times it was pernicious counsel to make use of councils." [246] And when a council became inevitable, the Curia had exerted every effort to keep it under control, to manage its agenda, and to limit discussion, though at the same time pretending (with a fine show of indignation at those who professed doubt on the point) that the Council enjoyed complete freedom.[247] But in fact the hand of the pope was everywhere at work behind the scenes, and one of Sarpi's motives was to expose the ultimate subservience of the Council to curial manipulation.

Thus he depicts the legates regularly soliciting instruction from Rome on questions both of substance and of tactics,[248] and Rome supplying it; couriers were constantly passing back and forth between Rome and Trent, to the indignation of many of the fathers.[249] The Spanish delegation complained at "this insupportable imposition, that every item of business should require not only consultation, but consultation and decision in Rome ... nothing was resolved by the fathers, but everything in Rome, to such a degree that a blasphemous proverb was on the lips of all: that the synod of Trent was guided by the Holy Spirit sent up periodically in the dispatch-cases from Rome." [250] Meanwhile the legates used every device to inhibit debate, above all when it threatened to touch on papal authority. Denunciations sent to Rome, threats, veiled charges of heresy, pressure from secular governments reminded by the pope of the danger of conciliar freedom to themselves: all were invoked against any man bold enough to demand more open discussion or more vigorous reform. The function of the Council was to be kept as narrow as possible; as one of the legates informed the assembled fathers, they had been convened "only to condemn heresies." [251] We may detect in Sarpi's emphasis on this point not only religious indignation but also a hint of republican outrage.

Already apparent here is a third important result of the decline of the church into a species of government: that its affairs, as became peculiarly

---

[246] I, 55. Cf. pp. 78–79: "Ma il pontefice, che di nessuna cosa più temeva che di un concilio, e massime quando fosse celebrato di là da'monti, libero e con l'intervento di quelli che già apertamente avevano scosso il giogo dell'obedienza."

[247] Cf. II, 380–381; III, 322.

[248] Cf. II, 169, 268.

[249] See the complaint of the cardinal of Lorraine, III, 202.

[250] II, 371.

[251] III, 92

evident at Trent, were now conducted largely by political techniques, by pressure and manipulation. Sarpi's history of the Council of Trent is thus necessarily a political history, and it was appropriate for this reason for him to draw on the methods and attitudes of his Florentine and Venetian predecessors in this genre. Not only does Sarpi treat the popes of the Council much like Machiavellian princes, although deprived of military force and compelled to struggle to maintain a vast tyranny with the arts of peace. In addition his conception of their predicament may be seen as an illustration of a problem with which Renaissance political speculation was centrally concerned: the predicament of the man of *virtù* (here clearly *virtuosity* rather than *virtue*) contending with circumstances that threaten to destroy him. Sarpi is even more ambivalent, in his depiction of papal action at Trent, than in his attitude to earlier popes as political leaders; because the cynical maneuvering that Sarpi must deplore for its invasion of the church he is compelled to admire, as a student of politics, for its finesse and finally for its success.

His focus is thus finally on the popes themselves, master politicians in the end, though in so bad a cause; and a better illustration could hardly be found than the Council of Trent to display how they had fallen into this role and how well they managed to fill it. Their long success in holding off the Council had been impressive,[252] and so too their skill in playing on Italian fears that a foreign power might come to dominate the papacy, the only honor now left to Italy,[253] and in balancing between France and the Habsburg powers;[254] for Sarpi the papacy had been notably successful in carrying out a policy that had also seemed the best way to protect the independence of Venice. Much of the story he tells thus takes place not in Trent but in Rome and the other great power centers of Europe. Meanwhile, at the Council itself, the pope and his able lieutenants were displaying remarkable skill in another type of political manipulation, controlling the numbers of fathers,[255] sending reinforcements for the papalist faction at strategic moments, keeping the Council too busy with dogmatic questions to discuss reform,[256] gaining information from spies among the opposition,[257] controlling votes by

[252] Cf. the guile Sarpi attributes to the Curia, I, 92–93.
[253] Cf. III, 43, for example.
[254] *Passim:* II, 169, for example.
[255] As I, 175, 225.
[256] Cf. II, 143–144.
[257] III, 84–85.

promises of preferment,[258] spreading rumors.[259] The effectiveness of both kinds of maneuver in the unpromising situation confronting the papacy suggests in the end, perhaps, that Sarpi took a more positive view than some of his other writings may indicate of what can be accomplished in the political world by a man of skill and determination.

The political virtuosity of the papacy reached its great climax, for Sarpi, in the final group of sessions at Trent in 1562–1563. At no point had the situation looked so unpromising for the Curia, and the pope had agreed to reconvene the Council only because the alternative would have brought a general decline in the support of the major secular powers, a further movement toward Protestantism, the recourse to national councils: in short, a complete disintegration of the papal system.[260] Yet it seemed likely that to call the Council together once again might produce an even worse result. The resentment of many of its members at curial manipulation, the resistance of bishops to papal centralization, suspicion by the secular powers of the pope's intentions, pressure for basic reform, everything that for Sarpi expressed the health of the church, were now stronger than ever; and for once, with the major states at peace, it seemed unlikely that the pope could play off one against another. The Spanish ambassador had joined the bishops of his nation in demanding a genuinely free council, and the latter were openly denouncing the Curia as the source of every abuse and calling for restrictions on the authority of the pope.[261] The emperor took the same position and threatened to intervene to force the Council to enact real reforms.[262] The French were even more radical and outspoken. They demanded not only "opportune remedies" and an end to "clear and manifest abuses" but also a strong collective affirmation of the superiority of a general council to the pope.[263] Worst of all, these various enemies of the Curia now seemed disposed to work together.

The situation looked black indeed for the future of the papal tyranny; and for a moment, Sarpi seems to have believed, the constitutional deformity that supported every other abuse might have received a fundamental remedy. Apprehension at the Curia mounted as the fathers in Trent discussed

[258] As III, 127.
[259] As I, 428–431.
[260] II, 250ff.
[261] II, 317, 388; III, 11.
[262] III, 168–169.
[263] III, 71–72, 95.

one reform after another, and above all at the demand that episcopal residence be identified as an obligation of divine law. On the surface the proposal merely attacked the dispensing power of the pope, but Sarpi recognized that it hit at the root of hierarchy and centralization in the church. Thus, he reported, the followers of the pope foresaw that, if this should be allowed to stand, Rome would be "emptied of prelates and deprived of every prerogative and eminence." [264] The papal legate, Cardinal Seripando, was reduced to bitter remonstrations at the "excessive liberty" of the fathers "in entering on these questions and the boldness of discussing the power of the pope, all vainly and immoderately, repeating the same things ten times and more, and by some with shallow arguments and unsuitable manners unworthy of that assembly." [265] The temper of the Council grew increasingly unruly.

This comprehensive challenge brought the Council, for Sarpi to its great climax, and in describing it he revealed both a considerable dramatic skill and his ambivalence in the presence of political art. The artist in this case was Pius IV, who had done his best to avoid reconvening the Council and then (like any good statesman) had chosen what seemed the lesser of evils and made the best of what could no longer be prevented.[266] He was "a person of great intelligence and much experience in affairs" [267] and, as Sarpi presents him, a master of guile. On one occasion, Sarpi reported, he had made a series of apparently wild charges in his consistory, attacking (among others) the French ambassador in Trent as no better than a Huguenot, the Venetian ambassadors for obstructing his wishes, and even his own legates to the Council as unworthy of their responsibilities. But, Sarpi observed, "the whole thing was done and said by him (although it would not all have been believed) not through incontinence of the tongue but with art, to force each one through fear, shame, and courtesy, to make his own defense to him. This he received with the greatest facility and readily believed; and it is incredible how much he advanced his own interests in this way. He won over some, and he made others proceed more cautiously and more submissively." [268]

Faced with the prospect of a revolt in the Council which threatened to destroy the political achievement of centuries, the situation of the papacy,

[264] II, 379.
[265] III, 87.
[266] Cf. II, 245.
[267] III, 180.
[268] II, 402–403.

as Sarpi represented it, was delicate. The pope had somehow to frustrate reform, though he could not appear publicly opposed to it, and to bring the Council as quickly as possible to an end.[269] To obtain these goals he pursued a double strategy, in which he was assisted by men as politically astute as himself. In the sessions of the Council, while staunch papalists like Lainez denounced the presumption of those who proposed to reform the Curia, defended the propriety (or at least the utility) of much that was generally condemned as abuse, criticized the primitive model of reform, and proclaimed that the pope's tribunal was that of Christ himself,[270] Simonetta held the Italian fathers together by playing on their resentment of foreigners and above all by his extraordinary knowledge of men, whose various native talents, perfected by experience at the Curia, he exploited "to oppose those in the congregations contrary to his aims." These men "were skilled in the trick of jesting knowingly to irritate or make fun of the others, preserving their own dignity and not allowing themselves to be disconcerted." [271] Sarpi's own experience with the tricks by which men accomplish their purposes in the disputes of committees and assemblies, one suspects, has contributed to this aspect of his account.

At the same time the diplomatic Morone was at work behind the scenes attempting to break up the antipapal coalition. His first target was the emperor, whom the pope had identified as the easiest of his enemies to influence;[272] and accordingly Morone was dispatched to the imperial court at Innsbruck. What exactly transpired there, Sarpi admitted, was "among those things to which my knowledge has not arrived." But rumor had it that Morone succeeded in persuading the emperor of the futility of continuing the Council, the likelihood that it would result in some great scandal, and the desirability of concluding it as quickly as possible; and it seemed to Sarpi that from this point the emperor gradually began to withdraw his support from the Council. In any event, he concluded, "the catastrophe had its beginning in this time." [273]

Next, Morone turned his considerable powers of persuasion on the cardinal of Lorraine, leader of the French delegation. His flattery was not enough,[274] but now there intervened a series of unpredictable events in

[269] III, 33, 59, 60, 177, 293, 305, 307.
[270] III, 230–231.
[271] II, 317–318, 418.
[272] III, 180–181.
[273] III, 205–206.
[274] III, 214.

France, of the kind that for Sarpi so often arise to frustrate the calculations of men. Already beginning to doubt that reform could be expected at Trent, Lorraine's attention was completely diverted from the Council during the summer of 1563 by developments at home, especially the death of his brother, the duke of Guise, at the hands of the Huguenots. Henceforth "he saw clearly that there was no other way to support religion and his family in France than union with the Apostolic See"; and he wanted only the benevolence of the pope and a quick end to the Council so that he could return home. In addition the pope promised him great influence at the Curia and even hinted that he might expect to become the next pope.[275]

Thus, within a few months, the reform alliance had totally collapsed. The pope had triumphed in everything; and, Sarpi wrote ironically as though describing a miracle, where previously he had described "variety of minds and opinions, the designs of the one in conflict with those of another, and delays obstructing decisions," and had therefore needed frequent pauses "to explain the counsels of different men, often repugnant to each other," from this point on he would "narrate a single purpose, and harmonious operations which appeared rather to fly than to run to a single end." All sides now desired only to rush the Council to a finish. Decrees acceptable to the pope, meaningless for the cause of a true reform but ominous for Christianity, were rapidly pushed through the assembly; and the pope, the crisis surmounted, ordered his legates to dissolve the Council.[276] But the miracle was of a singularly secular kind. It was the miracle of the fox who outwits and triumphs over a band of ferocious lions resolved upon his destruction.

But in spite of his reluctant admiration, on one level, for this accomplishment, Sarpi's abomination of the Council on religious grounds is clear throughout. Its operations and decisions, in his view, had been defective in every respect; and thus, instead of achieving the reformation of the church, it had confirmed the church's deformation. He had made the point at the beginning of his account;[277] but now, instead of reiterating this judgment in his conclusion, thereby giving it a limited and merely personal significance, he preferred to hint, by reporting the reactions to the work of the Council in various parts of Europe, that this was the common opinion of contemporaries.

[275] III, 307.
[276] III, 331.
[277] This is, of course, the judgment Sarpi offers at the outset, I, 4.

In the first place, Sarpi suggested (as an opinion common in Germany during the earlier stages of the Council), the assembly at Trent had been incompetent, for technical and other reasons, to deal with the problems it had presumed to settle. The argument evidently rested on theories of representation advanced in the previous century, with which Sarpi may have felt some sympathy. The German view was that those in attendance at Trent had been too few and too narrowly chosen properly to represent the church universal. Most had been "bishops of cities so small that, each representing his own people, it could not be said that they represented a thousandth part of Christendom"; and not a single German had been present.[278] The French, Sarpi noted, later developed similar objections; they had further insisted that no council could bind a people without its consent.[279] The attention he gave to the question of Protestant representation also suggests that he considered the exclusion of the Lutherans a serious defect in the universality of the Council.[280] In addition, as he makes the Germans remark, the Council had been incompetent in another respect. Few of its members, at least during the early stages when so much had been settled theologically, were theologians. Some were lawyers, "learned perhaps in that profession but not competent in religion," but "the greater number gentlemen or curialists." [281]

A consequence of this circumstance was that, although (as "those learned in ecclesiastical history" observed) the Council decided more theological questions in its first sessions alone than all previous councils of the church together,[282] its dogmatic decrees were unintelligible and meaningless. This outcome Sarpi represented as in some degree calculated, and a further consequence of the political nature of the Council. Concerned to make a show of unity where in fact there was great diversity of opinion, the legates had worked, with considerable success, to conceal division by devising deliberately ambiguous doctrinal formulas.[283] The result, as Sarpi remarked, was a curious combination of "unity of words and contrariety of minds," in spite of which, he remarked sardonically, there had been no difficulty in

[278] I, 259.

[279] II, 82–85, 388–389.

[280] Cf. such passages as II, 97, 149–164. It seems clear that Sarpi also regarded the restrictions on Protestant participation as a further infringement on the freedom of the Council.

[281] I, 259. Cf. pp. 284, 286.

[282] I, 365.

[283] Cf. I, 342–343.

condemning the Lutherans, on which "all agreed with exquisite una-nimity." [284] Eventually, as he noted in a letter to Leschassier, the ambiguity of the Tridentine decrees had the further advantage of allowing the Curia to interpret them in any sense it pleased.[285]

But their essential meaninglessness, he suggested, had been equally the result of theological incompetence, and more specifically of scholastic obfuscation. In Germany "facetious" observers had suggested "that if the astronomers, not knowing the true causes of the celestial motions, have propounded eccentrics and epicycles to save appearances, it was hardly astonishing if, wishing to save appearances with the super-celestial motions, [the Council] gave itself to eccentricity of opinion." For a man of Sarpi's scientific culture, the witticism could not have appeared altogether frivolous. It pointed to a profound connection between medieval cosmology (now largely discredited) and the assumptions of the schoolmen whom he also despised; it implied that the theology of the Counter Reformation was as backward as its science, and for much the same reasons. The "German" critics of the Council attacked its decrees on the ground that "the best expression is the simplest," a proposition fundamental to the new astron-omy;[286] and they objected strongly to their reliance on an Aristotelian terminology.[287] Even so the decisions of the Council were riddled with logical inconsistencies;[288] and thus, from every standpoint it had failed to solve the problems of belief.

The vanity of its dogmatic decrees had meanwhile been paralleled by the ineffectuality of its disciplinary decrees. Even when desirable, they had made little difference:[289] the Council, according to the proverb, was a mountain that had labored and brought forth a mouse.[290] The reason for this small effect was, of course, that the attention of the fathers had been confined to trivialities; the essential defects of the church had been ignored. The Council had behaved like a doctor ("it was generally said") who "treats con-sumption by curing the itching." [291] The reservation that no reform should

[284] I, 368.
[285] Sept. 1, 1609, Ulianich, pp. 53–54. Cf. Sarpi's remark in his letter of Sept. 29, p. 56: ". . . attamen cavete vobis, ne concilium illud recipiatis ea spe, quod ad bonum sensum trahi possit." For further comment on the ambiguity of the decrees of Trent, see Concilio di Trento, I, 260, 343–344; II, 500; III, 68–69, 254.
[286] I, 363.
[287] II, 146.
[288] Cf. II, 122–123.
[289] III, 296, 347, for example.
[290] III, 264.
[291] II, 438.

be interpreted as an infringement on the authority of the pope meant, quite simply, that there could be no fundamental reform. "Any fool would have known where it aimed," Sarpi wrote of the reservation: "that it merely implied a pertinacious obstinacy in abuses when it proposed to remedy them while preserving their causes." [292] And he noted the curious absence of a sermon to celebrate the first set of disciplinary reforms, as though to suggest that the fathers were ashamed of what they had done.[293]

But the crucial defect of the Council, in Sarpi's judgment, the reason for both the futility of its decrees and its lack of authority, was the patent absence from its proceedings of the Holy Spirit. The Council of Trent, in short, had not been a spiritual body. It had throughout been cleverly manipulated with the techniques appropriate to the political world, and it had also been deprived of liberty by the machinations of the Curia. Authority had constantly been exerted to inhibit that free discussion by devout and responsible men which is the necessary condition of any genuinely spiritual work. The councils of antiquity had been spiritual assemblies, and they had therefore achieved the spiritual ends for which they had been called: in the case of the Council of Jerusalem, for example, "the reunion of divisions and the reconciliation of contrary opinions." [294] But Trent, according to one of the wittier fathers at the Council, "favored and chosen as the city in which to establish a general concord of Christendom," had proved unworthy of that honor, and "must shortly incur universal hatred as a seminary of greater discords." [295] Sarpi's *Istoria del Concilio Tridentino* was a fulfillment of this lugubrious prophecy.

The work is full of interest as an interpretation of the past. But it was by no means conceived merely as the expression of a vision and an attitude. Sarpi was an activist as well as a contemplative; he conceived of historiography not only as an account of past politics but as an instrument for present and future action. A late *consulto* addressed to the Venetian government perhaps suggests the frame of mind in which he composed his history of the Council of Trent: "Not only in private questions and armed battles but also in literary affairs there is no greater misery than to remain only on the defensive; and he who takes such a role will necessarily succumb since the enemy, certain that he will be respected and not attacked, will boldly pass

[292] I, 419.
[293] I, 423.
[294] I, 5.
[295] III, 194.

on to new and more insolent injuries." [296] The advice suggests a fundamental confidence in the future and invites comparison with the disillusionment of Guicciardini, who had written history for the most part only to understand a catastrophe long past mending.

Sarpi wrote, therefore, in the expectation that a use for his work lay somewhere ahead; God could not allow his church to be forever degraded. But the effectiveness of literary, as of other kinds of action, depended for Sarpi on the occasion; and much of the time it seemed to him that the occasion for striking at the church of Rome was lacking. He often felt that only a remote posterity was likely to benefit from his work.[297] Although he had finished his history of the Council of Trent by the summer of 1616, he waited, as though for a sign from heaven that the moment of action had arrived.[298] But at last it came, not from Italy, where conditions were now hopeless, but from the Netherlands: Sarpi seems to have found it in the Synod of Dort, whose proceedings were followed with keen interest by many still in the Roman communion and widely interpreted as a bitter reverse to the hopes of the papacy.

Sarpi's *Istoria del Concilio Tridentino*, smuggled out of Italy by his English friends, was accordingly published in London, early in the summer of 1619, by the exiled and now Protestant archbishop of Spalato, Marcantonio de Dominis, with whom Sarpi had been acquainted before his flight from Italy.[299] De Dominis printed Sarpi's work much as he had received it, although making some attempt to polish its style.[300] But he indicated its source by identifying the author anagrammatically on the title page as *Pietro Soave Polano*. He also attached to it a dedication of his own composition to the heretical king of England. And, worst of all, he gave it a polemical subtitle: *History of the Council of Trent In Which Are Revealed All the Artifices of the Roman Curia to Prevent Either the Truth of Dogmas From Being Revealed or the Reform of the Papacy and of the Church From Being Discussed.* Sarpi's indignation at these indiscretions was probably genuine.

---

[296] *Sulla publicazione di scritture malediche contra il governo, SG*, p. 223. This work was composed no earlier than 1620, and Sarpi may well have had in mind his own recent history, published a year or more in the past.

[297] Cf. his letter to Groslot Sept. 25, 1612, Busnelli, I, 243.

[298] For what follows see Cozzi, "Sarpi, l'anglicanesimo, e la *Historia*."

[299] See Sarpi's account of de Dominis in his letter to Simone Contarini, Dec. 13, 1615, *Letter inedite del Sarpi al Senator Contarini*, ed. C. Castellani (Venice, 1892), pp. 61–63. Cf. his letter to Gillot, Feb. 17, 1617, Ulianich, p. 159.

[300] For what follows see the acute work of Luigi Salvatorelli, "La prima edizione autentica della *Istoria del Concilio Tridentino*," *Pan*, VI (1935), 353–355.

So open a challenge to ecclesiastical authority was deeply repugnant to the calculated subtlety of his own manner. In addition it seemed likely both to endanger his position in Venice and (by arousing resistance at the outset) to reduce the impact of his attack.[301]

Few historical compositions, nevertheless, can have become so quickly and widely popular. Within a decade Sarpi's history had been published in Latin, German, French, and English as well as Italian. The Latin edition alone went through four editions by 1622. And although it was put on the Index within a few months of its appearance in England, within a short time few literate men even in Rome had failed to read Sarpi's work. Its popularity was destined to persist, in Catholic as well as Protestant Europe, until well into the nineteenth century.[302]

But the extraordinary appeal of the *Istoria del Concilio Tridentino* did not derive solely from the fact that it presented an argument of such evident utility for religious controversy. Sarpi's work retained its influence because it was a historiographical masterpiece on a subject of great general interest. It was a masterpiece because it maintained the fruitful tension between the two essential elements of any vital historiography: empirical investigation, the product of a powerful impulse to comprehend the concrete world in all its actuality and immediacy, and an imaginative vision which reflects living needs and values. Both the method and the vision had deep roots in the republicanism of Italy, and Sarpi's great work has thus some claim to be considered the last major literary achievement of the Italian Renaissance.

[301] For the objections of Micanzio, see Gabrielli, pp. 226ff.

[302] Jedin, *Konzil von Trient, ein Überblick*, p. 93. See also Cozzi, "Sarpi, l'anglicanesimo, e la *Historia*," pp. 561. 584.

Epilogue

FRA Paolo Sarpi, the last great spokesman of the Venetian Republic, died on January 15, 1623.[1] His career, its moments of greatest influence and the decline of his practical authority after the interdict, had long reflected the transformations in the political vigor of his beloved Venice; and so also did the immediate sequel to his death. The government was sufficiently moved to announce the event promptly to its representatives abroad, a gesture normally reserved for the passing of a doge;[2] and within a few days reports of miracles performed by the dead monk were circulating among the populace. But, although the government reacted directly with indignation to the demand from Rome that Sarpi's remains should be disinterred for the trial that had proved impossible during his lifetime, it gave up its plans for a handsome memorial to its deceased champion.[3]

A few gestures expressed the honor in which he was still held. Fulgenzio Micanzio was appointed to succeed Sarpi as *consultore* to the Republic; Sarpi's *consulti* were copied out into great and well-indexed parchment volumes that were closely studied for generations;[4] and the government still felt bold enough in 1658 to refuse to permit the sale of Cardinal Pallavicino's *Istoria del Concilio di Trento* in Venetian territory, on the ground that its author had attacked "the memory of a faithful subject and servant of

---

[1] Cf. Gaetano Cozzi, "Sulla morte di fra Paolo Sarpi," *Miscellanea in onore di Roberto Cessi* (Rome, 1958), II, 387–396, which gives particular attention to Micanzio's idealized account of the event.

[2] See Camillo Manfroni, "Paolo Sarpi," in *Paolo Sarpi ed i suoi tempi*, (Città di Castello, 1923) p. 1, which quotes the official announcement: "Il padre maestro Paolo da Venezia servita, è stato dal Signor Iddio chiamato a sè: soggetto a noi carissimo per le sue degne qualità, e per aver in tutti i tempi ed occasioni, con pari fede, virtù e devozione mostrato grande amore per il servizio delle cose nostre."

[3] Dispatch of Sismondo d'Este to Savoy, Feb. 11, 1623, in Luzio, pp. 52–53. Cf. Battistella, *Repubblica di Venezia*, p. 636, on the effort of the Holy Office as late as 1722 to have Sarpi's remains removed from the Addolorata where he was first buried and dumped indiscriminately with the bones of other anonymous Venetian dead. His body was finally reburied in 1828 in San Michele di Murano.

[4] Gambarin, *Scritti*, III, 276.

the Republic." [5] But it was increasingly impossible for Venice to identify herself openly or in a general way with Sarpi's views, as the position of the Republic continued to deteriorate through the steady erosion of her Mediterranean commerce, the terrible plague of 1630, and the loss of Crete in the long and expensive conflict with the Turks during the middle decades of the century. Under these pressures Venice slowly weakened, both as a respected European power and as a source of vital republican energies; the oligarchic tendencies already apparent in her aristocratic government intensified; and her libertarian traditions chiefly survived as a calculated permissiveness that made her, in the later seventeenth and eighteenth centuries, a city of pleasure, the gaudiest stop on the Grand Tour of the European upper classes.

But the importance of Venice and of the ideals and attitudes whose development has been the subject of this book was by no means ended with the political decline of the Republic. The complex of values, immediately political but ultimately so much more, that had first been clearly enunciated in Renaissance Florence and then elaborated in Venice a century later, had meanwhile been taking root in other parts of Europe; and to this process the nourishment contributed by the political and historical literature of Venice was as significant as the stimulus supplied by the writings of the great Florentines. The fact that Venice had survived as a working republic, whatever the decline in her actual power and its moral foundations, undoubtedly contributed to her continuing influence. Men could visit Venice still, not only to marvel at her location and her beauty but also to enjoy her good order and to experience its persistent combination with a unique degree of personal freedom. The literature of Venice, unlike that of Florence, seemed to express an enduring tradition; Venice was not, like Florence, merely a monument to past glory but a living demonstration of fundamental truths about life in society.

The major Venetian writers were thus widely studied abroad and frequently translated. Gasparo Contarini's *Republica venetorum*, for example, so important for explaining the peculiar durability of Venetian institutions, was made available to English readers in 1598 in a translation by Sir Lewes Lewkenor,[6] which was prefaced by a sonnet of Spenser celebrating Venice

---

[5] Cecchetti, *Venezia e la Corte di Roma*, I, 78. Even so the position was based on Pallavicino's allegedly erroneous identification of Sarpi with the pseudonymous Pietro Soave.

[6] Under the title *Commonwealth and Government of Venice* (London, 1598).

as heir to Babylon and Rome:

> Fayre *Venice*, flower of the last world's delight,
> And next to them in beauty draweth neare,
> But farre exceedes in policie of right.

Eventually the polity of Venice, as Contarini had depicted it, was to leave a mark both on such theoretical works as Harrington's *Oceana* and on the practical constitutional discussions carried on in Cromwell's England and the Holland of de Witt.[7] And even in France (in spite of the growth of an absolutist tradition which discerned in Venice a principle quite antithetical to its own) Pierre d'Avity, in his popular survey of the world's political geography, cited Contarini shortly after the interdict and paraphrased his work in order to explain the superiority of the Venetian government over all others known to man.[8]

Meanwhile other Venetians found an audience abroad. The works of Paolo Paruta were translated, the *Perfezione della vita civile* into French (1582) and English (1658), and the *Discorsi* into German (1666); and their author was widely esteemed as one of the greatest political thinkers of his century.[9] Davila's history went into numerous Italian editions and was also made available in French, Spanish, English, and Latin;[10] Bolingbroke compared him to Livy.[11] But Sarpi was the most popular among the Venetian writers. Much of the interest in his work derived from its obvious value for religious polemic, Gallican as well as Protestant. Translations of his *consulti* circulated among Frenchmen, and of his letters among Anglicans;[12] his history of the Council of Trent was read everywhere, as we have seen, and its English translation was carried to the New World by William Brewster, spiritual leader of the Plymouth colony.[13]

But the larger political and historiographical significance of Sarpi's

---

[7] Gaeta, "Mito," p. 71; Fink, pp. 28ff. On Harrington see also W. H. Greenleaf, *Order, Empiricism and Politics: Two Traditions of English Political Thought* (London, 1964), pp. 236–237.

[8] *Les estats empires royaumes et principautes du monde* (Paris, 1635), pp. 476–477. This was first published in 1614.

[9] Curcio, p. 211 n. 1; Fink, p. 19 n. 77.

[10] See the introduction to the translation by Ellis Farnsworth, *The History of the Civil Wars of France* (London, 1758), I, v, for a list.

[11] *Letters on the Study and Use of History* (London, 1770), pp. 136–37.

[12] Cf. Francescon, p. 103; Taucci, pp. 2–3.

[13] Giorgio Spini, "Riforma italiana e mediazioni ginevrine nella Nuova Inghilterra puritana," *Ginevra e l'Italia* (Florence, 1959), pp. 454–455.

thought, with which his religious and jurisdictional position was so closely connected, also did not escape attention. The Enlightenment in particular recognized (like the Curia a century earlier, but in a different spirit) his affinities with the Renaissance. In the Berlin of Frederick the Great a book of worldly political counsel was attached to his name bearing the title, *Le Prince de F. Paolo;*[14] the attribution was spurious, but the instinct behind it was not altogether inappropriate. Above all, however, in an age whose importance for the evolution of modern historiography is now growing clearer, Sarpi was recognized as one of the great examples for a modern historian to follow. The *Encyclopédie* praised his "immortal history" of the Council of Trent: "The style and the narration of this work are so natural and so energetic, the intrigues are so well developed in it, and the author has sown everywhere in it reflections so judicious, that it is generally regarded as the most excellent piece of Italian history." [15] Hume listed him (with Machiavelli, Davila, and Bentivoglio) among the best modern historians whom he had tried to imitate.[16] For Gibbon Sarpi (with Guicciardini, Machiavelli, and Davila) was one of the four supreme "historians of modern languages" before his own time.[17] Both evidently found Venetian models of peculiar importance.

And it was left to the Enlightenment to celebrate most effusively, and to be most profoundly impressed by, the general achievement of Venice. The *Squittinio della libertà veneta* aroused indignation in many western Europeans,[18] and even Voltaire felt moved to take issue with it, as though an attack on Venice obscurely threatened his own most cherished ideals; the Venetian conception of liberty was evidently identical with his own. "No power can reproach the Venetians with having acquired their liberty by revolt; none can say to them, I have freed you—here is the diploma of your manumission," he wrote. "They have not usurped their rights, as Caesar usurped empire,or as so many bishops, commencing with that of Rome, have usurped royal rights. They are lords of Venice—if we dare use the audacious comparison—as God is Lord of the earth because he founded it. ... Rome lost, by Caesar, at the end of five hundred years, its liberty

[14] Griselini, p. 260.

[15] In the article, "Venise," *Encyclopédie, ou Dictionnaire raisonné des sciences, des arts et des métiers* (Paris, 1751–1765), XVII, 8. The article is by Jaucourt.

[16] Letter to Walpole, Aug. 2, 1758, in David Hume, *Letters*, ed. J. Y. T. Grieg (Oxford, 1932), I, 152. This passage was called to my attention by Peter Gay.

[17] *The History of the Decline and Fall of the Roman Empire*, Ch. LXX, n. 89.

[18] Cf. Foscarini, pp. 105–106.

acquired by Brutus. Venice has preserved hers for eleven centuries, and I hope she will always do so." [19] And the *Encyclopédie*, in describing Venice, seemed to echo Botero nearly two centuries before in its association of a splendid culture with the liberty (and the order) supported by her republican government. Jaucourt wrote of her: "The Republic of Venice enjoyed, after the League of Cambray, an internal tranquility that has never altered. The arts of the mind were cultivated in the capital of their state. One tasted there both liberty and pleasure." [20]

It was only after Venice had disappeared as an independent republic that she ceased to conjure up an ideal for man's life in society and became no more than the glorious but fading memory of Wordsworth's sonnet:

> ... Venice, the eldest Child of Liberty.
> She was a maiden City, bright and free;
> No guile seduced, no force could violate;
> And, when she took unto herself a mate,
> She must espouse the everlasting Sea.
>
> And what if she had seen those glories fade,
> Those titles vanish, and that strength decay;
> Yet shall some tribute of regret be paid
> When her long life hath reached its final day:
> Men are we, and must grieve when even the Shade
> Of that which once was great, is passed away.

This book has been concerned with the contribution of the Venetians themselves to the formation and development of the powerful myth of Venice as the ideal combination of liberty and order, and with the broad implications of the myth for European political and historical culture.

[19] From the article "Venise, et, par occasion, de la liberté," in *Oeuvres complètes*, ed Louis Moland (Paris, 1877–1885), XX, 552–554. This piece is actually one of Voltaire's *Questions sur l'Encyclopédie*, though it has often been included in editions of the *Dictionnaire philosophique*.

[20] XVII, 12.

Bibliography

1. Collections of sources

Briefe und Akten zur Geschichte des 30 jährigen Krieges. M. Ritter et al., eds. 11 vols. Munich, 1870–1909.

Carlo Emanuele I e la contesa fra la Repubblica Veneta e Paolo V (1605–1607): Documenti. Carlo de Magistris, ed. Venice, 1906.

Controversiae memorabiles inter Paulum V Pontificem Max. et Venetos: De excommunicatione contra eosdem Venetos Romae promulgata XVII. Aprilis anno 1606. Acta et scripta varia controversiae inter Paulum V et Venetos. Vicenza, 1607.

Documents Illustrative of the Continental Reformation. B. J. Kidd, ed. Oxford, 1911.

"Dokumente zum Ausgleich zwischen Paul V und Venedig," A. Nürnberger, ed. *Römische Quartalschrift für christliche Alterthumskunde und für Kirchengeschichte,* II (1888), 64–80, 248–276, 354–367.

"Fra Paolo Sarpi, documenti inediti dell'Archivio di Stato di Torino," Alessandro Luzio, ed., *Atti della R. Accademia delle Scienze di Torino,* LXIII (1927–1928), 24–60.

L'Interdetto di Venezia del 1606 e i Gesuiti. Silloge di documenti con introduzione. P. Pirri, ed. Rome, 1959.

Le Mercure Iesuite: ou recueil des pieces concernant le Progrès des Iesuites, leurs Escrits, & Differents: Depuis l'an 1620. iusqu'à la presente annee 1626. Le Tout Fidelement rapporté par Pieces publiques & Actes authentiques selon l'ordre des temps. Jacques Godefroy, ed. Geneva, 1626.

Nunziature di Venezia. Vol. I (1533–1535), Franco Gaeta, ed. Rome, 1958.

"Nuovi documenti su Fra Paolo Sarpi e Fulgenzio Micanzio," Achille de Rubertis, ed., *Civiltà Moderna,* XI (1939), 382–390.

"Nuovi documenti sulla vertenza tra lo studio di Padova e la Compagnia di Gesù sul finire del secolo decimosesto," Antonio Favaro, ed., *AV,* Ser. 3, XXI, Part 1 (1911), 89–100.

Paolo V e la Repubblica Veneta: Giornale del 22. Ottobre 1605–9. Giugno 1607. Enrico Cornet, ed. Vienna, 1859.

"Paolo V e la Repubblica Veneta. Nuova serie di documenti (MDCV–MDCVII). Tratti dalle deliberazioni secrete (Roma) del Consiglio dei Dieci," Enrico Cornet, ed., *AV*, Ser. 1, V (1873), 27–96, 222–318; VI (1873), 68–131.

Per la storia del componimento della contesa tra la Repubblica Veneta e Paolo V (1605–1607): Documenti. Carlo de Magistris, ed. Turin, 1941.

"Per l'epistolario di Paolo Sarpi," Pietro Savio, ed., *Aevum*, X (1936), 1–104; XI (1937), 13–74, 275–322; XIII (1939), 558–622; XIV (1940), 3–84; XVI (1942), 3–43, 105–138.

Pieces du memorable proces esmeu l'an M.DC.VI. entre le pape Paul V et les seigneurs de Venise. Saint Vincent, 1607.

Politici e moralisti del Seicento. S. Caramella, ed. Bari, 1930.

Raccolta degli Scritti usciti fuori in istampa, e scritti a mano, nella causa del P. Paolo V. co' signori venetiani. Secondo le stampe di Venetia, di Roma, & d'altri luoghi. 2 vols. Coira, 1607.

Relazioni degli ambasciatori veneti al senato. Eugenio Albèri, ed. 15 vols. Florence, 1839–1863.

Relazioni degli ambasciatori veneti al senato. Arnaldo Segarizzi, ed. 3 vols. in 4. Bari, 1912–1916.

Thesaurus antiquitatum et historiarum Italiae. J. G. Graevius, ed. 10 vols. in 45. Leyden, 1704–1725.

2. Individual sources

Ad Paulum V. Pontificem Maximum epistolae duorum clarissimorum iurisconsultorum, anno MDCVI. Venice, 1606. Included in the *Raccolta*, I, 127–135.

Amato, Giovanni. *Breve discorso del principio della Republica di Venetia.* n.p., n.d.

Avity, Pierre d'. *Les estats empires royaumes et principautes du monde.* Paris, 1635.

Baglioni, Lelio. *Apologia contro le considerazioni di F. Paolo.* Perugia, 1606.

Barbaro, Daniele. *Storia Veneziana.* Tommaso Gar, ed., *Archivio Storico Italiano*, VII, Part 2 (1844), 949–1137.

Bardi, Girolamo. *Dichiaratione di tutte le istorie, che si contengono ne i quadri posti novamente nelle Salle dello Scrutinio, & del Gran Consiglio, del Palagio Ducale della Serenissima Republica di Vinegia, nella quale si ha piena intelligenza delle più segnalate vittorie; conseguite di varie nationi del mondo da i Vinitiani.* Venice, 1587.

Baronio, Cesare. *Annales ecclesiastici*. 37 vols. Bar-le-Duc, 1864–1883.

———. *Paraenesis ad rempublicam venetam*. Rome, 1606. Included in the *Raccolta*, I, 96–126.

———. *Sententia super excommunicatione venetorum*. Rome, 1606. Included in the *Raccolta*, I, 135.

Bedmar, Count. "Una relazione del Marchese di Bedmar sui Veneziani," ed. I. Raulich, *AV*, Ser. 2, XVI (1898), 5–32.

Bellarmino, Roberto. *Avviso alli sudditi del Dominio Veneto di Matteo Torti Sacerdote e Teologo di Pavia*. Rome, 1607. Included in the *Raccolta*, II, 121–129.

———. *Opera*. 7 vols. Venice, 1721–1728.

———. *Risposta ad un libretto intitolato 'Trattato et resolutione sopra la validità delle scommuniche, di Gio. Gersone Theologo e Cancellier Parisino'*. Rome, 1606. Included in the *Raccolta*, I, 308–323.

———. *Risposta alla difesa delle otto propositioni di Giovan Marsilio Napolitano*. Rome, 1606.

———. *Risposta al trattato dei sette teologi di Venetia, sopra l'Interdetto della Santità di Nostro Signore Papa Paolo Quinto. Et all'oppositioni di P. Paolo servita, contro la prima scrittura contro Gersone dell'istesso cardinale*. Rome, 1606.

———. *Risposta alle oppositioni di fra'Paulo servita contra la scrittura del cardinale Bellarmino*. Rome, 1606.

———. *Risposta a un libretto intitolato Risposta di un dottore di Theologia* Rome, 1606. Included in the *Raccolta*, I, 149–182.

Bembo, Pietro. *Della istoria viniziana libri dodici*. 2 vols. Milan, 1809.

Beneficio di Cristo, Ruth Prelowski, trans. In *Italian Reformation Studies in Honor of Laelius Socinus*, John A. Tedeschi, ed. (Florence, 1965), pp. 21–102.

Biondi, Giovanfrancesco. *Storia delle guerre civili di Inghilterra*. 3 vols. Venice, 1637.

Bolingbroke, Henry St. John. *Letters on the Study and Use of History*. London, 1770.

Botero, Giovanni. *The Reason of State*. P. J. and D. P. Waley, trans. New Haven, 1956.

———. *Relationi universali. Divise in Quattro Parti. Arricchite di molte cose rare, e memorabili, E con l'ultima mano dell'Autore. Aggiuntovi di Nuovo La Ragione di Stato del medesimo*. Venice, 1640.

Bovio, Giovanni Antonio. *Lettera al R. P. M. Paolo Rocca nella quale si discorre sopra a due lettere del Doge e Senato di Vinetia al clero e populo del suo stato et sopra a due altre scritture intorno alla validità delle censure da Papa Paolo V pubblicate contra li Signori Venitiani.* Milan, 1606.

————. *Risposta alle considerationi del P. Maestro Paolo de Venetia.* Rome, 1606. In the *Raccolta,* II, 19–87.

Bruto, Giovanmichele. *Delle istorie fiorentine.* Stanislao Gatteschi, ed. 2 vols. Florence, 1838.

Campanella, Tommaso. *Antiveneti.* Luigi Firpo, ed. Florence, 1945.

Canaye, Philippe, Seigneur de Fresne. *Lettres et ambassade.* 3 vols. Paris, 1635–1636.

Capello, Marc'Antonio. *Delle controversie tra il sommo pontefice Paulo Quinto, et la serenissima republica di Venetia parere.* Venice, 1606.

Comitolo, Paolo. *Confutatione del libro de'sette teologi, contra l'Interdetto apostolico.* Bologna, 1607.

Commynes, Philippe de. *Mémoires.* Joseph Calmette, ed. 3 vols. Paris, 1925.

Contarini, Gasparo. *Commonwealth and Government of Venice.* Lewes Lewkenor, trans. London, 1598.

————. "Die Correspondenz des Cardinals Contarini während seiner deutschen Legation," Ludwig von Pastor, ed., *Historisches Jahrbuch,* I (1880), 321–392.

————. *De magistratibus et republica venetorum.* Leyden, 1628.

————. *Gegenreformatorische Schriften (1530c.–1542).* Friedrich Hünermann, ed. Münster in Westfalen, 1923.

————. "Lettere del Cardinale Gasparo Contarini durante la sua legazione di Bologna (1542)." Alfredo Casadei, ed., *ASI,* CXVIII (1960), 77–130, 220–285.

————. "La lettera del Cardinale Contarini sulla predestinazione," Aldo Stella ed., *Rivista di Storia della Chiesa in Italia,* XV (1961), 411–441.

————. *Opera.* Luigi Contarini, ed. Paris, 1571.

Contarini, Pier'Maria. *Compendio universal di republica.* Venice, 1602.

Coryat, Thomas. *Crudities.* 2 vols. Glasgow, 1905.

Crasso, Nicolò. *Antiparaenesis ad Cesarem Baronium Cardinalem, pro Sereniss. Veneta Republica.* Padua, 1606. Included in the *Raccolta,* II, 281–320.

Davila, Enrico. *The Historie of the Civill Warres of France.* Charles Cotterell and William Aylesbury, trans. London, 1647.

————. *The History of the Civil Wars of France.* 2 vols. Ellis Farneworth, trans. London, 1758.

————. *Istoria delle guerre civili di Francia.* 6 vols. Milan, 1807.

Dei, Benedetto. "Un frammento inedito della Cronaca di Benedetto Dei," Giustiniano Degli Azzi, ed., *ASI*, CX (1952), 99–113.

Del Bene, Girolamo. *Risposta alla dimanda fattagli circa l'essito di quel che passa al presente fra la Santità di Paolo V e la Serenissima Republica.* Bologna, 1606.

Difesa delle censure pubblicate da N. S. Paolo Papa V nella causa de' Signori Venetiani fatta da alcuni theologi della religione de' Servi in risposta alle considerationi di F. Paolo da Venetia. Perugia, 1607.

Discorso, sotto nome di sentenza d'un clariss. senator Veneto, esposta nel consiglio de' pregadi, sopra le contentioni prese contro la Chiesa. n. p., n.d. Included in the *Raccolta*, II, 273–280.

Donà, Leonardo. *La legazione di Madrid. Dispacci dal 1570 al 1573.* Mario Brunetti and Eligio Vitale, eds. 2 vols. Venice, 1963.

Du Perron, Jacques Davy. *Les ambassades et negotiations.* C. de Ligny, ed. Paris, 1623.

Encyclopédie, ou Dictionnaire raisonné des sciences, des arts et des métiers. 17 vols. Paris, 1751–1765.

Galilei, Galileo. *Opere.* Antonio Favaro, ed. 20 vols. Florence, 1890–1909.

Giannotti, Donato. *Lettere a Piero Vettori.* Roberto Ridolfi and Cecil Roth, eds. Florence, 1932.

———. *Opere.* 3 vols. Pisa, 1819.

Gibbon, Edward. *The History of the Decline and Fall of the Roman Empire.* H. H. Milman, ed. 5 vols. Philadelphia, n.d.

Giustinian, Antonio. *Dispacci di Antonio Giustinian.* Pasquale Villari, ed. 3 vols. Florence, 1876.

Giustiniani, Bernardo. *De origine urbis gestisque venetorum historiae.* In Graevius, *Thesaurus*, V, cols.

Giustiniani, Pietro. *Le historie venetiane.* Gioseppe Horologgi and Remigio Fiorentino, trans. Venice, 1576.

Guicciardini, Francesco. *Maxims and Reflections of a Renaissance Statesman.* Mario Domandi, trans. New York, 1965.

———. *Opere.* Vittorio de Caprariis, ed. Milan, n.d.

Henri IV, King of France. *Recueil des lettres missives.* M. Berger de Xivrey, ed. 9 vols. Paris, 1843–1876.

Hume, David. *Letters.* J. Y. T. Grieg, ed. 2 vols. Oxford, 1932.

———. "Leggenda veneziana di Alessandro III," D. Urbani de Gheltof, ed., *AV*, Ser. 1, XIII, Part 2 (1877), 361–369.

Le Jay, L'Avocat. *Tocsin au Roy, à la Royne régente aux Princes du sang contre le livre della puissance temporelle du Pape par le Cardinal Bellarmin.* Paris, 1610.

Leoni, Giovanni Battista. *Considerationi sopra l'Historia d'Italia di messer Francesco Guicciardini.* Venice, 1583.

Leschassier, Jacques. *Consultatio Parisii cujusdam de controversia inter sanctitatem Pauli V et Serenis. Rempublicam Venetam, ad virum Venetum.* Paris, 1606.

L'Estoile, Pierre de. *Mémoires-Journaux.* G. Brunet, ed. 12 vols. Paris, 1875–1896.

Lettera sotto nome della Repubblica di Genova (falsa) alla Repubblica di Venezia. Milan, 1606. In the *Raccolta,* II, 89–95.

Machiavelli, Niccolò. *The Chief Works and Others.* Allan Gilbert, trans. 3 vols. Durham, 1965.

———. *The Discourses.* Leslie J. Walker, trans. 2 vols. New Haven, 1950.

———. *Opere.* 7 vols. Florence, 1960–1964.

Manuzio, Aldo. *Il perfetto gentilhuomo.* Venice, 1584.

Marcello, Pietro. *De vita, moribus, et rebus gestis omnium ducum venetorum.* Venice, 1574.

———. *Vite de' prencipi di Vinegia.* Ludovico Domenichi, trans. Venice, 1557.

Marsilio, Giovanni. *Difesa a favore della risposta dell'otto propositioni contro la quale ha scritto l'illustrissimo et reverendissimo sig. cardinal Bellarmino.* Venice, 1606. Included in the *Raccolta,* I, 183–291.

———. *Essame sopra tutte quelle scritture, che sin hora sono state mandate alle stampe da alcuni, parte senza nome d'Autore, parte sotto nomi finti, e suppositi, parte con i proprii nomi di essi Autori contro la giustissima causa della Serenissima Repubblica di Venetia.* Venice, 1607.

———. *Risposta d'un Dottore in theologia ad una lettera scrittagli da un reverendo suo amico, sopra il breve di censure della Santità di Papa Paolo V publicate contro li signori venetiani: et sopra le nullità di dette censure, cavata dalla Sacra Scrittura, dalli Santi Padri, e da altri cattolici dottori.* n.p., n.d. Included in the *Raccolta,* I, 137–147.

———. *Votum excellentissimi, pro Serenissima Republica Veneta.* n.p., n.d.

Medici, Lelio. *Discorso sopra i fondamenti e le ragioni delli ss. Veneziani, per le quali pensano di essere scusati della disubbidienza, che fanno alle censure, e interdetto della santità di nostro signor Papa Paolo.* Bologna, 1606. Included in the *Raccolta,* II, 183–210.

Mercure François, Le. I (Paris, 1614).

Micanzio, Fulgenzio. *Confirmatione delle considerationi del P. M. Paulo di Venetia, contra le oppositioni del R. P. M. Gio. Antonio Bovio.* Venice, 1606.

————. *Vita del Padre Paolo dell'ordine de' Servi e theologo della Serenissima Republica di Venetia.* n.p., 1658.

Mornay, Philippe Du Plessis de. *Mémoires et correspondance.* A. D. de La Fontenelle de Vaudoré and P. R. Auguis, eds. 12 vols. Paris, 1824–1825.

Morosini, Andrea. *Historia veneta ab anno MDXXI usque ad annum MDCXV.* Apostolo Zeno, ed. 3 vols. Venice, 1719.

————. *L'imprese et espeditioni di Terra Santa, et l'acquisto fatto dell'Imperio di Constantinopoli dalla Serenissima Republica di Venetia.* Venice, 1627.

Nores, Iason de. *Panegirico in laude della Serenissima Republica di Venetia.* Padua, 1590.

Offman, Pandolfo. *Avvertimento, et ammonitione catolica. Al padre Antonio Possevino Giesuito. Contenuta in una lettera, scrittagli da un Gentil'huomo Alemano, allevo del collegio germanico di Roma.* Venice, 1607. Included in the *Raccolta,* II, 97–109.

Palmerio, Gio. Battista. *Lettera alli fedeli sudditi del dominio Venetiano.* n.p., 1607.

Paruta, Paolo. *Historia vinetiana.* Venice, 1703.

————. *La legazione di Roma, 1592–1595.* Giuseppe de Leva, ed. 3 vols. Venice, 1887.

————. "Lettere passate tra Antonio Riccobono et il Procuratore Paruta d'intorno allo scrivere le historie venete," Antonio Favaro, ed., in *AV,* II (1891), 169–180.

————. *Opere politiche.* C. Monzani, ed. 2 vols. Florence, 1852.

Patrizi, Francesco, *Della historia diece dialoghi ne' quali si ragiona di tutte le cose appartenenti all'historia, & allo scriverla, & all'osservarla.* Venice, 1560.

Pisanio di Pizzoni. *Copia d'una lettera a Papa Paulo V.* n.p., n.d. Included in the *Raccolta,* I, 406–408.

Pius II. *The Commentaries.* Florence A. Gragg, trans. Smith College Studies in History, XXII, XXV, XXX, XXXV, XLIII. Northampton, 1937–1957.

Ponte, Nicolò da. "Ricordi del doge Nicolò da Ponte per il buon governo della Patria in pace ed in guerra," N. Barozzi, ed., in *Raccolta veneta. Collezione di documenti relativi alla storia, all'archeologia, alla numismatica,* I (Venice, 1866), 5–17.

Porto, Luigi da. *Lettere storiche dall'anno 1509 al 1528.* Bartolommeo Bressan, ed. Florence, 1857.

Possevino, Antonio. *Lettera al maestro Marc'Antonio Cappello Minor Conventuale.* Bologna, 1606. In the *Raccolta,* II, 235–246.

————. *Nuova risposta di Giovanni Filoteo di Asti alla lettera di un Theologo incognito scritta ad un Sacerdote suo amico.* Florence, 1606.

————. *Risposta del Sig. Paolo Anafesto all'Avviso del Sig. Antonio Quirino.* n.p., n.d.

————. *Risposta di Teodoro Eugenio di Famagosta all'aviso mandato fuori dal sig. Antonio Quirino senatore veneto, circa le ragioni che hanno mosso la Santità di Paolo V pontefice a publicare l'Interdetto sopra tutto il dominio venetiano.* Bologna, 1607.

Priuli, Girolamo. *I Diarii.* Roberto Cessi, ed. *Rerum italicarum scriptores,* XXXIV: III. 4 vols. Bologna, 1912–1938.

Przvovski, Stanislao. *Condoglienza di S. P. Sublinessense studente in Padova. Col padre Antonio Possevino, Giesuita.* n.p., n.d. Included in the Raccolta, II, 228–233.

Querini, Antonio. *Avviso delle ragioni della serenissima repubblica di Venezia intorno alle difficoltà, che le sono promosse dalla Santità di Papa Paolo V.* Venice, 1606. In the *Raccolta,* I, 11–33.

Sabellico, Marco Antonio. *Le historie vinitiane.* Lodovico Dolce, trans. Venice, 1554.

Sansovino, Francesco. *Del governo et amministratione di diversi regni, et republiche, così antiche, come moderne.* Venice, 1607.

————. *Venetia città nobilissima, et singolare; Descritta già in XIIII libri.* Venice, 1604.

Sardi, Giovanni Simone. *Due discorsi sopra la libertà ecclesiastica.* n.p., n.d. Included in the Raccolta, II, 211–227.

Sarpi, Paolo. *Istoria del Concilio Tridentino.* Giovanni Gambarin, ed. 3 vols. Bari, 1935.

————. *Istoria dell'Interdetto e altri scritti editi ed inediti.* Giovanni Gambarin, ed. 3 vols. Bari, 1940.

————. *Lettere ai Gallicani.* Boris Ulianich, ed. Wiesbaden, 1961.

————. *Lettere ai Protestanti.* Manlio Diulio Busnelli, ed. 2 vols. Bari, 1931.

————. *Lettere inedite di fra Paolo Sarpi a Simone Contarini ambasciatore veneto in Roma, 1615.* C. Castellani, ed. Venice, 1892.

————. *Opere.* 8 vols. Helmstadt-Verona, 1761–1766.

————. *La Repubblica di Venezia, la casa d'Austria, e gli Uscocchi.* Gaetano and Luisa Cozzi, eds. Bari, 1965.

————. *Scritti filosofici e teologici.* Romano Amerio, ed. Bari, 1951.

————. *Scritti giurisdizionalistici.* Giovanni Gambarin, ed. Bari, 1958.

Servin, Louis. *Pro libertate status et reipublicae Venetorum Gallofranci ad Philenetum epistola.* Paris, 1606. In the *Raccolta* II, 1–17.

Sosa, Francesco di. *Discorso contro due trattati stampati senza nome d'auttore, intorno le censure che N. Signore Papa Paolo V pronuntiò contro la republica di Venetia.* Ambrosio Cordova, trans. Naples, 1607.

Squitinio della libertà veneta nel quale si adducono anche le ragioni dell'Impero Romano sopra la città e Signoria di Venezia. Mirandola, 1612.

Theologorum Venetorum Io. Marsilii, Pauli Veneti, Fulgentii, Ad excommunicationis, citationis, & monitionis Romanae. Sententiam in ipsos latam Responsio. n.p., 1607. In the *Raccolta*, II, 257–271.

Tomaselli, Fulgentio. *Le mentite Filoteane, overo Invettiva di Giovanni Filoteo d'Asti contra la Republica Serenissima di Venetia, confutata.* Padua, 1607. Included in the *Raccolta*, II, 389–405.

Two Biographies of William Bedell. E. S. Shuckburgh, ed. Cambridge, 1902.

Valier, Agostino. *Dell'utilità che si puo ritrarre delle cose operate dai Veneziani libri XIV.* Padua, 1787.

Vendramin, Hieronymo. *Assertiones contra Venetae Reipublicae Detractores ac Maledicos.* Venice, 1606.

Venturi, Ventura. *Della maiestà pontificia parte prima. Nell'occasione, del giusto risentimento, fatto dalla Santità di N. S. Paolo quinto, verso la Republica di Venetia.* Siena, 1607.

Voltaire, François-Marie Arouet. *Oeuvres complètes.* Louis Moland, ed. 52 vols. Paris, 1877–1885.

Wotton, Henry. *The Life and Letters of Sir Henry Wotton.* Logan Pearsall Smith, ed. 2 vols. Oxford, 1907.

Zeno, Niccolò. *Dell'origine de'barbari, che distrussero per tutto'l mondo l'imperio di Roma, onde hebbe principio la città di Venetia libri undici.* Venice, 1557.

3. Secondary Works

Abbagnano, Nicola. "Italian Renaissance Humanism," *Journal of World History*, XI (1963), 267–283.

Addio, Mario d'. *Il pensiero politico di Gaspare Scioppio e il Machiavellismo del Seicento.* Milan, 1962.

Adorno, Francesco. "La crisi dell'umanesimo civile fiorentino da Alamanno Rinuccini al Machiavelli," *Rivista critica di storia della filosofia*, VII (1952), 19–40.

Alberigo, Giuseppe. *I vescovi italiani al Concilio di Trento (1545–1547)* Florence, 1959.

Albertini, Rudolph von. *Das florentinische Staatsbewusstsein im Übergang von der Republik zum Principat.* Bern, 1955.

Amerio, Romano. *Il Sarpi dei pensieri filosofici inediti.* Turin, 1950.

Ancona, A. d'. "Saggi polemica e di poesia politica del sec. XVII (da una Miscellanea veneta)," *AV*, Ser. 1, III (1872), 386–412.

Bacchion, Eugenio. "Le vicende trivigiane dell'interdetto di Paolo V," *AV*, Ser. 5, XV (1934), 156–174.

Barblan, Guglielmo. "Aspetti e figure del cinquecento musicale veneziano," CVR, pp. 57–80.

Baron, Hans. *The Crisis of the Early Italian Renaissance: Civic Humanism and Republican Liberty in an Age of Classicism and Tyranny.* Rev. ed. Princeton, 1966.

———. "A Forgotten Chronicle of Early Fifteenth Century Venice," *Essays in History and Literature Presented to Stanley Pargellis* (Chicago, 1965), pp. 19–36.

———. *Humanistic and Political Literature in Florence and Venice at the Beginning of the Quattrocento.* Cambridge, Mass., 1955.

Baschet, A. *Les archives de Venise: histoire de la Chancellerie secrète.* Paris, 1870.

Battistella, Antonio. "Il dominio del Golfo," *AV*, Ser. 3, XXXV (1918), 5–102.

———. "Un'eco in Friuli della contesa dell'Interdetto," *Paolo Sarpi ed i suoi tempi: Studi storici* (Città di Castello, 1923), pp. 105–118.

———. "La politica ecclesiastica della Repubblica Veneta," *AV*, Ser. 2, XVI (1898), 386–420.

———. *La Repubblica di Venezia ne' suoi undici secoli di vita.* Venice, 1921.

———. "Venezia e l'Austria durante la vita della Repubblica," *AV*, Ser. 3, XXXI (1916), 279–320.

Battistini, Mario. "Jean Michel Bruto, humaniste, historiographe, pédagogue au XVIe siècle," *De Gulden Passer*, XXXII (1954), 29–153.

Becker, Marvin B. "Church and State in Florence on the Eve of the Renaissance (1343–1382)," *Speculum*, XXXVII (1962), 509–527.

———. "Florentine Politics and the Diffusion of Heresy in the Trecento: A Socio-Economic Inquiry," *Speculum*, XXXIV (1959), 60–75.

Belloni, A. *Il Seicento.* Rev. ed. Milan, 1929.

Beltrami, Daniele. "Lineamenti di storia della popolazione di Venezia dal Cinquecento al Settecento," in *Storia dell'economia italiana* (Turin, 1959), I, 501–531.

———. *La penetrazione economica dei veneziani in Terraferma. Le forze di lavoro e la distribuzione della proprietà fondiaria nelle campagne venete dei secoli XVII e XVIII.* Venice and Rome, 1961.

————. *Saggio di storia dell'agricoltura nella Repubblica di Venezia durante l'età moderna.* Florence, 1956.

Bennato, F. "La partecipazione militare di Venezia alla lega di Cognac," *AV*, Ser. 5, LVIII–LIX (1956), 70–87.

Bénoist, Charles. *Le machiavélisme.* 3 vols. Paris, 1907–1936.

Benzoni, Gino. "Una controversia tra Roma e Venezia all'inizio del'600: la conferma del patriarca," *BSV*, III (1961), 121–138.

Berenson, Bernard. *Italian Painters of the Renaissance.* London, 1952.

Bersi, Ruggero. "Le fonti della prima decade delle *Historiae rerum venetarum* di Marcantonio Sabellico," *AV*, Ser. 3, XIX (1910), 422–460; XX (1910), 115–162.

Besta, E. *Il senato veneziano.* Venice, 1899.

Beutin, Ludwig. "La décadence économique de Venise considérée du point de vue nord-européen," in *Aspetti e cause della decadenza economica veneziana nel secolo XVII* (Venice, 1961), pp. 87–108.

Bianchi-Giovini, A. *Biografia di Frà Paolo Sarpi teologo e consultore di stato della Repubblica Veneta.* 2 vols. Zurich, 1836.

Bonardi, Antonio. *I padovani ribelli alla Repubblica di Venezia (a. 1500–1530).* Miscellanea di storia venetiana. Ser. 2, VIII (Venice, 1902), 303–614.

————. "Venezia città libera dell'Impero nell'immaginazione di Massimiliano I d'Asburgo," *Atti e memorie della R. Accademia di Scienze, Lettere ed Arti in Padova*, Ser. 2, XXXI (1915), 127–147.

————. "Venezia e la lega di Cambrai," *AV*, Ser. 3, VII (1904), 209–244.

Branca, Vittore. "Ermolao Barbaro e l'umanesimo veneziano," in *Umanesimo europeo e umanesimo veneziano* (Venice, 1963), pp. 193–212.

Braudel, Fernand. *La Méditerranée et le monde méditerranéen a l'époque de Philippe II.* Paris, 1949.

————. "La vita economica di Venezia nel secolo XVI," *La civiltà veneziana del Rinascimento* (Florence, 1958), pp. 81–102.

Braudel, Fernand; Pierre Jeannin; Jean Meuvret; and Ruggiero Romano. "Le déclin de Venise au XVIIème siècle," in *Aspetti e cause della decadenza economica veneziana nel secolo XVII* (Venice, 1961), pp. 23–86.

Brentano, Robert J. *Two Churches: England and Italy in the Thirteenth Century.* Princeton, 1968.

Brodrick, James. *Robert Bellarmine, Saint and Scholar.* London, 1961.

Brown, Horatio. *Venice: An Historical Sketch of the Republic.* Rev. ed. London, 1895.

Brucker, Gene A. *Florentine Politics and Society, 1343–1378.* Princeton, 1962.

Brunetti, Mario. "Il Diario di Leonardo Donà procuratore di S. Marco de Citra (1591–1605)," *AV*, Ser. 5, XXI (1937), 101–123.

———. "Le istruzioni di un nunzio pontificio a Venezia al successore," in *Scritti storici in onore di Camillo Manfroni nel XL anno di insegnamento* (Padua, 1925), pp. 369–379.

———. "Schermaglie veneto-pontificie prima dell'interdetto. Leonardo Donà avanti il Dogado," in *Paolo Sarpi ed i suoi tempi: Studi storici* (Città di Castello, 1923), pp. 119–142.

Bueno de Mesquita, D. M. "The Place of Despotism in Italian Politics," in *Europe in the Late Middle Ages* (Evanston, 1965), pp. 301–331.

Buffon, Vincenzo M. *Chiesa di Cristo e Chiesa romana nelle opere e nelle lettere di fra Paolo Sarpi*. Louvain, 1941.

Burckhardt, Jacob. *Die Kultur der Renaissance in Italien: Ein Versuch*. 10th ed. 2 vols. Leipzig, 1908.

Calenzio, Generoso. *La vita e gli scritti del Cardinale Cesare Baronio*. Rome, 1907.

Candeloro, Giorgio. "Paolo Paruta," *RSI*, Ser. 5, I (1936), Fasc. III, 70–97, Fasc. IV, 51–79.

Cantimori, Delio. *Eretici italiani del Cinquecento*. Florence, 1939.

———. "Su M. A. de Dominis," *Archiv für Reformationsgeschichte*, IL (1958), 245–258.

———. "L'utopia ecclesiologica di M. A. de Dominis," in *Problemi di vita religiosa in Italia nel Cinquecento* (Padua, 1960), pp. 103–122.

Caretti, Lanfranco. "Giovanni Della Casa, uomo pubblico e scrittore," *Studi urbinati*, XXVII (1953), 30–45.

Carocci, Giampiero. *Lo Stato della Chiesa nella seconda metà del secolo XVI*. Milan, 1961.

Carotti, Natale. "Un politico umanista del Quattrocento: Francesco Barbaro," *RSI*, Ser. 5, II (1937), 18–37.

Cassani, Pietro. "Paolo Sarpi e le scienze naturali," *Ateneo Veneto*, Ser. 6, III (1882), 204–229, 284–327.

Cassirer, Ernst. *The Individual and the Cosmos in Renaissance Philosophy*. Mario Domandi, trans. Oxford, 1963.

Catalano, Franco. "La crisi italiana alla fine del secolo XV," *Belfagor*, XI (1956), 393–414, 505–527.

Cattaneo, Enrico. "Influenze veronesi nella legislazione di san Carlo Borromeo," in *Problemi di vita religiosa in Italia nel Cinquecento* (Padua, 1960), pp. 132–166.

Cauchie, A. "Témoignages d'estime rendus en Belgique au Cardinal Baronius spécialement à l'occasion du conflit de Paul V avec Venise," in *Per Cesare Baronio: Scritti vari nel terzo centenario della sua morte* (Rome, 1911), pp. 17–25.

Cecchetti, Bartolomeo. *La Repubblica di Venezia e la Corte di Roma nei rapporti della religione.* 2 vols. Venice, 1874.

Celani, Enrico. "Documenti per la storia del dissidio tra la Repubblica di Venezia e Paolo V," *AV,* Ser. 2, XVII (1899), 243–267.

Cessi, Benvenuto. "Il taglio del Po a Porto Viro," *AV,* Ser. 3, XXX (1915), 319–368.

Cessi, Roberto. *Le origini del ducato veneziano.* Naples, 1951.

———. "Paolinismo preluterano," *Rendiconti dell'Accademia Nazionale dei Lincei: Classe di scienze morali, storiche e filologiche,* Ser. 8, XII (1957), 3–30.

———. "Paolo Sarpi ed il problema Adriatico," in *Paolo Sarpi ed i suoi tempi: Studi storici* (Città di Castello, 1923), pp. 143–169.

———. *La Repubblica di Venezia e il problema Adriatico.* Naples, 1953.

———. "Sarpi novellista," *Rendiconti dell'Accademia Nazionale dei Lincei: Classe di scienze morali, storiche e filologiche,* Ser. 8, IX (1954), 361–388.

———. *Storia della Repubblica di Venezia.* 2 vols. Milan, 1944.

Chabod, Federico, *Giovanni Botero.* Rome, 1934.

———. *Per la storia religiosa dello Stato di Milano durante il dominio di Carlo V: Note e documenti.* 2nd ed. Rome, 1962.

———. *La politica di Paolo Sarpi.* Venice, 1962.

———. "Venezia nella politica italiana ed europea del Cinquecento," in *La civiltà veneziana del Rinascimento* (Florence, 1958), pp. 27–55.

Cian, V. "Paolo Paruta, spigolature," *AV,* XXXVII (1889), 109–131.

Cicogna, Emmanuele Antonio. *Saggio di bibliografia veneziana.* Venice, 1847.

Cipolla, Carlo M. "Comment s'est perdue la propriété ecclésiastique dans l'Italie du Nord entre le XIᵉ et le XVIᵉ siècle," *Annales,* II (1947), 317–327.

Clancy, Thomas H. *Papist Pamphleteers. The Allen-Persons Party and the Political Thought of the Counter-Reformation in England, 1572–1615.* Chicago, 1964.

Collingwood, R. G. *The Idea of History.* Oxford, 1946.

"Come Paolo Sarpi non fu vescovo di Nona," *Civiltà Cattolica,* Quaderno 2073 (Nov. 7, 1936), 196–205.

Cozzi, Gaetano. "Appunti sul teatro e i teatri a Venezia agli inizi del Seicento. L'interdetto e il teatro," *BSV,* I (1959), 187–192.

————. "Cultura politica e religione nella 'pubblica storiografia' veneziana del '500," *BSV*, V–VI (1963–1964), 215–294.

————. *Il doge Nicolò Contarini: Ricerche sul patriziato veneziano agli inizi del Seicento*. Venice, 1958.

————. "Federico Contarini: un antiquario veneziano tra Rinascimento e Controriforma," *BSV*, III (1961), 190–220.

————. "Fra Paolo Sarpi, l'anglicanesimo, e la Historia del Concilio Tridentino," *RSI*, LXVIII (1956), 559–619.

————. "L'interdetto di Venezia e i Gesuiti," *AV*, Ser. 5, LXVI (1960), 163–175.

————. "Paolo Paruta, Paolo Sarpi e la questione della sovranità su Ceneda," *BSV*, IV (1962), 176–237.

————. "Paolo Sarpi e Jan van Meurs," *BSV*, I (1959), 3–11.

————. "Paolo Sarpi: il suo problema storico, religioso e giuridico nella recente letteratura," *Il diritto ecclesiastico*, LXIII (1952), 52–88.

————. "Paolo Sarpi tra il cattolico Philippe Canaye de Fresnes e il calvinista Isaac Casaubon," *BSV*, I (1959), 1–125.

————. "Politica e diritto in alcune controversie confinarie tra lo Stato di Milano e la Repubblica di Venezia (1564–1622)," *Archivio storico lombardo*, LXXVIII–LXXIX (1951–1952), 7–44.

————. "Sulla morte di fra Paolo Sarpi," *Miscellanea in onore di Roberto Cessi* (Rome, 1958), II, 387–396.

————. "Traiano Boccalini, il Cardinale Borghese e la Spagna, secondo le riferte di un confidente degli Inquisitori di Stato," *RSI*, LXVIII (1956), 230–254.

————. "Una vicenda della Venezia barocca: Marco Trevisan e la sua 'eroica amicizia'," *BSV*, II (1960), 61–154.

Croce, Benedetto. *Storia della età barocca in Italia*. 2nd ed. Bari, 1946.

Curcio, Carlo. *Dal Rinascimento alla Controriforma. Contributo alla storia del pensiero politico italiano da Guicciardini a Botero*. Rome, 1934.

Cutolo, Alessandro. "Un diario inedito del doge Leonardo Donà," *Nuova antologia*, CDLVII (1953), 270–281.

Dalla Santa, Giuseppe. "Le appellazioni della Repubblica di Venezia dalle scomuniche di Sisto IV e Giulio II," *AV*, Ser. 2, XVII (1899), 216–242.

————. "Il vero testo dell'appellazione di Venezia dalla scommunica di Giulio II," *AV*, Ser. 2, XIX (1900), 349–361.

Davis, James Cushman. *The Decline of the Venetian Nobility as a Ruling Class*. Baltimore, 1962.

Dazzi, Manlio. "Il Mussato storico," *AV*, Ser. 5, VI (1929), 357–471.

Deane, Herbert A. *The Political and Social Ideas of St. Augustine.* New York, 1963.

Delaruelle, E., E. R. Labande, and Paul Ourliac. *L'Église au temps du Grand Schisme et de la crise conciliare.* Histoire de l'Église, XIV. 2 vols. Paris, 1962.

Della Torre, Arnaldo. "La prima ambasceria di Bernardo Bembo a Firenze," *Giornale storico della letteratura italiana*, XXXV (1900), 258–333.

Delumeau, Jean. *Vie économique et sociale de Rome dans la seconde moitié du XVIe siècle.* 2 vols. Paris, 1957–1959.

Dionisotti, Carlo. "Chierici e laici nella letteratura italiana del primo Cinquecento," *Problemi di vita religiosa in Italia nel Cinquecento* (Padua, 1960), pp. 167–185.

Elwert, W. Theodor. "Pietro Bembo e la vita letteraria del suo tempo," *La civiltà veneziana del Rinascimento* (Florence, 1958), pp. 125–176.

———. *Studi di letteratura veneziana.* Venice, 1958.

Emery, Luigi. "Religione e politica nella mente di fra Paolo Sarpi," *Nuova rivista storica*, VIII (1924), 304–329, 443–475.

Ercole, Francesco. *Dal comune al principato: saggi sulla storia del diritto publico del rinascimento italiano.* Florence, 1929.

Ettlinger, L. D. *The Sistine Chapel before Michelangelo: Religious Imagery and Papal Primacy.* Oxford, 1965.

Fasoli, Gina. "Nascita di un mito," *Studi storici in onore di Gioacchino Volpe* (Florence, 1958), I, 445–479.

———. "Sulle ripercussioni italiane della crisi dinastica francese del 1589–95 e sull'opera mediatrice della Repubblica di Venezia e del Granduca di Toscana," *Memorie dell'Accademia della Scienze dell'Istituto di Bologna: classe di scienze*, Ser. 4, IX (1949), 1–64.

Favaro, Antonio. "Fra Fulgenzio Micanzio e Galileo Galilei," *AV*, Ser. 3, XIII, Part 1 (1907), 34–67.

———. "Giovan Francesco Sagredo e la vita scientifica in Venezia al principio del sec. XVII," *AV*, Ser. 3, IV (1902), 313–442.

———. "Un ridotto scientifico a Venezia al tempo di Galileo Galilei," *AV*, Ser. 2, V (1893), 199–209.

———. "Lo Studio di Padova e la Compagnia di Gesù sul finire del secolo decimosesto: narrazione documentata," *Atti del R. Istituto Veneto di Scienze, Lettere ed Arti*, Ser. 5, IV (1878), 401–535.

Febvre, Lucien. *Au coeur religieux du XVIe siècle.* Paris, 1957.

Ferguson, Wallace. *The Renaissance in Historical Thought.* Boston, 1948.

Fink, Zera S. *The Classical Republicans: An Essay in the Recovery of a Pattern of Thought in Seventeenth-Century England.* 2nd ed. Evanston, 1962.

Firpo, Luigi. *Appunti e testi per la storia dell'antimacchiavellismo. Corso di storia delle dottrine politiche.* Turin, n.d.

————. "Filosofia italiana e Controriforma," *Rivista di filosofia*, XLI (1950), 150–173, 390–401; XLII (1951), 30–47.

————. "Il processo di Giordano Bruno," *RSI*, LX (1948), 542–597.

————. "L'utopia politica nella Controriforma," *Contributi alla storia del Concilio di Trento e della Controriforma* (Florence, 1948), pp. 78–108.

Foscarini, Marco. *Della letteratura veneziana ed altri scritti intorno essa.* 2nd ed. Venice, 1854.

Francescon, Clemente Maria. *Chiesa e Stato nei consulti di fra Paolo Sarpi.* Vicenza, 1942.

Franklin, Julian H. *Jean Bodin and the Sixteenth-Century Revolution in the Methodology of Law and History.* New York, 1963.

Fueter, Eduard. *Histoire de l'historiographie moderne.* Émile Jeanmaire, tr. Paris, 1914.

Gabrielli, V. "Bacone, la riforma e Roma nella versione hobbesiana d'un carteggio di Fulgenzio Micanzio," *English Miscellany*, VIII (1957), 195–250.

Gadaleta, Antonio. "Di un diario dell'interdetto di Venezia del secolo XVII," *ASI*, Ser. 5, XVIII (1896), 98–108.

Gaeta, Franco. "Alcune considerazioni sul mito di Venezia," *Bibliothèque d'Humanisme et Renaissance*, XXIII (1961), 58–75.

————. *Un nunzio pontificio a Venezia nel Cinquecento (Girolamo Aleandro).* Venice and Rome, 1960.

————. "Origini e sviluppo della rappresentanza stabile pontificia in Venezia (1485–1533)," *Annuario dell'Istituto Storico Italiano per l'Età Moderna e Contemporanea*, IX–X (1957–1958), 5–281.

————. *Il vescovo Pietro Barozzi e il trattato "De factionibus extinguendis".* Venice and Rome, 1958.

Gambarin, Giovanni. "Il Sarpi alla luce di studi recenti," *AV*, L–LI (1953), 78–105.

Garin, Eugenio. "I cancellieri umanisti della Repubblica Fiorentina da Caluccio Salutati a Bartolomeo Scala," *RSI*, LXXI (1959), 185–208.

————. "Cultura filosofica toscana e veneta nel Quattrocento," *Umanesimo europeo e umanesimo veneziano* (Venice, 1963), pp. 11–30.

————. *Medioevo e Rinascimento: studi e ricerche.* Bari, 1961.

————. *L'umanesimo italiano.* Bari, 1958.

Geanakoplos, Deno J. *Greek Scholars in Venice: Studies in the Dissemination of Greek Learning from Byzantium to Western Europe*. Cambridge, Mass., 1962.

Getto, Giovanni. *Paolo Sarpi*. Pisa and Rome, 1941.

Gilbert, Felix. "The Date of the Composition of Contarini's and Giannotti's Books on Venice," *Studies in the Renaissance*, XIV (1967).

———. "Florentine Political Assumptions in the Period of Savonarola and Soderini," *Journal of the Warburg and Courtauld Institutes*, XX (1957), 187–214.

———. "The Humanist Concept of the Prince and the 'Prince' of Machiavelli," *Journal of Modern History*, XI (1939), 449–483.

———. *Machiavelli and Guicciardini: Politics and History in Sixteenth Century Florence*. Princeton, 1965.

———. "The 'New Diplomacy' of the Eighteenth Century," *World Politics*, IV (1951), 1–38.

———. "Religion and Politics in the Thought of Gasparo Contarini," in *Action and Conviction in Early Modern Europe: Essays in Memory of E. H. Harbison*, ed. Theodore K. Rabb and Jerrold E. Seigel (Princeton, 1968).

———. "The Venetian Constitution in Florentine Political Thought," in *Florentine Studies*, ed. Nicolai Rubinstein (London, 1968),

Gilmore, Myron P., "Freedom and Determinism in Renaissance Historians," *Studies in the Renaissance*, III (1956), 49–60.

———. *Humanists and Jurists: Six Studies in the Renaissance*. Cambridge, Mass., 1963.

Gilson, Étienne. "L'affaire de l'immortalité de l'âme à Venise au début du XVIe siècle," in *Umanesimo europeo e umanesimo veneziano* (Venice, 1963), pp. 31–61.

Gleason, Elisabeth G. "Cardinal Gasparo Contarini (1483–1542) and the Beginning of Catholic Reform". Unpublished doctoral dissertation, Berkeley, 1963.

Godefroy, L. "Interdit," *Dictionnaire de Théologie Catholique*, VII:2 (Paris, 1930), cols. 2280–2290.

Govi, Gilberto. "La partenza dei Gesuiti dal Dominio Veneto," *Memorie della R. Accademia dei Lincei: classe di scienze fisiche, matematiche e naturali*, Ser. IV, I (1884–1885), 622–640.

Grazioli, Angelo. *Gian Matteo Giberti vescovo di Verona precursore della riforma del Concilio di Trento*. Verona, 1955.

Greenleaf, W. H. *Order, Empiricism and Politics: Two Traditions of English Political Thought*. London, 1964.

Griselini, Francesco. *Memorie anedote spettanti alla vita ed agli studi del sommo filosofo e giureconsulto F. Paolo Servita.* Lausanne, 1760.

Haas, Alban. *Das Interdikt nach geltendem Recht, mit einem geschichtlichen Überblick.* Amsterdam, 1929.

Heiler, F. *Altkirchliche Autonomie und päpstlicher Zentralismus.* Munich, 1941.

Hochschild, Patricia. "Bernardo Giustiniani: a Venetian of the Quattrocento," Unpublished doctoral dissertation, Cambridge, Mass., 1957.

Jedin, Hubert. "Contarini und Camaldoli," *Archivio italiano per la storia della pietà* II (1959), 51–117.

———. "Gasparo Contarini e il contributo veneziano alla riforma cattolica," in *Là civiltà veneziana del Rinascimento* (Florence, 1958), pp. 103–124.

———. *Geschichte des Konzils von Trient.* 2nd ed. 2 vols. Freiburg, 1951–1957.

———. *Das Konzil von Trient, ein Überblick über die Erforschung seiner Geschichte.* Storia e letteratura, 19. Rome, 1948.

———. *Papal Legate at the Council of Trent: Cardinal Seripando.* Frederic C. Eckhoff, trans. London and St. Louis, 1947.

———. *Studien über Domenico de' Domenichi (1416–1478).* Mainz, 1958.

———. "Ein 'Turmerlebnis' des jungen Contarini," *Historisches Jahrbuch,* LXX (1950), 115–130.

———. "V. Quirini und P. Bembo," *Miscellanea Giovanni Mercati* (Vatican City, 1946), IV, 407–424.

Jemolo, Arturo Carlo. *Stato e Chiesa negli scrittori politici italiani del Seicento e del Settecento.* Turin, 1914.

Jung, Eva-Marie. "On the Nature of Evangelism in Sixteenth Century Italy," *Journal of the History of Ideas,* XIV (1953), 511–527.

Kellenbenz, Hermann. "Le déclin de Venise et les relations économiques de Venise avec les marchés au nord des Alpes," in *Aspetti e cause della decadenza economica veneziana nel secolo XVII* (Venice, 1961), pp. 109–183.

Koenigsberger, H. G. "Decadence or Shift? Changes in the Civilization of Italy and Europe in the Sixteenth and Seventeenth Centuries," *Transactions of the Royal Historical Society,* Ser. 5, X (1960), 1–18.

Krebs, Richard. *Die politische Publizistik der Jesuiten und ihrer Gegner in den letzten Jahrzehnten vor Ausbruch des dreissigjährigen Krieges.* Halle, 1890.

Krehbiel, Edward B. *The Interdict: Its History and Operation, with Special Attention to the Time of Pope Innocent III, 1198–1216.* Washington, 1909.

Kristeller, Paul Oskar. *Eight Philosophers of the Italian Renaissance.* Stanford, 1964.

————. "Il Petrarca, l'umanesimo e la scolastica a Venezia," in *La civiltà veneziana del Trecento* (Florence, 1956), pp. 147–178.

Lagomaggiore, Carlo. "*L'Istoria Veneziana di M. Pietro Bembo*," *AV*, Ser. 3, VII (1904), 5–31, 334–372; VIII (1904), 162–180, 317–346; IX (1905), 33–113, 308–340.

Lane, Frederic C. "Recent Studies on the Economic History of Venice," *Journal of Economic History*, XXIII (1963), 312–334.

————. *Venice and History*. Baltimore, 1966.

La Servière, J. de. *La théologie de Bellarmin*. Paris, 1909.

Lazzarini, Lino. "Francesco Petrarca e il primo umanesimo a Venezia," in *Umanesimo europeo e umanesimo veneziano* (Venice, 1963), pp. 63–92.

————. *Paolo de Bernardo e i primordi dell'umanesimo in Venezia*. Geneva, 1930.

Lazzarini, Vittorio. "Antiche leggi venete intorno ai proprietari nella terraferma," *AV*, Ser. 3, XXXVIII (1920), 5–31.

Lecler, Joseph. "L'argument des deux glaives (Luc XXII, 38)," *Recherches de science religieuse*, XXI (1931), 229–339; XXII (1932), 151–177, 280–303.

Leicht, Pier Silverio. "Lo stato veneziano ed il diritto comune," in *Miscellanea in onore di R. Cessi* (Rome, 1958), I, 203–211.

Lewy, Guenter. *Constitutionalism and Statecraft during the Golden Age of Spain: A Study of the Political Philosophy of Juan de Mariana, S.J.* Geneva, 1960.

Lievsay, John L. "Paolo Sarpi's Appraisal of James I," *Essays in History and Literature Presented by Fellows of the Newberry Library to Stanley Pargellis* (Chicago, 1965), pp. 109–117.

Longo, Raffaele Giura. "La bolla *In Coena Domini* e le franchigie al clero meridionale," *Archivio storico per la Calabria e la Lucania*, XXXII (1963), 275–295.

Lopez, Roberto. "Il principio della guerra veneto-turca nel 1463," *AV*, Ser. 5, XV (1934), 45–131.

Lortz, Joseph. *Die Reformation in Deutschland*. 3rd ed. 2 vols. Freiburg, 1948.

Luca, Giuseppe de. "Della pietà veneziana nel Seicento e d'un prete ven-. eziano quietista," in *La civiltà veneziana nell'età barocca* (Florence, 1959), pp. 215–234.

————. "Letteratura di pietà," in *La civiltà veneziana del Trecento* (Florence, 1956), pp. 207–230.

Luca, Luigi de. *Stato e Chiesa nel pensiero politico di G. Botero*. Rome, 1946.

Luciani, V. *Francesco Guicciardini and His European Reputation*. New York, 1936.

Luzio, A. "Fra Paolo Sarpi," *RSI*, XLV (1928), 1–23.

Luzzatto, Gino. "La decadenza di Venezia dopo le scoperte geografiche nella tradizione e nella realtá," *AV*, Ser. 5, LIV–LV (1954), 162–181.

———. "L'economia," in *La civiltà veneziana del Trecento* (Florence, 1956), pp. 85–109.

———. *Storia economica di Venezia del XI al XVI secolo*. Venice, 1961.

Magalhães-Godinho, Vitorino. "Le repli vénitien et égyptien et la route du Cap," in *Hommage à Lucien Febvre: éventail de l'histoire vivante* (Paris, 1953), II, 283–300.

Mancini, Augusto. *Storia di Lucca*. Florence, 1950.

Manfroni, Camillo. "Paolo Sarpi," in *Paolo Sarpi ed i suoi tempi: studi storici* (Città di Castello, 1923), pp. 1–16.

Maranini, Giuseppe. *La costituzione di Venezia dalle origini alla serrata del Maggior Consiglio*. Venice, 1927.

———. *La costituzione di Venezia dopo la serrata del Maggior Consiglio*. Venice, 1931.

Martin, Victor. *Les origines du gallicanisme*. 2 vols. Paris, 1939.

Martines, Lauro. *The Social World of the Florentine Humanists, 1390–1460*. Princeton, 1963.

Mattei, Rodolfo de. "La concezione monocratica negli scrittori politici italiani del Seicento," *Studi storici in onore di Giocchino Volpe* (Florence, 1958), I, 315–360.

———. "Contenuto ed origini dell'ideale universalista nel Seicento," *Rivista internazionale di filosofia del diritto*, IX (1930), 391–401.

———. "Contenuto ed origini dell'utopia cittadina nel Seicento," *Rivista internazaionale di filosofia del diritto*, IX (1929), 414–425.

———. *Dal premachiavellismo all'antimachiavellismo europeo del Cinquecento*. Rome, 1956.

Mattingly, Garrett. *Renaissance Diplomacy*. Boston, 1955.

Medin, Antonio, "Il culto del Petrarca nel Veneto fino alla dittatura del Bembo," *AV*, Ser. 3, VIII (1904), 421–465.

———. *La storia della Repubblica di Venezia nella poesia*. Milan, 1904.

Merores, Margarete. "Der venezianische Adel," *Vierteljahrschrift für Sozial- und Wirtschaftsgeschichte*, XIX (1926), 193–237.

Molmenti, Pompeo. "La corruzione dei costumi veneziani nel Rinascimento," *ASI*, Ser. 5, XXXI (1903), 281–307.

———. *Storia di Venezia nella vita privata dalle origini alla caduta della Repubblica*. 7th ed. 3 vols. Bergamo, 1927–1929.

Mor, Carlo Guido. "Problemi organizzativi e politica veneziana nei riguardi dei nuovi acquisti di terraferma," in *Umanesimo europeo e umanesimo veneziano* (Venice, 1963), pp. 1–10.

Morandi, Carlo. "Il concetto della politica di equilibrio nell'Europa moderna," *ASI*, XCVIII (1940), 3–19.

Nadel, George H. "Philosophy of History before Historicism," *History and Theory*, III (1964), 291–315.

Nani Mocenigo, Filippo. *Agostino, Battista e Giacomo Nani.* Venice, 1917.

Nardi, Bruno. "Letteratura e cultura veneziana del Quattrocento," in *La civiltà veneziana del Quattrocento* (Venice, 1956), pp. 99–145.

———. "La scuola di Rialto e l'umanesimo veneziano," in *Umanesimo europeo e umanesimo veneziano* (Venice, 1963), pp. 93–139.

Nicolini, Benedetto. *Aspetti della vita religiosa, politica e letteraria del Cinquecento.* Bologna, 1963.

Niebuhr, Reinhold. *Christian Realism and Political Problems.* New York, 1953.

Niero, Antonio. *I patriarchi di Venezia da Lorenzo Giustiniani ai nostri giorni.* Venice, 1961.

Nürnberger, A. "Papst Paul V und das venezianische Interdikt," *Historisches Jahrbuch*, IV (1883), 189–209, 473–515.

Oberman, Heiko A. "Some Notes on the Theology of Nominalism, with Attention to Its Relation to the Renaissance," *Harvard Theological Review*, LIII (1960), 47–76.

Odorici, Federigo. "Paolo V e le città di terraferma. Note istoriche in appendice al Giornale pubblicato dal Cornet," *ASI*, Ser. 2, X (1859), 171–180.

Pallucchini, Rodolfo. "L'arte a Venezia nel Quattrocento," in *La civiltà veneziana nel Quattrocento* (Venice, 1956), pp. 147–177.

Partner, Peter. "Florence and the Papacy, 1300–1375," in *Europe in the Late Middle Ages* (Evanston, 1965), pp. 76–121.

Paschini, Pio. "Daniele Barbaro letterato e prelato veneziano nel Cinquecento," *Rivista di storia della Chiesa in Italia*, XV (1961), 73–107.

———. "L'Inquisizione a Venezia ed il nunzio Ludovico Beccadelli, 1550–1554," *Archivio della R. Deputazione Romana di Storia Patria*, LXV (1942), 63–152.

———. "La nomina del patriarca di Aquileia e la Repubblica di Venezia nel secolo XVI," *Rivista di storia della Chiesa in Italia*, II (1948), 61–76.

———. *Tre illustre prelati del Rinascimento.* Rome, 1957.

————. *Tre ricerche sulla storia della Chiesa nel Cinquecento*. Rome, 1945.

Pastor, Ludwig von. *The History of the Popes*. F. I. Antrobus et al., trans. 40 vols. London and St. Louis, 1898–1953.

Pecchioli, Renzo. "Il 'mito' di Venezia e la crisi fiorentina intorno al 1500," *Studi storici*, III (1962), 451–492.

Pieri, Piero. *Intorno alla politica estera di Venezia al principio del Cinquecento*. Naples, 1934.

Pintard, René. *Le libertinage érudit dans la première moitié du XVIIe siècle*. 2 vols. Paris, 1943.

Piovene, Guido. "Anacronismo della Venezia quattrocentesca," in *La civiltà veneziana del Quattrocento* (Venice, 1956), pp. 1–21.

Polman, Pontien. *L'élément historique dans la controverse religieuse au XVIe siècle*. Gembloux, 1932.

Pommier, Edouard. "La société vénitienne et la Réforme protestante au XVIe siècle," *BSV*, I (1959), 3–26.

Pompeati, Arturo. "Le dottrine politiche di Paolo Paruta," *Giornale storico della letteratura italiana*, XLVI (1905), 286–358.

————. "Per la biografia di Paolo Paruta," *Giornale storico della letteratura italiana*, XLV (1905), 48–66.

Ponti, Giovanni. *Paolo Sarpi*. Turin, 1938.

Pozzo, Giovanni da. "Per il testo dei 'Pensieri' del Sarpi," *BSV*, III (1961), 139–176.

Procacci, Giuliano. "La 'fortuna' nella realtà politica e sociale del primo Cinquecento," *Belfagor*, VI (1951), 407–421.

Prodi, Paolo. "San Carlo Borromeo e la trattative tra Gregorio XIII e Filippo II sulla giurisdizione ecclesiastica," *Rivista storica della Chiesa in in Italia*, XI (1957), 195–240.

Prost, August. "Les chroniques vénetiennes," *Revue des questions historiques*, XXXI (1882), 512–555.

Pullan, Brian. "Poverty, Charity and the Reason of State: Some Venetian Examples," *BSV*, II (1960), 17–60.

Putelli, Raffaello. "Il duca Vincenzo Gonzaga e l'interdetto di Paolo V a Venezia," *AV*, Ser. 3, XXI (1911), 255–352; XXII (1911), 6–280, 481–658.

Quazza, Romolo. *Preponderanza spagnuola (1559–1700)*. 2nd ed. Milan, 1950.

Raulich, Italo. "La contesa fra Sisto V e Venezia per Enrico IV di Francia, con documenti," *AV*, Ser. 2, IV (1892), 243–318.

Reynold, Gonzague de. "La conception catholique de l'État au temps de la Contre-Réforme et du Baroque," *Barock in der Schweiz* (Einsiedeln, 1930), pp. 7–43.

Reynolds, Beatrice. "Shifting Currents in Historical Criticism," *Journal of the History of Ideas*, XIV (1953), 471–492.

Rhodes, Dennis E. "Roberto Meietti e alcuni documenti della controversia fra Papa Paolo V e Venezia," *Studi secenteschi*, I (1960), 165–174.

Ricci, Pier Giorgio. "Umanesimo filologico in Toscana e nel Veneto," in *Umanesimo europeo e umanesimo veneziano* (Venice, 1963), pp. 159–172.

Rivkin, Ellis. *Leon da Modena and the 'Kol Sakhal'*. Cincinnati, 1952.

Roberti, Melchiorre. "Il collegio padovano dei dottori giuristi," *Rivista italiana per le scienze giuridiche*, XXV (1903), 171–234.

Romanin, S. *Storia documentata di Venezia*. 10 vols. Venice, 1853–1869.

Romano, Ruggiero. "La marine marchande vénitienne au XVIᵉ siècle," in *Les sources de l'histoire maritime en Europe, du moyen âge au XVIIIᵉ siècle* (Paris, 1962), pp. 33–68.

Ronga, Luigi. "La musica," in *La civiltà veneziana nell'eta barocca* (Florence, 1959), pp. 123–144.

Rothenberg, Gunther. "Venice and the Uskoks of Senj, 1537–1618," *Journal of Modern History*, XXXIII (1961), 148–156.

Rubertis, Achille de. *Ferdinando I dei Medici e la contesa fra Paolo V e la Repubblica Veneta*. Reale Deputazione di Storia Patria per le Venezie: Miscellanea di studi e memorie, vol. II. Venice, 1933.

———. "Francesco Maria II della Rovere e la contesa fra Paolo V e la Repubblica Veneta," *AV*, Ser. 5, XXII (1938), 207–260; XXIII (1939), 1–55.

Rubinstein, Nicolai. "Florence and the Despots in the Fourteenth Century," *Transactions of the Royal Historical Society*, Ser. 5, II (1952), 21–45.

———. "Marsilius of Padua and Italian Political Thought of His Time," *Europe in the Late Middle Ages* (Evanston, 1965), pp. 44–75.

Ruffini, F. *Perché Cesare Baronio non fu papa*. Perugia, 1910.

Ryan, E. A. *The Historical Scholarship of Saint Robert Bellarmine*. Louvain, 1936.

Sagredo, A. "Leggi venete intorno agli ecclesiastici sino al secolo XVIII," *ASI*, Ser. 3, II (1865), 92–133.

Salvatorelli, Luigi. "Le idee religiose di fra Paolo Sarpi," *Atti della Accademia Nazionale dei Lincei: classe di scienze morali, storiche e filologiche: memorie*, Ser. 8, V (1953), 311–360.

———. "Paolo Sarpi," in *Contributi alla storia del Concilio di Trento e della Controriforma* (Florence, 1949).

———. "La prima edizione autentica della *Istoria del Concilio Tridentino* di Paolo Sarpi," *Pan*, VI (1935), 351–360.

———. "Profilo di una storia religiosa d'Italia," *RSI*, LXIII (1951), 153–161.

————. "Venezia, Paolo V, e fra Paolo Sarpi," in *La civiltà veneziana nell'età barocca* (Venice, 1959), pp. 67–95.

Sandi, Vettore. *Principi di storia civile della Repubblica di Venezia dalla sua fondazione sino all'anno di N.S. 1700.* 6 vols. Venice, 1755–1756.

Sanesi, Giuseppe. *La vita e le opere di Donato Giannotti.* Pistoia, 1899.

Santillana, Giorgio de. *The Crime of Galileo.* Chicago, 1955.

Sapori, Armando. *L'Età della Rinascita: secoli XIII–XVI.* Milan, 1958.

Sasso, Gennaro. *Niccolò Machiavelli, Storia del suo pensiero politico.* Naples, 1958.

Savio, Pietro. "Il nunzio a Venezia dopo l'interdetto," *AV*, Ser. 5, LVI–LVII (1955), 55–110.

Saxl, Fritz. "Veritas Filia Temporis," in *Philosophy and History: the Ernst Cassirer Festschrift.* Raymond Klibansky and H. J. Paton. ed. New ed. (New York, 1963), pp. 197–222.

Scaduto, Francesco. *Stato e Chiesa secondo fra Paolo Sarpi e la coscienza pubblica durante l'interdetto di Venezia del 1606–1607.* Florence, 1885.

Segre, Arturo. "Di alcune relazioni tra la Repubblica di Venezia e la S. Sede ai tempi di Urbano V e di Gregorio XI," *AV*, Ser. 3, IX (1905), 200–214.

Seigel, Jerrold E. "Civic Humanism or Ciceronian Rhetoric? The Culture of Petrarch and Bruni," *Past and Present*, No. 34 (1966), 3–48.

————. *Rhetoric and Philosophy in Renaissance Humanism: the Union of Eloquence and Wisdom, Petrarch to Valla.* Princeton, 1968.

Sella, Domenico. *Commerci e industrie a Venezia nel secolo XVII.* Venice, 1961.

————. "L'industria della lana in Venezia nei secoli sedicesimo e diciassettesimo," in *Storia dell'economia italiana* (Turin, 1959), I, 533–556.

Seneca, Federico. *Il doge Leonardo Donà: la sua vita e la sua preparazione politica prima del dogado.* Padua, 1959.

————. *La politica veneziana dopo l'interdetto.* Padua, 1957.

————. *Venezia e Papa Giulio II.* Padua, 1962.

Sestan, Ernesto. "La politica veneziana del Seicento," in *La civiltà veneziana nell'età barocca* (Venice, 1959), pp. 35–66.

Sforza, Giovanni. "Riflessi della Controriforma nella Repubblica di Venezia," *ASI*, XCIII (1935), 5–34, 189–215; XCIV (1936), 25–52, 173–186.

Simeoni, Luigi. *Le signorie.* 2 vols. Milan, 1950.

Simonsfeld, Enrico. "Andrea Dandolo e le sue opere storiche," *AV*, Ser. 1, XIV (1877), Pt. 1, 49–149.

Smalley, Beryl. "Church and State, 1300–1377: Theory and Fact," in *Europe in the Late Middle Ages* (Evanston, 1965), pp. 15–43.

Soranzo, Giovanni. *Bibliografia veneziana*. Venice, 1885.

———. *La guerra fra Venezia e la S. Sede per il dominio di Ferrara (1308–1313)*. Città di Castello, 1905.

Spini, Giorgio. "La congiura degli spagnoli contro Venezia del 1618," *ASI*, CVII (1949), 17–53; CVIII (1950), 159–174.

———. *Ricerca dei libertini. La teoria dell'impostura delle religioni nel Seicento italiano*. Rome, 1950.

———. "Riforma italiana e mediazioni ginevrine nella Nuova Inghilterra puritana," in *Ginevra e l'Italia* (Florence, 1959), pp. 451–489.

———. *Tra Rinascimento e Riforma: Antonio Brucioli*. Florence, 1940.

———. "I trattatisti dell'arte storica nella Controriforma italiana," in *Contributi alla storia del Concilio di Trento e della Controriforma* (Florence, 1948), pp. 109–136.

Starn, Randolph. *Donato Giannotti and His Epistolae*. Geneva, 1968.

Stefani, F. "Andrea Morosini," *AV*, Ser. 1, II (1871), 220–222.

Stella, Aldo. *Chiesa e Stato nelle relazioni dei nunzi pontifici a Venezia: Ricerche sul giurisdizionalismo veneziano del XVI al XVIII secolo*. Studi e Testi, No. 239. Vatican City, 1964.

———. "La crisi economica veneziana della seconda metà del secolo XVI," *AV*, Ser. 5, LVIII–LIX (1956), 17–69.

———. "Guido da Fano, eretico del secolo XVI al servizio dei re d'Inghilterra," *Rivista di storia della Chiesa in Italia*, XIII (1959), 196–238.

———. "La proprietà ecclesiastica nella Repubblica di Venezia dal secolo XV al XVII," *Nuova rivista storica*, XLII (1958), 50–77.

———. "La regolazione delle pubbliche entrate e la crisi politica veneziana del 1582," *Miscellanea in onore di Roberto Cessi* (Rome, 1958), II, 157–171.

———. "Ricerche sul socinianesimo: il processo di Cornelio Sozzini e Claudio Textor (Banière)," *BSV*, III (1961), 77–120.

Taucci, R. *Intorno alle lettere di fra Paolo Sarpi ad Antonio Foscarini*. Florence, 1939.

Tenenti, Alberto. *Cristoforo da Canal. La marine vénitienne avant Lépante*. Paris, 1962.

———. "Il 'De perfectione rerum' di Nicolò Contarini," *BSV*, I (1959), 155–166.

———. *Venezia e i corsari, 1580–1615*. Bari, 1961.

Teza, E. "Correzioni alla Istoria Veneziana di P. Bembo proposte dal Consiglio dei Dieci nel 1548," *Annali delle Università toscane*, XVIII (1888), 75–93.

Toffanin, Giuseppe. *Machiavelli e il tacitismo: la politica storica della Controriforma*. Padua, 1921.

Tolnay, Charles de. "Tintoretto's Salotto Dorato Cycle in the Doge Palace," in *Scritti di storia dell'arte in onore di Mario Salmi* (Rome, 1963), III, 117–131.

Trexler, Richard C. *Economic, Political and Religious Effects of the Papal Interdict on Florence, 1376–1378*. Frankfurt am Main, 1964.

Ulianich, Boris. "Appunti e documenti: Sarpiana: la lettera del Sarpi allo Heinsius, *RSI*, LXVIII (1956), 425–446.

———. "Considerazioni e documenti per una ecclesiologia di Paolo Sarpi," in *Festgabe Joseph Lortz* (Baden-Baden, 1957), II, 363–444.

Ullman, Berthold L. *The Humanism of Coluccio Salutati*. Padua, 1963.

Ullmann, Walter. *The Growth of Papal Government in the Middle Ages. A Study in the Ideological Relation of Clerical to Lay Power*. London, 1955.

———. *The Individual and Society in the Middle Ages*. Baltimore, 1966.

———. *Principles of Government and Politics in the Middle Ages*. New York, 1961.

Valeri, Nino. "Venezia nella crisi italiana del Rinascimento," in *La civiltà veneziana del Quattrocento* (Florence, 1956), pp. 23–48.

Ventura, Angelo. *Nobiltà e popolo nella società veneta del '400 e '500*. Bari, 1964.

Veress, Andrea. "Il veneziano Giovanni Michele Bruto e la sua storia d'Ungheria," *AV*, Ser. 5, VI (1929), 148–178.

Viscardi, Antonio. "Lingua e letteratura," in *La civiltà veneziana del Trecento* (Florence, 1956), pp. 179–205.

Volpati, Carlo. "Paolo Giovio e Venezia," *AV*, Ser. 5, XV (1934), 132–156.

Volpe, Gioacchino. "L'Italia e Venezia," in *La civiltà veneziana del Trecento* (Florence, 1956), pp. 23–83.

Weinstein, Donald. "Savonarola, Florence, and the Millenarian Tradition," *Church History*, XXVII (1958), 291–311.

Weiss, Roberto. *The Spread of Italian Humanism*. London, 1964.

Welliver, Warman. *L'impero fiorentino*. Florence, 1957.

Wickhoff, Franz. "Der Saal des Grossen Rats zu Venedig in seinem alten Schmucke," *Repertorium für Kunstwissenschaft*, VI (1883), 1–37.

Wilks, M. J. *The Problem of Sovereignty in the Later Middle Ages*. Cambridge, 1962.

Willaert, Leopold. *Après le concile de Trente: la restauration catholique (1563-1648)*. Histoire de l'Église, vol. XVIII. Paris, 1960.

Williams, George. *The Radical Reformation*. Philadelphia, 1962.

Wind, Edgar. *Pagan Mysteries in the Renaissance*. New Haven, 1958.

Woolf, Stuart J. "Venice and the Terraferma: Problems of the Change from Commercial to Landed Activities," *BSV*, IV (1962), 415–441.

Yates, Frances A. *The Art of Memory*. Chicago, 1966.

———. "Paolo Sarpi's *History of the Council of Trent*," *Journal of the Warburg and Courtauld Institutes*, VII (1944), 123–144.

Yriarte, Charles. *La vie d'un patricien de Venise au XVIᵉ siècle*. Paris, 1874.

Zanella, G. "Della vita e degli scritti di Celio Magno, poeta veneziano del secolo XVI," *Atti del Regio Istituto Veneto*, Ser. 5, VII (1880–1881), 1063–1075.

Zanelli, Agostino. "Di alcune controversie tra la Repubblica di Venezia e il S. Officio nei primi anni del pontificato di Urbano VIII," *AV*, Ser. 5, VI (1929), 186–235.

Zanetti, Polibio. "L'assedio di Padova del 1509 in correlazione alla guerra combattuta nel Veneto del maggio all'ottobre," *AV*, Ser. 2, II (1891), 5–168.

Zippel, Gianni. "Lorenzo Valla e le origini della storiografia umanistica a Venezia," *Rinascimento*, VII (1956), 93–133.

Zonta, Gasparo. "Un conflitto tra la Repubblica Veneta e la Curia Romana per l'episcopato di Padova (1459–1460)," *Atti e memorie della R. Accademia di Scienze, Lettere ed Arti in Padova*, XL (1924), 221–238.

Index